IC3® Internet and Computing Core Certification Guide

Global Standard 4

Using Windows 7 &
Microsoft® Office 2013

D0478105

Computing Fundamentals

Key Applications

Living Online

 **CCI Learning**™

Internet and Computing Core Certification Guide

This courseware is one in a series prepared by CCI Learning Solutions Inc. for use by students and instructors in courses on computer software applications. CCI designed these materials to assist students and instructors in making the learning process both effective and enjoyable.

This training manual is copyrighted and all rights are reserved by CCI Learning Solutions Inc. No part of this publication may be reproduced, transmitted, stored in a retrieval system, modified, or translated into any language or computer language, in any form or by any means, electronic, mechanical, magnetic, optical, chemical, manual or otherwise without written permission of CCI Learning Solutions, Canada: 1-800-668-1669.

The information in this courseware is distributed on an "as is" basis, without warranty. While every precaution has been taken in the preparation of this courseware, neither the author nor CCI Learning Solutions Inc. shall have any liability to any person or entity with respect to any liability, loss, or damage caused or alleged to be caused directly or indirectly by the instructions contained in this courseware or by the computer software and hardware products described therein.

CCI Learning Solutions Inc. would like to acknowledge the financial support of the Government of Canada through the Canada Book Fund for our publishing activities.

Courseware Development Team: Sue Wong, Irina Heer, Kelly Hegedus, Kevin Yulo

Copyright © 2014 CCI Learning Solutions Inc.

ISBN: 978-1-55332-440-9
All rights reserved.
Printed in Canada.
CCI Courseware#: 7318-1-00-00

Any brand name or product mentioned in this publication is a trademark or registered trademark of their respective companies and are used for identification purposes only.

Working With the Data Files

The exercises in this courseware require you to use the data files provided for the book. Follow the instructions shown to download the data files for this courseware.

1. Launch your browser and navigate to the CCI Web site location http://www.ccilearning.com/data.

2. Enter: 7318 in the Courseware # box and click [Find Data].

3. Click **Run** in the File Download – Security Warning window. (Alternatively, you can choose to Save the file to a location on your computer.)

4. In the Internet Explorer – Security Warning window click **Run** again.

5. In the WinZip Self-Extractor dialog box, use the **Browse** button to specify the Windows Desktop as the location to unzip the file and then click **Unzip**.

6. The *7318 Student Files* folder containing the required student work files has now been downloaded to your desktop. It is recommended that you rename the folder using your own name before starting the exercises in this courseware. You can reinstall and use the work files as many times as you like.

Approved by Certiport

We are pleased to announce that our courseware has been approved for the IC³ Certification. This book fulfills the basic requirements for all three IC³ Internet and Computing Core Certification exams. Please refer to the IC³ Courseware Mapping at the back of this book to see where each of the features is covered. Passing these exams demonstrates a level of proficiency to employers and customers. The exams are available through participating IQ test centers.

IC³ . . . What Is It?

IC³, or the Internet and Computing Core Certification program, is a global training and certification program providing proof to the world that you are:

- Equipped with the needed computer skills to excel in a digital world.
- Capable of using a broad range of computer technology – from basic hardware and software, to operating systems, applications and the Internet.
- Ready for what the work employers, colleges and universities want to throw your way.
- Positioned to advance your career through additional computer certifications such as CompTIA's A+, and other desktop application exams.

IC³ . . . Why Do You Need It?

Employers, Colleges and Universities now understand that exposure to computers does not equal understanding computers. So, more than ever, basic computer and Internet skills are being considered prerequisites for employment and higher education.

This is Where IC³ Helps!

IC³ provides specific guidelines for the knowledge and skills required to be a functional user of computer hardware, software, networks, and the Internet. It does this through three exams:

- Computing Fundamentals
- Key Applications
- Living Online

By passing the three IC³ exams, you have initiated yourself into today's digital world. You have also given yourself a globally accepted and validated credential that provides the proof employers or higher education institutions need. To learn more about IC³, visit www.certiport.com/ic3

To find a testing center near you, visit www.certiport.com/iQcenterLocator

CERTĬPORT

About Certiport:

Certiport, Inc. is the leading provider of global, performance-based certification programs and services designed to enable individual success and lifetime advancement through certification. For more information about Certiport's offerings, visit www.certiport.com

Certiport is a registered trademark of Certiport, Inc. in the United States and other countries.

Table of Contents

About This Courseware

Courseware Description xiii
    Course Series xiii
    Course Prerequisites xiii
    System Requirements xiv
    Classroom Setup xiv
Course Design...xv
Course Objectives...xvi
Conventions and Graphics xvii

Computing Fundamentals

Lesson 1: Operating Systems

Lesson Objectives...1
What is an Operating System? 1
    Modern Operating Systems 3
Common Operating System Features 6
    Power On / Power Off...6
Looking at the Windows Desktop 11
    Navigating Around the Desktop...12
    Using the Start Button 12
    Working with an Application Program...14
    Using the Taskbar..14
The Software/Hardware Relationship...18
Understanding Updates...18
    Automatic Updating 19
Lesson Summary 21
Review Questions 21

Lesson 2: Files and Folders

Lesson Objectives..23
Looking at a Typical Window..23
    Moving a Window 25
    Sizing a Window 25
    Using Scroll Bars 25
Understanding Files and Folders...27
    Creating Folders 29
    Renaming a Folder 32
    Changing Folder Options 32
    Changing the View 33
    Understanding File Name Extensions 35
    Selecting Files or Folders 41
    Copying and Moving Files or Folders 42
    Renaming Files 45
    Finding Files..46
    Looking at the Recycle Bin 47
    Points to Keep in Mind when Working with Files 49
Lesson Summary 49
Review Questions 50

Lesson 3: Hardware

Lesson Objectives 51
Identifying Computers 51
    Desktop Computers...51
    Notebooks or Laptop Computers...52
    Tablet PCs..52
    Servers...52
    Hand-held or Mobile Computers...53
    Music or Media Players 53
    Electronic Book Readers 54
Looking Inside a Computer..54
    The Microprocessor Chip...55
    Looking at System Memory 56
    Understanding Storage Systems 57
    Factors that Affect Performance 60
Recognizing Input/Output Devices 61
    Using the Keyboard..61
    Using Pointing Devices 63
    Using Microphones..64
    Looking at the Monitor...65
    Using Printers 65
    Using Projectors 65
    Using Speakers...66
Understanding How It Works Together...66
Lesson Summary 68
Review Questions 68

Lesson 4: Control Panel

Lesson Objectives 69
Using the Control Panel 69
    Customizing the Desktop Display 71
    Changing the Date and Time..74
    Changing the Language 76
    Accessibility Settings 79
Understanding Power Options 81
    Shutting Down..81
    Sleep...81
    Hibernate 81
    Working with Power Settings...82
Understanding User Accounts and Rights 84
    User Account Control (UAC) 85
    Creating a New User Account...86
    Rights and Access 88
    Group Policy 89
Lesson Summary 89
Review Questions 90

Lesson 5: Software

Lesson Objectives 91
What is a Software Program? 91
Obtaining Software 91
    Checking the System Requirements 93

Choosing an Application Program..95
    Hardware Implications 95
    Application Types..95
    Integrated Suites 96
    Desktop Publishing..96
    Spreadsheets..97
    Database Management 97
    Presentations..103
    Content Creation 104
    Multimedia 105
    Entertainment 109
    System Protection Tools 112
Disk Management Programs 114
    File Compression Utilities 114
Managing Software...120
    Installing a New Program 120
    Uninstalling a Program 130
    Reinstalling a Program 133
    Updating Software 136
Lesson Summary 139
Review Questions 139

Lesson 6: Troubleshooting

Lesson Objectives..141
What is Troubleshooting?...141
    Managing the Hardware...142
    Keeping Copies of Your Data 145
    Managing the Software 155
    Dealing with Viruses or Malware 157
    Using the Safe Mode 166
Getting Windows Help and Support...167
    Using the Table of Contents 168
    Getting Additional Technical Support..169
    Using the Windows Knowledge Base 171
Using Task Manager 173
Lesson Summary 175
Review Questions 175

Key Applications

Lesson 7: Common Features

Lesson Objectives..177
Getting Started 177
    Starting a Program 177
    Exiting a Program 178
Looking at the Screen 179
    Microsoft Word 2013..179
    Microsoft Excel 2013..180
    Microsoft PowerPoint 2013 180
    Microsoft Access 2013 181
    Accessing Commands and Features...183
Getting Help 187
    Getting Additional Help 190

Manipulating Files 191
    Changing the Program Options 191
    Using Basic Editing Tools..192
    Collaborating with Others 198
    Saving to the Cloud...200
    Using a Network 201
Lesson Summary 205
Review Questions 205

Lesson 8: Microsoft Word

Lesson Objectives..207
Entering and Editing Text 207
    Displaying Formatting Codes 208
    Using the Ruler...208
    Moving Around the Document 208
    Selecting Text...209
    Saving Documents 210
    Starting a New Document...213
    Closing a Document 215
    Opening a Document 216
Customizing the View 217
    Adjusting the Zoom..218
Editing Text 220
    Using Undo...220
    Using Repeat 221
    Using Cut, Copy, and Paste...221
Formatting Text Characters 223
    Using the Font Command 224
    Aligning Text..224
Understanding Tab Settings 226
Working with Indents...230
    Organizing List Information 231
Working with Paragraphs 234
    Changing Line Spacing 234
    Setting Paragraph Spacing..234
    Working with Styles 235
    Using Quick Styles 237
Proofing the Document..241
    Finding and Replacing Items 243
    Using Research Tools...246
Changing the Page Setup 248
    Changing the Paper Size 248
    Changing the Orientation 249
    Changing Margins 250
    Inserting Page Breaks...251
    Adding Page Numbering..252
    Applying Columns 253
Previewing and Printing the Document..256
Using Multimedia Files 260
    Inserting Images 260
    Inserting Multimedia Objects 264
    Manipulating Graphics 264
Using Tables 271
    Inserting a Table...272
    Selecting Items in the Table 273
    Formatting the Table 273

Working with Comments 279
    Tracking Changes 280
Lesson Summary 282
Review Questions 282

Lesson 9: Microsoft Excel

Lesson Objectives 285
Understanding Basic Terminology 285
Managing Workbooks 286
    Creating a New Blank Workbook 286
    Creating a New Workbook from a Template 286
    Entering Data in the Worksheet 288
    Moving Around the Worksheet 289
    Saving Workbooks 289
    Opening Workbooks 290
    Closing Workbooks 291
Manipulating the Contents 293
    Selecting Cells 293
    Using Undo or Repeat 294
    Copying and Moving Data 294
    Changing the Column Widths 297
    Adjusting the Row Height 298
    Manipulating Rows, Columns, or Cells 298
    Managing Worksheets 300
Creating Simple Formulas 303
    Using Common Built-In Functions 305
    Using Absolute and Relative Addresses 306
What Does Formatting Mean? 309
    Formatting Numbers and Decimal Digits 309
    Changing Cell Alignment 310
    Changing Fonts and Sizes 312
    Applying Cell Borders 312
    Applying Colors and Patterns 314
    Using Cell Styles 314
Using the Spell Checker 318
Sorting or Filtering Data 319
    Sorting Data 319
    Filtering Information 322
Working with Charts 324
Getting Ready to Print 330
    Customizing the Printout 331
    Printing the Worksheet 336
Lesson Summary 339
Review Questions 339

Lesson 10: Microsoft PowerPoint

Lesson Objectives 341
What is PowerPoint? 341
    What Does a Presentation Include? 342
Working with Presentations 343
    Creating Presentations 343
    Saving a Presentation 345
    Closing a Presentation 347
    Opening a Presentation 347
    Displaying Information in the Presentation 350
    Moving Around in the Presentation 351

Managing the Slides 354
    Inserting New Slides...354
    Changing the Slide Layout 354
    Deleting Slides...355
    Rearranging the Slides 355
    Changing the Theme 355
    Modifying Themes..355
Managing Slide Objects..359
    Using Select Versus Edit Mode 359
    Manipulating Text...360
    Creating and Using Tables 363
    Creating a Chart...365
    Inserting Pictures or Clip Art Images 372
    Inserting Multimedia Objects 377
Creating a Master Slide 381
    Inserting Headers and Footers 381
Animating Objects 383
    Customizing the Animation 385
    Applying Slide Transitions 387
Running the Slide Show 390
    Setting Up the Presentation 390
    Viewing the Slide Show 390
Previewing or Printing the Presentation 393
    Creating Notes 393
    Creating Handouts 395
    Printing Items 395
Lesson Summary 398
Review Questions 398

Lesson 11: Microsoft Access

Lesson Objectives...401
What is Access?...401
    Access Database File..401
Database Objects...401
    Tables 402
    Forms...402
    Reports 403
    Queries 403
    Object Views..403
Interface Components 403
    The Navigation Pane 404
    Backstage View 404
Managing Database Files...405
    Creating a New Blank Database 405
    Creating a Database from a Template...406
    Saving a Database..407
    Closing a Database 407
    Opening an Existing Database 407
Table Basics 411
    Working with Records 412
Adjusting the View...414
    Switching between Open Objects 415
    Manipulating a Datasheet...415

Finding the Data You Want 416
    Finding Records 417
    Sorting Records 418
    Filtering Records 418
    Using Queries to Find Data 422
Working with Data in Form View 424
What is a Report? 424
    Report Views 425
Designing Reports 428
    Report Layouts 428
    Creating Reports 428
Lesson Summary 432
Review Questions 432

Living Online

Lesson 12: World Wide Web

Lesson Objectives 433
The Internet, Browsers and the World Wide Web 433
    The Internet 433
    The World Wide Web 435
    Web Browsers 436
Understanding Web Site Addresses 437
    Web Site Protocols 437
    Resource Names 437
Common Web Site/Page Elements 438
Browser Features and Functions 440
    Browser Functions 441
    Browser Features 445
Lesson Summary 455
Review Questions 456

Lesson 13: Getting Connected

Lesson Objectives 457
Defining a Network 457
    Advantages of Using a Network 457
    Network Speeds 458
Networking Models 458
    Client/Server Model 458
    Peer-to-Peer Model 459
    Web-based Model 459
TCP/IP and Networking 459
Local Area Networks (LANs) 459
    Connecting to the LAN 459
    Common LAN Devices 460
    Addressing on the LAN 461
    Reserved Address Ranges 463
    Connecting LANs Together 464
Wide Area Networks (WANs) 464
Public Switched Networks 465
    The Public Switched Telephone Network (PSTN) 465
    Circuit Switching 466
    Packet Switching 466

Connecting to the Internet 466
    Dial-Up Connections 466
    Direct Connections – Broadband 467
    Other Factors Affecting Performance 470
Addressing on the Internet 470
    Domain Name System (DNS) 471
The Need for Security 471
    Private vs. Public 472
    Authentication and Access Control 472
    Firewalls/Gateways 472
    Virtual Private Networks (VPN) 474
    Wireless Security 474
Network Troubleshooting 475
    Reviewing the Basics 476
    Troubleshooting Hardware Issues 478
    Troubleshooting Addressing Issues 480
    Troubleshooting Security Settings 481
Lesson Summary 483
Review Questions 483

Lesson 14: Digital Communication

Lesson Objectives 485
How Can I Communicate with Others? 485
    Electronic Mail (Email) 485
    Instant Messages 486
    Text Messages 488
    VoIP 489
    Video Conferencing 490
    Chat Rooms 491
    Social Networking Sites 491
    Blogs 493
    Presence 496
    Standards for Electronic Communication 496
Working with Email 498
    Usernames, Passwords and Credentials 499
Using Microsoft Outlook 503
    Creating New Messages 505
    Receiving Messages 511
    Working with Attachments 516
    Managing Spam 519
    Emptying the Junk E-mail Folder 523
    Automating Outlook 525
Lesson Summary 530
Review Questions 530

Lesson 15: Digital Citizenship

Lesson Objectives 533
Identifying Ethical Issues 533
    Understanding Intellectual Property, Copyrights and Licensing 533
    Censorship and Filtering 538
    Practices to Avoid 539
    Inappropriate Behavior 540
Practicing Good Online Citizenship 541

Protecting Your Data or Computer 542
    Identifying Software Threats 544
    Understanding Viruses 547
Preventing Personal Injuries 551
    Working Safely and Comfortably 552
Protecting Yourself While Online..553
    Buying Online 554
    How Much Information Should I Share?...556
    Protecting Your Privacy...557
Lesson Summary 560
Review Questions 560

Lesson 16: Finding Information

Lesson Objectives...563
Searching for Information...563
    Using Search Engine Technology 567
    Evaluating the Information 574
Lesson Summary 579
Review Questions 579

Appendices

Appendix A: Courseware Mapping ....A 2
Appendix B: Glossary of Terms ....A 5
Appendix C: Index ....A 15

Course Description

This courseware is designed to introduce what digital literacy means and what can be accomplished using a computer. The participant will progress to using popular software application programs to process typical documents found in a business or school environment. Participants are also introduced to what the Internet is and what makes it so popular for communicating and sharing information with others.

This courseware is targeted towards people who are new to computers or have limited exposure to a computer prior to taking this course. The intent of this courseware is to introduce computer knowledge and skill sets that a participant can acquire and then apply to tasks he/she may want to perform using a computing device.

Note: To recognize some of the components that make up a computer, it is preferable to have access to these actual components, wherever possible.

Course Series

This courseware is a composite of three different modules targeting specific skill sets:

- Computing Fundamentals
- Key Applications
- Living Online

The IC[3] Global Standard 4 (GS4) courseware contains exercises that students can use to learn each of the topics and features discussed. Additional resources to practice and apply the skill sets are available from the CCI IC[3] GS4 Microsite. Students are encouraged to register at http://7318.ccilearning.com in order to access these additional activities both during and after completing the course.

Instructor Resources are available and are produced specifically to help and assist an instructor in preparing to deliver the course using the CCI materials. Contact your coordinator or administrator, or call your CCI Account Manager for information on how to access these resources.

Course Prerequisites

This courseware was designed to provide the essential skills for computer literacy, using application programs commonly found in school and business environments. It is intended for those who have not used a web browser, word processor, spreadsheet, presentations, database or email program previously, or have minimal experience. Some familiarity with using a mouse and keyboard can be helpful.

System Requirements

This courseware was developed using specific software and hardware configurations. In order to complete this courseware, you will require the following minimum requirements:

Hardware Requirements

- 1-gigahertz (GHz) 32-bit (x86) processor or 1-GHz 64-bit (x64) processor
- 1 GB (32-bit) or 2 GB (64-bit) of RAM system memory
- Windows Aero-capable graphics card
- 128 MB of graphics memory (minimum)
- 60 GB hard disk that has 16 GB (32-bit) or 20 GB (64-bit) of free hard disk space (the 15GB of free space provides room for temporary file storage during the install or upgrade.)
- Blank DVD or minimum 1GB flash drive to perform backup exercise
- Internet access capability
- Mouse or other compatible pointing device
- 101 enhanced keyboard
- Printer (must have access rights to print)

Software Requirements

- Microsoft® Windows 7 Professional
- Microsoft® Office 2013 Professional
- Windows® Internet Explorer 10.0

The objectives outlined in each lesson can be achieved by properly using the material and exercises in this courseware, and by paying close attention to your instructor. You should not hesitate to ask questions if you have problems in working through the material. To help you understand how some tasks or actions are performed or required in a business environment, CCI builds many of the exercises around a fictional company named Tolano.

All software programs used in this courseware are large and powerful programs, with more features than you can master in a single course. This courseware presents a tremendous amount of material in a simple, easy-to-learn format. You should read ahead during the course; you should also reread regularly. This will increase your retention of important concepts and skills, and will help you cope with the size and power of these programs as you continue to learn.

Classroom Setup

The explanations in this courseware are based on the default settings established during the installation of the Microsoft Windows 7 and Microsoft Office 2013 programs on a networked computer. Your computer (or the computers in the classroom lab) may be configured differently. If so, please check with your instructor (where applicable), or consult the appropriate User's Guide to change the setup.

If you are using another version of Word, Excel, PowerPoint, Access or Outlook, or a different office suite such as Open Office or Google Docs, you will find that all of the concepts are the same; what will change may be some of the steps required to accomplish the task.

To assist with the learning process, CCI has designed exercises for a fictional company called Tolano, consisting of a division named Tolano Environmental Consulting and another division named Tolano Adventures. Typical business documents have been modified to address the type of business that Tolano conducts. All names of employees, vendors and customers of Tolano are fictional and created for the purpose of the CCI Learning solutions only.

Course Design

This courseware was developed for instructor-led training and will assist you during class. Together with comprehensive instructional text and objectives checklists, this courseware provides easy-to-follow hands-on lab exercises and a glossary of course-specific terms.

This course book is organized in the following manner:

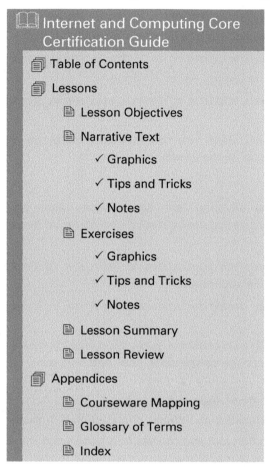

When you return to your home or office, you will find this course book to be a valuable resource for reviewing exercises and applying the skills you have learned. Each lesson concludes with questions that review the material. Lesson review questions are provided as a study resource only and in no way guarantee a passing score on a certification exam. Appendices in the back of this course book provide additional information.

Course Objectives
Computing Fundamentals

The Computing Fundamentals exam covers subjects needed for a foundational understanding of computing, including knowledge and use of computer hardware, software, and operating systems. In this module you will:

- learn how to start a computer and access the operating system.

- look at the different ways files or folders display and explore how to manipulate them.

- look at the different types of computers available, and learn basic hardware terminology.

- learn how to customize your computer using the Control Panel in Windows.

- be introduced to software, and how it is created, and look at different application programs and explore the typical ways software can be used.

- look at what troubleshooting means and what steps you can take to ensure the maximum performance of the hardware and software set up on the computer.

Key Applications

The Key Applications exam includes questions covering four applications (word processing, spreadsheet, presentation, and database software) and includes questions on common features of all applications. In this module you will:

- examine the common features shared between the applications in Microsoft Office 2013 and explore basic techniques for working in an Office application.

- learn some of the basic skills required to create simple documents using Word, including letters, reports, and a brochure.

- be introduced to the basic skills for working with a spreadsheet application, including how to enter and format text and formulas, navigate and manage worksheets, filter and sort data, create and modify charts and set printing options.

- learn basic skills for working with an application designed to manage presentations, set up presentations, and create and edit slides that include text, images, charts, tables, or multimedia.

- be introduced to a relational database management tool you can use to organize and retrieve large amounts of information.

Living Online

The Living Online exam covers aspects of working in an Internet or networked environment, including basic knowledge of networks and the Internet, skills in specific applications such as electronic mail software and Web browsers, skills required to find and evaluate information, and an understanding of issues related to computing and the Internet being used at work, home and school. In the module you will:

- prepare to browse the Internet by reviewing how web sites are organized, and identify common web page elements, and then learn how to perform basic tasks using a web browser.

- examine the hardware, media and configuration settings that are required to connect to an organization's network or to the Internet.

- be introduced to different communication methods and means of sharing information, with an emphasis on using electronic mail.

- examine the practices of good digital citizenship and online safety.

- conduct research and evaluate the information you find on the Internet.

Conventions and Graphics

The following conventions are used in CCI learning materials.

File Names or Database Field Names	File names or database field names are indicated in *italic* font style.
Exercise Text	Content to be entered by the student during an exercise appears in `Courier` font.
Procedures	Procedures and commands you are instructed to activate are indicated in **bold** font style.
Features or Command Options	Menu options and features are listed in the left hand column and corresponding descriptions are in the right hand column.

The following graphics are used in CCI learning materials.

 Specific Keyboard Graphics to easily identify the key to press on the keyboard.

 This icon indicates the numbered objective from the IC3 GS4 exam being covered in this topic. Refer to the Appendix for a complete listing of exam objectives.

Tips are provided when there may be another way to perform a task, or a reminder on how to complete the task.

Notes point out exceptions or special circumstances that you may find when working with a particular procedure, or may indicate there is another method to complete the task.

 When you see this icon, navigate to http://7318.ccilearning.com for **M**ore **M**aterials on the **M**icrosite. These additional activities include online exercises, creative application exercises, fun activities and additional review. They're designed to give you more practice and review of the IC3 GS4 topics and features. Use the microsite in class or at home to practice some of the skills you are having trouble mastering, or to try your skills using different materials.

EXERCISE

Exercise graphics signal the start of step-by-step, hands-on exercises or other activities.

Lesson 1: Operating Systems

Lesson Objectives

In this lesson you will learn how to start a computer and access the operating system. You will also be introduced to Windows. On completion you will be familiar with:

☐ how an operating system works

☐ how to start and exit Windows

☐ what the Windows desktop is

☐ how applications differ from operating systems

☐ how to use the Start button

☐ how to navigate around the desktop

☐ how to use the taskbar

☐ understand the relationship between software and hardware

☐ understand software updates

What is an Operating System?

 Exam 1 - Objective 1.1

Throughout this course, you will learn about using computers. A computer is essentially a collection of connected components and devices which must be able to communicate with each other and with the user in order to function correctly and efficiently.

Communication is made possible through collections of computer code known as programs, operating systems, and device drivers. The components and devices described above are known collectively as hardware. Programs, operating systems and device drivers are known as software.

As you work through this course, you will become familiar and comfortable with various types of hardware and software. In this lesson, you will be introduced to operating systems.

An *operating system* or *environment* is a collection of programs designed to control all the hardware and application software on the computer, and to manage the computer's interaction and communication with the user. It performs two important functions:

- manages the input devices (keyboard and mouse), output devices (monitor and printer), and storage devices (hard, flash, and optical drives)
- manages the files stored on the computer

Every computer requires an operating system to function. A computer must load the operating system into memory before it can load any application software or interact with the user. Examples of operating systems include DOS, Windows, UNIX, Linux, and Mac OS.

Disk Operating System (DOS) was the original operating system developed for the PC. DOS is a text-based software; you enter single line commands to perform such tasks as managing files, starting programs, or sending output to the printer.

Most operating systems (except UNIX) use an integrated *graphical user interface (GUI)*, or "gooey" for interacting with users. In a GUI, many functions and commands are represented by menus and clickable buttons or icons (pictures or symbols which are shortcuts for launching a program or wizard). The GUI makes it possible for a user to "point and click" in order to perform most tasks. This makes it easy for novice users to work with the operating system.

Software programs designed to run on a particular operating system use the same buttons, symbols, or pictures for common functions (such as copy, paste, bold, save, print, and so on) as those used in the operating system. This consistency reduces the time required to learn new software.

The operating system manages hardware, programs and files. For example, you would use the operating system to copy a file.

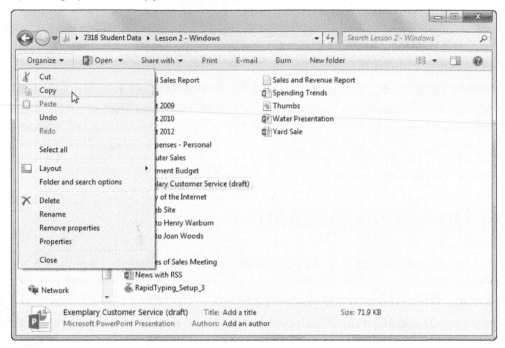

Application software, on the other hand, allows a user to be productive – to create documents or complete specific tasks such as writing a report, creating a budget, removing red-eye from a photograph, watching a movie, or searching the Internet. Examples of application programs you may use include Microsoft Word, Adobe Photoshop, Windows Media Center, or Internet Explorer. For example, you would use an application program such as Microsoft Word to create a letter.

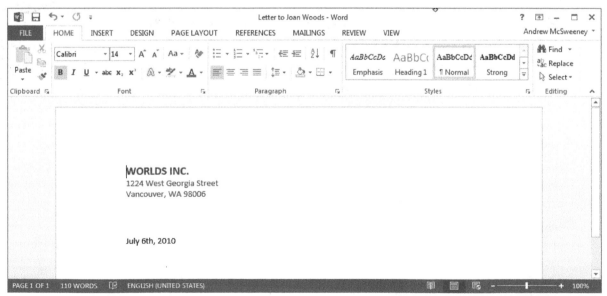

While a user works in an application program, the application program interacts with the operating system behind the scenes.

Modern Operating Systems

There are several operating systems in wide use today and it is not uncommon for an organization to include computers which run different operating systems. Consequently, operating systems are designed with a certain amount of interoperability, which is the ability for different operating systems to communicate and share/exchange information with one another.

The following screens are examples of the first screen that appears when you start the computer and the operating system loads into memory. This screen is commonly known as the Desktop.

Microsoft Windows 8.1

Microsoft released this edition of the Windows operating system in October 2012. Major changes were made to the functions of the operating system and how items display on the screen were drawn from consumer experiences with mobile operating systems. For instance, you can now select items on the screen by touching the item, similar to how you can select items on your mobile phone or tablet. The 8.1 upgrade was released in October 2013 which included a Start button on the desktop. The screen is an example of how Windows 8 appears after you start it, before accessing the desktop:

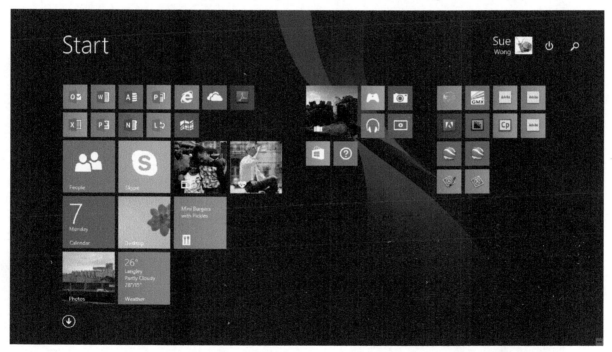

Microsoft Windows 7

Windows 7 is an operating system for PCs released in October 2009. Like earlier Windows products, it includes a *WYSIWYG (What You See Is What You Get)* screen display, which provides an instant preview of what is available. Windows 7 is designed to make computing simple and easy.

Mac OS

Mac OS is designed by Apple Inc. for the Macintosh computers. It was one of the original graphic user interface systems and set the standard for true WYSIWYG programs. Newer versions of the Macintosh operating systems use UNIX as the underlying structure, providing a very secure and stable operating environment. The most recent version is OS X Mavericks.

UNIX

UNIX was one of the first multi-tasking, multi-user operating systems and was originally developed in 1969. Unlike Windows or Mac OS which were designed for desktop systems, UNIX was originally developed for use on large mainframe computers and servers. Modern versions are available for desktop systems, and include a GUI; however, the GUI is separate from the operating system. (You can uninstall the GUI and still have a completely functional UNIX system.) UNIX is widely used in universities and scientific or research organizations, and is often used on machines which support engineering or computer-aided design (CAD) applications.

Linux

First developed in 1991, Linux is a UNIX-like operating system which is freely available and modifiable. Linux is packaged into formats called distributions. A distribution includes the operating system, various utilities and libraries, and even some application software. Distributions available for servers and desktop systems usually include a GUI desktop. Linux is widely used on supercomputers and high-end servers, and is very popular with entrepreneurial software developers.

Handheld Operating Systems

These operating systems are used on PDAs and Smartphones; the options for each system vary depending on the type of handheld device. Popular handheld operating systems include Windows Phone, Android, iOS and Blackberry.

Embedded Operating Systems

Embedded operating systems manage and control operations on the specific type of equipment for which they are designed, such as a vehicle, a machine that controls robotic manufacturing, or a piece of medical equipment. When the equipment is turned on, the embedded operating system loads into memory. Embedded operating systems are designed to be compact and are highly specialized; they include only the functions that are required by the specific devices for which they are developed.

EXERCISE

In this activity, your instructor will show one or two short videos that introduce the power and flexibility of modern operating systems. If there is insufficient class time to view both videos, your instructor will select one. The first video compares Windows 7 to Linux, giving you a glimpse into how another operating system works. The second video demonstrates some features of an operating system for an Apple machine.

1. **Instructor:** Open a web browser and play one or both of the following videos:

    - **Windows 7 vs. Linux: The Desktop Comparison** (approx. 8 minutes)
      http://www.youtube.com/watch?v=QHCDU-CUoaQ&feature=related

    - **Mac OS X Lion Demo** (approx. 5 minutes)
      http://www.youtube.com/watch?v=BlPjQ6a6Dal

2. **Instructor:** After showing the video(s), close the browser and lead a short discussion on the following questions:

    a. How do the operating systems compare to one another?

    b. Does either one of them seem significantly more feature-rich or powerful than the other?

    c. What factors might be considered when deciding which operating system to use?

    d. Which one looked most intriguing to you?

Operating System Capabilities and Limitations

Operating systems provide specific capabilities and limitations. Following are some examples:

- You can save files using names that are up to 255 characters long, enabling a detailed description of a file's contents.

- If you are using a PC (that is, running a Windows operating system), you cannot include certain characters (\ / : * < > ? |) in a file name, whereas with a Mac only the colon cannot be used in file names.

- You can open multiple programs at the same time; the number of simultaneous programs you can run is restricted only by the amount of memory available to support each program. (You will learn more about memory later in the course.)

- You can customize an operating system to suit your personal preferences by changing the desktop background, the color, or the screensaver. In a corporate network environment, your customization options may be restricted; for example, you may not be allowed to change certain system settings, or you may be forced to adhere to company standards for colors, background picture, and so on. In some school environments, the network is set to provide a standard format for the operating system so that any custom changes revert to the default settings when the computer is shut down.

- On a stand-alone computer, you may be able to install programs or download items from the Internet. On a system within an organization, you may not have sufficient rights to perform such tasks. (You may also be restricted from activities on a stand-alone computer if you do not have administrative rights for that computer.)

- Your access to files located on a network could be restricted. For example, you may be able to view the contents of folders for other departments but be unable to move or delete any of these files.

Common Operating System Features

IC³ Exam 1 - Objective 1.1

Modern operating systems not only interact with hardware and programs, but also allow for multiple users to use the same computer. The operating system can maintain separate accounts for each user, keep track of each user's documents and settings, and keep user accounts secure.

When you first turn on a Windows 7 computer, one of two things can happen. If you are the only user on the computer and your user account does not require a password, then you will be automatically logged on to your account and the Desktop appears.

If you are using a computer on which multiple user accounts have been set up, or if your user account requires a password, then Windows displays an icon and account name for each user account and you must log on to your account by clicking your account icon and entering your password.

> MMM
> Recognizing
> Valid Files

Power On / Power Off

Powering on and powering off a computer are two different processes. When you first power on (start) the computer, you press the power button. The computer runs a set of self-diagnostic programs to ensure that critical hardware is working properly, and then it loads the operating system into memory. Once the operating system is loaded, you are either logged on to your account automatically or you must log on manually.

Although you simply press the power button to turn the system on, you should never simply press the power button to turn the system off. You should always use the operating system's Power Off or Shut Down option. This option ensures that any changes you have made to the system are properly saved, and that any temporary files, which are no longer needed, are deleted.

Starting the Computer

On many desktop computers, the power switch is located at the front or top of the system case. The power switch for the monitor is usually located at the lower right corner. Do not try to feel for the switches the first time you want to start the computer – locate them visually.

Some desktop systems include a Reset button. Pushing the Reset button causes the system to restart without powering all the way down.

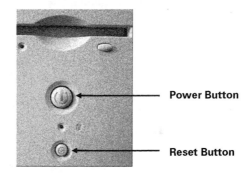

Power Button

Reset Button

The location of the power button on a notebook will vary from the outside left or front side of the notebook to the top of the notebook, usually above the keyboard. Perform the following steps to correctly power on a computer:

1. Turn on everything connected to the system unit (such as the monitor and printer) first. This ensures a steady flow of power to the system unit when it is finally turned on. Otherwise, the power to the system unit could be interrupted each time one of these devices is turned on.

2. Turn on the system unit. Make sure that this is the last power switch you turn on.

Several lines of information are displayed to the screen; this is the diagnostic part of the operating system checking that everything is working. The computer then starts to look for the operating system files.

What is Happening in the Background?

The process of turning on the computer and loading the operating system is called *booting* the computer. The term is derived from the phrase *to pull oneself up by one's bootstraps*, and calls to mind the paradox that a computer cannot run without first loading software but some software must run before any software can be loaded.

Special computer chips called ROM-BIOS chips are used to make the bootup procedure possible. When the computer is powered on, it loads the instructions stored in ROM-BIOS into memory and then executes the instructions. (You will learn about ROM-BIOS in a later lesson.) The computer then takes an inventory of its internal and external equipment and performs several self-tests collectively known as the power on self-test (POST). The BIOS program checks and counts the memory, and then the computer looks for and loads the operating system into memory. Messages may display on the screen, or the text "Starting Windows" may appear on screen.

When the operating system is loaded, Windows will display a Welcome screen, quickly followed by the Windows desktop.

If the computer is connected to a network or set up for multiple users, Windows will display a logon screen. In this case, you must enter the appropriate account information to log on to the computer before you can access the Desktop. A sample logon screen is shown here.

If a logon screen displays, click the icon for your user account or enter your login ID, type your password and press (Enter). When you have logged on successfully, the Windows 7 Desktop displays.

Exiting the Computer Properly

It is important that you save your files, close open programs, and either log off or shut down the computer when you finish working in order to prevent unauthorized access to your files and, more importantly, to your company's network.

Never turn off your computer without closing your files and open software programs in the correct manner; always shut down or log off properly. This will protect the software and data files from being corrupted or lost.

In Windows 7, you click the Start button to access the Shut Down options. You can click the **Shut down** button to turn off the system, or you can select one of the options in the menu that appears to the right of the Shut down button. When you shut down, the computer closes all open files, closes all programs, exits the operating system and then completely turns off the computer.

Shut down   **Shut down options**

Click the ▶ to display several options including:

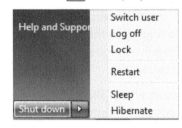

Switch user	Switches to another user account without logging out of the current account. Clicking this option takes you to the log on screen.
Log off	Closes all open items, logs out of the current user account, and returns to the log on screen.
Lock	Hides the desktop behind a log on screen. You can use this option if you need to walk away from your desk. When you lock the system, all your programs and files remain open and ready, but only the log on screen displays and you must enter the log on password before you can resume working. If you are working on your company network, you may be required to press (Ctrl)+(Alt)+(Delete) to enter a login ID and password to identify your account. Once your network account has been validated, the computer will unlock. In cases where there is no password associated with the currently logged on account, the user need only press (Enter).

Restart	Closes all open items and restarts the computer without powering down; also called a reboot or warm boot. Restarting the system in this manner clears the memory and reloads the operating system, but does not cause the system to perform the self-diagnostic tests.
Sleep	Puts the computer in a state called sleep mode, where it consumes less power. When a computer is in sleep mode, the display turns off and often the computer fan stops. A light on the outside of the case may blink or turn yellow to indicate that the computer is asleep. Windows puts your work and settings into memory and then draws only a low amount of power. When you wake the computer, the screen will look exactly as it did when you put it to sleep. If you are using a desktop computer, the Sleep command may appear as Standby.
Hibernate	Available only on notebooks; click this option to put a notebook into a mode where it draws no power. Hibernation is like sleep mode, except that instead of maintaining the current state of all programs and files in memory, the computer writes them to the hard disk and then turns off the system. When you press the power button on a notebook that is in hibernation, the system starts back up and resumes the state it was in when you put it into hibernation. That is, your programs and files are read back into memory from the hard disk, and you can resume where you left off. Hibernate mode is designed to save battery power on notebooks and is not available on desktop systems.

Always allow Windows to complete the Shut down or Restart process properly. Reactivating the computer before Windows has completed these processes may cause files to be corrupted and result in a message, the next time you turn on the computer, indicating the machine was not shut down properly.

If a power failure occurs while a computer is in Sleep or Standby mode, you will lose any unsaved information, so be sure to save your work every time you leave the computer, even if you will not be gone for long. To turn off Standby and return to normal mode, simply move the mouse or press a key on the keyboard.

To turn off hibernation, press the Power button on the notebook.

EXERCISE

In this exercise you will turn on the computer to start the operating system. You will also log on to Windows and explore various Shut down options. If you require assistance identifying/locating objects on the screen, ask your instructor for assistance. Navigating the Desktop will be covered in detail later in this lesson. For now, you will simply explore power on and power off techniques.

1. Identify where the power buttons are located on your computer and the monitor.
2. Turn on the monitor, then press the power button to turn the computer on.
3. Watch the monitor and note any messages or prompts that display.
4. If a Windows logon screen appears, click the icon for your user account and enter your password to log on to Windows. (Ask your instructor for assistance if necessary.) When you have successfully logged on to Windows, the Desktop displays.
5. Click the **Start** button in the lower left corner of the desktop to open the Start menu.

6. Point the mouse pointer over the **Shut down** options arrow to view the Shut down options menu. (Ask your instructor for assistance if necessary.)

7. In the Shut down options menu, click **Switch user** to access the log on screen. If there are multiple accounts on the computer, an icon will display for each user account.

8. Click the icon for your user account and enter your password if necessary to return to the Desktop.

9. Point the mouse pointer over the **Shut down** options arrow to view the Shut down options menu again.

10. In the Shut down options menu, click **Log off** to log out of your account and return to the Windows log on screen. Again, if there are multiple accounts on the computer, an icon will display for each user account.

11. Click the icon for your user account and enter your password, if necessary, to return to the Desktop.

12. Display the Shut down options menu.

13. In the Shut down options menu, click **Lock** to lock the system.

    Notice that the Desktop is hidden by a log on screen that displays only the account which is currently logged on.

14. Click the icon for your user account or enter your password if necessary to return to the Desktop.

15. Display the Shut down options menu, then click **Sleep** (or Standby) to put the computer to sleep.

    Notice that the screen goes dark. Has the power light changed color?

16. Press a key on the keyboard or press the power button to wake the computer. If your system has been configured to require a password upon waking, then putting the system to sleep also locks it and you will have to click the icon for your user account or enter your password to return to the Desktop. If your system has not been configured to require a password upon waking, then you are returned to the Desktop immediately.

17. If necessary, click the icon for your user account or enter your password to return to the Desktop.

18. Display the Shut down options menu, then click **Restart** to restart the system.

    Notice that Windows shuts down, and then starts again without performing the self-diagnostic tests that run when you first power on the system.

19. When the log on screen displays, click the icon for your user account and enter your password if necessary to access the Desktop.

20. Click the **Start** button, then click the **Shut down** button to power off the system.

    Notice that Windows shuts down, and then the system turns off.

21. Press the power button on the computer to start the system.

22. Log on to Windows.

Looking at the Windows Desktop

 Exam 1 - Objective 1.2

The Windows 7 Desktop will look similar to the following screen. You will notice several objects or icons on the desktop; these vary from one system to another depending on how the system was set up.

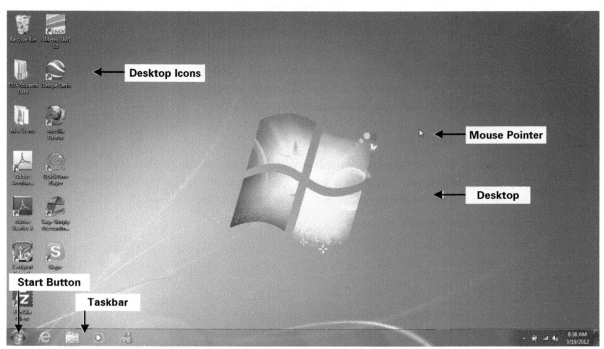

Desktop Icons	These are "shortcuts" you can select to open frequently used programs, folders, or files.
Mouse Pointer	The arrow that follows the movement of the mouse. Use the mouse pointer to identify which option you want to select or activate.
Desktop	This is the work area or screen on which windows, icons, menus, and dialog boxes appear. You can customize the appearance of the desktop using features such as wallpaper, themes, pictures, or solid colors, and you can create shortcuts that will take you directly to frequently used folders, files, programs, or web pages.
Start Button	Use the Start button to start programs, open documents, find items on your computer, and get help, as well as log off and shut down your computer.
Taskbar	The Taskbar is the long horizontal bar at the bottom of the screen. It includes three main sections: the Start button, the middle section (which displays the taskbar buttons for open programs and files), and the notification area (which includes a clock and icons that communicate the status of certain programs and computer settings). The taskbar is an integral part of Windows' multitasking features.

Navigating Around the Desktop

Using a Pointing Device

You can use a pointing device such as a mouse or the touchpad to move the mouse pointer on the desktop, or to select or activate items. Using a pointing device is faster than using the keyboard to navigate to different areas or options on the screen.

- To select an item, move the mouse pointer (arrow) over top the item and then click the left mouse button once. This action is called a **single-click**.

- To activate an item, point the arrow at the item and then press the left mouse button twice in quick succession; this action is called a **double-click**.

- To display a shortcut menu with more options, point the arrow at the item and then click the right mouse button once; this action is called a **right-click**.

Using the Keyboard

A number of features can be accessed through keyboard shortcuts. For instance, to display the Start button, you can press the 🪟 button on the keyboard, press (Esc) to cancel an action, or press (Tab) to move to the next field in a dialog box. Many keyboard shortcuts are standardized between applications, and are listed in this courseware when applicable.

Using the Start Button

 The Start button is the primary means of starting programs, finding files, accessing online help, logging off Windows, switching between users, or shutting down the computer. You can use the mouse or the keyboard to navigate through the Start menu.

To activate the Start button, you can:

- Click the **Start** button, or

- press 🪟, or

- press (Ctrl)+(Esc).

When you click the Start button, the Start menu opens:

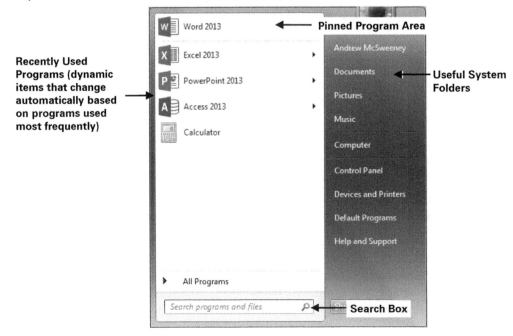

A ▶ (triangle) with a command beside it indicates that a submenu will display when you click or point to an item. For example, when you point to the All Programs command, Windows displays a list of all programs available on your system.

To return to the main Start menu, point to or click the **Back** command.

Items with a ▨ (folder) icon indicate there is sub list of options (in alphabetical order) that you can choose to start.

Items can be selected from the Start menu using the mouse or keyboard.

- If using the mouse, click the **Start** button once. Point to **All Programs** to display a list of programs you can click to start. If a program name appears in a folder, click the folder to open it and display a list of options for the program, then click the option you want to start.

- If using the keyboard, press the ⊞ key to display the Start menu. Then press the arrow directional keys to navigate to the required command, and when it is highlighted, press ⏎Enter⏎ to activate it. To move quickly to a main area such as the Shut Down button, press ⎋Tab⎋ until the item is highlighted and press ⏎Enter⏎ to activate it.

EXERCISE

In this exercise you will explore the Desktop and navigate the Start menu.

1. If necessary, start the computer and log on to Windows.

2. When the Desktop is visible, put your hand on the mouse appropriately and then slide the mouse along your desk and watch how the mouse pointer (⌕) follows the movements you make with the mouse.

3. On the keyboard, press ⊞ to open the Start menu.

4. On the keyboard, press ⎋Esc⎋ to close the Start menu.

5. Click the **Start** button to display the Start menu again.

6. In the Search field near the bottom of the Start menu, type: `windows experience`.

    A list of possible matches for the term you typed displays at the top of the menu.

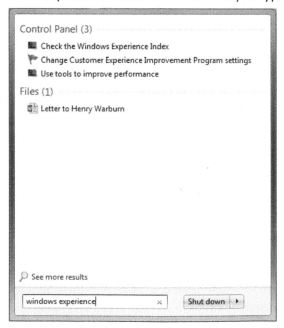

7. At the top of the menu, click **Check the Windows Experience Index**. Windows opens the Performance Information and Tools window on the Desktop.

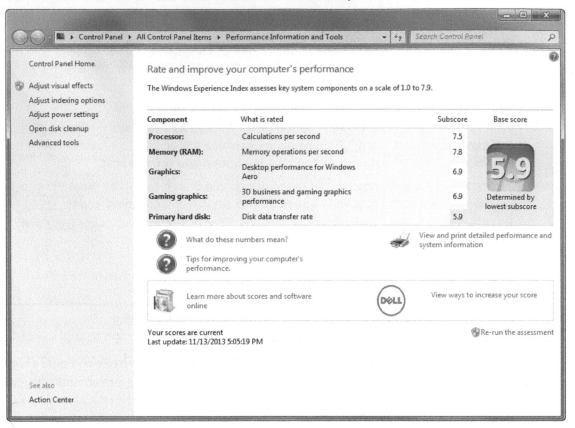

The information displayed in this window will vary from system to system. This feature calculates a rating of how your system will perform based the installed hardware and software.

8. Click the **X** **(Close)** button at the top right corner of the window to close the window.

Working with an Application Program

Application programs are the packages such as Microsoft Word or Windows Notepad that you use to create documents or presentations or spreadsheets. These are the programs that allow people to perform productive work using computers. Every operating system provides a method for starting application programs. In Windows, you can use the **Start** button at the lower left corner of the screen or click an icon on the Desktop.

When you start an application program, Windows (the operating system) loads a copy of the program into memory. When you close the application program, the memory that was used by the application is released and available for the operating system to reallocate to another task.

As you work with application programs, the operating system monitors your work in order to identify specific requirements. For example, if you attempt to close a file that has not been saved, the operating system will notify you and ask if you would first like to save your changes.

Using the Taskbar

By default, the taskbar appears at the bottom of the Windows desktop. It includes the Start button, a notification area, the clock, and a taskbar button for each open program. Windows also automatically installs some commonly-used programs in the taskbar for easy access, as an example, File Explorer.

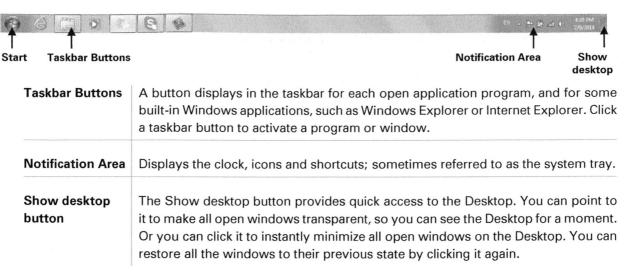

Start   Taskbar Buttons   Notification Area   Show
                                                                                           desktop

Taskbar Buttons	A button displays in the taskbar for each open application program, and for some built-in Windows applications, such as Windows Explorer or Internet Explorer. Click a taskbar button to activate a program or window.
Notification Area	Displays the clock, icons and shortcuts; sometimes referred to as the system tray.
Show desktop button	The Show desktop button provides quick access to the Desktop. You can point to it to make all open windows transparent, so you can see the Desktop for a moment. Or you can click it to instantly minimize all open windows on the Desktop. You can restore all the windows to their previous state by clicking it again.

The notification area displays the time and provides quick access to items such as the volume control or a wireless network connection. It can also display information about the status of the power level of a laptop battery or whether operating system updates are available. You can also control which icons are visible.

You can move the taskbar or change the way it displays as follows:

- Position the mouse pointer over a blank area of the taskbar and drag it to any side of the screen.

- To prevent changes to the taskbar, right-click any blank area of the taskbar and ensure that the **Lock the taskbar** feature is active. (The feature is active if its check box is checked.)

- To customize the properties for the taskbar, right-click the area you want to customize or right-click the **Start** button, and then click **Properties**.

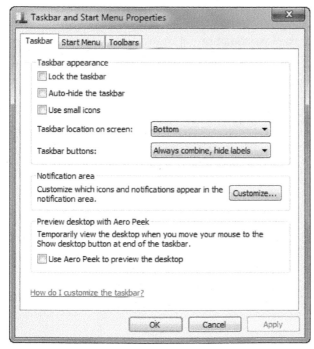

- To reduce clutter, Windows hides icons in the notification area when you haven't used them in a while. If icons become hidden, click the Show hidden icons button  to temporarily display the hidden icons.

When you open a program, a button appears in the taskbar as a visual clue that program is running. As you open or create files within that program, a preview window appears for each file when you point at the program button on the taskbar.

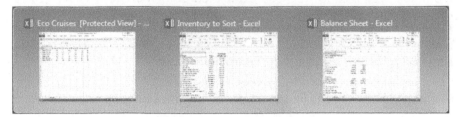

EXERCISE

In this exercise, you will practice using the pointing device to activate different items on the desktop, and you will work with the Start menu and the Taskbar.

1. Right-click the time in the notification area and review the items on the shortcut menu.

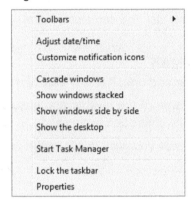

2. Click in an empty area of the Desktop to close the shortcut menu.

3. Right-click the time in the notification area, then select **Properties** from the shortcut menu to open a window that allows you to control system icons.

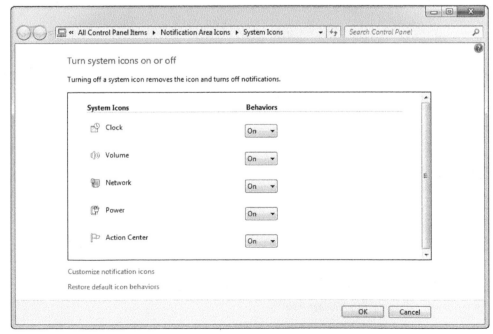

4. Scroll through the list of items to see what you can adjust, and then click **Cancel** to close the window.

5. Click the  in the notification area to view any hidden icons, then click in an empty area of the Desktop to close the hidden icon window.

You will now start a program using the Start menu.

6. Click **Start**, point to **All Programs**, scroll and click **Accessories**, and then click **WordPad**. Windows opens the WordPad application in its own application window. All application programs run inside their own dedicated application window.

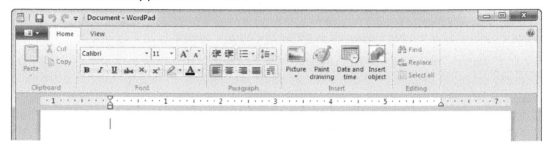

Now try using the taskbar.

7. Click the **Internet Explorer** button in the taskbar to open a web browser. (Ask your instructor for assistance if you cannot locate the Internet Explorer button.)

8. Point at the Internet Explorer button in the taskbar.

    Windows displays a small preview window of the web page you currently have displayed on the screen. Notice also that the button now has a border around it to indicate this program is active.

9. Click the folder button to the right of Internet Explorer to open Windows Explorer.

    Windows Explorer is the file management tool for Windows. (Windows Explorer is covered later in this courseware).

10. Click the **Show desktop** button at the right edge of the taskbar to make the open windows invisible and display only the Desktop.

11. Click the **Show desktop** button again to redisplay the open windows.

12. Point at the Internet Explorer button in the taskbar.

    Notice that the web browser is still open even though you started additional programs from the taskbar.

13. With the web page preview window displayed, click the **Close** button in the preview window to close Internet Explorer without having to make the browser window active.

14. Click the **Close** button for Windows Explorer to close this program. Now only the WordPad window remains open.

15. Click the **Close** button in the WordPad window to close the application.

The Software/Hardware Relationship

 Exam 1 - Objective 1.1

As you have learned, the physical components and devices that comprise the computer are called hardware. The operating system and application programs that run on the computer are called software. Although you have been only very briefly introduced to operating systems and application programs, you should understand the nature of the relationship between hardware and software.

All software, whether operating system software or application program software, is designed to work with specific types of computer hardware. As computers have evolved over time, their speed and storage capacity have steadily increased. Software is designed to take advantage of the speed and capacity offered by modern systems as these become available.

For this reason, new software (designed with modern computing systems in mind) may not run correctly on older systems if those older systems are not fast enough or cannot provide the required capacity. This situation creates an interesting dynamic: if you must use a particular version of software in order to perform a task, then that choice of software may dictate which type of computer system you can use. You may have to replace an old desktop system with a new one. On the other hand, if you do not have a choice regarding your system hardware (that is, perhaps you were given an older system and you cannot change it), then you must select software that will run on the system you have available.

As you progress through this course, you will learn more about hardware and software, and you will revisit and re-examine the software/hardware relationship.

Understanding Updates

 Exam 1 - Objective 1.1

Operating systems are routinely updated for the purposes of increasing security, fixing bugs and adapting to new hardware. Application programs and plug-ins (specialized programs that run inside web browsers) are updated as well. Updates can be released in various forms. These include:

- **Patches** – a patch is a file of programming code that is inserted into an existing program to fix a known problem, or bug. Patches are designed to provide an immediate solution to a particular programming problem. Patches are intended to be only temporary solutions until problems can be permanently repaired.

- **Updates** – an update is a file or collection of software tools that resolves security issues and improves performance. Updates are released when necessary.

- **Service Packs** – a service pack is a collection of updates that is typically released after enough updates have accumulated to warrant the release. Service packs typically contain all previous updates, which include security patches, bug fixes, and new features.

Microsoft provides updates for the Windows operating system (and the Internet Explorer web browser) through a service called Windows Updates. The updates can be downloaded from the Windows Update web site.

There are different kinds of updates. Security updates or critical updates protect against security vulnerabilities and viruses and spyware. Other updates correct errors that are not related to security, or enhance functionality.

Automatic Updating

Windows Update can be set to automatically check for and install the latest updates. You can also set Windows Update to check for and download updates and then alert you that updates are ready to be installed. You can even set it not to check for updates at all.

You can manually check for (and install) available updates at any time.

Update Categories

Updates are categorized based on their importance. There are three categories for updates:

- **Important** – these updates include security and critical updates.

- **Recommended** – these updates include software updates and new or improved features. Depending on how you set up Windows Updates, recommended updates can be shown together with important updates, or with optional updates.

- **Optional** – these updates include software that you can install manually, such as new or trial Microsoft software or optional device drivers from Microsoft partners.

EXERCISE

In this exercise you will examine the settings for Windows Update. The following steps assume that you are logged on to a Windows 7 computer. If you are using a different version or different operating system, please check with your instructor on how to access the update feature for the operating system appropriately.

1. Click the **Start** button.

2. In the search field at the bottom, type: `windows update`.

3. Click **Windows Update** at the top of the menu.

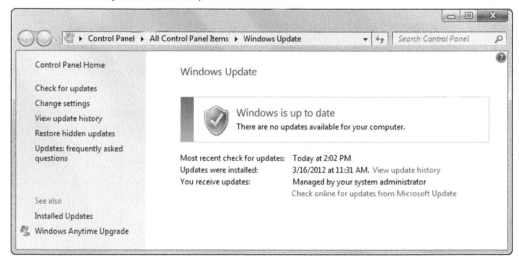

The panel at the left provides links for working with updates.

4. In the panel at the left, click **Change settings**.

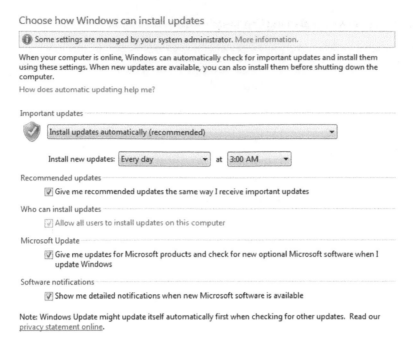

The preceding figure indicates that updates are currently set to be installed automatically each day at 3:00 AM. This is the default setting, but may be different on your system.

5.   Click the drop-down arrow to view the options for how and when to install updates.

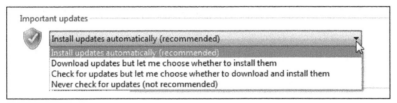

6.   Click in a blank area of the screen to close the drop-down list.

7.   Click **Cancel** to exit the window without changing any settings.

You can also check for updates manually at any time, as long as your computer is connected to the Internet.

8.   In the left pane, click **Check for updates**. It may take a few minutes for Windows to check for available updates. If any new updates are available, Windows may display a screen similar to the one shown below:

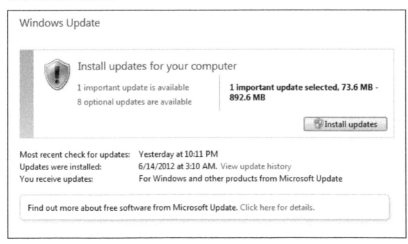

You can manually install updates by clicking the **Install updates** button.

If no new updates are available, Windows will indicate that as well.

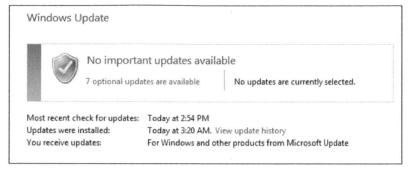

9. Regardless of whether updates are available, click the close button at the upper-right corner of the window to close the Windows Update screen.

Lesson Summary

In this lesson you learned how to start a computer and log on to the operating system. You also explored the Windows environment. You should now be familiar with:

- ☑ how an operating system works
- ☑ how to start and exit Windows
- ☑ what the Windows desktop is
- ☑ how applications differ from operating systems
- ☑ how to use the Start button

- ☑ how to navigate around the desktop
- ☑ how to use the taskbar
- ☑ understand the relationship between software and hardware
- ☑ understand software updates

Review Questions

1. For which of the following tasks would you use an operating system?
   a. To create a Contacts list.
   b. To delete files from a folder.
   c. To calculate the return on an investment.
   d. To edit audio and video files.

2. How can you tell where the cursor is on the Windows desktop?
   a. The Start button.
   b. Press the Spacebar to view it.
   c. The white arrow.
   d. The last button on the Windows taskbar.

3. How do you display a shortcut menu for an item on the Windows desktop?
   a. Click the left mouse button.
   b. Click the right mouse button.
   c. Double-click either mouse button.
   d. Tap the scroll wheel.

4. To see the programs installed on your system, which option from the Start button would you use?
   a. Documents
   b. All Programs
   c. Search
   d. List of Quick Start items

5. Circle in the following image which button you would use in the notification area to display the desktop immediately:

6. What is the best way to shut down the computer?
   a. Press the power switch on the computer case.
   b. Click Shut down from the Start button and let it complete the process.
   c. Press Ctrl + Alt + Delete twice.
   d. Press Esc.

7. What is a service pack?
   a. A collection of software updates.
   b. A form of spyware.
   c. A shut down mode designed to conserve battery power.
   d. An embedded operating system.

MMM
Go online for
Additional
Review

Lesson 2: Files and Folders

Lesson Objectives

In this lesson, you will look at the different ways files or folders display and explore how to manipulate them. On completion you will be familiar with:

☐ how to work with a typical window

☐ what a file or folder is

☐ selecting files or folders

☐ copying or moving files or folders

☐ changing the view for drives, files or folders

☐ how to view or modify file or folder properties

☐ renaming files or folders

☐ finding files

Looking at a Typical Window

 Exam 1 - Objective 1.2

When programs or folders are opened, they appear on the desktop in individual "windows." You can have multiple windows displayed on the screen, and each may appear different from the others, but each window shares similar features.

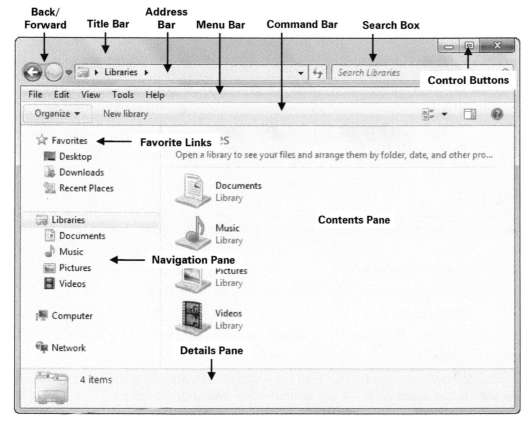

Back / Forward	Use to navigate back or forward to display previous views of files or folders.
Title Bar	Displays the name of the currently active feature or application program. (In the example shown above, the name of the window appears in the Address Bar, instead of the Title bar.

Menu Bar	Displays the names of pull-down menus which contain commands for performing specific tasks. By default the menu bar is not displayed, but you can set it to display all the time using the **Organize** menu options. You can also press (Alt) or (F10) to temporarily display the menu bar.
Command Bar	Provides commands you can use to organize, view, or protect your data.
Address Bar	Indicates the current location and facilitates quick and easy navigation. This feature allows you to click the name of any folder visible in the trail so that you can go to that folder, or click the arrow that appears next to any item and see other items at the same level in the folder hierarchy.
Search Box	Provides an area into which you can enter criteria to search for a file or folder.
Control Buttons	Change the way currently open windows are displayed, as follows:
	▢ **(Minimize)** Temporarily closes the window, replacing it as a button on the taskbar. Click the button on the taskbar to open or restore the window.
	▢ **(Maximize)** Displays the window full screen.
	▢ **(Restore Down)** Restores the window to the size it was before it was maximized.
	▢ **(Close)** Closes the window. (If you see a box that only displays a ▢ **(Close)** or ▢ **(Help)** button, you are viewing a *feature window,* with a message about what you must do before being able to do anything else.)
Favorite Links	Displays links to folders or locations you use often. Click a link to go directly to a location.
Navigation Pane	Displays folders and drives that you can double-click in order to see their contents. The navigation pane is also commonly referred to as the Folders list. You can expand or collapse folders using the ▷ or ◢ arrows at the left of the Navigation pane item.
Contents Pane	Displays the contents of the folder or drive selected in the Navigation pane.
Details Pane	Displays properties or details about the selected file or folder in the Contents pane.

EXERCISE

In this exercise you will practice working with the Minimize, Maximize, Restore Down, and Close buttons.

1. Click **Start**, and then click **Computer**.

2. Click the ▢ **(Maximize)** button at the top right corner of the window.

3. Click the ▢ **(Minimize)** button.

    Notice that the window disappears from the screen, but is represented by a button on the taskbar.

4. Click the **Computer** button on the taskbar to redisplay the window.

    The window is now maximized, occupying the entire screen, and the ▢ **(Restore Down)** button now appears in the control buttons, replacing the ▢ **(Maximize)** button.

5. Press (Alt) to display the menu bar.

6. Click **View** to see the menu options.

7. Click **Refresh**.

    Notice how the moment you selected this command, the entire menu bar disappeared. This is an example of how you can activate the menu bar as needed.

8. Click the ▢ **(Restore Down)** button.

9. Click the ▓▓ x ▓▓ **(Close)** button.

The Computer window is now removed from the screen.

Moving a Window

You can move a window anywhere on the desktop using the mouse or keyboard.

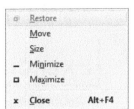

- Position the mouse pointer anywhere on the title bar and then drag the window to a new location.

    With the keyboard, press (Alt)+(Spacebar) to activate the control icon; it is not visible on the screen but the menu appears once it's activated.

    Press the (↓) key to select the **Move** command and press (Enter). Using the arrow direction keys, move the window to the new location and then press (Enter) to exit the action.

Maximized windows cannot be moved because they occupy the entire screen. You can only move a restored (that is, not maximized) window.

Sizing a Window

On occasion you may want to change the size of the window so that you can see more or less of the information inside it, or so that you can view that information in multiple windows. You can use the mouse or the keyboard to size a window.

- Position the mouse pointer anywhere on the border (side) to be sized. When you see the mouse cursor change to a ⬍ (vertical double-headed arrow) for the top or bottom border, or ⬌ (horizontal double-headed arrow) for the left or right border, drag the mouse to the desired size.

- To size the vertical and horizontal sides at the same time, position the mouse cursor on any corner of the window, and then drag to the desired size for the window when you see ⬊ or ⬈ (diagonal double-headed arrow). Some windows are set to a specific size and cannot be altered.

- With the keyboard, press (Alt)+(Spacebar) to activate the control icon; it is not visible on the screen but the menu appears once it's activated. Press the (↓) key to select the **Size** command and press (Enter). Using the appropriate arrow direction key for the side you want to size, press that direction key until the window is the size you want, and then press (Enter) to exit the action. You will need to repeat this action for every side to be sized.

Using Scroll Bars

If a window is too small to display all the contents, scroll bars will automatically appear vertically on the right side of a window, or horizontally at the bottom.

A scroll bar consists of three parts: an arrow button at each end of the scroll bar, a scroll box, and the scroll area. The scroll box is also called a *thumb* or an *elevator*. The position of the scroll box within the scroll area provides an approximate gauge of where the information currently displayed in the window is in relation to the entire window's contents.

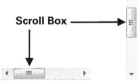

Use one of the following methods to move around with the scroll bars:

- Click in the lighter shaded area above or below the scroll box to display the previous or subsequent screen of information.

- Click the arrow at either end of the vertical scroll bar once to display a line of information in that direction.

- Click the arrow at either end of the horizontal scroll bar once to display a column of information in that direction.

- Click and hold down the mouse button on the arrow at either end of the scroll bar to have the screen scroll in that direction.

- Drag the scroll box to a specific area in the scroll area to move directly to that location. Depending on the program, you may also see a tip showing where the cursor will be placed when you release the mouse button.

EXERCISE

In this exercise, you will move a window around the screen and then resize it.

1. Click **Start**, and then click **Computer**.

2. If the window appears full screen, click the middle button at the top right corner (Restore Down) for the Computer window.

3. Position the mouse pointer on the title bar of the Computer window.

4. Click and drag the window to a new position on the desktop.

5. Practice moving the window around to several different locations.

6. Move the mouse pointer to the right edge of the window and hold the mouse over the border until the pointer changes to a  (horizontal double-headed arrow).

7. Drag the border to approximately one inch (2.5 cm) from the right side of the screen.

8. Move the mouse pointer to the lower right corner of the window and drag the corner of the window until the window is approximately half the current size.

9. Resize the window to approximately the size it was originally.

   Notice that the window was resized vertically and horizontally at the same time.

10. Click the arrow button at the bottom of the vertical scroll bar in the Folders list.

11. Click the arrow button at the top of the scroll bar.

12. Drag the scroll box up and down to view the information in the window.

13. Resize the window so that all of the contents are visible and the scroll bars disappear.

    It is not necessary to perform step 13 before closing the window; the step is provided here for you to practice sizing windows as well as to prepare for forthcoming exercises.

14. Click ▨ **x** ▨ **(Close)** to close the Computer window.

Understanding Files and Folders

 Exam 1 - Objective 1.2

A *file* is created using a specific program; the type of program determines what type of file it is.

Application File	This type of file includes very detailed instructions for the microprocessor on what tasks to perform (such as read, write, calculate) and is usually stored in a folder named for that program, which in turn resides in the Program Files folder on your hard drive.
Data File	This type of file contains information you have entered and saved in one of the applications you have on your computer. For example, you might have created a budget file in Excel, a letter file in Word, a database in Access, and so on. These files can be stored anywhere.
System File	This type of file also contains detailed instructions for the microprocessor on what tasks to perform, except that they are part of the operating system. Many of these files are hidden to protect them from being changed or deleted.

Regardless of the file type, all files appear with an icon that includes a symbol of the associated program. Shown are examples of icons that appear beside an application file (Publisher), a data file (Excel), and a system file (Windows).

mspub.exe   Balance Sheet   win32k.sys

A *folder* is a container for programs and files and provides a method for organizing information; it's something like a hanging folder in a file cabinet within which you can organize other folders and files. A *subfolder* is simply a folder contained within another folder, and the terms folder and subfolder are often used interchangeably. A folder that you create is represented by a yellow icon that looks like a file folder. You can create folders using Windows or an application program.

The organization of files and folders on a disk is called a *directory* or a directory tree. The highest level of any directory on a disk is called the root folder, or the root directory. The root directory is always represented by the disk drive letter followed by a colon (:) and a backslash (\). For example, the root directory of the hard drive is represented as C:\.

Every file on a computer is stored in a particular location on a disk, and that location is described by its *path*. A path indicates the exact route to follow to get to the location of a file. When you write a path, you separate each folder level with a backslash.

Consider the directory structure shown at the right. The structure shows a folder named Libraries with a folder underneath called Documents, and another folder below that called My Documents. Within the My Documents folder is a subfolder called Annual Reports, which contains two folders for previous years and a folder for the current year. Stored within the 2014 folder are several reports: two files saved in a Word file format, five files saved in an Excel file format, and one text file.

If you were to verbally describe how to find the Balance Sheet file, you could say, "Go to Libraries, then Documents, then My Documents, then Annual Reports, then the Balance Sheet document is inside the 2014 folder."

If you were to write your description of how to find the file in "path notation", it would appear as follows: Libraries\Documents\My Documents\Annual Reports\2014\Balance Sheet. However, this is not the actual path to the file – and we will return to this point in a minute.

Windows provides a feature called libraries to help you access your files quickly and easily. A library is a collection of items, such as files and folders, assembled from various locations and presented in one central location.

A library looks and acts like a folder – you can see and use files when you open a library – but the files that appear in a library are actually stored in other locations on the disk. For example, if you have picture files stored in various folders on your hard disk you can access all of them in one place using the Pictures library.

Windows provides four libraries as a start: Documents, Music, Pictures, and Videos.

While libraries make it easy to find folders and files, they can make finding the true path to a file a little confusing.

📚 Libraries
📄 Documents
♪ Music
🖼 Pictures
🎞 Videos

A Windows computer accommodates multiple user accounts and creates a unique user folder for each account. Windows also automatically creates a My Documents folder within each user folder. The files you create while logged on to an account are automatically stored under the account's user folder. For example, if you were logged on as a user named Student01, and you created the directory structure for the annual reports described in the previous example, the actual path to the Balance Sheet file would be: C:\Users\Student01\My Documents\Annual Reports\2014\Balance Sheet.

There are no limitations on where you can store a file, or to the number of folders you can create. Think again about a filing cabinet where you keep hard copies of your documentation. Keeping all your documents in one folder called "My Documents" could seem simple, but without some kind of organization or hierarchy it could take a lot of time to find any particular file within that folder. On the other hand, if you set up too many levels, you would spend all your time "drilling down" through the levels to find what you require.

There is no one correct method for setting up a filing system on your computer; just be sure to follow the company's standards or create a structure that is logical to you and to others who are sharing the computer.

As you've already learned, Windows creates separate My Documents folders for each user account on the system, so if each user logs on using his or her own account, then each user's files are saved to the appropriate folder automatically. If you are saving files to a network drive where others may share this file, you may need to create your own folder structure on that drive for you and others to use.

To begin working with files and folders, use one of the following methods:

- Click **Start** and then click **Computer**, or
- click **Start**, point at **All Programs**, click **Accessories**, and then click **Windows Explorer**, or
- click **Start**, type: `expl` in the **Search** box, and click **Windows Explorer**, or
- right-click the **Start** button and click **Open Windows Explorer**, or
- press 🪟+Ｅ.

Both the Computer window and Windows Explorer allow you to perform the same functions when managing your files and folders. The only difference is what appears when you start Computer versus Windows Explorer: Computer displays the storage devices in the right pane, whereas Windows Explorer displays the contents of the Library folder or area where you may be storing your work.

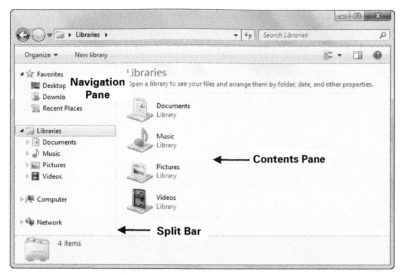

Navigation Pane	Displays several lists. The **Favorites** list contains links to locations you navigate to frequently. The Libraries or Folder List provide shortcuts to locations where the majority of user files stored on the local drive. The Computer or Network areas provide access to all storage devices available on the computer such as the local hard drive, the optical drive, and any network drive(s).
▷ **(Expand)**	Displays more folders or items at this level; you may see several of these arrows depending on the way the structure is set up.
◢ **(Collapse)**	Allows you to hide items or "collapse" the structure at this level; you may see several of these arrows based on the structure set up.
Split Bar	Click and drag this bar to show more or less of the Folders list.
Contents Pane	Displays all files and folders stored in the selected folder at the left in the Navigation Pane.

Files or folders can be saved and displayed anywhere in Windows, including on the Desktop for quick access. Consider the following when viewing files or folders:

 An icon similar to one of these indicates that a data file or folder is saved in this location. If a file is a data file, the miniature icon in the upper left corner represents the program needed to view or modify the document. The text below the icon is the file or folder name. If you delete an icon, you will delete the actual file or folder.

 A similar icon with a small arrow at the lower left corner represents a shortcut to the location where this data file or folder is saved. The arrow indicates that the icon is a shortcut only. If you delete a shortcut icon from the desktop, only the shortcut is deleted not the actual file.

 An icon with a program symbol on it indicates that it is a shortcut to an application program file. If you delete the icon, you are deleting only the shortcut, not the actual file that starts the program.

Creating Folders

You can create folders at any level, including directly on the Windows Desktop. To create a folder, use one of the following methods:

- On the Command bar, click 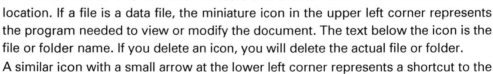 , or

- right-click the location (drive or folder) in the Folders list for the new folder, click **New**, and then click **Folder**, or

- right-click a blank area of the Contents pane, click **New**, and then click **Folder**.

Navigate to the location for the new folder before activating the New Folder command. The Address bar (also known as the Breadcrumb bar) displays the path or current location as a reminder.

Windows does not restrict where you create folders, or whether another folder shares the same name in another location. It is recommended, however, that you keep folder names unique to prevent accidental deletion or replacement of files and folders. You can rename or move any file or folder to another location, as appropriate.

To create a shortcut to a folder, use one of the following methods:

- Right-click the location (drive or folder) in the Folders list for the new shortcut, click **New**, and then click **Shortcut**, or

- right-click a blank area of the Contents pane and then click **New**, and then click **Shortcut**.

EXERCISE

> **Note:** The following exercises require that you have downloaded the student data files. If you have not already done so, please follow the data file instructions in the Preface before proceeding.

In this exercise you will create some folders.

1. On the desktop, double-click the *7318 Student Files* folder.

   Review the screen so you can identify the structure of the folders on the left side of the window. Notice that there are no Collapse arrows displayed in the Folders list.

Try creating some folders in different locations.

2. In the Contents pane, double-click *Lesson 2 - Windows*.

3. On the Command bar, click **New folder**.

   You should now have a new item in the Contents pane similar to the following:

   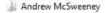

4. Type your first and last name for the new folder and press (Enter).

   You have created a new folder within the *Lesson 2 - Windows* folder. The new folder should look similar to this:

5. Double-click your new folder to view the contents (it should be empty).

6. In the Contents pane, right-click to display the shortcut menu, click **New**, and then click **Folder**.

7. Type: `Personal` and press (Enter).

   You have created a new folder that resides within the folder with your name in the *Lesson 2 - Windows* folder.

8. Move up one level by clicking *Lesson 2 - Windows* in the Address bar, as shown in the following:

   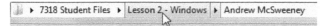

   You should now be looking at the contents of the Lesson 2 folder. Use the path in the Address bar to help you navigate quickly to a specific location. Alternatively, click the last item to move up one level at a time.

Try creating a shortcut to the Student Files folder as a quick method to navigate to the entire set of data files for this courseware. For the purpose of this exercise and to demonstrate how to create a shortcut, you will create this shortcut inside your new folder. For practical application however, you would likely create this shortcut on the desktop to provide quick access on a regular basis to a folder on a local or network drive.

9. Double-click on your folder again to move down to this level. Then in the Contents pane, right-click to display the shortcut menu, click **New**, and click **Shortcut**.

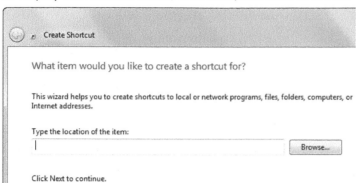

10. Click the **Browse** button.

11. If necessary, scroll until you can see the *7318 Student Files* folder, click to select it, and then click **OK**.

12. Click **Next**.

13. Click **Finish** to keep the name suggested by Windows as the name for the shortcut.

    The contents of your folder should appear similar to:

Now create some subfolders in your folder.

14. In the Contents pane, right-click, click **New**, and then **Folder**.

15. Type: `Worksheets` as the name of the new folder and press (Enter).

16. Repeat steps 14 and 15 to create the *Documents*, *Misc*, and *Slide Shows* folders. When you are finished, your folders should display as shown:

> **Tip:** When adding new folders, be sure to right-click in a blank area of the Contents pane to select **New**, **Folder**. If necessary, make the Computer window larger to show a blank area.

Renaming a Folder

The name of a folder can be as long or short as required (up to 255 characters), although with longer names, the entire name may not be visible in certain views.

To change a folder's name, use one of the following methods:

- Click the folder icon to select it and then press (F2) to activate the Edit mode, or
- click the folder icon, then click inside the folder name to activate the Edit mode, or
- right-click the folder and then click **Rename** from the shortcut menu, or
- on the Command bar, click [Organize ▾] and then click **Rename**.

Whenever you see the folder name highlighted as shown here, you are in Edit mode. Once the name is highlighted, you can type in a new name for the folder. Alternatively, you can use the mouse pointer or arrow keys to move the cursor to the exact location in the folder name where you would like to insert or delete characters.

EXERCISE

In this exercise you will rename folders.

1. Ensure you are viewing your folder and the items appear in the Contents pane.

You will now rename the Documents folder created in the previous exercise to prevent confusion between this folder and the Windows folder that shares the same name.

2. Click the *Documents* folder in the Contents pane to select it. Then point at the name *Documents* and click once more to activate the Edit mode.

3. Press the (Home) key to move quickly to the beginning of the highlighted name. Type: General (include a space) to rename this folder to General Documents and then press (Enter).

    You have now successfully changed the name of this folder.

Changing Folder Options

You can change the appearance of the folder to suit your preferences by changing its properties. You can also change the way you view folders and files, and display file types or extensions.

To change the properties for a folder, select the folder and on the Command bar, click [Organize ▾] and then click **Folder and search options** to open the Folder Options dialog box. This dialog box includes three tabs. The General tab (shown in the following figure) includes three sections:

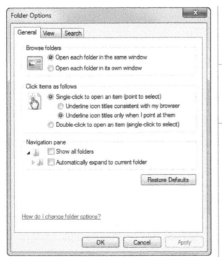

Browse folders

Specifies whether each folder will open in the same window, or in a different window so you can switch between the windows.

Click items as follows

Provides options on whether to single- or double-click to open items.

Navigation pane

Choose which folders should appear in the Navigation pane, or if you want Windows to automatically expand the current folder.

Changing the View

There are different ways to display information for files or folders. Occasionally you may want to sort files in a specific order, or to see more information for the files or folders. Select the view options using one of the following methods:

- Click the arrow of the Views button on the Command bar, or

- right-click in a blank area of the Contents pane and then click **View**, or

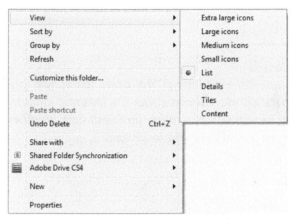

- on the Command bar, click the Views button to cycle through the different views.

Extra Large Icons

Shows files and folders as very large icons, which can be helpful for visually impaired users; file and folder names display below the icon.

Large Icons

Displays files and folders as large icons with file or folder names below the icon. This is helpful when you want to preview the contents of picture files.

Medium Icons

Displays files and folders as medium-sized icons with the names below the icons, and is helpful when you want an overview of folders or files in a certain location.

Small Icons

Lists files and folders as smaller icons with the names displayed to the right. The main difference between this view and the List view is how the contents are sorted. In this view, the contents are sorted alphabetically in multiple columns from left to right. In the List view, the contents are sorted alphabetically from top to bottom in multiple columns starting with the left-most column.

List

Displays the contents of a folder as a list of names preceded by small icons. This view is useful if your folder contains many files and you want to scan the list for a file name. Files and folders can be arranged in the same options as with other views.

Details

Lists the contents of the open folder and provides detailed information about the files and folders inside it, including name, type, size, and date modified; this view also shows files in groups.

Tiles

Displays files and folders as medium-sized icons with the file names to the right of the icon. The file format and file size also display.

Content

Displays any properties or reference information about the contents of the file.

Whenever you can see the column headings in the Contents pane, you can use these buttons to sort the contents or to manipulate the view further, as follows:

- To adjust the width of a column, position the mouse pointer over the vertical line at the right edge of the column you want to adjust; the mouse pointer changes to display ╬ (thick cross hair with double horizontal arrows). Click and drag to the left or right to make the column narrower or wider.

- To sort the contents by item type, click the Type column heading. An ▲ arrow symbol indicates the items are sorted in ascending order (that is, A–Z or 0–9); a ▼ arrow symbol indicates the items are sorted in descending order (that is, Z–A or 9–0).

Understanding File Name Extensions

A file name extension is a suffix added to the base name of a computer file, and separated from the base name by a dot (.). Operating systems and application programs use file name extensions to recognize the format of a file and to identify which program created the file and which program may be used to open the file successfully.

Most operating systems automatically recognize common file name extensions, and associate particular application programs with particular extensions. These associations make it possible for you to double-click a file in order to open it. The operating system launches the necessary application and then opens the file within the application.

Additionally, Windows displays an application icon to the left of the file name, indicating which application is associated with the file type. In general, the icon is a visual reminder of the software program used to create or access the file. If Windows displays a generic file icon, then it does not know which application to use to open the program. In most cases, this is because you do not have an application installed that is capable of opening and editing the specific type of file.

There are thousands of file types and applications. The following section introduces a few of the most common types, and the applications often associated with them.

Audio Files

Audio files are generally produced using specialized applications, but can be played through freely available applications called "players." Common audio players include Windows Media Player, RealNetworks RealPlayer, Winamp2, Winamp3, and XXMS (for UNIX-based systems). When you double-click an audio file, the associated player opens and begins playback of the file. Common audio types include:

.au	Audio format used on UNIX servers.
.aiff	Audio Interchange File Format – developed by Apple Computer, but most browsers can play AIFF files.
.mp3 and m4a	Motion Picture Experts Group MPEG – requires a player application such as iTunes, Apple QuickTime or Windows Media Player.
.ra	RealAudio – audio files that require the RealPlayer application for playback.
.wav	Waveform Audio File Format – this is the native sound format for Windows. Most browsers include built-in support for WAV files.
XMMS	File format used on UNIX-based systems. The XXMS player is available as a free download.

Video Files

Video files are generally produced using specialized applications, but can be played through freely available applications called "players." Common video players include Windows Media Player, RealNetworks RealPlayer, and Apple QuickTime. When you double-click a video file, the associated player opens and begins playback of the file. Commonly-used video file formats include:

.avi	Audio Video Interleave – standard video files for Windows. AVI files play in Internet Explorer through the Windows Media Player.
.mov and .qt	Standard video formats for Apple QuickTime movies, and the native format for Macintosh operating systems.
.mpg or .mpeg	Motion Picture Experts Group – standard format for video files on the Internet.

.ram	Real Audio Metadata file – video format used by RealNetworks RealPlayer or any browser with the RealPlayer plug-in.
.swf	Animation file created with Adobe Flash and played in web browsers through the Flash Player plug-in.

Graphics Files

Graphics files are images. Many graphics formats are supported in web browsers and most operating systems include built-in graphics viewers. Graphics can be imported to a system from a digital camera or scanner, or can be created on a computer using a dedicated graphics creation and manipulation program such as Microsoft Paint, PaintShop Pro, Adobe Illustrator, etc. When you double-click a graphics file, the image displays in either a dedicated graphics editing program, or in a viewer. If the file is not supported, Windows will prompt you to select an application to use to open the file. Common graphics formats include:

.gif	Graphics Interchange Format – graphics format used for line drawings and illustrations.
.jpg or .jpeg	Joint Photographic Experts Group – graphics format used for photographs and complex graphics.
.png	Portable Network Graphics – graphics format commonly used on web pages.
.tif or.tiff	Tagged Image File Format – graphics format commonly used for desktop publishing and medical imaging.

Document Files

Document files can be created using specialized applications, such as those found in the Microsoft Office suite, or in OpenOffice. Some formats, such as PDF and RTF, are designed to be cross-platform compatible. That is, you can open them on Windows systems or Apple systems, or UNIX systems. Double-clicking a document file opens it in an application that can support it (if one is installed on the system). Document file formats include:

.asc	ASCII – a standard text format for all computers, regardless of operating system.
.doc	The default document format for Microsoft Word (prior to version 2007) or Windows WordPad.
.docx	The default document format for Microsoft Word 2007 and above.
.htm or .html	Hypertext Markup Language – the document format used in web pages and supported by all web browsers.
.pdf	Portable Document Format – document format supported on all operating systems through the use of the Adobe Reader plug-in. A full version of Adobe Acrobat is required to edit a PDF file. Microsoft Office files can be saved to PDF format to make them cross-platform compatible.
.ppt	The default presentation format Microsoft PowerPoint (prior to version 2007).
.pptx	The default presentation format Microsoft PowerPoint 2007 and above.
.rtf	Rich Text Format – a document format that supports text and images. This format is supported by most word processing applications across many operating systems.
.txt or .text	Document format that supports text only, without formatting. Double-clicking a .txt file on a Windows system will open the file in either NotePad or WordPad.

.xls	The default spreadsheet format for Microsoft Excel (prior to version 2007).
.xlsx	The default spreadsheet format for Microsoft Excel 2007 and above.
.one	The default format for Microsoft OneNote.

Executable Files

Executable files are files that launch a program or procedure. Take great care when opening executable files that you receive via email or that you download from web sites with which you are not familiar. When you open an executable file, your PC can automatically run any number of operations without your explicit approval. Executable file formats include:

.bat	Batch file – found on old DOS systems.
.cgi	Common Gateway Interface – script file used to generate web content.
.cmd	Windows command file.
.com	DOS command file.
.dll	Dynamic Link Library – these files are not executables, but are libraries of code that are called by executable programs.
.exe	Windows executable program; these files are typically self-extracting compressed files.
.msi	Windows installer file – these executables are used to automate software installation on Windows systems.
.vbs	Visual Basic – script files created in the Visual Basic programming language. VBS scripts have been used to spread viruses.

Archive/Compressed File Formats

Archives are compressed file formats. Used primarily on the Internet, the compressed file format reduces the amount of time necessary to download a file. Archives can contain any type of file – images, documents, executables, etc. A compression utility is required to compress and decompress the files. Archived file formats include:

.bz or .bz2	Archive files used by the Bzip/Bunzip application.
.rar	A compression standard that is platform-neutral (can be used on various operating systems). On UNIX systems, the RAR application is used. On Windows systems, the WinRAR application is used.
.tar	Compressed file used on UNIX systems.
.zip	Compressed file used by the PKZIP and WinZip applications.

Windows automatically recognizes common file name extensions, and associates particular application programs with particular extensions. For example, if you are using a file management tool such as Windows Explorer, and you double-click a file with a .pdf file name extension, Windows will try to open the file in Adobe Reader, which is the program used to read PDF files. The operating system launches the necessary application and then opens the file within the application.

If you try to open a file for which there is no associated application installed, Windows displays a window similar to the one shown:

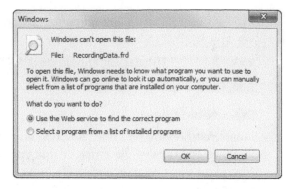

Click the appropriate selection to locate a program that will open the file.

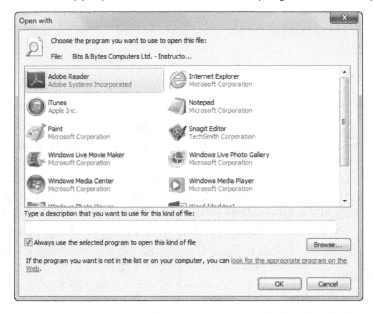

In some cases you can choose a program that is already installed on the computer to try and open the file. If you are unsure which program to use, check with your network administrator or a technical specialist prior to selecting a program in this dialog box.

Sometimes the associations set in Windows between file name extensions and application programs open files in an application other than the one you want to use. For example, if you double-click a text file, Windows will automatically open the file in Notepad (which is installed with Windows). However, you might want to open the file in Microsoft Word.

To open a file in an application other than the one which is presently associated with its file name extension, you can open the application and then use the application's Open command to open the file; or you can right-click the file in Windows Explorer, and click Open within the shortcut menu to display the Open with dialog box shown in the preceding figure.

EXERCISE

In this exercise you will try to match the file type with an appropriate software program that could be used to view or edit the file.

a.	.docx	_____	iTunes
b.	.swf	_____	Operating system
c.	.pptx	_____	Internet Explorer
d.	.jpg	_____	Windows Media Center
e.	.mp3	_____	Word
f.	.avi	_____	PowerPoint
g.	.htm	_____	PhotoShop
h.	.exe	_____	Flash Reader

Viewing the File Extensions

In order to keep things simple and keep the display uncluttered, the default setting in Windows is to hide file name extensions. Displaying file name extensions can be useful, however. For example, you can display extensions to show which picture files use the .jpg, .gif, or .tif format. Viewing file extensions is also useful for differentiating between two files with the same name but different file formats, such as .xlsx versus .csv; both file types can be opened in a spreadsheet program but the first one opens as an Excel workbook whereas the latter will prompt you to import the file into Excel. By viewing the file name extension of audio or video files, you can quickly identify which program you can use to open the file. Another good reason for displaying the file types is to help you easily identify executable files. These files are used to launch a program (or other code that will carry out commands). You should take care before launching any executable file. While in most cases these files launch legitimate programs, they can also be used to install a virus on your computer.

To display the file extensions at all times, open a Windows Explorer window and on the Command bar, click ⎡ Organize ▾ ⎤. Click **Folder and search options** and then on the **View** tab, in the **Advanced settings** list, uncheck **Hide extensions for known file types**.

When you need to see hidden files, you can uncheck the **Hide protected operating system files (Recommended)** option. Important files such as system files or the data file for your email program are hidden to prevent them from being deleted or changed inadvertently. Protected system files may be displayed when a technical support person is working on your computer and needs to view them; it is recommended that you hide the system files once he/she has finished.

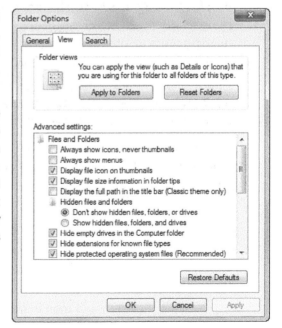

EXERCISE

In this exercise you will change the setting to open items with a single click and you will apply different views in Windows Explorer.

1.   From the Command bar, click Organize ▾ and then **Folder and search options**.

2.   On the **General** tab, in the **Click items as follows** area, click **Single-click to open an item (point to select)**.

3.   Ensure **Underline icon titles only when I point at them** is selected and then click **OK**.

4.   In the Contents pane, position the mouse pointer over the *General Documents* folder.

     Notice that the folder is now highlighted and the name is underlined. This is a visual indicator that you can single-click this folder to open it. Simply pointing to an item selects it, and everything that used to require a double-click now requires only a single-click. Changing the number of clicks to select an item is really a personal preference on how to select or access items, and can be changed at any time to suit the user.

5.   In the Contents pane, point at the **Slide Shows** folder and then click to open it.

6.   Click the 🔙 **(Back)** button to return to the previous level.

Now set the file extensions to display for all files.

7.   On the Command bar, click Organize ▾ and then click **Folder and search options**.

8.   Click the **View** tab and then in the **Advanced settings** list, click **Hide extensions for known file types** to turn this feature off. Then click **OK**.

9.   Click **Lesson 2 – Windows** in the Address bar. Then on the Command bar, click the down arrow for ▤ ▾ and click **Medium Icons**.

     Notice that Windows now displays larger icons for the files and your folder, and also displays the file name extensions.

10. On the Command bar, click the down arrow for ▤ ▾ and then click **Details**.

11. Click the **Type** column heading to sort the contents by the file type.

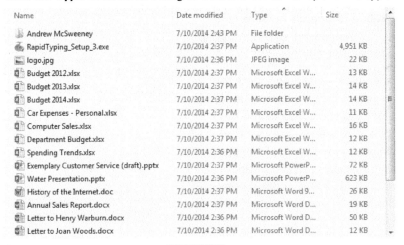

Name	Date modified	Type	Size
Andrew McSweeney	7/10/2014 2:43 PM	File folder	
RapidTyping_Setup_3.exe	7/10/2014 2:37 PM	Application	4,951 KB
logo.jpg	7/10/2014 2:36 PM	JPEG image	22 KB
Budget 2012.xlsx	7/10/2014 2:37 PM	Microsoft Excel W...	13 KB
Budget 2013.xlsx	7/10/2014 2:37 PM	Microsoft Excel W...	14 KB
Budget 2014.xlsx	7/10/2014 2:37 PM	Microsoft Excel W...	14 KB
Car Expenses - Personal.xlsx	7/10/2014 2:37 PM	Microsoft Excel W...	11 KB
Computer Sales.xlsx	7/10/2014 2:37 PM	Microsoft Excel W...	16 KB
Department Budget.xlsx	7/10/2014 2:37 PM	Microsoft Excel W...	12 KB
Spending Trends.xlsx	7/10/2014 2:36 PM	Microsoft Excel W...	12 KB
Exemplary Customer Service (draft).pptx	7/10/2014 2:37 PM	Microsoft PowerP...	72 KB
Water Presentation.pptx	7/10/2014 2:36 PM	Microsoft PowerP...	623 KB
History of the Internet.doc	7/10/2014 2:37 PM	Microsoft Word 9...	26 KB
Annual Sales Report.docx	7/10/2014 2:37 PM	Microsoft Word D...	19 KB
Letter to Henry Warburn.docx	7/10/2014 2:36 PM	Microsoft Word D...	50 KB
Letter to Joan Woods.docx	7/10/2014 2:36 PM	Microsoft Word D...	12 KB

12. On the Command bar, click Organize ▾ and then click **Folder and search options**.

13. Click the **View** tab and then in the **Advanced settings** area, click **Hide extensions for known file types** to turn this feature back on. Then click **OK**.

     The files are still listed in alphabetical order by file type, even though the file name extensions are not visible.

14. Place the mouse pointer on the vertical line between the **Name** column and the **Date modified** column. When the mouse pointer turns into a ↔, drag it to adjust the width of the column until you can see the full name for every file.

15. Try changing the view to small icons, then to tiles to see how this affects the view. Make **List** the last view style you use.

Selecting Files or Folders

Before performing any actions such as copying, moving, or deleting, you must select the file or folder.

Consider the following methods of selecting files or folders:

- To select one file or folder, point to that file or folder.

- To select all files and folders in this location, click Organize ▼ and click **Select all**, or press Ctrl + A .

- To select multiple files or folders that are consecutive, point to the first file or folder in the list, press and hold the Shift key, and then point to the last file or folder in the list.

- To select files using the *lasso* method, point at the right of the first file or folder to be selected, then click and drag up or down to select the rest of the files or folders in the selection. A box will appear as confirmation of the selection, along with the files or folders being highlighted.

- To select multiple files or folders that are non-consecutive, point to the first file or folder to be selected, press and hold the Ctrl key, and then point at each file or folder to be selected.

- At any time files or folders are selected, if you need to change any part of the selection, use either the Shift or Ctrl key to deselect specific parts of the selection.

To de-select or turn off the selection of any files or folders, click anywhere away from the selection.

EXERCISE

> **Note**: Every exercise in this lesson from this point forward uses the single-click option for working with files and folders. If you have not performed the previous exercise, please go back and perform steps 1 through 3, 11 and 15 before proceeding with this exercise.

In this exercise, you will use different methods to select files.

1. Ensure the *Lesson 2 - Windows* folder is active.

2. In the Contents pane, point the mouse pointer at the first file (the *RapidTyping* file) to select it, press Shift and then point to the *Letter to Henry Warburn* file. This action selects all the files between the RapidTyping file and the Letter to Henry Warburn file.

3. Click in a blank area of the Contents pane to de-select the list.

You will now select files in random order.

4. Position the mouse pointer over the *Letter to Joan Woods* file to select it, press and hold the (Ctrl) key, and then point at the *History of the Internet* file.

These two files are now selected.

5. Click in a blank area to deselect the list.

Now try the lasso technique to select files.

6. Position the mouse pointer over a blank space to the right of the *Water Presentation* file, and then press the left mouse button as you drag down and slightly to the left of the *News with RSS* file.

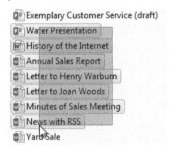

7. When the files are selected, release the mouse.

8. Click anywhere away from the selection to de-select the list.

You will now select all contents in this location.

9. Press (Ctrl)+(A).

10. Click anywhere away from the selection to de-select the list.

Copying and Moving Files or Folders

Files or folders may be copied or moved from one drive location to another, from one folder to another, or to the desktop. Use the Folders list to view the hierarchical structure of the folders and subfolders, and to quickly navigate between the different folders or drives.

Copying Files or Folders

When you copy a file or folder, the original remains in the source location and a copy is placed in the destination location—the same information will be in both locations. For example, suppose you want a copy of a file from the network to edit. The new file, with your edits, should be the version everyone in the office uses from now on, so you must make a copy of your file to replace the network copy.

To do this, you must first select the files or folders. Then, to copy a file or folder, use one of the following methods:

*   Click Organize ▾ and then **Copy**, navigate to the new location and then click Organize ▾ , **Paste**, or

*   press (Ctrl)+(C), move to the new location and then press (Ctrl)+(V), or

- right-click the selection and then click **Copy**, navigate to the new location, right-click and then click **Paste**, or

- if you are copying files from one drive to another, Windows will automatically copy the selection as you drag the selection to the new location, or

- if you are copying files in the same drive, press Ctrl as you drag the selected file or folder to the new location.

As Windows copies the files from the source location to the destination location, it will check to see if there are files with the same name already in the destination location. If so, you will see a message similar to the screen shown:

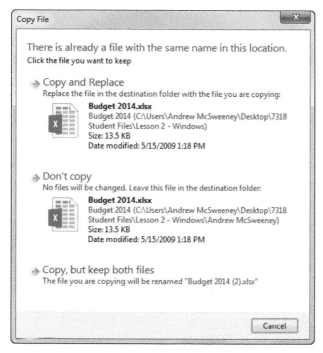

Always double-check whether you want the new file to be copied over the existing file. You can choose to keep both copies and let Windows create a file with a number at the end of the filename to indicate that it is a copy. In this example, the original file will be named Budget 2014.xlsx and the copy in the same location will be named Budget 2014 (2).xlsx.

EXERCISE

In this exercise you will use the copy and paste feature to copy files to another folder.

1. Ensure you are viewing the contents of the *Lesson 2 - Windows* folder.

2. Press Ctrl+A to select everything in this folder. Then press Ctrl and point at the folder with your name to deselect this folder.

3. On the Command bar, click Organize ▾ and then **Copy**.

4. In the Contents pane, click the the folder with your name.

5. On the Command bar, click Organize ▾ and then **Paste**.

    The files are now copied from the student files folder to your folder.

Moving Files or Folders

When you move a file or folder, it is cut (deleted) from its original location and copied into the destination location. When you move a folder, all the contents within that folder (subfolders and files) move as well.

After selecting the files or folders to move, use one of the following methods:

- Click Organize ▼ and then click **Cut**, move to the new location, click Organize ▼ and then click **Paste**, or
- press Ctrl + X , move to the new location and then press Ctrl + V , or
- right-click the selection and then click **Cut**, move to the new location, right-click, and then click **Paste**, or
- drag the selected files or folders to the new location on the same drive. For different drives, Windows will automatically copy the selection unless you press the Shift key as you drag.

If after completing the move action the file or folder is not in the location you intended, it is possible you may have moved the file or folder to the folder above or below the one you wanted. Click in the folder on either side to see if the file or folder is there, then move it into the appropriate location.

EXERCISE

In this exercise, you will try moving files to different locations.

1. Ensure you are in your folder. If necessary, change the view to **Details**. Then click the **Type** column to sort the files by file format.

   > **Tip:** Resize the **Type** column to see the names of the programs.

2. Select all the Microsoft Word files and then press Ctrl + X .

3. In the Contents pane, click the *General Documents* folder and then press Ctrl + V .

   The Microsoft Word data files are moved to this folder.

4. Click your folder in the Address bar, and then repeat steps 2 and 3 moving the Microsoft Excel files into *Worksheets*, Microsoft PowerPoint files into *Slide Shows*, and the remaining data files into the *Misc* folder.

   Your folder should then display the folders and shortcut only, as all files are organized into appropriate folders.

Suppose you now want to move your folder to another location, such as the Documents library.

5. Click *Lesson 2 – Windows* in the Address bar to go to this level, then point to and drag your folder so it hovers over *Documents* in the Libraries area. (If the individual libraries are not visible, click the expansion arrow to the left of Libraries in the Folders list.)

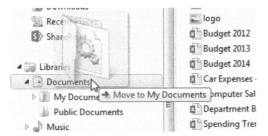

6. Release the mouse when *Documents* is highlighted as seen in the above screen.

You have now successfully moved your folder to the Documents library.

Now move it back to where the data files are.

7. In the Folders list, click **Documents** and if necessary, click the **Expand** arrow for *My Documents*.

8. Select your folder in the Contents pane and press (Ctrl)+(X).

9. Under Favorites, click **Desktop** and then in the Contents pane, click *7318 Student Files*.

10. In the Contents pane, click *Lesson 2 – Windows* and then press (Ctrl)+(V) to paste your folder into this location.

Renaming Files

As with folders you can rename a file to make it more descriptive using the Edit mode.

To activate the Rename feature use one of the following methods:

- Select the file and then press (F2).
- Select the file and then click once in the file name.
- Right-click the file and then click **Rename**.

Remember the two limitations of file and folder naming conventions: a maximum of 255 characters; and the following characters \ / : * " < > | cannot be used in the file or folder name.

Be very careful not to rename any program files or folders, or the application program may not be able to find them.

You should take care not change the file name extension when you rename a file. If you change a file name extension, Windows may display the following message.

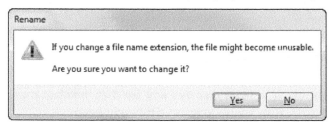

If you accept the change, you may make the file unrecognizable and unusable. Check the name and make changes accordingly.

EXERCISE

In this exercise, you will rename files in different folders.

1. In the *Lesson 2 – Windows* folder, click your folder and then click the *Misc* folder.

2. In the Contents pane, point at the *logo* file to select it and press (F2).

3. Click at the beginning of the file name, type: TEC (include a space) and then press (Enter).

   The file is renamed as "TEC logo" and is listed alphabetically.

4. Point at the *Sales and Revenue Report* file to select it.

5. Right-click and then click **Rename**.

6. Double-click the word "and", type: & (include a space) and press (Enter).

   The file is renamed.

7.   Navigate up one level and click the *Worksheets* folder.

8.   Right-click the *Budget 2014* file and click **Rename**.

9.   Make sure the cursor is at the end of the file name and change the year from 2014 to 2015. Press ⎡Enter⎤.

You have now successfully changed the name of this file.

Finding Files

You can search for a file or folder in various disk drives or folders on your system using specific criteria, such as name, type, size, date created, date last modified, and so on.

To activate the Search feature, enter the search criteria in _____ 🔍.

Click the ✕ in the **Search** field to clear all search results.

EXERCISE

In this exercise you will search for files using different criteria to narrow the search.

1.   Click the *General Documents* folder in your folder.

2.   Click in the **Search** field in the top-right corner of the window and type: letter.

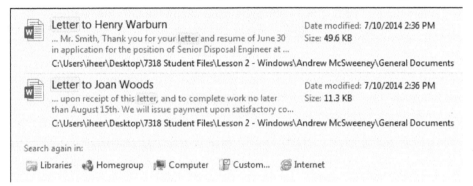

Notice that, as you begin entering the text, Windows displays any file that matches the criteria, including any subfolders within your folder. Now try performing a different search.

3.   Click in the **Search** field and then click ✕ to clear the search results.

4.   In the **Search** field, click in the field and then click **Date modified**.

> **Note:** To move from one month to another, click the appropriate arrow on either side of the current month.

5.   Click **Earlier this month**.

Notice that no files are listed. Windows did not find any files that matched the criteria.

6. Click to clear the search criteria.

7. In the **Search** field, type `sale`. Windows displays three files: *Annual Sales Report*, *Minutes of Sales Meeting* and *Yard Sale*.

8. Click to clear the search results.

Looking at the Recycle Bin

The Recycle Bin is a temporary storage area for files and folders that you delete from the local hard disk. Files and folders deleted from an external disk (such as a flash drive, memory card, or virtual storage device) or from a network drive are <u>permanently</u> deleted and cannot be restored from the Recycle Bin.

The Recycle Bin has an icon on the desktop for easy access, but is also accessible from Windows Explorer and the Computer window. Two icons are used to represent the Recycle Bin:

Indicates there are files in the Recycle Bin that can be restored or the Recycle Bin can be emptied.

Indicates the Recycle Bin is empty.

If the computer is shared by multiple users, a separate Recycle Bin exists for each user account on the computer.

To permanently delete a file and bypass the Recycle Bin, press and hold the (Shift) key while deleting the file.

Deleting Files and Folders

When you no longer need files or folders, you can delete them.

Always check the contents of a folder before you delete the entire folder. This is especially crucial if the folder is stored on a network drive or external disk, as these are not moved to the Recycle Bin.

To delete a file or folder, select the file or folder and then use one of the following methods:

- Click Organize ▾ and then click **Delete**, or
- select the file or folder and then press (Delete), or
- right-click and click **Delete**, or
- drag the item to the Recycle Bin icon on the Desktop.

MMM
Organizing
Your Files

EXERCISE

In this exercise you will delete files and folders.

1. Click the *Misc* folder in your folder to open it, point at the *IC3 Web Site* file and press (Delete).

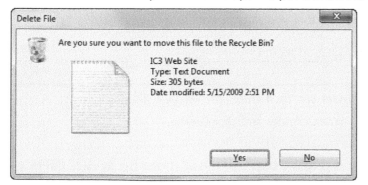

2. Click **Yes** to delete this file and move it to the Recycle Bin.

3. Navigate to your folder once more. Right-click the *Misc* folder in the Folders list and then click **Delete**. Click **Yes** to confirm the deletion.

    The entire folder is deleted, including all the folder contents.

Restoring a File or Folder

You can restore a deleted file or folder to its original location. You can only restore an entire folder (including all its contents), not individual items that were deleted with the folder.

To restore a file or folder from the Recycle Bin, use one of the following methods:

- Select the file or folder to be restored, and then click `Restore this item` , or

- to restore multiple files or folders, select the appropriate files or folders, and then click `Restore the selected items` , or

- if you want to restore all items, click `Restore all items` , or

- right-click the selected files or folders, and then click **Restore**.

EXERCISE

In this exercise you will restore the file and folder deleted previously.

1. On the desktop, click the Recycle Bin icon to open the Recycle Bin.

2. Select the *Misc* folder, and then on the Command bar, click `Restore this item` .

3. Point at the *IC3 Web Site* file, and then on the Command bar, click `Restore this item` .

4. Close the Recycle Bin.

5. In Windows Explorer, navigate to your folder.

    The *Misc* folder appears in the Contents list.

6. Click *Misc* to verify that the IC3 Web Site file has been restored.

Emptying the Recycle Bin

Deleted files remain in the Recycle Bin until you empty it or it becomes full; in the latter case, Windows will automatically delete older files and folders to free up space for new items. When a file or folder is deleted from the Recycle Bin, it is permanently deleted.

To empty the Recycle Bin, use one of the following methods:

- On the Command bar, click `Empty the Recycle Bin` , or

- right-click in a blank area of the Recycle Bin window and click **Empty Recycle Bin**, or

- right-click the **Recycle Bin** icon on the desktop and then click **Empty Recycle Bin**.

Use this option only when you are sure that you will not want to restore anything from the Recycle Bin.

EXERCISE

In this exercise you will delete a folder and then empty the Recycle Bin.

1. In Windows Explorer, right-click your folder and click **Delete**.

2. Click **Yes**.

3. At the far right of the taskbar, click **Show Desktop**, and then click the **Recycle Bin** to open it.

4. On the Command bar, click [Empty the Recycle Bin].

> **Note:** The number of items that display in the prompt will vary depending on what other items have been deleted to the Recycle Bin on the system you are using.

5. Click **Yes**.

Notice the Contents pane is now blank, and the Recycle Bin icon on the Desktop is also empty.

6. Close Windows Explorer.

Points to Keep in Mind when Working with Files

Following are some points to keep in mind when working with files:

☐ Use a standard naming convention when saving files. Try to ensure each file name is unique and do not overwrite a file unless you are sure you do not need the original version. Try to adhere to any file management standards that have been set so others can find files and folders easily. For example, if you are working with network files that you have copied to your hard drive, be sure to copy the files back out to the appropriate folders on the network when you are done so that others can access them.

☐ Use file names that will help you identify a file's contents later. Refrain from saving a file using the generic file name provided by the program when you create a new file (Document1, Document2, Book1, Book3). If you rename a file, be careful not to change the file name extension.

☐ When moving files, take extra care to ensure that you are moving the correct files and to the correct location. You don't want to leave other users guessing as to where a file has gone. It is recommended you copy and paste the files to the new location and then delete the files from the original location once you have confirmed the copied files are in the new location.

☐ Make backup copies of your files in case a file becomes lost, or damaged.

☐ Do not bypass the Recycle Bin when deleting files, especially if there is a possibility you may need them at a later date. If you plan to delete a file from a network drive, copy it first to your hard drive. Network files are not sent to the Recycle Bin.

☐ An error message similar to the following indicates you do not have sufficient access to view or open the item. You may need to contact your manager/supervisor or the network administrator to obtain access to the file or folder item.

Lesson Summary

In this lesson, you looked at the different ways files or folders display and explored ways of manipulating them. You should now be familiar with:

☑ how to work with a typical window	☑ changing the view for drives, files or folders
☑ what a file or folder is	☑ how to view or modify file or folder properties
☑ selecting files or folders	☑ renaming files or folders
☑ copying or moving files or folders	☑ finding files

Review Questions

1. How can viewing the path for a folder or file be helpful?
   a. It tells you which drive the file or folder is stored on.
   b. It tells you whether the file or folder is stored on a network.
   c. It tells you the name of the folder and how many levels you must go through to get to it.
   d. Any of the above.

2. Which arrow indicates you can resize two borders of a window at the same time?

   a.   b. [icon]   c. [icon]

3. What is a library in Windows Explorer?
   a. Same as a folder.
   b. Name of the disk drive.
   c. A folder to keep track of your Internet files.
   d. A collection of items, such as files and folders, assembled from various locations and presented in one central location.

4. On the following image, mark the location of the Navigation pane (Folder list) and Contents pane.

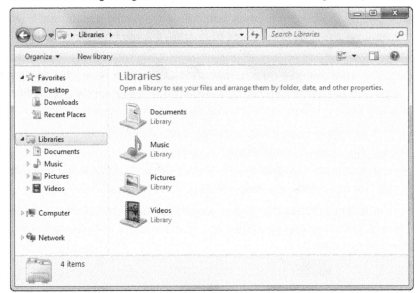

5. When you see a file or folder appear similar to the following, what does it mean?

   [icon: New folder]

   a. The file or folder will be deleted.
   b. The file or folder will be renamed.
   c. The file or folder will be copied.
   d. The file or folder will be printed.

6. How long are items stored in the Recycle Bin once you delete them?
   a. 30 days
   b. 60 days
   c. Until you delete selected items or empty the Recycle Bin.
   d. Forever

MMM
Go online for
Additional
Review

Lesson 3: Hardware

Lesson Objectives

In this lesson, you will look at the different types of computers available, and learn some basic hardware terminology, including the following items:

- ☐ bits and bytes
- ☐ mega, giga, tera, or peta
- ☐ hertz and gigahertz
- ☐ CPU

- ☐ microprocessor chip
- ☐ ROM and RAM memory
- ☐ volatile and non-volatile storage
- ☐ types of devices

Identifying Computers

 Exam 1 - Objective 2.2, 2.3

Computers are integrated into our work, home, and social environments and perform a multitude of tasks. Many organizations use a combination of large and small systems to manage the flow of information, and it is crucial that these systems be well maintained if companies such as banks, insurance agencies, or schools are required to keep histories of customer transactions.

Many computers are designed to be used specifically as computing devices, while others are embedded in products such as automobile engines, medical or industrial equipment, household appliances, or calculators.

Desktop Computers

Desktop computers (also called personal computers) sit on, beside, or under a desk. These machines process data quickly and are typically used in small businesses, schools, and homes.

There are generally two types of personal computer: the *PC* or personal computer, based on the original IBM machine, and the Mac, designed by Apple.

Windows compatible desktop

iMac desktop

Apple MacBook

Windows compatible Notebook

Desktop computers are designed to process data quickly and almost always include the ability to render or play rich multimedia (sound and video). While desktop systems are stable and powerful, they are not portable.

Notebooks or Laptop Computers

Notebook or laptop computers are designed to be small and light enough to sit on the user's lap. These systems are self-contained and include most of the components found in a desktop model, such as a display, keyboard, pointing device (touchpad and/or pointing stick), speakers, and usually a rechargeable battery that is charged from an AC adapter.

A laptop includes the same components as a desktop, but all the components are contained in a single unit, which makes it easy to carry. These systems are generally similar to desktop models in terms of speed, performance, and usage. The primary advantage in using a notebook is its portability. Also, in some cases, a laptop's power consumption is considered a "greener" alternative to desktops. You can purchase a number of accessories to enhance your notebook computing experience, such as a bigger hard drive for storage, a larger screen, a wireless external mouse or keyboard, or more memory. A disadvantage to laptops is that they are generally not as powerful as desktop systems.

As with desktop models, you can purchase a notebook for either the PC or the Apple environments.

Netbook

A *netbook* is similar to a notebook, but is smaller and less expensive. Netbooks are generally less powerful, provide less storage capacity and have smaller screens and keyboards than laptops. Most do not include all the standard peripheral ports that a laptop offers and many do not include a CD-ROM drive because they rely on the Internet to transfer files. Netbooks are designed for people who want wireless communications or access to the Internet, but are not interested in using the computer for storing data files.

Tablet PCs

A *tablet PC* is a mobile computing device that is larger than a mobile phone or personal digital assistant (PDA) and integrated into a flat touch screen. The Tablet PC is primarily operated by touching the screen – users can "type" on an onscreen virtual keyboard rather than using a physical keyboard.

Tablet PC

All tablets have "touch screen" capability, which means you can touch a pen or pointing device to an item on the screen to select it. Most provide an option for connecting devices such as a monitor, a keyboard or a pointing device. Some popular tablet models include the Apple iPad, Asus Transformer, Samsung Galaxy, Motorola Zoom, or Windows Surface. Tablets are light and ultra-portable. On the downside, tablets are expensive and quite fragile and very few include optical media drives. Because tablets do not include keyboards, they can be uncomfortable to use for long periods of time.

Servers

A server is a computer that functions primarily to provide files or services to other systems on a network. Typically a server runs specialized software that enables it to perform specific functions, and in many cases a server may be dedicated to providing only one or two specific functions. For example, one server may be designated as a database server that stores huge amounts of data such as an organization's customer list or order history; another server may be dedicated to handle electronic mail only; or a web server may be dedicated to store data for an organization's web site as well as manage commercial transactions electronically.

Servers

Systems marketed for use as servers are built differently from end-user desktop systems. They are designed to be highly reliable and must have a low failure rate. Servers should be able to run continually, and are shut down or restarted only when software or hardware upgrades are being installed. They often include redundant power supplies, and because their main function is to communicate with other systems on a network, they are often designed to transfer data quickly. In a server system, there is generally more focus on the processor power, memory and hard drive size than there is on features such as video and graphics capability. Because of their increased power, server systems are considerably more expensive than desktop systems.

Hand-held or Mobile Computers

A hand-held computer is any portable computing device that fits within the palm of your hand. Depending on the model, these devices can be used to make telephone calls, send or receive voice or electronic messages, take pictures or videos, browse the web or perform personal computing tasks.

Smart phones are hand-held devices that also offer the option to copy or download music or electronic books from the Internet. Smart phones come complete with built-in system memory and support for memory cards, which can store data, and include software for organizing appointments and contact lists, or for writing simple notes. Many individuals who do not require the full capabilities of a notebook or desktop system use smart phones as their main computing device. Most models incorporate touch screen technology as well as the option to connect and synchronize the data from the hand-held/mobile device to a personal computer or vice versa. Synchronizing is an example of how the hand-held device such as a smart phone can accept or send instructions from or to a computer to update data files.

You can also download and install specialized applications that enable you to synchronize files (such as contact lists or music files) between your hand-held device and your desktop or laptop computer.

The number and type of services you require will determine the type of hand-held computer you will use. For example, a realtor may choose a smart phone to handle numerous incoming and outgoing calls, keep track of open house viewings, and update his/her web site with new homes listed or sold. On the other hand, a parent purchasing a hand-held device for a child might opt for a cellular phone with text messaging, photo and video capabilities.

Music or Media Players

A music player (also called an *MP3 player* or a *digital audio player*) is a device that stores, organizes and plays audio files. MP3 refers to the specific type of audio file supported by the player. MP3 players play back audio only; they do not support video files.

A media player allows you to view other types of media files such as movies, videos, or books. These players provide both audio and video capabilities and, occasionally, the option to search the Internet. Some players allow you to store pictures and play games, and some offer WiFi connectivity as well. Popular models include iPod and iPod Touch (or iTouch).

The iPod can be used on Windows or Macintosh computers, and uses an application called iTunes to establish communication between the computer and the player. The iPod Touch uses a touchscreen display (like an iPhone) and includes WiFi connectivity for surfing the Web.

Electronic Book Readers

An electronic book reader (e-reader) is a specialized hand-held computing device that enables you to download and view electronic copies of published works. Many publishers offer the option of joining their online clubs in order to purchase books in electronic form. Some e-readers have similar features to tablets such as the iPad to play games or include touch-screen technology.

In some cases, you can find software that will add e-book reading capabilities to your smart phone, media player, notebook or desktop system.

> ┌─────────────┐
> │ **MMM**   │
> │ Picking a   │
> │ Computing   │
> │ Device   │
> └─────────────┘

EXERCISE

In this exercise, you will determine which type of computer would be best suited for two new employees who will be joining the team in the new Seattle location. Read about the position and role the person plays and decide which computer type would be best for the employee.

Name	Position	Computing Device
Ji Mai Kim	Administration / General Office Ji Mai will be in the office most of the time but may be required to travel to take notes or check email when offsite with a Tour Director. She will manage the office supplies and coordinate with consultants for items such as new telephone lines or Internet access. In addition, she'll be the main contact between Seattle and Head Office for handling administration documents such as expense reports.	
Brooke Lakewood	New Tour Development – West Brooke will be responsible for finding tours throughout the Pacific Rim. She is expected to be working outside the office seeking new tours to propose to Andrew and Lawrence. In some cases, she may need to investigate a tour in place of a Tour Director. Photos and testimonials will be key for her proposals, as will Word and Excel.	

Looking Inside a Computer

 Exam 1 - Objective 2.1, 2.3

Personal computers are complete "systems" which include many components and attached devices. These components and attached devices are referred to collectively as hardware. *Hardware* consists of the pieces you can actually see and touch; hardware performs the physical work of the computer. In contrast, *software* refers to the programs (applications and operating systems) you install and use in order to be productive. Software allows you to create spreadsheets or check email or manipulate images. In this lesson, you will learn about hardware.

Hardware can be divided into two basic types – internal components and peripheral devices. Internal components are housed within the case and peripheral devices are attached to the computer through special connection locations called ports.

The case (or chassis) of the computer houses the power supply for the system and all the internal components. These components (which include the microprocessor, memory chips and hard drive) are seated on or otherwise attached to a large printed circuit board called the motherboard or system board.

The system board contains most of the computer's circuitry and provides pathways for communication among all the components and connected devices. It also provides ports for connecting external (peripheral) devices, such as a mouse, keyboard, speakers, flash drive, etc.

Collectively, the chassis and the internal components are called the *system unit* or *box*. The chassis on a desktop system is easily opened, allowing access to the internal components. If an internal component in a desktop system fails, for example, it is an easy task to open the case and replace the component.

Notebooks and hand-held computing devices include many of the same internal components as desktop systems, but because of the extremely tight working space, replacing failed components on a portable system is considerably more complicated than replacing them inside a desktop system. Repairs or component upgrades must usually be handled by professionals.

The Microprocessor Chip

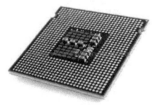

The microprocessor is a silicon chip and is often called the "brain" of the computer because it is where calculations and logical operations are performed. The microprocessor is also referred to as the *Central Processing Unit (CPU)* or simply as the processor.

Different CPUs process information and instructions at different speeds, and processor speed is measured in units called hertz (Hz). The hertz (Hz) is the unit of frequency or cycles per second and is usually represented with the prefixes shown in the following table.

Name	Abbreviation	Multiplies by	Equal to
Hertz	Hz		1 cycle per second
Kilohertz	KHz	One thousand	1,000 cycles per second
Megahertz	MHz	One million	1,000,000 cycles per second
Gigahertz	GHz	One billion	1,000,000,000 cycles per second
Terahertz	THz	One trillion	1,000,000,000,000 cycles per second

The speed or power of the processor is one of the factors that determine overall system performance (the amount of system memory is also a major factor in making this determination). Operating systems and application programs require a minimum processor speed to run successfully.

A processor is sometimes referred to by its architecture, which determines how much memory it can address and control. Common architectures found in modern systems include 32-bit processors (which are referred to using the term x86) and 64-bit processors (referred to using the term x64).

Processors are also commonly described by the number of cores they possess. Every processor includes one or more cores which process instructions and data. A dual-core processor has two cores; a quad-core processor has four cores. Multi-core processors are common today and all the cores in a multi-core processor are combined onto a single silicon chip.

Looking at System Memory

In order for a computer to process information, it must include a certain amount of installed system memory. System memory is used for temporary storage of programs and data. Data and programs are read into memory from a hard disk or CD-ROM and then passed from memory to the microprocessor.

Memory capacity and disk storage space are measured in bits and bytes. A *bit*, or binary digit, is the smallest unit of data a computer can understand—and it is represented by the value of either 0 or 1.

A group of eight bits is called a *byte*. The smallest unit of data humans can understand is represented by one alphanumeric character ('a' to 'z', or 0 to 9); an alphanumeric character requires a full byte of computer memory.

Because a byte represents such a small amount of data, these capacities are measured in thousands, millions, billions and trillions of bytes. The following table shows standard capacity measurements:

Measurement	Abbreviation	Equal to...	About the same as...
bit		A single binary digit	
byte		Eight bits	One character
kilobyte	KB	1,024 bytes (a thousand bytes)	Half a typewritten page
megabyte	MB	1,024 KB (a million bytes)	One 500-page novel
gigabyte	GB	1,024 MB (a billion bytes)	One thousand 500-page novels
terabyte	TB	1,024 GB (a trillion bytes)	One million 500-page novels
petabyte	PB	1,024 TB (a quadrillion bytes)	Twenty million four-drawer filing cabinets filled with text

Every file used by the computer has a specific byte size, and in order for the computer to use or process the file in any way, there must be sufficient memory to "hold" the file. Without system memory, a computer could not run programs or be used to create or edit files.

Physically, memory consists of chips located inside the system unit. The number of memory chips in the computer and the capacity of each chip determine the amount of available memory. Computers use two basic kinds of memory:

- Read-only memory (ROM)
- Random-access memory (RAM)

Read Only Memory (ROM)

Read Only Memory (ROM) stores data that can be read and used, but not changed. ROM chips store instructions that control the basic functions of the computer, and these instructions remain in ROM regardless of whether the power is on or off. For this reason, ROM is referred to as non-volatile memory.

Read Only Memory (ROM) BIOS

Read Only Memory Basic Input/Output System (ROM BIOS) refers to a group of integrated circuits and chips responsible for starting your computer, checking system memory, and loading the operating system. The computer executes the instructions in ROM-BIOS only when you turn the computer on or each time you have to restart or "reboot" it. ROM is also used to control input and output devices such as disk drives, keyboards, and monitors while the computer is running.

Random Access Memory (RAM)

Random Access Memory (RAM) is provided through RAM chips which are installed inside the system unit. RAM is the main memory of a PC and functions as an electronic memory pool where your computer holds "working copies" of programs and data. RAM is also commonly referred to as system memory or RAM memory.

RAM is volatile; any data stored within it exists there only while the computer is on. Any information stored in RAM "vanishes" when the computer is turned off. As you have learned, data and programs are read into memory from a hard disk or CD-ROM and then passed from memory to the microprocessor, where the information can be modified and returned to memory. When you close a program or save and close a file, the information is cleared from memory, and the memory becomes available to store other information.

Aside from being used for system memory, RAM chips are used in video display cards to increase how quickly a picture appears on your monitor. RAM is also used to buffer information sent to the printer, thereby freeing the computer to perform other operations while a document is being printed (multi-tasking).

Understanding Storage Systems

Even though a computer loads software programs into RAM while you are working, the software must reside permanently on a hard disk or optical disk. Also, because data stored in RAM is lost when you turn off the computer, you must save your work to a storage device before exiting the software program or turning off the power.

Technically, storage media refers to the physical components on which you store data. Storage devices refer to the physical components by which data is transferred back and forth between storage media and RAM. Storage devices can use magnetic or flash-based technology. Commonly-used storage devices include hard drives, optical drives, flash drives and memory cards.

The storage device you use will depend on the amount of storage space you require as well as the desired *data transfer rate* (the speed at which a computer can move data from one place to another). Hard disk drives are used most often to store and retrieve software programs and data due to their speed and storage capacities. You can also use other media such as a flash drive or optical disc to store copies of the data for backup or portability purposes. Hard drives come in traditional (magnetic) or flash-based (solid state) varieties.

Using Traditional Drives

A traditional hard drive includes metal or plastic disks called platters that are covered with a magnetic coating. Hard drive platters rotate around a spindle. A motor turns the spindle at a constant speed, and common speeds include 5,400, 7,200 or 10,000 revolutions per minute (rpm). As the platters spin, one or more pairs of read/write heads (small recording/playback devices) hover close to the surface of the platters and read or write data to the magnetic surface.

Internal Hard Drive

Each platter is prepared for data storage and retrieval through a process called *formatting*, which creates a set of circles called tracks on each side of the disk. Each track is divided into *sectors*, which are the smallest units of data storage with which read/write heads can work. Each piece of data is stored in a specific sector on a specific track. As data is read or written, the read/write heads move to the sector in which the data is stored.

Hard drives are the primary storage location for both data and programs. Software programs must be installed on a hard drive before you can use them. The operating system must also be installed on a hard drive. Hard drives may be internal (housed inside the computer) or external (sitting on the desk beside the computer).

The data transfer rate (or *throughput*) of a hard drive is a function of the hard drive rotation speed and the number of read/write heads per surface; the higher the rotation speed and/or the number of heads, the less time it takes to retrieve a particular piece of data. Hard drives are faster than removable storage devices and can store enormous amounts of data.

A drawback of traditional hard disks is that the read/write heads must float extremely close to the platter surfaces without actually touching them. If any contaminant comes between a platter surface and a read/write head, the head will make contact with the surface of the platter. Contact of this sort can destroy the data stored in the affected sector(s) and damage the read/write head itself.

External Hard Drive

Advantages of magnetic drives are that they offer greater storage capacity than what is available in solid state drives and that they are substantially less expensive that solid state drives.

Using Solid State Drives

Solid state hard drives (SSD) use memory chips to read and write data. There are no moving parts in solid state drives, which makes them less fragile than traditional drives, and also silent. However, they require constant power to maintain their data, so they include backup batteries.

Solid state drives use flash memory, which is a transistor-based silicon memory technology that can store information permanently by trapping electrons into specialized transistors. Flash transistors eventually become worn out with use after between 1 million and 2 million write cycles. Wear-leveling algorithms are used to ensure that all cells are worn evenly to maximize the lifespan, but the performance of solid state drives degrades with use.

Although solid state drives are becoming increasingly available in portable products, they are more expensive than their traditional counterparts and are only now becoming available in competitive storage capacities.

Advantages of solid state drives include:

- Faster startup times (because the drive does not need to get up to speed like magnetic drives do).
- Faster read speeds because the drives do not have to move a read/write head.
- Less heat generated.
- Less risk of failure because there are no moving parts.

Working with Optical Drives

Optical disc drives are designed to read a flat, circular disc commonly referred to as a *Compact Disc (CD)* or *Digital Versatile/video Disc (DVD)*. The optical drive spins the disc at speeds from 200 revolutions per minute (rpm) or higher and a laser reads the data stored on the disc. The higher the speed, the faster the information is read and transferred to the computer.

A *CD-ROM (Compact Disc Read Only Memory)* or *DVD-ROM* drive is similar to a player in an audio/video entertainment system. The information is written (or burned) onto the surface and retrieved with a laser beam and you can only read the data.

New computers are usually equipped with at least one optical drive, usually a DVD optical drive or a CD/DVD optical writer drive.

Optical Writers

An *optical writer drive,* also known as a *burner drive,* has the ability to record information onto a blank disc. These drives use special software which allows you to "burn" or write data onto a disc. Formats for optical drives include:

CD-R/ DVD-R	You can write once only to a blank disc, but the disc can be read multiple times. This format can be read in a DVD player or a DVD burner drive.
CD-RW/ DVD-RW	You can read and write multiple times to the same disc. This format can be read in a DVD drive and some DVD players that support the RW format.
DVD-RAM	This is similar to a DVD-RW but can be used only on devices that support this format. These types of DVDs usually come in the form of cartridges.

Blank discs are relatively inexpensive, and -R disks are cheaper than -RW discs. The capacity of a CD can be 650 or 700 MB, while DVDs can provide from 4.7GB to 17+GB of storage space. DVDs also feature rapid access speeds.

The special software that comes with the DVD burner often includes tools for manipulating or editing video before burning it to a DVD.

USB Storage

A USB flash drive is a flash memory data storage device integrated with a USB connector. These types of storage devices may also be referred to as jump or thumb drives. The drive consists of a small circuit board and a standard type-A USB connector, tucked inside a plastic or rubberized case. The connector may include a protective cap, or may retract into the case.

USB Flash Drive

The USB (universal serial bus) standard has been in use for several years, and three versions of USB exist: 1.1, 2.0 and 3.0. Version 2.0 is much faster than 1.1 and is in wide use today. Version 3.0 is newer and even faster, and is found on new computer systems.

Flash drives are small (averaging between 2½" (60mm) and 2¾" (70mm) long and around ½" (16mm) to ¾" (20mm) wide), weigh less than 1 oz. (28g) and can store gigabytes of information. They are durable and reliable because they do not contain moving parts and can last for several years. Most computer systems today come equipped with two, four or six USB ports.

The USB mass storage standard used by flash drives is supported by modern operating systems such as Windows, Mac OS X, and Linux. Flash drives with USB 2.0 support can store more data and transfer data faster than optical drives, and they are easier to use. When you plug the drive into a USB port, the operating system automatically recognizes it and assigns it a drive letter.

It is recommended that you right-click the drive icon and select **Eject** before removing the flash drive. You should also ensure that the activity light on the flash drive itself is not blinking when you remove the drive. Removing the flash drive while the activity light is blinking may cause the data to be lost or damaged.

Most USB flash drives draw their power from the USB connection, and do not require a battery. However, devices such as MP3 players, which combine the functionality of a digital audio player with flash-drive-type storage, require a battery for the player to function.

Card Readers and Writers

You can use a memory card reader to read flash memory cards and transfer their contents to your computer. Flash memory cards are popular storage devices for digital cameras, cell phones, camcorders and MP3 players. A single memory card reader can read a single memory card type, while a multiple memory card reader can read a variety of memory card formats (for example, PCMCIA, CompactFlash1, SmartMedia, or xD-PictureCard). The following figures show a few memory card formats.

Some card readers are standalone devices that connect to the computer; and others are designed to be installed inside the system. Many new computers come with a memory card reader built in. Many photo-quality printers also include card readers.

Without a memory card reader, you would need to directly connect the device that uses memory cards to the computer (generally by using a special connection cable). The card reader allows you to simply remove the card from the device that uses it, and insert the  card into the card reader so that you can work with the contents. Most card readers also offer write capability. The figure at right shows an external card reader with a memory card installed.

Many people own a variety of devices that use flash memory cards, and each device may use a different type of card. Multiple card readers accept numerous formats and commonly feature two or more slots that allow you to insert different sized cards simultaneously.

On a multiple card reader, each card slot is assigned its own drive letter and activity light. When you insert the media, the Safely Remove Hardware window may appear. Once a card has been inserted, you can select a program (such as a photo editing application) to access your files. It is recommended that you right-click the drive icon and select **Eject** before removing the media. You should also ensure that the activity light is not blinking when you remove the card. Removing the card while the activity light is blinking may cause the data to be lost or damaged.

Factors that Affect Performance

After reading about processor speed, RAM and storage devices, you might think that one or another of these components determines how well a system performs. In fact, all these components (CPU, system board, RAM and storage devices) affect the overall performance of a computer because all of these components must interact as a system, and a system is only as efficient as its weakest component. For example, if you purchase a system with a blazing faster processor, but you don't include enough RAM, performance will be disappointing. The same is true if you install the maximum amount of RAM, but skimp on the processor.

If you look for a system that includes processing power (CPU) and memory (RAM) that exceeds the listed minimum requirements for the programs you want to run, and you ensure that you have a hard drive with sufficient access speed and storage capacity, you will likely be pleased with the overall performance.

Recognizing Input/Output Devices

 Exam 1 - Objective 2.1

You learned earlier that the two basic types of hardware are internal components and peripheral devices. While internal components are housed within the case, peripheral devices are attached to the computer through special connection locations called ports.

Peripheral devices add functionality to the computer, and can generally be classified as input devices, or output devices. Input or output (I/O) devices enable communication between the user and the computer. There are three classifications of I/O devices you can use to:

- send information to the computer (for example, the keyboard, mouse, trackball, or scanner).
- display or transmit information from the computer (examples include the monitor, printer, and speakers).
- communicate between computers (for example, modems and networks).

Note that devices such as modems or network interface cards perform both input and output functions – they send information from a computer onto a network, and they receive information from a network and bring that information into a computer.

In simple terms, anything used to enter information into a computer is an input device. Anything that can display information from a computer is an output device. This is true for devices that are both internal (installed inside the computer) and external (connected outside the computer).

Standard input devices include a keyboard, mouse, and microphone. Common output devices are a monitor, printer, and speakers.

Using the Keyboard

The keyboard is an input device that allows you to send information to the computer. It is the primary tool for inputting data. You can also use the keyboard to input commands for a task in an application program.

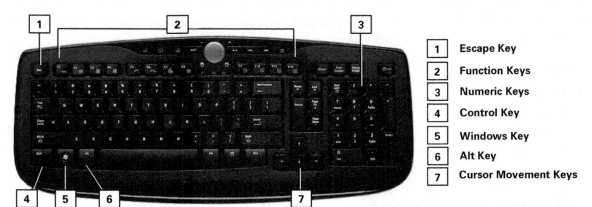

1	Escape Key
2	Function Keys
3	Numeric Keys
4	Control Key
5	Windows Key
6	Alt Key
7	Cursor Movement Keys

The previous graphic shows a traditional keyboard. Some keyboards are ergonomically designed to reduce or prevent stress on the wrists (i.e., carpal tunnel syndrome) or eyestrain. Many newer keyboards also contain buttons to enhance the multimedia experience while using your computer.

Regardless of keyboard type, the same keys are available for document processing. Special keyboards can be purchased for game enthusiasts or for people with disabilities.

Typewriter Keys

These keys enter text or commands into the computer.

You can combine some keys with others to perform a function by pressing the first key and holding it down while you press the second key once. After you release the second key, you may release the first key. The following provides a basic description of the more commonly used keys:

Key	Description
Enter	Executes a typed command or a selected option from a menu, marks the end of a line, or creates a blank line.
Backspace	Deletes one character to the left of the cursor each time you press it. When held down, the computer continuously deletes characters to the left of the cursor until you release the key. This key may also be shown with a left pointing (←) arrow.
Delete	Deletes the character to the right of the cursor each time it is pressed. When held down, it continuously deletes characters to the right of the cursor until released.
Spacebar	Inserts a blank space between words, and is the safest key to press when a software program prompts you to press any key.
Esc	Cancels a current selection or generates a special code for the computer; also referred to as the *Escape* key.
Tab	Advances the cursor to the right by a set number of spaces or to the next cell in a spreadsheet program. When pressed while holding down the Shift key, you can move the cursor a similar distance to the left.
Shift	Displays uppercase letters for the alphabetic keys or the punctuation symbols that share the number keys. Use this key with other keys to perform a function in a program; for example, Shift+F7 activates the thesaurus in Word.
Caps Lock	Locks the letter keys to produce only uppercase versions of each letter.
Ctrl	Provides a secondary meaning or function for almost every other key on the keyboard. You can press and hold down the Ctrl or *Control* key and press another key at the same time to perform a specific task in an application program, such as adding boldface to the text by pressing Ctrl+B.
⊞	Displays the Start menu.
🗐	Displays a shortcut menu—similar to right-clicking an item. Options available in the menu depend on where the mouse pointer is at the time the key is pressed.
Alt	Provides an alternate meaning or function for almost every other key on the keyboard. Press and hold down the Alt or *Alternate* key and press another key to send a command to the computer or to perform a specific task in an application program; for example, Alt+F activates the File menu.
↑ ↓ ← →	Moves the cursor up, down, left, or right, and is usually located between the typewriter keys and the numeric keypad.
Print Scrn	Captures the information on the screen and sends it to the Windows Clipboard.
Scroll Lock	Toggles (starts and stops) the scrolling display of data on the screen.
Ctrl+Pause	Stops or freezes the computer. The computer will continue when any key is pressed. This key combination sends a Break code to unfreeze a computer.

Function Keys

These are located across the top of the keyboard and are labeled (F1) through (F12). Each application program assigns a special meaning or function to each key, generally to provide a shortcut for commonly used commands.

Cursor/Numeric Keypad

This is located at the far right of the keyboard, and can be toggled on and off by pressing the (Num Lock) key in the pad. When the toggle light is on, the pad becomes a calculator or numeric pad; when off, the pad becomes an arrow or cursor movement pad.

Using Pointing Devices

A pointing device enables you to select or activate items on the screen by placing the pointer arrow on the item and performing the required action; for example, you can click to select a file or click and drag to select text. Pointing devices come in many forms but the traditional pointing device is a mouse.

Mouse

This device moves the pointer around on the monitor. Sliding or dragging the mouse across a flat surface such as a desk causes the mouse to initiate movement reflected by the pointer on the monitor. The traditional mouse used a ball that rotated to initiate this movement as you moved the mouse device on the desk. Newer mouse models use an optical light or diode technology to move the pointer on the screen. A trackball has the ball on the side where your thumb rests; you rotate the ball to move the pointer.

A mouse usually has two buttons that are used to select and activate features on the screen. As mentioned previously items can be selected using a single mouse click, activated using a double-click and a shortcut menu displayed using a right-click. Additionally the following actions are available:

Left Drag	Press and hold the left mouse button as you move the mouse to move or select multiple items on the screen.
Right Drag	Press and hold the right mouse button as you move the mouse to move or copy items. On release of the mouse button, a shortcut menu appears with further options.
Scroll Wheel	Roll the wheel between the buttons to scroll through the contents on the screen. Most software applications will zoom in or out when you press the (Ctrl) key while rolling the scroll wheel.
Thumb Button	An additional button on the side of the device where your thumb would rest. This can be set to perform specific tasks, such as starting a program or working as an alternate (Ctrl) key.

To use the mouse pointer to select items, grasp the mouse with your palm down and your index finger gently resting on the first button. As you slide the mouse flat along the desk, the mouse pointer will move in the same direction on the screen. If you run out of space on the desk, lift the mouse and place it in a new position on the desk, and continue moving.

To cancel any option, click the left button anywhere on the screen away from the item being selected.

Mouse devices are available in the traditional style or as wireless devices. The traditional mouse has a cord that extends from the base of the mouse to a plug or port on the computer. A wireless mouse has a separate connector that plugs into the computer and recognizes the commands from the mouse; it may look like a memory key that plugs directly into your computer or may have a connector box with a cord that plugs into the computer. A wireless mouse requires batteries, whereas a traditional mouse needs only to be plugged into a computer.

Touchpad

A touchpad device enables you to use your finger to move the mouse pointer around on the screen. This is common on a notebook, although these devices can be purchased separately for a desktop. A touchpad has two buttons that work in the same manner as the left and right buttons on a mouse.

- To move the mouse pointer around on the screen, place your finger anywhere on the touchpad and then glide your finger around the touchpad in the direction you want to move the mouse pointer.

- To select an item, position the mouse pointer over the item and then tap the touchpad once or click the left button below the touchpad.

- To activate an item, position the mouse pointer over the item and then tap the touchpad twice in quick succession or double-click the left button below the touchpad.

- To drag an item, position the mouse pointer over the item, press (Ctrl), and then glide your finger on the touchpad to the required location.

- To display a shortcut menu, position the mouse pointer over the item and then click the right button below the touchpad.

Stylus

A stylus is an input device that looks similar to a pen and can be used instead of your finger to select or activate an item on a device that includes touch-screen capabilities. Press the stylus lightly on the option on the screen you want to select or activate. For example, on a smart phone or a tablet you may use the stylus to "type" the digits of a phone number, start an application, or write text. Depending on the system and the programs available for that device, you can use the stylus to draw shapes or diagrams.

Pointing devices of this type are typically designed in a pen format but are also available in various designs and can be referred to as a digital writer.

Using Microphones

Microphones allow you to record sounds and convert them into a digital format for use on the computer. Specialized software can even recognize your voice as you speak into a microphone and convert what you say into text characters that appear on the screen. Specialized software of this type is very beneficial for users with special needs.

Microphones are not usually included with a desktop computer although many newer notebooks include a built-in microphone. There are also many microphones of varied quality available for separate purchase.

Looking at the Monitor

The monitor is an output device that enables you to view information the computer displays. All monitors include a power switch as well as brightness and contrast controls to adjust the screen image.

Monitors come in a variety of sizes, resolutions, and types; the larger the screen, the larger the image will be on the screen and the more expensive the monitor will be. *Resolution,* or the monitor's ability to display images, is a measurement based on particular mathematical levels of sharpness and clarity, and is a factor in the price.

Flat screen monitors are popular due to their size as well as for touch screen technology. A touch screen allows you to select an option on the screen using your finger instead of a mouse or keyboard.

Using Printers

Printers convert what was on the screen into print when you activate the print command. All applications allow you to choose different print options, such as landscape or portrait orientation, paper size, and manual or automatic feed.

A number of different types of printers are available, such as inkjet printers, laser printers, photo printers, and all-in-one printers; what you choose will depend on your needs.

- Many home users have inkjet-type printers for printing simple documents. Inkjet printers, ink cartridges, and paper are lower in cost as compared to laser printer cartridges, the print quality is quite good and they can print several pages per minute. This is an appropriate choice for home users who have very low printing volumes.

- If a large amount of printing is required, for schools or businesses, a laser printer can be set up on a network so multiple users can share this device. You can choose from black-and-white or color laser printers. A laser printer may contain several trays of varying paper sizes, including one that holds large pieces of paper for printing booklets, posters, or flow charts.

- Other types of printers available for specific uses include plotters to print large posters or architectural plans, photo printers to print high quality photographs, or all-in-one printers that enable you to print, copy, and scan items from one machine.

Using Projectors

While gathering around a notebook computer to view a presentation may be suitable for co-workers collaborating on a project, most professional presentations are delivered to an audience using a projector connected to the computer. Projectors display the presentation on a large surface, such as a screen or a wall. Output can be directed to both the notebook screen and a projector, allowing the presenter to annotate and navigate slides directly on the notebook while the audience's attention is focused on the screen. Projectors of varying size, portability and resolution are widely available for purchase and generally connect to a notebook or desktop system using a standard video cable.

Using Speakers

Speakers play sounds saved as digital files on the computer. Different forms of sound files, such as .mp3, .wav, or .wma can be used to store sounds, and the file format used directly determines the sound quality of the audio file. However, the quality of the speakers also affects the user experience.

A set of speakers may be included with the computer as a separate device to plug in, or may be incorporated into the computer (as with notebooks). A variety of speakers of different qualities can be purchased separately.

Understanding How It Works Together

 Exam 1 - Objective 1.1, 2.3

As you have learned, the ROM-BIOS chips are responsible for starting your computer, checking system memory, and loading the operating system. The process of starting up and loading the operating system is referred to as "booting." The computer executes the instructions in ROM-BIOS only when you first boot up by powering on the computer or when you restart or "reboot" the computer.

Once the instructions in ROM-BIOS are loaded, the computer looks for a valid operating system. An operating system can be loaded into memory from a bootable disk or from a hard drive onto which the operating system has been installed. A bootable disk is a removable medium from which a computer can load and run an operating system or utility program. A boot disk can be created on a CD, DVD, or flash drive. (In the early days of computing, a boot disk was created on a floppy disk.)

Most computers boot (load the operating system) from the hard drive. However, a computer can also load an operating system from a CD-ROM, DVD, or flash drive, and if the computer cannot find a valid operating system on the hard drive, it will search these other storage drives.

The boot sequence determines the order in which each drive is accessed when the computer is looking for the operating system files. Most systems check the hard drive (usually drive C) first, then they may search optical drives or USB devices. If a system checks the hard drive before any other drive, and a valid operating system is installed on the hard drive, then the system will boot from the hard drive regardless of whether bootable media exists in an optical drive or USB port.

When the operating system files are found, the operating system is loaded into RAM and occupies a specific amount of RAM the entire time the system is up and running. If a valid operating system cannot be found, the computer will not boot up.

When the computer loads the Windows 7 operating system and passes control over to it, the first screen you will see is the Windows welcome screen, identified by the Windows logo and confirmation of the version of Windows you are using. In most setups, you log on to Windows at the welcome screen.

When you log on to your Windows account, the Desktop appears. On systems where there is only one user account on the machine, and that account does not require a password, the user is automatically logged on and the Desktop appears automatically.

As you begin to perform tasks, the computer will use as much RAM as it needs to complete those tasks.

Software application programs are typically stored on the hard disk drive, thereby taking a specific amount of space for storage. Each installed application program requires a certain amount of storage space on the hard disk drive. This amount of space does not change once the application program is installed unless you change or remove the program on the hard disk drive. As you create and save files in your application programs, more disk space is required to store those files. The software vendor for each program will indicate how much storage space is required to install the software, and you must take into account the requirements for each program you want to install when determining if you will have sufficient disk space.

When you start an application program, the computer loads a copy of the program's instructions into RAM. The program remains in RAM until you close it. As you perform work within an application program, your work is also stored in RAM until you specifically save your file. The software vendor for each program will indicate how much RAM is required for the program to run properly, and you must take into account the requirements for running the program and the operating system simultaneously when determining if you will have sufficient memory.

You should always close an application program when you have finished using it, as this frees up RAM for other application programs to run.

EXERCISE

Now that you have been introduced to different types of computers, try the following activity to review some of the concepts.

You would like to purchase a portable computer device, but are unsure which one might suit your needs. You also want to consider purchasing a printer so you can make hard copies of items, when needed. Use a newspaper advertisement or visit a retail store to create notes on some of the different items available for purchase. Include the following for comparison purposes when you complete the notes:

- Name of product or brand of the device
- Version of product or brand, if applicable
- Microprocessor speed
- Amount of RAM memory included
- Amount of storage space included
- Size of the monitor
- Built-in or external Keyboard
- Pointing devices (e.g., is this a device that uses touch-screen or do you need a traditional pointing device)
- Type of power devices (e.g., how do you charge or recharge this device)
- If the device has a battery, how long does the battery last between charging
- Printer options (included or purchase separately)
- Length of warranty
- Sale price

Lesson Summary

In this lesson, you looked at the different types of computers available, and were introduced to some basic hardware terminology, including the following items:

☑ bits and bytes   ☑ microprocessor chip

☑ mega, giga, tera, or peta   ☑ ROM and RAM memory

☑ hertz and gigahertz   ☑ volatile and non-volatile storage

☑ CPU   ☑ types of devices

Review Questions

1. What would be considered an advantage of using a notebook to keep class notes if you are a student?
    a. Cost   c. Speed
    b. Portability   d. Size

2. Which hand-held device could be considered a productivity tool to manage your messages and music?
    a. Cellular phone   c. Smart phone
    b. MP3 device   d. e-reader

3. What are binary numbers?
    a. 1s and ls   c. 1 to 9
    b. 0s and Os   d. 1s and 0s

4. Why is RAM considered volatile?
    a. It disappears when the computer is shut down or restarted.
    b. It is unstable.
    c. Its contents cannot be changed.
    d. The amount of RAM cannot be changed.

5. Imagine you work for ABC Company and you need to purchase a computer that will store the company's customer and order information and make it accessible to several users within the company. Which type of system should you consider purchasing?
    a. A notebook   c. A server
    b. A desktop PC   d. A PDA

6. Which internal component performs calculations and logical operations?
    a. Microprocessor   c. RAM chips
    b. ROM-BIOS   d. System board

7. Which statement about solid state drives is accurate?
    a. Solid state drives are less expensive than comparably sized magnetic drives.
    b. Solid state drives are available in larger capacities than magnetic drives.
    c. Solid state drives have no moving parts.
    d. Solid state drives never wear out.

MMM
Go online for
Additional
Review

Lesson 4: Control Panel

Lesson Objectives

In this lesson you will learn how to customize your computer using the Control Panel in Windows. On completion you should be familiar with how to:

☐ start the Control Panel

☐ change the view

☐ change the display of the desktop

☐ change the date and time

☐ change to view or input with a different language

☐ find settings for accessibility options

☐ set different power options

☐ identify different account types and restrictions

Using the Control Panel

 Exam 1 - Objective 1.3.1

The Control Panel is the area in Windows where you can access features to either install or customize the settings for devices on your system.

Use one of the following methods to access the Control Panel:

- Click **Start**, **Control Panel**; or
- in Windows Explorer, click **Computer** in the Navigation pane, then click Open Control Panel in the Command bar.

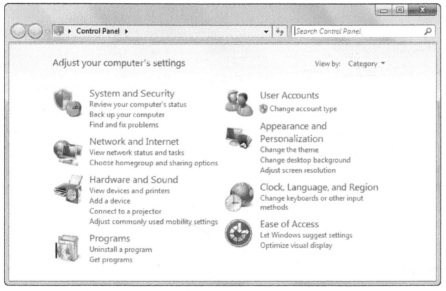

System and Security	Provides options for maintaining system integrity, performing data backups, checking for updates and scanning downloads.
Network and Internet	Allows you to set up or modify how your system connects to a network or the Internet, and to share files with others.
Hardware and Sound	Enables you to set up or modify the way hardware items such as sound devices will work.
Programs	Provides access to system management tasks such as installing and uninstalling programs.

User Accounts	Provides options for setting the computer up to be used by more than one person.
Appearance and Personalization	Allows you to customize your screen with screen savers, desktop backgrounds, and so on.
Clock, Language, and Region	Provides access so you can change the format of dates, times, currency, or numbers to reflect regional standards or languages.
Ease of Access	Provides options for changing accessibility specifications, such as turning on voice recognition or altering visual displays.

Some of the more commonly used features in Control Panel include changing options for the:

- desktop background
- screen saver
- mouse or keyboard

- date or time
- sounds that accompany specific actions in Windows
- audio volume

If you prefer to see icons for Control Panel items, you can switch the display to **Large icons** or **Small icons**:

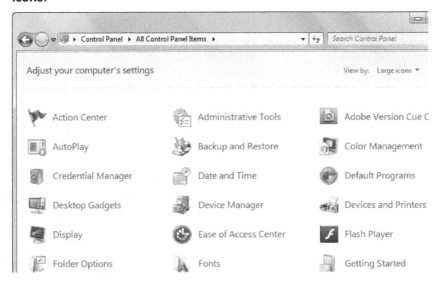

The Control Panel includes a number of features that you should not use unless you are very comfortable with the computer. Be sure you fully understand what each option can do and when you might want to use it before attempting any changes. If you choose not to work with someone who has advanced knowledge, record the original settings before making any changes so that you will have the option of returning to them if the changes you make do not work. For example, if you change the device driver for an output device such as a printer, be sure to record what the original device driver was in case the printer does not work after you make the change. This is very important if you choose to change any of the security options such as the firewall or Internet settings.

Some features, specifically those that affect how the computer functions or those that can affect other users, may not display in the Control Panel if you are using a system that belongs to a company or school. Your network administrator will set access to these features according to organization standards. For example, a school administrator may allow students to customize the background for the system but the User Accounts feature never appears in the Control Panel window, or a retail store may set the background so that it will always display the company logo and cannot be changed in the Control Panel.

Customizing the Desktop Display

Customizing the desktop display includes changing the background, screen saver, desktop appearance, or screen resolution. To change the display, use one of the following options:

- Click **Start**, **Control Panel**, **Appearance and Personalization**, **Personalization** or

- right-click a blank area of the desktop, click **Personalize**, and then click the display option to change, or

- if in one of the icon views, click **Personalization** in the Control Panel window.

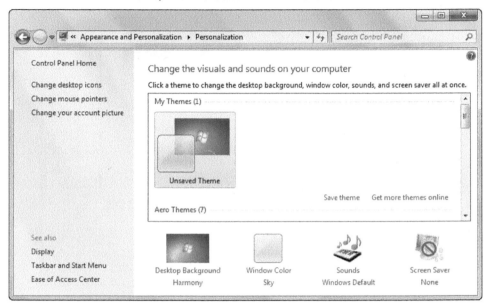

You can now apply a theme to the desktop, customize an existing theme, or create your own theme. A theme is a combination of pictures, colors and sounds. Each theme includes a Desktop background, a window border color, sounds and a screensaver.

My Themes	Themes you have customized, saved or downloaded. When you make changes to a theme, the new settings appear in this section as an unsaved theme.
Aero Themes	Themes include Aero glass effects and many include a desktop background slide show.
Installed Themes	Themes that are created by computer manufacturers or non-Microsoft providers. Not every system includes installed themes.
Basic and High Contrast Themes	Themes are designed to improve computer performance or to make items easier to see. These themes do not include Aero glass effects and therefore do not support all of the Aero features.

Click any theme in the dialog box to select it. For the selected theme, you can change the window color, sounds and screen saver settings. Simply click the theme component at the bottom of the Personalization window to access the configuration settings.

Note that supporting the Aero features can impact the performance of the system, especially if the system only barely meets the hardware requirements.

To customize the desktop:

- Use the **Desktop Background** option to apply a theme or to customize how the themes will display in the list for selection, or

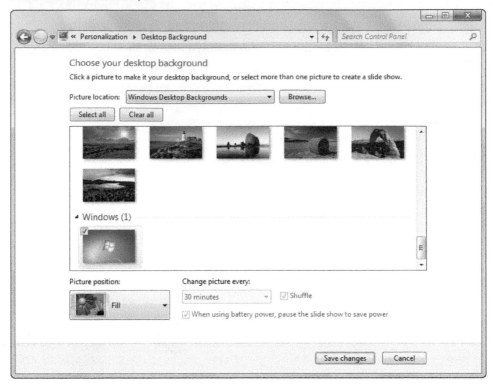

- use the **Window Color** option to choose a specific color for the window borders, Start menu, or taskbar. You can also use this option to control the color intensity and to enable or disable window transparency.

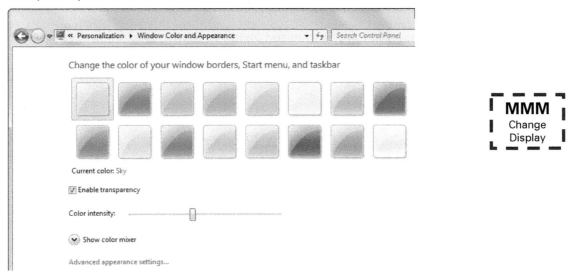

- use the **Sounds** option to apply a specific sound scheme to the theme. The sound scheme determines which sounds play when particular Windows events (such as closing a program or minimizing a window) occur.

┌─────────────┐
│   **MMM**   │
│ Using the │
│   Screen   │
│   Saver   │
└─────────────┘

- use the **Screen Saver** option to select and apply a screen saver. If the screen saver includes configurable options, you can set those too.

EXERCISE

In this exercise you will customize the desktop by changing the display to a solid color and then applying a screen saver.

1. Close any open windows if necessary, then right-click a blank area of the desktop, and click **Personalize**.

2. Click **Desktop Background** in the area below the list of themes.

3. Click the **Picture location** field and then click **Solid Colors**. Pick a light color such as the light grey in the first row. Click **Save changes**.

   The background, behind the Personalization window, changes to the color you've chosen.

4. Click **Screen Saver**.

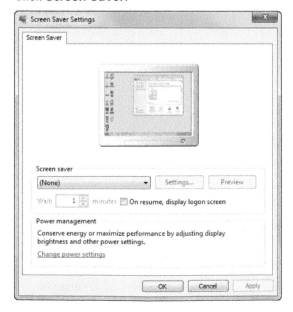

5. Click the arrow for the **Screen saver** field and click **Bubbles**.

   Windows displays a preview of this screen saver. Take note that some screen savers (such as this one) are transparent and will still allow you to see what you were working on before the screen saver activated.

6. Ensure the **Wait** time is 1 minute. Click **OK**.

7. Do not touch your mouse for at least 1 minute so you can view the screen saver.

8. Move the mouse slightly and notice that the screen saver disappears.

9. In the list of background options, locate the Aero Themes section, then click the **Windows 7** theme to return your display to its default setting.

10. Click **Window Color** to customize this a bit more.

11. Click any color other than the default color and notice how certain elements in the windows change in color.

12. Click another color and then click the **Enable Transparency** option to see the changes.

   Not only did certain screen elements change to the new color, you should notice that they appear more solid in color. In the previous version, you could see through the color.

13. Click the **Enable transparency** option once more to view the screen changes.

14. Click **Cancel** to exit the customization options here.

15. Close the Personalization window.

Changing the Date and Time

By default, the current date and time displays in the notification area; when you point the mouse pointer at the time, a screen tip also displays the current date in the default format set up on the computer. The operating system uses the date and time settings to identify when you create or modify files. These date and time settings are obtained from a battery-operated clock inside the computer (its internal clock), which should be current. If you are connected to a network, the time may be determined by the server and only the network administrator can change it permanently. If you are connected to the Internet, your computer will synchronize its clock with a time server on the Internet. You can set this by selecting the Internet Time tab in the Date and Time window.

To view the current date and time, click the time in the notification area:

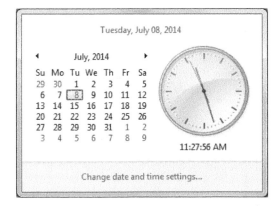

You can change the date or time using one of the following methods:

- Click **Start, Control Panel, Clock, Language, and Region**, and then click **Date and Time** or **Set the time and date**, or

- click **Start, Control Panel**, and if in an icon view, then click **Date and Time**, or

- click the time in the notification area and then click **Change date and time settings**.

Date and Time

Changes the existing time and date, or the existing time zone.

Additional Clocks

Displays additional clocks in the notification area so you can see the time in different parts of the world.

Internet Time

Provides access to settings that you can use to configure your computer to automatically synchronize with an Internet time server.

EXERCISE

In this exercise you will add a clock for another location so you can view the time for both locations directly from the taskbar notification area.

1. Click the time in the notification area and then click **Change date and time settings**.

2. Click the **Additional Clocks** tab.

3. Click the first **Show this clock** option to turn it on and then change the time zone to somewhere far away from your current location.

4. In the **Enter display name** field, type the name of a large city in that time zone, such as Seattle, Toronto, Edinburgh, or Beijing.

5. Click **OK**.

6. Point at the time in the notification area to view the current time for the two locations.

7. Click the time in the notification area and then click **Change date and time settings**.

8. Click the **Additional Clocks** tab and then click **Show this clock** to turn this clock off. Click **OK**.

Changing the Language

When you first receive your computer, the language has been preset for you based on the location where the computer is purchased. However, you can install or uninstall other languages and change the display or the input option.

To change, add or remove a language, click **Start**, **Control Panel**, and click **Clock, Language, and Region**. Then click **Change keyboards or other input methods**.

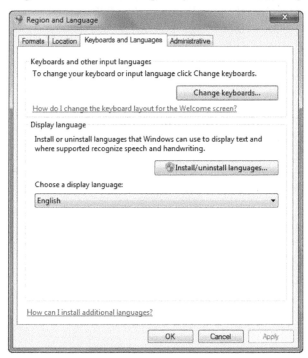

To change the display of items on the screen to another language, click the arrow for **Choose a display language** and click the appropriate language. Alternatively, if you need to install or uninstall a language, click the **Install/uninstall languages** button.

The Display language section will be visible only if a language interface pack (LIP) or multilingual user interface pack (MUI) has been installed. If this section is not visible, contact your system administrator or click the **How can I install additional languages** link to read more about installing or changing a display language.

To change the keyboard so you can input characters in another language, click **Change keyboards**.

To add another keyboard to the list, click **Add**; alternatively, to remove a keyboard, select it in the list and then click **Remove**.

You can change the format for the dates as required by clicking the **Formats** tab.

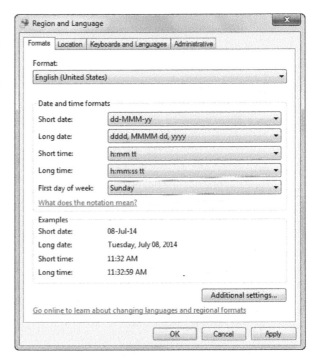

EXERCISE

In this exercise you will add a keyboard layout with a different language and then remove it.

1. Click **Start** and then click **Control Panel**.

2. Click **Clock, Language, and Region**. Then click **Region and Language**.

3. In the Region and Language dialog box, ensure you are viewing the Formats tab and try clicking the down arrow for the different date formats. Check with your instructor before making any changes here.

4. Click the **Keyboards and Languages** tab and then click the **Change keyboards** button.

5.   In the Installed services area, click **Add**.

6.   Pick a language that is different than yours, or select one as indicated by your instructor. Click the
     ⊞ symbol at the left to expand the layout choices available for this language (we have chosen
     Greenlandic as our example) and select one of the layouts.

7.   Click **OK** once the keyboard layout has been selected.

At this point you would click **Apply** and then switch the keyboard layouts as needed. In this
demonstration, you will now delete the keyboard layout as it is not needed.

8.   Click to select the new keyboard layout you just added to the list. Then click **Remove**.

The keyboard layout should no longer be visible in the list.

9. Click **OK** to close the Text Services and Input Languages dialog box, then click **Cancel** to close the Region and Language dialog box.

10. Close the Control Panel window.

Accessibility Settings

Windows 7 includes accessibility options and programs that make it easier for people with disabilities to see, hear and use the computer. Additionally, Windows 7 supports assistive devices for people with impairments. You can use the Ease of Access option to customize accessibility settings and devices.

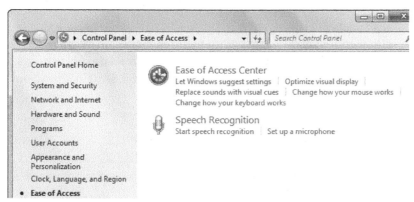

You can choose one of these options or click **Ease of Access Center** to see the list of options.

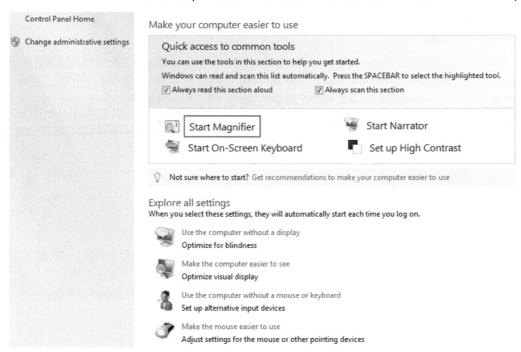

Built-in accessibility options include:

Magnifier	Enlarges portions of the screen making it easier to view text and images and see the whole screen more easily. In Windows 7, Magnifier includes full-screen mode, lens mode and docked mode. You can set the magnification level up to 16 times the original size.

Narrator	A basic screen reader which reads aloud the text on the screen and describes some events (such as the appearance of error messages) to let you know what is happening as you use the computer.
On-Screen Keyboard	Displays a visual keyboard on the screen which you can use with a mouse or other pointing device.
High Contrast display settings	Increases the contrast of colors to reduce eyestrain and make things easier to read.

If you have installed special assistive devices, the type of device will determine which settings can be modified.

Be aware that other operating systems include accessibility features similar to Windows to address certain disabilities. For instance, all Apple computing devices include the following features: screen magnification, a simplified user interface that uses rewards for exploring learning, and options to change how the keys work.

EXERCISE

In this exercise you explore accessibility options to see how these can make the computer easier to use.

1. Click **Start** and then click **Control Panel**.

2. Click **Ease of Access** and then click **Ease of Access Center**.

3. Click **Start Magnifier**.

    How the screen appears depends on whether this option was activated previously. If the text and images appear quite large at the top of the screen, the view is set to Docked Mode; this can be advantageous for someone with a visual impairment. Alternatively, the view may be set for Full Screen if the only change to the screen is a small window with icons. The Magnifier toolbar can be used to manipulate the zoom or magnification of the screen. If the Magnifier toolbar is not visible, click **Start Magnifier** again.

    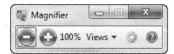

4. In the Magnifier toolbar, click **Views** and then click **Lens**.

    You should now have a small box that you can drag around the screen in order to magnify specific portions of the screen. Using lens mode is just like using a hand-held magnifying glass.

5. In the Magnifier toolbar, click the ⊕ sign to increase the zoom and then move the lens box around so you can see how it magnifies areas of the screen.

6. In the Magnifier toolbar, click **Views** and then click **Full screen**.

7. If the screen displays very large, in the Magnifier toolbar, click ⊖ to reduce the zoom.

8. In the Magnifier toolbar, click **Close** to close the toolbar and turn off screen magnification. Then close the Ease of Access window.

Understanding Power Options

 Exam 1 - Objective 1.3

Every computer has a power supply that converts the AC power from an outlet into DC power that the computer can use. The computer receives power using a power cord that is plugged into a standard electrical outlet. All portable computing devices include an internal or additional battery that allows you to use the computer without plugging it into an electrical outlet.

As you learned in Lesson 1, there are various methods for properly exiting Windows. These include shutting down, going into sleep or standby mode, and going into hibernation mode. These modes are reviewed here. Windows also provides power options and power plans that allow you to specify how power is used, and when the display and/or hard disks are put into sleep mode.

Shutting Down

When you are finished using your computer, turning it off properly is important, not only to save energy, but also to ensure that your data is saved. The three ways to turn off your computer are pressing the power button, using the Shut down button on the Start menu, and, on a notebook, closing the lid.

To shut down, click the **Start** button, then in the lower-right corner of the Start menu, click **Shut down**. When you shut down, the computer closes all open files, applications and the operating system, then completely turns off the computer and display. Shutting down does not save files. You must save your work before you shut down. Restarting your computer after shutting down takes longer than waking the computer from sleep/standby or from hibernation.

Sleep

As an alternative to shutting the system down, you can put the computer to sleep. When a computer is in sleep mode, the display turns off and often the computer's fan stops. The whole process takes only a few seconds.

When you put the computer into sleep mode, Windows puts your work and settings into memory and then draws only a low amount of power. It is not necessary to close programs and files before putting the computer into sleep mode. However, it is always a good idea to save your work before putting the computer into any low-power mode (to prevent data loss in the event of a power failure). When you wake the computer, the screen will look exactly as it did when you put it to sleep.

To wake the computer from sleep, move the mouse or press a key. Because you do not have to wait for Windows to start, your computer wakes within seconds and you can resume work almost immediately.

When the computer is in sleep mode, it uses very little power to maintain all current work in memory. After a computer has been asleep for several hours, or if the battery is running low, your work is automatically saved to the hard disk and the computer turns itself off completely. This can also be adjusted to your preferences using the Power Options.

Hibernate

Hibernation is a power-saving state designed primarily for notebooks. In hibernation mode, the computer puts your open documents and programs on the hard disk and then turns off the computer. Of all the power-saving states in Windows, hibernation uses the least amount of power.

On a notebook, use hibernation when you know that you will not use your laptop for an extended period and will not have an opportunity to charge the battery during that time. Hibernation is also useful when you need to close the lid and move the computer to a different location. When you restart the computer and log on, the desktop returns to where you left it.

To wake a computer from hibernation, press the power button.

Working with Power Settings

The operating system allows you to customize how much power is used for specific tasks. That is, you can configure and apply power plans that will automatically turn off the display and put a computer into sleep after a specified amount of time.

> **Note:** We are using Windows 7 installed on a notebook to discuss power options. Please adjust the following information to match your computing device (such as with an Apple iPad or iPhone, use the **General** option in **Settings**).

To change the power state for a portable device, click **Start**, **Control Panel**, **Hardware and Sound**. You can then access the power options, similar to the following:

Power Options
Change battery settings | Require a password when the computer wakes
Change what the power buttons do | Change when the computer sleeps

To view all configurable options, click **Power Options**. Be aware that if you are connected to a network or do not have full administrative rights, some options may be restricted to you. You will then need to work with your network administrator to assist with the power options.

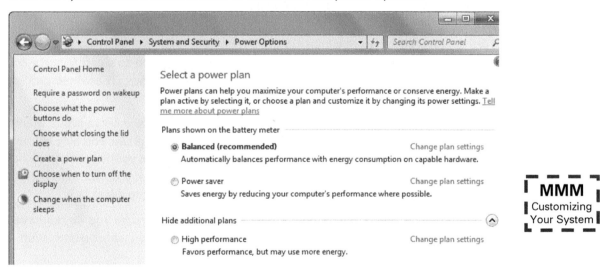

Windows includes several built-in power plans. You can apply these, modify their settings, or create custom power plans based on the built-in power plans. To view or change the settings for a power plan, click **Change plan settings** to open the Edit Plan Settings window.

Change settings for the plan: Balanced

Choose the sleep and display settings that you want your computer to use.

> ⊘ Some settings are managed by your system administrator. Why can't I change some settings?

	On battery	Plugged in
Dim the display:	2 minutes ▾	5 minutes ▾
Turn off the display:	5 minutes ▾	10 minutes ▾
Put the computer to sleep:	15 minutes ▾	Never ▾
Adjust plan brightness:	○ ────────🔆	○ ────────🔆

Change advanced power settings

Restore default settings for this plan

- To choose how the power buttons will react or what happens when you close the lid of the notebook, click the **Choose what the power buttons do** or **Choose what closing the lid does** option from the panel at the left of the main Power Options window. Options set here determine what happens with the power for Standby/Sleep, Hibernation, or Shut Down mode.

Define power buttons and turn on password protection

Choose the power settings that you want for your computer. The changes you make to the settings on this page apply to all of your power plans.

Power and sleep buttons and lid settings

	On battery	Plugged in
When I press the power button:	Sleep ▾	Sleep ▾
When I press the sleep button:	Sleep ▾	Sleep ▾
When I close the lid:	Sleep ▾	Sleep ▾

Password protection on wakeup

🛡 Change settings that are currently unavailable

◉ Require a password (recommended)
   When your computer wakes from sleep, no one can access your data without entering the correct password to unlock the computer. Create or change your user account password

○ Don't require a password
   When your computer wakes from sleep, anyone can access your data because the computer isn't locked.

EXERCISE

In this exercise you will look at the power options for the computer system you are currently using.

1. Click **Start** and then click **Control Panel.**

2. Click **Hardware and Sound**. Then click **Power Options**.

3. Review the options set up for the computer system you are currently using.

---

4. Click the **Change plan settings** link for the Balanced power option.

    The number of items that display will depend on the type of computer you are using and what rights you have on that computer. For example someone with a notebook will have the option to change the power settings when using a battery, whereas if you are using a desktop, you may see only one option set. Check with the instructor prior to changing anything.

5. Click **Close** to exit this window.

Understanding User Accounts and Rights

 Exam 1 - Objective 1.3.6

As you already know, Windows 7 computers can support multiple users, and each user must log on with a specific user account.

There are three different types of user accounts in Windows 7: standard user accounts, administrator accounts, and a guest account. (The guest account has very limited permissions. People using the guest account have limited access and cannot change settings, install hardware or software or create a password. The guest account is turned off by default.)

Each type of account has a specific level of permission associated with it. *Permissions* are rules associated with objects on a computer, such as files, folders and settings. Permissions determine whether you can access an object and what you can do with it. Everyone has permission to read/write (create, edit, view or print) files for their own account; only someone with an Administrator account can see files created by all users on the system.

The two account types you deal with most often on a Windows 7 system are:

Administrator account	Enables you to make changes to the system that will affect other users. Administrators can change security settings, install and uninstall software and hardware, and create or make changes to other user accounts on the system.
Standard user account	Enables you to use most of the capabilities of the computer. You can use most programs that are installed on the computer and change settings that affect your user account. However, you can't install or uninstall some software and hardware, you can't delete files that are required for the computer to work, you can't access other users' files stored on the computer, and you can't change settings that affect other users or the security of the computer.

An administrator account is created automatically when Windows 7 is installed on a computer. If you are using a computer at your school or office, the system administrator will likely have already created a standard user account for you.

If you are the only person using the computer (such as a home or your own computer), it might seem like a good idea to simply use the administrator account for everyday computing. However, Microsoft recommends that you create and use a standard user account to perform your day-to-day computing tasks because when you use a standard account you are much less likely to inadvertently make significant changes to the system.

When you use a standard user account, you will be prompted to enter an administrator password before you can perform certain tasks, such as changing the security settings or updating device drivers. Prompting you to enter a password is Windows' way of bringing to your attention the fact that you are about to make a significant change to the system.

In previous versions of Windows, it was inconvenient to work as a standard user because every time you needed to make substantial configuration changes, or wanted to install software or drivers, you had to log off as the standard user and then log on as an administrator in order to perform the desired tasks.

To view the type of account you are using, click **Start**, **Control Panel**, **User Accounts and Family Safety**, then click the **User Accounts** link.

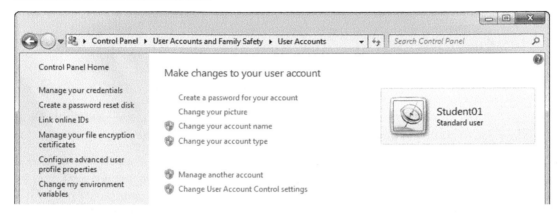

Depending on whether you are using a stand-alone system or a system that is part of an organization's network, certain options may not appear as shown in the figure above. For example, you may not be able to create or change your password.

Options that display with an icon to the left require an administrator password. The icon is part of the user account control (UAC) feature, discussed in the next section.

User Account Control (UAC)

In Windows 7, User Account Control (UAC) adjusts permission levels so that you have permissions appropriate to the tasks you are performing. This means you can log on as a standard user, and when you want to perform tasks that require administrator-level permissions, Windows 7 will prompt you for an administrator password and you can proceed. You no longer need to log off, and log back on as an administrator.

User account control issues notices when a user or program is about to make a change that requires administrator-level permission. For example, when you or programs you are using need to make changes that require administrator-level permission, UAC gives you options for proceeding:

- If you are logged on as an administrator, you can click **Yes** to continue.

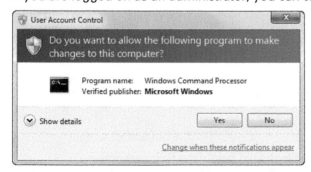

- If you are logged on as a standard user, you must select an administrator account presented in the dialog box and enter the administrator password.

- If you click **Yes**, or enter the administrator password, your permission level is temporarily elevated to allow you to complete the task, then your permission level is returned to that of a standard user.

UAC works by adjusting the permission level of your user account. If you are performing tasks that can be accomplished as a standard user (such as reading email, or creating documents), you have the permissions of a standard user, even if you are logged on as an administrator.

Creating a New User Account

You must have administrator rights before you can create a new user account. The following steps demonstrate how to create a new account on a stand-alone computer; if you are in a networked environment and require a new account, please ask your network administrator for assistance with this procedure.

To create a new user account on a stand-alone computer:

1. Log on using an administrator account.

2. Click **Start**, **Control Panel**, and then click **User Accounts and Family Safety**, then under the User Accounts link, click **Add or remove user accounts**.

3. Click **Create a new account**.

4. Type the name of the new user in the blank field below the first paragraph.

5. Select which access level you want this user to have (Standard user is recommeneded) and then click **Create Account**.

Choose the account you would like to change

Create a new account

What is a user account?

At this point you can choose to create another user account, change options for the new user just created, or exit this feature.

We will now look at some of the options you can set for the new user.

6.   Click the new account to access it.

Make changes to Allison's account

Change the account name
Create a password
Change the picture
Set up Parental Controls
Change the account type
Delete the account

Manage another account

7.   Click **Create a password.**

Create a password for Allison's account

Allison
Standard user

You are creating a password for Allison.

If you do this, Allison will lose all EFS-encrypted files, personal certificates and stored passwords for Web sites or network resources.

To avoid losing data in the future, ask Allison to make a password reset floppy disk.

New password

Confirm new password

If the password contains capital letters, they must be typed the same way every time.

How to create a strong password

Type a password hint

The password hint will be visible to everyone who uses this computer.

What is a password hint?

Create password   Cancel

8.   Type a password for this user in the New password and Confirm new password fields and then click **Create password.**

To delete a user account, you will need to access the user's account and then click **Delete the account.**

Do you want to keep Allison's files?

Before you delete Allison's account, Windows can automatically save the contents of Allison's desktop and
Documents, Favorites, Music, Pictures and Videos folders to a new folder called 'Allison' on your desktop.
However, Windows cannot save Allison's e-mail messages and other settings.

As each user can read or write their own files, when you delete the account all data files associated
with this account can be deleted at the same time. You are encouraged to make a backup of these files,
should you need them later, prior to proceeding. Click **Delete Files** to continue.

If you are sure you want to delete the account, click **Delete Account** to proceed.

Rights and Access

As you have learned, each type of account (administrator versus standard) has a specific level of
permission associated with it. Additionally, each individual user account can have specific permissions
associated with it.

Permissions determine whether you can access an object and what you can do with it. For example,
you might have access to a document in a network folder, but even though you can read the
document, you might not have permissions to make changes to it.

Two basic permissions you should be aware of are:

Read	You can view the names of files and folders on the network, view the contents of files, and execute application program files.
Write	You can view the names and contents of files and folders, and can create new files and folders, modify the contents of files, and delete files and folders.

When you work on a standalone system, you automatically have both read and write permissions to
all folders (and the files contained within them) associated with your user account. In order to access
folders associated with other user accounts on the computer, you must supply an administrator
password.

If you work on a network (for example, within a
company or at a school), the network administrator
controls which users can access specific network
resources, such as printers, or servers or files stored in
network folders. You may be able to view the contents
of some network folders, but not be able to create or
save files to those folders. There might also be some
folders that you cannot access at all.

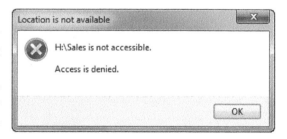

To keep their network resources secure, most network administrators provide the least amount of
access privileges required for users to perform their daily tasks. For example, a user in data entry who
spends all day entering customer orders into the company database does not require access to the
company web server, except perhaps to request web pages on the company intranet. The web server
administrator on the other hand, requires access to the web server, but does not require access to
confidential documents handled by the Human Resources department.

While each user account can have specific permissions associated with it, most system and network
administrators find it much more efficient to define specific user groups in a network, associate specific
permissions to each defined group, and then add individual users to those user groups. System
administrators often assign particular users membership in one or more groups. Often, a user belongs
to several groups.

If you have limited administrative rights, you can edit the rights on a file or folder to add or remove read/write/control rights. You will need to use the **Advanced** button in the **Security** tab of the file or folder's properties to view who currently has access to the file or folder; to add (or remove) rights, you will need to select the **Owner** tab and make the appropriate changes.

Any computing device owned by a school or organization is the responsibility of the network and system administrators. These administrators set up accounts, determine who can access what, and determine which features a user can access on a computer.

In many cases, the system administrator will configure computers so that users can perform their assigned job tasks, but cannot install programs, load additional device drivers, change network configuration settings, or interrupt or turn off scheduled virus scans or virus software updates. Often, the system administrator sets up scheduled tasks (such as performing virus scans and installing updates) on a company computer to ensure that the system is kept secure and up to date.

Group Policy

Large networks such as school or corporate networks, use a network organization and management system called Active Directory. Active Directory treats all network resources (servers, workstations, printers, users, files, etc.) as objects. Network objects are stored in a central hierarchical directory, allowing the administrator to manage all network objects from a central location.

Group policy is a feature in Active Directory networks that administrators can use to control the working environment of user accounts and computer accounts. Administrators can use group policy to manage and configure operating systems, applications, and users' settings.

As described earlier, administrators usually configure systems to run virus scans and update software as part of a regular maintenance schedule. While the administrator could sit at every machine and configure it individually, it is more efficient to use group policy to configure the computers. When an administrator uses group policy, he or she can create a policy once, then apply that policy to computers and user accounts throughout the organization automatically. Group policies are most commonly applied to groups of users or groups of computers. For example, an administrator can create a policy specifically for the users and computers in the accounting department, and then apply the policy. Whenever employees in the accounting department log on to their computers, the group policy is automatically applied and enforced.

Group policy is especially useful for helping administrators control and manage portable (mobile or remote) computing devices. Whenever these users connect to the company network (for example, when checking their email), any group policy the administrator has created for the mobile computer is automatically applied and enforced.

Lesson Summary

In this lesson you looked at how to customize your computer using the Control Panel feature in Windows. You should now be familiar with how to:

☑ start the Control Panel	☑ change to view or input with a different language
☑ change the view in the Control Panel to find an item to customize	☑ find settings for those who are physically challenged to access the computer
☑ change the display of the desktop	☑ set different power options
☑ change the date and time	☑ identify different account types and restrictions

Review Questions

1. How can you access the Control Panel?
   a. From the Start menu.
   b. From a file management tool such as Windows Explorer.
   c. By pressing ⊞+ⓒ .
   d. Any of the above.
   e. Only a or b.

2. If you cannot access certain commands in Control Panel, what is the most likely cause?
   a. You do not have access rights to these commands.
   b. You have selected the wrong command.
   c. Your version of Windows does not include the Control Panel feature.
   d. Any of the above.

3. What determines the date and time settings on a computer that is not connected to a network?
   a. Settings in RAM.
   b. A battery-operated clock inside the computer.
   c. The network server.
   d. A time server on the Internet.

4. Why might you want to change the formats for the dates on your computer?
   a. To comply with company standards.
   b. To comply with country standards.
   c. To suit your personal preferences.
   d. Any of the above.

5. Which of the following options can be accessed through the Ease of Access Center?
   a. Magnifier   c. Date and Time settings
   b. User Account Control   d. Power options

6. When might you set the power to Standby?
   a. When you need to take the notebook to another location.
   b. When you are waiting to connect to a network.
   c. When you want to continue working where you left off prior to going to a meeting.
   d. When you want to conserve power and your Desktop system is not plugged in.

7. To what does group policy refer?
   a. The logon ID and password you need to connect to the network.
   b. The group you have been assigned to by the network administrator.
   c. Set of rules for your office or department only.
   d. A feature that network administrators can use to control the working environment of user and computer accounts.

8. Which account type enables you to create additional user accounts?
   a. Administrator   c. Standard User
   b. Guest   d. a and c only

MMM
Go online for
Additional
Review

Lesson 5: Software

Lesson Objectives

In this lesson you will be introduced to software, and how it is created. You will also have a chance to look at different application programs and explore the typical ways software can be used. Upon completion you will be familiar with the following:

☐ different software applications
☐ installing a new program
☐ uninstalling a program
☐ reinstalling a program
☐ updating a program

What is a Software Program?

The term *computer software* refers to everything that makes a computer run, including operating systems, programming software, and application programs.

A computer program is a sequence of instructions written to perform a specified task. The instructions which constitute a program are written by computer programmers who use special programming languages. A programming language allows the programmer to write instructions and calculations in a human-readable form called source code.

In order to prepare a program for use by a computer, the programming language compiles the source code into an executable form. That is, the source code is changed into machine code – a form that the computer can use.

While creating the source code for a program can be a very complex process, using the finished program is generally as easy as clicking a button or entering text. The program's code works "behind the scenes" to interpret mouse clicks, keystrokes and menu selections or to display messages and text on the screen.

Software programs can create documents, record sounds, manipulate images, carry out complex calculations, and perform an enormous variety of other tasks. You have an almost infinite number of choices when selecting software. Your choice should be based on what you need to accomplish, the degree of detail and features you need, and what is most cost-effective.

Obtaining Software

 Exam 1 - Objective 3.2

All retail software programs are thoroughly tested before they are released to the public. Software vendors perform quality control tests on their software to minimize problems that can occur once you install the program. The cost of software often includes future updates to the program.

When you purchase a software program, you are purchasing a license to install and use that program on one computer only. This is also known as a *single seat* license. The traditional method of purchasing software is to obtain the program on CD or DVD in a package which may include a booklet with instructions on how to install and use the program.

You can also purchase and download software online. In such cases, you pay for the program, usually with a credit card, and then receive separate emails from the vendor confirming the purchase and providing a license number, often called the *product code* or *key code.*

An organization or company with a large number of users for a software program will usually purchase a *network* or *volume license* instead of individual copies. The network administrator will receive one media set (for example, a set of CDs) that contains the software, as well as additional files such as drivers. The network administrator then copies the program into a folder on the network, from which he/she can install it onto multiple computers and enter the key code to activate the program. The number of systems onto which the software can be installed is determined by the terms of the volume license. This option is cost-effective by reducing the amount of time needed to install a program on many computers. The network administrator can also perform installations from a remote site without needing to carry the software media around, thereby reducing the possibility of damage or loss as well as reducing the carbon footprint.

A *site* license grants the purchaser permission to use the software on a network at a single location (site), with an unlimited number of end users. A site license usually allows you to copy and use the software on multiple computers at a single site. It is more expensive than purchasing a single copy but less expensive than purchasing a copy for each computer at the site. There may be a maximum specified number of simultaneous users.

Software as a Service (SaaS) or Application Service Provider (ASP) licensing enables you to access and use a software program from your system via a network, the organization intranet, or the Internet. You are required to log on to the appropriate network using a valid ID and password before you can access the software. Once a SaaS contract expires, you can no longer access that software until you renew the license. Managing the licenses can be done by a network administrator in an organization or by an ASP.

Although these are the most common ways to obtain software, there are other legitimate means as well. Other methods of distributing or obtaining software include *shareware, freeware, bundling, premium* and *Open Source.* These software types are also considered to be copyrighted or owned by the software developer, and there may be restrictions on their use even though you may not have to pay for use of the software. Shareware are trial versions of software that you can download for free, but usually these programs have limited functionality or provide a limited amount of time that you can access the program. If you like the program though, you pay a nominal fee which removes these restrictions. Freeware programs do not charge a fee and may be shared with others at no charge. A potential drawback to using Shareware of Freeware is that support is often limited or non-existent and you are not automatically entitled to updates.

Software can also be "bundled" with a computer purchase. For example, when you purchase a new PC, the purchase price includes the license for the operating system, and may include a trial version of Microsoft Office, or an evaluation copy of Norton Utilities. Some of these programs may require you to purchase a full version of the program or to register online before you have access to the program, while others may include the full version and require no further action on your part.

Premium software refers to a special bundle of software you can purchase where one license key gives you access to the other programs included in the bundle; for example, you can purchase annual subscriptions to one or more of the fourteen desktop applications available in the Adobe Creative Cloud release. When you purchase the subscription, you are paying a set fee per user per month for each program those users will install on their systems.

Another type of software is Open Source. As the name implies, open source refers to applications where the source code is "open," meaning it can be accessed, customized and changed. Open source applications (and their source code) are generally freely available, and you can modify the program to suit your needs or to enhance it in some form, and then share your modified version of the code with others. However, certain restrictions apply: you cannot copyright your modified version of the source code, nor can you apply any type of distribution terms that would make the software proprietary, nor can you charge other users for your modified version. These restrictions are called "copyleft" restrictions (as opposed to copyright restrictions). While they offer more freedom than copyright restrictions, they still impose limits on how source code can be used. These restrictions distinguish open source software from public domain software.

Public domain software is not copyrighted. Anyone can use it for free, without restrictions. Public domain software does not necessarily allow a user to access, use, or alter source codes, but in some cases, it may.

Whichever way you obtain software, it is your responsibility to ensure you are observing the licensing rules. When you purchase licensed software, you will be notified by the vendor of updates and you will be able to obtain them at no additional cost. If you do not have a valid license, you will be violating the vendor's copyright and could be subject to legal action. A network administrator is aware of this responsibility and should take the necessary steps to ensure there are enough licenses for each computer in the organization. By accepting the End User License Agreement (EULA) at the time of installation, you further agree to abide by the rules for using this software on the computer.

Checking the System Requirements

System requirements identify the type of hardware (and operating system version) required to successfully run the program. All software, whether operating system software or application program software, is designed to work with hardware that can be expected to function at a specific speed and capacity. The software vendor lists these expectations so you can determine whether your computer is compatible and meets (and hopefully exceeds) all the requirements before purchasing the program. System requirements always appear on the software package if you purchase it in a retail store; if you purchase a license or other electronic means such as downloading from the software vendor's web site, the system requirements are listed on the site, usually before you click the Download or Purchase button.

A system requirements checklist may appear similar to the following:

Required Processor	1 gigahertz (Ghz) or faster x86- or x64-bit processor with SSE2 instruction set
Required Operating System	Windows 8, Windows 7, Windows Server 2008 R2, or Windows Server 2012
Required Memory	1 GB RAM (32 bit); 2 GB RAM (64 bit)
Required Hard Disk Space	2.0 GB available
Required Display	Graphics hardware acceleration requires a DirectX 10 graphics card and 1024 x 576 resolution
Required .NET Version	3.5, 4.0, or 4.5
Multi-touch	A touch-enabled device is required to use any multi-touch functionality. However, all features and functionality are always available by using a keyboard, mouse, or other standard or accessible input device. Note that new touch features are optimized for use with Windows 8.
Additional System Requirements	Some functionality may vary, based on the system configuration. Some features may require additional or advanced hardware or server connectivity.

If you are unsure of the type of hardware installed in your computer, check with a technical specialist before purchasing the software.

On a Windows 7 system, you can click **Start**, right-click **Computer**, and then click **Properties** to display the system properties.

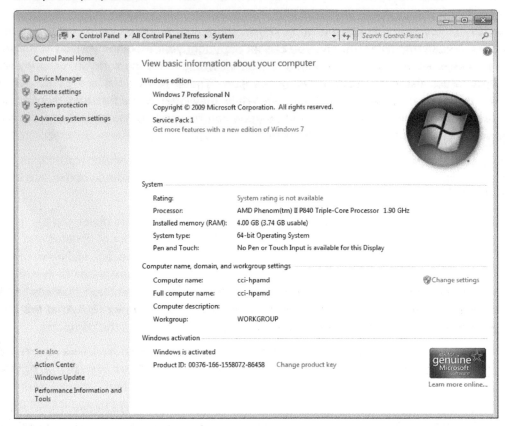

Notice that the displayed properties indicate the speed of the processor, the operating system version and the amount of RAM. Another method of checking the system requirements or performance rating is to use the Windows Experience Index; you can access this feature using the search field in the Start menu.

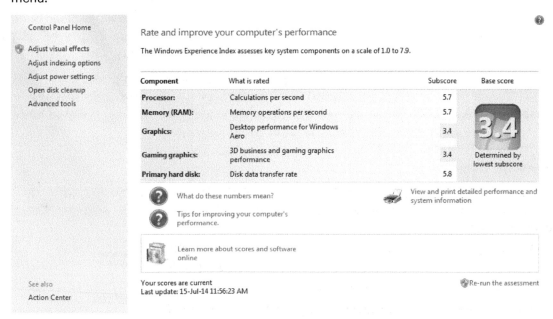

Some computers will have a sticker on the front of the case or on the area where you rest your palms on a notebook listing various system specifications.

Choosing an Application Program

IC³ Exam 1 - Objective 3.3, 3.4

Before you install any application software, an operating system must be installed on the system. The operating system controls the computer hardware and acts as a host for any application program you want to run on the computer. Application software programs are designed to be compatible with specific versions of an operating system. For example, a program may be designed to work with Windows 7 or higher. You should always check the box (if you purchase software from a retailer) or check the specifications listed on the web site (if you purchase and download an application program over the Internet) to ensure that the program you are purchasing is compatible with your operating system.

Hardware Implications

As discussed earlier, application software is written with the assumption that specific types of hardware will be used. This means that the hardware in your system can determine which operating system and application software you can install, and your operating system and application software can determine which hardware you can use.

For example, some systems use 32-bit processors and others use 64-bit processors. Systems with 64-bit processors can run either a 32-bit or a 64-bit version of Windows; but systems with 32-bit processors can run only a 32-bit version of Windows.

Computers running 64-bit versions of Windows can run 32-bit or 64-bit versions of application software. Computers running 32-bit versions of Windows can run only 32-bit versions of application software.

Additionally, operating systems require small programs called device drivers to communicate with installed hardware devices. A computer running a 64-bit version of Windows requires 64-bit device drivers. If you have some older hardware, such as a scanner or wireless network card, and you purchase a new computer that runs 64-bit Windows, you will need 64-bit drivers to enable the new computer to work with your older scanner or wireless network card. If 64-bit drivers are not available for these devices, you will not be able to use them with the new computer.

Software vendors will list the minimum requirements for processor speed, amount of available RAM, amount of available hard disk space, and sometimes the amount of video memory.

If your hardware does not meet or exceed the minimum requirements, the software will not run, or will perform poorly. In some situations you may be able to adjust your hardware; for example, you can clear off some disk space or add more RAM to the system. In other cases, you should probably look for different software that will work with your current hardware setup.

Application Types

While operating systems control hardware and manage files, an application program performs a specific function such as accounting, word processing, or drafting. Standard categories of application programs include:

Word Processing	Utility	Multimedia
Presentations	Accounting	Web Browsers
Graphics	Spreadsheets	Suite
Electronic Mail	Database Management	Customized

Within each category, there are several available software programs with industry-wide acceptance.

It is important to select the appropriate software program for the task at hand. Many programs share a number of features; to choose the one that best suits your needs, you must look closely at what you want to accomplish. Make a list of all the tasks you need to perform, and check off items as you compare different software programs. Look for a program that can handle at least eighty percent of the desired tasks, and factor in the amount of training time you'll need to learn the program when making your choice.

The following sections explore some of the standard types of application software.

Integrated Suites

An integrated suite is a group of programs packaged together for purchase as a bundle. Purchasing a suite is often much more cost effective than purchasing separate products. For example, an office business suite such as Microsoft Office, OpenOffice or Google Docs consist of word processing, spreadsheet, presentation, and email programs, and perhaps a database or graphics program. The programs within the suite are integrated or compatible with each other, so that data from one program can be used in any other program without difficulty.

The following suites are examples of software you install using an installation CD or DVD; this option enables you to select which programs in the suite you want to use.

Adobe Creative Cloud:
InDesign®
Photoshop®
Illustrator®
After Effects
Dreamweaver®
Lightroom
Premier Pro

**Microsoft Office
2013 Professional:**
Word
Excel
PowerPoint
OneNote
Outlook
Publisher
Access

You can also access Web-based versions of integrated suites using a web browser and a valid login ID and password. All programs in the suite will be available to you whether you use them or not, and can be referred to as *Web applications*. For instance, if you purchase Microsoft Office 365, you have access to a "light" version of Office 2013 commonly referred to as Office Online. If you purchased a subscription that includes Office 2013, users will then have the option to create or edit documents using the online (Web) version in a browser or directly in the full program installed on the computer.

Desktop Publishing

A desktop publishing (DTP) program enables you to manipulate large amounts of text and graphics that require a specialized page layout or structure, and then send the finished product to be printed by a dedicated printing service. In general, when you need to print professional documents that cannot be handled with a word processor, a desktop publishing application is suitable. For instance, to create a 9.5"x6" (24.1cm x 15.3cm) booklet with 10 pages would require you to use a booklet layout that allows content to appear in the proper order as the separate pages of the booklet are printed. You might also use a desktop publishing application to create a multi-color magazine or newspaper.

Most desktop publishing programs contain the same features and functions available in a word processing program but are more flexible for manipulating items such as pictures, drawn objects, or long documents.

Some popular desktop publishing programs include Microsoft Publisher, Adobe InDesign, or Scribus.

The following figure shows a layout for a multi-page booklet in a desktop publishing application.

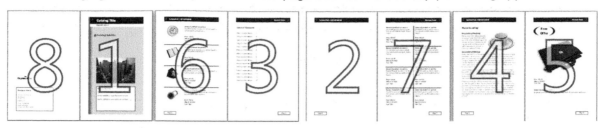

Spreadsheets

Spreadsheet programs perform mathematical calculations, produce "what-if" analyses, and display graphs, charts, and diagrams. If you need to track numbers or analyze information for trends or patterns, a spreadsheet is a good choice. A spreadsheet file is called a workbook and you can have any number of worksheets or reports within a workbook. For example, an entire workbook may be called *Sales Projections* and the workbook might include a worksheet of estimated revenue figures for each product the company sells.

Spreadsheets provide the ability to sort, find or filter information, and are very useful for managing and manipulating large amounts of data. You can use spreadsheets to track information such as bank reconciliations, travel expenses, assignment or report marks, and so on, and you can sort information by almost any criteria.

The spreadsheet documents shown in the following figure include a pricing report, a contacts list created with appropriate headings but no sort order, and the same contact list with filters applied wherein it can be sorted by any of the column headings such as Last Name or County.

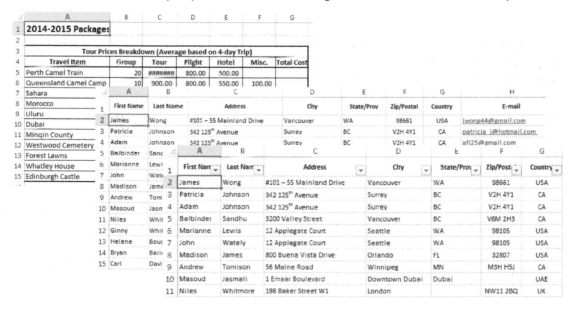

Database Management

A database is an organized collection of related information such as a phone book, inventory list, student grades, price list, or personnel files. A *Database Management Software (DBMS)* program organizes, stores, tracks, and retrieves the information in a database.

The basic function of a database application is to store data and organize data. If the database is well organized, retrieving the data you want is easy.

In addition to storing and retrieving data, database programs can generate reports, create specialized forms to make data entry easy and accurate, and control and verify the type of data that is entered.

Databases are identified by their structure:

- Fields contain individual pieces of data, such as names, addresses, and customer types

- A collection of related fields make up a record (for example, all the information for one contact is considered a record)

- A collection of records make up a table

- Multiple tables of related records make up a database

Many web sites use databases "behind the scenes" to help you find and purchase items on the site. They may also use databases to collect information about you when you subscribe or register as a user for the site. The collected information in this type of database can then be sorted or filtered to meet specific criteria, such as sending emails to those people who want information on a particular product, or contacting those customers who have not purchased in the past year.

Some popular database or database management systems include Microsoft Access, Microsoft SQL, or Oracle.

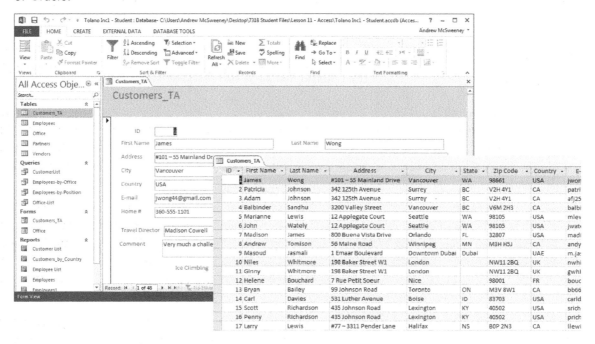

Database versus Spreadsheet

Many users are comfortable with spreadsheets, and many databases begin as data entered into a spreadsheet. Spreadsheets display rows and columns of data in a table format. It is easy to understand and visualize the data in a spreadsheet because the data is stored in one location.

A database in Excel is a single table that cannot include any blank rows or columns.

Consider the scenario of a gardening supply store that needs to track orders. A spreadsheet database solution created in Microsoft Excel 2013 might appear as shown below:

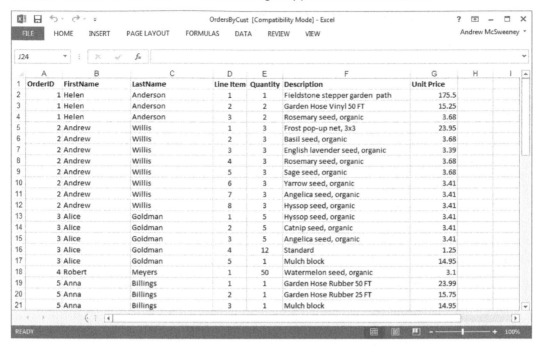

Although it is easy to visualize and understand the data shown in the spreadsheet, notice that there is considerable repetition in the table. In this database, a single order requires a record for every line item. This type of database will take longer and longer to search as it grows.

The large size and repetitive nature of the data reflect the complexities of the data itself. At first thought, tracking orders might seem a simple task; but consider how the various pieces of data are related: a customer may place one or more orders, each order will consist of one or more line items, and each line item must reflect a particular product that is available in inventory. These relationships are quite complex.

The true power of databases lies in their ability to represent complex data relationships. Instead of all the information being stored in a single table (as it is in a spreadsheet), the data in a database is most often stored in multiple tables. Each table stores information about a specific aspect of the information. In the case of the gardening supply company, for example, there might be a table that contains customer information, a table that contains order information, a table that contains detail information for each order and a table that contains product information.

Because the data stored in each table is "related" to data in the other tables of the database, a complete set of information can be retrieved for a desired entity. For example, you could retrieve complete information for an order from several separate tables using a query.

EXERCISE

In this exercise, you will start two Microsoft office programs to compare how they are set up for the type of data they are designed to handle.

1.   Click the **Start** button and then point at **All Programs**.

2.   In the menu that appears, scroll and then click **Microsoft Office 2013**.

3.   In the submenu that appears for Microsoft Office, click **Excel 2013**.

Excel opens in a view called Backstage where you can specify to create a new workbook or to open an existing one. Notice how Excel provides you with templates that consist of various business documents that can be created or modified using the worksheet format.

4. From the list of templates, click **Retirement financial planner**.

> **Note:** (If the Retirement financial planner template does not appear in the list of templates, click in the search box at the top of the page, type: `retirement`, click the Search button (🔎), then click the **Retirement financial planner** template when it appears.

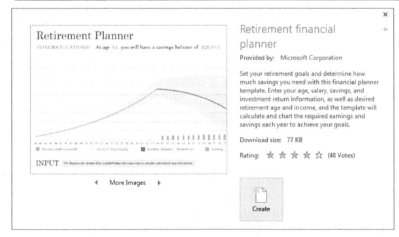

5. Click **Create**.

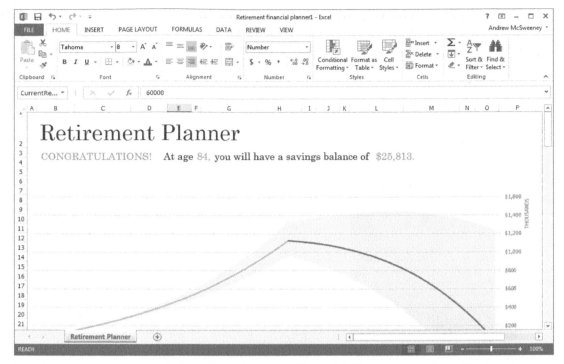

Excel creates a new worksheet based on the Financial Planner template. Notice that the new worksheet includes text, titles and a chart, followed by the data that makes up the chart is organized into specific columns. You can now enter data into individual cells to create this list.

6.   Scroll to view the type of data that has been entered as part of the sample.

Now try entering data to change the sample data to a more realistic value for what increases may be.

7.   Click in cell **E28** (the cell next to the Annual Inflation and income Increases cell) and type: 1 for the percentage and press (Enter).

The cursor should now be in cell E29. When you press (Enter), Excel moves the cursor to the next cell below the one where you just entered data. To enter data into another cell that is not adjacent to this one, you can click in that cell or use the arrow keys to move the cursor to that cell.

Look how the values have changed in cells B36 downward. This is an example of how a formula was set up to calculate values for a specific calculation, thereby saving you time and effort to change every line of data.

8.   Scroll up to view the chart to see how the values and chart line changed when the percentage increase was changed.

This report is an example of how you can enter information into a worksheet that can help your financial planning, whether it be a budget, cash flow analysis, savings-plan to purchase a home or as in this case, to retire. Once you've had a chance to enter all the values, you can then analyze the report to see those areas that may need revision; in this case, you may find you will need to increase the amount you place in a retirement fund, increase your income, or increase your savings.

Now try using a database to enter information and see how it compares to using a spreadsheet application.

9.   Click the **Start** button and then point at **All Programs**.

10. In the menu that appears, scroll and then click **Microsoft Office 2013**. In the submenu that appears for Microsoft Office, click **Access 2013**.

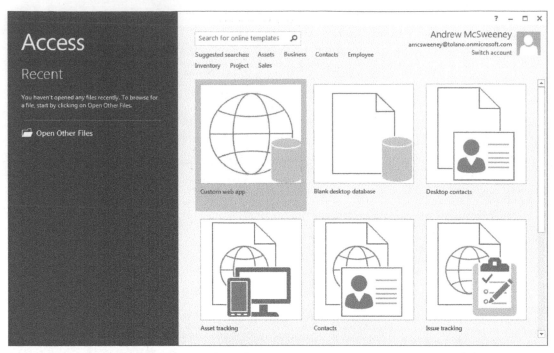

As with Excel, Access started in Backstage view, giving you the opportunity to create a new database or open an existing one.

11. From the list of templates, click **Desktop contacts**.

Note: (If the Desktop contacts template does not appear in the list of templates, click **Contacts** in the Suggested searches area at the top of the window, then click the **Desktop contacts** template when it appears.

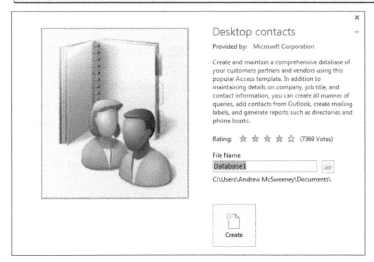

12. Type: 7318 Contacts as the name of the new database and then click **Create**.

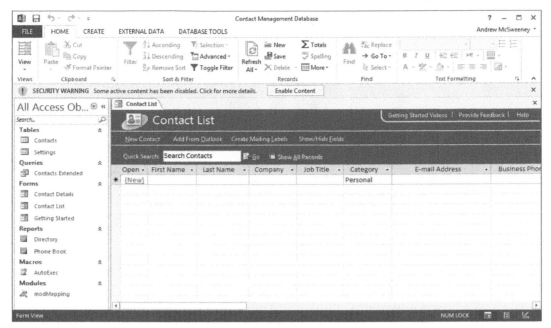

Access has just created a new database for you to enter information about contacts. Notice in the Navigation Pane how Access has also created a number of objects that can be used to help you generate specific reports or queries to find data.

13. Click in the first blank box or field below the First Name field name. Type: `Andrew` and then press (Tab) to move the cursor to the next field.

14. Type: `McSweeney` as the entry for the Last Name field. Press (Tab) twice and type: `Travel Director` for the Job Title field.

   Notice how entering data into Access is similar to how you entered data using Excel, structuring the values to match the field names, and navigating from one field to the next. Each program has advantages and disadvantages. For example, Excel is easier to use when you are first learning because you can see all the data at once. On the other hand, you cannot easily represent complex relationships in Excel. While Access can represent complex relationships, it is difficult for new users to understand where the data is actually stored and why it is separated into several tables. Now that you've seen an example of how the same type of information can be captured in a database and spreadsheet program, you can also determine which program, you might want to use for specific purposes.

15. Click the **Close** button at the far top right of the screen for Access.

16. Repeat step 15 to also close Excel. Click **Don't Save** when asked if you want to save the file.

Presentations

Presentation programs allow you to create slides or handouts for either speaker-delivered or self-running presentations. Most allow you to add special effects such as animations, slide transitions, and theme designs, and slides can contain any type of content such as text, graphics, diagrams, charts, or tables. Examples of presentation programs are Microsoft PowerPoint, Corel Presentations and Apple Keynote.

You can also create speaker notes and handouts for the audience, and you can set up presentations to be broadcast over the Internet, delivered to a live audience, or played automatically as a self-running slide show on a computer or kiosk for training or education purposes.

The following is a sample of files you can create with a presentation program including an award certificate, and an entire presentation shown in slide sorter view.

Content Creation

Content creation has traditionally involved creating text documents with a word processing program and then passing the documents to someone else for desktop publishing. In most cases, creating and managing professional documents of this type lead to frustration due to limitations of a word processing program's limited ability to handle a number of graphics items such as pictures, shapes, tables, etc. Word processing programs are now commonly used to create more design-intensive documents such as flyers, brochures, or long reports in addition to simple office documents.

Creating professional quality digital content for any purpose is easier than ever. Many application programs provide quick start aids or templates that automate much of the content creation process. For example, Microsoft PowerPoint includes built-in templates for creating targeted presentations such as training presentations, or presentations geared for academic, business or healthcare audiences. Microsoft Word includes built-in templates for memos, business letters, faxes, legal pleadings, flyers, schedules or newsletters. These templates are created by Microsoft based on the common types of designs or layouts used for published documents, thereby making it much easier for any user to create more professional looking documents.

Content Creation Programs

Digital content creation software programs perform similar tasks and provide the flexibility of managing different types of content for a variety of media. For example, content that may have originally been developed for print can now be combined with animation, audio, video and graphics for a web page, an electronic book (e-book), applications for use on mobile devices or as an online learning tool (e-learning).

The power of these programs comes from the fact that you can insert the content elements in a central repository (project folders) and then generate the content using any combination of these elements for an article, blog, online learning tool, or printed book. Files you include in the central repository can be in any number of electronic standard formats such as word processing files, .jpg or .gif pictures, .mp4 or .avi videos, etc. These programs also provide a variety of templates or pre-designed structure and layouts for a variety of content delivery.

You can also purchase content creation programs that are specific to a particular purpose, such as for developing web pages or e-learning. These programs include features and commands that help the user create content for a specific medium. For instance, a web authoring tool enables a user to create the content directly into the program, in a similar manner to a word processing program, import these into the web authoring program, and then use HTML and style sheets to format the text for any web browser.

Examples of content creation programs include Adobe FrameMaker for print/online Web/Help media, Microsoft Learning Content Development System (LCDS) for e-learning, and Adobe Dreamweaver or Microsoft Expression Web for web pages:

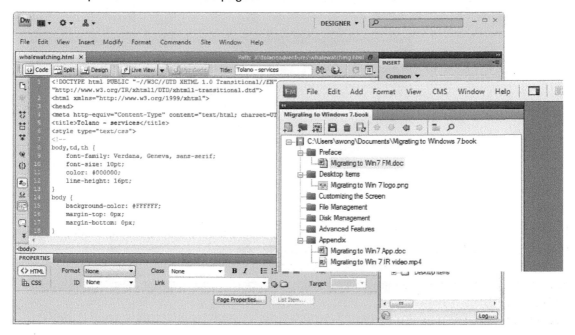

Multimedia

Multimedia programs enable you to extend the capabilities of graphic design by adding elements such as video, music, or animation. These programs are becoming so much easier to use that multimedia elements are now commonly included in web pages on the Internet or an intranet.

The term "multimedia" encompasses any content that incorporates graphics, music, or video. You must save multimedia files in a recognized file format in order for the computer to play them.

- The file formats most commonly used for video are .mpg/mpeg (Moving Picture Experts Group), or .mov, or .avi (includes animation), which is also used for still graphics.

- Music files are most commonly saved as .mp3 files. Music files can also be saved in the .wav (Waveform Audio Format or Audio for Windows) format. Files in this format can be played on any computer with an installed media player program.

- Graphic design programs may be grouped with multimedia software programs so that, in addition to manipulating pictures, you can create or edit sounds or video. A dedicated graphic design program is different from a software program with built-in drawing features, which may offer similar tools, but is generally not as flexible as a dedicated graphic design program. The most common file formats used for pictures include:

.tiff (Tagged Image File Format)	.wmf (Windows Metafile Format)
.bmp (Bitmap)	.jpeg/jpg (Joint Photographic Experts Group)
.gif (Graphics Interface Format)	.png (Portable Network Graphics)

The following figure shows a song being played in Windows Media Player, and a media file being edited in Adobe Flash.

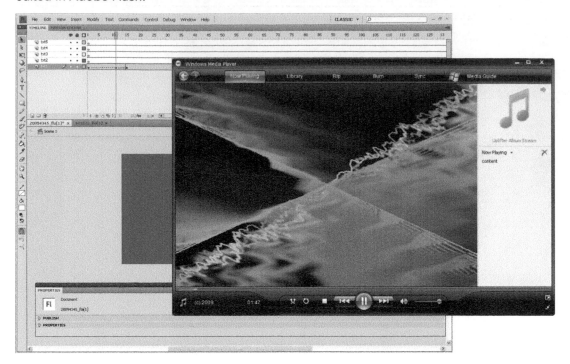

The following figure shows Microsoft Paint and Adobe Photoshop – each a drawing/graphics design program you can use to create simple diagrams or manipulate photographs:

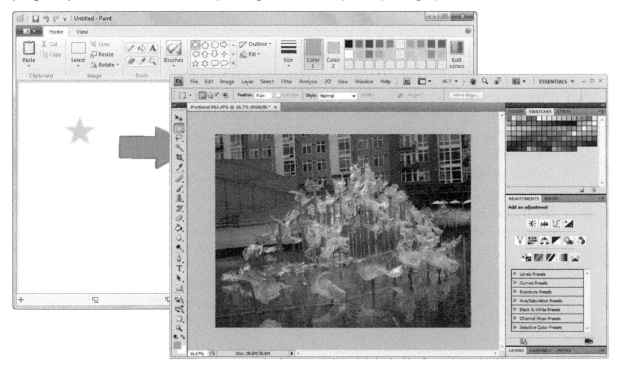

Something to be careful of when using multimedia programs is to ensure the file format is compatible with different operating platforms before distributing to others. For example, Adobe Flash files (file type is .swf) may not work on Apple computers when viewed online via the Internet. When you are using this program type, remember who your audience is, and how it will be viewed.

EXERCISE

In this exercise you will try using a simple drawing program called Paint that is included with Windows and which enables you to manipulate graphics for certain effects. It is not as flexible or powerful as a dedicated graphics design program such as Illustrator or Photoshop but can be useful to save a picture to a different file format or to create a simple drawing.

1. Click the **Start** button, point at **All Programs**, click **Accessories**, and then click **Paint**.

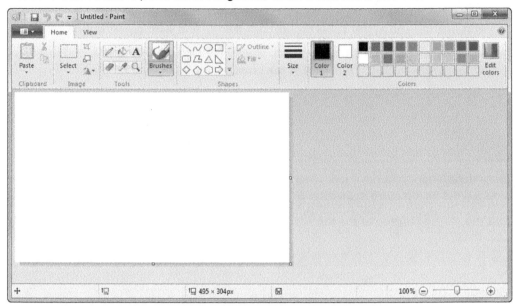

You will now create a small drawing of a mountain peak to practice using a drawing program.

2. On the **Home** tab, in the **Shapes** group, click the △ **(Triangle)** shape.

   The cursor changes to show ⌖ indicating you can now draw the shape. You will create the shape by clicking at where the top of the triangle will be and then drag to set the height and width of the shape.

3. Click and drag to create a triangle shape similar to the following:

   You have just drawn a shape and we will now modify it by changing its outline color.

4. On the **Home** tab and in the **Colors** group, click a blue of your choice (we chose indigo).

   The outline color has changed and we will now add a line to make it look more like a mountain.

5. On the **Home** tab and in the **Shapes** group, click the arrow for **Brushes** and then click the 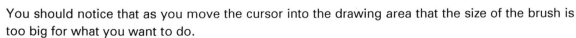 **(Crayon)** brush.

   You should notice that as you move the cursor into the drawing area that the size of the brush is too big for what you want to do.

6. On the **Home** tab and in the **Size** group, click the **Size** command and then click the first one in the list.

7. Starting somewhere on the left side of the triangle, click to create a curved line to simulate a snowcap on the mountain, similar to the following:

Note: Be sure that your snowcap line connects to both sides of the triangle, completely separating the top of the triangle from the bottom.

Suppose we now want to fill in the bottom portion of the triangle so it looks more like a mountain.

8. On the **Home** tab and in the **Tools** group, click the **(Fill with color)** button.

9. On the **Home** tab and in the **Colors** group, ensure the same blue you selected for the outline color of the triangle is selected. Then click in the bottom portion of the triangle.

Congratulations – you have just used drawing tools to create a mountain that can now be saved and inserted as a picture in another program.

10. Click the [button] button at the top left corner of the Paint window, and point at **Save as**.

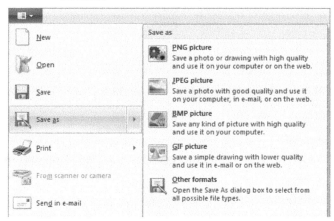

Notice the list for the different types of file formats available and which one might be suitable for what you plan to do with this drawing. In this case, we will choose JPEG as this drawing could be used somewhere on the Tolano intranet.

11. Click **JPEG picture**, and navigate to the location for the student data files.

12. In the **Save as** field, type: `Mountain - Student` for the file name and then click **Save**.

Now try opening a picture in Paint and reducing its size for use in an online flyer.

13. Click the [button] button and then click **Open**. Navigate to the student data files and in the Lesson 2 – Windows folder, select to open the *logo* file.

14. On the **Home** tab, click the **Resize** button.

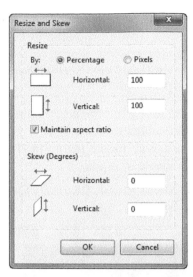

15. Change the percentage to **50** for both horizontal and vertical. Then click **OK**.

At this point, you decide you would like to save this smaller version with a different name than the original.

16. Click ▣▼ and then point at **Save As**.

    Each file type gives you a quick summary of how it can be used or the type of document for which this format is best suited.

17. Click **PNG picture** and type: `logo - student` as the new file name. Click **Save**.

18. Right-click the Start button and click **Open Windows Explorer**. Navigate to the *Lesson 2 - Windows* folder of the student data files and notice the file sizes for the two logo files. If necessary, change the view to be **Details**.

    You should notice that the PNG file is slightly larger than the original JPG format; this is because even though you reduced the size of the picture you saved the file using the higher quality PNG file format.

19. Close Windows Explorer and then close Paint.

Entertainment

You can find entertainment software suitable for personal or business purposes. This software type usually includes tools to help you with animation elements, be it in a video, audio, or a gaming environment. Many education programs include an entertainment aspect to challenge the learners in a variety of ways to keep the interest in the learning object. For example, a number of classrooms today include the use of computing devices such as the Microsoft Kinect or Apple iPad as part of the curriculum to teach topics such as programming games, practicing the piano in music class, watching documentaries of historical events, and so on.

Entertainment software can be purchased and installed on your own computer, game console or mobile device, and are also made available as web applications. These programs include features similar to those on physical audio and video players such as play, rewind, repeat, or shuffle (use a random order to play items). They also include the ability to create your own playlist that consists of songs you want to listen to, in the order you want to hear them.

One advantage of entertainment and multimedia systems is the ability to connect to other devices to share the information. For example, you can purchase special cables to connect your PC to a high definition (HD) television so you can share photos with others, play music stored in iTunes in the background prior to a presentation event, or simply to watch a movie or event.

Some examples of entertainment software include Windows Media Player, Windows Media Center, iTunes, GarageBand, iPhoto, iMovie.

EXERCISE

In this exercise you will be introduced to a multimedia program included with Windows, and you will go online to view an entertainment environment. If you do not have sound available on the system, the instructor may provide a demonstration to the class instead.

1. Click the **Start** button and point at **All Programs**. When the menu appears, scroll in the list and click **Window Media Player**.

The number and type of albums or audio that appears in the list will depend on what has been saved on your system. The screen here shows only the default sounds that were included with Windows 7.

2. Click the first item in the list and then click the **Play** button at the bottom.

    You should now be listening to the sample song for this album.

3. Click the **Stop** button to end the audio.

4. Click the **Play** tab near the top right corner of the window.

> **Note:** This panel may already be displayed if someone has used Windows Media Player prior to this exercise.

Notice how Windows Media Player now shows a playlist based on the listed items. You can choose to save the playlist as shown, drag the audio items up or down the list to change the play order, or click **Clear list** to remove the list. You can also use the **Create playlist** button to create a new playlist for audio or video items.

Let's now look at an Internet site that offers online games for entertainment and education.

5. Close the Windows Media Player window and then click the **Internet Explorer** icon on the taskbar.

6. In the Address Bar at the top, type: `www.disney.com` and press (Enter).

7. Click **Games** from the navigation bar near the top of the screen.

8. Click a game of your choice to play it and view what options are available for this online entertainment game.

9. When finished, close the web browser.

System Protection Tools

System protection programs can be indispensable if your computer stops working or behaves erratically due to some type of malicious attack from an external source.

Some popular types of system protection utilities you should consider installing include:

Antivirus Protection	One of the best investments you can make is to purchase an antivirus program which is updated frequently to protect your system from viruses that may disrupt, erase or corrupt information on your computer. Viruses are created every day and can range from being an annoyance to causing serious damage or data loss on your system.
Adware/Spyware Protection	Many vendors include a utility with antivirus software to find and block unwanted items from the Internet such as *spam, spyware,* and *adware.* Spam refers to unwanted messages, usually selling something; spyware refers to programs that gather information about your Internet use; and adware are programs that display advertisements automatically.
Malware Protection	Malware, or malicious software, can include viruses, adware/spyware, or code that disrupts a computer's operations, gives unauthorized access to an outsider, or gathers confidential or sensitive information.

The following are examples of antivirus programs that also contain protection for spyware or malware, AVG Internet Security, Windows Defender, and Microsoft Security Essentials.

EXERCISE

In this exercise, you will now look at Windows Defender, the system protection program that comes installed with Microsoft Windows. If there is a different antivirus or other system protection program installed in the classroom or computer, please activate that program through the Start menu to view the options available with that program.

1. Click **Start** and in the search field, type: `windows defender`.

2. Click the **Windows Defender** item at the top portion of the Start menu.

If Windows Defender is turned off, the message box shown will appear.

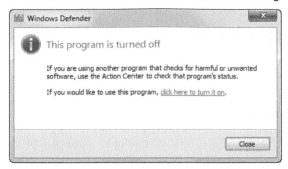

3. If necessary, click the **click here to turn it on** link to open Windows Defender.

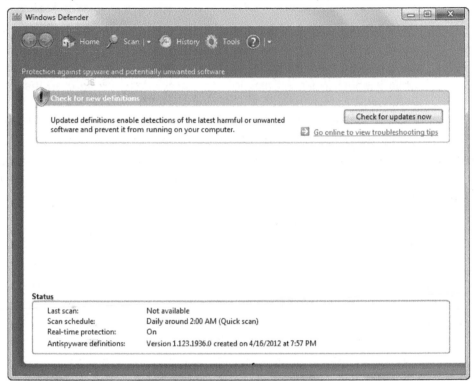

If Windows Defender had not previously been turned on, or has not been used for a while and is not configured to automatically search for updates, you can check for any updates.

4. Click the **Check for updates now** button.

    If the **Check for updates now** button is not visible, you can still manually check for updates. In the toolbar at the top of the window, click the drop-down arrow to the right of the **Help** button and select **Check for updates**.

    It may take several minutes for updates to be downloaded and installed. When Windows Defender is up to date, the Status will indicate either that the program is up-to-date or that no new definitions or updates are available.

5. To begin a scan, click the **Scan** button in the toolbar.

    The scan may take a few minutes. When complete, Windows Defender will display the scan results.

6. Click **Tools**, and in the Settings area click **Options**.

7. In the left pane of the Options window, click the **Administrator** link, then clear the **Use this program** check box. Clearing this check box turns Windows Defender off.

> **Note:** You should clear this check box only if Windows Defender was turned off when you began this exercise. If Windows Defender was on, then simply click the **Close** button and skip the remaining steps in this exercise.

8. Click the **Save** button.
9. When the notification that Windows Defender has been turned off appears, click the **Close** button.

Disk Management Programs

Disk management programs help you maintain your hard disk and data to ensure that your system operates efficiently. In some cases this type of utility can help to reduce the amount of space taken up by the data by removing unnecessary files such as temporary files created when you install a program or use a web browser.

Disk Compression	Compressing files on a hard disk is like taking rarely-used files out of the top drawer of the filing cabinet and squeezing them tightly into the bottom drawer. Compression frees up space to store more files in the most accessible drawer, while keeping less-used files in a less accessible spot in case they need to be retrieved.
	You can compress files and folders on the hard disk using Windows Explorer. Compressed files and folders display in blue.
Defragmentation	Over time, as files are created and deleted, a hard disk can become fragmented. This means that individual files are not stored in one contiguous location on the disk, but rather, are scattered over several regions of the disk. Fragmentation causes poor performance because the read/write heads have to jump from location to location to retrieve the file. The Disk Defragmenter utility defragments hard disks and puts fragmented files back together in a contiguous format.
	In Windows 7 the Disk Defragmenter runs automatically when the computer is idle. By default, Disk Defragmenter is scheduled to run every Wednesday at 1:00 a.m. You can also start the Disk Defragmenter manually at any time.
Disk Cleanup	Software programs create many temporary files, such as automatic saves in your word processing program or copies of attachments in your email program. Disk cleanup is a way of reducing the number of these temporary files, which can take up space and cause conflicts between programs. Disk cleanup recovers the disk space used by temporary files, unused applications, files in the Recycle Bin, and files you downloaded as part of web pages.

File Compression Utilities

A file compression utility can be very useful when you need to reduce the size of one or more files, usually for the purpose of transferring the file(s) from one location to another (for example, as an email attachment). Compressing one or more files is also referred to as *zipping,* much like when you stuff a tote bag as full as possible and then press everything down to make it fit prior to zipping (closing) the bag.

Some files are larger than others, simply by the nature of the type of file. For example, video files are usually very large and should be converted to a compressed format (such as .avi) so they can be shared. Music files in .wav format are generally converted to .mp3 format to make them smaller for sharing. Picture files with a .tif or .bmp file type tend to be large in size and are compressed to a .png or .jpg format. The image, audio and video files you encounter on the Internet are already in a compressed format, which reduces the time required to download them to a web browser.

You are probably already familiar with popular "zip" programs that compress text and images. WinZip and PKZIP are third-party utilities that have been used to easily and successfully compress and uncompress files for decades, and a built-in zip utility has been included with Windows since Windows XP.

Compressed files for Windows computers have a .zip file name extension, and you can often find zipped files on web sites that offer downloads. Compressed files for UNIX/Linux computers have a .rar file name extension. You can, however open a compressed file with a .rar extension in Windows by using a program called WinRAR.

To compress (zip) a file or folder:

- Locate the file or folder that you want to compress.

- Right-click the file or folder, point to **Send to**, and then click **Compressed (zipped) folder**.

To extract (unzip) compressed files and folders:

- Locate the compressed folder from which you want to extract files or folders.

- To extract a single file or folder, double-click the compressed folder to open it. Then drag the file or folder from the compressed folder to a new location.

- To extract the entire contents of the compressed folder, right-click the folder, click **Extract All**, and then follow the instructions.

Note that some types of files, such as JPEG image files, are already highly compressed. If you compress several JPEG pictures into a folder, the total size of the folder will be about the same as the original collection of pictures.

The following images show examples of disk management and file compression tools that are included with Windows:

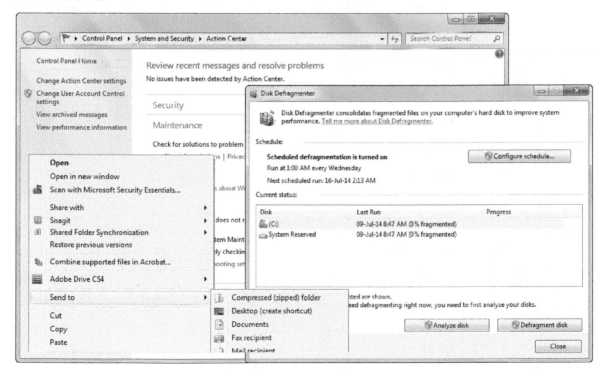

EXERCISE

In this exercise you are introduced to Disk Defragmenter, Disk Cleanup and file compression tools.

1. Press ⊞+E to start the file management tool.

2. In the panel at the left, right-click the **Local Disk (C:)** location under **Computer** and then click **Properties**.

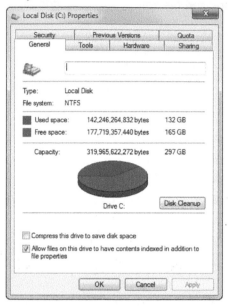

You will notice that this tab contains the **Compress this drive to save disk space** command that you can turn on, as needed. As Windows 7 is very efficient in managing the files on the hard drive, we will not use this option.

3. Click the **Tools** tab.

4. Click the **Defragment now** button.

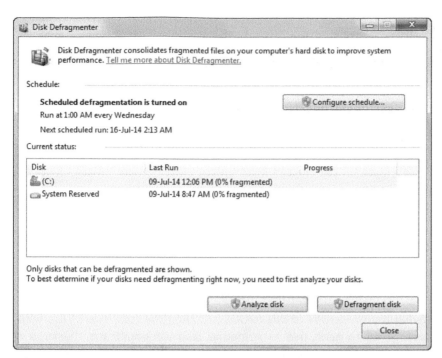

This window displays a summary of the disk drives available to you and how necessary it may be to perform a defragmentation of the files on the disk. The screen shows a low defragment rate which should prompt the user to have Windows analyze the drive to see how much space can be saved prior to running the command.

5. Click **Analyze disk**.

Windows now begins the analysis; how long this takes will depend on how big the drive is and the defragment rate. When the analysis is complete, Windows displays how much space can be saved.

> **Note:** If you do not have the access rights to perform this utility, click **Stop operation**, read the following steps that would occur when you run a defragmentation, and then proceed to step 7.

In this demonstration, no further space could be saved so we will opt not to run the defragment tool. However, depending on the system you are using, you can determine whether this procedure is necessary.

6. Click the **Close** button to exit this tool and then close the Properties window.

Now take a look at how a file compression tool works.

7. Click the local drive location and navigate to the location of the student data files. Click to view the Lesson folders.

8. Right-click the *Lesson 8 – Word* folder in the Contents pane to display the menu.

9. Click **Properties**.

You are now viewing the properties of this folder, including the total size of the contents of this folder. If you were going to send this to someone else via email, the message may not be deliverable if there are size restrictions on attachments at your end or the recipient's end.

10. Click **OK**. Then right-click the *Lesson 8 – Word* folder once more and click **Send to**.

11. Click **Compressed (zipped) folder**.

    You should now have a folder similar to the following:

12. Press (Enter) to keep the same name.

13. Right-click this zipped file and click **Properties**.

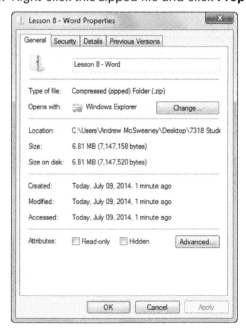

You should notice that the file has been compressed and is smaller by almost 2MB. In this case the attachment might still be too large to send via email, but you can see how compressing the folder has reduced its size.

14. Click **OK** and then click the **Close** button to exit the file management tool.

Let's take a look at how Windows can help to remove unwanted files from the hard drive.

15. Click the **Start** button, type: `disk cleanup` in the search field and press (Enter).

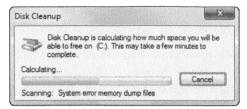

Windows will now check the hard drive to find specific types of files that can be deleted safely from the hard drive. When it has calculated this information, a screen similar to the following appears:

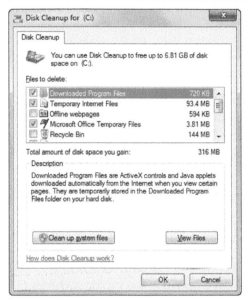

The amount of space that can be saved will vary, depending on what exists on your computer. Notice that you can specify the locations in which Windows can delete unnecessary files in order to save space.

Note that there is an additional button called **Clean up system files** that you can use to have Windows safely delete specific system files that are no longer in use.

16. Click **OK** to accept the currently selected locations.

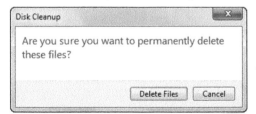

17. Click **Delete Files** to proceed with this task.

18. Close any open windows when the files have been deleted.

Managing Software

 Exam 1 - Objective 1.1, 3.1, 3.4

Once you decide which application program you want to use, you will need to purchase the program and then install it on the hard disk of your computer before you can use it. Once a program has been installed, it can be removed (uninstalled), modified, or re-installed as required.

Note that *Web apps* and *Cloud solutions* are examples of software that are designed to be accessed and used over the Internet. These applications do not need to be installed; in fact, you cannot download and install them. These applications run on a dedicated server owned by the vendor and are made available to subscribers as a service. For this reason, these solutions are referred to as Software as a Service (SaaS).

Users purchase the rights to access and use these applications on a subscription basis and log in to these applications with a registered account. TurboTax Online, Office 365, and Google Apps are examples of cloud solutions.

EXERCISE

In this exercise you will navigate to a specific web address to view a page and some videos from customers that describe how Microsoft Office 365 can help you be more productive in your daily tasks. The instructor may do this as a demonstration to the entire class.

1. Start a web browser on your computer.

2. In the address bar, type: `office.microsoft.com/en-us/business/why-office-365-for-business-FX104138860.aspx#proMobility` and press `Enter`.

3. Click the Play (▶) button and watch the first video on the page.

4. When complete, scroll through the page and click other videos, as time allows.

5. When finished visiting this page, click the ▬▬x▬▬ **Close** button at the top right corner of the screen.

Installing a New Program

You can install programs from a number of different locations such as a hard drive, an optical drive, a USB drive, or the Internet. How you purchase the software will determine the installation process.

Some programs will automatically start the installation process when you insert the installation CD or DVD; other programs may require you to start the installation process yourself. Most installation routines lead you step by step through the installation process.

Programs from the Internet fall into one of two categories: either you can download the program file for installation, or you can subscribe to a Software as a Service (SaaS) option with the software vendor. Each option entitles you to updates just as if you purchased the software from a retail outlet and installed it from a CD.

One consideration with software from any source is to make a backup or copy of the original. As the licensed owner of the software, you are allowed to make one copy for backup purposes. You may want to use the backup copy to install the software so that you can keep the original media intact and store it in a safe location. Software can be costly and it makes sense to protect your investment.

If you are downloading software from the Internet, always save it to a designated location such as the desktop and scan it for viruses prior to installing it. It is rare that software from a reputable vendor will have problems; however, if you download software from a site that is not the vendor's official web site, there could be spyware or viruses included in the download file.

Once the installation process begins, within a few moments you will be asked to agree to an End User License Agreement (EULA); depending on the vendor, this may appear in a separate screen or it may be a link you should click to read the contents of the License Agreement. Items in this type of agreement will vary between software vendors but the main purpose of the EULA is to protect the software vendor. In a typical EULA, you agree not to make illegal copies of the software to distribute to others, and you agree not to hold the software vendor liable for any damage or expenses that may occur from misuse or improper use of the software, such as incorrect entries into an income tax preparation program that leads to an audit of your income tax report, or installing another program that corrupts the operating system and causes your computer to stop working.

When the installation is complete, you will be asked to register or activate your copy of the program. Performing this last step ensures that you will be notified of any updates to the program. It also usually provides the option to call technical support should you require technical assistance.

Once the software program is installed, it can be configured for your operating environment, as needed. For example, if you need to install more languages than the standard or default language for the computer, you can likely add the new item using the Control Panel. Another requirement may be to customize how the program will work with a connected device such as a specific type of pointing device. In most cases, the software vendor will include files within the setup file to identify and make adjustments for hardware devices commonly connected on a computer.

In the situation where the program being installed is for a new device, such as a new printer, the process to install the new device follows a similar procedure to installing a software program. This type of install will be different in that the prompts you see will deal specifically with the hardware connected on your computer before installing and then configuring the appropriate device drivers for your operating environment.

When you receive a notification that an update to a program or device is available, it is usually not critical for you to install the update immediately; however, be sure to read the notice in order to decide whether you want to install the update. Security updates for software programs are generally considered to be critical; you should install security updates.

You might receive notices from the vendor in one of the following ways:

- an email with a link to the web site where you can download the update to your system.

- a CD or other media that you can install in much the same way as you installed the program initially.

- a command, button, or link in the program that enables you to check for updates. (Usually this option links you to the vendor's web site; once you are connected to the site, a check for updates begins and a list of update options is displayed. You can then choose what you want to install.)

- a pop-up box appears in the Task Notification area informing you of an update's availability. In these instances, you can usually click the box to read more information about the update, or click the X at the top right corner of the box to close the notification and delay any action. Notices of this type generally deal with the operating system or a program that is required to view items on the Internet.

EXERCISE

In the following exercise, you will install a program provided with the student data files, and then uninstall it later. This exercise presumes you have sufficient rights to install software on your system. If not, please read the steps to gain some familiarity with installing and uninstalling programs on your system, or watch the demonstration provided by the instructor.

1. Right-click the **Start** button and then click **Open Windows Explorer**.

2. Navigate to where the student data files are located and then click the *Lesson 2 – Windows* folder to view the contents.

3. Click the *RapidTyping_Setup_3* file.

4. When prompted with the User Account Control window, click **Yes** or, if necessary, enter log on information provided by the instructor to enable the installation to continue.

> **Note:** The type of action that appears will depend on the level of security set up for the computer in your location.

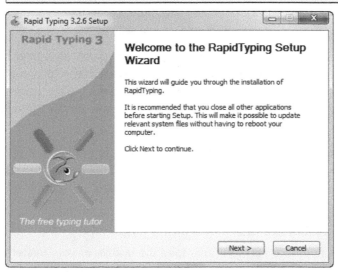

5. Click **Next**.

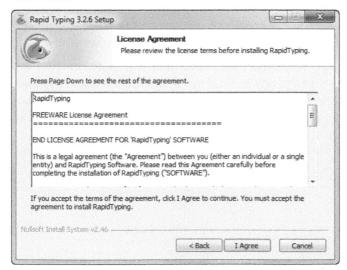

6. Scroll through and read the License Agreement and then click **I Agree**.

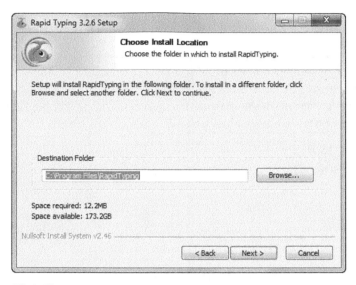

7. Click **Next**.

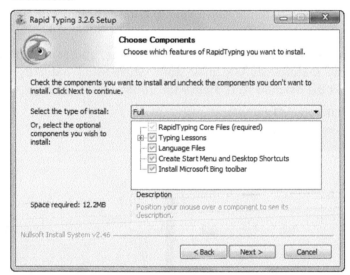

8. Click **Install Microsoft Bing toolbar** to turn off this option, leave the other options as shown, and click **Next**.

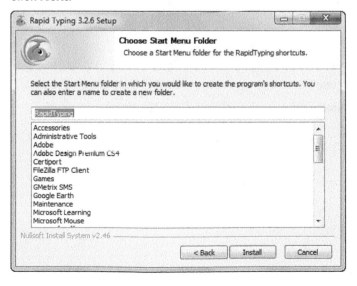

9. Accept this default setting by clicking **Install**.

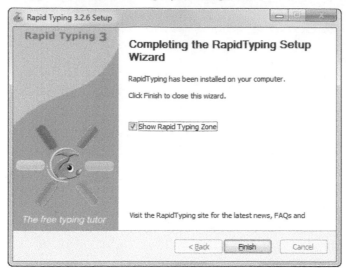

10. When the installation has completed, click **Show Rapid Typing Zone** to turn this off and then click **Finish**.

While the installation of the program onto the computer is complete, you still need to change settings in the software to any preferences you may want when using the program. Some programs may ask you to restart the machine to complete the configuration settings.

11. On the Windows desktop, click the **RapidTyping** icon.

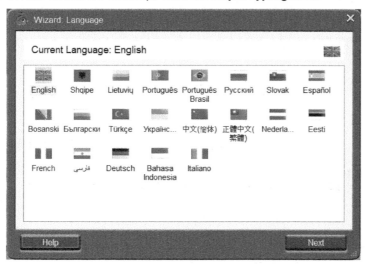

12. Click the language you want to use for this program (we selected English) and then click **Next**.

13. Enter a name to track your statistics or leave it as Guest. Click **Next**.

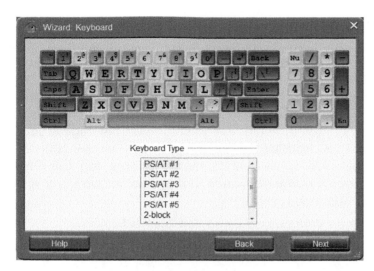

14. Click the keyboard layout, if required, and then click **Next**.

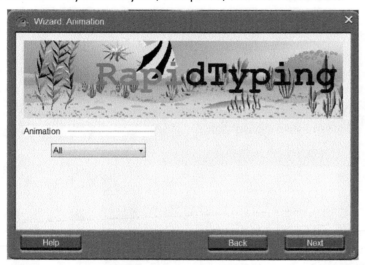

15. Choose whether you want animation with the program (having all the animation may cause the program to run slower), and then click **Next**.

16. Choose whether you want the program to measure the speed you type by the number of characters or words per minute. Then click **Next**.

Tip: If the keyboard does not appear when you start the program, click the grey arrow at the far right of the bottom green bar.

17. You can now begin testing your typing speed or click **Close** to exit the program.

EXERCISE

This exercise will demonstrate how to access OneNote with a Windows account and then download and install the Microsoft OneNote application to a mobile device, in this case an iPhone. You will then see how you can work with a program in one location and easily have it available and updated for you on another device. The instructor may choose to provide a demonstration for the class; OneNote is available for various smartphones so if you do not have an iPhone, review the steps so you are familiar with what is required prior to installing it on your own mobile phone, or visit http://office.mirosoft.com/en-us/onenote/ to view which mobile devices can use OneNote. This exercise includes the steps to create a Microsoft account ID if you do not have one already. If you already have an account, you can skip ahead to step 11).

1. Click the web browser icon on the Windows taskbar to start Internet Explorer.

2. In the Address bar, type: `www.onedrive.com` and press `Enter`.

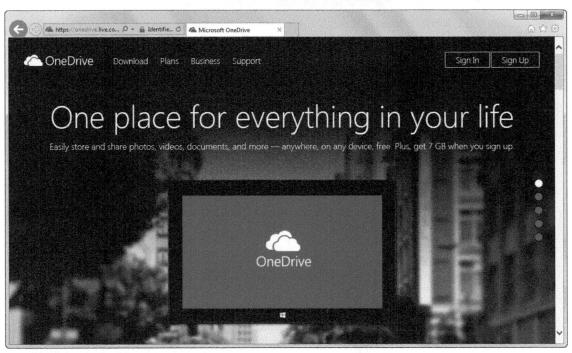

3. Click **Sign Up** to create a new account.

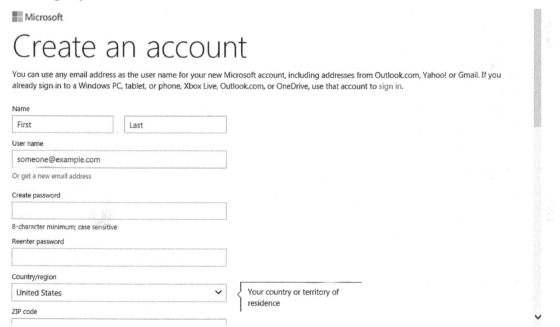

4. Click **Sign up now**.

5. Fill in the first two fields to begin creating your new account.

6. Enter an existing email account name or click **Or get a new email address** to enter a new name that will be set up with @outlook.com as the domain.

7. Create a password and reenter the password to confirm what was entered in the first password field.

8. Continue entering information for each of the fields on this page and then enter the validation code at the bottom. Click **I accept**.

9. Click the **Create** menu at the top of the window.

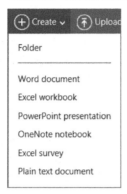

Notice how you have a number of the popular Office apps that you can use to quickly create or manipulate a document online from wherever you may be (provided you have access to the Internet). OneNote is an application that enables you to gather information in the form of notes from a variety of sources in an undefined manner, and then organize these into pages or sections. This is similar to gathering pages of hard copy notes and diagrams and then adding them to a binder, using dividers to separate the information.

10. Click **OneNote notebook**.

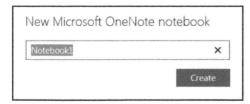

11. Type: `Marketing Project` and then click **Create**.

The OneNote application is now active and you are ready to begin typing text for the Marketing Project notebook.

12. In the area where the cursor is blinking, type: `Marketing Project` for the title.

13. Click anywhere below the title and type the following, pressing (Enter) to end the lines as shown:

14. Starting at the text, *more*, click and drag to the end of the last point. On the **Home** tab, in the Basic Text group, click **Bullets**.

Statistics needed on customer preferences for booking tours
- more offered through Web?
- prefer interaction with Travel Director?
- combination of both?

An advantage of using OneNote to keep track of notes, ideas, or pictures in one location is that you don't need to constantly save the file to ensure the file is up to date. In fact, when you finish entering information, you need only to exit the program – OneNote saves the work you've done to that point automatically.

15. Click **Sign out** to exit OneDrive.

The following screens demonstrate how to install Microsoft OneNote to an iPhone device. This program is available for various other hand-held devices such as the Android Phone, Windows Phone, or iPad. If you do not have an iPhone available, review the steps as they will be similar for whichever hand-held device you may be using.

16. Start the iPhone and tap the **App Store** icon.

17. Tap the **Search** icon at the bottom of the phone.

18. Tap in the field to begin typing: `onenote` to have the store search for this application.

19. Tap the **Microsoft OneNote** option.

20. Tap the **cloud** icon to download the Microsoft OneNote app.

The circle next to the name of this app is a progress bar and shows you how soon the download will be completed. When the program is installed, it will have its own icon on the screen, similar to:

You can now start OneNote on the phone to keep track of notes, pictures, and other items. You can also synchronize with OneDrive to have a copy of the Marketing Project notebook stored on the phone.

21. Tap **OneNote** to start the application.

22. Tap **Sign In**, enter your Microsoft account information and tap the **Sign in** button.

You will need to do this only on the first time you use OneNote on your phone, wherein you will need to enter the information for your Microsoft account (that is, email address). Each time you use OneNote on the phone after this, OneNote will automatically display your notebooks.

By default OneNote will display any items you have entered in the Personal notebook available with a mobile installation of OneNote. You can then use the icon at the top right of the screen to close this notebook, share a notebook, or synchronize the account on the phone with any notebooks you have on OneDrive. Alternatively click the icon at the top left to see a list of all notebooks

When the Sync is complete, you should be returned to the Home page in OneNote with a copy of the Marketing Project notebook. At this point you can make updates to the notebook on the phone or from OneDrive. If you share this notebook with others, you will also be notified on the phone when someone makes a change to the notebook.

23. Press the Home button to exit OneNote.

> **MMM**
> Downloading
> iTunes

Uninstalling a Program

You can uninstall a program when you no longer need it. Usually, the best way to uninstall a program is to use the **Uninstall a program** command using the Control Panel. Once you select the program you want to uninstall, click the Uninstall/Change button in Control Panel.

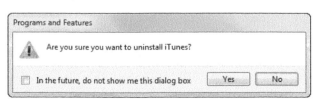

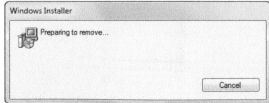

Alternatively, you can use the program's uninstall option (if one is included). Most antivirus applications are best uninstalled using the included uninstall routine. Either of these options helps ensure that the program is properly and completely removed from the system.

You should never simply delete program files using the Windows Explorer. When you install a program, configuration information is added to the Windows Registry so that the operating system will identify this program. If you delete program files improperly, the obsolete configuration information is left in the Registry. This can lead to problems with other software programs if you re-install this program at a later date, or if you upgrade this program with a new version.

Conversely, uninstalling applications (apps) from a smart phone is simplified.

To uninstall an application from a Windows Phone, from the applications list, tap and hold the app you wish to uninstall and from the menu tap "uninstall".

To uninstall an application from an iPhone, tap and hold the icon for the app you wish to uninstall until the icon begins to shake, then click the **X** in the top left hand corner of this icon to uninstall it.

EXERCISE

In this exercise you will uninstall the typing program installed previously.

1. Click **Start** and then click **Control Panel**.
2. Click **Uninstall a program** under the Programs group heading.

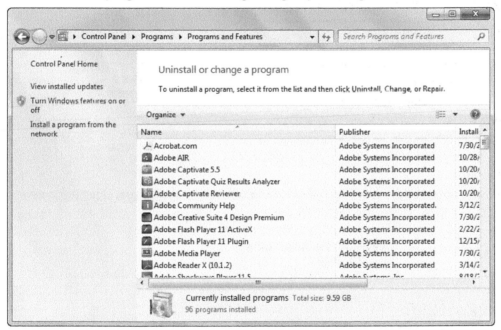

3. Scroll in the list until you see the RapidTyping program and then point at it to select it.
4. Click the **Uninstall** button on the command bar above the list of programs.

5. Click **Next**.

6. Click **Uninstall**.

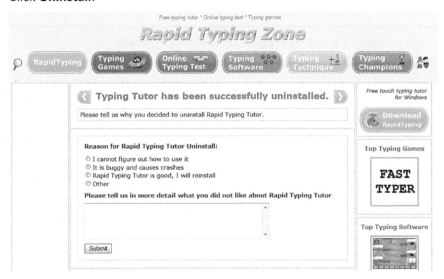

7. You can choose to provide information to the software maker or just close the browser window.

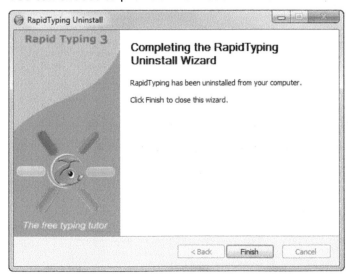

8. Click **Finish**.

Reinstalling a Program

Sometimes, a program may not work correctly (or at all) after installation, or problems may occur during installation. In most cases, you will need to uninstall the program, restart the computer, and then try the installation process again. You may also want to research through user groups, knowledge bases or blog sites to determine if other users have had similar issues. This type of information can often help you determine if the issue is related to hardware or software, and if this can be resolved before another installation attempt.

There may also be occasion when you need to reinstall a program that had been previously uninstalled. In scenarios such as this, complete the installation as if you were installing the program for the first time. Based on the software and vendor's requirements you may also be required to activate the software once more with the vendor.

Following are some examples of why you might need to reinstall a program:

- You can start the installation or download of a program to your system, but are unable to complete the installation. Usually this indicates that you do not have sufficient rights to install the software. Contact your network administrator to have your rights adjusted or to request that the administrator install it for you.

- A program may stop working after you install new software. Not all software programs are compatible with one another, even if they are all designed for the Windows environment. If you install a new program and an older program stops working, the two programs may share a system file. You will need to uninstall the new program, then check to see if the older program works again. If such is the case, you will likely need to check with a technical specialist on how you can get both programs to work.

- Sometimes Windows detects that a program is running improperly, or detects that a program has been installed improperly. In such cases, Windows will display the Program Compatibility Assistant. The assistant gives you the option to reinstall or to verify that the program has been installed correctly.

Some vendors let you download to install or re-install their program numerous times without any fees, such as iTunes, Adobe Reader or Flash Player. Generally once you have paid for a software program, you can re-install a program as often as needed.

Whenever you need to reinstall a program, follow these steps:

1. Uninstall the program from your system.
2. Restart the computer to ensure all remnants of that program are removed from the computer.
3. Ensure all other applications are closed.
4. Start the installation process again.

The following procedure is a demonstration of how you can add or reinstall a program to Microsoft Office:

1. Click **Start** and click **Control Panel**. Then click **Uninstall a program**.
2. Scroll in the list and then select the Microsoft Office 2013 edition on your system.

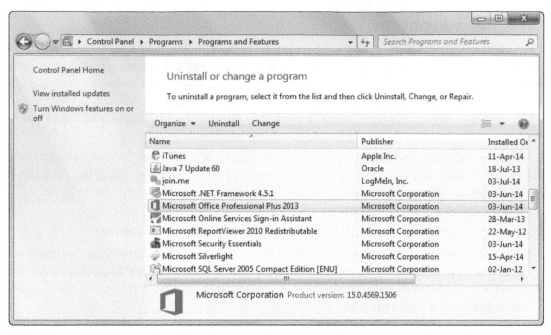

Notice how in this case, there is a command to enable you to change the configuration setup for this program.

3. Click the **Change** button.

Windows now begins the preparation for Office 2013 so you can add, remove, or repair an item. When complete, you see the following screen:

Microsoft provides the list of options for you based on what you can do with Office 2013. If you were experiencing consistent problems with an Office 2013 program, you would use this feature to repair the program; alternatively, if you will not be using a particular program, you can remove or uninstall it from the Microsoft Office setup on your system.

4. Make sure **Add or Remove Features** is selected and then click **Continue**.

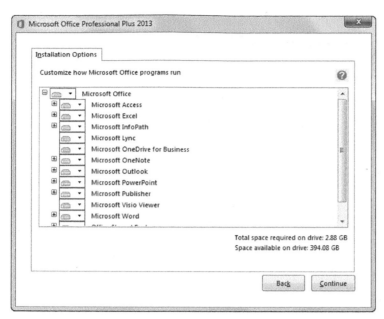

A list of programs and features available for Office 2013 appears. Any option that displays with a red X in the icon box indicates this component is not currently available from your system. Some components are configured to run from the computer but require the Office installation DVD to access additional items such as templates or pictures. Generally, you can re-configure these components so that they do not require the Office DVD. You can also use the Add or Remove Features option to remove particular programs in the Office suite from the hard disk.

5.   Click the icon box for the program you want to modify and choose the appropriate command:

6.   Click **Continue**.

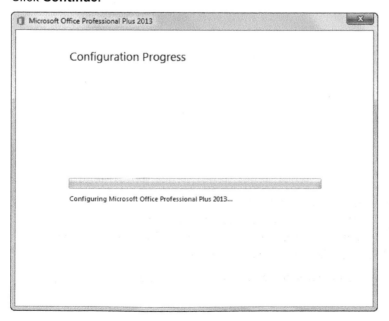

The change occurs now; the length of time for the installation/re-configuration will depend on what was selected. When complete, you will see the following:

7.   Click **Close** to exit.

Updating Software

It is very unusual for software programs to be error free in their first release. Many of the *bugs* (errors) that occur are issues that the software company cannot predict because they are based on how customers use the program. Software companies develop programs for the most commonly used or requested features and later provide updates or "patches" to address bugs. A patch is a file of programming code that you can insert into an existing program to fix a particular problem, or bug. Patches are designed to be only temporary fixes until problems can be permanently repaired.

Updates are not always created to address problems with the software; they may be required due to changes in government regulations (such as a new tax table for accounting programs) or other external factors beyond their control (such as additional security settings against new viruses).

These known issues should not prevent users from purchasing software. Whether you purchase software as soon as it is released or a few months later should be dictated by your own requirements.

When you register your copy (license) of the software, you become entitled to receive notification about updates or upgrades, usually via a link in an email that you can use to download the update. Some software vendors build a feature into the program to schedule or automatically check for online updates, and display messages to indicate when a new update is ready for download and installation. Microsoft and Adobe provide this type of service for their products.

Users can generally perform software updates, regardless of whether the computer is a stand-alone model or connected to a network. Most network administrators provide access to users to perform software updates; but restrict changes to configuration or to critical software such as antivirus programs.

Web applications such as web browsers may be updated more often than other applications in order to address security issues. You will usually be informed that an update has become available when you next visit the site or start the program from your system.

Always register your software to ensure you receive notices about available updates. A number of organizations, groups, and newsgroups share information about updates such as why they're being provided, and whether you should install them. If you find you've missed something, you can check the software vendor's web site to find specific updates. Once you receive notice of an update's availability, you have the option of saving a copy of the update file onto your system instead of automatically installing it from the vendor's web site.

Installing the Update

If you receive notification of an update in an email, open the message to read the contents. The vendor will have set up a hyperlink that when clicked will navigate you directly to the correct page to download the update for the software.

You can follow the instructions on the screen to download the update and have Windows install it onto the system. Update files are generally set up as an executable file which means once it is downloaded, Windows detects that it is a setup file and then prompts you to run and install the program file.

If the program has an option to check for updates automatically, you will be notified to install the update in one of the following methods:

- A message box appears when you log on the system indicating there is an update available for the specified program. You can then proceed to do the update at that time or choose a different time.

- A colored icon (usually yellow) appears with the program icon in the taskbar notification area as an identifier that some action is needed for this program. Double-click the icon to open the program and follow the instructions to update the program.

- Updates to the antivirus program will vary from a networked environment to a standalone computer. A network is generally set up to check for updates on a regular basis and if found, updates the program on the main server and as each person logs on, the update is then applied on that workstation. On an individual system the update may occur in the background when you start the computer, or you may need to open the program and check for updates manually.

- If the update is for Windows, you may see a yellow icon or a small message in the taskbar notification area indicating an update is available for install.

A method to check manually for any updates is to start the application program and navigate to the Help menu. Vendors often include a check for updates command in this menu, and you need only click the command to have the program check for updates. If updates are available you can then follow the instructions to update the program.

The following steps demonstrate how to install an update for a Microsoft IntelliPoint mouse:

1. In a web browser, navigate to `www.microsoft.com` and then click **Downloads**.

2. Click **Download Center**. In the search field, type: `microsoft intellipoint mouse` and press Enter .

3. Scroll through the list and click to select the appropriate update for the mouse and the system.

4. Click **Download**.

Do you want to run or save **IPx64_1033_8.0.225.0.exe** (16.3 MB) from **download.microsoft.com**? | Run | Save ▼ | Cancel | ×

5. Click **Save** to save the file after Windows has scanned it to ensure it can be safely used.

6. Click **Run** to begin the installation. If the User Account Control window appears, click **Yes**.

The program file is now extracting the compressed files so it can begin the installation of the update. When it has completed the extraction, you will a screen similar to the following:

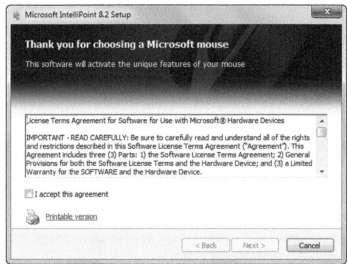

Notice how even though this is a device driver update for a pointing device, the process to install the update follows the same procedure as when installing an application. You should read the End User License Agreement prior to starting the installation.

7. Click the checkbox for **I accept this agreement** and then click **Next**.

8. Determine whether you want to select either of these options and then click **Next**.

    The program now begins the installation and update of the pointing device. When complete, you see a screen similar to:

9. Click **Finish**.

Lesson Summary

In this lesson you were introduced to software and how it is created. You also had a chance to look at different application programs and explore the typical ways software can be used. You should also be familiar with the following:

☑ different software applications   ☑ reinstalling a program

☑ installing a new program   ☑ updating a program

☑ uninstalling a program

Review Questions

1. Before program source code can be used by a computer, it must be:
    - a. compiled
    - b. compressed
    - c. patched
    - d. converted to a web app

2. Which is the most cost-effective method for a network administrator to purchase licenses for 25 computers in an organization?
    - a. Purchase 25 licenses from a retail store.
    - b. Purchase a network license for 25 computers.
    - c. Purchase SaaS subscriptions for 25 computers.
    - d. Purchase 25 new systems with the software already bundled.
    - e. b or c

3. Tim is on a tight budget, but needs to purchase software for keeping track of expense reports on his personal laptop. Which of the following factors should he consider most heavily when deciding on what to purchase?
    a. Finding software that supports site licensing.
    b. Finding software that he can purchase on the Internet as a download.
    c. Finding software that works with his current hardware and operating system.
    d. Finding a software suite that will perform a wide variety of functions.

4. Which type of application software is best suited for storing and organizing large amounts of information that includes complex data relationships?
    a. A word processing program.
    b. An accounting program.
    c. A database management program.
    d. A spreadsheet program.

5. If you are downloading a program from the Internet, what process should you take before installing the program?
    a. Check that the purchase of the software is complete.
    b. Save the file and run the installation from the web site.
    c. Save the file and run a virus/spyware scan on the file.
    d. Compress the file.

6. Which of the following is a potential drawback to using freeware?
    a. Freeware is usually defective.
    b. There is usually very limited support for freeware.
    c. Freeware is not compatible with Windows 7.
    d. Freeware will only run for thirty days.

7. How can you guarantee you will get notices of any updates for a specific software?

Lesson 6: Troubleshooting

Lesson Objectives

In this lesson you will look at what troubleshooting means and what steps you can take to ensure the maximum performance of the hardware and software set up on the computer. On completion you should be familiar with:

☐ what troubleshooting means

☐ how to identify a problem for resolution

☐ looking at how you can manage the hardware

☐ recognizing what may cause software issues

☐ identifying potential solutions for software issues

☐ how to find and use Help resources

What is Troubleshooting?

In general, computers are efficient and run well on their own. As you add or remove devices and software, you may experience errors or performance problems, or have general queries on how to manage the computer.

Prevention is always preferable to repair. In a corporate environment, the Information and Technology (IT) department is responsible for the secure functioning of each company system, whether a desktop system within the company office space, or a portable system outside the office. Two simple ways to keep these systems secure is to schedule regular maintenance and to ensure that application and operating system updates are installed as required.

Obviously, to keep track of several systems, a complete log that provides details about each corporate system (for example, hardware components, operating system version, processor, RAM, installed applications, installed updates and patches) must be created and kept up to date.

As you encounter a potential problem, there are standard troubleshooting steps you can follow to isolate the problem and resolve it. You may not need to use all the troubleshooting steps for every problem, but knowing and following them will help you gather the information necessary to resolve the issue, whether you resolve it yourself or refer it to a technical specialist.

Depending on the problem and its resolution, you can assess whether you can resolve the issue yourself, or if you require assistance. Any time you are uncomfortable upgrading or replacing items in your computer, ask for help from a specialist. For instance, adding more RAM to your system is relatively easy and you may not require anyone's help. However, adding a hard drive may require a specialist to help you connect it and change the system settings so the operating system can identify the new drive. A specialist has the appropriate tools, knowledge and experience to handle changes to any internal component of a computer.

Take care when applying updates for software or hardware. Not all updates are necessary, and some may slow system performance or introduce new problems. Always read the release notes and make sure that the update will be compatible with your existing hardware and software. If you are unable to determine whether an update should be installed, ask a specialist.

Managing the Hardware

 Exam 1 - Objective 4.2, 4.3

Most computer hardware does not require maintenance until you notice such things as unusual noises or a decrease in performance. In instances such as these, it could mean the hardware needs to be replaced, as with a damaged fan, or the hard drive is close to its maximum storage capacity and takes longer to find or store files or folders. On other occasions it may be a simple solution of ensuring all the cables are connected or that you need to turn on the power.

In general, problems that arise with hardware can fall into one of the following categories:

Replacing Hardware

As with most things, hardware devices have a useful life cycle and will deteriorate with time and usage. There also is the possibility that the item may have been defective from the start and will have to be replaced. When you purchase a hardware item, there is a limited warranty on the use of that item, and depending on the product, you may want to purchase a service agreement or an extended warranty. An example of when a replacement is needed could be a hard drive in an older computer that was large enough to accommodate applications and data files at that time, but has become limited in free space for new items. Another example of when you may need to replace an item could be the power supply box in a desktop computer – this item may have worn out from poor air circulation, dust accumulation, or a power surge. One other example of when you may need to replace the hardware is when you purchase a new computer system but connect an older monitor to it. The monitor may display the output but the display may appear blurry or dull due to the limitations of the monitor. The monitor may not even work if it is not compatible with the new video display card in the new system.

Checking the Connections or Cables

Whenever a device doesn't seem to work, check that all the connections for the device are secure and that there is nothing wrong with the cables, such as a broken connector or frayed wires. Cables provide the pathway for computers and peripheral devices to send signals to one another; a broken or intermittent connection will make communication impossible. You may find you have to replace the entire cable to test whether the original cable is faulty or if the connection needs to be fixed. Check that you have the right cable connector type as well; for instance, the jack at the end of a network cable looks very similar to the end of a telephone cable but the telephone jack is slightly smaller than the network cable and the wiring within the cable is designed for different purposes and they are not interchangeable. Another example could be when nothing appears on your screen to indicate there may be an error with the printer, but the document doesn't print. You may need to check that the printer is connected, with power (plugged into the wall outlet or power button is on), and with a cable securely connected to the local machine or the network.

Updating the Hardware

As with software updates, occasionally a vendor will release a *firmware* update for a device. *Firmware* is built-in programmable logic (software) that is embedded in a piece of hardware and controls how the device functions. Firmware updates become available as new computing and networking technologies and standards emerge. However, there is no automated system for updating firmware as there is for updating operating systems and application software. If an old hardware device (such as a network card or an optical media burner) stops working or doesn't work in the same way it used to, it could be that updates to the operating system are not compatible with the device. You can check the manufacturer's website for any available firmware updates. Firmware updates tend to be smaller than software updates because they target a specific device, and usually contain fixes or improvements for that device only.

You can check to find new versions of firmware by navigating to the vendor's website and looking on their Support page. You may be required to enter a serial or model number of the device to narrow the search for any updates. Be sure before installing any firmware the you have the correct model and type of the device; check the date for the release as the company may list more than one update for a particular product (this is usually to address different operating systems or platforms where the device is used).

Updating Device Drivers

A driver is software that allows your computer to communicate with and control the devices connected to it. Device drivers actually control the hardware, and the operating system communicates with the device drivers. Without drivers, devices will not function properly.

Device drivers are designed to work with specific operating system architectures. For example, 32-bit device drivers are not compatible with a 64-bit operating system. To check whether a device includes 64-bit drivers you can check the product documentation, visit the manufacturer website, or visit the Windows 7 Compatibility website at
http://windows.microsoft.com/en-us/windows/hardware-compatible-windows#1TC=windows-7.

If you have recently upgraded your operating system or connected old hardware to a new system and some of your devices are not functioning properly, you may want to check the device drivers. You can find a device's driver name and version by right-clicking the device in the Device Manager window, clicking **Properties**, then clicking the **Driver** tab.

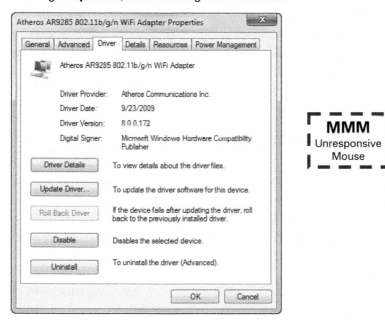

MMM
Unresponsive
Mouse

Notice that you can click the **Update Driver** button to find an updated driver directly from within Windows.

In most cases, Windows includes drivers for the devices you may want to connect. These generic drivers will provide basic functionality, but to utilize the full features of a device, you should install the drivers that ship with the device, or download and install drivers from the manufacturer's website. As you update your programs and operating system over the course of time, it is also important to keep your drivers up to date.

When updating drivers keep the following points in mind:

- Check for drivers at the computer manufacturer's site first. Even though manufacturers use third-party brands of devices, in many cases the manufacturer modifies the drivers for use with your specific model of computer. Many manufacturers include driver update utilities on their websites – you need only visit the site and enter your computer make and model. In many cases, the manufacturer includes driver update utilities built right into the computer and you need only start up the utility and it will evaluate the currently installed drivers and alert and advise you of available and/or recommended updates.

- You can also configure Windows Update to automatically download recommended drivers for your hardware and devices.

Updating the Operating System

Updates to an operating system include fixes for a variety of issues. Occasionally you may find something goes wrong after or even during an update. These include:

- A hardware device no longer works; this is usually a result of a conflict in a system file used by the operating system or the device. You may need to check for an updated device driver for the hardware device before the device will work again.

- A software program no longer works as it used to; this could result from a conflict in a system file used by the operating system and the application program. Depending on the program, you may need to check for updates to the software program, or possibly uninstall the update to enable the software program to work. This issue may require the assistance of a technical specialist to determine which solution is best.

- The computer stops responding while you are installing the update. This could be a result of numerous issues such as your internet connection is no longer active, or you do not have enough hard disk space for the operating system to process the update. With this scenario, you may want to work with a technical specialist to determine the best course to take. Alternatively, you can choose to restart the computer and try the update again once you ensure all connections are active or you have appropriate space to handle all the updates.

- You are asked for a product key or activation code for Windows; when you purchase a computer, the version of Windows on the computer will have been registered or activated during the setup process. However, if the computer required hardware changes such as replacing the hard drive, Windows may have been reinstalled and the registration process wasn't completed properly. When prompted for a code, check the sides of the computer to find the official sticker for Windows; this sticker should have a product key code that you can use to validate the version of Windows on your computer.

It is important to keep the computer updated with the latest updates to Windows to ensure the best performance; however, not all updates are necessary. When you have Windows check for updates and there are a large number of updates, you can choose which ones to apply. It is important to install security updates and updates that are marked as critical.

Handling Other Hardware Issues

Not all hardware problems involve the updates or changes. Consider some minor issues that may require troubleshooting on your part:

- If you cannot read files from media such as CDs or DVDs, check the disk for scratches or dirt. Clean the disk using an appropriate cloth and try again. Also, ensure that you are using the correct type of media for the driver. For example, you cannot play Blu-ray disks on a standard DVD disk drive without installing special software.

- If you cannot print, ensure that the printer is connected and turned on. If this is not the problem, check the cable connections from the printer to your computer to ensure they are securely connected. If you are on a network or using a wireless connection for the printer, ensure that the network connections are operational and then try printing again.

- If the connections are active but the printer does not print, check the printer for any possible error messages such as a paper jam or low toner. These problems can easily be resolved by reading the screen on the printer. Turn the printer off before clearing any paper jams or changing the toner cartridge. Check to ensure the correct cables are used.

- Occasionally, you may need to clean the computer or printer of dust or paper particles. You can buy items to clean the keyboard, mouse, monitor, and other peripheral devices. Be very careful when removing devices for cleaning or replacement, and take your time putting them back into place. For instance, if you are removing a toner cartridge, take note of how you removed it and how you need to insert the new cartridge so the printer will recognize and use the new cartridge.

- If you are using an optical mouse and it is not responding when you move or click it, check to see if there is a light on the mouse. A red light indicates the battery charge is low and you will need to replace the battery. This may also be true of a wireless keyboard if you notice characters you type do not appear on the screen, or pressing the direction keys does not move the mouse cursor.

- If a key on the keyboard, or a button on the mouse, is not working properly, try cleaning the device. In addition to purchasing cleaning kits for the keyboard, you can also purchase vacuums or cans of compressed air to help disperse any dust. In the case of liquid spilled on the keyboard, cleaning may not help – you may need to replace the item.

Keeping Copies of Your Data

 Exam 1 - Objective 4.4

A system is useful only if the data it contains is valid and accessible. You can take several steps to ensure the safety of data. Perhaps the most obvious way to protect data is to schedule regular backups and to closely follow corporate guidelines regarding backup procedures. Backups are crucial if data is lost or damaged. Data that has been properly backed up can easily be restored onto a system or the network.

A backup is a duplicate copy of files and folders. When you make a backup of the files on your computer, you store a copy of those files on another computer on the network or on an external storage device, such as a tape, CD, DVD, flash drive or to the cloud. You can use specialized software to handle backups such as the Windows Backup and Restore utility, or you can simply copy the files. The advantage of using a dedicated program for backups is that the program can be set to create various types of backups.

Full	Copies every selected file on the system to whatever backup device you are using. This version should be used the first time you run the Backup command for all the data files. This type of backup requires the most storage space and the most time to perform. It is also necessary to perform a full backup before you can perform differential or incremental backups.
Differential	Copies all files which have changed since the last time the program performed a full backup. The storage size and time requirement increase with each differential backup because each subsequent backup includes the changes made on the previous day(s).

Incremental	Copies only the files that have changed since the last backup. If an incremental backup is performed every day, then each day's backup contains only the changes made on that day. An incremental backup method uses several sets of backup media to backup only those files created or modified since the last backup. A new set of media is used for each day. Each new set of media contains only files created or changed that day.

Most companies use a backup strategy that combines either full and differential backups, or full and incremental backups.

In a full and differential strategy, backups occur as follows:

1. A full backup occurs on Friday night at 2:00am to capture all data for the company.

2. Differential backups are performed each night from Monday to Thursday at 2:00am to capture all data that has changed since the full backup on the previous Friday. The differential backup performed on Monday includes all changes made on Monday. The differential backup performed on Tuesday includes all the changes made on both Monday and Tuesday. The differential backup performed on Wednesday includes all the changes made on Monday, Tuesday and Wednesday, and so on. The media used for Thursday's differential backup would contain all the data that has changed since last Friday.

3. On Friday, a full backup occurs at 2:00am to capture all current data for the company, including the changes made after the differential backup on Thursday.

This method requires more time to back up than the full and incremental combination, but less time to restore. Because a differential backup copies everything that has changed since the last full backup, if the system fails on a Thursday, only the previous Friday's full backup and Wednesday's backup (containing all changes since Friday) would be required to restore the system (two days' backups).

In a full and incremental strategy, backups occur as follows:

1. A full backup occurs on Friday night at 2:00am to capture all data for the company.

2. Incremental backups are performed each night from Monday to Thursday at 2:00am to capture each day's changes on separate backup media.

3. On Friday, a full backup occurs at 2:00am to capture all current data for the company, including the changes made after the incremental backup on Thursday.

This method requires less time to back up than the full and differential method, but more time to restore. Incremental backups copy only the changes made each day, so if a system fails on Thursday, the previous Friday's full backup must be restored, and then each day's incremental backup (Monday, Tuesday, and Wednesday) must be restored in turn (four days' backups).

Because incremental backups must be restored in chronological order, it is extremely important to ensure that they are identified fully and correctly.

It is important to understand that backup tapes (or other storage media) can become expensive and bulky, depending upon the amount of data generated. If you use the full and incremental strategy and performed backups every weekday, you would have 260 tapes at the end of the year.

Tapes and CDs can be reused to reduce expenses and reduce the amount of space required to store the backup media. However, many companies maintain an entire year's worth of backups and then take the entire set of media offsite and store it for a year or more. Some organizations have contracts in place that require them to store data for five, 10 or 15 years and even longer.

Storing backup media off-site is key in planning for disaster recovery. If an entire office complex were destroyed by fire or earthquake, a new set of servers could be set up elsewhere and the company's data could be restored using backup media that had been safely stored in a separate location. (If backup media were stored in the same location as the company systems, and disaster were to strike, the backup media would be lost along with the company computers.)

You may wonder why you would want to save an entire year's worth of incremental backups, especially since changes are backed up every day. Consider this scenario: your company maintains incremental backup media for one month, and then reuses the media. Suppose in February, someone accidentally deletes an important document. The deletion, however, is not noticed until May when someone needs to look at the file. February's backup set has been overwritten with data from March, and March's backup set has been overwritten with data from April. A file that was deleted in February will not be included on any of the backup media, and is now unrecoverable.

Storing the Backup Copies

In addition to completing backups, it is important to consider where the copies of the data will be stored. For example, you cannot create a backup on the same drive that contains the files that you want to back up. You must select a different drive or storage location for the backup file. This location can be on another hard drive within the computer, on removable media such as a USB drive or optical disc, or even on a remote location.

Backup methods and their associated storage locations are described in the following table:

External (or Local) Backup	A very cost efficient method for creating backups is to save them to an external hard drive or optical media of sufficient size to store the data. Once the backup is complete, you can store the external hard drive or media in a location separate from the computer.
Offsite (or Online) Backup	These are backups stored to a remote location on the network, or stored to the servers or storage locations provided through an Internet-based backup service provider. There are companies who offer the service to create backups of your data and store it at their site, thereby ensuring you can get access to these files when you need them. This can be for the purpose of restoring a file that has been accidentally deleted, or in the case of a disaster such as theft or fire at your location.
Cloud Backup	A cloud backup is a variation of an online backup wherein data is saved to a cloud location such as Microsoft OneDrive. Cloud computing is the practice of using applications or storage space on the Internet rather than on your own computer or server. That is, you can use hosted applications and services offered by a third party and run almost entirely from one or more servers that reside on the Internet. All that is required to use cloud computing services is a web browser and an Internet connection; no other software needs to be installed.
	To perform a cloud backup, you need to set up an account with a cloud service such as Microsoft OneDrive or Apple iCloud. Using a web browser, log into the service using your account information and then copy files to the remote storage location, thereby creating your backup copy.

Windows provides you with two different backup methods: one where you select the data to be backed up, and one where important system information and registry settings are saved automatically to a file called a restore point. A restore point is like a snapshot of the system configuration at a particular point in time. In Windows 7, if the system protection feature is turned on, Windows automatically creates restore points whenever significant changes are made to the system, such as when new application software or device drivers are installed. The restore option provides a way to undo system changes without affecting personal files such as documents or email. System Protection/Restore is beyond the scope of this courseware; please refer to Windows Help for more information on this feature.

EXERCISE

In this exercise you will look at how to copy data files on an external source or to the cloud, specifically OneDrive. We will also look at how to use the Backup and Restore feature although this may be demonstrated by the instructor if the feature or resources are not available.

1. In a web browser, navigate to www.onedrive.com and sign in with your Microsoft account ID.

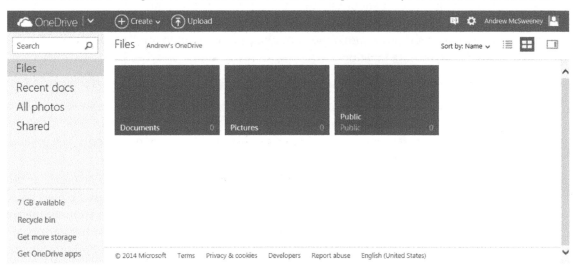

2. Click **Documents** to open this folder. Click **Create** from the top and then click **Folder** to create a new folder for the backup copy you will make of the data files.

3. Type: 7318 Backup as the name of the new folder and press (Enter).

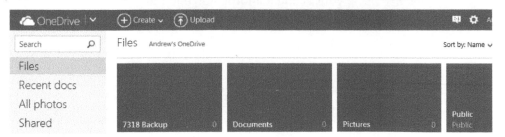

4. Click the new folder to display its contents.

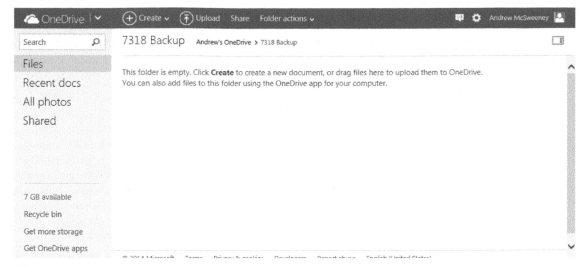

5. Click **Upload**.

6. In the Choose File to Upload window, navigate to where the student data files are located and click *Lesson 2 - Windows* to view the contents of this folder.

7. Press Ctrl+A to select all the files in this folder and click **Open**.

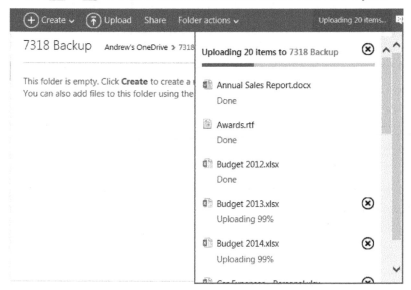

The selected files are copied to your OneDrive folder. Instead of using the Open command, you could also have dragged the selected files into the OneDrive screen to upload a copy of the files into the folder in OneDrive.

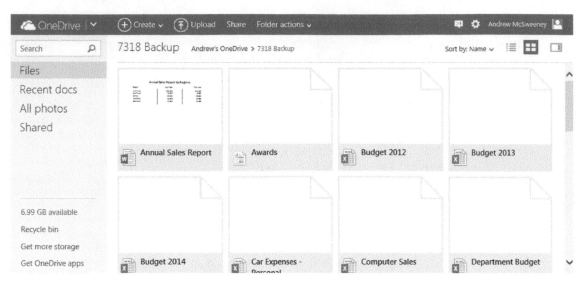

You now have a duplicate copy of the student data files in the cloud so you can access them anywhere you may be, provided you have Internet access. These files are also a backup in case the ones on your computer become damaged or lost.

8. Click your name at the top right to exit OneDrive and in the drop-down menu, click **Sign out**. Click the **Close** button to exit the web browser.

Now let's try doing a backup using the Windows Backup and Restore command. Check with your instructor before continuing to determine if you have access to this command, and if so, ensure a flash drive or blank DVD is available for use with this exercise. Otherwise, the instructor may provide a demonstration of how to perform this exercise. We will be using a flash drive for this exercise.

9. Click the **Start** button, in the search field, type: `backup`. Then click the **Backup and Restore** command at the top of the Start menu.

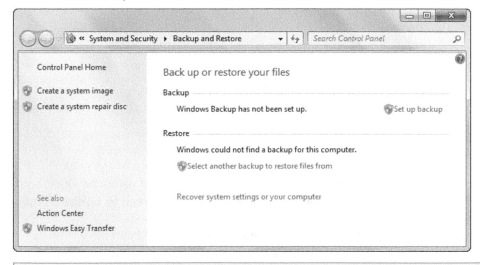

> **Note:** If this is the first time you have activated this command you will see a screen similar to the previous image; however, if a Windows backup has already been setup, the Set up backup link will not be visible, and instead you can click the **Change settings** link.

10. Click **Set up backup** if the link is visible; otherwise, click **Change settings**.

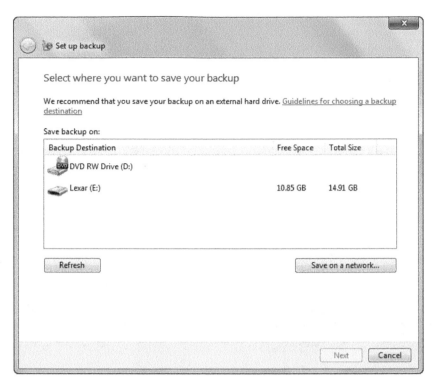

You are now required to select the destination where the backup copy will be stored. If you have access to a location on a network, click **Save on a network**.

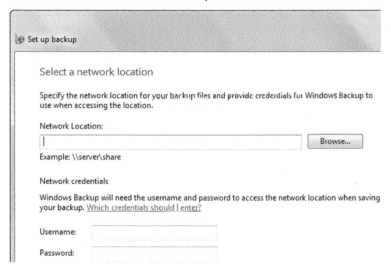

For the purpose of this demonstration, you will specify to back up files onto a DVD or flash drive that can be stored in another location for reference. In practical application, you will likely use a storage device that has a larger capacity than a DVD or flash drive. In this exercise, you will be selecting a small amount of data to backup which should fit onto either media.

11. Click the drive in the list to select it as the destination location and then click **Next**.

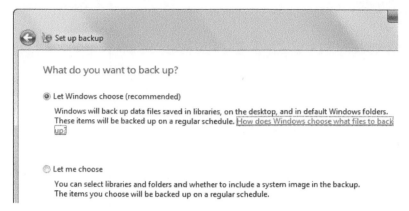

Choose which files will be backed up – if you were performing a backup of the system files for archival purposes, choose the first option which backs up the files saved in libraries, on the Desktop and in default Windows folders; otherwise, you can specify which files you want to back up, such as personal documents, photographs or email file. For this demonstration, we will choose the second option to make a backup of specific files.

12. Click **Let me choose** and then click **Next**.

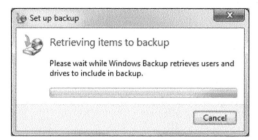

Windows now searches for which items which can be included in the backup.

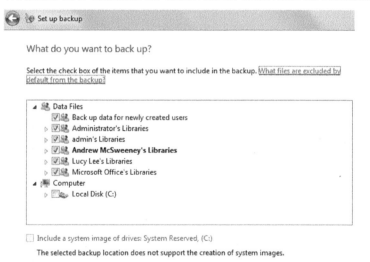

13. Uncheck all options, then expand the option with your name or login id used for this course. In the expanded list, clear the check boxes for the default libraries (Documents, Music, Pictures, Videos) if necessary, so that only the check box for Additional Locations remains checked.

Normally, you would include all the default libraries in the backup, but we are simplifying the backup here in this exercise for the sake of simplicity.

Click **Next**.

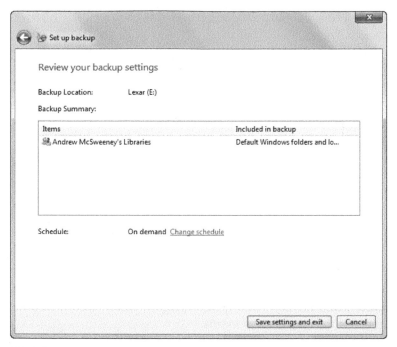

14. Click **Save settings and exit**.

    Windows now saves the settings created for where the backup will be stored.

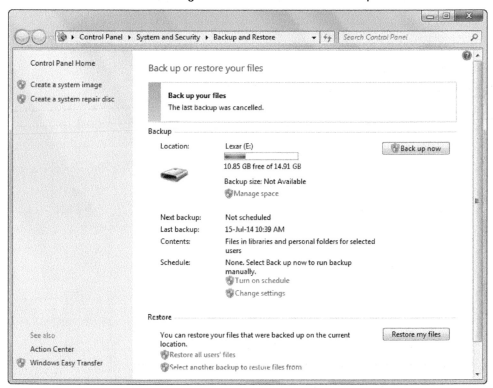

    Ensure you have a blank DVD in the drive appropriately. If you are prompted to specify a disc title, accept the suggested title. If asked how you want to use the disc, select the **Like a USB flash drive** option (Live File System). You may be prompted to format the media, or Windows may format it automatically. In our demonstration, we are using a flash drive so you will need to ensure you use one that has enough space to copy the selected files and folders for the backup.

15. Click **Back up now**.

Notice the backup icon 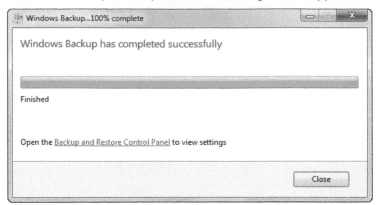 in the taskbar notification area that indicates the backup process is active.

When the backup is complete, the following screen appears:

16. Click **Close** to exit the backup process.

Let's assume time has passed and you now need a file that was inadvertently deleted from the computer. You can restore this file from the backup media.

17. In the Restore area, click **Restore my files**.

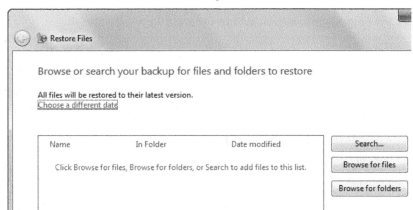

18. Click **Browse for files** to choose the file from a previous backup.

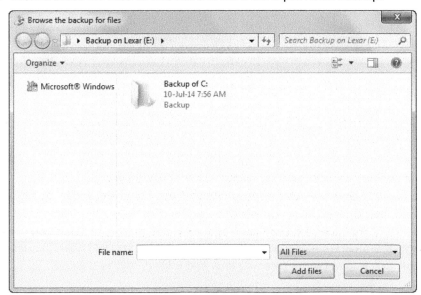

19. Double-click **Backup of C:** and then drill down through the folders to find a particular file to restore. Click the file that you want to restore, then click the **Add files** button. Then click **Next**.

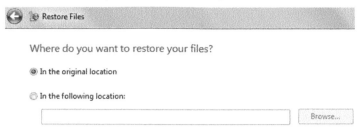

20. Choose the location to restore the files to (in most cases you will want to restore to its original location but you do have the option to save in a different location, as needed). Click **Restore**.

21. Click **Finish** when the restore is complete, then close the Backup and Restore window.

Managing the Software

 Exam 1 - Objective 3.4, 4.1, 4.3

Problems with using a software program often result in lost productivity and wasted time. Software issues are often related to incompatibility with the operating system, incompatibility with changes to the operating system, or exposure to a virus or malware.

Updating the Software

Application software updates are released for a variety of reasons – adding or improving functionality, updating built-in data, or improving security. When you are notified that an update is available, be sure you understand the purpose of the update and then decide whether you need to install it. For instance, an update indicating there is a new additional feature that you may not use in the program does not warrant immediate action; however, an update that resolves a potential security risk would warrant a closer look. If an update is a service pack, it usually contains a combination of fixes and additional features, and should be installed if you are experiencing any issues with the software.

Update notices may appear in an email, a prompt box when the Desktop appears (usually in the Task Notification area), or possibly in a social media post such as on Twitter. If you are unsure about whether to proceed with the update, check with the network administrator or another technical specialist for more information.

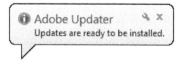

If you installed the update and encounter problems with the software, consider taking steps similar to the following:

- Uninstall the update to return to the previous version of the software. It may not resolve any issues you had previously with the software but you will have a working version of the software. It is rare that a service pack will cause problems with the software.

- Close all other applications before trying to install the update again. This ensures there are no common files in use at the time you start the update that may create conflicts during the update installation.

- Restart the computer and try using the software program again. In some cases the update may not be active until you restart the computer.

Upgrading the Operating System

There are many reasons you may want (or need) to upgrade or change the version of your operating system. These include:

┌─ ─ ─ ─ ┐
│ **MMM** │
│ Finding a │
│ Solution │
└ ─ ─ ─ ─ ┘

- Improved performance.
- Support for new technologies.
- Equipment upgrades making new OS possible.
- Improved security features.
- Improved support for wireless networking, file sharing, resource sharing, etc.

There are several versions of the Windows operating system in current use around the world. Currently, the most common versions of Windows operating systems are:

Version	Home (Student or Home Use)	Professional (General Office/ Business User)	Ultimate (Includes Security and Backup Features)
Windows XP	✓	✓	
Windows Vista	✓	✓	✓
Windows 7	✓	✓	✓
Windows 8	✓	✓	✓

Upgrading an operating system is different than updating it.

Upgrade	When you purchase and install another version of the operating system, for example changing from Windows XP to Windows 7.
Update	When you install fixes or product enhancements for the existing operating system.

Each operating system version is designed to work with specific hardware. Be sure to check the minimum system requirements before purchasing. Be sure your system meets or exceeds the minimum requirements for processor speed, RAM, video capacity and available disk space.

Remember that if you change from a 32-bit operating system to a 64-bit operating system, you will need 64-bit device drivers for all your devices.

You should also keep in mind that some older versions of application software may not be compatible with an upgraded operating system. For example, some programs that run in Windows XP will not run in Windows 7. If there are old application programs you must use, check the Windows 7 Compatibility website, or the software vendor website, to ensure that the program will be compatible with the operating system version you want to use.

You can also use the *Upgrade Advisor* (also called the Windows 7 Upgrade Advisor) to determine if a particular system is capable of running Windows 7 and to generate a report of any potential compatibility issues with installed programs and connected devices. This program is available on the Microsoft website at: http://windows.microsoft.com/en-us/windows/downloads/upgrade-advisor. It is supported on Windows 7, Windows Vista, and Windows XP Service Pack 2.

Upgrading the operating system may cause problems such as the following:

- Forgetting to activate – Windows uses Windows Genuine Advantage (WGA) technology, which requires activation after installation. Remember to activate your upgraded copy of Windows. All versions of Windows must be activated after being installed on the computer.

- Wrong OS edition – Each operating system version comes in various editions, and each edition provides specific features. You should determine the features you want and need before selecting an edition for installation. However, if you install the wrong edition, you can use Windows Anytime Upgrade to upgrade to the edition you need.

- Conflict with applications – In some instances you may find that an application no longer runs after upgrading the operating system. In this case you can check the vendor's website to check for updates to the application program. Sometimes, you may need to purchase a new version of the application software in order to enable it to work with the upgraded operating system.

If at any time you are unsure or uncomfortable with how to resolve issues that occur after upgrading/updating, always refer to a technical specialist for assistance. They are much more familiar with these types of issues and can narrow down the possibilities of what is causing the issues and then how to correct them.

Dealing with Viruses or Malware

One of the most important software programs installed on a computer is an antivirus or antimalware program. *Malware*, or malicious software, refers to programs or files whose purpose is to harm computer systems. Malware includes computer viruses, worms and Trojan horses. Generally, a virus destroys files and data, a worm consumes system resources, and Trojan horses are designed to provide unauthorized users illicit access to a computer.

Spyware is also considered a form of malware. *Spyware* is a software application that is secretly placed on your system and gathers personal or private information without your consent or knowledge. Spyware can be placed on your system by a virus or by an application downloaded from the Internet. Many Internet-based applications contain spyware. Once installed, spyware monitors your activity on the Internet and conveys the information to the spyware originator who can then gather website usage, email and even password information from you, then use it for advertising purposes or malicious activities.

Regularly scheduled scans (or checks) for malware should be configured on computers, regardless of whether the computer is used for personal or corporate purposes.

In the case of a corporate computer, this is crucial as you want to protect the company against any malicious attacks. To avoid interfering with an employee's ability to work, scans can be scheduled to occur after normal working hours (for example, you can schedule a scan to begin at midnight).

A member of the IT staff should periodically view the quarantine files on corporate systems to see how much virus activity has been discovered and possibly to identify systems that are more at risk than others. If it is discovered that employees are turning off scheduled scans, the rights on the system can be adjusted as appropriate. Limiting a user's rights on a computer can be a sensitive area, however, and increasing user awareness and education may be necessary.

To keep track of portables, the IT staff may require employees to periodically bring in their laptops for routine maintenance. The IT staff can also create group policies for portables that automatically download antivirus updates and start system scans any time the portable connects to the corporate network (even over the Internet).

As soon as you install antivirus software, scan the computer for any possible viruses that could already be resident, and subscribe immediately to automatic updates (or notices of updates) for the virus definition files and patches for the program. It is generally a good practice to scan the system again after updates are installed. It is important to schedule regular system scans and to configure the application to automatically scan email messages as they are delivered to your Inbox.

If and when a virus is detected, you can use the antivirus software to disinfect the system. Antivirus software that is kept current knows the signatures of the latest viruses, and works by scanning the infected file or program for these known signatures. If the virus is found, your hard drive can often be disinfected immediately so that the virus cannot infect other files or cause more damage.

It bears repeating that it is extremely important to keep your antivirus software up to date and configured to automatically download updates. It is equally important to keep the email scanner and resident scanner portions of the application turned on. Regular system scans are recommended, and these can be scheduled. You can also manually start a scan at any time.

Avoiding Viruses or Malware

Conducting regular scheduled scans, and enabling the resident scanner and email scanner portions of the application can give you peace of mind that your system is not infected. Other steps you can take to avoid infection include:

- Save all files you download from the Internet to a folder other than your data folder. Scan all downloaded files before opening them, especially if they are executable files or from a file sharing application (such as Kazaa, Grokster or Limewire) that may be known to have suspicious files embedded in its downloads.
- Scan any removable media (CD, DVD or flash drive) before copying or opening files contained on the media.
- If you share files with other people using portable devices, scan any files you plan to give to others to ensure you do not inadvertently pass a virus on to them.
- Because email is the most common method for spreading viruses, always set your antivirus program to automatically scan all incoming and outgoing messages.
- Always scan email attachments before opening them, even if they come from someone you know.
- Be suspicious of any unexpected attachments you receive with email or instant message transmissions. If you receive an attachment you did not expect or do not recognize:
  - Do not open the attachment.
  - Try to contact the message sender (using a method other than email) and determine whether the attachment is legitimate.
  - If you are unable to contact the sender or the sender is unaware of the attachment, delete the attachment from the message, or if you no longer need the message, delete the entire message from your email program.

The best protection is prevention, but you should understand that most viruses can be removed without permanent damage to your system.

Consider the following symptoms that might indicate that your system has been infected with a virus:

- You see messages or prompts you have never seen before.
- You notice the computer seems to be running slower or you are suddenly having problems with programs.
- Certain software applications no longer work.
- You see files you do not recognize on your hard disk.
- You see error messages indicating that a file is missing, usually a program file.

If you notice any of these symptoms, perform a system scan. When an antivirus program is running, it will scan the files you select; when it finds a virus or threat, it will give you the option to quarantine or remove the threat. Quarantine is an isolated area on the PC designed to hold potentially dangerous files to keep them from running and harming the system. Files remain in quarantine until you remove or restore them.

- If you elect to quarantine the infected files, the antivirus program will place the infected files in a quarantined or vault area where they cannot infect other files. Quarantined files can usually be deleted at any time. While your first response might be to delete the infected file, it may be helpful to alert someone in the IT department so they can view the quarantined file and be made known of its presence. Check with your IT department regarding their policy on discovered viruses.

- If you elect to remove the file, the antivirus program will permanently delete this file from your system. You usually do not need to do anything else.

- If the antivirus program finds a virus that cannot be removed, it will still quarantine the infected file. The matter should then be escalated to the IT department.

- If the virus is in active memory and you are not able to launch the antivirus software, notify the IT department. A member of IT will most likely turn off the computer and reboot from a known, clean bootable disk to start the system without the virus in memory. You should then be able to launch the antivirus software and begin the disinfection process

- If you find a virus on your home system that your antivirus software cannot remove, make a note of the virus name and, when the scan is complete, go to the antivirus program's website to find a removal tool for this virus. Generally you will need to download a file and then follow the instructions for removing the virus from your system.

- Remember to check all your disks and backup files with the antivirus software, and remove the virus from them if necessary.

- Replace any file or programs that have been damaged or changed by the virus with backup copies or reinstall programs from original installation media.

EXERCISE

In this exercise, you will download and install the Microsoft Security Essentials free antivirus protection program.

> **Note:** Due to the length of time required for this lab, your instructor may have installed the program on your system before class began. If so, read through the steps of this exercise to get an idea of how simple it is to load good antivirus protection on your system, then move on to the next part of the exercise.

1. Open a web browser and visit: `www.microsoft.com/downloads`.

2. Locate and click in the search field, and type: `security essentials`.

3. In the drop-down suggestion list, click **security essentials download** and then press ⌷Enter⌷ or click the magnifying glass.

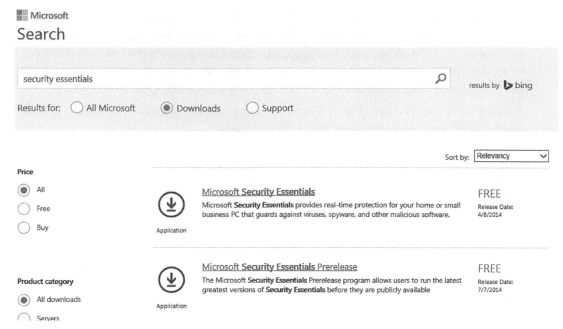

4. Click **Microsoft Security Essentials**.

5. Click **Download** button and then click the appropriate version for the type of computer you are using. Ask your instructor for assistance in selecting the appropriate version. We are using the ENUS\x86 version.

    The following information box should appear at the bottom of the screen:

6. Click **Save** to save this file to the *Downloads* folder, set as the default location to store files from the Internet.

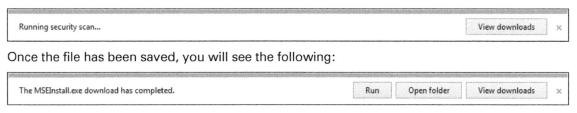

    Once the file has been saved, you will see the following:

7. Click **Run** to begin the installation.

    If a User Account Control dialog box appears, click **Yes** or ask the instructor to provide you with the required information.

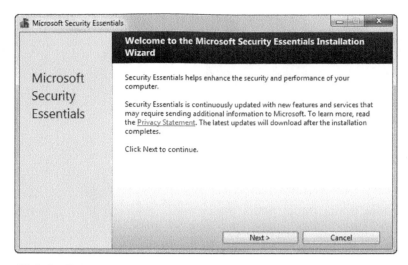

8. Click the link to read the Privacy Statement and then click **Next** in the Microsoft Security Essentials window.

9. Read the License Terms and then click **I accept**.

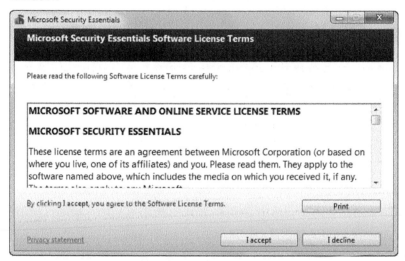

10. You can choose to join the program to help improve the product, if desired. For the purpose of this exercise, click **I do not want to join the program at this time**. Then click **Next**.

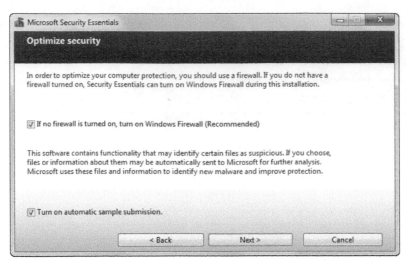

11. Click **Next**.

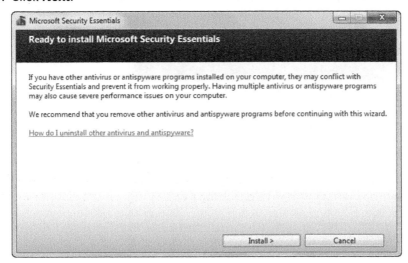

12. Click **Install**.

At this point, the program will begin to install and give you a bar to show the progress. When the installation is complete, you will see a screen similar to the following:

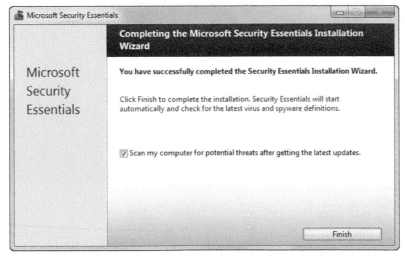

13. Click **Finish**.

The installation process will complete and then display a screen you can use to configure the program to protect your system.

14. Close the web browser in the background while Microsoft Security Essentials checks for any updates to the program (the updates here will be for any new virus, spyware, or malware definition files since this release of the program).

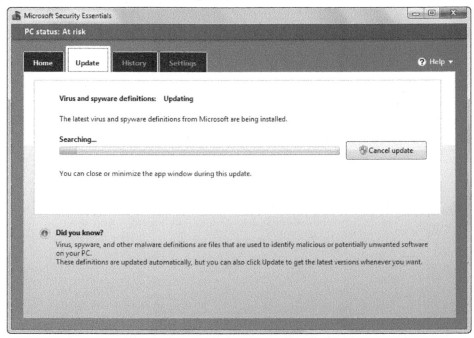

15. If there are any updates, allow the program to complete the update. Otherwise, Microsoft Security Essentials will begin a scan of your system to check for any existing viruses, spyware, or malware.

> **Note:** This length of time for this process will vary based on what has been installed or stored on the system.

When the scan is complete, you will see a screen similar to the following:

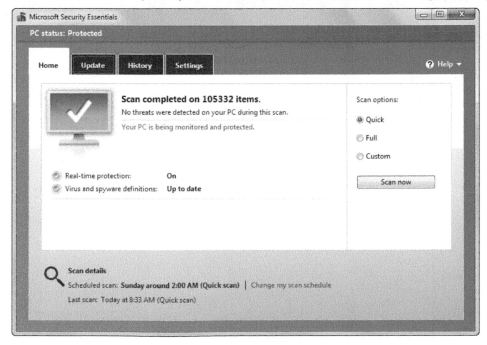

Let's now explore the program interface and take a look at options you can set to have this program automatically protect your system.

16. Click the **Update** tab.

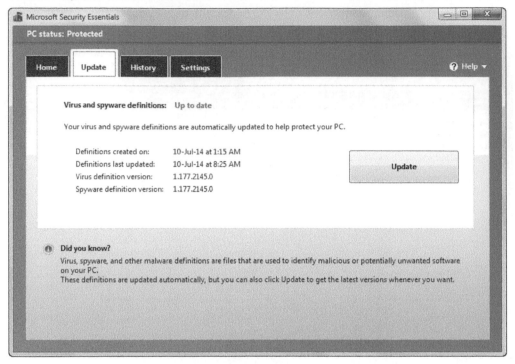

You can use this tab to manually update the virus definitions at any time. In our exercise, updates were automatically installed when you installed Security Essentials. You should check this tab occasionally to ensure that you have the latest updates, especially if you choose to ignore any prompts that may appear in the Task Notification area.

17. Click the **History** tab.

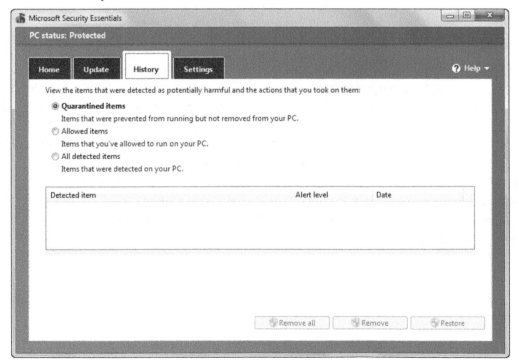

Use this tab to view which files, if any, have been detected and removed or quarantined during a scan. Some files are removed automatically, and others are placed into quarantine.

18. Click the **Settings** tab.

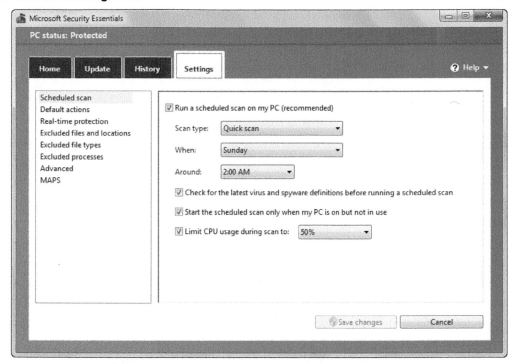

Use this tab to set when you want a scan to be performed on your system. It is important that you configure these settings so that scans are set to occur when the computer is turned on. For example, leaving the settings as shown in the above screen is useful only if the computer is still turned on at 2:00AM. A more appropriate setting might be Monday morning when you are preparing for the week, (or any weekday evening if you leave the computer on when you leave the office) thereby giving the computer time to perform the scan.

If Microsoft Security Essentials detects malicious or potentially unwanted software on your PC, it notifies you about the detected item by displaying a message in the notification area at the right edge of the taskbar.

In some cases, Microsoft Security Essentials takes automatic action to remove malicious software from your PC, and will notify you that it is doing so. In other cases, Microsoft Security Essentials will show you a notification that malicious or potentially unwanted software has been detected. Click **Clean computer** to remove the software, or click **Show details** to open the Potential threat details window and get additional information about the detected item.

You can specify to remove, quarantine or allow the software. Removing permanently deletes the software from the computer. Quarantining moves the software to the quarantine area and prevents it from running. Allowing the software allows it to run on the computer.

19. Close the Microsoft Security Essentials window.

Using the Safe Mode

If your computer does not start up properly or won't start at all, you can use a troubleshooting tool called *Safe Mode* to load only the core services of the operating system. This allows you to try and diagnose what specific problem is preventing the system from starting up normally. There are many possible reasons why an operating system won't start properly; the most common reasons include the accidental deletion or corruption of a system file, or the installation of a system, application or driver update that is not compatible with the rest of the system. When Safe Mode is activated, the operating system loads with reduced functionality, disabling any devices that are not crucial to the operating system. Usually, this means that the offending driver or file is not loaded (and therefore cannot crash the system), but you can still adjust some settings and back up files if necessary.

The following are examples of when Safe Mode may be required or appears during the startup process:

- Windows was not shut down properly, for example, you experience a power failure where the computer loses all power, or someone turned the power off to the computer when Windows was still active.

- Windows displays the desktop but then freezes.

- You cannot launch your antivirus software, but suspect you may have a virus and need to run a scan.

- An input or output device stops working once Windows starts and you want to see which device driver could be causing the conflict.

Sometimes when the system can't start normally, a menu appears, allowing you to choose how you want to start the system.

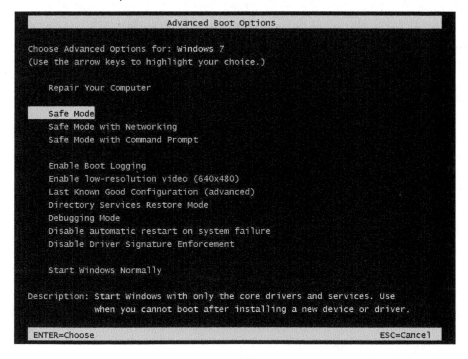

Use the arrow key to move to the option you want to use and then press (Enter). Most users select one of the following options:

Safe Mode	Starts the system using the minimum number of drivers and services possible. Networking is not available.
Safe Mode with Networking	Starts the system in the same manner as safe mode, but also includes the network drivers and services necessary to access the Internet or another computer on the network.
Start Windows Normally	Start Windows normally, using all drivers and services.

> **Note:** The other options in the menu such as Safe Mode with Command Prompt, Directory Services Restore Mode, or Debugging Mode, are best handled by a technical specialist who fully understands how the computer is configured.

You can also force a system to boot into Safe Mode; press and hold (F8) as the system is powering up until the menu appears, then select one of the Safe Mode options.

To use Safe Mode:

1. Turn the computer on.
2. As soon as the computer starts, press and hold (F8) until you see the menu of startup modes.
3. Use the arrow key to move down to the Safe Mode you want to use and then press (Enter).
4. After a few moments the Windows desktop appears and the text Safe Mode appears on the four corners of the screen.
5. You can then use the resources you have available to resolve the problems you are experiencing with the computer, such as running a scan to check for viruses.
6. Once you have determined what is causing Windows to malfunction you can correct the problem and then restart the computer. If it is able to start normally, then the problem has been resolved.

Depending on what is wrong with the computer, you may find you need to run Safe Mode a few more times to isolate and correct the problem. If the problem persists, obtain assistance from a technical specialist.

Getting Windows Help and Support

 Exam 1 - Objective 4.1

Windows provides an extensive online Help system that displays step-by-step procedures, definitions for terms, and hypertext links to other related topics. Web Help is available for additional online support via the Internet.

To activate Help, use one of the following methods:

- select **Help and Support** from the **Start** menu, or
- press (F1), or
- click the 🔘 (**Help**) button in any dialog box, if available.

The Windows Help and Support window contains navigation and search tools, as well as links to a variety of resources, such as assistance in Finding an Answer, Asking Someone, or Obtaining Information from Microsoft.

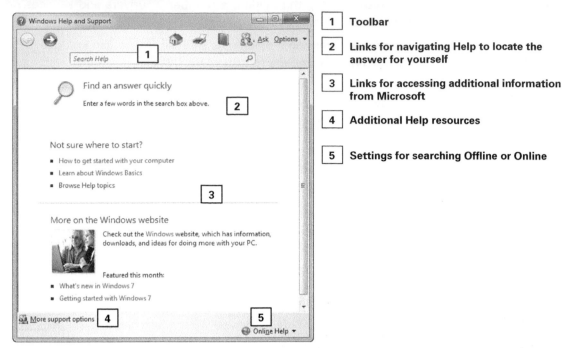

1	Toolbar
2	Links for navigating Help to locate the answer for yourself
3	Links for accessing additional information from Microsoft
4	Additional Help resources
5	Settings for searching Offline or Online

The toolbar at the top of each Help window includes buttons that assist when working with the Help system.

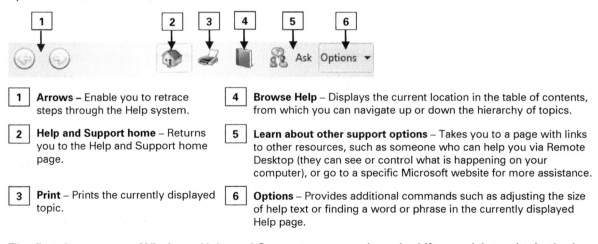

1	**Arrows** – Enable you to retrace steps through the Help system.	4	**Browse Help** – Displays the current location in the table of contents, from which you can navigate up or down the hierarchy of topics.
2	**Help and Support home** – Returns you to the Help and Support home page.	5	**Learn about other support options** – Takes you to a page with links to other resources, such as someone who can help you via Remote Desktop (they can see or control what is happening on your computer), or go to a specific Microsoft website for more assistance.
3	**Print** – Prints the currently displayed topic.	6	**Options** – Provides additional commands such as adjusting the size of help text or finding a word or phrase in the currently displayed Help page.

The first time you use Windows Help and Support, you may be asked if you wish to obtain the latest online content. Unless you are using a dial-up connection, you should accept this option. Remember that online help content is not stored on your computer; it is only available when you are connected to the Internet.

Using the Table of Contents

Windows provides an option to use a table of contents to find help on specific topics. Here, the topics are grouped by the type of task or activity. To activate the Help Contents, do one of the following:

- In the Windows Help and Support window, click the **Browse Help topics** link, or
- on the Help toolbar, click ▓ (**Browse Help**).

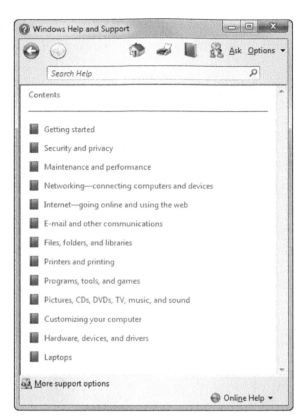

These categories will link you to information about specific features or options available in Windows. As you move from one page to another, you will see symbols similar to the following:

a link that opens an article with further information for this topic

a link that displays a list of articles for this topic.

Getting Additional Technical Support

If you cannot find help on a specific topic online, a number of other options for technical support are available:

- Contact Microsoft. A list of numbers and ways to contact them are available in the Help menu from within any Microsoft application program; you can also use the online help option to find technical support information.

- Go to a computer retailer that provides technical support. This does not have to be the store where you purchased the computer. Technicians charge an hourly fee for repairs or training.

- Hire a consultant who can come to your site to fix the computer or provide you with training or assistance on a problem. Consultants also charge an hourly fee, which may include travel time.

- Take additional courses on Windows to study advanced skills and troubleshooting techniques. Check your Yellow Pages or go online to locate courses offered in your area. Pricing for courses will vary depending on the training facility.

- Search the Internet for any groups that specialize in Windows or host a community area such as a blog or forum where they share information with each other. The following is a list of common sites where you can research or ask for assistance:

  www.techrepublic.com – provides articles and reviews about the latest technologies

  www.cnet.com – provides downloadable tools and utilities, and reviews about popular technologies www.howstuffworks.com – provides informative articles about how particular technologies work.

technet.microsoft.com – provides technical information about all versions of the Windows operating systems

When you require technical support, you may be asked which version of Windows you are using. It is important to tell technical support the version you are using so they can provide you with the correct support. Windows 7 is fairly easy to identify as the taskbar is large and the Start button is an icon only and does not contain the word "Start" as with earlier versions.

To display the version of Windows for technical support:

- click the **Start** button and click **Control Panel**. In the Control Panel window, click **System and Security**, and then click **System**, or

- click the **Start** button, right-click **Computer** and then click **Properties**.

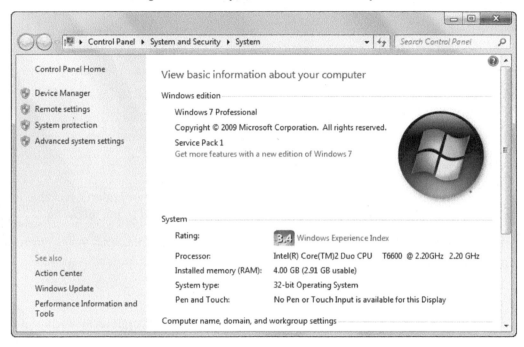

EXERCISE

In this exercise you will learn how to use the Help feature in Windows and how to use the Help system.

1. Click **Start** and then click **Help and Support**.

   The Windows Help and Support window displays.

2. Type: `Windows 7` in the **Search Help** field and click the 🔍 button, or press ⏎ Enter .

   The search results will display the top 30 results on the term "Windows 7." Notice that Windows breaks the results down by category to help you identify the area about which you may want more assistance.

3. In the list of topics, click a link of interest to you, such as **Share files with someone**.

   The information appears in the window with a variety of links for more help on specific topics.

4. In the window, click a text item that appears in green with underline (if one is displayed).

   Text links in green will display a definition of the text for easy reference.

   Text links in blue will move quickly to another page with more information on the clicked item.

Up to this point, you have been moving forward to find and read more information on specific topics. As you move from page to page, the **Back** and **Forward** buttons appear.

5. Click ⊙ **(Back)** to go back one page.

6. Click another link of your choice in the Top 30 results list.

    Notice that Windows now displays this article. You can continue to look for help on items, as needed, or go back to previous Help screens as necessary.

7. In the Windows Help and Support toolbar, click ▉ **(Browse Help)**.

    You should now be viewing additional links regarding the result topic you chose in step 6.

8. Click ⊙ **(Back)** to return to the previous help page.

9. Click ⊙ **(Forward)** to return to the previous page.

10. Click ⊙ **(Home)** to return to the Windows Help and Support page.

11. Close the Windows Help and Support window.

Let's now try searching for a topic using some of the other technical support web sites commonly used by others.

12. Open a web browser and in the Address bar, type: `techrepublic.com` and press ⌈Enter⌋.

13. Scroll and review the different topics listed. Then click the one of most interest to you.

14. Read the information and then click **Back**.

15. If there is another topic of interest, click that to read more about that topic.

    TechRepublic is a popular site for people to register to receive email on a variety of topics related to both technical and non-technical topics such as how to deal with different personalities in the team, why spelling matters when you send a resume, new benefits of a specific new product.

Now try looking at a different web site for researching information on a specific topic.

16. In the Address bar, type: `howstuffworks.com` and press ⌈Enter⌋.

17. Click in the search field and type: `search engine`. Press ⌈Enter⌋.

18. Scroll the page to view some of the information listed here and if desired, click a link to view further details on this topic.

    You should notice that the information on both sites can be valuable when you want to find help on a topic, and both sites contain documents for technical and non-technical topics.

19. Close the web browser.

Using the Windows Knowledge Base

You may find that the Help feature in Windows may not contain the necessary information or as much detail as you need in order to resolve an issue with the computer. You can use one of the other resources mentioned earlier, or you can try to find the answer yourself using the *Knowledge Base* on Microsoft's website. Microsoft maintains an extensive list of issues relating to hardware and software for the different versions of Windows. This list has been compiled into a database that is available for searching.

To access the Knowledge Base, use the following steps:

1. Start a web browser and in the Address Bar, type: `support.microsoft.com` and press ⌈Enter⌋.

Choose your product so we can help:

2.   Enter the text you want Microsoft to search the Knowledge Base for and press (Enter).

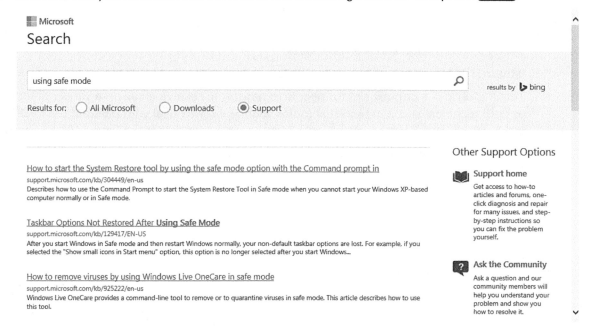

3.   Click the link you would like to read from the list.

4.   Review the contents and continue to search as needed, or

   •   click the appropriate action for the feedback at the bottom left corner, or

   •   click **Back** to move back one screen at a time.

> **Tip:** Feedback provided to Microsoft helps to keep the Knowledge Base current or to update their files, and as needed, points you in the right direction for the search text.

5.   Continue with the search for information or close the web browser.

Using Task Manager

You can use the Task Manager to switch programs, start a program, check which programs are running and view their status, or safely close a program when problems are occurring, such as it is no longer responding. The Task Manager is an advanced application that can be used to troubleshoot specific issues on the computer, and should only be handled by an experienced user or network administrator.

To display the Task Manager, use one of the following methods:

- Press the (Ctrl)+(Alt)+(Delete) key combination to display a screen with options to lock the computer, switch user, log off, change the password, or start the Task Manager. Click **Start Task Manager**, or

- press (Ctrl)+(Shift)+(Esc), or

- right-click the taskbar and then click **Start Task Manager**.

When managing tasks on the computer, you will likely use one of the first three tabs to determine what may be happening on the computer and what action to take next.

Applications

Displays a list of open programs and their status. Use the Status column to help determine which program may need to be ended. Use the buttons on this tab to end a program, switch to another program or start a new task.

You can also right-click on the program task to choose one of these actions.

If you have multiple tasks in the list, you can sort the list by clicking the appropriate column heading.

When you choose to end a task here, you are asking Windows to close the entire application, including the last document you were working on prior to activating the Task Manager.

Processes

Displays a list of all processes currently running on the system, including any processes by other user accounts on this system.

This tab is the most helpful when troubleshooting an issue on the computer. For instance, if there appears to be no problem with an application but it is running slowly, use this tab to see if another program may be consuming a large amount of RAM. In fact, if you see a large number of processes running with high memory usage and you don't recognize the process names, you may be able to identify any suspicious or malicious activity.

When you need to end a process, click it from the list and then click **End Process**.

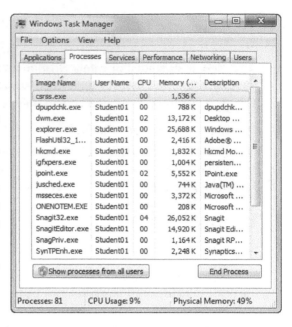

To sort the information, click the appropriate column header, currently this list is sorted by the Image Name.

To see more details on the process, resize the window and then resize the columns. The Description column will display the name of or indicate the purpose of this process.

Services

Displays a list of services currently active on the system. A service is a program that performs a function that runs without any user involvement.

To stop or start a process, right-click the process and click the appropriate command. You can also choose to go to the process to view more information about that process.

Alternatively, click the **Services** button to view the Services management console to manage the service accordingly. Be careful to not change anything in this area if you are new to computers. Turning off a service will also turn off any other activities related to this service. Wherever possible, work with a technical specialist to stop or start processes and services.

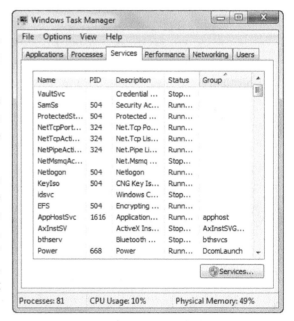

EXERCISE

In this exercise, you will start programs and then use the Task Manager to end one of them.

1. Click the **Start** button, point at **All Programs**, and then click **Windows Media Center**.
2. Click the **Start** button once more, point at **All Programs**, click **Accessories** and then click **Paint**.
3. Click the **Start** button, point at **All Programs**, and click another program from the list at the top, such as Windows Live Movie Maker or Windows Media Player.

4. Click the **Start** button, point at **All Programs**, click **Microsoft Office 2013**, and then click **Excel 2013**.

5. On the taskbar, click the web browser to start that program.

Suppose you notice there seems to be a problem with one of the applications you have started. You decide you will look at Task Manager to see if there is a problem.

6. Press $\boxed{\text{Ctrl}}+\boxed{\text{Alt}}+\boxed{\text{Delete}}$ once to display the Task Manager menu choices.

7. Click **Start Task Manager**.

8. Ensure you are viewing the Applications tab and then click the program activated in step 3 to select it in the list.

9. Click **End Task**.

10. Close Task Manager.

11. Close each open application using its own **Close** button

Lesson Summary

In this lesson you learned about what troubleshooting means and what steps you can take to ensure the maximum performance of the hardware and software on the computer. You should now be familiar with:

☑ what troubleshooting means

☑ how to identify a problem for resolution

☑ looking at how you can manage the hardware

☑ recognizing what may cause software issues

☑ identifying potential solutions for software issues

☑ how to find and use Help resources

Review Questions

1. John is beginning to see numerous messages regarding the lack of space on his hard drive. What should he do next?
    a. Write down what the error messages display.
    b. Call technical support to fix the problem.
    c. Shut down the computer until technical support arrives.
    d. Buy a new computer.

2. What does firmware refer to?
    a. Built-in software that controls how a device functions.
    b. Software that allows an operating system to communicate with a device.
    c. A type of storage media.
    d. A standard that a company wants to enforce on every company computer.

3. What could cause an update to the operating system to fail 75% through the installation?
    a. You no longer have permission to continue the installation.
    b. You have run out of time to complete the full installation.
    c. You have insufficient hard disk space to install all the files.
    d. You realize you already have the program installed.

4. If you store a backup of your data to the Cloud, where is the data located?
    a. On a local network drive.
    b. At an offsite location such as your home.
    c. On your local hard drive.
    d. On a service provider's computer in an offsite location, such as a OneDrive folder.

5. If an application program update causes the program to stop working, what steps can you take before trying to reinstall the update?
    a. Uninstall the entire application program.
    b. Close all open applications, including your email program, and reboot the computer.
    c. Reinstall the operating system.
    d. Any of the above

6. In the list of operating system updates listed below, which is critical to install?
    a. An update that corrects a known security flaw.
    b. An update that recognizes new BlueTooth devices.
    c. An update that includes experimental (beta) software.
    d. All the listed updates are critical

7. What can you do to minimize the possibility of infecting your computer with a virus?
    a. Save and scan any attachments from email before opening them.
    b. Never open a file with an .exe file type sent via email without scanning it first.
    c. If downloading a file from the Internet, save and scan the file before using it.
    d. Any of the above
    e. a or c

8. Where can you find help or advice for fixing a problem on your computer?
    a. IT department
    b. Online sources, such as a Knowledge Base.
    c. Offline sources, such as the library or textbooks.
    d. Any of the above
    e. a or b

MMM
Go online for
Additional
Review

Lesson 7: Common Features

Lesson Objectives

In this lesson you will examine some of the common features shared among the applications in Microsoft Office 2013. You will also explore basic techniques for working in an Office application. On completion of the lesson, you should be familiar with:

- ☐ identifying similar layouts and features on the screen between applications
- ☐ recognizing tips and tools on the screen for easy access
- ☐ how to start or exit a Microsoft Office program
- ☐ how to use and customize the Quick Access Toolbar
- ☐ using commands and navigating around the Ribbon
- ☐ how to navigate around the screen
- ☐ getting help in Microsoft Office
- ☐ using the File tab and Backstage
- ☐ changing program options and defaults
- ☐ common methods to manipulate data

Getting Started

As you begin working with different application programs in the Windows environment, you will notice consistency between programs. This consistency reduces the amount of time required to learn the basics of a new program.

You will also find that concepts and fundamental skills are the same for similar types of application programs (such as Word and WordPerfect); the majority of differences involve the location of various commands in each program. For example, changing margins refers to the process of setting a measurement for the amount of space from the edge of a sheet of paper to where text begins. In Word, you set margins using the Margins command, whereas in WordPerfect, you use the Layout command.

Microsoft Office is one of the most popular suite programs; Word, Excel, PowerPoint and Access are some of the most commonly used programs within the Office suite. The following lessons demonstrate how to accomplish common tasks required in an office environment using these programs.

Starting a Program

To start a Microsoft Office 2013 program, click **Start**, point at **All Programs**, click **Microsoft Office 2013** and then click the appropriate program.

If shortcut icons for any of the programs appear on the desktop or the taskbar, you can start the program by clicking the icon.

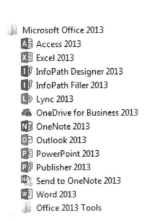

Exiting a Program

When you finish using a program, always exit it properly. Properly closing a program will prevent possible corruption of program files and free up memory for another program. Use one of the following methods to exit the program:

- Click the ✕ **(Close)** button at the far right corner of the title bar for the application program to exit the program, or

- press (Alt) + (F4).

If you have made any changes to an open document, you will be prompted by the application to save the document or abandon the changes. This gives you a last chance to save your files before exiting the program.

EXERCISE

In this exercise you will practice starting and then exiting Microsoft Office programs.

1. Click the **Start** button and then point at **All Programs**.

2. Click **Microsoft Office 2013** in the submenu, and then **Excel 2013**.

   Microsoft Excel opens and appears on your screen.

3. Click the **Start** button and then **All Programs**.

4. Click **Microsoft Office 2013**, and then **Word 2013**.

   Microsoft Word opens.

5. Click the **Start** button and then **All Programs**.

6. Click **Microsoft Office 2013**, and then **PowerPoint 2013**.

7. Click the **Start** button and then **All Programs**.

8. Click **Microsoft Office 2013**, and then **Access 2013**.

   As each new program opens, a button for the program appears on the taskbar. Remember that you can switch among different programs or files by clicking the appropriate button on the taskbar.

9. Switch to Excel by clicking its button in the taskbar.

10. Switch to Word by clicking its button in the taskbar.

11. Switch to PowerPoint by clicking its button in the taskbar.

12. Switch to Access by clicking its button in the taskbar.

13. Click the ✕ **(Close)** button at the far top right corner of the Access screen.

    Access closes. The buttons for Excel, PowerPoint, and Word remain on the taskbar.

14. Click the ✕ **(Close)** button at the far top right corner of each of the remaining programs to close them.

    When all the programs are closed, you are back at the desktop.

Looking at the Screen

 Exam 2 - Objective 1.1, 1.3

Microsoft Office programs share a number of common elements in the application window, such as the ribbon and Zoom buttons. You can see the changes you make in the document window where the contents of the file display (that is, below the ribbon and above the status bar).

When you start a Microsoft Office program, Office 2013 displays a page where you can choose to create a new blank document type for the program, create a new document using a template or document style, or open an existing file. The following screens show the main editing screen you will use to work with files in the various Microsoft Office programs.

Microsoft Word 2013

When you start a new blank document in Word, it appears similar to the following:

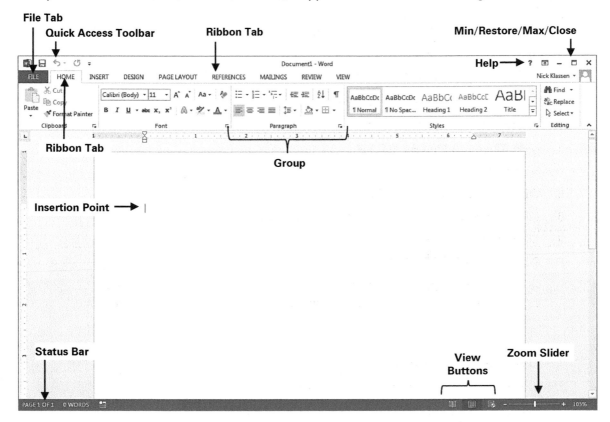

Microsoft Excel 2013

When you open a new blank workbook in Excel, the application window looks much like the following:

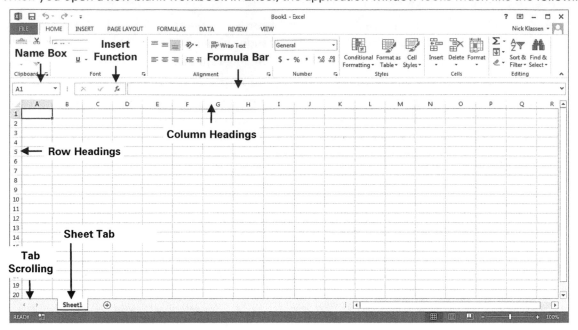

Microsoft PowerPoint 2013

When you create a new blank presentation in PowerPoint, the application window looks much like the following:

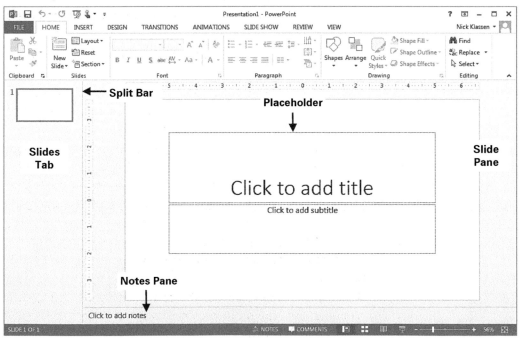

Microsoft Access 2013

When you start Access and create a new file or open a file, a screen similar to the following appears:

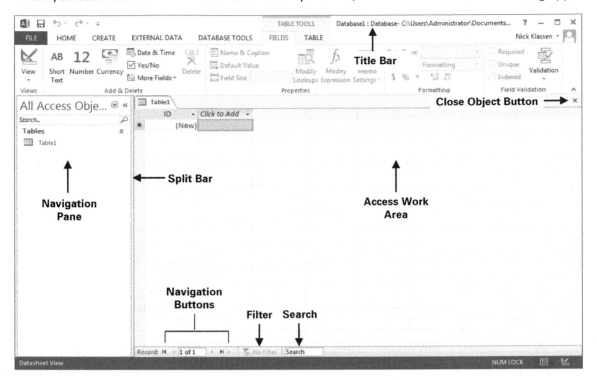

The most common elements found on these screens include:

File Tab	Click the **File** tab to display the Backstage view, which you use to create, open, save, print and manage files. In Backstage view you do things *to* a file, as opposed to doing things *in* a file. Use the ⬅ **(Back)** icon to return to the document.
Quick Access Toolbar	Use the Quick Access toolbar to gain quick access to frequently used commands. You can customize the Quick Access toolbar to include the commands and macros that you use regularly.
Title Bar	Look at the title bar to see what files or programs are currently displayed in the window. For example, it might read "Document 2 - Word", "2014 Qtr Sales - Excel", "Waterford Estates – PowerPoint", or "Customers – Access".
Minimize/Maximize/ Restore Down/Close	Use these buttons to affect how much of the application window displays on the screen: Minimize closes the program temporarily to the Windows taskbar, Maximize fills the entire screen with the application window, Restore Down reduces the screen to the size it was before it was maximized, and Close will exit the program.
Ribbon	Use the tabs on the ribbon to access the commands you need to complete a task. For example, the Home tab provides access to commands grouped in categories such as Clipboard, Font, and Paragraph.
Microsoft [Program] Help	Click the Help button to open the Help window when you have a question. In the Help window, you can search online on Microsoft's Office web site to get the latest help on a feature. If you do not have access to the Internet, you can use the offline Help feature but it will not be as comprehensive as when you search Microsoft's live help center.

Status Bar	Look at the status bar to find information about the document currently displayed, such as which page or slide you are viewing out of the total number, the total number of words in the document, or the number of words in a selected section. You can also see the View buttons and the Zoom slider on the status bar.
View Buttons	Use these buttons to quickly change between different document views, such as **Print Layout, Read Mode**, or **Web Layout**. Each view in each program provides its own advantages.
Zoom Slider	Click the buttons at either side of the Zoom slider to increase or decrease the zoom level (percentage) of the document currently on screen. Alternatively, you can drag the slider button to increase or decrease the zoom level. The program displays the current zoom level to the right of the Zoom slider. You can also click this button to set a custom or specific zoom level.

The following is specific to Microsoft Word only:

Insertion Point	Look for the Insertion Point to see where the cursor is currently located in a document. The Insertion Point displays as a flashing vertical line. In a new document, it displays at the top left of the page just inside the margins.

The following items are specific to Microsoft Excel only:

Name Box	Look in the Name box for the address of the active cell. For example, if the Name box displays A21, this indicates the active cell is the one that resides where column A and row 21 intersect. In the example displayed previously, cell A1 is selected and the cell address is displayed in the Name box.
Insert Function	Use the Insert Function to open a dialog box that will help you choose and insert a built-in function.
Formula Bar	Look at the Formula Bar to see the contents of the active cell. Under certain circumstances, you can use this bar to make entries in the worksheet.
Column Headings	The sequential letters at the top of each column enable you to identify columns.
Row Headings	The sequential numbers on the left side of each row enable you to identify rows.
Tab Scrolling Buttons	Use these buttons to move between worksheet tabs. A button with a single triangle moves the view one sheet per click in the corresponding direction. A button with a vertical line before or after the triangle moves the view to the first or last worksheet in the workbook. This does not change the sheet you are viewing, only the tabs displayed at the bottom of the screen.
Horizontal and Vertical Split Bars	Use these bars to split the worksheet window into two or more panes. There is also a split bar at the left of the horizontal scroll bar that you can use to adjust the width of the horizontal scroll bar.

The following are specific to Microsoft PowerPoint only:

Slides Tab	Refer to the thumbnail or miniature picture of the slide in this area to quickly view the contents of slides or the flow of the slides in a presentation. You can also use this view to move quickly to a particular slide.
Outline Tab	By default, does not appear on the screen but will display in the same area as the Slides tab when this view is activated. This view shows a list of the text content only per slide for quick review of the topic flow.
Placeholder	Use these dash-lined boxes on the slides for hints on the type of content you might insert into different areas of the slide.

Split Bar	Drag this bar to increase or decrease the size of the Outline or Slides tab, or to increase or decrease the size of the Slide or Notes pane.
Notes Pane	Type presentation notes such as speaker notes, reminders of actions you need to perform during the presentation, and so on into the Notes pane. These notes are for the presenter's use and are not visible to the audience.
Slide Pane	Use this primarily for entering or viewing the contents of the slide. (Note that the Slide pane displays all the slide contents, whereas the Slides tab displays only a miniature of the slides and the Outline tab, when active, displays only the text for each slide.)

The following items are specific to Microsoft Access only:

Access Work Area	When objects in the Navigation Pane are opened, they appear in the Access work area so you can work with them.
Split Bar	Drag this bar to increase or decrease the size of the Navigation Pane, or to increase or decrease the size of the object you are viewing to the right of the Navigation Pane.
Navigation Buttons	Enable you to move between records in a table or form. The first button moves you to the first record; the second button moves you to the previous record; the third button moves you to the next record; the fourth button moves you to the last record; and the last button creates a new blank record.
Filter	Enables you to remove or re-apply a filter.
Search	Enables you to search and find characters in the table records.

Accessing Commands and Features

The images displayed on the previous pages show various commonly used components of the program screen. You can customize the appearance of your screen so that not all components display. For example, you can turn the ruler on or off as needed for precise alignment of text, or you can set up a default font that will automatically apply to every new blank document.

Use *ScreenTips* to help you identify buttons or elements on the tabs of the ribbon and the screen. To view a ScreenTip, position the mouse pointer over the item. A tip displays the name of the button or feature and sometimes a brief description of its purpose. In some cases, the ScreenTip will provide a keyboard shortcut as an alternative way to activate the feature.

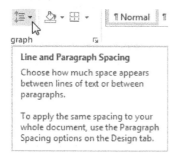

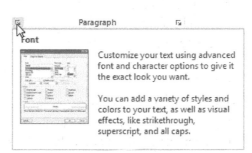

Note that a number of the elements shown in this section can be configured to display or to be hidden, based on your preference. In most cases, you configure elements by clicking **File** and then **Options**.

Using the Quick Access Toolbar

The Quick Access toolbar is located above the File tab and includes buttons for frequently used commands. By default, this toolbar includes the Save, Undo, and Redo buttons. You can customize the Quick Access toolbar to include additional commands you want to access quickly, such as opening a new blank document, printing a document, or running a spell check.

To customize the Quick Access toolbar, use one of the following methods:

- At the right of the Quick Access toolbar, click **Customize Quick Access Toolbar** and click a button in the list or click **More Commands**; or

- click **File**, **Options**, and then click **Quick Access Toolbar**; or

- right-click the ribbon, and click **Customize Quick Access Toolbar**.

You can also move the Quick Access toolbar to below the ribbon using one of the following methods:

- At the right of the Quick Access toolbar, click **Customize Quick Access Toolbar** and then click **Show Below the Ribbon**; or

- right-click the ribbon, and then click **Show Quick Access Toolbar Below the Ribbon**; or

- right-click the ribbon, click **Customize Quick Access Toolbar**, and then click **Show Quick Access Toolbar below the Ribbon**.

Using the Ribbon

The ribbon helps you quickly find the command buttons you require to complete a task. Command buttons are grouped logically on each tab, with each tab relating to a type of activity, such as inserting pictures into a document. Some tabs appear only when they are applicable.

Buttons that appear in a different color or have an outline around them are active; many of these deactivate when you click the button again or click another choice. For instance, the Bold command can be applied to text by clicking the **Bold** button and then typing the text; to turn off the boldface, click the **Bold** button again. Alternatively, you can select the text to which you want to apply boldface, and then click the Bold button once. If you want to increase the font size, select the text, then click the down arrow for the Font Size button and choose the size you want.

Each tab on the ribbon includes groups of related commands; for example, the Home tab includes a Font group that includes buttons for formatting text characters, while the Insert tab includes an Illustrations group from which you can select different types of graphics to insert into a document.

If a group includes a feature with a scroll bar, you will also find the ⊽ **More** button, below the bottom scroll button. Click the **More** button to display the full list or gallery of choices for that feature.

When you position the mouse pointer over an option in a gallery, the program displays a live preview of how the selected item will appear if you apply the gallery option. You can turn off the preview option in **File**, **Options** if you prefer.

Some groups on the ribbon include a **Dialog box launcher** button at the lower right of the group. Click the dialog box launcher to open the corresponding dialog box or window associated with the feature you want to apply. Within a dialog box, you can select items from the lists, use the arrow for a list box to display more choices for that list, or click a command to turn the feature on or off. A dialog box may also display a preview of the changes that will be applied.

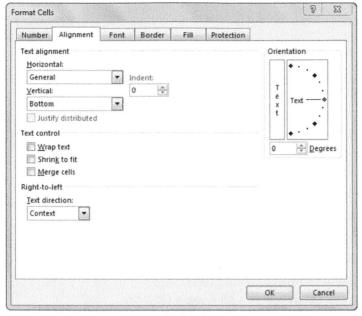

Dialog Box   **Window/Task Pane**

A dialog box is a special type of window; it contains options specific to applying a feature (as seen in the Page Setup dialog box above), and it must be closed before you can access any other items on the screen. Another type of window is the Office Clipboard, also shown above, which will display items that have been cut or copied from a document.

The ribbon can be hidden or minimized temporarily to make more space for the document, worksheet, or slide you are working with. To minimize the ribbon, use one of the following:

- Double-click one of the tabs, or

- click ∧ on the ribbon.

To redisplay the ribbon, click ⊞ **(Ribbon Display Options)** button at the top right of the screen and then select the display type from the menu.

Access Navigation Pane

Located on the left side of the screen, the Navigation Pane is a central location from which you can create and use any type of database object. It replaces the Database window found in versions of Access prior to 2007. The Navigation Pane is shown at the right.

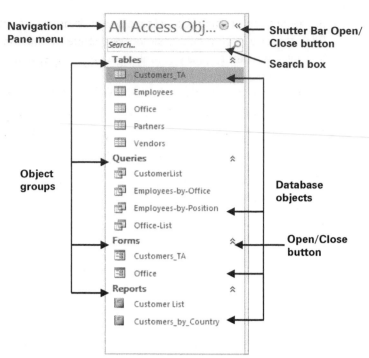

The Navigation Pane includes the following components:

Navigation Pane menu	Click the arrow to open a menu that allows you to specify which objects to show. The default selection is All Access Objects.
Open/Close buttons	Collapses the Navigation Pane so only its Open/Close button and shutter bar display. Collapsing the pane provides more space on the screen for working with an object. To reopen the Navigation Pane, click its shutter bar.
Object groups	Organize the objects in a database, allowing you to find what you are looking for. Each object group includes an Open/Close button, which you can use to collapse or expand the list.
Database objects	The tables, queries, forms and other objects that exist in the database. Each object appears in its appropriate group.
Search box	You can type the name of an object you want to find and the objects that display in the Navigation Pane are filtered to match the name you enter.

The Navigation Pane shown in the figure above shows all the objects in the database and does not display empty object groups. Access databases include Macros and Modules groups; however, these groups do not appear in the Navigation Pane in the figure because the database does not contain any of these objects.

To open an object, double-click it in the Navigation Pane. You can also right-click an object to display a shortcut menu. For example, you can right-click a table and specify to open it in a particular view.

EXERCISE

In this exercise you will start a program and work with various items on the Ribbon.

1.   Click **Start**, **All Programs**, **Microsoft Office 2013**, and **Word 2013**.

2.   Take a few moments to review how Backstage appears as well as some of the different types of new documents that can be created. Then click **Blank document** to create this document so you can identify the screen elements discussed on the previous pages.

3. Move your mouse pointer slowly over of any of the buttons on the ribbon and note the tips and messages that display. Move the mouse pointer slowly over the buttons on the status bar.

4. Click the **File** tab and review the options in Backstage view.

5. Click the ⊘ (**Back**) button to return to the blank document.

6. Click the **Page Layout** tab to view the commands there.

7. Point at the dialog box launcher for the Page Setup group to view the ScreenTip.

8. Click the **Home** tab to move to this tab.

9. In the Clipboard group, click the **Clipboard** dialog box launcher to display the Clipboard task pane.

10. Click the ✕ (**Close**) button on the Clipboard task pane to close it.

11. Click **Start, All Programs, Microsoft Office 2013**, and **PowerPoint 2013**.

12. Click the **File** tab to review the contents of the Backstage. Then click **Blank presentation** to view the slide.

    Notice that many of the commands here are similar to those you saw in Word.

13. Click ⊘ to return to the presentation.

14. On the Design tab, in the Themes group, point at one of the options in the gallery.

    Even though there is nothing on the slide, notice that PowerPoint displays a preview of this theme.

15. Click the **More** button to display all the themes available.

16. Click anywhere away from the gallery to close it.

17. Close PowerPoint and then close Word.

Getting Help

 Exam 2 - Objective 1.1

The Help feature in Microsoft Office is linked to the Office Online web site. Although you can obtain help without being connected to the Internet, you will not have access to the latest information or updates when you are working offline.

To access the Help feature in Office, use one of the following methods:

- Click the ? (**Microsoft Word Help**) button; or
- press F1.

> **Tip:** The Help feature works the same in all Microsoft Office programs. For demonstration, we are using Word.

Help Toolbar	Notice that the buttons in the Help toolbar are similar to the navigation tools available in a web browser. These buttons will help you move from one Help page to another.
Search	Use the **Search online help** field to search for a specific topic. 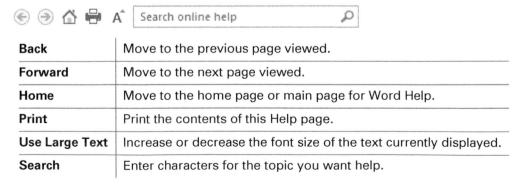
Popular searches	Click a topic from the list of items that are searched often by most users. A separate screen then appears with more explanation on the topic.
Getting started	Click an item to open a new page from the Office web site for this item. You can then click links on the page to view more information or view training on that topic.

To access one of the listed Help topics, click the link. Depending on the item selected, you may see another list of items to choose from, or you may see a window with information on that feature.

Using the Help Toolbar

Back	Move to the previous page viewed.
Forward	Move to the next page viewed.
Home	Move to the home page or main page for Word Help.
Print	Print the contents of this Help page.
Use Large Text	Increase or decrease the font size of the text currently displayed.
Search	Enter characters for the topic you want help.

When you have entered the search criteria, Word displays a list containing various articles with information for that topic in separate windows, as seen in the following:

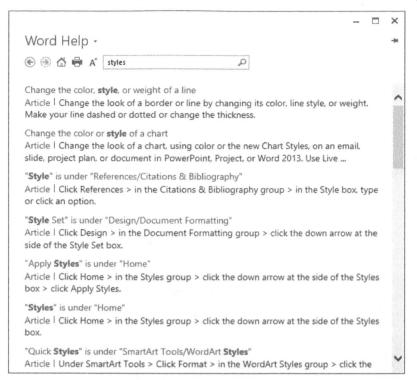

Scroll through the list items to view all the results found that match the search criteria. In some cases, there may be videos available to show you a particular task. If there are more items for the search criteria, the program displays a link to go to the next (or previous) screens.

To access the item you wish to view, click the heading link.

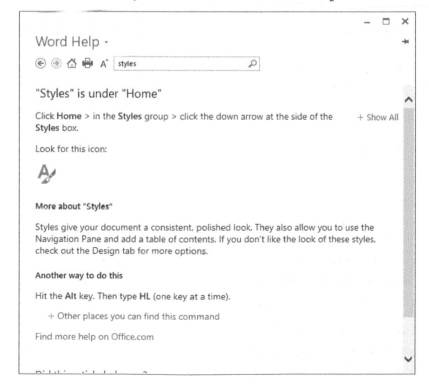

Depending on the link topic, Office displays various items on a page to assist you in finding the help you want. Anything in the same color as the program title (in this case, Word Help) is considered a link and will take you to a new location for further help. If you have touch technology available to you on the device in use, you can use the following icon to navigate to the Microsoft Office site for more information on how to use touch technology to move around the program.

 Touch
Guide

This will open a page on the Office web site regarding how to work with Office programs on a tablet:

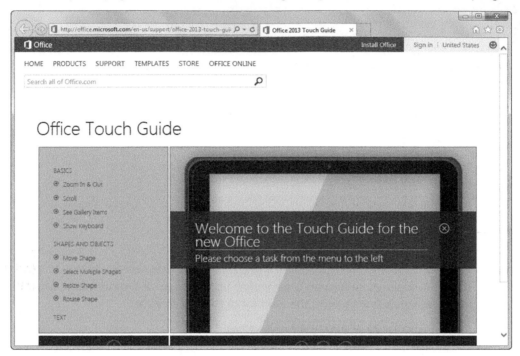

If you see a picture similar to the following, you can start a video from this page to watch this feature in action.

Use the navigation tools in the video window to play, pause, stop, or exit the video.

If you want the Help feature to be available at all times, click the ⇥ at the top right of the Help screen. Help will then stay on the screen as a window and you can switch between this screen and other programs.

Getting Additional Help

The Help feature in the Microsoft Office programs is quite extensive; occasionally you may want to access other sources for further details or to view how others may resolve an issue. Additional resources include:

• Speaking with a colleague or calling the internal Help Desk Support department.

- Calling Microsoft and speaking to a help support representative, using an online chat service or sending them an email with your query.

- Subscribing to a dedicated site for users to share their knowledge and experiences, such as a forum or blog where you can post a question.

- Research the Internet on this topic for possible resolutions, including technical support sites, online articles or Frequently Asked Questions (FAQs) pages.

Manipulating Files

 Exam 2 - Objective 1.3

Each Microsoft Office program uses the **File** tab to manage files, whether to save a new file, save an existing file, open a file, or create a new file. In general, any task that involves an entire file can be accomplished using Backstage view, including printing and setting program preferences.

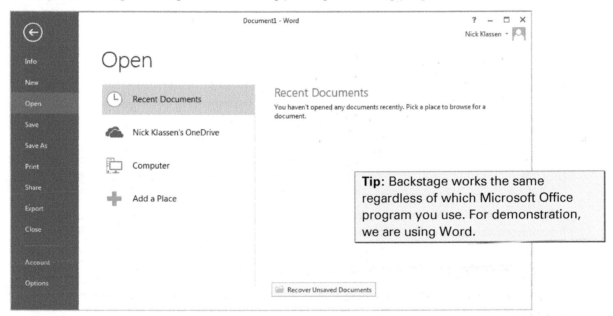

The left panel contains a set of commands that can assist you when working with new or existing files in this program. Each of these tabs includes commands and options that appear in the right pane of the window when the tab is selected. Most of the commands and options are standard to Microsoft Office but may vary based on the program, as in the case with Outlook or OneNote.

Backstage view also includes the Options button which opens the Program Options dialog box, and the Account option to set up or modify account settings on this computer (usually already handled by an organization's network administrator).

Changing the Program Options

 Exam 2 - Objective 1.1

You can customize each Office program to meet your specific requirements or preferences. For example, you can specify the unit of measurement you want to use such as inches or centimeters. Some options are shared among Office programs, and if you make a change in one program, it will be applied to other Office programs installed on your computer. For instance, if you make changes to the Spelling feature in Word, the same changes will be applied in Excel and PowerPoint. You can also reset some features to their default settings, such as with the Quick Access toolbar or the ribbon.

To change or view the program options, click the **File** tab and then click **Options**.

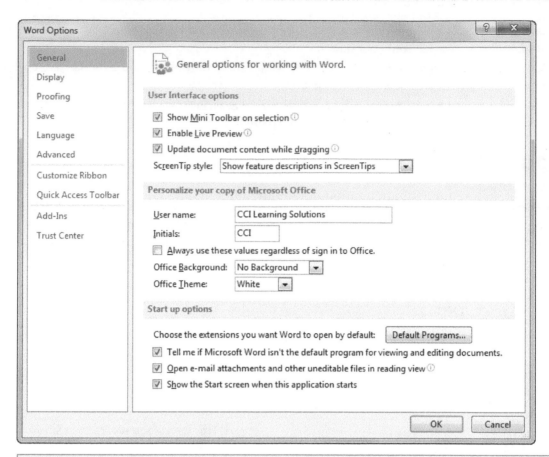

Tip: The options will vary between the programs based on the purpose of that program, such as displaying formulas in Excel, changing the display of cells in Access, or changing units of measurement in Word or PowerPoint. Other options such as Customize the Ribbon or Quick Access Toolbar, Add-Ins, or the Trust Center offer the same features, regardless of the Office application.

Using Basic Editing Tools

 Exam 2 - Objective 1.1, 1.3

Some tasks are common to a number of programs, not just Microsoft Office. For instance, to access the Copy command using the keyboard shortcut or right-click method is the same regardless of whether you are using Word, Excel, or a Web browser. If you want to delete text from a file, you must first select it no matter which program you are using.

Sharing common tasks and commands such as these can help to reduce the learning curve for different programs. There will be some tasks where you may be required to perform an extra step but this step would be specific to the program; for example, selecting cells in Excel versus selecting placeholders in PowerPoint. You may also find that options in a dialog box are similar, and vary only on points that apply to a specific program. The following screens show the Print panel for Word and Excel. Notice that each contain options to change a printer or the page setup, and that the number of options varies based on what is available in the application.

Print

The following table lists common tasks, a description of the task, and how to access the appropriate command in Microsoft Office to perform the task:

Task	Purpose	How to Access the Command
Close	Close a file	• Click the **File** tab and then click **Close** • Click the **Close** button for the application, or if the file is in Restore Down mode, click the **Close** button for the document window • Press Ctrl+W or Ctrl+F4
Copy	Make a duplicate or copy of a selected item	• On the Home tab, in the Clipboard group, click **Copy** • Press Ctrl+C • Right-click the selection and click **Copy**
Drag and Drop	Move a selected item from its current location to a new location using the mouse	• Position the mouse pointer overtop the selection and then drag it to the new location
Find	Search for or find an item in the current file	• On the Home tab, in the Editing group, click **Find** • Press Ctrl+F
Move	Cut or move a selected item from its current location	• On the Home tab, in the Clipboard group, click **Cut** • Press Ctrl+X

New Blank File	Create a new blank file	• Press ⟨Ctrl⟩+⟨N⟩
Open	Open an existing file	• Click the **File** tab and then click **Open** • Press ⟨Ctrl⟩+⟨O⟩ or ⟨Ctrl⟩+⟨F12⟩
Paste	Paste a copied or cut item into a new location	• On the Home tab, in the Clipboard group, click **Paste** • Press ⟨Ctrl⟩+⟨V⟩ • Right-click the destination area and click **Paste**
Print or Preview	Print or preview the selected contents or the entire file	• Click the **File** tab, and then click **Print** • Press ⟨Ctrl⟩+⟨P⟩
Redo	Repeat or redo the last action that was reversed	• On the Quick Access Toolbar, click **Redo** • Press ⟨Ctrl⟩+⟨Y⟩
Replace	Replace a particular (searched for) item with another item	• On the Home tab, in the Editing group, click **Replace** • Press ⟨Ctrl⟩+⟨H⟩
Save As	Save the active file with a new file name	• Click the **File** tab and then click **Save As** • Press ⟨F12⟩
Save	Save changes to the current file	• On the Quick Access Toolbar, click **Save** • Press ⟨Ctrl⟩+⟨S⟩
Select	Highlight items using a variety of different methods in order to perform an action on the selection	• On the Home tab, in the Editing group, click **Select** • Drag the mouse over the text you want to select • To select all text, press ⟨Ctrl⟩+⟨A⟩
Spell Check	Check the spelling in the file	• On the Review tab, in the Proofing group, click **Spelling & Grammar**
Undo	Reverse or undo the last action performed	• On the Quick Access Toolbar, click **Undo** (or click the arrow for Undo to display the last 100 items you can undo sequentially) • Press ⟨Ctrl⟩+⟨Z⟩
Views	Change the view to display the file contents in a different layout	• Click the **View** tab and click the appropriate view • Click the View mode button from the lower right corner of the screen

EXERCISE

In this exercise you will use some of the basic editing tools to insert and edit text or data in an application program.

1. Click **Start, All Programs, Microsoft Office 2013**, and then **Word 2013**. Click **Blank document** to create a new blank document.

2. Type your full name on the first line and press (Enter).

3. Type your street address on this line and press (Enter).

4. Type the city you live in, the state or province, and then the zip or postal code. Press (Enter) when done.

    You have entered some simple text into a word processing program. Pressing (Enter) at the end of each line will end the line at the current cursor location, moving you to the beginning of the next line.

5. Press (Enter) once more to enter a blank line. Then type the following:

    ```
    When typing text into a word processing program, you do not have to
    worry about running out of space at the right side of the page. The
    word processing program includes a feature called word wrap to determine
    automatically when the line is full and text wraps or flows to the next
    line.
    ```

6. Press the (Ctrl) key and hold it as you tap the (S) key.

    Notice that Word displays Backstage with the Save As option active, waiting you to indicate where you would like to save the document. You won't save the document right now.

7. Press (Esc) once to return to the document.

8. Press (Ctrl) + (W) to close this document.

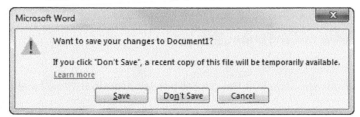

9. Click **Don't Save** to close the document without saving.

    Let's now take a look at some of the program options available.

10. Click the **File** tab and then click **Options**.

    A list of categories appears in the left panel for you to select the program option you want to change. For instance, when the General category is selected, you can change the color scheme or the user name. Many of the program options are available in the same category within each of the Microsoft Office applications, thereby reducing the learning curve or time spent searching for a specific feature.

11. Click **Advanced** in the left panel.

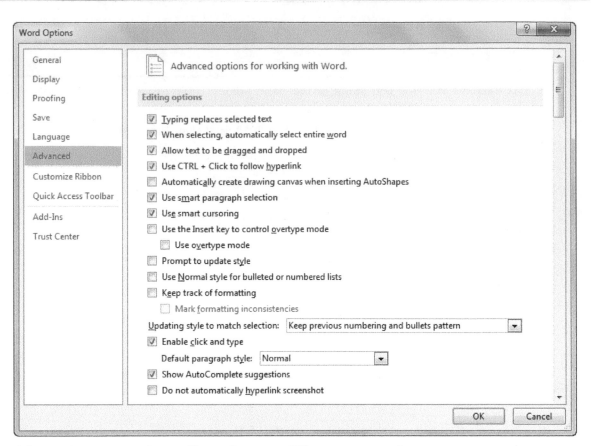

Advanced program options will vary from one Office program to the next.

12. Click **Cancel** to exit the program options.

13 Click the **Close** button to close Word.

Now take a look at some of these options and editing tools for Excel.

14. Click **Start**, **All Programs**, **Microsoft Office 2013**, and then **Excel 2013**. Click **Blank workbook**.

15. Type your name in the first cell or box and press Enter.

16. Press Tab.

The cell or box in column B now appears with the darker border around it. You have just moved to this cell.

17. Type: Microsoft Excel 2013 and press Tab.

Notice how even though the text is longer than the width of the cell, Excel still displays it completely in the cell.

18. Press Ctrl + S.

Excel displays Backstage with the Save As command active, in a similar manner to how it appeared when you pressed this key sequence in Word.

19. Press Esc to cancel the Save as command.

20. Press Ctrl + W to close this workbook.

As with Word, you should see a dialog box asking if you want to save this workbook.

21. Click **Don't Save**.

22. Click the **File** tab and then click **Options**.

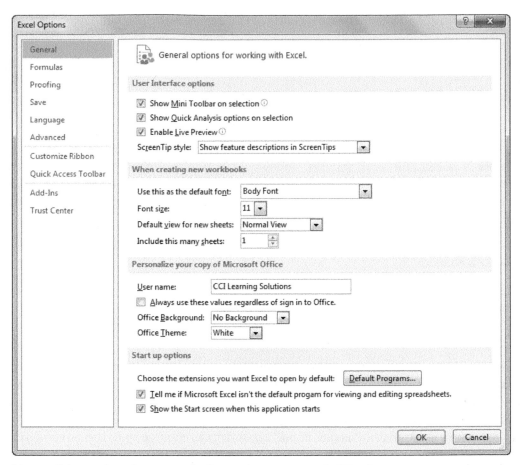

Many of the options here are similar to those we saw in Word.

23. Click the **Advanced** category.

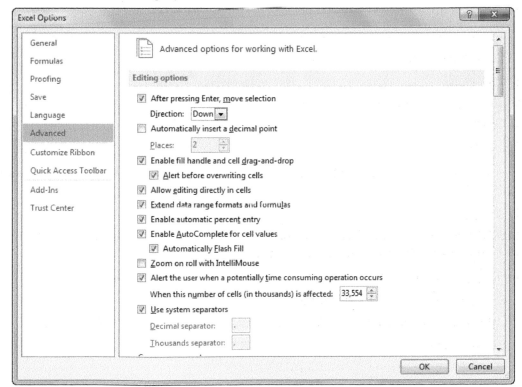

Notice that the options here relate specifically to a spreadsheet program.

24. Click **Cancel** to exit the program options.

25. Click **Close** to exit this application.

Collaborating with Others

 Exam 2 - Objective 6.2

The rapid adoption of the Internet into everyday life demonstrates how communication helps people to connect in social and work settings. Today's workplace leverages the power of technology to increase worker productivity in creating, analyzing and sharing data, leading to faster and more informed decision-making. Most office workers now have at least one computer, and almost every one of them connects to the others using a corporate local area network.

Word taps into this connectivity with its built-in ability to send documents to others using email, the Internet, or a network.

> **Tip**: Sharing documents with others works the same regardless of which Microsoft Office program you use. For demonstration, we are using Word.

Using Email

One way of sharing documents quickly with others is to send them by email. The email message is sent using the default email program installed on the system. If Microsoft Outlook is installed, then it will be used to send the email, but other email programs such as Mozilla Thunderbird, can be used as well. The downside of using email is that every recipient gets his or her own copy of the document. These individuals often make changes or add comments to their copy of the document and send it back. The originator must then merge these copies together.

To send a document using email:

1. Open the document.

2. On the **File** tab, click **Share**.

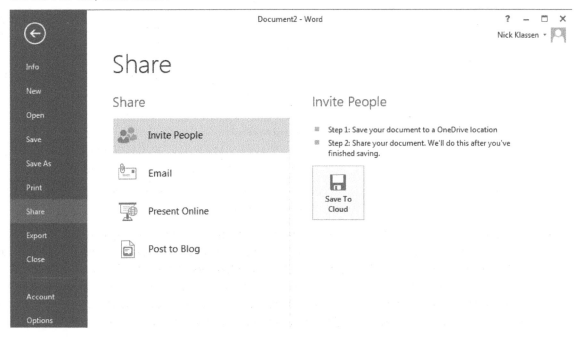

3. Click **Email** and then click one of the following options:
   a. Send as Attachment
   b. Send a Link
   c. Send as PDF
   d. Send as XPS
   e. Send as Internet Fax

Send as Attachment	Creates a new email message with your document included as an attachment: 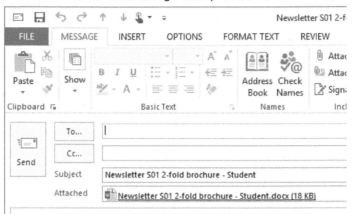 When you click the **Send** button, Outlook sends the email and the attached document to the intended recipient. The recipient can edit the document if he or she has Microsoft Word installed.
Send a Link	Launches Outlook and opens a new email message containing a hyperlink to your document. Unlike **Send as Attachment**, **Send as PDF** or **Send as XPS**, your recipients do not receive the file; instead, they open the original document by clicking on the hyperlink in the email. Note that your document must be stored in a shared location, such as a network drive, where your recipients can access it from wherever they are located.
Send as PDF	Converts the document into a PDF (Portable Document Format) before you send it. Outlook then creates a new email message with the PDF file included as an attachment. The PDF format allows the recipients to view and print the document, but it does not permit them to make changes.
Send as XPS	Converts the document into XML Paper Specification (XPS) format before sending. As with **Send as PDF**, Word converts the document and then Outlook creates a new email message with the XPS file included as an attachment; recipients can view and print the document but they cannot make changes to it.
Send as Internet Fax	Converts the document into an electronic fax file and sends it to the internet fax software installed on your local computer.

You should select **Send a Link** as your preferred method when sharing with co-workers within the same organization. Avoid sending a document as an attachment because you will simply create more work for yourself; your co-workers may each make changes to their copies of the document, possibly at the same time that you are working on the document. Ultimately, you will have to incorporate changes from several documents into one version. If instead you put the document into a shared location and send a link, everyone (including you) is always updating the same document.

The **Send as PDF** or **Send as XPS** are useful selections if you want to prevent the recipients from making changes to the document.

Saving to the Cloud

Another way of sharing documents with others is to use a web-based storage or Cloud service such as Microsoft OneDrive or iCloud. The service will provide a specified amount of storage at no cost and you can pay for more storage or additional services if you need them. The benefit of using cloud storage is that you can access your files from wherever you may be, provided you have a connection to the Internet and can log into your account on the Cloud service. You can copy or upload files of any type to the Cloud and view them on your computer with the appropriate software installed. This makes sharing files and collaborating with others much easier than using email to share documents. Saving to the cloud also allows you to assign permissions to others to view only, or edit the files. Any changes made by others are marked and tracked in the program with a different color for each person.

An advantage of using a Microsoft Office program is that storage space on OneDrive is automatically included. OneDrive is one of the components of Microsoft's group of online services. Every registered Microsoft user has a OneDrive with a certain amount of storage space at no cost. By default, you have two main folders: My Documents and Public. Anyone with a Microsoft Account can access any files in the Public folder at any time; any files you put into the My Documents folder are accessible only by you, unless you designate that you want to share them with one or more of your contacts.

To save a document to the OneDrive:

1. Open the document.

2. Click the **File** tab, and then click **Save As**.

3. Ensure **[User Name] OneDrive** is selected.

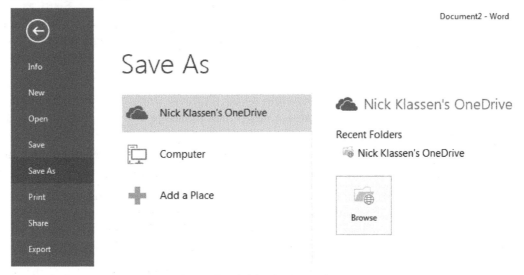

4. Double-click the User Name OneDrive folder in the right pane.

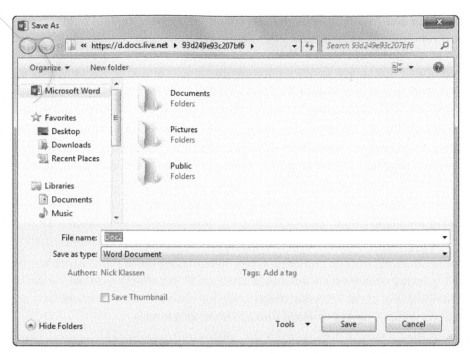

The Save As dialog box appears (there may be a short wait while the connection is completed with the OneDrive server). Although it looks like any other folder on your computer or a network drive, it is actually a remote drive provided as part of your Microsoft Account. If you want to share your document with others, be sure to select the *Public* folder.

5.   If desired, change the file name.

6.   Click **Save.**

7.   If necessary, make any other changes to the document and save these changes. Note that any time you save changes you are saving them directly to the document in the OneDrive, not to your local computer.

8.   Close the document.

The document is now accessible from the OneDrive.

Using a Network

Another method of sharing documents with others is by saving or copying files to designated network drives or using a collaboration tool such as SharePoint. Depending on how the organization or school has structured the network, you may be required to save files only on network drives. While this ensures that the files are available to others to view or edit, it requires that the user activate a command to track any changes or comments made by others. It usually does not allow for multiple users to make changes simultaneously to the file and then merge the changes when everyone is done.

Recognizing that people working together are more productive than people working alone, Microsoft designed SharePoint to facilitate document sharing within an organization and with authorized users in partner organizations. The term *web-based collaborative environment* refers to this kind of online sharing.

SharePoint brings together the many different tools that people use to share, including:

*   **Shared network drives to store files and documents** – In the past, a company or IT department would designate specific computers to store these files. Access security quickly followed to ensure protection of confidential files. However, the demand for shared storage space in an organization usually exceeds the space available after a period of time, representing an ongoing administrative nightmare for most IT departments.

- **Document version control** – A collaborative environment brings a new set of challenges; primarily the dispersal of ownership and loss of control over changes made, which often leads to uncontrolled and haphazard changes. For example, a user may delete a document accidentally or make changes that conflict with another person's changes. Version control ensures that only one person enters changes at any one time. If someone accidentally deletes a document or makes unwanted changes, the version control feature allows you to easily restore a previous version.

- **Workflow control** – You can designate that documents be funneled through workflow processes, such as approving purchase requisitions or media releases. The system automatically routes the document to the next person in the workflow when the current approver has completed his or her work.

- **Social networking** – You can post comments as well as share text and multimedia files in a manner similar to using a bulletin board, except these programs share the information on a global scale. Links to these sites can be set up in a common area to allow users to share information quickly.

- **Email** – Announcements, notices and other types of team communication, which are often sent by email, can be quickly lost in the daily volume of other email. An effective collaboration site provides an area containing the most relevant communications, and team members can access these communications without having to wade through unrelated emails.

- **Other shared communications** – SharePoint also allows you to set up corporate or team calendars, surveys and polls.

To save a document to SharePoint:

1. Open the document.

2. Click the **File** tab, click **Save As**.

3. Click **[Company Name]**.

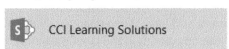

4. If necessary, click **Browse**.

The Save As dialog box appears, allowing you to navigate to the SharePoint site where the document is to be stored.

A SharePoint site can be structured in many different ways; the following example shows documents of various types in a shared folder.

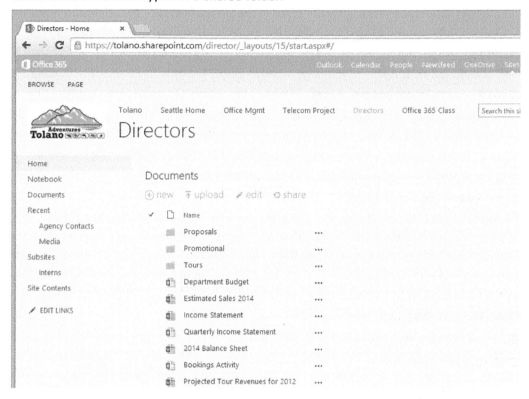

EXERCISE

In this exercise, you will change some program preferences and then use tools to manipulate the text in a document.

1. Click **Start, All Programs, Microsoft Office 2013**, and then **PowerPoint 2013**. Click **Blank presentation**.
2. Click the **File** tab and then click **Options**.
3. With the General category active, click **Enable Live Preview** to turn this feature off.
4. Click **OK**.
5. Click the **Design** tab, in the Themes group, point at any of the themes in the gallery.
   Notice that there is no preview of how the theme will affect the slide.
6. Click the **File** tab and then click **Options**.
7. With the General category active, click **Enable Live Preview** to turn this feature on. Click **OK**.
8. On the **Design** tab, in the Themes group, point at any of the themes in the gallery.
   This time when you point at a theme, the slide displays a preview of the theme.
9. Click **Start, All Programs, Microsoft Office 2013**, and **Excel 2013**. Click **Blank workbook**.
10. Click **File, Options**.
11. With the General category active, click the arrow for **Office Theme**, and click a color that is different from what is currently selected.

12. Click the **Advanced** category at the left, and then scroll down to the **Display options for this worksheet** area.

13. Click **Show gridlines** to turn off this option. Click **OK**.

    Notice that Excel no longer displays the gridlines in the main worksheet area. You should also notice that the screen has a different color in the background for the application, for example, the background color might have changed from white to dark gray.

14. To show how changing the color scheme affects other programs, switch to Microsoft PowerPoint

    You should notice the Office theme selected in step 11 is now the theme for PowerPoint as well.

15. Close PowerPoint to return to Excel.

16. Click **File** and then click **Options**. Change the Office Theme in the General category back to its original setting (that is, back to what it was before making the change in step 11). Click **OK**.

17. Type your name in the current cursor location in the main worksheet area and click ⟨Enter⟩. (You may need to click in the worksheet area to activate a cell.)

18. Click **File** and then click **Print**.

    Changes made here affect only the active file open in this program; however, the types of settings are very similar for all the Microsoft Office programs. For instance, you can select a specific printer from the available printers, or you can define page margins, the size of the paper, and so on. Notice that Excel displays a preview of how your file will print, giving you a chance to make any last minute changes to the page setup or the file contents prior to clicking the **Print** button.

19. Click ⬅ to go back to the file contents.

You will now explore some basic editing techniques. The box with the dark line around it is called the active cell. The active cell is affected by any action you take, such as delete, copy, or paste.

20. Ensure the active cell is still the one with your name in it. Then on the Home tab, in the Clipboard group, click **Copy**.

21. Click in the box formed by the intersection of **column B** and **row 6** (the column heading and row heading will change color to confirm that this is the box or cell you have clicked). On the Home tab, in the Clipboard group, click **Paste**.

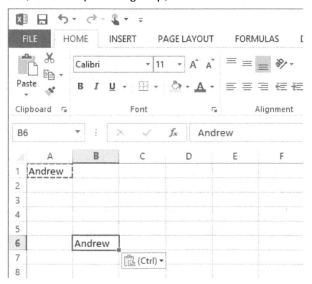

A copy of your name should now appear in two places on the screen. We will discuss the other elements on the screen in Lesson 9 – Using Microsoft Excel.

22. Click **Close** to exit this program.

This window appears to prompt you to save the changes you have made to the workbook. When you want to save your changes, click the Save button. In this exercise, you will not save any changes.

23. Click **Don't Save**.

Excel closes without saving the file.

Lesson Summary

In this lesson you examined some common features shared among Microsoft Office 2013 applications. You also explored a few basic techniques for working in an Office application. You should now be familiar with:

☑ identifying similar layouts and features on the screen between applications

☑ recognizing tips and tools on the screen for easy access

☑ how to start or exit a Microsoft Office program

☑ how to use and customize the Quick Access Toolbar

☑ how to use commands and navigate around the Ribbon

☑ how to navigate around the screen

☑ getting help in Microsoft Office

☑ using the File tab and Backstage

☑ changing program options and defaults

☑ common methods to manipulate data

Review Questions

1. Why is it important to close an application program when you no longer need to use it?
   a. To prevent any possible corruption of program files.
   b. To free memory for another program.
   c. To see a simplified desktop.
   d. Any of the above.
   e. a or b

2. What is Backstage view?
   a. A view accessed through the File tab that enables you to manage files and settings for the program.
   b. A dialog box that appears when you choose to open or save a file.
   c. The name of the feature where you can customize options for the program.
   d. A window that enables you to organize your files, similar to File Manager.

3. What is the name of the toolbar located immediately above the ribbon in a Microsoft Office program?
   a. Standard   c. Quick Access
   b. Page Setup   d. File

4. What is the purpose of each of the following ribbon options?
   a. ⌐⌐
   c. ⌐⌐
   b. ⌐⌐

5. Identify the split bar in the following figure:

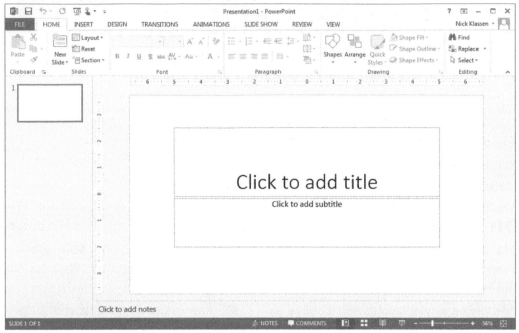

6. What does the following symbol represent in the Help feature for a Microsoft Office program?

 Touch
Guide

7. When might you want to click a link in the Popular Searches area instead of the Search field in the Help feature?

   a. To show only the most popular topics.
   b. To get a specific type of help for a topic such as creating a resume or adjusting the margins.
   c. To navigate quickly to the Microsoft web site to enter the search criteria.
   d. To change from online to offline Help mode.

```
MMM
Go online for
 Additional
  Review
```

8. Identify which option in the left panel you would use to change the preferences for this program:

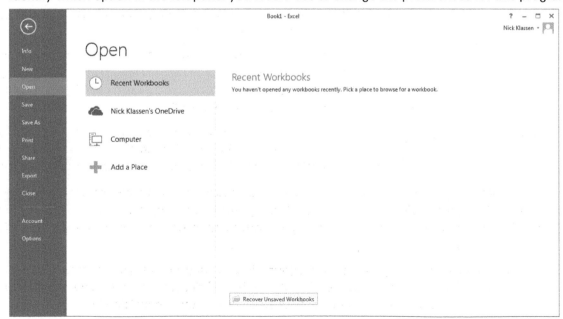

Lesson 8: Microsoft Word

Lesson Objectives

In this lesson you will learn some of the basic skills required to create simple documents, including letters, reports, and a brochure. On completion of this lesson, you should be familiar with how to:

- [ ] enter and edit text
- [ ] move around in the document
- [ ] create new, save, close and open files
- [ ] select specific types of text
- [ ] change the view mode

- [ ] format text, paragraphs, or the page
- [ ] organize data
- [ ] work with pictures in a document
- [ ] track changes and comments in a document

Entering and Editing Text

 Exam 2 - Objective 1.1, 1.3

Typing involves using the keyboard to input text that is shown on screen. Editing includes actions such as inserting and deleting single characters, words, or multiple lines of text, correcting typographical errors, and inserting or deleting blank lines between paragraphs.

The following are basic concepts related to typing and editing text:

Insertion Point	The insertion point displays as a vertical blinking bar that shows where Word will insert typed text and pasted items. It moves to the right as you type. The insertion point is commonly referred to as the cursor.
Typing Text	Word is set by default to insert text; this means you can move the insertion point anywhere in the document and Word will insert the text you type to the right of that point. As you type, any existing text will be "pushed" to the right.
Deleting Text	There are two ways to delete text one character at a time. You can press the (Delete) key to delete one character to the right of the cursor, or the (Backspace) key to delete one character to the left.
Word Wrap	When you have typed enough words to fill a line, Word will automatically shift the insertion point to the beginning of the next line. This is called *wrapping* text. If you are in the middle of a word that is too long for the line, Word will shift the entire word to the beginning of the next line.
Ending Word Wrap/ Blank Lines	When you are finished typing text for a line or paragraph, you can press the (Enter) key one or more times. Word will insert as many blank lines as you want and shift the insertion point to the beginning of the line below the last blank line.

These basic concepts are applicable to all word processing programs, regardless of the software vendor. A major benefit of word processing programs is that they can be used to create documents ranging from short letters or memos to larger, more complex documents like manuscripts, Web pages, and brochures.

Another benefit of word processing programs is that they enable you to give your documents a professional look through the application of a variety of design elements. You can also incorporate design elements into a style or template to ensure you use them consistently.

Well-planned design elements can also help you organize information and allow the reader to identify different components of your document at a glance. For instance, headers and footers that include page or section numbers can help the reader identify where they are in a large document. You can also use white space to make reading large amounts of text easier, apply bullets to make lists more "scanable," or create numbered lists to indicate the priority of items. You can also use the Table feature to create forms, add borders or shading, and set up the form for online data entry.

Another way to organize topics in the document is to create an *outline,* which is similar to a table of contents. The Outline feature in Word provides an overview of your document helping you ensure that your information is organized in a logical order; this feature also provides the flexibility for you to move topics around in a document.

Displaying Formatting Codes

The ¶ (**Show/Hide ¶**) button allows you to show or hide non-printing characters, which can help you identify what you have inserted into the document. These characters appear only on the screen; they do not print. Some common non-printing characters include:

¶	Represents a hard return and is inserted every time you press Enter.
→	Represents a tab and is inserted every time you press Tab.
·	Represents a space and is inserted every time you press Spacebar.
....	Represents a *soft page break* (this code is inserted automatically when you type enough text to fill a page); a soft page break is visible only in Draft view.
·········Page Break·········	Represents a *manual* or *hard page break* (you manually insert this code when you want to end the page at the current location and move to the next page).

Using the Ruler

The Ruler helps you identify where to position text. The width of the ruler depends on the view or magnification factor.

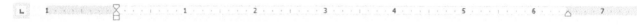

The ruler uses the default measurement for your location, e.g., English US is set to inches, English/French Canada is set to centimeters. You can change the unit of measurement in the **Display** area of the **Advanced** category in **Word Options**. You can select from inches, centimeters, millimeters, points, or picas.

To turn the ruler on or off, on the View tab, in the Show group, click **Ruler**.

Moving Around the Document

You can move quickly to another area in the document by moving the mouse pointer to the new location and clicking, or by using one of the following keyboard methods:

Movement Desired	Press	Movement Desired	Press
Next Character	→	Next Line	↓
Previous Character	←	Previous Line	↑
Next Word	Ctrl+→	Next Paragraph	Ctrl+↓
Previous Word	Ctrl+←	Previous Paragraph	Ctrl+↑
Beginning of Line	Home	Next Screen	PgDn
End of Line	End	Previous Screen	PgUp
Beginning of Document	Ctrl+Home	End of Document	Ctrl+End

You can also use the **Go To** command to move quickly to a particular item using one of the following methods:

- On the Home tab, in the Editing group, click the down arrow for **Find**, and then click **Go To**; or
- press Ctrl+G; or
- press F5; or
- on the status bar, click the PAGE 9 OF 16 (**Page number in document**) box.

Using the Scroll Bar

The *vertical scroll bar* is used to move (or scroll) the view of the screen up or down in the document. The *horizontal scroll bar* is used to move (or scroll) the view to the left or right in the document.

There are three methods of moving around the document using the scroll bars:

- Click the scroll bar arrows to move the scroll box up and down or left and right; or
- click the arrow either side of the scroll box; or
- drag the scroll box.

If you are working in a document with numerous pages, or with headings, a ScreenTip will appear showing the page numbers or heading text as you move the vertical scroll box up or down.

Selecting Text

Selecting or *highlighting* text enables you to tell Word exactly which portions of text you want to work on. Once text has been selected, the selection stays in place until you de-select it; this allows you to apply multiple actions to that selection. The only exception is when you delete or replace the selection with new text.

If you inadvertently make the wrong selection or you wish to remove the selection, click anywhere in the document window or press any arrow direction key to de-select, and then begin the selection procedure again.

Selecting Consecutive Text

You can select text using the mouse or keyboard, and occasionally you may want to use a combination of mouse and keyboard to select larger pieces of text.

To select text using the mouse, position the mouse pointer at the beginning of the text to be selected and then drag to highlight the text. You can increase or decrease the selection as long as you hold down the mouse button. You can highlight forwards or backwards from the starting point.

To select text using the keyboard, position the insertion point, hold down Shift, and then press the arrow keys to move the insertion point to highlight the text. Release Shift when the text is highlighted.

To select a word, double-click the word. To select a sentence, hold Ctrl and click anywhere in the sentence. To select a paragraph, triple-click anywhere in that paragraph.

To select the entire document, use one of the following methods:

- On the Home tab, in the Editing group, click **Select** and then click **Select All**; or

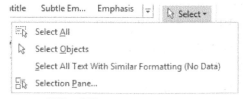

- press Ctrl+A.

Selecting Non-Consecutive Text

You can select text anywhere in the document, regardless of whether the text is consecutive or not. To select multiple pieces of text, you must select the first piece of text and then press and hold (Ctrl) as you select the next piece of text. Press and hold (Ctrl) to continue selecting more pieces of text anywhere in the document. The following screen shows an example of non-consecutive text selected in a document.

> customers and new vendors. We are also exploring new opportunities and services we can offer with the focus to the Pacific / Asian coast lines.
>
> **Please Fill In the Blanks ...**
>
> After a few delays, we are pleased to announce that we have finalized our first tour offering using the camel trains!
>
> To make a long story short, we have now selected and confirmed the vendor who is partnering with Tolano Adventures to offer you some spectacular tours in the Middle East and Australia! Call your Travel Director for more details on these tours, or check out the details at www.tolanoadventures.com.
>
> We are also excited to announce that the Haunted Tours have taken off with great success, with many customers enjoying the tours in Scotland, especially at Edinburgh Castle where there have been many sightings of a woman sitting on a bench outside the Castle!
>
> We seem to be receiving a lot of requests from our Tokyo office for special group tours to visit the resting places of infamous Hollywood stars. We have reached out to our partner in California to make special arrangements for the groups so we can offer a truly spectacular package. We hope to have the detailed form out to all offices to review very soon.
>
> **Calling All Customers**

Using the Selection Bar

Another way to select larger amounts of text is with the selection bar. The selection bar is located in the white area at the left edge of the text, in the area that constitutes the left margin. When the mouse pointer is positioned within the selection bar, it changes to a right pointing arrow as shown in the following:

> beautiful state of Washington!
>
> With more resources on the West Coast, we will be able to offer more service and faster communications with customers and new vendors. We are also exploring new opportunities and services we can offer with the focus to the Pacific / Asian coast lines.
>
> **Please Fill In the Blanks ...**
>
> After a few delays, we are pleased to announce that we have finalized our first tour offering using the camel trains!
>
> To make a long story short, we have now selected and confirmed the vendor who is partnering with Tolano Adventures to offer you some spectacular tours in the Middle East and Australia! Call your Travel Director for more details on these tours, or check out the details at www.tolanoadventures.com.
>
> We are also excited to announce that the Haunted Tours have taken off with great success, with many customers enjoying the tours in Scotland, especially at Edinburgh Castle where there have been many sightings of a woman

You can use any of the following methods to make selections using the selection bar:

- To select a line of text, click at the left of the line of text.
- To select a paragraph, double-click at the left of the paragraph.
- To select an entire document, triple-click anywhere in the selection bar, or press the (Ctrl) key and click anywhere in the selection bar.

Saving Documents

It is important to save your documents frequently as you work on them. This ensures that if an unexpected problem arises, such as a power outage, you will have a recently-saved version of your work and not be forced to recreate all of it. You can save files to any location on the local drive, a network drive, or a portable media device such as a USB flash drive. Once you have saved a file, you can retrieve or open it from any of these locations. You can have multiple documents open on the screen, including new documents that you have not saved yet.

When you save a document, Word automatically assigns a *.docx* extension to the end of the file name; however, you can save the file in a different format, if necessary. By default, Word selects the *My Documents* folder within the *Documents* library the first time you use the Save command in a new document. You can save the document to that location or any other location you choose. If you specify to save the document in a different location, Word will display that location each time you save or open a file, until you change locations or exit Word.

To save a document, use one of the following methods:

- Click the **File** tab and then click **Save** or **Save As**; or
- on the Quick Access toolbar, click the ⊟ **(Save)** button; or
- press Ctrl + S .

To save an existing document with a different name, use **Save As** in the **File** tab.

The first time you save a document, you will see the Save As dialog box. Word will also automatically insert the first line of text in the document into the File name field, on the assumption that you want to use this string of text as the file name. Type over this selection to specify the file name you want.

File names can be up to 255 characters long, including the drive and path (such as C:\Documents\Draft Proposals\January 29 Proposal to ABC Company.docx). Consider that using descriptive file names helps you locate what you want easily, but excessively long file names will not fully display in most dialog boxes. If your organization enforces a file naming convention, be sure to adhere to the guidelines.

How often you save a document depends on how much work you put into it. If you make a large number of changes, save the document frequently as you work to preserve your changes. If you're not sure whether you'll need a certain document again, err on the side of caution and save it.

On occasion you may find that Word displays a prompt indicating there may be a compatibility issue to address. This can occur when you want to save a document that was saved in a previous version of Word, or if you try to open a file that has a file format that Word does not recognize as a default file type that can be opened automatically in Word. When this occurs, give some thought as to which file format you want to use and select it appropriately from the Save as type field in Word.

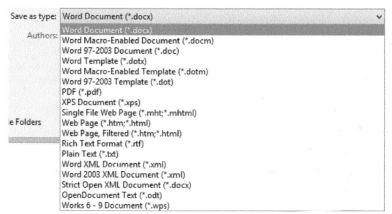

Another message box you may see when dealing with compatibility is similar to:

When this message appears, be very sure you want to save the document to Word 2013 as some objects you create and place in a Word 2013 document are converted to a different format when you open the file in an earlier version. For instance, a SmartArt diagram created in Word 2013 will be converted to a single diagram when the document is saved as an earlier version of Word.

EXERCISE

In this exercise you will create a new document and then save it for future use.

1. Start Microsoft Word, if necessary, and then type the following text pressing (Enter) whenever you see the ¶ symbol:

   ```
   Seattle Move¶
   Get copy of signed lease contract to Amar in Accounting for safekeeping¶
   Finalize office furniture rentals¶
   Confirm purchase of computer equipment from Seattle vendor¶
   Confirm implementation of telephone and Internet services before month-end,
   including the long distance offer¶
   Sign and fax rental agreement for condo to realtor for strata approval¶
   ```

2. On the Home tab, in the Paragraph group, click the ¶ **Show/Hide ¶** button.

   You should now see the ¶ or paragraph markers, indicating every time the (Enter) key was pressed to end the paragraph. A paragraph can be one or more lines of text; you need only press (Enter) whenever you want to insert a blank line or tell Word to end the paragraph at the current location.

3. On the Quick Access Toolbar, click **Save**.

4. Click **Computer** in the first pane and then click **Browse**. Navigate to the *7318 Student Data* folder on the Desktop (or to an alternate location where you have been saving your data files for this course) and click *Lesson 8 – Word* to view the contents of this folder.

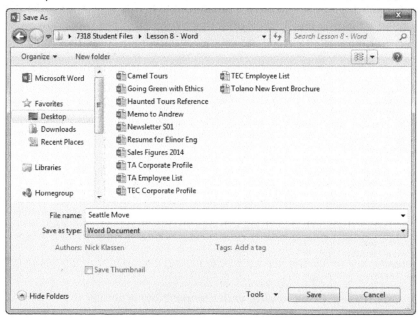

Notice that Word highlights the title in the document for you, saving you time.

5. Click at the end of the name, type: `- Student` (use your own name or initials in the place of "Student") and press (Enter).

   The document has now been saved. You can also confirm the document has been saved by looking at the title bar which should now show Seattle Move - Student - Word.

Starting a New Document

When you start Word, a blank document appears on the screen. Once Word is open, you can easily create additional new blank documents with no formatting, or choose from a variety of built-in templates that will help you lay out particular types of documents, such as invitations, meeting agendas, or business memos.

To create a new document, use one of the following methods:

- For a new blank document, click the **File** tab, click **New**, and then click **Blank document**, or

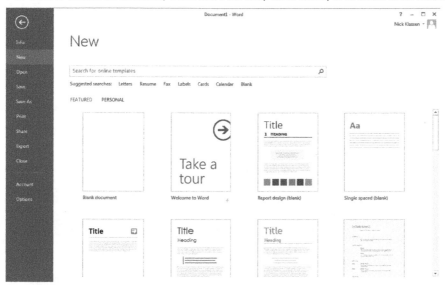

- press ⌨Ctrl+⌨N.

To choose from the variety of pre-designed templates for the new document, click the **File** tab, click **New**, choose one of the templates displayed, and click **Create**.

Each time you create a new document, a document number will automatically appear in the title bar. For example, if you have three new Word documents open and you create another new one, Word will assign it the number "4" and the title bar will display "Document4." Document numbering resets back to Document1 each time you start a new session of Word. Use this generic name as a reminder that you have not yet saved the file with a descriptive and memorable name.

EXERCISE

In this exercise you will create a new blank document and then try creating a new document from a template provided by Microsoft.

1. Press ⌨Ctrl+⌨N to create a new document.

   A new blank document displays on the screen (the Document # will vary depending on how often you press ⌨Ctrl+⌨N before or during this exercise).

2. Click **File** and click **New**.

3. In the search field, type: memos and click the **Search** icon.

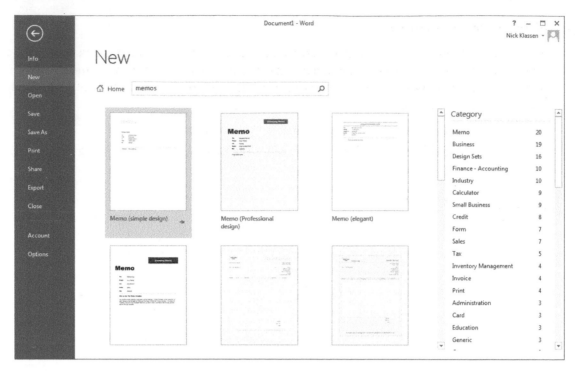

A list of memo templates appears on the screen for selection. A list of categories for documents appears in a pane at the right for quick reference and access.

4. Double-click **Memo (Elegant)**.

Word creates a new document based on the template. The template includes placeholders in which you can enter your personal information. These placeholders are field codes.

5. Click the **[RECIPIENT NAME]** field code for the **To** field and type: Nick Klassen.

    Notice that each letter you type is displayed as a capital letter. This format is set in the template.

6. Click the **[YOUR NAME]** field code for the **From** field and type: Andrew McSweeney.

7. Click the **[SUBJECT]** field code for the **Subject** field and type: Computer Purchases.

8. Click the arrow for the [CLICK TO SELECT DATE] code and click today's date.

9. Click the [Type your memo text here] and type the following:

    Can you confirm that the purchases of the following items have been made?¶

    Two notebooks with Windows 7 Professional installed¶

    One desktop with Windows 7 Professional installed¶

    One color laser printer¶

    We will also need Office 2013 to be installed on the computers. Is David handling this or making arrangements for this requirement?¶

    The new office will be ready by the end of the month with the furniture arriving a day or two before. We would like the equipment to be installed and set up before we arrive the following week.¶

    Thank you.¶

10. Press `Ctrl`+`S` to save the document.

11. Click **Computer** and then click **Lesson 8 - Word** from the list of Recent Folders. Replace the file name with: Memo to Nick for confirmation of computer purchases - Student and click **Save**.

12. When prompted that the file will be saved in the new file format, click **OK**.

Closing a Document

Once you have finished editing a document, close the document to clear the screen and memory; this enables you to start or open another document without old documents cluttering up your screen. Think of closing your document in much the same way that you think of closing a book and putting it back on the shelf before opening another book; it helps keep your desktop organized and ensures you have adequate work space.

As Word displays each document in its own window, use one of the following methods to close a document:

- Click the **File** tab and then **Close**; or
- press Ctrl + W or Ctrl + F4.

These methods keep the Word application open after you close the last document on screen. When there are no open documents, the Word application window appears as shown in the following:

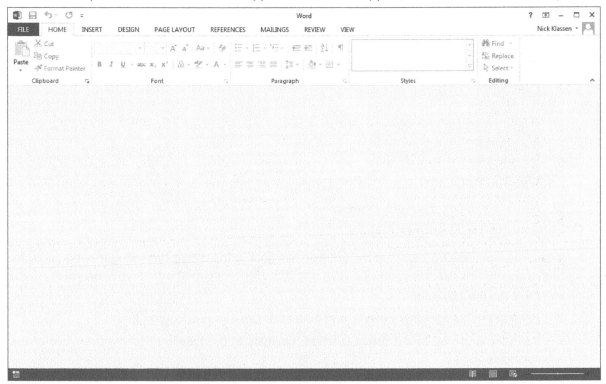

If you want to close the Word application completely, click ⊠ **(Close).**

If you add or change something in a new or existing document and then try to close it without saving, Word will provide the following prompt to give you the option of saving before you close:

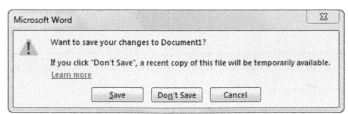

Opening a Document

Once a file is saved, you can open it from wherever it is located; the document is presented on the screen for further processing. You can open as many documents as needed; only the amount of available memory on your system limits the number of documents you can have open simultaneously.

Use one of the following methods to open a document:

- Click the **File** tab, click **Open**, and then click the file name from the list of Recent Documents; or

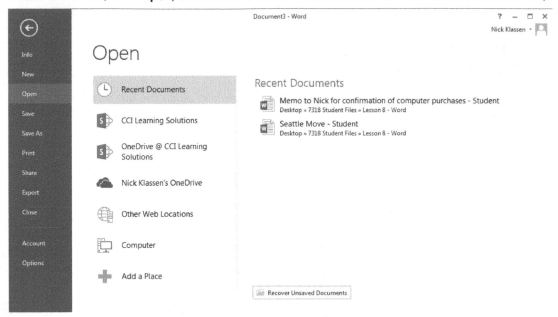

- click the **File** tab, then click **Open**; or
- press (Ctrl)+(O) or (Ctrl)+(F12).

When the Open dialog box appears, you can navigate in the dialog box using the mouse or keyboard to display the files or folders, and then use one of the following methods to open one of the documents:

- Click the file name; or
- point at the file name to select it, and then click **Open** or press (Enter); or
- if the file is stored in a different location, navigate to the location and then use one of the above methods.

As you open documents, Word will display the files in the same order as you opened them, with the most recent at the top of the list. As you reach the maximum number of files that show in this list, the oldest will be dropped from the list. You can click the pin icon at the right of a file name to keep a particular file on the list, no matter how many files are opened.

EXERCISE

In this exercise you will close documents on the screen and then use different methods to open files.

1. Click the **Close** button at the top right corner of the *Memo* document.

   The document should no longer be visible on the screen.

2. Using the Windows taskbar, point at the Word icon to display the preview windows for each document. Move to the one with the new blank document and click the **Close** button in the preview window to close this document.

3. Press (Ctrl)+(W) to close the *Seattle Move* document, and any other documents you may have on the screen.

   The screen should now display with a grey background (depending on your color scheme) with only the **File** tab active.

4. Click the **File** tab.

   The list should show the Word documents you recently worked on (the list may also show other documents if you share the computer with others).

5. Click *Seattle Move - Student*.

   This document opens and displays on the screen.

6. Click the **File** tab and click **Open**.

7. Click **Computer** and then **Lesson 8 - Word** from the list of folders, and then click the *Camel Tours* file.

   This document now appears on the screen.

Now try a different method of opening a file.

8. Press (Ctrl)+(O), click **Computer**, and then **Lesson 8 – Word** from the list of folders. Point at *Newsletter S01* and click **Open**.

9. On the Windows taskbar, point at the Word icon and click the *Seattle Move – Student* preview window to switch to this document.

   This document should appear on the screen. Remember that Windows gives you the advantage of previewing the contents by clicking (or pointing at) the preview window for the application in the Windows taskbar.

10. Point at the Word icon and click the **Newsletter S01** window to display it. Then press (Ctrl)+(W) to close this file.

11. Repeat step 10 for the *Camel Tours* document and any blank documents.

    You should now have only the *Seattle Move* document open.

12. On the Home tab, in the Paragraph group, click **Show/Hide ¶** to turn off the display of non-printing characters.

Customizing the View

 Exam 2 - Objective 1.3

You can adjust how a document displays by selecting the appropriate option using the **View** tab.

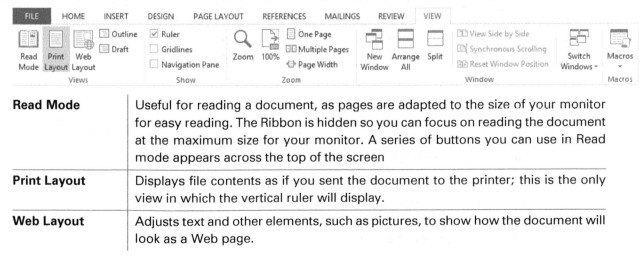

Read Mode	Useful for reading a document, as pages are adapted to the size of your monitor for easy reading. The Ribbon is hidden so you can focus on reading the document at the maximum size for your monitor. A series of buttons you can use in Read mode appears across the top of the screen
Print Layout	Displays file contents as if you sent the document to the printer; this is the only view in which the vertical ruler will display.
Web Layout	Adjusts text and other elements, such as pictures, to show how the document will look as a Web page.

Outline	Collapses a document to display certain types of text, such as headings or body text, to assist you in organizing content flow.
Draft	Displays the document to the full width of the screen with only the horizontal ruler visible; this is the best view for manipulating text through editing and simple formatting.
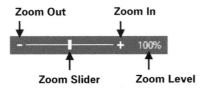	An alternative to using the View tab for the most common views is to use one of the view buttons located at the bottom right of the screen.

Adjusting the Zoom

You can adjust the text display on the screen using the Zoom feature, the View tab, Zoom level, or the Zoom slider on the status bar.

The ability to enlarge the text display can be very useful when you are working with a small font size, whereas the ability to reduce the display is useful when you are working with landscape or horizontal orientation.

You can set the zoom percentage anywhere from 10% to 500%, or you can have Word automatically adjust the magnification so that you can see the entire width of the page of text on screen. When changing the view, the position of the insertion point will determine the zoom area.

Keep in mind that the Zoom feature controls only the screen display. The amount of text that displays when you change the zoom percentage is based on the display settings and size of your monitor. For example, if you have a 19" monitor or larger, you may see more of a document at 50% magnification than someone who has a 17", monitor, but less than someone using a 21" monitor. Changing the magnification level has no effect on the size of the text when it is printed.

Using Protected View

A protection feature that you may encounter when working with documents, especially documents received from outside sources, is Protected View. Protected View applies the read-only attribute to the file until you specify otherwise, thereby protecting you from content that may potentially contain viruses, malware, or other items that can be harmful to your computer.

You can identify a file that is in Protected View the moment you attempt to open it. When the file is opened, Word displays a message similar to the following below the ribbon:

Alternatively, you can choose to open a file with this mode if you want to ensure no changes are made inadvertently to the file while you are viewing it. To activate this mode, click **File** and **Open** to locate the file, then click the arrow for the Open button and click **Open in Protected View**.

A file opened in Protected View is in read-only mode; you will not be able to do anything with the file until you click **Enable Editing**. When you go to Backstage to view the properties for this file, the following screen displays:

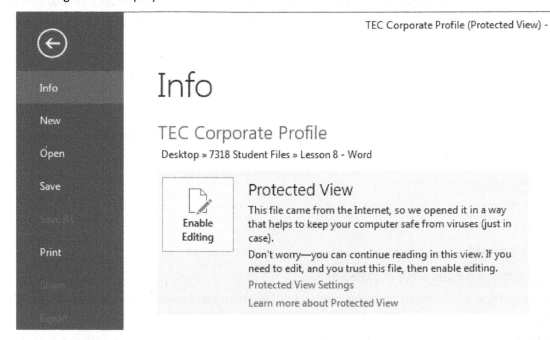

Notice that Word reminds you that you are still in Protected View. You can then choose to view more information about this mode, or choose another action.

If you try to save the file without turning the Protected View mode off, the following message displays:

Word will keep the file in Protected View until you choose to enable other actions.

EXERCISE

In this exercise you will practice using the zoom buttons, apply different views and open a file in Protected mode.

1. With the *Seattle Move – Student* document active, click the ➕ button on the zoom bar at the lower right corner of the screen.

   The magnification level of the document contents increases by 10%. Remember that changing the zoom affects only the display; not the actual size of the characters when the document is printed.

2. Click the ➕ button two more times.

3. Click the 100% (**Zoom level**) button and then change the **Percent** to **75** and click **OK**.

4. Click the **View** tab in the Ribbon if necessary, then click **Draft** view mode to see how the document appears.

Notice that the page now fills from one edge of the screen to the other and that the vertical ruler is no longer visible.

5. Click the **(Read Mode)** view mode and notice how the view now changes for you.

6. Click the **View** menu to see what options are available to you while in this view.

7. Click **Edit Document** to exit this view mode.

8. Close the document without saving it.

Now try opening a document that was sent previously as an attachment from the New York office. As it is an original file sent from Marketing, you want to protect it from any possible changes so you will open it using Protected View.

9. Click **File** and then click **Open** if necessary.

10. From the student data files, select *TEC Corporate Profile* and click the arrow for **Open**. Then click **Open in Protected View**.

    The warning prompt should appear across the top of the document, indicating that this document is now in protected view, preventing any changes to be made to the file.

11. Click **File** and read the information in Backstage, indicating the file has been protected from any changes until you enable editing.

12. Click **Save** from the panel in the left.

13. In the window, click **Enable Saving** to save the document.

    Notice that the warning prompt about the protected view mode no longer appears.

14. Click **File** and click **Close**.

Editing Text

IC³ Exam 2 - Objective 1.1

Editing is the process of adding, deleting, or changing text. In many cases, you will select text before you edit it. Be careful when making changes to selected text. The moment you press a key or click on an option, all the selected text is affected.

Using Undo

Any time you perform an action and then need to reverse the action (such as adding, deleting, or formatting text, inserting page breaks, etc.) you can undo the action by using one of the following methods:

*   In the Quick Access toolbar, click ↺ **(Undo)** to undo the last action or command performed; or

- press (Ctrl)+(Z); or
- click the arrow for the **Undo** button to display a list of the last 100 consecutive actions performed. You can undo sequential actions only. For example, in the illustration shown, if you want to undo the "Bold", then you must also undo the three actions before this action.

Using Repeat

If you change your mind after undoing an action, you can redo or repeat the action using one of the following methods:

- In the Quick Access toolbar, click ↻ **(Repeat)**; or
- press (Ctrl)+(Y) or press (F4).

This feature is the reverse of the Undo feature. It will repeat actions in the same sequence as they were performed, although it will repeat only one action at a time.

Using Cut, Copy, and Paste

Occasionally you may want to insert text into a document from another document, or from another location in the current document. Instead of retyping the text, use one of the following tools:

Cut	Cuts or removes the item from its current location and places it in the Clipboard.
Copy	Copies the item from its current location and places it in the Clipboard.
Paste	Inserts an item from the Clipboard into a document to the left of the Insertion Point.

Word uses the Clipboard to temporarily store any cut or copied items such as text or graphics. You can then paste these items into place wherever you choose.

To cut or move an item, select the item first and then use one of the following methods:

- On the Home tab, in the Clipboard group, click ✄ Cut ; or
- press (Ctrl)+(X); or
- right-click the item and then click **Cut** in the shortcut menu; or
- drag the selected item to the new location.

To copy an item, first select the item and then use one of the following methods:

- On the Home tab, in the Clipboard group, click ▤ Copy ; or
- press (Ctrl)+(C); or
- right-click the item and then click **Copy** in the shortcut menu.

To paste an item, first place the insertion point where you want to paste the item and then use one of the following methods:

- On the Home tab, in the Clipboard group, click **Paste**; or
- press (Ctrl)+(V); or
- right-click and then click **Paste** in the shortcut menu.

Once you paste an item, the ▤ (Ctrl) ▾ **(Paste Options)** button appears at the bottom right of the pasted item with choices for pasting the selected item. For example, you can specify to match the formatting in the destination area, keep the source formatting, or paste only text if text and graphics were copied.

Using the Office Clipboard

While the traditional Windows Clipboard offers the ability to store only one item, Office offers the ability to store and retrieve up to 24 items. It also shows you the contents of the Clipboard, along with an icon representing the software program that was used to create each item.

To display the Clipboard task pane, on the Home tab, in the Clipboard group, click the **Clipboard** dialog box launcher.

Paste All	Pastes all items currently in the Clipboard in the same order as they appear in the Clipboard.
Clear All	Clears all items from the Clipboard.
Options	Allows you to select options that control how the Clipboard will work.

The Clipboard can collect up to 24 items, making this useful if you need data from several files. For instance, perhaps you are working on a report in Word and you want to insert some text from a company Web site page, as well as a chart from an Excel file, and some other content from a recent presentation created in PowerPoint. You can collect items from any of these programs (up to the maximum of 24 items) and then paste them into the Word report. As you collect new items, previous items accumulated on the Clipboard will be replaced by the newer ones. To paste an item into the current location in the document, click that item on the Clipboard.

Point at various items on the Clipboard to display a drop-down arrow at the right of the item; click that arrow to display a menu offering various options. Use **Delete** to delete only this item from the Clipboard. If you want to paste only this item into the current location, use **Paste** in this shortcut menu or click the item on the Clipboard.

EXERCISE

In this exercise you will learn to copy information from one document and paste it into a new document.

1. Press (Ctrl)+(N) to create a new blank document. Type: Estimated Sales 2015 and press (Enter).

2. Click **File** and then click **Open**. Navigate to the student data files location and click **Sales Figures 2014** to open it.

3. Move the cursor to the beginning of the table, starting with the text *Popular Tours*.

4. Click and drag to highlight the figures in the entire table and then on the Home tab, in the Clipboard group, click **Copy**.

5. Switch to the new document and in the blank line below the title, on the Home tab, in the Clipboard group, click **Paste**.

    The table of figures has been copied from one document to another.

6. On the Quick Access toolbar, click the **Undo** button.

The pasted item is cleared, giving you the option to undo or reverse an action as needed.

7. On the Home tab, in the Clipboard group, click **Paste** once more.

   The information is pasted into the document again, and in fact, you could paste this information into other areas of the same document or to another document, as needed.

8. Save the new document as `Estimated Sales 2015 - Student` and then close it.

9. Close the *Sales Figures* document without saving.

Formatting Text Characters

 Exam 2 - Objective 1.2, 2.2

Character formatting refers to any feature that changes the appearance of characters on the screen and in print. You can control the following aspects of character formatting:

Font	Describes the typeface of characters on the screen and in print.
Font Size	Refers to the height of the characters (as characters get taller, they also grow wider.)
Character Formatting	Refers to the special stylized variations applied to plain characters to make them stand out from other text. They include bold, italics, and various kinds of underlines.
Effects	Refers to special effects you can add to the text, such as ~~strikethrough~~, superscript or subscript, shadow, SMALL CAPS, and so on.

You can apply formatting to text as you type it or after you have typed it. It can be easier and faster to wait until all the text in your document has been typed and edited before you format it. This way, you do not need to remember to turn formatting features on and off (often finding afterward that you need to go through the document again and check that you have done everything consistently).

There are several ways to apply formatting to text characters:

- On the Home tab, in the Font group, click the appropriate formatting button; or
- use the formatting options in the Font dialog box; or
- press the appropriate keyboard shortcut for the formatting option you want to use; or
- right-click in the document, and then click **Font**; or
- on the Mini toolbar, click the appropriate option.

Many common character formatting features are located on the Home tab, in the Font group. The Mini toolbar appears only when text is selected; it contains buttons for applying specific, common features for formatting characters and paragraphs.

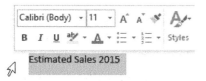

You can turn most formatting features on and off by clicking the corresponding button. When a feature is active, it appears in a different color from the other buttons. An arrow beside any button indicates that you can select additional options for the feature. The **Font** group includes only text formatting features while the Mini toolbar includes features that affect paragraphs and pages of text, such as centering text between the left and right margins, increasing and decreasing indents, and so on. The Mini toolbar includes the most common or frequently used formatting features.

When you want to remove all formatting options from selected text, on the Home tab, in the Font group, click **Clear Formatting**.

Using the Font Command

The Font dialog box contains both basic and additional choices to enhance text. Use this dialog box to access formatting options not available in the Font group or the Mini toolbar, or to apply several options at the same time. These formatting options can be applied to selected text or as you type.

To access the Font dialog box, use one of the following methods:

- On the Home tab, in the Font group, click the **Font** dialog box launcher; or
- press Ctrl + D .

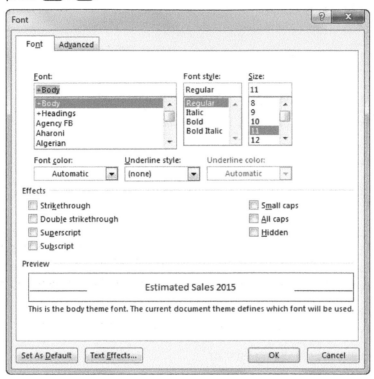

Aligning Text

Alignment refers to the way the left and right edges of a paragraph line up horizontally on the page. You can easily change the alignment in your document using one of the following four options:

Align Left	Aligns text to the left margin with a ragged or uneven edge on the right side of the text; this is commonly known as *ragged-right* alignment.
Center	Aligns text exactly between the left and right margins to an imaginary line down the middle of the page; the text has ragged edges on both the left and right sides.
Align Right	Aligns text to the right margin with ragged left edges.
Justify	Aligns text so the left and right edges of the text are flush with the margins and each line of text is evenly spaced out between the margins, except for the last line of each paragraph.

Note that all paragraph formatting affects the entire paragraph.

As with other types of formatting, text alignment formatting can be applied as you type, or it can be applied to existing text. When changing the alignment of existing text, position the mouse pointer anywhere within the paragraph and then choose the alignment you want to apply to the entire paragraph.

You can select alignment options using one of the following methods:

- On the Home tab, in the Paragraph group, click the **Paragraph** dialog box launcher to display the Paragraph dialog box. Select the **Indents and Spacing** tab, click the arrow for **Alignment**, and click the appropriate alignment; or

- on the Home tab, in the Paragraph group, click the appropriate alignment button; or

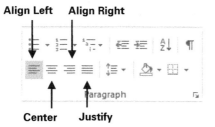

Align Left   Align Right

Center   Justify

- press one of the following keyboard shortcuts:

Align Left	Ctrl + L
Center	Ctrl + E
Align Right	Ctrl + R
Justify	Ctrl + J

EXERCISE

In this exercise, you will apply simple formatting options to text in a memo.

1. Click **File** and then **Open**. From the student data files location, select the *Memo to Andrew* file to open it.

2. Click **File** and then **Save As.** Type: `Memo to expand cemetery tours - Student` and press `Enter`.

   The cursor should be at the Interoffice Memorandum title.

3. On the Home group, in the Paragraph group, click **Align Left**.

4. Select the entire title and then on the Home tab, in the Font group, click the arrow for **Font Size** and change this to **12**.

5. Near the end of the first paragraph, select the text *Forest Lawn at Glendale*. Press the `Ctrl` key and then select *Holy Cross Cemetery*.

6. On the Home tab in the Font group, click **Bold** and then click the down arrow for **Font Color** to select a green of your choice.

7. Near the end of the third paragraph, select *10-day package* and press `Ctrl` + `D` to display the Font dialog box.

8. In the Font style list, click **Bold Italic**. In the Font color list, click a red color of your choice.

9. In the Effects area, click **Small caps**.

   Notice how Word displays a preview for you as you select different formatting options. The preview will change as you add or remove effects on the text.

10. Click **OK** to apply the changes.

11. Save the document and then close it.

Understanding Tab Settings

 Exam 2 - Objective 2.2

Setting tabs or stops is similar to aligning text; the difference is that setting tabs allows you to align information at specific intervals across the document so that text is lined up in columns.

Most font types are proportionally spaced; that is, they only use as much space for each character as needed, which makes it difficult to create aligned columns using spaces. Using the appropriate tab alignment options in Word is faster and produces better results than aligning columns using spaces.

Click in the Tab Selector box to choose the alignment type; a ScreenTip appears defining each character and how it will align your tabbed columns:

Left Tab	Center Tab	Right Tab	Bar Tab	Decimal.Tab
T. Jones	VP, Computers	Data Processing		$65,082.3009
J. Martinez	VP, Supplies	Purchasing		64,376.08
A. Chan	VP, Manufacturing	Manufacturing		62,000.152
D. Arcosa	VP, Operations	Administration		$61,705.297

Left	Aligns text along the left edge of the column with characters shifting right as you type; this is the default setting.
Center	Centers text along an imaginary line down the middle of the column, with characters shifting evenly to the left and right as you type.
Right	Aligns all text along the right edge of the column with characters shifting left as you type.
Decimal	Aligns columns of numbers to a decimal point: text shifts to the left of the decimal point until you type the decimal point, and then text shifts to the right of the decimal point.
Bar	Displays a small vertical line as a separator between the previous and next column of information.

Left tab settings exist at every 0.5" by default. Press the (Tab) key to move from one column to the next when typing text.

You can set new tab stops before typing, or apply them to existing text. Select the text first before adding or changing tab settings to existing text. Tab settings remain in effect until you change them.

Use the ¶ (**Show/Hide ¶**) feature to display → every time you press the (Tab) key. If text doesn't line up with the tab stops you've set, seeing your tab stops can help you determine why and how to correct the problem.

Using the ruler is the fastest way of setting and adjusting tabs; however, you can use the Tabs dialog box to set precise tab positions or *dot leaders.* To set and adjust tab positions or dot leaders using the Tabs dialog box, use one of the following methods:

- On the Home tab, in the Paragraph group click the **Paragraph** dialog box launcher and then click the **Tabs** button in the lower left corner; or

- double-click a tab character on the ruler to take you directly to the Tabs dialog box.

For precise positioning of the tab stop on the ruler, press and hold the (Alt) key as you click on the ruler to position the tab stop.

To set tabs using the ruler, click the Tab Selector box until the desired tab alignment character displays and then click in the ruler where the tab stop is to be placed.

The items in the Tab Selector box will cycle through each time you click on the box. Click as necessary until the desired character appears.

When clicking on the ruler to place the tab stop, position your mouse close to the measurement mark in the ruler. A vertical dash line will appear to verify the tab stop as you click in the ruler to set the tab stop.

To remove an undesired tab stop, click the tab character on the ruler and drag it down off the ruler.

If you need to adjust the position of a tab stop, click the tab character on the ruler and drag it to the new position.

If you need to set a new tab alignment character, click the Tab Selector box to choose the required tab alignment character, and then click in the ruler where you want to place the new tab stop. You may need to delete existing tab stops, as required.

When you need to edit a tab setting that is currently applied to existing text, be sure to select the text first; otherwise, the revised tab setting is applied only to the current line. For example, to adjust a tab setting in a list of 20 names, select the 20 lines of text and then drag the tab character to its new location on the ruler.

EXERCISE

In this exercise you will create an itinerary by setting tabs on the ruler.

1. Create a new blank document and then save it as Seattle Restaurants Itinerary - Student.

2. Type: Seattle Restaurants Itinerary as the title and press Enter.

3. On the ruler, ensure the Left Alignment character is displayed in the Tab Selector box and then click the **0.8" (1.8 cm)** measurement on the ruler.

> **Tip:** It isn't necessary to be precise when setting the measurements for the tab settings as it is very easy to adjust these once you enter the text and see how much space may be needed between the columns of text.

4. With the Left Alignment character still active, click the **2.5" (6.3 cm)** measurement and then the **4.5" (11.5 cm)** measurement.

5. Click the Tab Selector box until the Decimal Alignment character appears and then click the **5.5" (14.3 cm)** measurement.

6. Click the Tab Selector box until the Center Alignment character appears and then click the **6.3" (15.8 cm)** measurement.

You will now enter the column titles for your itinerary.

7. Type: Date and press Tab. Type: Site/Location and press Tab. Continue entering each column title as shown, pressing Tab between the columns. At the last entry, press Enter.

Seattle Restaurants Itinerary

Date	Site/Location	Entrée		Meal	Cost	Show

Now try entering the data for the report.

8. Type: `Jun 12`, press (Tab), type: `Georgia's Greek`, press (Tab), type: `Lamb Souvlaki`, press (Tab), type: `Lunch`, press (Tab), type: `$7.85`, press (Tab), type: `DDD` and then press (Shift)+(Enter).

9. Enter the rest of the table as shown in the following; press (Shift)+(Enter) when you get to the end of the line in order to enter a text wrapping break, then enter the address for the restaurant (and/or additional entree information).

Date	Site/Location	Entrée	Meal	Cost	Show
Jun 12	Georgia's Greek 323 NW 85th St	Lamb Souvlaki Vegetarian Mousaka	Lunch Dinner	$7.85 $12.95	DDD
Jun 14	Red Mill Burgers 312 N. 67th St	Red Mill Deluxe with Cheese	Lunch	$6.95	MvF
Jun 16	Beth's Café 7311 Aurora Ave N	The Triple Bypass Omelet Mondo Burger	Breakfast Lunch	$17.95 $9.95	MvF
Jun 20	Le Pichet 1933 1st Ave	Crepinettes au porc, a l'agneau (Rustic pork & lamb meatballs)	Dinner	$19.00	Crave
Jun 25	Revel 403 N. 36th St	Roasted duck, smoked noodle	Dinner	$14.00	TBT
Jun 30	Beechers 1601 5th Ave NW	World's Best Mac n Cheese 2 6"x9" Pans – Take Home	Dinner (Side)	$29.00	Crave
Jul 3	Toulouse Petit 601 Queen Anne Ave N	Toulouse Eggs Benedict	Brunch	$8.00	TBT

10. At the end of the table, be sure to press (Enter) and then type the following, pressing (Tab) once between the columns (don't worry about the text being in the wrong location as you will change it in a later step):

Show: DDD – Diners, Drive-ins & Dives   MvF – Man vs Food   TBT – The
Best Thing I Ever Ate

11. Save the document.

You will now adjust the tab settings to align items appropriately.

12. Click anywhere in the column headings line.

13. Click the decimal tab alignment character and drag it to the right by one increment.

Notice how only the Cost text was affected and not the entire column. This is what we want in this instance as we are adjusting the appearance of the column title only. If you wanted to adjust the setting for the restaurant items, you would need to select these lines.

14. Starting from Jun 12, select all the text to the last line for the Jul 3 restaurant entry.

15. Drag the first left tab alignment character to the left to reduce the amount of space between the date and the location.

16. Drag the second left tab alignment character to the left to increase the amount of space between the Entrée and Meal columns. Adjust the decimal tab by one character as well to "center" the values under the Cost heading.

Your itinerary should appear similar to the following:

Seattle Restaurants Itinerary

Date	Site/Location	Entrée	Meal	Cost	Show
Jun 12	Georgia's Greek 323 NW 85th St	Lamb Souvlaki Vegetarian Moussaka	Lunch Dinner	$7.85 $12.95	DDD
Jun 14	Red Mill Burgers 312 N. 67th St	Red Mill Deluxe with Cheese	Lunch	$6.95	MvF
Jun 16	Beth's Café 7311 Aurora Ave N	The Triple Bypass Omelet Mondo Burger	Breakfast Lunch	$17.95 $9.95	MvF
Jun 20	Le Pichet 1933 1st Ave	Crepinettes au porc, a l'agneau (Rustic pork & lamb meatballs)	Dinner	$19.00	Crave
Jun 25	Revel 403 N. 36th St	Roasted duck, smoked noodle	Dinner	$14.00	TBT
Jun 30	Beechers 1601 5th Ave NW	World's Best Mac n Cheese 2 6"x9" Pans - Take Home	Dinner	$29.00	Crave
Jul 3	Toulouse Petit 601 Queen Ave N	Toulouse Eggs Benedict	Brunch	$8.00	TBT

Show: DDD - Diners, Drive-ins & Dives   MvF - Man vs Food   TBT - The Best Thing I Ever Ate

Let's now adjust the tab settings for the last line of text.

17. Select the last line beginning with the Show text.

18. Drag the first left tab alignment character to **0.5" (1.3 cm)**. Drag the next left tab alignment to **2.9" (7.4 cm)**. Drag the last left tab alignment to **4.5" (11.4 cm)** if necessary.

19. Drag the decimal tab alignment character down from the ruler to delete it. Repeat for the center tab alignment character.

The line of text should appear similar to:

Jun 30	Beechers 1601 5th Ave NW	World's Best Mac n Cheese 2 6"x9" Pans - Take Home	Dinner	$29.00	Crave
Jul 3	Toulouse Petit 601 Queen Ave N	Toulouse Eggs Benedict	Brunch	$8.00	TBT

Show: DDD - Diners, Drive-ins & Dives   MvF - Man vs Food   TBT - The Best Thing I Ever Ate

20. With the line still selected, change the font to size **9**.

21. Format the document, enhancing the titles as well as any other formatting you may want to apply in the itinerary. Make any adjustments to the tabs for the headings as necessary.

22. Save and close the document.

Working with Indents

 Exam 2 - Objective 2.1, 2.2

An indented paragraph is one that aligns along a temporary left and/or right margin. Indents are useful for identifying new paragraphs, or emphasizing items such as quotations or subparagraphs. You can create the following kinds of indents:

Left Indent	Indents from the left margin; often used with lists.
Right Indent	Indents from the right margin; often used with left indents to set off block quotations.
First Line Indent	Indents only the first line of the paragraph by a set amount from the left margin.
Hanging Indent	Aligns the first line of a paragraph with the margin while the rest of the paragraph aligns to a position further in from the left margin. This style is commonly used for bibliographies and for bulleted and numbered lists.

Using the Indent Markers

Just as you can use the ruler to set tab stops quickly and easily, you can use it to set and adjust indents:

ScreenTips identify the different indent types as you hover over the corresponding markers.

To create a specific type of indent on the ruler, click the Tab Selector box until the appropriate indent marker displays, and then click the ruler at the desired location.

Using the Paragraph Command

You can set precise paragraph indents using one of two methods:

- On the Page Layout tab, in the Paragraph group, set the indent measurement from the **Left** or **Right** margin; or

- on the Home tab, in the Paragraph group, click the **Paragraph** dialog box launcher.

In the Indentation area, select **Left** to indent text from the left margin, similar to using the □ marker on the ruler; or select **Right** to indent text from the right margin, similar to using the △ marker on the ruler; or select **Special** to display a list from which you can choose either **First Line**, similar to using the ▽ marker on the ruler, or **Hanging**, similar to using the △ marker on the ruler.

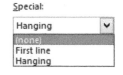

Once you select one of these items, the **By** option becomes available and you can enter precise measurements for your indentations.

In the Indentation area, you can also select the **Mirror indents** option to ensure that your left and right indents will be adjusted appropriately for odd and even pages.

The Preview box at the bottom of the Paragraph dialog box shows how the indent measurements you've entered will affect the appearance of the document.

Adjusting Indents

Once a text indent is defined, you can adjust it using one of the following methods:

- Drag the appropriate indent marker to the new measurement on the ruler, or
- on the Home tab, in the Paragraph group, click the **Paragraph** dialog box launcher, and make the appropriate changes in the **Indentation** area.

You can increase or decrease the amount of space in an indent on the ruler using the default tab stop at 0.5" (1.3 cm). On the Home tab, in the Paragraph group, click ⁝≣ **(Increase Indent)** or ≣⁝ **(Decrease Indent)** to increase or decrease the indent from its current location.

Organizing List Information

There are a number of different ways to emphasize or separate list information. You can use bullets if there is no priority for the list items, or apply numbers to prioritize the list. You can also use the Outline feature to show a progression:

Popular Tours	**Popular Tours**	**Popular Tours**
• Cycling trips	1. Rock climbing	1. Cycling trips
• Whale watching	2. Cycling trips	a. Copenhagen
• Rock climbing	3. Ice climbing	b. Bogotá
• Heli skiing	4. Whale watching	2. Whale watching
• Hot air ballooning	5. Heli skiing	a. Victoria
• Ice climbing	6. Hot air ballooning	b. Perth
		3. Rock climbing
		a. Kilimanjaro
		b. North Carolina
		4. Heli skiing
		a. Rockies
		b. Colorado

Word provides a variety of the most commonly used bulleting and numbering styles. You can also customize these styles to create a different look for any document.

To apply a list style to your text, on the Home tab, in the Paragraph group, click the arrow for the appropriate list button.

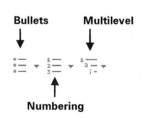

Bullets   **Multilevel**

Numbering

By default, the bullet or number style that appears when you click the button is the same style that was used last. If you want to choose a new style, click the arrow beside the button to view the range of options shown in the Library.

An advantage of using the automatic list feature to organize information is that, when you need to move or copy an item in a numbered or multilevel list, Word reorganizes the information and adjusts the bullets or renumbers the points accordingly.

Customizing Lists

As noted, using the Bullets or Numbering button automatically applies the last used style of bullets or numbers to your new list. However, once you have applied one of these features, you can easily change it using the options in the Library.

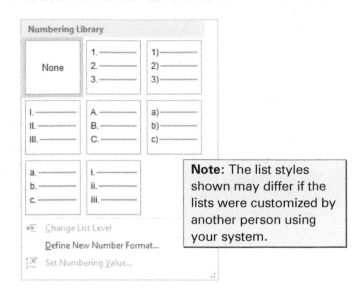

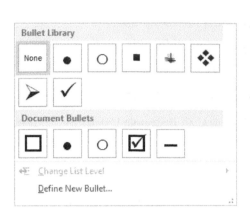

Alternatively, you can define a new style for the bullet or numbering.

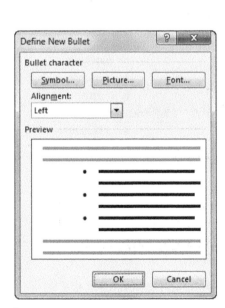

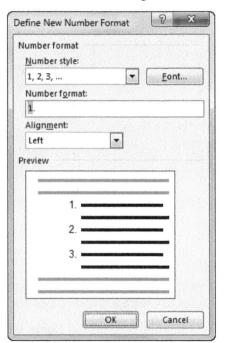

EXERCISE

In this exercise you will organize your lists by applying a list format. You will also set indents to emphasize the text.

1. Click **File** and then **Open**. From the student data files, select the *Haunted Tours Reference* file.

2. Click **File** and then **Save as**. Type: - Student at the end of the file name and press (Enter).

3. Click in the *Whaley House* line immediately below the Haunted Sites subheading.

4. On the Home tab, in the Paragraph group, click **Bullets**.

Haunted Sites

- The Whaley House, California, USA

http://whaleyhouse.org/haunted.htm

5. On the Home tab in the Paragraph group, click the **Decrease Indent** button.

   Notice how the bullet point now aligns with the left margin instead of being indented.

6. Select the three Web address links below this bullet point.

7. On the ruler, click the ▱ **(Left Indent)** marker and drag to the **0.5" (1.3 cm)** mark on the ruler.

8. Select the next two points below the links. On the Home tab in the Paragraph group, click the arrow for **Bullets** and choose another bullet of your choice.

Haunted·Sites¶

- → The·Whaley·House,·California,·USA¶

     http://whaleyhouse.org/haunted.htm¶

     http://www.sdparanormal.com/page/page/199234.htm¶

     http://paranormalphotos.tripod.com/id30.html¶

   o→ Appeared·in·the·American's·Most·Haunted·and·Ghost·Hunters·International·TV·shows¶
   o→ Paranormal·sightings·random;·range·from·seeing·woman·in·the·courtroom·or·garden·to·Mr.· Whaley·on·upper·landing,·and·unexplained·footsteps·and·movement·of·windows¶

Word has applied the new bullet symbol.

9. Repeat steps 3 to 8 for the remaining two categories, adjusting the indents as required.

   When complete the bullet points should appear similar to the following:

Haunted Adventure Tours

The following tours have been approved and will be managed primarily by the Seattle office:

Haunted Sites

- The Whaley House, California, USA

     http://whaleyhouse.org/haunted.htm

     http://www.sdparanormal.com/page/page/199234.htm

     http://paranormalphotos.tripod.com/id30.html

Note: Remember to change the bullet for the appropriate level.

- Appeared in the American's Most Haunted and Ghost Hunters International TV shows
- Paranormal sightings random; range from seeing woman in the courtroom or garden to Mr. Whaley on upper landing, and unexplained footsteps and movement of windows

Celebrity Burial Sites

- Pierce Brothers Westwood Village Memorial Park Cemetery, Los Angeles, USA (Marilyn Monroe, Burt Lancaster, Jack Lemmon, Rodney Dangerfield, etc.)

     http://en.wikipedia.org/wiki/Westwood_Village_Memorial_Park_Cemetery

     http://www.pbwvmortuary.com/dm20/en_US/locations/47/4798/index.page

     http://www.seeing-stars.com/maps/piercebrosmap.shtml

- Hugh Hefner has reserved spot, next to Marilyn Monroe
- Dominique Dunne buried here; death part of supernatural myth from Poltergeist movie that saw three deaths of actors (stems supposedly from using real human skeleton in first movie)
- Very popular tourist site – map provided of where celebrity headstones are

10. Save the document.

Working with Paragraphs

 Exam 2 - Objective 1.2, 2.2

Word provides you with a number of tools to change the entire paragraph to best suit the message in your document. Many of the following items will affect the amount of white space vertically between the lines of text and paragraphs, as well as assist in maintaining the look and consistency in order to produce a professional-looking document.

Changing Line Spacing

Line spacing refers to the amount of space between lines of typed text, measured from the baseline of one line to the baseline of the next. Word automatically adjusts the amount of space between lines according to the size of the characters being used. However, you can also specify that line spacing be set to an exact point size.

It's important to note that a precise line spacing setting will not adjust to accommodate larger text if the font size is changed. It's also important to note that, if you decrease line spacing too much, the lines of text may overwrite each other, or the text may not display.

You can set line spacing using one of the following methods:

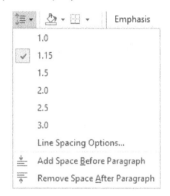

- On the Home tab, in the Paragraph group, click ⬆≡ ▾ (**Line and Paragraph Spacing**); or

- on the Home tab, in the Paragraph group, click the **Paragraph** dialog box launcher. Then, in the Indents and Spacing tab of the Paragraph dialog box, click the arrow for **Line spacing** to choose the spacing you require; or

- press the shortcut key for the following commonly used line spacing options:

  Single   Ctrl + 1
  One-and-a-Half   Ctrl + 5
  Double   Ctrl + 2

Setting Paragraph Spacing

Paragraph spacing refers to the amount of space between paragraphs of text. Although it is possible to create extra space between paragraphs by pressing Enter to insert blank lines, most published documents are set up to insert a specific amount of space between paragraphs. This enables you to set spacing slightly smaller than a full line, which reduces the amount of white space on a page and ensures consistency throughout a document.

To set or change the paragraph spacing, use one of the following methods:

- On the Home tab, in the Paragraph group, click the **Paragraph** dialog box launcher. Then, in the **Spacing** area, set the appropriate measurement for the spacing. You can set the spacing for **Before**, **After**, or both.

- Alternatively, on the Page Layout tab, in the Paragraph group, set the spacing as required:

EXERCISE

In this exercise, you will change the line spacing on the document to try and fit the text onto one page.

1. Ensure the *Haunted Tours Reference – Student* document is active.

2. Press ⌈Ctrl⌉+⌈A⌉ to select all text in the document.

3. On the Home tab, in the Paragraph group, click the **Line and Paragraph Spacing** button. Then click **1.0**.

    It will appear as if the line spacing changed for some text but not others. This is a result of the default settings for bullets versus normal text.

4. Click the **Page Layout** tab, and in the Paragraph group, click the Up incremental button for **After** to display **0** (zero).

    You should have noticed that there was no spacing amount indicated for the After measurement when you accessed the Page Layout tab of the Ribbon. Because the spacing in the document varied between paragraphs, Word leaves the value in this field empty, indicating that spacing was inconsistent for the selected text.

5. Click the Up incremental button for **After** once more to change this to **6**.

    All of the text for the document should now fit on one page.

6. Save and close the document.

Working with Styles

A *style* is a combination of character and paragraph formatting that you create and save with a unique name. Styles save time when formatting documents, as you can create a style and then apply it to multiple selections of text. When you change the formatting attributes of a style, all text formatted with that style will automatically update to reflect the new attributes.

There are two main types of styles:

Character Style	Affects the selected text only and includes any character formatting attributes found in the Font dialog box.
Paragraph Style	Affects the appearance and position of the entire paragraph and can include both paragraph and character formatting. Note that applying a paragraph style to a paragraph with character formatting may turn off that character formatting.

Word includes several standard built-in styles to help you format typical portions of a document, such as headings. The Normal style contains the default formatting for all new documents.

The Styles task pane lists the styles used in the current document. Styles created for a particular template will appear in all new documents created from the template to make it easy for you to standardize the appearance of all the reports, newsletters, and memos you might need to publish in that particular style. You can apply styles before or after you type the text.

To create a style, you must first determine how you want your text to appear, and then create a naming structure or hierarchy for the style.

Properties	Lists the types of properties you can enter or change for this style.
Formatting	Identifies the attributes used in a style.
Add to the Styles gallery	Adds this style to the Normal template which contains the list of styles displayed in the gallery on the Home tab for quick access. If you do not select this feature, the style appears in the Styles pane only.
Automatically update	Updates the style whenever you change attributes of this style manually in the text.
Format	Displays a list of formatting commands available to you when you are creating the style.

Consider the following points about naming a style:

- You can use any combination of characters and spaces for the style name, with the exception of the backslash (\\), semicolon (;) or brace ({ }) characters.

- Style names are case sensitive.

- Each style name within a document must be unique.

Using Quick Styles

Microsoft created and designed a set of styles called Quick Styles that contain common formatting options for common types of text. For instance, the Normal style uses 11-point Calibri font; the Heading 1 style is set to highlight a major heading in the document. You can also add any style you create to the Styles gallery.

Once you select text, point to a style option; the Styles feature will display a preview of how the selected text will look when you apply the style.

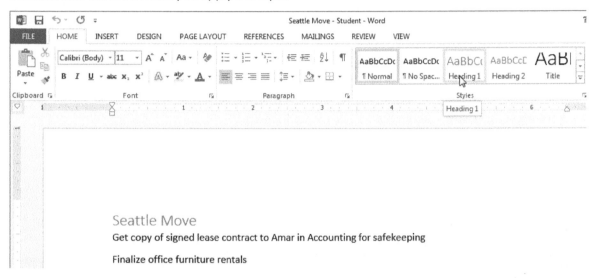

As you point from one style to another, the preview of the selected text will change accordingly, although Word will keep the original style highlighted. The graphic above shows Normal as the original style while indicating a preview of the Heading 1 style.

Click **More** in the Styles list to display the full gallery of Quick Styles.

Create a Style	Create a new style for the selected text, as required.
Clear Formatting	Removes the style and all formatting from the selection of text.
Apply Styles	Displays a window where you can select from a list of styles. You can also press Ctrl + Shift + S to display this window.

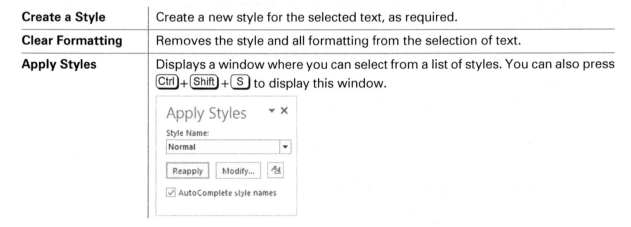

Understanding the Styles Window

When you click the **Styles** dialog box launcher, the Styles pane appears with further options:

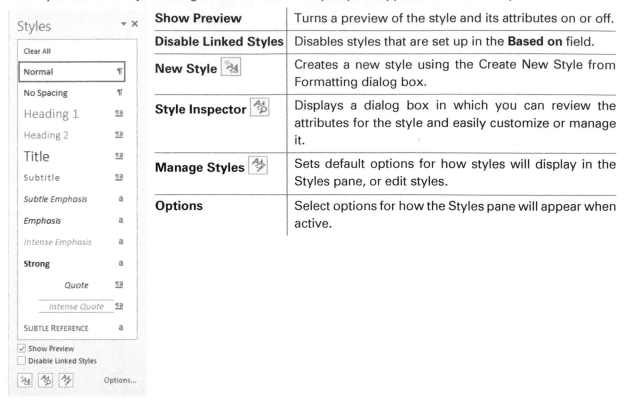

Show Preview	Turns a preview of the style and its attributes on or off.
Disable Linked Styles	Disables styles that are set up in the **Based on** field.
New Style	Creates a new style using the Create New Style from Formatting dialog box.
Style Inspector	Displays a dialog box in which you can review the attributes for the style and easily customize or manage it.
Manage Styles	Sets default options for how styles will display in the Styles pane, or edit styles.
Options	Select options for how the Styles pane will appear when active.

If you want to view the formatting options for a style, point at its name in the Styles list; a ScreenTip will list the formatting attributes associated with this style.

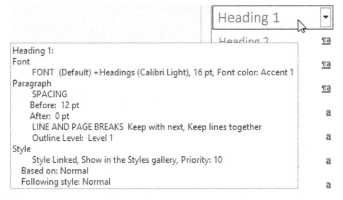

If you want to make changes to the way the style is used, click the down arrow beside the style name; a dialog box will list several options for managing the usage of this style in the document:

Modifying Styles

One of the major advantages of using styles becomes evident when you want to make formatting changes to your document. When you redefine the formatting of a style, Word automatically changes all paragraphs in the document formatted with that style.

Styles can be based on an existing style, or you can create a style from scratch. All new styles are based on the Normal style, unless you specify to base them on another style. Consequently, if you change the base style, all variations of that style will reflect that change. You can modify the attributes for a style at any time.

To modify a style, use one of the following methods:

- On the Home tab, in the Styles group, click the **Styles** dialog box launcher to display the Styles pane. Point at the style to be changed, click the down arrow for the style, and then click **Modify**; or

- on the Home tab, in the Styles group, click **More** for the Quick Styles gallery, click **Apply Styles**, and then click **Modify**. When the Modify Style dialog box appears, you can make changes as required.

You can also use the **Automatically update** option to modify a style by changing existing text to which the style is currently applied. Alternatively, in the Styles pane, you can click the down arrow for the style and then click **Update [Style Name] to Match Selection**.

EXERCISE

In this exercise, you will apply styles that are built into Word and then create a new style to apply in the document.

1. Open *TA Employee List* and save as `TA Employee List - Student`.

2. With the cursor on the main title, on the Home tab, in the Styles group, click **Heading 1**.

3. Click anywhere in the next line "New York" text and in the Styles group, click **Heading 2**.

4. Scroll through the rest of the document and apply the **Heading 2** style to all the city names.

Now create a style for the branch office information and another style for the contact information.

5. Click in the first line of text for the New York address. On the Home tab, in the Styles group, click the **Styles** dialog box launcher button.

6. At the lower left corner of the task pane, click 🔲 (**New Style**).

7. Type: `Branch` as the name of the new style.

8. In the Formatting area, change the font size to **12** and then the font color to a blue similar to the one used in the Heading 2 heading style (we used the medium Blue in the Standard Colors row).

9. Click **OK**.

    Word automatically applies the new style to the line where the mouse cursor is positioned.

10. Click anywhere in the Nick Klassen line of text.

11. Click **New Style** once more from the Styles task pane.

12. Type: `Contact` as the name of the new style.

13. Change the size of the font to **10** and then click **OK**.

Tolano Adventures

New York

300 171st Street, New York, NY 98032

(540) 555-4321 (Head Office)

Nick Klassen
Vice President
nklassen@tolano.com

Madison Cowell
Travel Director
mcowell@tolano.com

Amar Boutros
Accountant
aboutros@tolano.com

Cape Town

14. To reduce some of the spacing between the branch address and the first contact, in the Styles task pane, click the arrow for **Branch**, then click **Modify**. In the Modify Style dialog box, click the **Format** button, then click **Paragraph**. In the Paragraph dialog box, click the down arrow for **After** and change the setting to **6pt**.

15. Click **OK** twice to return to the document.

16. Apply the new styles appropriately.

Your document should appear similar to the following:

Tolano Adventures

New York

300 171st Street, New York, NY 98032

(540) 555-4321 (Head Office)

Nick Klassen
Vice President
nklassen@tolano.com

Madison Cowell
Travel Director
mcowell@tolano.com

Amar Boutros
Accountant
aboutros@tolano.com

Cape Town

#47 212 Pine Road, Cape Town 4002

555 456 1234

Jamie Gibson
Travel Director
jgibson@tolano.com

Robin Black
Administrative Assistant
rblack@tolano.com

Let's now change the color of the contact style so the names can be emphasized.

17. Click in one of the lines with a contact name such as Nick Klassen or Lawrence Jang. In the Styles pane, point at the Contact style and then click the arrow to display the menu. Click **Modify**.

18. Click the arrow for the **Font Color** and change it to a color of your choice. Click **OK**.

You probably would not distribute a business list with as many different colors; the steps in this exercise are intended to demonstrate how quickly and easily you can modify a style.

19. Save and close the document.

Proofing the Document

 Exam 2 - Objective 1.1, 1.3

Before sending your document to print, you should always proof it for correct spelling, grammar, and context as you want your document to reflect a professional image of you and your company. Word provides tools to automate proofing and also displays visual hints if it encounters an item that should be reviewed.

contrat Red wavy lines indicate the word is not recognized in either the current or custom Word dictionary.

there Blue wavy lines indicate a grammatical or structural error or a potential contextual error.

The Spelling and Grammar feature provides options, such as the ability to create custom dictionaries for special terms you may use in your work, to help you check for spelling and grammatical errors. The spelling portion checks for incorrect spelling, duplicate words, and occurrences of incorrect capitalization. The grammar portion detects sentences with grammatical errors or weak writing style, based on widely accepted standards in the language overall as well as some regional variations (such as American versus British English).

The Spelling and Grammar feature works in the background to check for mistakes as you type. This enables you to correct mistakes immediately or when you are finished creating the document.

To activate the automatic Spelling and Grammar feature, use one of the following methods:

* On the Review tab, in the Proofing group, click **Spelling & Grammar**; or
* press F7.

When Word finds the first misspelled word in the document, it displays the item in the Spelling and Grammar pane at the top.

Ignore	Ignores this occurrence of this spelling but continues to search for other occurrences of this spelling.
Ignore All	Ignores all occurrences of this spelling; this might apply to a person's name or some technical jargon.

Add	Adds this spelling to your custom dictionary. In addition to providing a regular dictionary, Word allows you to build a custom dictionary so that it will not identify names, jargon, slang, or regional spellings you use often as misspelled words.
Suggestions	Displays a list of alternatives for the misspelled word. If the correct word is in the list, click it and then click **Change**, or **Change All**, or double-click the word to change it immediately.
Change	Changes this occurrence with the selected word in the suggestions box.
Change All	Changes all words with this spelling with the selected word in the suggestions box.

Towards the bottom of the pane is a definition for the word, displaying a list of possible words to use to replace this word. This is especially helpful if you find yourself repeating the word several times on a page. The types of words that appear will depend on the type of word, for example, if it is a noun, verb or adjective. If you have sound available on your device, you can also click the speaker icon to hear the pronunciation of the word.

Grammatical or contextual errors appear in the Spelling and Grammar dialog box as the spell check encounters them. Grammatical errors occur when Word has detected there is a structural error in the text such as too many spaces, an incorrect or lack of punctuation, or the wrong tense may have been used or a passive versus active voice in the sentence.

Contextual error refers to words that have the same sound but different spellings and meanings depending on the context. Some words that often give rise to contextual errors include:

- there (refers to a place), their (possessive form), or they're (contraction for they are)
- its (possessive form) and it's (contraction for it is)
- where (refers to a location), ware (goods or services), and wear (attire or clothing)
- bear (could be the animal, or to endure or support) and bare (plain or empty)

Contextual errors, as with spelling or grammar errors, appear in at the top of the Spelling and Grammar pane for quick reference.

Suggestions	Provides a list of suggestions as to how to fix this error.
Ignore	Ignores this occurrence but continues to find other occurrences of the same grammatical error.
Change	Changes the error identified in the top box with the highlighted option in the Suggestions box.

In the lower half of the pane you will see an explanation as to the reason why the text was marked as an error; the text in this box changes to reflect the grammatical error identified.

Finding and Replacing Items

You can use the Find feature to locate occurrences of specific words, phrases, symbols, codes, or any combination of these items in your document. You might use the Find feature as a quick way to find a word you think you may have misspelled or to refer back to a particular piece of information. Once you've found what you're looking for, you can replace it, check other occurrences, or continue working with your document.

To activate the Find feature, use one of the following methods:

- On the Home tab, in the Editing group, click **Find**; or

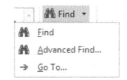

- click the page number box on the status bar; or

- press (Ctrl)+(F), to display the Navigation pane.

With the Navigation pane, you need only enter the search criteria and click 🔍 (or press (Enter)) to have Word search your document. Word lists any matches it finds in the tab as summaries where you can see some of the text around the found occurrence to determine if this is an item you want to view or change. When you click a result in the list, Word moves automatically to where that result is in the document so you can make a change, as needed.

Each time you activate the Find feature within any given Word session, Word will display the last search criteria entered. When you exit Word, all the boxes in the Find and Replace dialog box will clear.

To activate the Replace feature, use one of the following methods:

- On the Home tab, in the Editing group, click **Replace**; or

- press (Ctrl)+(H); or

- if the Find and Replace dialog box is open, click the **Replace** tab.

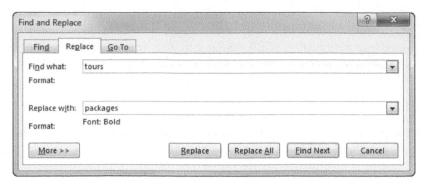

This tab is very similar to the Find tab, but also has a **Replace with** box in which you can enter the text you want to use to replace occurrences of found text. Use the **More** button to view options you can set for the find or replace options:

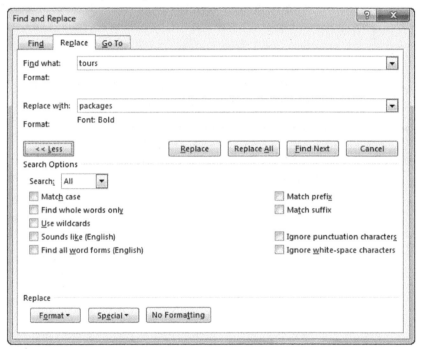

Find what	Provides a field to enter the word, phrase, symbol, or code you want to find.
More	Displays additional criteria you can select to help Word narrow the search. By default, Word does not display the options for **More**; once active, you can turn this display off using **Less**.
Match case	Searches for any text with exactly the same casing (capitalized or lowercase characters) as typed in the **Find what** box.
Find whole words only	Ignores all words where the search text is only a part of that word. For instance, if you type "red" in the **Find what** box without setting this option, Word will find all occurrences of these characters, including those that are buried in other, unrelated words, such as "hundred," "bred," "credible."
Use wildcards	Use the ? (question mark) character to represent one character at a time within another word; for example, entering "c?t" will find words like "cat," "cot," or "cut," but not "cart," "chat," or "crater." You can also use the * (asterisk) character to represent any number of characters regardless of the length of the word; for example, entering "br*d*" will find words like "broad", "bred", "broaden", "breed", "breeder", "bride."

Sounds like	Enables you to use a phonetic spelling to narrow the search criteria.
Find all word forms	Searches for all forms of a word, whether it is being used as a noun, verb, adjective, or adverb, whether it is singular or plural, and regardless of verb tense.
Match prefix	Enables you to search for all words beginning with certain characters, even when you do not know what the rest of the letters are or how many more letters there are. You can insert as many characters as you know for the beginning of the item to find. Word then matches only those words that begin with these characters, for example, if you enter "psyc," Word will find "psychology," "psychic," "psyche," "psychometrics."
Match suffix	Enables you to search for as many characters as you know appearing at the end of the item to search. Word will then match only those words in the document ending with these characters; for example, entering "try" would yield results such as "symmetry," "try," "poetry."
Ignore punctuation characters	Ignores any punctuation characters such as commas, colons, semi-colons, and periods.
Ignore white-space characters	Ignores regular or non-breaking spaces or tab characters. Select this to ignore characters in the document such as double-spaces.
Format	Include formatting attributes applied to text in the search criteria. You could also use the corresponding buttons or shortcut keys to enter a formatting attribute to find. Format ▾ — Font… / Paragraph… / Tabs… / Language… / Frame… / Style… / Highlight
Special	Searches for special characters, such as paragraph marks, page breaks, or tab marks. Paragraph Mark / Tab Character / Any Character / Any Digit / Any Letter / Caret Character / § Section Character / ¶ Paragraph Character / Column Break / Em Dash / En Dash / Endnote Mark / Field / Footnote Mark / Graphic / Manual Line Break / Manual Page Break / Nonbreaking Hyphen / Nonbreaking Space / Optional Hyphen / Section Break / White Space — Format ▾ Special ▾
No Formatting	Clears any options previously selected with the **Format** button in the **Find what** box.

Using Research Tools

You can use the Research feature to search for facts and other information, much as you would use encyclopedias or other reference materials. Word includes some specific reference tools and sites you can use for research purposes.

- To activate the Research option, press (Alt) and then click in the document to display the Research pane.

Search for	Provides a field into which you can enter the text you want to use as your search criteria.
Reference	Provides a list of sources you can search to find matches for your search criteria; click the down arrow to display the list. 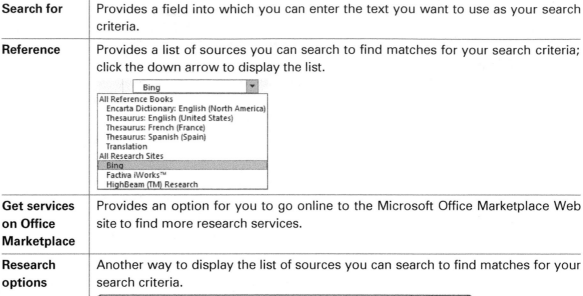
Get services on Office Marketplace	Provides an option for you to go online to the Microsoft Office Marketplace Web site to find more research services.
Research options	Another way to display the list of sources you can search to find matches for your search criteria. 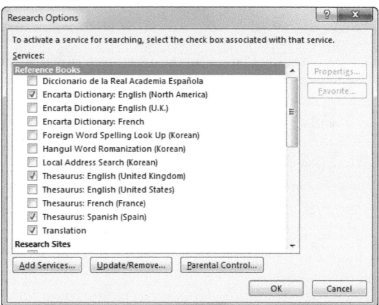

Once you have performed a search and retrieved results matching your criteria, you can use the ▷ **(Expand)** or ◢ **(Collapse)** buttons at the left of the titles to show more or less information for each topic; alternatively, you can click the links for each article or Web address to preview the item. Depending on which research service you use, your Web browser may display the information within the Research task pane at the left—similar to using the Search feature within a Web browser.

Many online research services are available only by subscription and, in most cases, there is a cost. If you are interested in third-party research services, use the **Get services on Office Marketplace** link to obtain further information.

Once you find the information you need, you can copy and paste it into your documents. Keep in mind when doing so that the copyright for information on a Web site belongs to the Web site owner; find out if you need to obtain permission to use the information and, regardless, cite your sources.

EXERCISE

In this exercise, you will proof a document in order to emphasize how important it is to ensure there are no errors in any document you will be distributing to the public.

1. Open *TA Corporate Profile* and save as `TA Corporate - Student`.

2. Click the **Review** tab and in the Proofing group, click **Spelling & Grammar**.

3. When the first error is found, click the correct spelling from the **Suggestions** list and then click **Change**.

4. Continue with the spelling and grammar check.

5. When you encounter the "yor" error, double-click the word in the paragraph and type: `you` to replace the word.

   The Spelling pane will still display the error but now also shows Resume as the command, as you moved into edit mode when you changed the text directly in the document.

   > **Tip:** Be sure to read the text around the proposed error to ensure you are selecting the correct word for the context.

6. Click **Resume** to continue with the spelling and grammar check. When Word has finished, click **OK**. Save the document.

There is still one error in the document which was not detected by Word. It appears in the second bullet point and is a contextual error. That is, the wrong form of the word is used.

7. In the second bullet point in the document, change the second occurrence of the word *there* to `their`.

   This is an example of why you should still read over the document even after a spelling and grammar check has been completed to ensure the document has no errors.

8. Save and close the document.

Let's begin a proof by checking if there is a word we use repetitively in the document.

9. Open the *Camel Tours* document from the student data files and save as `Camel Tours - Student`.

10. On the Home tab, in the Editing group, click **Find**. In the search field, type: `tours`

    Notice as you begin to enter the characters in the Search field, Word displays all matches for the characters by highlighting them in the document.

11. Close the Navigation pane and press Ctrl+H to display the Find and Replace dialog box.

    Word automatically places the word *tours* in the **Find what** field.

12. Click in the **Replace with** field, type: `packages` and then click **Replace**.

    Word highlights the first occurrence of the word tours that it finds, but does not replace it immediately. Word begins with the Find command first, then requires that you specify whether to replace one or all occurrences of the found word at a time.

13. Click **Replace All** to have Word replace all occurrences.

14. Click **OK**, then close the Find and Replace dialog box.

In an office setting, you would likely proceed to formatting the document appropriately, turning it into a flyer you can send to customers as a promotional piece. For the purpose of this exercise, we will focus on the proofing options only.

Suppose now you want to add more information about one of the cities mentioned in the flyer.

15. Press the (Alt) key and then click anywhere in the *camel* text.

The Research pane opens and Word displays information it has gathered from the Internet about this city so you can read a bit more about it. The Research feature can be handy if you need to verify facts or items in the document; the Research feature is available at any time to help you accomplish this task.

16. Close the Research task pane and then save and close this document.

Changing the Page Setup

 Exam 2 - Objective 2.2

There are several options you can use to alter the way pages are laid out for different types of documents. Options can include setting the margins to print differently for odd and even pages or changing the paper size in order to print an envelope. Take note that some options, such as collating the pages or printing single- or double-sided are set in the Settings section of the Print tab in Backstage view.

Changing the Paper Size

The default paper size is determined by the Language and Regional settings for your system (the example at the right is set for English US which uses 8½" by 11" or standard Letter size in this region); you can change this for any document using the **Page Layout** tab. To change the paper size for a document, use one of the following methods:

- On the **Page Layout** tab, in the Page Setup group, click **Size**; or

- double-click anywhere in the darker area of the ruler to open the Page Setup dialog box, and then click the **Paper** tab.

Paper size	Lists standard paper sizes such as Letter or Legal (used in North America), or A4 and B5 (used in other regions, such as Europe and Australia). You can also specify envelope sizes.
	To create a document of another size, click **Custom size** and type the horizontal and vertical measurements for custom paper, such as personalized note paper. The paper sizes described will vary depending on the printer installed on your system.
Paper source	Selects the tray that contains the paper you want to use for printing this document. Depending on the number of trays your printer offers, you may be able to use one paper tray for the first page, perhaps for letterhead, and a different tray filled with plain paper for subsequent pages in the document.
Preview	Displays a thumbnail preview of the way your document will look once it's printed. Use **Apply to** to indicate whether you want changes to apply to the entire document, the current section, selected text, or from this point forward.
Print Options	Set various options for how the printer(s) connected to your system will print documents. For example, you can choose to print the Document Properties or hidden text for a document.

Changing the Orientation

Orientation refers to the way the document will print on the page. **Portrait** refers to a vertical orientation, while **Landscape** refers to a horizontal orientation. To change the orientation for a document, use one of the following methods:

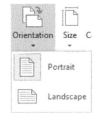

- On the Page Layout tab, in the Page Setup group, click **Orientation**; or

- double-click a darker area of the active ruler to open the Page Setup dialog box, click the **Margins** tab, and then select the orientation you want to use.

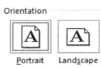

Changing Margins

Margins determine the amount of space between the edge of the paper and the area where the text is printed. You can adjust the margin settings for the entire document or for specific parts of the document.

You must be in Print Layout view in order for the arrows that adjust the margins to appear on the horizontal and vertical rulers. The Draft view does not include the vertical ruler.

The boundaries for the top and bottom margins are easy to see; they appear as the divider line between the lighter (inside margins) and darker (outside margins) shades on the ruler. When you position the mouse pointer at the divider line, a ScreenTip appears similar to those shown at the right:

The margin boundaries for the left and right margins appear on the top ruler, although the indent markers may obscure the left margin markers. You can access the left margin marker by pointing precisely between the Left Indent and First Line Indent markers. You can access the right margin marker by pointing above the Right Indent marker.

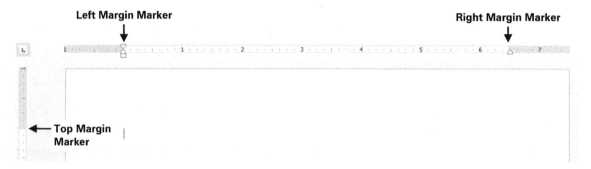

To change your margins, use one of the following methods:

- On the Page Layout tab, in the Page Setup group, click **Margins**; or

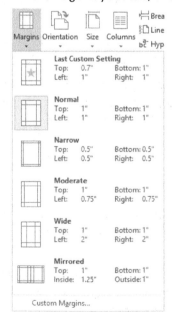

- to adjust the margins using the ruler, point the mouse pointer at the margin and, when the appropriate arrow appears, drag to the measurement you want for the margin; or

---

- double-click one of the darker areas of the horizontal or vertical ruler to open the Page Layout dialog box. Click the **Margins** tab, then set options in the Margins section.

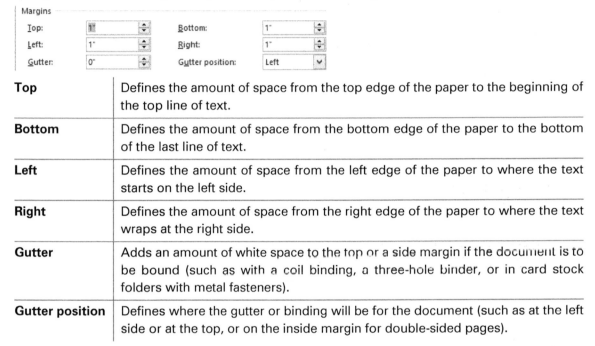

Top	Defines the amount of space from the top edge of the paper to the beginning of the top line of text.
Bottom	Defines the amount of space from the bottom edge of the paper to the bottom of the last line of text.
Left	Defines the amount of space from the left edge of the paper to where the text starts on the left side.
Right	Defines the amount of space from the right edge of the paper to where the text wraps at the right side.
Gutter	Adds an amount of white space to the top or a side margin if the document is to be bound (such as with a coil binding, a three-hole binder, or in card stock folders with metal fasteners).
Gutter position	Defines where the gutter or binding will be for the document (such as at the left side or at the top, or on the inside margin for double-sided pages).

Each method of changing the margins provides the flexibility to change some or all of the margins at the same time. The **Margins** command lists the most common measurements for margins, but you can also click **Custom Margins** to set different measurements. When using the Page Setup dialog box, you can set the measurements by typing them into the appropriate boxes or by clicking the up or down arrows at the right of each box to increase or decrease the measurements incrementally.

Inserting Page Breaks

When Word calculates the amount of text that will fill a page in your document, it inserts a *soft page break*—a break that occurs automatically. If you are in Draft view with non-printing characters set to display, a soft page break will be represented by a dotted line.

When you want to break a page at a specific location, you need to insert a *hard* or *manual page break*. This is preferable to pressing (Enter) continuously until you reach a new page, as any change in the text may require that you go back and change or remove these. A hard page break will break text in the same place, no matter what other changes you make. A hard page break displays with the break type in a dashed line whenever Show/Hide ¶ is active, regardless of the view mode.

Calling·All·Customers¶

If·you·haven't·had·a·chance·to·visit·our·Web·site·as·yet,·please·take·a·few·moments·now·to·check·and·update·your· account·with·us.·As·we·expand,·we·want·to·ensure·that·the·information·stays·current·and·accurate·so·we·can· include·you·in·all·our·new·offerings·and·services.·Click·here·to·check·your·account·with·us.¶

Share·Your·Adventures¶

Check·out·this·video·showing·a·customer·who·showed·us·how·much·fun·taking·your·bike·onto·the·beach·can·be.· This·was·taken·on·one·of·the·beaches·in·Perth—this·isn't·part·of·the·tour·but·the·customer·wanted·to·share·how· beautiful·the·sunset·is·while·having·a·different·bike·adventure·also!¶

·····················Page Break·····················¶

If·you·are·interested·in·sharing·videos·or·pictures·from·your·adventures,·please·let·Shauna·Adams·know.·You·can· reach·her·using·sadams@tolano.com,·or·call·her·using·our·new·toll-free·number,·1-888-555-1001.¶

To enter a manual or hard page break, use one of the following methods:

- On the **Insert** tab, in the **Pages** group, click **Page Break**; or
- press Ctrl + Enter ; or
- on the Page Layout tab, in the Page Setup group, click **Breaks**, and then click **Page**.

You can remove a manual page break in the same way as you would delete a text character.

Adding Page Numbering

You can add page numbers to a document at any time. The page number is automatically inserted into the footer, or the location in the bottom margin area where you insert items to repeat on every page. To insert page numbers into your document, on the Insert tab, in the Header & Footer group, click **Page Number**.

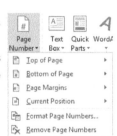

Top of Page	Displays possible positions from a gallery of top-of-page numbering options.
Bottom of Page	Displays possible positions from a gallery of bottom-of-page numbering options.
Page Margins	Displays possible positions from a gallery of margin numbering options.
Current Position	Displays numbering options (page number only, page # of #, and so on) to apply to the current page number location.
Format Page Numbers	Displays various numbering styles (1, 2, 3; i, ii, iii), as well as the option to begin numbering at a digit other than the number 1.

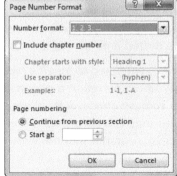

Applying Columns

Word allows you to set up newspaper-style columns in a document using the Columns feature. In a newspaper-style column, text from the bottom of one column flows to the top of the next; this makes it an ideal layout for documents such as newsletters and reports. The number of columns you create depends on factors such as paper size and orientation, font size, and document layout (for example, for print or the Web), as well as the column width and margins you choose.

You can apply columns to text before or after you type. You may find it easier to type and edit the text first, and then apply multiple columns formatting. Note that when you are working with multiple columns, Draft view will display the appropriate column widths but the columns will not display side by side; to view columns side by side, use Print Layout view.

To create columns, on the Page Layout tab, in the Page Setup group, click **Columns**.

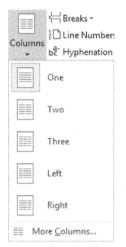

To set up additional options for the columns, click **More Columns**.

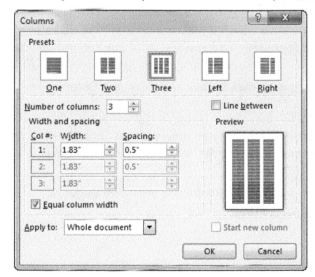

Presets	Offers options for a number of different column layouts. The **One**, **Two**, and **Three** options provide columns of equal width and are generally used for newspaper-style columns. The Left and Right column layouts are used for Web pages or for print publications with columns of uneven widths; for example, a software manual might be laid out with a wide column for body text and a narrow column or *sidebar* for additional tips or keywords that help you quickly find topics in the main text.
Number of columns	Provides incremental buttons you can use to set the number of columns you want.
Width and spacing	Alters the width and spacing between one column and the next. Use the **Equal column width** option to create columns of the same width; when this box is selected, only the options for column 1 will display, as any changes you make will affect the other columns equally.
Apply to	Identifies which text you want the column structure applied to; options include **Whole document**, **From this point forward**, and **Selected text**.
Line between	Inserts a vertical line between each of the columns in the document.
Start new column	Becomes available when you choose **From this point forward** in the **Apply to** field.

Once you have your columns set up, you can make a variety of changes to them. For example:

- To change the number of columns, select the text and use the **Columns** command to change the number.
- To insert or turn off vertical lines between each column, in the Columns dialog box, click **Line between**.
- To adjust column width or the spacing between columns, use the Columns dialog box or simply drag the appropriate markers in the ruler to adjust each side of a column.
- To apply indents to the text within columns, adjust that column's indent markers on the ruler.

If the text from one column to the next is breaking in a way that makes it difficult to read, you can insert a column break and force some text into the next column. To force text from one column into the next, use one of the following methods:

- On the Page Layout tab, in the Page Setup group, click **Breaks** and then click **Column**; or
- press (Ctrl)+(Shift)+(Enter).

Similarly, if your columns run across more than one page, you may want to control where the text breaks between pages to ensure that it makes sense to the reader. To force a page break in your column layout, use one of the following methods:

- On the Page Layout tab, in the Page Setup group, click **Breaks** and then click **Page**; or
- on the Insert tab, in the Pages group, click **Page Break**; or
- press (Ctrl)+(Enter).

Sometimes, you may need to change the column layout to more or fewer columns in the middle of a page. To have two different column layouts on a page, insert a Continuous section break between the two different layouts.

Note that when you change the column layout of a document, the entire document changes unless you specify otherwise. To change the column layout for only a portion of the document, select that portion of text and make the appropriate column layout change. Word automatically inserts the appropriate section breaks for this selection.

EXERCISE

In this exercise, you will change some settings for a document that will be turned into a flyer.

1. Open the *Newsletter S01* file and save as `Newsletter S01 2-fold brochure - Student`.

This document is a draft of the newsletter that will be sent to customers to update them on the company and our new offerings. You will now make changes to the portion of the document that will be printed on the inside of a two-fold brochure.

2. Click the Page Layout tab and in the Page Setup group, click **Orientation**. Then click **Landscape**.

The document is now set with a landscape orientation and as such, the content flows onto two pages instead of one (as it did when it was portrait orientation). Although a full paragraph sits on the next page, it is best to keep the information together when there is a small amount of data.

3. Click at the beginning of the heading *Share Your Adventures*. Then on the Page Layout tab, in the Page Setup group, click **Breaks** and then click **Page**.

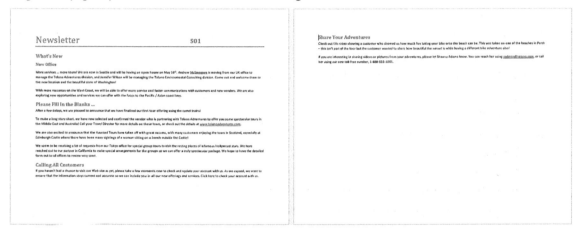

The entire heading and its paragraphs are now on the second page.

4. On the Home tab, in the Paragraph group, click **Show/Hide ¶** to turn on this feature so you can view the page break code.

> • Calling·All·Customers¶
> If·you·haven't·had·a·chance·to·visit·our·Web·site·as·yet,·please·take·a·few·mon
> ensure·that·the·information·stays·current·and·accurate·so·we·can·include·you·
>
> ············Page Break············¶

The page break code appears with the dash lines and the name of the break for quick reference. You can delete or move this code as if it were a text character.

Let's try changing the margins to see how the text flows for our brochure.

5. On the Page Layout tab, click Margins. Then click **Narrow**.

Notice how the document could fit on one page, which means you could delete the page break to reflow the text on one page.

6. Move the cursor to the beginning of the page break code and press ⌨(Delete). Also delete the extra blank line and then on the Home tab, in the Paragraph group, click **Show/Hide ¶** to turn this feature off.

Now that the text flows on one page, change the layout to use columns so that the text flows on what will become the inside page of the brochure.

7. On the Page Layout tab, click Columns and then click **Two**.

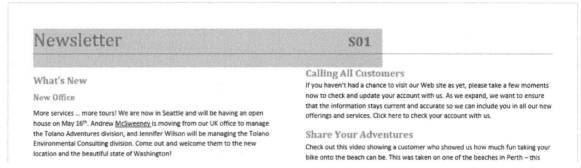

The document is now laid out in two columns but you may want the title to span across the entire page instead of just one column.

8. Select the Newsletter title line. Then on the Page Layout tab, click **Columns** and click **One**.

The title now spans across the two columns. You could manipulate the title to include pictures or align the text to suit the two-fold brochure.

9. Save and close this document.

Previewing and Printing the Document

IC³   **Exam 2 - Objective 1.1**

The Print feature allows you preview the document as it will appear when printed. This gives you an opportunity to review the document before you print or distribute it in order to discover if there are problems with the appearance or layout. You can also use some of the print options to adjust or change the margins or orientation, or display one or more pages at a time.

To preview or print a document, use one of the following methods:

- Click the **File** tab and click **Print**; or
- press (Ctrl)+(P).

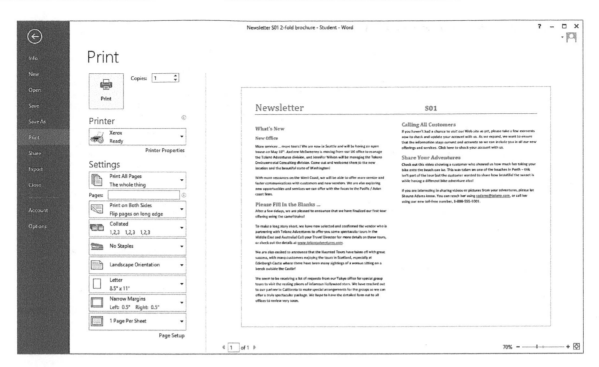

Use the options in the bottom to adjust the zoom of the document, as well as move between pages in the document, as applicable. Use the options in the middle panel to adjust items as needed for the document prior to printing.

Print	Print the document with the settings shown.
Copies	Enables you to specify the number of copies to be printed.
Printer	Select a printer from the list of installed printers. Use the **Printer Properties** link to choose options for how the output is printed, such as single- or double-sided, or color. Some of the options in the properties for your printer may also be available in specific print options.
Settings	Select how much of the document or which specific pages or items to print.

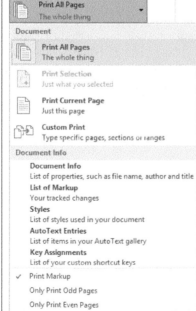

Alternatively, use the Pages: [   ] ⓘ field to enter specific pages to print:

\# - #   Print from one page to another, inclusive (for example 5-7)

\#,#,#   Print only the following pages (for example 3,7,10)

\- #   Print from page 1 to a specific page (for example 1-6)

\# -   Print from a specific page to the end of the document (for example 13-)

Print Sides	Specify whether to print on one or both sides of each sheet of paper.
	Print on Both Sides / Flip pages on long edge
	Print One Sided — Only print on one side of the page
	Print on Both Sides — Flip pages on long edge
	Print on Both Sides — Flip pages on short edge
	Manually Print on Both Sides — Reload paper when prompted to print the second side
Collated	If printing multiple copies, choose how each page is printed, for example a copy of the full document, or copies of each page individually.
	Collated — 1,2,3 1,2,3 1,2,3
	Collated — 1,2,3 1,2,3 1,2,3
	Uncollated — 1,1,1 2,2,2 3,3,3
Orientation	Choose which orientation should be used for printing this document.
	Landscape Orientation
	Portrait Orientation
	Landscape Orientation
Paper Size	Choose the paper size to use for printing this document.
	Postcard (148 x 200 mm) — 5.83" x 7.87"
	JIS B6 (128 x 182 mm) — 5.04" x 7.17"
	B6 (125 x 176 mm) — 4.92" x 6.93"
	SRA3 (320 x 450 mm) — 12.6" x 17.72"
	A4 Oversized (223 x 297 mm) — 8.78" x 11.69"
	215 x 315 mm — 8.47" x 12.4"
	C5 Envelope (162 x 229 mm) — 6.38" x 9.02"
	C4 Envelope (229 x 324 mm) — 9.02" x 12.76"
	Letter — 8.5" x 11"
	More Paper Sizes...
	Letter — 8.5" x 11"

Margins	Choose the margins to apply when printing this document.

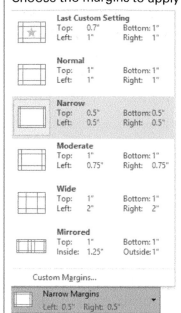

Pages per Sheet	Select the number of pages to print per sheet.

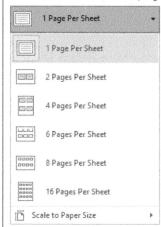

EXERCISE

In this exercise, you will practice using the Preview feature

1. Open the *TEC Corporate Profile* file. Then click **File** and **Print**.

2. Use the zoom bar at the bottom right corner to increase or decrease the zoom. Try clicking the ▬ and ➕ buttons to change the zoom.

3. Take a few moments to view the options for printing.

4. Click the **Back** button to return to the document.

5. Close the document without saving it.

Using Multimedia Files

 Exam 2 - Objective 1.4

Multimedia refers to any type of visual or audio content that you can insert into a document. These include photographs, clip art pictures, text boxes, charts, diagrams, videos, music, or object shapes. To insert a multimedia object into a document, click the **Insert** tab and then select the appropriate illustration type or use the **Object** command.

Any objects you insert will appear with eight handles when it is selected in the document, as shown in the following image. *Handles* are the small circles or squares that appear around the perimeter of the object; they confirm that the object has been selected and that you can now make changes to it. These handles may vary in appearance but always appear around the selected object.

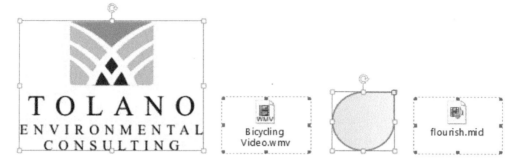

Inserting Images

You can add pictures to any document from sources such as digital photographs, graphics files, scanned images, or you can go online to find pictures on the Office.com site. Microsoft provides the facility to insert picture files in a wide variety of file formats; some commonly used formats are Windows Metafile (*.wmf), JPEG File Interchangeable format (*.jpg, *jpeg), Portable Network Graphics (*.png), Windows Bitmap (*.bmp), or Graphics Interchange format (*.gif).

To insert a picture, position the mouse pointer in the document where you want the picture to be placed, and then on the Insert tab, in the Illustrations group, click **Picture**.

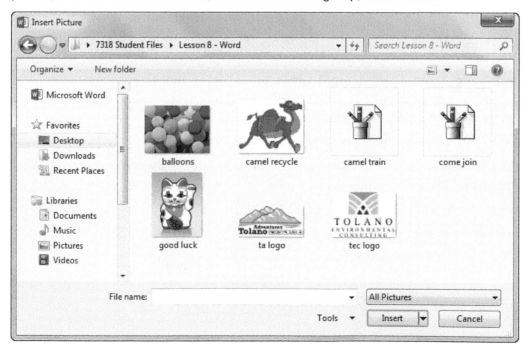

Word displays a dialog box to select the picture file, similar to opening a text file. Navigate to where the picture file is located, select it and then insert it into the document.

Microsoft provides a number of Clip Art graphics you can use in your documents. These are available online from the Office.com web site and can be downloaded to your computer. To insert Clip Art, position the mouse pointer where you want the graphic to be placed, and then on the Insert tab, in the Illustrations group, click **Online Pictures**.

Office.com Clip Art	Enter search criteria to find royalty-free images on the Office.com web site. Select an image from the search results page and then insert it into the document.
Bing Image Search	Allow Bing to search the web for matches to the search criteria you enter. It is your responsibility to ensure you are not violating copyright laws when you insert images returned in the search results page.

After a search has been conducted, the search results window displays images that match the criteria:

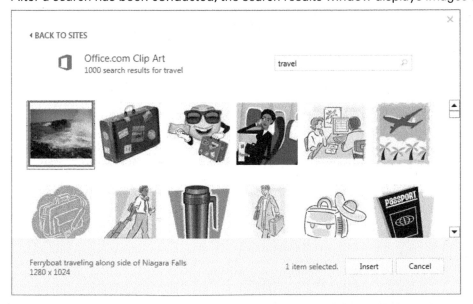

A brief summary of the currently selected image also appears at the lower left corner of the window.

To look at keywords you can use to narrow or expand the search, point at the image – a ScreenTip appears with some keywords for reference. This is useful when you want to search for other pictures that may be more appropriate for your document.

airliners, airplanes, computers, flights, jetliners, jets, laptop computers, online reservations, online travel planning, PCs, photographs, technology, transportation, travel, travel planning

- To enlarge the preview, click the  at the lower right corner of the image.

- To close this enlarged image preview, click the ｘ at the top right corner of the image.

- To insert the image, click the image and then click **Insert**.

If there is more than one image on the search results page that you would like to insert into the document, click the first image, hold down the Ctrl key and click on the required images. The images will be inserted into the current cursor location, but can then be moved to other parts of the document.

> **Hint:** You can also double-click the image or press Enter after selecting the image to insert it into the document.

To return to the search fields, click **Back to Sites** at the top of the search results page.

Using Bing to Search for Images

You can also use Bing to search the web for more images that match the search criteria.

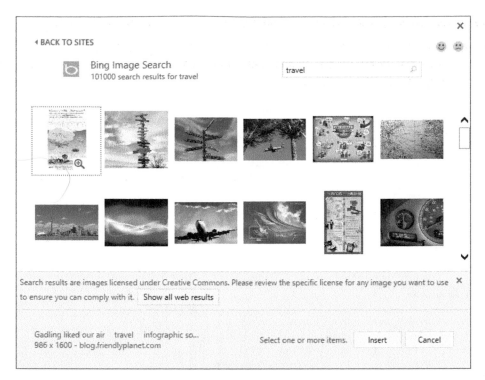

Notice that Microsoft displays a reminder about the use of the images displayed from the search criteria. If you agree to comply with the rules of Creative Commons, you can click **Show all web results** to view all the results for the search criteria.

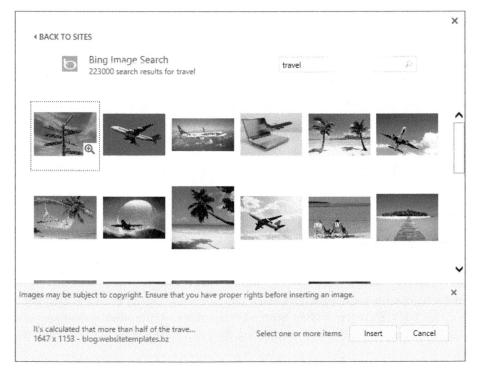

Clicking this link increases the number of results shown in the search results page and Microsoft displays another reminder that some pictures are copyrighted. The lower left corner displays the URL of the web site where you can find more information about the owner of this image.

Inserting Multimedia Objects

In addition to pictures, you can insert multimedia objects such as audio or video files. Inserting a multimedia object is effective when the document is viewed online, as the audience can click the file to view or listen to the content.

To insert an object, on the Insert tab, in the Text group, click **Object**.

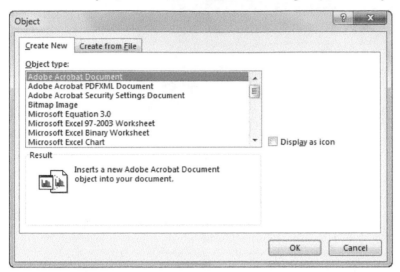

You can choose to create a new object using one of the programs in the list, or create (insert) the item using an existing file.

If you use this option, you can then specify whether the file should be set up as a link, which means any updates you make to the object in this document will automatically update the original file, for example sales figures for the quarter, or a slide from a presentation. Alternatively, you can specify to display the item as an icon only, indicating to the audience they can click it to view or hear the contents.

Manipulating Graphics

You can insert pictures into a document as *inline objects* (the default setting) or as *floating objects*.

- An inline object acts as a text character in a paragraph.
- A floating object can be placed anywhere (it floats) in the document.

Regardless of which way you insert a picture initially, you will be able to switch from inline to floating or vice versa, as you wish.

You must select a picture before you can manipulate it. Once selected, the picture displays the eight handles, as shown in the following:

Once you insert a picture, the **Picture Tools** ribbon appears and offers you a variety of ways to manipulate it.

Sizing a Picture

When you insert a picture into a document, it appears at its original size, or the largest size that the page will accommodate. You can resize or *scale* the picture to any proportions you want. You use the same method to size a picture whether it is inline or floating.

You can use the handles to size a picture:

- Vertically, by dragging the middle horizontal handle at the top or bottom edge in or out.
- Horizontally, by dragging the middle vertical handle at the left or right edge in or out.
- On two adjacent sides at once, by dragging one of the corner handles in or out.

If you want to ensure that your resized picture remains in proportion, press (Shift) before you drag the appropriate handle.

To enter precise measurements for the size of the picture, use the options in the **Size** group.

Cropping a Picture

Cropping refers to the ability to "cut off" certain portions of the picture. Using this feature, you can crop pictures horizontally (at the top or bottom) or vertically (at the sides); for more precise cropping, you must use a dedicated graphics program.

- When the Cropping feature is active, the cursor changes to ⊹.
- To crop the top or bottom of the picture, drag the top or bottom ▬.
- To crop the left or right side of the picture, drag the left or right ▎.
- To adjust two adjacent sides of a picture, drag one of the corners ⌊ (the angle displayed will change depending on which corner handle you select).
- You can crop the picture to a shape; however, the picture remains in its original form and you are able to move the picture within the shape to emphasize a specific area of the picture.

Rotating a Picture

You can rotate pictures by 90° at a time, or you can set the rotation to a specific angle. Each object rotates based on its center point. Note that not all images can be rotated. When you select an image, if there is a white circle at the top of the image you can rotate the picture to any angle required.

To rotate a picture, select it and then:

* Drag the white circular handle to rotate the object. When you point at the handle, Word displays a circular arrow to show this is the rotation direction. As you click the handle, it displays a circular motion on the symbol as a reminder, or

> **Note:** To rotate the object 15° at a time, press the (Shift) key as you drag the object.

* under Picture Tools, on the Format tab, in the Arrange group, click **Rotate**, or

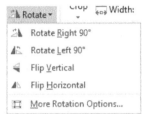

* under Picture Tools, on the Format tab, in the Arrange group, click **Rotate** and then **More Rotation Options**. In the Rotation area, enter the measurements for the rotation.

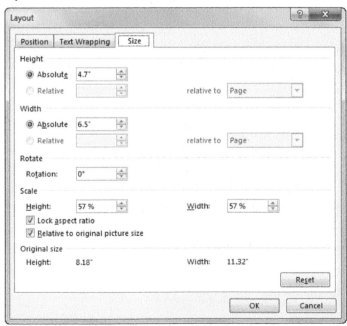

Wrapping Text Around a Picture

Wrapping styles affect the way the text flows around pictures and change the way pictures are positioned in relation to the surrounding text.

By default, the picture wrapping style is *In Line with Text*, which places the graphic at the insertion point on a line of text in the document. The graphic then moves with the text, so that if text is added before the graphic, the graphic moves down to make room for the new text.

Changing the wrapping style can give the document a completely different look and enables the picture to "float" or be positioned anywhere in the document. Word provides a number of tools to achieve this effect including a method that uses the most common types of layout for pictures in a document.

To change the text wrapping style for a picture object, after selecting the picture:

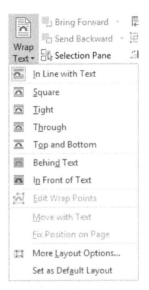

- Under Picture Tools, on the Format tab, in the Arrange group, click **Wrap Text** to choose the appropriate text wrapping style.

Each text wrapping style provides a different effect for the picture and the text in the document. Use the previews to see which text wrap style is suitable for the picture and the document. You can also use a combination of these methods to achieve the desired effect.

Changing the Properties for a Picture

The way a picture displays in a document depends on the picture's properties. You can adjust these properties to achieve the effect you want in the document. Some of these properties include:

- Adding or changing the line style, fill, or arrow options of the picture.
- Changing the size of the picture.
- Changing the layout of the picture in relation to the text, or having text *wrap* around the picture.
- Setting precise measurements for the position of the cropped picture in the document, or where the picture appears within the cropped area.
- Altering color options for the overall appearance of the picture.
- Changing options for the appearance of text in a text box.

Many properties can be modified using commands such as Wrap Text or Picture Effects on the Picture Tools Format ribbon or from an option with a drop-down list. Alternatively, you can use one of the following methods to display the appropriate dialog box for multiple changes:

- Click the picture and under Picture Tools, on the Format tab, click the **Format Shape** dialog box launcher; or
- right-click the picture and then click **Format Picture**.

 Fill & Line

Set options to adjust the fill or line of the selected object.

 Picture Effects

Choose from a variety of effects you can add to the selected object, such as shadow, reflection, glow, soft edges, 3-D format, 3-D rotation, or artistic effects.

 Layout & Properties

Choose options for any text that may appear in the selected object, such as a text box, or to add Alt Text to add global accessibility to this document.

 Picture

Choose options to correct or adjust the color or clarity of the picture. You can also select this option to crop the picture, as needed.

You can also click the ▦ **Layout & Properties** icon at the right of the picture to display the pull-out menu to quickly adjust the picture (the options displayed in this menu will vary with the type of picture or object that is selected). Once you click **See more**, you will see the Format Picture pane, as shown above.

Moving a Picture

The drag-and-drop method is the easiest way to move a picture. However, take note of whether the picture is inline or floating before you try to move it, as this determines how and where you can move the picture:

- If it is an inline object, the mouse pointer displays as ▨ when you drag it.

- If it is a floating object, the mouse pointer displays as ⁂ when you drag it.

EXERCISE

In this exercise, you will add pictures to a document and then manipulate the graphics. This exercise uses pictures available at the Office.com Web site. The pictures that you will insert into documents are also included in the student data files folder in case you do not have access to the Internet. If these pictures are not available to you, insert any image you have available.

1. Open the *Newsletter S01* file and save it as `Newsletter S01 - Student`.

2. Click at the beginning of the first paragraph of text, starting with *More services ...*

3. Click the Insert tab and in the Illustrations group, click **Pictures**.

4. Navigate to the student data files location and then select the **come join** file and then click **Insert** to insert the picture.

What's New

New Office

house on May 16th. Andrew McSweeney is mo

A new tools group called Picture Tools appears on the ribbon. Use the options in Picture Tools to manipulate pictures.

5. Under Picture Tools, on the Format tab in the Arrange group, click **Wrap Text** and click **Tight**.

6. Position the mouse cursor anywhere inside the picture and drag it to the right side of the paragraph.

Newsletter
S01

What's New

New Office

More services ... more tours! We are now in Seattle and will be having an open house on May 16th. Andrew McSweeney is moving from our UK office to manage the Tolano Adventures division, and Jennifer Wilson will be managing the Tolano Environmental Consulting division. Come out and welcome them to the new location and the beautiful state of Washington!

With more resources on the West Coast, we will be able to offer more service and faster communications with customers and new vendors. We are also exploring new opportunities and services we can offer with the focus to

Notice as you drag the picture that Word displays guides to assist you in placing the picture based on the existing margins – in this case, at the right of the paragraph and aligns with the top of the paragraph.

7. Position the mouse cursor on the bottom left corner of the picture and drag the handle to re-size it to approximately one half of its original size. Make sure the right edge of the picture is close to the right margin.

8. Move the picture to align it your preference.

   Your document should then appear similar to the following:

   New Office

   More services ... more tours! We are now in Seattle and will be having an open house on May 16th. Andrew McSweeney is moving from our UK office to manage the Tolano Adventures division, and Jennifer Wilson will be managing the Tolano Environmental Consulting division. Come out and welcome them to the new location and the beautiful state of Washington!

   With more resources on the West Coast, we will be able to offer more service and faster communications with customers and new vendors. We are also exploring new opportunities and services we can offer with the focus to the Pacific / Asian coast lines.

9. Click at the beginning of the second paragraph under *Please Fill In ....*

10. Click the Insert tab, and in the Illustrations group, click **Online Pictures**.

11. In the Search Office.com field, type: `camel` and then click the Search icon.

12. Scroll through the pictures and then click one of your choice and click **Insert**.

13. Under Picture Tools, on the Format tab in the Arrange group, click **Wrap Text** and then click **Square**.

14. Using one of the corner handles, resize the picture so it is approximately the same height as the paragraph. Move the picture as necessary to position the picture (if preferred, you can make the picture bigger and then place the picture between the two paragraphs, as shown in the following example):

   Please Fill In the Blanks ...

   After a few delays, we are pleased to announce that we have finalized our first tour offering using the camel trains!

    make a long story short, we have now selected and confirmed the vendor who is partnering with Tolano Adventures to offer you some spectacular tours in the Middle East and Australia! Call your Travel Director for more details on these tours, or check out the details at www.tolanoadventures.com.

   We are also excited to announce that the Haunted Tours have taken off with great success, with many customers

15. Click the white circular handle for the camel picture and rotate it slightly to make it appear as if the camel is walking up hill.

   Please Fill In the Blanks ...

   After a few delays, we are pleased to announce that we have fir

    Take a long story short, we have now se with Tolano Adventures to offer you some s Call your Travel Director for more details or www.tolanoadventures.com.

   We are also excited to announce that the Haunted Tours have t

16. Move the cursor to the beginning of the last paragraph in the newsletter and click the Insert tab, then in the Text group, click **Object**.

17. Click the **Create from File** tab and then click **Browse**.

18. Navigate to the student data files location and then select the **Bicycling Video** file. Click **Insert** and then click **OK**. Click away from the object to view it on the page.

Share Your Adventures

Check out this video showing a customer who
This was taken on one of the beaches in Perth
beautiful the sunset is while having a different

Bicycling Video.wmv

Notice how the document is now two pages. If you were preparing a newsletter for actual distribution, you would need to decide how you want the newsletter to look. For instance, if this is all the text that will be entered for the newsletter, you may want to resize the pictures or change the text size until the document is only one page. On the other hand, even if there will be no more text, you can add pictures or other formatting options to stretch the newsletter onto two pages.

19. Decide how you want to modify your newsletter. If you choose to add more pictures, be sure to move and resize them accordingly to best suit the layout of the newsletter.

20. Save and close the document.

Using Tables

 Exam 2 - Objective 1.1, 2.1

Use the Table feature to arrange columns of text and numbers, group paragraphs side by side, or create forms. Each horizontal line in a table is a row, each vertical block is a column, and the intersection of each row and column is a cell. When working with a table, you are working with cells within the table. You can create a table before or after you type the text.

You can enter text, numbers or graphics into each cell. Text longer than the width of the cell will automatically wrap to the next line in the same cell. End of cell markers display by default to make it easier to see where you are working in the table. To show or hide markers, on the Home tab, in the Paragraph group, click ¶ **(Show/Hide¶)**.

You create a table based on the default settings. You can apply many design features to a table. Design the overall appearance and layout of the table first; then make detailed adjustments later. By default, Word adds a single line border to the table, but you can adjust this as required.

You can apply alignment and formatting to the cell contents, as well as to the cell itself, merge adjacent cells horizontally or vertically, and rotate text in a cell by 90 degrees.

Use the ⊞ **(Table Selector)** to select the entire table; it appears at the top left corner of a table when your cursor is in or near the table.

Once you create a table, the Table Tools ribbon appears providing further options for the design or layout of the table:

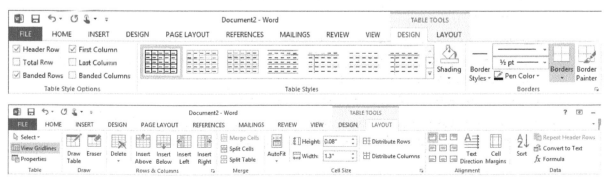

Inserting a Table

Use the **Insert Table** command when you want to create a simple table with even column widths and row heights. You can adjust these at any time during or after text entry.

To insert a table, use one of the following methods:

┌─────────────┐
╎ **MMM**   ╎
╎ A New   ╎
╎ Addition   ╎
└─────────────┘

- On the Insert tab, in the Tables group, click **Table**.

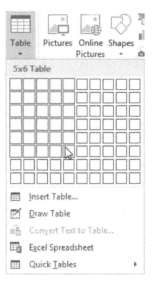

In the drop-down menu, position your mouse pointer over the box in the upper left corner and begin dragging across, down, or diagonally over the grid to specify the number of columns and rows you want. As you drag, Word will display the number of columns and rows for reference in the title area of this list. Use this feature to create a table of up to 10 columns by 8 rows.

- If you need a table larger than 8×10, use the **Insert Table** feature. You can also use this feature to display a dialog box with more options:

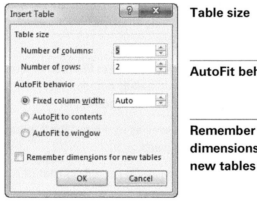

Table size	Enter the number of columns and rows by typing the number into the box or using the incremental buttons.
AutoFit behavior	Selects options for specifying an exact cell size or adjusting cell size to accommodate contents.
Remember dimensions for new tables	Remembers the options you've selected as the default settings for all new tables you create. You can adjust column widths or row heights as needed after the table is created.

Once you create a table layout, Word places the insertion point in the first cell of the table for you to begin typing. You can use the following methods to move within a table:

- Press (Enter) to add more lines of text in the same cell. This will increase the row height.
- Use the arrow keys to move through the text in the cell.
- Use the (Tab) key to jump forward to the next cell.
- Use the (Shift) + (Tab) combination to jump backward to the previous cell.
- Press (Ctrl) + (Tab) to insert a tab character.

Selecting Items in the Table

To make changes to anything in the table, you must first select it. Following are shortcuts for selecting several items at once:

- To select an entire column, click at the top of the column when you see ↓.
- To select an entire row, click in the selection bar for the row.
- To select multiple columns or rows, click and drag across the columns or rows.
- To select one cell, move the cursor to the left border of that cell and then click when you see ↗.
- To select multiple adjacent cells, click and drag across those cells.

Formatting the Table

You can format the text in a table in the same manner as you format regular text. You can also apply formatting options to the entire table or parts of it.

You may find it easier to format or adjust items once there is text in the table, especially if there are large pieces of text. Having the text in the cells will help you determine the best width for columns, styles for headings and titles, and so on.

Many of the formatting options you will be introduced to shortly are accessible from one of the tabs in the Table Tools ribbon. You can also right-click selected cells, rows or columns to display a shortcut menu for more options. On occasion you may find that a formatting feature is also available from the Home tab, such as borders.

Modifying the Borders and Shading

When Word creates a table for the first time, the table appears with single line borders around every cell. You can modify these lines to display different colors, styles, and widths, or to not show at all. You can also modify the lines or borders for specific cells. Under Table Tools, on the Design tab, in the Borders group, click the arrow for **Borders**.

You can also change the look of your table by adding shading to the cells. Under Table Tools, on the Design tab, in the Table Styles group, click the arrow for **Shading**.

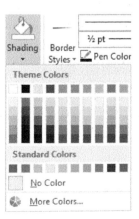

In addition to changing the colors of your borders, you can modify the properties using features in the **Borders** group. For instance, you can select a color for the border and then draw the border in the table, or change the border color and then draw over an existing line to change the color for that border. Under Table Tools, on the Design tab, in the Borders group, click the appropriate option to draw borders in the table.

> **Note:** You can also use the Borders or Shading feature on the **Home** tab, in the **Paragraph** group.

Changing the Alignment

Table alignment refers to the position of the table relative to the left and right margins of the document. You can also change the alignment of text vertically within the table.

To change the alignment for the table, under Table Tools, on the Layout tab, in the Table group, click **Properties** and click the desired alignment from options in the **Table** tab.

To change the vertical alignment of text in the table, select the cells and then under Table Tools, on the Layout tab, in the Alignment group, click the appropriate alignment option.

To change the horizontal alignment of text in the table, select the cells and then on the Home tab, in the Paragraph group, click the appropriate alignment option.

Inserting & Deleting Rows/Columns/Cells

You can insert additional rows and columns into a table after you have created it. New rows may be inserted above or below the current row location; new columns may be inserted to the left or right of the current column. You can insert rows, columns, or cells individually or several at a time by selecting the appropriate number of units in the table first before activating the Insert tab.

- To insert a single row or column, position the mouse pointer where you want the new row or column inserted. Under Table Tools, on the Layout tab, in the Rows & Columns group, click the appropriate option.

Cells can also be inserted into specific locations of the table. Use caution with this option as you can change the structure of your table quickly if you select the wrong option. In some cases, it may be easier to split or merge cells and modify the text instead of inserting or deleting individual cells.

- To insert cells, under Table Tools, on the Layout tab, in the Rows & Columns group, click the **Table Insert Cells** dialog box launcher.

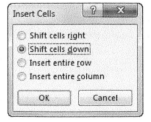

- To delete cells, rows, columns, or an entire table, under Table Tools, on the Layout tab, in the Rows & Columns group, click the arrow for **Delete** and then the appropriate option.

- To delete specific individual cells, under Table Tools, on the Layout tab, in the Rows & Columns group, click the arrow for **Delete**, click **Delete Cells**, and then click the appropriate option.

Adjusting the Width or Height

You can adjust the width of each column, the height of each row, and the overall alignment of your table. You can also evenly space selected rows or columns in a table.

Use one of the following methods to adjust the column width or row height:

- Under Table Tools, on the Layout tab, in the Table group, click **Properties**, then click the appropriate tab for the item to adjust; or
- under Table Tools, on the Layout tab, in the Cell Size group, click the incremental buttons or type a measurement to change the **Height** or **Width** accordingly; or
- place the mouse pointer on a vertical line on either side of the column to adjust and, when you see ⁺‖⁺, drag left or right to the desired column width; or
- place the mouse pointer on a horizontal line for the row to adjust and, when you see ⁜, drag up or down to the desired row height; or
- click the ▦ in the ruler for the column to be adjusted and drag it to the desired width.

To distribute the width for each column or height of each row evenly, use one of the following methods:

- Under Table Tools, on the Layout tab, in the Cell Size group, click ⊞ Distribute Rows or ⊞ Distribute Columns ; or
- under Table Tools, on the Layout tab, in the Cell Size group, click **AutoFit**.

Merging and Splitting Cells

Table cells can be merged to create a single cell, or a cell can be split into multiple columns or rows. Merging cells is particularly useful when creating a title row for your table. To merge cells, select the cells and then under Table Tools, on the Layout tab, in the Merge group, click **Merge Cells**.

To split a cell into multiple cells, select the cell and then under Table Tools, on the Layout tab, in the Merge group, click **Split Cells**. Specify the appropriate number of columns and rows, then click OK.

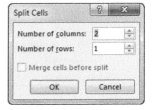

EXERCISE

In this exercise you will create a simple table to record some expenses for the new office. You will then format the table.

1. Press `Ctrl`+`N` to create a new blank document. Then click the **Insert** tab, and in the Tables group, click **Table**.

2. Starting at the top left box in the grid, drag over to select **4 columns** and then down to select **5 rows**. When the correct number of columns and rows has been selected, click to insert the new table into the document.

   You should now have a table similar to the following:

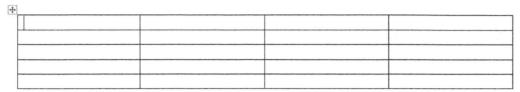

3. Ensure the mouse cursor is in the first box (cell) at the top left corner of the new table. Type: `Expenses` and then press `Tab`.

4. Type: `Actual` and press `Tab`. Type: `Quote` and press `Tab`. Type: `Budget` for the last column and press `Tab`.

   The mouse cursor should now be in the first cell of the second row.

5. Enter text for the rest of the table as shown:

Expenses	Actual	Quote	Budget
Rent	1500	1500	1500
Utilities	375	350	400
Office Supplies	750	700	1000
Furniture	2500	2550	3000

6. At the end of the 3000, press `Tab`.

   You have just inserted a new row in the table for another expense item.

7. Type: `Parking`, press `Tab`, type: `200`, press `Tab`, type: `150`, press `Tab`, and type: `400`.

8. Save the file as `First Month Expenses - Student`.

Now try changing the appearance of the table data by using some simple formatting attributes.

9. Move the mouse cursor to the Selection bar directly to the left of the first row where the column headings are. Click to select the entire row.

10. Press `Ctrl`+`B` to apply the bold attribute to the selected text.

11. Move the mouse cursor to above the Actual column. When you see ↓, click and drag to select the three columns (Actual to Budget).

12. On the Home tab, in the Paragraph group, click **Align Right**.

Expenses	Actual	Quote	Budget
Rent	1500	1500	1500
Utilities	375	350	400
Office Supplies	750	700	1000
Furniture	2500	2550	3000
Parking	200	150	400

13. Position the mouse cursor on the vertical line between the Expenses and Actual columns. When you see ◄‖►, click and drag the line approximately five characters to the right.

   The width of the Actual column is now smaller than the other two columns. This allows for longer text entries in the Expenses column, as required.

14. Ensure all three columns are selected and then under Table Tools, click the **Layout** tab and in the Cell Size group, click **Distribute Columns** to resize the selected columns evenly.

Expenses	Actual	Quote	Budget
Rent	1500	1500	1500
Utilities	375	350	400
Office Supplies	750	700	1000
Furniture	2500	2550	3000
Parking	200	150	400

15. Save the document again.

Organizing Table Lists

You can organize or sort information in a table format in ascending (for example, A-Z or 0-9) or descending (for example, Z-A or 9-0) order. The type of data determines the type of sort that is required to achieve the order you want. For example, you may want to sort a list of names alphabetically by the last name but you notice the list contains people with the same last name. You could sort the data first in ascending order by the last name, and then in ascending order by first name. In cases where you use more than one field (column) to determine the sort order, the first field you sort by is referred to as the primary sort key, the second field is the secondary sort key, and so on. In the example cited, the last name field would be the primary sort key, and the first name field would be the secondary sort key.

You can activate the Sort command quickly by selecting the cells (or table) and then using one of the following methods:

- Under Table Tools, on the Layout tab, in the Data group, click **Sort**; or

- on the Home tab, in the Paragraph group, click ↓ₐ𝓏 **(Sort)**.

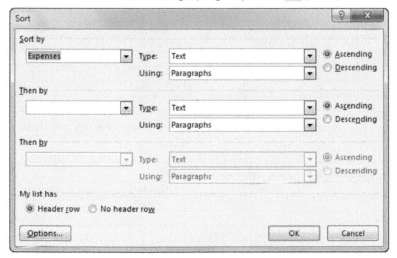

Sort by	Selects the column that will serve as the primary sort key and determines the type of content to be sorted.
Then by	Selects the secondary and tertiary sort keys, if applicable.
My list has	Indicates whether you have a row of column headings; this prevents the column title row from being included in the sort.

EXERCISE

In this exercise you will sort the data in the expenses report by different criteria.

1.   Ensure the *First Month Expenses – Student* document is active and that the mouse cursor is in the row with the column headings.

2.   Under Table Tools, on the Layout tab and in the Data group, click **Sort**.

3.   Click the arrow for the **Sort by** field and click **Actual**. Leave the other options as is. Click **OK**.

     The table items should now be sorted by the smallest to largest figures in the Actual column, allowing you to easily determine which items cost the least and which cost the most.

4.   On the Layout tab, click **Sort** again.

5.   Click the arrow for **Sort by** and change this to **Expenses**.

6.   Click the arrow for **Then by** and click **Budget**. Click **OK**.

Expenses	Actual	Quote	Budget
Furniture	2500	2550	3000
Office Supplies	750	700	1000
Parking	200	150	400
Rent	1500	1500	1500
Utilities	375	350	400

Notice this time the table is sorted by the expense type alphabetically and then by the budget figure. If there had been two expense items with the same label, Word would have then sorted these by the smallest to largest figure.

Now add a title to the table.

7.   Click anywhere in the first row (column headings). Under Table Tools, on the Layout tab and in the Rows & Columns group, click **Insert Above**.

8.   With the row still selected, in the **Merge** group, click **Merge Cells**.

Expenses	**Actual**	**Quote**	**Budget**
Furniture	2500	2550	3000
Office Supplies	750	700	1000
Parking	200	150	400
Rent	1500	1500	1500
Utilities	375	350	400

9.   Type: `New Office - First Month Expenses`. Select the title and change the size to **14**. Center the text in the row.

New Office – First Month Expenses			
Expenses	**Actual**	**Quote**	**Budget**
Furniture	2500	2550	3000
Office Supplies	750	700	1000
Parking	200	150	400
Rent	1500	1500	1500
Utilities	375	350	400

10. Save and close the document.

Working with Comments

 Exam 2 - Objective 6.1

Comments are similar to sticky notes and can be set to display in balloon objects, within the document, or in the Reviewing Pane. Comments display on screen and by default, will also print with your document, unless you specify otherwise. Use comments when you want to make a suggestion to change something in the content of the document. This feature is often used when you are reviewing a shared document with others.

When reviewing comments, you can choose to hide or display them on the screen. You can also record your own audio comment and insert it into the document.

Take note of the following when using comments:

- To insert a comment, on the Review tab, in the Comments group, click **New Comment**.

- To navigate backward and forward through comments in a document, on the Review tab, in the Comments group, click **Previous** or **Next**.

- To delete a comment, use one of the following methods:

  - On the Review tab, in the Comments group, click **Delete**; or

  - on the Review tab, in the Changes group, click **Reject and Move to Next**.

- To see all the comments or changes in a separate window, on the Review tab, in the Tracking group, click the arrow for Reviewing Pane ▾ , and then:

  - Click **Reviewing Pane Vertical** to open a window at the left side of the screen; or

  - click **Reviewing Pane Horizontal** to open a window at the bottom of the screen.

  You can then navigate through all the comments and other markups in the document.

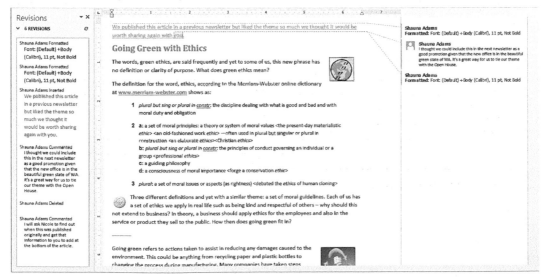

You can print the markup items in the document as part of the document or as a separate list. Click the **File** tab, click **Print**, and click the **Print All Pages** field to choose **List of Markup**.

Tracking Changes

When you want others to review a document and yet still want to maintain control over the final changes, distribute copies to others with the **Track Changes** feature activated. The Track Changes feature "keeps track" of edits made by other people and highlights them for you when you review the documents after others have made their changes. You can also track your own changes in a document.

- You can view tracked changes in a variety of formats, including balloons to the right of the text, a reviewing pane to the left of or below the text, or with a line through deleted text in the body of the document, depending on what you find most readable.

- If a document has been reviewed by several different individuals, you can distinguish one person's changes from another's by displaying each person's changes in a different color.

- You can combine comments and changes made separately by different reviewers and then accept the changes you want to keep and reject the changes that you do not want.

- You can password-protect your document so that only certain people can make changes, restrict the type of changes reviewers can make, or ensure that no changes can be made to a document at all once it's been finalized.

To turn on Track Changes, use one of the following methods:

- On the Review tab, in the Tracking group, click **Track Changes**; or
- press (Ctrl)+(Shift)+(E).

In a document that contains tracked changes, Word will move to the next change or comment once you accept or reject a change:

- To accept a change, click the change and then on the Review tab, in the Changes group, click **Accept** or **Accept and Move to Next**.

- To accept all changes in the document, click the arrow for **Accept** and then **Accept All Changes** or **Accept All Changes and Stop Tracking**.

- To reject a change, click the change and then **Reject** or **Reject and Move to Next**

- To reject all changes in the document, click the arrow for **Reject** and then **Reject All Changes** or **Reject All Changes and Stop Tracking**.

To show all marked items in a document, on the Review tab, in the Tracking group, click ⊟ Show Markup ▾ to select which options to display:

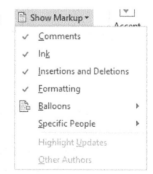

Use the Reviewing Pane if you find viewing all the balloons on screen too distracting. Be aware of the following when working with the Reviewing Pane:

- Make changes or insertions as if the Reviewing Pane were not there. When you make a change to the document, it will be inserted in the Reviewing Pane automatically in the appropriate location.

- Control what displays on screen by clicking the arrow for the ▦ All Markup ▾ **(Display for Review)** button. If you select **No Markup**, then the tracked changes are hidden and applied (as if you had accepted them) to the screen output. If you select **Show All**, the tracked changes are displayed.
- To delete an item in the Reviewing Pane, click on the heading for that item and then click **Reject**.

Be sure to turn off the Track Changes option when you no longer need it.

EXERCISE

In this exercise, you will work with documents marked with changes and comments.

1. Open the *Going Green with Ethics* document and save it as Going Green with Ethics - Student.

2. Click the **Review** tab and in the Changes group, ensure **Track Changes** is active. Then in the Tracking group, click the **Reviewing Pane** button for the default vertical display.

3. Scroll through some of the changes in the pane.

   Using this view allows you to see what all the comments or changes are without having to scroll through the individual pages of the document.

4. In the Changes group, click **Next** to have Word highlight the first change for you.

5. In the Changes group, click **Accept** to accept the text entered by Shauna Adams.

6. In the Changes group, click **Accept** for the formatting change.

7. Read the comment and then in the **Comments** group, click **Delete** to remove the comment.

8. Continue accepting or rejecting the changes as you see fit.

   When you have reviewed the entire document, you should notice that you may still need to make some final changes to the document, such as removing the blank line in the middle of the document. If the document is final, be sure to turn the Tracked Changes option off before you delete this blank line. Otherwise, it will be considered another change to track for others to see.

9. In the Changes group, click **Track Changes** to turn the feature off.

10. You can delete the last comment, if required.

11. Save and close the document.

Now view a document that has been reviewed by more than one person.

12. Open the *Resume for Elinor Eng* and save it as Resume for Elinor Eng - Student.

13. Scroll through the document to read the comments and notice how the colors vary when the author changes (from Andrew McSweeney to Nick Klassen).

   When you share a document with others, they can add their own comments, and you will see each reviewer's comments displayed in a different color. This helps you determine who suggested a change as well as the type of change, such as formatting, or edited text).

14. Move to the top of the document if not already there. Click the **Review** tab and in the Comments group, click **New Comment**.

   You should notice that the color changed immediately to indicate you are a different author on this document.

15. Type: I'm very enthusiastic about interviewing this candidate. When do you think we can set this up? as the comment.

16. Save and close the document.

Lesson Summary

In this lesson you learned some of the basic skills required to create simple documents. You should now be familiar with how to:

- ☑ enter and edit text
- ☑ move around in the document
- ☑ create new, save, close and open files
- ☑ select specific types of text
- ☑ change the view mode

- ☑ format text, paragraphs, or the page
- ☑ organize data
- ☑ work with pictures in a document
- ☑ track changes and comments in a document

Review Questions

1. When you see ¶, what does this symbol indicate?
   a.   You pressed Enter.
   b.   You pressed Tab.
   c.   Word has applied word wrap on the text in the paragraph.
   d.   This symbol appears automatically when you create a new document.

2. To select an entire line of text, which method could you use?
   a.   Click and drag across the line of text.
   b.   Click at the left of the line of text in the Selection Bar.
   c.   Press Ctrl and then click in the line of text.
   d.   Double-click on the line of text.
   e.   Any of the above
   f.   a or b

3. Which of the following view modes allows you to see how a document will appear when it is printed?
   a.   [image]   c.   [image]
   b.   [image]

4. Which of the following alignment buttons would you use to center text?

a. 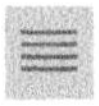   c.

b.   d.

MMM
Go online for
Additional
Review

5. Where are the margin boundaries on the ruler?
a. In the dark areas of the ruler.
b. At the divider line between the light and dark areas of the ruler.
c. At the far edge of left and right side of the ruler.
d. Underneath the indent markers in the light area of the ruler.

6. To insert a page break manually, you would:
a. Press (Shift)+(Enter).
b. Press (Ctrl)+(Enter).
c. Press (Enter) until you arrive at a new page.
d. On the Insert tab, in the Pages group, click Page Break.
e. Any of the above
f. b or d

7. How can you activate the Replace feature?
a. On the Home tab, in the Editing group, click Replace.
b. Press (Ctrl)+(H).
c. Double-click anywhere on the status bar and then select Replace.
d. Any of the above
e. a or b

8. A benefit of using styles to format a document is:
a. Changes to formatting are reflected automatically once they have been made in the style.
b. Styles ensure a consistent look throughout your document.
c. You can apply styles to any text in the document.
d. Any of the above
e. b or c

9. What types of pictures can be inserted into a Word document?
a. Clip art images   d. Any of the above
b. Photographs   e. a or b
c. Scanned images

10. To insert a video file you saved on your hard drive into a document, which command would you use?
a. Insert Clip Art   c. Insert Shape
b. Insert Picture   d. Insert Object

11. Which key would you press to create a new row when you are in the last cell of a table?
a. (Enter)
b. (Tab)
c. (Spacebar)
d. There is no quick method to create a new row using a key.

12. How does Word distinguish different reviewers who have suggested changes in your document?
a. Word automatically creates a new file to show changes from each reviewer.
b. The author names appear in the Reviewing Pane only.
c. Each reviewer's comments or changes appear in different colors.
d. There is no difference other than the text in the comment or suggested change.

Lesson 9: Microsoft Excel

Lesson Objectives

In this lesson you will be introduced to the basic skills for working with a spreadsheet application. You will learn to enter and format text and formulas, navigate and manage worksheets, filter and sort data, create and modify charts and set printing options. When you have completed this lesson, you will be familiar with:

- ☐ adding or changing numbers and labels
- ☐ entering simple formulas
- ☐ managing worksheets
- ☐ formatting data

- ☐ sorting or filtering data
- ☐ creating and manipulating charts
- ☐ customizing the page setup

Understanding Basic Terminology

 Exam 2 - Objective 3.1

An Excel worksheet is similar to a very large sheet of paper divided into rows and columns. Rows are numbered from 1 to 1,048,576; columns are assigned letters or letter combinations from A to Z, and then AA to ZZ, then AAA to AZZ, and so on up to XFD.

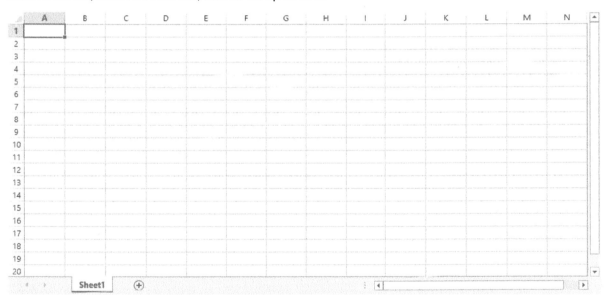

Workbook	A single Excel file containing one or more worksheets (Sheet1, Sheet2, Sheet3).
Worksheet	A single report or tab in a workbook; by default each new workbook includes only one worksheet but you can quickly add new worksheets as needed.
Cell	The intersection of a row and a column; can contain one single value (text or number), or formula.
Cell Address	The column-by-row intersection designated by the column letter and the row number, such as A1 in the figure above.
Active Cell	The cell currently displayed with a thick border, such as cell A1 in the figure above.

As discussed previously, worksheets are used whenever you need a report or document that tracks numerical information. Typical reports include budgets, cash flow analysis reports, revenue and expense reports, financial reports, an inventory analysis, or a document tracking data such as employee vacation time or student grades.

Organize the information on the worksheet in a way that will be clear to you and to anyone else who may be using or analyzing the content. Include appropriate labels and descriptions in the reports so the audience understands what they are viewing. As there are a large number of rows and columns available, you can structure your report to show individual data blocks. For example, you may want to set up an inventory report to track stock levels that change every month, but you may also want to view a two-year period at one time. To do this, you can set up columns to show levels for each of 24 months with each row representing an individual inventory item. You can also hide every month except the last six months of the previous year, or use a filter command to display information about specific inventory items.

You can use design elements to emphasize data areas such as labels, increases in sales or expenses, profit margins, highest or lowest grade, and so on. However, use discretion with design elements to ensure the report does not become difficult to read. Too much color and shading may be hard to read if it is printed on a black and white printer.

Managing Workbooks

 Exam 2 - Objective 1.3, 3.1

As you begin using workbooks and individual worksheets to generate reports, you need to understand basic file management to enable you to use the files again, such as save a file, open a file, create a new file from a template, close the file or open another file.

Creating a New Blank Workbook

When you start Excel, the Backstage view appears so you can create a new workbook or open an existing one. If you create a new blank workbook, it is automatically named Book1. Each time you create a new workbook during the same session, Excel will number it sequentially as Book2, Book3, and so on. When you exit Excel and start it later, the numbering begins at 1.

To create a new blank workbook, use one of the following methods:

- Click the **File** tab, click **New**, and double-click **Blank workbook**; or
- press (Ctrl)+(N).

Creating a New Workbook from a Template

You can create a workbook using a template or pre-designed workbook provided by Microsoft. This provides a consistent look for specific types of reports. The number of templates on your screen may vary, depending on what has been previously installed and on what is currently available from online Web sites.

To create a new workbook using a template, click the **File** tab, and click **New**.

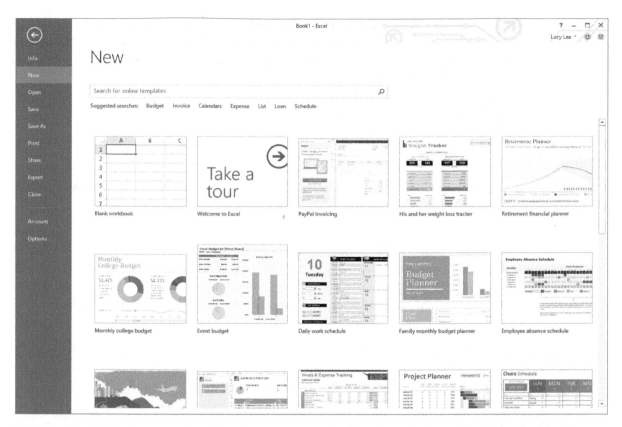

You can then click the type of workbook you want to display a larger view of the file contents.

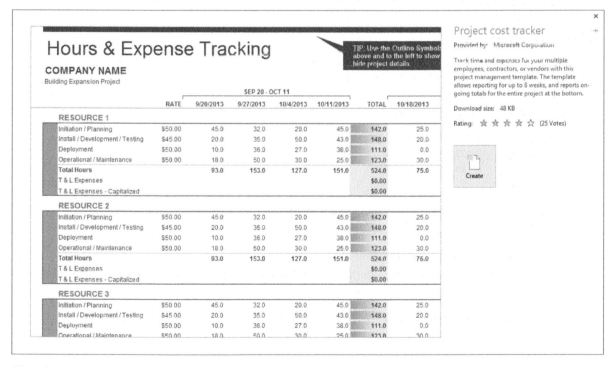

Click **Create** to have Excel create a new workbook based on the selected template. Alternatively, click the arrow at either side of the template to view other templates in the list on either side of this template. To exit the preview option, click the ✖ at the top right corner of the preview window.

You can also click one of the categories listed under the search field if there is a particular type of workbook you want to use from these categories. As noted, you can enter criteria in the search field to have Excel look for a specific type of workbook.

Entering Data in the Worksheet

You can insert three types of data into worksheet cells:

Labels	Text entries appear in the cells exactly as you enter them; default to left aligned.
Values	Numeric values; default to right aligned.
Formulas	Composed of cell references, arithmetic operators, and functions (calculation commands) that perform operations on data.

Entering these types of data into a single workbook with multiple worksheets allows you to organize the data into a three dimensional structure. For example, when you open a file the main worksheet may summarize company expenses from all departments for one year, but each individual entry may be a total of values from subsequent sheets for each department. Excel provides the flexibility to enter data into different worksheets that link to other worksheets in the same or other workbooks.

Entering Text or Labels

To enter information, click a cell to select it and then type the entry. Use the (Backspace) key or (Delete) key to correct any input errors. When you finish typing, press (Enter) to move to the next cell below, or press (Tab) to move to the next cell to the right. You can also click another cell or press any arrow key to accept the input in the current cell.

The best way to begin any worksheet is to enter labels to identify the values you will enter. Labels help outline the relationships you will represent mathematically. For example, the report shown here includes labels indicating each of four quarterly intervals. Each row beneath the column labels shows the revenue numbers for the given quarter in the noted region. You can see how the revenue figures fluctuate for Region 1 as you follow from Q1 to the Total column.

	A	B	C	D	E	F
1	ABC Company					
2		Q1	Q2	Q3	Q4	Total
3	Region 1	541,000	275,000	280,000	310,000	$ 1,406,000
4	Region 2	125,000	127,000	122,000	126,000	$ 500,000
5	Region 3	96,000	100,000	102,000	105,000	$ 403,000
6	Total	$ 762,000	$ 502,000	$ 504,000	$ 541,000	$ 2,309,000

When entering information, consider the following:

- You can enter or edit data directly in the active cell, or use the Formula bar for long data entries.
- Labels can be up to 32,767 characters long.
- If a label is longer than the width of the cell, it will display past the column border as long as the adjoining cells are empty. Entries in adjoining cells cut off the display at the column border. The long text label may not be visible, but it is still completely contained in the cell where it was entered.
- You can easily change the appearance and alignment of any label in any cell.
- The maximum length of formula contents is 8,192 characters.

Entering Numbers or Dates

Numbers are constant values such as dollars and percentages; by default, they align to the right side of a cell. If you enter characters other than numbers, Excel treats the entire entry as a label. Excel displays values with no formatting, allowing you to format them yourself.

When entering dates, you can enter them in a numeric form such as 2-26-05 or as text, Month day, year). When entering dates, note the following:

- The default format of the date value is m-d-yy, although you can change this using the Region and Language settings in the Control Panel.

- The date value does not have to be the full day, month, and year. It can be just the day and month (formatted mmm-dd), or the month and year (formatted mmm-yyyy).

When entering a date, Excel does its best to interpret what you enter, as with these acceptable date values:

> September 13, 2014 (include the comma and one space)
>
> Sep 13, 14
>
> 13-Sep-14
>
> 09/13/14(month, day, year sequence)
>
> 9-13-14
>
> Sep 2014
>
> Sep 14

If Excel cannot interpret the date value, it will appear as a text label and potentially cause problems in the worksheet if you want to use the date value in formulas or calculations.

Moving Around the Worksheet

You can move around the cells of a worksheet using one of the following methods:

Scroll Bars	Click the arrow buttons at either end to move one row or column at a time. Click and drag the scroll box to display another location in the worksheet.
(←) (→) (↑) (↓)	Press a direction key to move one cell at a time.
(Home)	Moves to column A in the current row.
(Ctrl)+(Home)	Moves to cell A1.
(Ctrl)+(End)	Moves to the last cell with data in your report.
(Ctrl)+(G) **or** (F5)	Displays the Go To dialog box which you can use to move quickly to a cell address, range name, or bookmark. You can also use the **Special** button in the Go To dialog box to find specific types of information.

Saving Workbooks

To use a file again, you must save the workbook. It is a good practice to save work frequently during a session, especially if the workbook is large, or if you are using a process you have not tried before.

To save the changes made to an existing file, use one of the following methods:

- Click the **File** tab and then **Save**; or

- on the Quick Access toolbar, click 🖫 **(Save)**; or

- press (Ctrl)+(S).

The first time you save a file, you will always see the Save As dialog box so that you can give the new workbook a distinct name and select the location where it will be stored, such as the hard drive, network drive, or portable media drive.

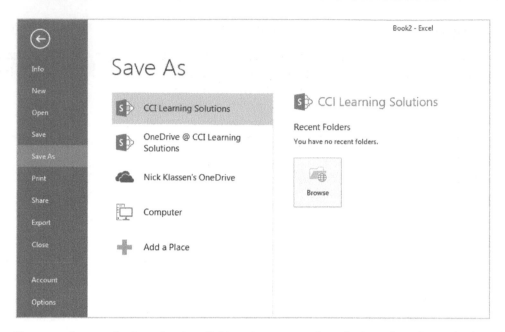

You can choose the location by clicking the appropriate designation. Once the location is selected, the right pane changes to display a list of recently accessed folders in which to save files.

From this screen you will click to select a folder to store the new file. Type the name in the File name field and click **Save** (or press Enter). File names can be up to 255 characters in length; you may need to follow the organization standards on how to name the file or where to save documents, such as a specific network drive. The default file type given to an Excel file is .xlsx, although you can save it in different file formats using the Save as type field in the Save As dialog box.

To save the changes made to an existing file and save it with a new name or in a different file format, click the **File** tab and then click **Save As**.

Opening Workbooks

To work with an existing workbook, you must first open it. You can have more than one workbook open in Excel at the same time.

To open a file, use one of the following methods:

- Click the **File** tab, click **Open**, click the location for the file, and then the folder where the file can be found, or click **Browse** to move to another folder or location. Select the file you want and click **Open**; or

- press Ctrl+O, click the location for the file, and then the folder where the file can be found, or click **Browse** to move to another folder or location. Select the file you want and click **Open**; or

- click the **File** tab, and click a file from the list of **Recent Workbooks** displayed on the right pane. This contains a list of the most recently used files; you can change the number of files that display in the list via **Options**.

When you try to open an Excel file that was saved from an email attachment, you will see a warning box, as shown in the following:

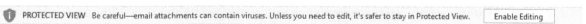

This is known as Protected View where Microsoft Office recognizes that a file was sent via the Internet. The warning is a reminder that the file should be scanned for malware before you begin to work with it. Once you know the file is safe to use, click **Enable Content** and make your changes. You may also want to save the file with a different name so you can keep the original file intact for future reference.

Closing Workbooks

When you no longer want to work with the current workbook, save the changes and then close it to protect it from accidental changes, or to free up system resources for other files. When you close a workbook, Excel displays any other open workbooks or a blank background screen if no workbooks are open.

To close a workbook, use one of the following methods:

- Click the **File** tab and click **Close**, or
- Press (Ctrl)+(W) or (Ctrl)+(F4), or
- Click the **Close** button for the application.

EXERCISE

In this exercise you will create new workbooks and enter data in one of them. You will also save some of the new files for future use.

1. Start Microsoft Excel, if necessary. Double-click **Blank workbook** to create a new workbook.

   Excel then displays a new blank workbook that contains a blank worksheet.

2. Press (Ctrl)+(N) to quickly create another new blank workbook.

   This new workbook should show Book2 in the title bar (the number may vary depending on how many times you pressed the shortcut key). Notice that the active cell is A1 – it should be highlighted with a darker border around it and both column A and row 1 change color to show this is the cell that is currently active. As you move the cursor or click in different cells, the column heading and row number will change color to confirm the current active cell.

3. In cell **A1** of Book2, type: `<Your Name> - Personal Budget` and press (Enter).

   The cursor should now be in cell A2 (you are still in column A but now in row 2).

4. Press (Tab) to move the cursor into cell **B2**. Type: `Apr` and press (Tab) to go to cell **C2**.

5. Type: `May` and press (Tab) to move to cell **D2**. Type: `Jun` and press (Enter).

   This time the cursor should be in cell A3.

6. Type: `Wages` and press (Tab). Continue entering the information as shown:

	A	B	C	D
1	Lucy Lee - Personal Budget			
2		Apr	May	Jun
3	Wages	2500	2500	2500
4				
5	Mortgage	1200	1200	1200
6	Utilities	250	250	250
7	Gas	300	300	300

7. On the Quick Access Toolbar, click **Save**.

8. Click **Computer** in the middle pane and click **Browse** in the right pane. Navigate to the *Lesson 9 - Excel* folder of the student data files, then in the **File name** field, type: `Personal Budget - Student` as the name of the file and click **Save**.

9. Click in cell **B1** and type in **today's date** using the mmm dd, yyyy format, for example, May 11, 2014 and press (Enter).

How did the date appear in your worksheet? Remember that the format we specified to enter the date may not be what has been set for your region. You should also notice that the title text has been cut off by the date. This is an example of why you want to watch where you are entering data and how it affects areas in the report. For instance, with this scenario, you may choose to delete the date and include it in the footer when printing the report so the title can display fully.

10. Save the workbook again.

Now create a new workbook using a template.

11. Click the **File** tab and then click **New**.

12. On the line below the search field, click the **Budget** category and click **Family budget**. Then click **Create** in the preview window.

    Notice how Excel created a new copy of this file for you using a similar name (Family budget1) to remind you of which template you used. If you were planning to use this form, you could click each field to enter the appropriate information. For the purpose of this demonstration, you will just save it.

13. Press Ctrl+S to save this file. Click **Computer** and then click **Lesson 9 – Excel** from the Recent Folders list.

14. Press the End key to move to the end of the existing file name, press Backspace to delete the 1 and type: from template - Student at the end of the file. Press Enter.

15. Press Ctrl+N to create a new blank workbook.

    You now have at least three workbooks open (the number will depend on the number of times you created a blank workbook or a new document from a template).

16. Point at the Excel icon on the Windows taskbar and you should have at least three preview windows displayed.

17. Click the *Personal Budget - Student* file.

    This file is now the active workbook on the screen.

18. Point at the Excel icon and then click the blank workbook created in step 15.

19. Close this workbook by pressing Ctrl+W.

20. Click the **File** tab and then click **Close** for the next workbook.

21. Press Ctrl+W to close the last workbook (or as many times as you need to close any open workbooks on the screen).

Now try opening a file.

22. Click **File** and then click **Recent Workbooks**, if necessary.

    There should be at least two files in the list of files most recently accessed.

23. Click *Personal Budget – Student* from the list.

24. Press Ctrl+O to go to Backstage and then navigate to the student data files location.

25. Click **Family budget from template – Student**.

26. Click **File**, click **Open**, and click **Computer**.

27. Click **Lesson 9 – Excel** from the Current Folder list, then click **Tour Prices** to open this file.

28. Click **File**, click **Open**, and click **Computer**.

29. Click **Lesson 9 – Excel** and then click *Eco Cruises* to open this file.

    Notice the warning bar across the top of the file informing you that this file was likely saved from an attachment in an email.

30. Press Ctrl+W as necessary to close all open files.

Manipulating the Contents

 Exam 2 - Objective 1.1, 3.1

The easiest way to change cell contents is to type the new content, press (Enter) and have Excel replace the old information with the new entry. To correct errors as you type, press (Backspace) or (Delete) prior to pressing (Enter) or moving to another cell.

If you want to add, delete, or change less than the entire contents of the cell, you can activate Excel's Edit mode by pressing (F2) or double-clicking on the cell; Excel will display the insertion point and you can proceed in one of the following ways:

- Select the text in the cell, type the replacement text, and press (Enter) to exit the Edit mode; or
- use the (Delete) key to remove any unwanted characters from the cell contents.

Selecting Cells

Prior to performing an action, you must indicate what *range* or part of the worksheet to affect with that action. A range can be a single cell, several cells, or the entire worksheet. Selected cells remain selected or highlighted until you click a cell or press an arrow key. The selected range appears in reverse color to the cells. The active cell in the selected range appears in normal color. You can highlight individual cells or any range of cells as follows:

Single cell	Click the cell.
Extend the selection	Click the first cell and drag to the end of the required range; or click the first cell, hold the (Shift) key, and click the end cell in the range.
Entire row	Click the row header when you see the ➡.
Entire column	Click the column header when you see the ⬇ .
Entire worksheet	Click the **Select All** button.
Non-adjacent cells, columns, or rows	Click the cell, column, or row, hold the (Ctrl) key, then click to select the next cell, column, or row.
Multiple rows	Click the first row number and drag for the number of rows to select.
Multiple columns	Click the first column letter and drag for the number of columns to select.

	A	B	C	D	E	F	G	H	I	J
1	ABC Company									
2		Q1		Q2		Q3		Q4		Total				
3	Region 1	541,000		275,000		280,000		310,000	$	1,406,000				
4	Region 2	125,000		127,000		122,000		126,000	$	500,000				
5	Region 3	96,000		100,000		102,000		105,000	$	403,000				
6	Total	$	762,000	$	502,000	$	504,000	$	541,000	$	2,309,000				
7										
8										
9										
10										
11										
12										
13										
14										
15										
16										
17										

Using Undo or Repeat

Excel includes an Undo function that enables you to undo commands executed in the worksheet.

Excel can undo up to a maximum of 100 recently-used commands; this "undo history" displays when you click the down arrow beside the **Undo** button. The Undo command can be performed only in the reverse sequence of the changes made to the worksheet; you cannot reverse the changes in a sequence of your choosing. Undo does not work for some commands such as saving the file.

If you need to reverse an undo, you can redo or repeat it. The Repeat function is available only if one or more commands were undone. Excel also keeps a history of the last 100 actions for the Repeat feature. To display the redo history, click the down arrow beside the **Redo** button. Like the Undo command, these commands must be performed in the reverse sequence of the actions that were undone.

Copying and Moving Data

Excel enables you to copy or move cell contents from a different part of the same worksheet, another worksheet in the same workbook, or a worksheet in a different workbook.

Cut	Removes the contents of a cell or a range of cells to the Office Clipboard.
Copy	Copies the contents of a cell or a range of cells to the Office Clipboard.
Paste	Pastes any or all contents from the Office Clipboard into one or more cell locations.

In addition to using the Copy or Cut command from the ribbon, Excel provides some tools you can use to copy or move cell contents:

- Point the mouse at the border of the cell whose contents you want to move and then drag the cell contents to its new location.
- Point the mouse at the border of the cell whose contents you want to copy, press (Ctrl) and then drag the cell contents to its new location.

Before you can activate the copy or cut command, you must select a range; when you do, a *marquee* (moving dotted rectangle) will appear around the selection after you active the Cut or Copy command, thereby identifying what you want to cut or copy. To remove the marquee, use one of the following methods:

- Press (Esc); or
- type the first letter, number, or symbol of a new entry; or
- press (Enter) to paste the cut or copied item into this location only.

Note that when you press (Delete) or use the Cut command, the information is removed, but any formatting applied to that data still exists in the original location. You must use the **Clear** command for more options regarding the deletion of formatting. This command is found on the Home tab, in the Editing group.

Using the Office Clipboard

You can cut or copy more than one cell range, and keep up to 24 cell ranges in the Office Clipboard at one time. You can then paste any or all these items in any sequence.

Activate the commands for cut, copy, and paste using the Home tab, in the Clipboard group, or with the keyboard shortcuts. Display the Office Clipboard at any time by clicking the **Clipboard** dialog box launcher in the Clipboard group of the Home tab.

EXERCISE

In this exercise you will copy and paste entries into cells of a worksheet in order to complete a descriptive listing of movies.

1. Click **File**, click **Open**, and click **Computer**. Navigate to the student data files location and then select the *Personal Movie Inventory List* file to open it.

2. Click **File**, click **Save As**, and click **Lesson 9 – Excel**. Type: - `Student` at the end of the file name and then click **Save**.

3. On the Home tab, in the Clipboard group, click the **Clipboard** dialog box launcher button.

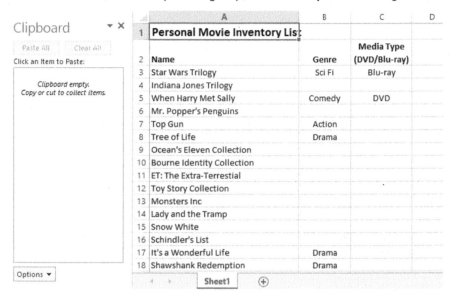

4. Click in cell **B8** where the word Drama is. Then on the Home tab, in the Clipboard group, click **Copy**.

    Notice how the Office Clipboard now shows an entry for the contents of this cell. You should also notice the marquee around cell B8, reminding you this is the original source for the copy action.

5. Click in cell **B4** and then click the entry in the Clipboard.

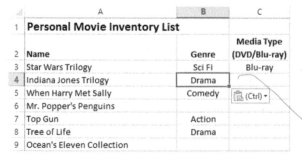

You have just successfully copied and pasted an entry from one cell to another (the marquee no longer appears around the original source). You will also notice the **Paste Options** button appears near the bottom right corner of cell B4 (where you pasted the content). You can click this button to display further actions you can apply to the pasted text. If you click the button in this case, two buttons display similar to the following:

These buttons allow you to keep the source formatting, or match the destination formatting. You can also dismiss the button by pressing the Esc key.

6. Click in cell **B5** and on the Home tab, in the Clipboard group, click **Copy**.

    You should now have two entries in the Office Clipboard and the marquee displays around cell B5. As you add items to the Clipboard, you expand your choice of items that can be pasted into the worksheet. Use the Clipboard to best suit your working style. In this exercise, you will copy all genre types to the Clipboard, and then paste them into the worksheet as appropriate.

7. Click in cell **B3** and press Ctrl+C to copy this genre type.

8. Repeat step 6 or 7 to copy the contents in cells **B7**, **B21**, **B32** and **B34**.

    The Office Clipboard should appear similar to the following:

9. Click in cell **C6** and then click **Comedy** in the Office Clipboard.

    The word Comedy is pasted into cell C6.

Suppose you realize this was copied into the wrong cell. You can choose to click Undo to reverse the paste action, or move the contents to the correct cell. In this case, we will move the cell contents by dragging it to the new location.

10. Point at dark border around cell **C6** and when the mouse pointer appears as ⛾ , click and drag the cell to cell **B6**.

    The cell contents, Comedy, are now in the correct location.

11. Click the appropriate category from the Clipboard to continue adding the genre to the rest of the titles in the list.

> **Tip:** It does matter if you don't know what the genre of a title is; the purpose here is to focus on using the copy and paste function.

12. As time permits, try the copy and paste option with the Clipboard for the Media type.

13. Click the **Clear All** button to remove all entries in the Clipboard, and click the **Close** button for the Clipboard task pane. Then save and close the workbook.

Changing the Column Widths

You can adjust column widths to display more characters. When an entry in a cell is longer than the standard column width, Excel displays the label by overflowing the entry into the next cells if they are empty. If you enter values that exceed the column width and there are entries in the adjoining cells, the text entry is truncated at the column boundary. Excel stores the complete cell entry, but displays only what will fit within the cell boundaries. If you enter a number or date that exceeds the column width, Excel displays # symbols within the cell, as shown in the following:

Once you change the width of the cell sufficiently, Excel shows the full value using the assigned cell formatting.

Column widths can be set between zero and 255 characters. When you change a column width, the stored contents of the cells do not change, only the number of the characters displayed.

To change the width of a column, use one of the following methods:

- On the Home tab, in the Cells group, click **Format**, and then **Column Width**; or

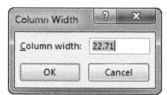

- position the mouse pointer on the line at the right edge of the column header to be adjusted; when you see ✛ (thick horizontal double-headed crosshair), click and drag to the required width for the column.

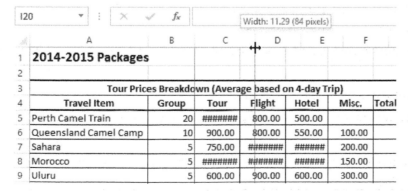

To check the width of a column, click the right edge of the column header. The width will be displayed in a screen tip above the mouse pointer.

Adjusting the Row Height

When you need to adjust the row height so the row is smaller or larger than others in the worksheet, use one of the following methods:

- On the Home tab, in the Cells group, click **Format**, and then **Row Height**; or

- Place the mouse pointer at the bottom edge of the row header to be adjusted. When it changes to ⬍ (thick vertical double-headed crosshair), click and drag to the height required.

Manipulating Rows, Columns, or Cells

Insert new rows, columns, or cells when you need to add information or separate parts of the worksheet. Delete rows, columns, or cells of data that you do not need in the worksheet.

Inserting Rows, Columns, or Cells

You can insert a new row above the current row, and a new column to the left of the current column. You can insert one or more rows or columns at the same time.

You can also insert cells in specific areas of the worksheet; use caution when activating this option as it can alter the structure of your worksheet.

Be careful using these commands as they affect the entire worksheet and may affect areas of the worksheet you are not viewing on the screen. For example, if you want to insert a row but only have one cell in the row selected, click the arrow for the Insert command to insert the row; do not click the Insert command on its own as Excel will insert a cell in the current cursor location only for that one column.

To insert a column to the left of the selected column, use one of the following methods:

- On the Home tab, in the Cells group, click the arrow for **Insert**, and then **Insert Sheet Columns**; or
- press (Ctrl)+(+) from the numeric keyboard; or
- right-click the selected column and then click **Insert**.

To insert a row above the selected row, use one of the following methods:

- On the Home tab, in the Cells group, click the arrow for **Insert**, and then **Insert Sheet Rows**; or
- press (Ctrl)+(+) from the numeric keyboard; or
- right-click the selected row and then click **Insert**.

To insert one or more cells in the current location, on the Home tab, in the Cells group, click the arrow for **Insert** and then click **Insert Cells**.

Note: If you select the entire row using the row heading or the entire column using its column heading, you can just click **Insert** on its own. Excel automatically recognizes what you want to insert based on the selection of the entire row or column.

Deleting Rows, Columns, or Cells

You can delete one or several rows or columns, or shift cells over in place of deleted cells. Deleting the contents of a cell affects only the contents, not the structure of the worksheet. Deleting a cell affects the structure of the worksheet.

Be careful when deleting entire rows or columns to ensure you do not accidentally delete valuable data not currently displayed on the screen.

To delete the selected column, use one of the following methods:

* On the Home tab, in the Cells group, click the arrow for **Delete**, and then **Delete Sheet Columns**; or
* press (Ctrl)+(-) from the numeric keyboard; or
* right-click the and then click **Delete**.

To delete the selected row, use one of the following methods:

* On the Home tab, in the Cells group, click the arrow for **Delete**, and then **Delete Sheet Rows**; or
* press (Ctrl)+(-) from the numeric keyboard; or
* right-click the selected row and then click **Delete**.

Note: If you select the entire row using the row heading or the entire column using its column heading, you can just click **Delete** on its own. Excel automatically recognizes what you want to delete based on the selection of the entire row or column.

To delete one or more cells in the current location, on the Home tab, in the Cells group, click the arrow for **Delete**, and then click **Delete Cells**.

EXERCISE

In this exercise you will change the column widths and row heights in the worksheet, as well as insert a row.

1. Open the *TEC Employee List* and save as `TEC Employee List - Student`.

2. Click **Column A** to select the entire column. Then on the Home tab, in the Cells group, click **Format** and click **Column Width**.

3. Type: `12` for the new column width and then click **OK**.

4. Click **Column B** to select the entire column. Then on the Home tab, in the Cells group, click **Format** and click **Column Width**. Type: `15` as the new width and press ⟨Enter⟩.

5. Point the cursor on the vertical line between the headings for columns C and D until you see ✛ and then drag to the right to change the column width (we chose 36 for the column width).

    As you drag you should notice a ScreenTip appear above the symbol indicating the current column width.

6. Using the method in step 4 or step 5, alter the column width for the remaining columns. Choose the width you consider most suitable for each column.

> **Tip:** For the two phone number columns, select both columns before adjusting the column width. Once you choose the required width, both columns adjust at the same time.

7. Click the **Row 1** heading to select the entire row.

8. On the Home tab, in the Cells group, click **Insert**.

    A new blank row appears above the column headings.

9. Type: `Tolano - Full Employee List` as the title for the report and then press ⟨Enter⟩.

10. Save the workbook.

Managing Worksheets

 Exam 2 - Objective 3.1.4

A workbook is a collection of worksheets. While each worksheet can be treated as an independent spreadsheet, information on the worksheets within a workbook is typically inter-related.

Worksheets can be renamed, added, deleted, copied, and moved within a workbook. Use the tab scrolling buttons to display more worksheet tabs as required.

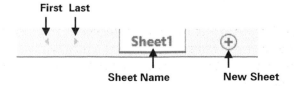

Naming Worksheets

Sheet1, Sheet2, Sheet3, and so on help to identify different sheets as you create them, but do not describe their contents, which can make it difficult for you to find what you want. Renaming tabs with more descriptive names makes locating data easier. Worksheet tab names can be up to 31 characters long.

To rename a worksheet tab, use one of the following methods:

- On the Home tab, in the Cells group, click **Format**, and then **Rename Sheet**; or
- double-click the sheet tab and then type the new name.

Another option you can apply to a worksheet to help identify tabs with similar names is to add a color to the worksheet tab.

To add a color to the worksheet tab, use one of the following methods:

- On the Home tab, in the Cells group, click **Format**, and then **Tab Color**; or
- right-click the sheet tab and click **Tab Color**.

Click a color to apply this to the worksheet tab. It then appears with a softer version of the color as the background fill in the worksheet tab. The name of the worksheet also appears in bold text. When the worksheet tab is not the active worksheet, it appears with the actual color as the background fill and the worksheet name appears in regular text.

Inserting or Deleting Worksheets

Excel automatically includes one worksheet with a new workbook, but you can add more. To insert a new worksheet, use one of the following methods:

- On the Home tab, in the Cells group, click **Insert**, and then **Insert Sheet**; or

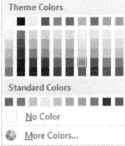

- in the sheet tabs area, click ⊕ **(New Sheet)** to automatically add a worksheet at the end of the current worksheet tabs; or
- press (Shift)+(F11); or
- right-click the tab where you want to place the new sheet, click **Insert**, **Worksheet**, and then click **OK**.

Use the tab scrolling buttons to display more worksheet tabs, or adjust the length of the horizontal scroll bar. The first and last buttons become active only when you have more worksheet tabs that can be seen across the bottom. Use either of these buttons to move to the first or last worksheet in the list; alternatively, you can resize the horizontal scroll bar to show more or less worksheet tabs.

Deleting worksheets that you no longer need can help keep your workbook easy to use, but consider saving the workbook before deleting a worksheet in case you need to revert to the previous version of the file. Note that the Undo command will not restore a deleted worksheet. Also, check every worksheet for any errors in case the deleted worksheet contained formulas that affect the values in the rest of the worksheets.

To delete a worksheet, select the sheet and then use one of the following methods:

- On the Home tab, in the Cells group, click the down arrow for **Delete**, and then **Delete Sheet**; or
- right-click the sheet tab and click **Delete**.

Moving or Copying Worksheets

When you add a new worksheet, Excel automatically places it to the right of the current worksheet in the workbook. This may not be the required position and you can easily move the worksheet to another location to best suit the workbook contents, such as the first worksheet to contain a summary of the data in the other department worksheets in the workbook.

To move a worksheet to another location, use one of the following methods:

- On the Home tab, in the Cells group, click **Format**, and then **Move or Copy Sheet**; or
- right-click the worksheet tab to be moved and click **Move or Copy**; or
- click and drag the worksheet tab to its new location.

If you use one of the first two methods, a dialog box appears for confirmation of where you want the worksheet to be placed. Notice in this dialog box you can also choose to make a copy of the selected worksheet for placement in this workbook. This can be useful when you want to set up a what-if scenario for the values without affecting the original worksheet.

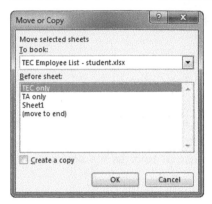

If you use the second method to move a worksheet, Excel displays the following symbols to confirm you are moving the worksheet and the black arrow confirms this is the location where the worksheet will be placed when you release the mouse.

EXERCISE

In this exercise you will edit a workbook and organize the worksheets to help you quickly identify the contents of each worksheet.

1. Ensure the *TEC Employee List – Student* file is active on the screen.

2. Double-click the **Sheet1** tab at the bottom of the worksheet.

3. Type: TEC only as the name for the tab and press (Enter).

4. Click the **Sheet2** tab.

   This sheet contains the listing for the Tolano Adventures group.

5. Double-click the **Sheet2** tab and type: TA only as the new name. Press (Enter).

6. Right-click the TA only tab and click **Tab Color**. Click a color of your choice from the palette.

   Once you select a color, it will appear as a line across the bottom of the tab.

7. Click the **TEC only** tab to make this worksheet active.

8. Right-click the **TEC only** tab, click **Tab Color** and then click another color of your choice.

9. Click the ⊕ (**New Sheet**) button.

You should now be able to see the color applied to both tabs. Using color to help identify the worksheet contents can be beneficial if the workbook contains a number of worksheets, or if you want to categorize the content in the worksheets, for example, Sales information should always be red while HR will be yellow, price lists are to be green whereas cost of goods could be blue.

10. Click **Sheet1** and drag it to the right of the TA only worksheet.

11. Save and close the worksheet.

Creating Simple Formulas

 Exam 2 - Objective 3.1, 3.2

A formula is a calculation using numbers (or other data) in a cell or from other cells, such as:

- automatically calculating sums horizontally and vertically
- performing "what-if" analyses by performing a calculation based on one or more changing input values, such as estimated profit for a business during the next year
- using one or more Excel functions to perform tedious or complex calculations, such as monthly mortgage payments.

Formulas can be linked from one worksheet to another, so that when you change values or amounts in the active worksheet, dependent cells in the other worksheet will be automatically updated. You can use a single cell as the reference point, or you can create complex formulas with many cell references as well as built-in functions.

To begin a formula in any cell, you must type an equal sign (=). You can enter a cell address into a formula either by typing it directly into the cell, or by clicking on the cells to be included. The cell into which you enter a formula will display the result of the formula; the formula itself will be visible in the Formula bar.

Some formulas are long and can include many calculations. If you need to change a formula, you can use the (F2) key to edit the formula in the cell, instead of re-entering the entire formula from scratch.

Cells containing formulas can be copied to other cells. If these formulas contain cell references, Excel will automatically adjust the cell references when you paste the formulas into a new location.

Excel calculates formulas in "natural order": exponents first, then multiplication and division, and then addition and subtraction. This order can be altered by inserting parentheses around portions of the formula; Excel will calculate the portions inside parentheses before calculating the other items in the formula.

The following symbols are used in Excel to represent standard mathematical operators:

*	Multiplication	+	Addition
/	Division	-	Subtraction

When Excel detects an error or inconsistency in a formula, it displays a suggestion for correcting it. The type of error message depends on the type of error, as indicated in the following examples:

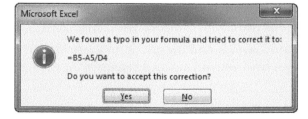

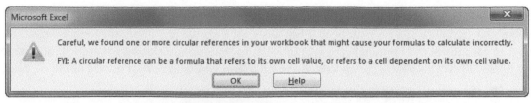

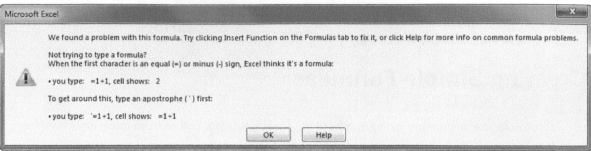

Excel displays ⌐ in the upper-left corner of a cell to alert you when a formula in that cell differs from the formulas used in surrounding cells that follow a particular pattern.

Excel can help you analyze the data in your worksheet by using formulas to identify trends or patterns in the data. For instance, when tracking sales figures over a period of time, an upward or downward pattern emerges; or in a budget, you may notice that office expenses are increasing. When Excel brings these trends to your attention, you can analyze when, why, and how the changes occurred, and take action if needed.

When data is used for analysis or comparison, you can display that information in a chart to show where any trends or patterns exist.

EXERCISE

In this exercise, you will enter a few simple formulas using math operators.

1. Open the *AM Personal Budget* file and save as AM Personal Budget - Student.

2. Click in cell **B5**. Type: =B3+B4 and press (Enter).

    You successfully entered a simple formula into cell B5 that adds the contents of cell B3 to the contents of cell B4.

3. Click cell **B5** once more and on the Home tab, in the Clipboard group, click **Copy**.

4. Select cells **C5** to **D5** and on the Home tab, in the Clipboard group, click **Paste**.

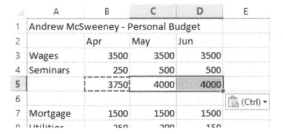

    You copied the formula from cell B5 to the other two columns that contain similar data.

Now try entering a formula to determine how much savings Andrew can accumulate for each month in this quarter. For the purpose of this exercise, we have entered the total expenses for each month in the report.

5.   Click in cell **B14** and type: =B5-B12 and press Enter .

6.   Click in cell **B14** again and then press Ctrl + C to start the copy process.

7.   Select cells **C14** and **D14**. Press Ctrl + V to paste the formula into these cells.

	A	B	C	D
1	Andrew McSweeney - Personal Budget			
2		Apr	May	Jun
3	Wages	3500	3500	3500
4	Seminars	250	500	500
5		3750	4000	4000
6				
7	Mortgage	1500	1500	1500
8	Utilities	250	200	150
9	Gas	200	200	200
10	Groceries	150	100	100
11	Meals Out	100	250	350
12		2200	2250	2300
13				
14	Savings	1550	1750	1700

8.   Save and close the budget report.

Using Common Built-In Functions

Excel provides over 300 built-in functions for mathematical and data operations. Functions accept numbers, values, and cell references as *arguments* within parentheses, following this format:

=FUNCTION(numbers or values or cell reference)

Some common functions you will use include:

=SUM	Calculates the sum of the values in the range of specified cells.
=AVERAGE	Calculates an average of the values in the specified cells (totals the range and divides the total by the number of entries).
=MIN	Displays the minimum value in the range of specified cells.
=MAX	Displays the maximum value in the range of specified cells.
=COUNT	Counts the number of values within the specified range.

Cell ranges in a function should be indicated as follows:

<first cell address>:<last cell address>

Examples:

A10:B15, C5:C25

You can specify the range by typing the cell reference directly or by using the "point-to" method, where you use the mouse to click and drag to select the cell range. The latter method allows you to visually identify the cell range, which reduces the chance that you will enter incorrect cell references.

When calculating totals, you can use Σ AutoSum ▾ on the Home tab in the Editing group. Excel then selects the range of cells immediately above or to the left of the current cell.

Be sure to verify that you have selected the correct cell range for the function. If there is even one blank cell between cells, the range may not include all cells.

Use the arrow next to the **AutoSum** tool to display other common built-in functions, or use **More Functions** to choose a different function.

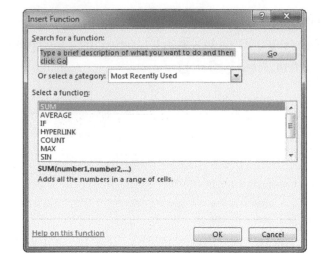

Using Absolute and Relative Addresses

Most formulas entered into an Excel worksheet refer to cell addresses which are *relative*. If you copy a formula with a relative cell address and paste it to another cell, Excel will automatically adjust the cell references in the pasted cell to reflect the new location. For example, suppose you have a formula that adds three rows together within one column; you can copy this formula to another column to add the same three rows in the new column. The cell addresses used in the formula are relative to the column in which you place the formula.

On the other hand, an *absolute* cell address refers to an exact or fixed location on the worksheet.

To change a relative cell address to an absolute (fixed) cell address in a formula or function:

- Enter a dollar sign before the row number and/or column letter; or
- press (F4) once you enter the cell address.

The (F4) key provides several options for absolute references: pressing (F4) the first time on a cell address makes both the column and row reference absolute; pressing it again results in only the row reference being absolute; pressing it a third time results in only the column reference being absolute; and a fourth press removes the absolute references on both the column and row.

Cell addresses can include a combination of relative and absolute references. The dollar sign ($) denotes an absolute reference. The cell address B6 is an entirely relative cell address reference. On the other hand, the cell address $B6 is a combination (or mixed) reference. In the cell address $B6, the column reference is absolute – that is, the cell address will always refer to Column B; the row reference is relative and will adjust depending on location.

The cell address B$6 is also a mixed reference. In the cell address B$6, the row reference is absolute – that is, the cell address will always refer to Row 6; the column reference is relative and will adjust depending on location.

The cell address B6 is an absolute cell address; both the column and row references are absolute. Any formula using this cell address will always refer to cell B6, no matter where the formula is located in the worksheet.

EXERCISE

In this exercise you will enter formulas into a worksheet to show totals for the pricing set on tours for the upcoming year.

1. Open the *Tour Prices* file and save as `Tour Prices - Student`.

2. Change the width for columns **C** to **G** to **11**.

3. Click in cell **G5**. Then on the Home tab, in the Editing group, click **AutoSum**.

	A	B	C	D	E	F	G	H	I
1	2014-2015 Packages								
2									
3		Tour Prices Breakdown (Average based on 4-day Trip)							
4	Travel Item	Group	Tour	Flight	Hotel	Misc.	Total Cost		
5	Perth Camel Train	20	1,000.00	800.00	500.00		=SUM(B5:F5)		
6	Queensland Camel Camp	10	900.00	800.00	550.00	100.00	SUM(number1, [number2], ...)		
7	Sahara	5	750.00	1,300.00	1,000.00	200.00			

Excel now identifies the cells you may want to sum or total. If these are correct, you need only accept the suggested cell range. If you need to change the range of cells, click to select the cells you want to be included in the formula.

4. Press (Enter) to accept the formula in this cell and move the cursor to the next cell below.

2014-2015 Packages

	Tour Prices Breakdown (Average based on 4-day Trip)					
Travel Item	Group	Tour	Flight	Hotel	Misc.	Total Cost
Perth Camel Train	20	1,000.00	800.00	500.00		$ 2,320.00
Queensland Camel Camp	10	900.00	800.00	550.00	100.00	
Sahara	5	750.00	1,300.00	1,000.00	200.00	

You will now insert the formula to total the remaining tours. You could choose to insert the AutoSum formula for each row, or recognizing that Excel uses relative addressing with formulas, you can copy this formula to the remaining cells.

5. Click in cell **G5** again and then on the Home tab, in the Clipboard group, click **Copy**.

6. Click cell **G6** and drag down to cell **G15**. Then on the Home tab, in the Clipboard group, click **Paste**.

	A	B	C	D	E	F	G	H
1	2014-2015 Packages							
2								
3		Tour Prices Breakdown (Average based on 4-day Trip)						
4	Travel Item	Group	Tour	Flight	Hotel	Misc.	Total Cost	
5	Perth Camel Train	20	1,000.00	800.00	500.00		$ 2,320.00	
6	Queensland Camel Camp	10	900.00	800.00	550.00	100.00	$ 2,360.00	
7	Sahara	5	750.00	1,300.00	1,000.00	200.00	$ 3,255.00	
8	Morocco	5	1,000.00	1,200.00	1,000.00	150.00	$ 3,355.00	
9	Uluru	5	600.00	900.00	600.00	300.00	$ 2,405.00	
10	Dubai	8	400.00	1,500.00	600.00	250.00	$ 2,758.00	
11	Minqin County	20	500.00	1,200.00	750.00	300.00	$ 2,770.00	
12	Westwood Cemetery	25	50.00	250.00	800.00	200.00	$ 1,325.00	
13	Forest Lawns	10	50.00	250.00	800.00	200.00	$ 1,310.00	
14	Whatley House	10	50.00	300.00	500.00	300.00	$ 1,160.00	
15	Edinburgh Castle	20	50.00	1,200.00	700.00	350.00	$ 2,320.00	
16								(Ctrl) ▾
17								

Excel has now copied the formula into each of the remaining cells.

7. Click cell **G6** to see how the formula appears.

You should notice that the cell references for the AutoSum range have adjusted to reflect the total for this row instead. That is, the range is B6:F6 for row 6, but will be B7:F7 for row 7 and so on.

8. Click in the remaining cells to see how the formula adjusted for each row.

9. Save the worksheet.

Suppose there is now a possibility that you may have to raise the tour prices by 15% to cover varying exchange rates.

10. Click cell **A20** and type: Exchange Rate as the label. Then press (Tab). In cell **B20**, type: 1.15 as the rate.

11. Click cell **I5**.

    We deliberately chose this column as we have no confirmation that the price will have to be increased. At this point, all you want to do is see what the tour prices would be if you had to raise them by 15%, and how much that would impact potential sales.

12. Type: = and then click cell **G5**.

    You are now going to use the point and click method to select the cells for the formula. If preferred, you can enter the cell addresses directly if you know all of them at the time you are entering the formula.

13. Type: * to set up a multiplication operator and then click cell **B20**. Press (Enter) to accept the formula.

14. Copy the results of this cell down to the cell **I15**.

Misc.	Total Cost	
	$ 2,320.00	$ 2,668.00
100.00	$ 2,360.00	$ -
200.00	$ 3,255.00	$ -
150.00	$ 3,355.00	$ -
300.00	$ 2,405.00	$ -
250.00	$ 2,758.00	$ -
300.00	$ 2,770.00	$ -
200.00	$ 1,325.00	$ -
200.00	$ 1,310.00	$ -
300.00	$ 1,160.00	$ -
350.00	$ 2,320.00	$ -

You should notice that the remaining cells have no results in them from the copying of the original formula. Remember that we used the relative addressing option to copy the original cell and paste it into the noted cells. What we need to do is set the appropriate cell in the original formula to be static or absolute so the new rate will be calculated correctly in the remaining cells.

15. Click in cell **I5** and press (F2) to activate the Edit mode.

16. With the cursor at the end of **B20** cell address reference, press (F4).

    =G5*B20

17. Press (Enter) to accept this change. You have specified that cell B20 is an absolute cell address. Neither the row nor the column will be adjusted as you copy and paste.

18. Now copy this formula down to cell **I15**.

$2,668.00
$2,714.00
$3,743.25
$3,858.25
$2,765.75
$3,171.70
$3,185.50
$1,523.75
$1,506.50
$1,334.00
$2,668.00

19. Save and close the workbook.

What Does Formatting Mean?

 Exam 2 - Objective 1.2, 3.1, 3.2

Formatting refers to changing the appearance of data to draw attention to parts of the worksheet, or to make the data easier to read. Formatting does not affect any underlying values.

You can format a cell or range of cells at any time, either before or after you enter the data. A cell remains formatted until you clear the format or reformat the cell. When you enter new data in the cell, Excel will display it in the existing format. When you copy or fill a cell, you copy its format along with the cell contents.

You can apply formatting using one of the following methods:

- On the Home tab, click the command to apply formatting from the appropriate group; or
- on the Home tab, in the Cells group click **Format** and then click **Format Cells**; or
- press (Ctrl)+(1); or
- right-click and then click **Format Cells**; or
- press the appropriate keyboard shortcut for specific formatting features, such as (Ctrl)+(B) for bold; or
- click the appropriate formatting option from the Mini toolbar, if active.

Formatting Numbers and Decimal Digits

When you enter numbers, Excel displays them exactly as you entered them except for any trailing zeros. Also, numbers larger than the width of the cell will display in scientific notation format.

Excel provides a rich set of standard formats with customizable options. Excel also provides a **Special** format category for commonly used formats.

To format selected cells that contain values, use one of the following methods:

- On the Home tab, in the Number group, click the **Number Format** dialog box launcher, and then choose the appropriate option from the **Category** list; or

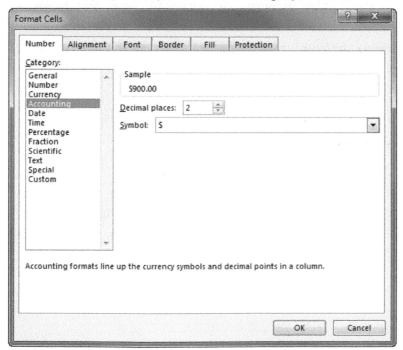

- to use the default options for values, on the Home tab, in the Number group, click the arrow for **Number Format**, and click the format required, or

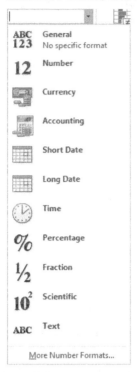

- click one of the commonly-used number format buttons in the Number group of the Home tab.

$ ▾ % ,

Changing Cell Alignment

Alignment refers to the position of data within a cell. You can align cell contents horizontally (column width) and vertically (row height). By default, new values entered into a worksheet use the **General** alignment option: numbers and dates automatically right-align, while text labels automatically left-align.

Use **Merge & Center** to center a text label across several cells. You can also wrap text in a cell or rotate it at a specific angle.

To change the alignment for selected cells, use one of the following methods:

- On the Home tab, in the Alignment group, click the alignment option required; or

- on the Home tab, in the Alignment group, click the **Alignment Settings** dialog box launcher and then choose the alignment option from the Alignment tab as shown:

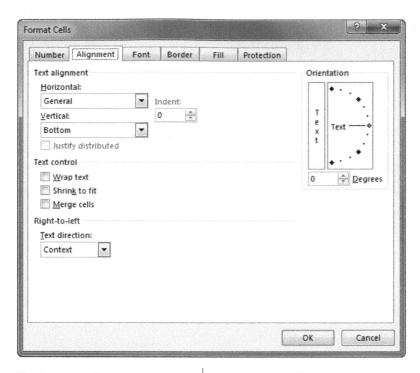

Horizontal - General, Left (Indent), Center, Right (Indent)	Changes the alignment of the contents of any cell to general (default), left, right, or center.
Horizontal - Fill	Duplicates the cell contents to completely fill the cell's width.
Horizontal - Justify	Justifies the text on both the left and right sides of the cell. Excel automatically wraps the text when justify is used.
Horizontal - Center Across Selection	Centers a title across multiple columns for headings.
Horizontal – Distributed (Indent)	Distributes the cell contents evenly between the remaining cell width after the indent.
Indent	Indents labels from the left of the cell by two characters (default) although you can set this to a larger or smaller indent.
Vertical - Top, Center, Bottom, Justify, or Distributed	Aligns cell contents at the top, middle (center), or bottom of the cell, regardless of the horizontal alignment. Using the **Justify** command will justify the contents between the top and bottom of the merged cell whereas using **Distributed** will distribute the cell contents evenly from top to bottom in the merged cell.
Orientation	Rotates the values to any angle from 90° up to -90° down, or displays the entry vertically. Excel adjusts the cell height automatically.
Wrap text	Fits a label in the existing column by creating additional lines and expanding the height of the row. This feature is also available on the Home tab in the Alignment group.
Shrink to fit	Automatically adjusts the text size to fit the available space.

Merge cells	Removes the borders between cells and treats the "new" cell as one large cell. Cells can be merged horizontally, vertically or both. This feature is also available on the Home tab in the Alignment group.
Text Direction	Displays characters from right to left when entering text in Hebrew, Arabic, etc., or leave it at **Context** to let Excel determine the text direction.

Changing Fonts and Sizes

A font is a typeface or text style. Changing fonts alters the way text and numbers appear. Keep the number of fonts in a worksheet to one or two, as the appearance of too many fonts can be distracting.

To format selected cells, use one of the following methods:

- On the Home tab, in the Font group, click the desired format; or

- on the Home tab, in the Font group, click the **Font Settings** dialog box launcher, and then choose the appropriate option from the Font tab; or

- press (Ctrl)+(Shift)+(F) and choose the appropriate option from the Font tab:

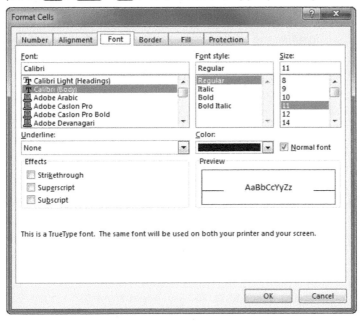

Applying Cell Borders

Borders separate groups of data to improve legibility, especially when the worksheet contains a large volume of numbers. This feature enables you to draw lines around any or all edges of a cell or range of cells. You can choose presets, line thickness, color/style options, and location of borders.

To apply a border to a cell, use one of the following methods:

- On the Home tab in the Font group, click the arrow for ⊞ ▾ **(Borders)**. This command also contains the **Draw Border** option to add the border around the cells you now select. This is useful when you want to draw lines or borders around several non-adjacent cells; or

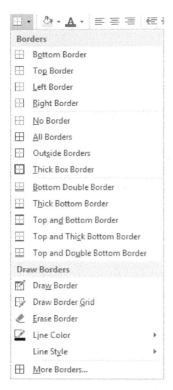

- on the Home tab, in the Font group, click the **Font Settings** dialog box launcher, click the **Border** tab, and then choose the option you prefer, as follows:

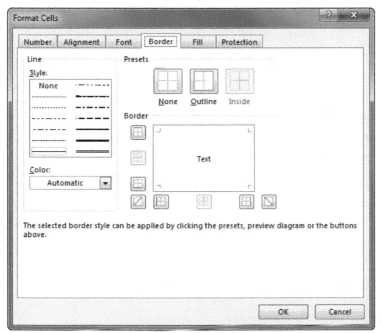

Line	Choose a line style or color for the border. For different border lines or colors, select the style or color, and then click in the **Border** area for the appropriate border.
Presets	Selects a pre-designed option for the borders of the selected cells.
Border	Adds or removes lines for the selected cells.

Applying Colors and Patterns

The Fill option sets the background color and pattern for a cell. Patterns and colors draw attention to certain parts of your worksheet, and can act as a visual divider of information.

Patterns and colors are different features. Patterns can make it harder to read the data than using a solid color; whenever possible, avoid dark colors and dense patterns that can obscure the information in the cells.

To apply a color or pattern to a cell, use one of the following methods:

- on the Home tab, in the Font group, click the arrow for ✎ ▾ **(Fill Color)**, or

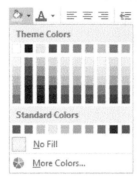

- On the Home tab, in the Font group, click the **Font Settings** dialog box launcher, and then click the **Fill** tab.

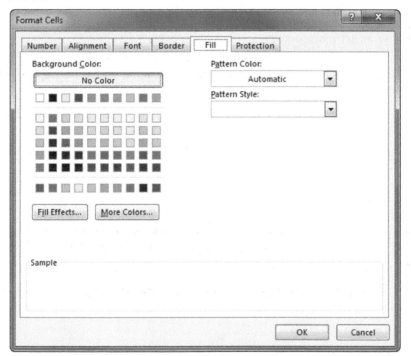

Using Cell Styles

You can use styles in Excel workbooks as a powerful formatting feature. As in Microsoft Word, a style in Excel is simply a grouping of specific format settings (such as font, size and color) for a cell. Every time you apply a style to a cell, Excel formats it the same way. If a style is changed, Excel applies the changes to all cells currently formatted with that style, maintaining a consistent look throughout the worksheet with minimal effort.

Excel provides you with a set of prebuilt styles you can access easily from the Styles group of the Home tab.

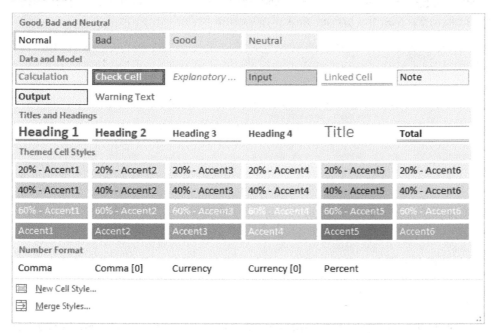

Styles here were created based on common formatting attributes used for general documents such as budgets, cash flows, etc.

Note the following restrictions:

- You define styles for a workbook. You cannot store them in a template file.
- If you change a style, Excel applies the changes to all cells using that style in every worksheet in the workbook.
- Unlike in Word, you cannot determine what style a cell is using because you cannot see the style name displayed on the Home tab.
- You base styles on the currently selected theme. If you change the theme or the formatting of the theme, the style also changes.

EXERCISE

In this exercise, you will format different parts of the worksheet to emphasize values and text.

1. Open the *Balance Sheet* file and save it as `Balance Sheet - Student`.
2. Select cells **A1** to **C1**. Then on the Home tab, in the Alignment group, click **Merge & Center**.
3. Repeat step 2 for cells **A2** to **C2** and **A3** to **C3**.

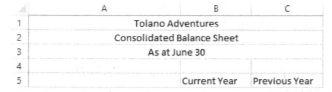

4. Select the three cells and on the Home tab, in the Font group, click **B**.
5. Click the arrow for **Font Size** and change this to **14**.
6. Click cell **B5** and drag to cell **C5**. Press Ctrl and then click cells **A6, A11, A13, A16, A18, A21** and **A23**.

7. Press (Ctrl)+(B) to add bold to all these cells.

8. Select cells **B7** to **C10**, press (Ctrl) and select cells **B14** to **C15** and also cells **B19** to **C20**.

9. On the Home tab in the Number group, click ' **(Comma Style)**.

	A	B	C
1		Tolano Adventures	
2		Consolidated Balance Sheet	
3		As at June 30	
4			
5		Current Year	Previous Year
6	Assets		
7	Cash	45,430.00	44,536.00
8	Customer Deposits	85,930.00	75,930.00
9	Equipment, Net	234,824.00	235,924.00
10	Buildings, Net	1,927,245.00	1,927,350.00
11	Total Assets	2293429	2283740
12			
13	Liabilities		
14	Accounts Payable	42,569.00	36,096.00
15	Mortgage Payable	1,592,742.00	1,592,850.00
16	Total Liabilities	1635311	1628946
17			
18	Shareholders' Equity		
19	Share Capital	100,000.00	100,000.00
20	Retained Earnings	558,118.00	554,794.00
21	Total Shareholders' Equity	658118	654794
22			
23	Total Liabilities and Equity	2293429	2283740
24			

10. Click cells **B11** to **C11**, press (Ctrl), then click **B16** to **C16**, **B21** to **C21**, and **B23** to **C23**.

11. On the Home tab, in the Number group, click $ ▾.

	A	B	C
1		Tolano Adventures	
2		Consolidated Balance Sheet	
3		As at June 30	
4			
5		Current Year	Previous Year
6	Assets		
7	Cash	45,430.00	44,536.00
8	Customer Deposits	85,930.00	75,930.00
9	Equipment, Net	234,824.00	235,924.00
10	Buildings, Net	1,927,245.00	1,927,350.00
11	Total Assets	$2,293,429.00	$2,283,740.00
12			
13	Liabilities		
14	Accounts Payable	42,569.00	36,096.00
15	Mortgage Payable	1,592,742.00	1,592,850.00
16	Total Liabilities	$1,635,311.00	$1,628,946.00
17			
18	Shareholders' Equity		
19	Share Capital	100,000.00	100,000.00
20	Retained Earnings	558,118.00	554,794.00
21	Total Shareholders' Equity	$ 658,118.00	$ 654,794.00
22			
23	Total Liabilities and Equity	$2,293,429.00	$2,283,740.00

You have successfully applied two different number styles to the report to reflect the different types of data, such as list items versus total values.

12. Select cells **B11** to **C11** and then **B23** to **C23**. On the Home tab in the Number group, click the **Number** dialog box launcher.

13. Click the **Font** tab. Click the arrow for the **Underline** option and click **Double**. In the field to the right, change the color to a **dark red**. Click **OK**.

234,824.00	235,924.00
1,927,245.00	1,927,350.00
$2,293,429.00	$2,283,740.00
42,569.00	36,096.00
1,592,742.00	1,592,850.00
$1,635,311.00	$1,628,946.00

> **Tip:** You could also have used the **Bottom Double Border** option from the **Borders** feature in the Font group of the Home tab.

	100,000.00	100,000.00
	558,118.00	554,794.00
iity	$ 658,118.00	$ 654,794.00
iity	$2,293,429.00	$2,283,740.00

14. Select cells **B5** to **B23**. Then on the Home tab, in the Numbers group, click the dialog box launcher and click the **Fill** tab.

   You want to apply a very light fill to emphasize the comparison between this year and last year.

15. In the first row below the horizontal line, click the first box (very light gray) for the fill color. Click **OK**.

16. Click anywhere away from the selected cell range to view the fill.

	A	B	C
1		Tolano Adventures	
2		Consolidated Balance Sheet	
3		As at June 30	
4			
5		Current Year	Previous Year
6	Assets		
7	Cash	45,430.00	44,536.00
8	Customer Deposits	85,930.00	75,930.00
9	Equipment, Net	234,824.00	235,924.00
10	Buildings, Net	1,927,245.00	1,927,350.00
11	Total Assets	$2,293,429.00	$2,283,740.00
12			
13	Liabilities		
14	Accounts Payable	42,569.00	36,096.00
15	Mortgage Payable	1,592,742.00	1,592,850.00
16	Total Liabilities	$1,635,311.00	$1,628,946.00
17			
18	Shareholders' Equity		
19	Share Capital	100,000.00	100,000.00
20	Retained Earnings	558,118.00	554,794.00
21	Total Shareholders' Equity	$ 658,118.00	$ 654,794.00
22			
23	Total Liabilities and Equity	$2,293,429.00	$2,283,740.00

When choosing a background color, try to choose one that does not make the values difficult to read or that emphasizes the wrong items or areas of the worksheet. On occasion you may find you need to adjust the colors accordingly.

Now apply cell styles to the worksheet to see how these work.

17. Select the first two cells (the titles on rows 1 and 2). On the Home tab, in the Styles group, click **Cell Styles**, and then click **Title**.

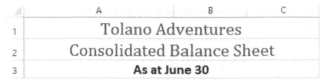
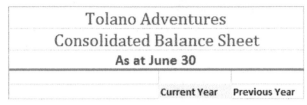

	A	B	C
1	Tolano Adventures		
2	Consolidated Balance Sheet		
3	**As at June 30**		

18. Move the cursor to the *June 30* title on row 3. On the Home tab, in the Styles group, click **Cell Styles**, and then click **Heading 1**.

Tolano Adventures		
Consolidated Balance Sheet		
As at June 30		
	Current Year	**Previous Year**

Notice how you can use the styles to apply formatting quickly for specific types of information. You can also blend them as we did in this exercise; Excel does not restrict you to using styles only, or manual formatting.

19. Save and close the workbook.

Using the Spell Checker

IC³ **Exam 2 - Objective 1.1**

Use the spell check feature on text labels as Excel cannot automatically verify the accuracy of numbers, dates, and time values. Note that using the spell checker does not eliminate the need for you to proof your worksheet.

To activate the Spelling feature, use one of the following methods:

- On the Review tab, in the Proofing group, click **Spelling**; or
- press (F7).

MMM
Pilot IT
Project
Budget

EXERCISE

In this exercise you will run a spell check on a report that was sent to Andrew from a friend who found this information to be very interesting.

1. Open the *International Backyard Olympics* file and save it as `International Backyard Olympics - Student`.

2. Click cell **A5**, then click the **Review** tab and in the Proofing group, click **Spelling**.

   When the first word appears in the Spelling dialog box, look at the word carefully before choosing to change it automatically. This is an example of when you will need to look at the data to determine if this is a proper name for an object or a misspelled word; in this scenario it is a misspelling.

3. In the Suggestions list, select **Leaf** and then click **Change**.

4. Continue with the spell check, changing words appropriately.

5. When complete, click **OK**.

6. If prompted to continue checking from the beginning of the sheet, click **No**.

7. Save and close the workbook.

Sorting or Filtering Data

 Exam 2 - Objective 3.2

Sorting Data

Excel provides a sorting tool that enables you to organize data in a worksheet based on the values in the selected columns or rows. Sorting makes data more readable. You can sort and re-sort data as many times as required, using different sort criteria each time. You can sort data by columns or rows. You may only need to sort by one column. Excel has two ready-to-use buttons for this:

- On the Data tab, in the Sort & Filter group, click **Sort A to Z** or **Sort Z to A**; or

- on the Home tab, in the Editing group, click **Sort & Filter**.

To activate the Sort dialog box for more than one sort option, on the Data tab, in the Sort & Filter group, click **Sort**.

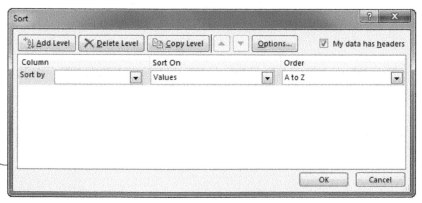

Add Level, Delete Level, Copy Level	Adds, deletes, or copies sort columns or rows. Note that the topmost sort key is the highest (primary) sorting level, followed by the remaining levels in descending order.
Move Up/Move Down	Moves the selected sort level higher or lower in the sorting sequence.

Options	Sort by columns or rows or left to right, and choose whether the sort criteria will be case sensitive. 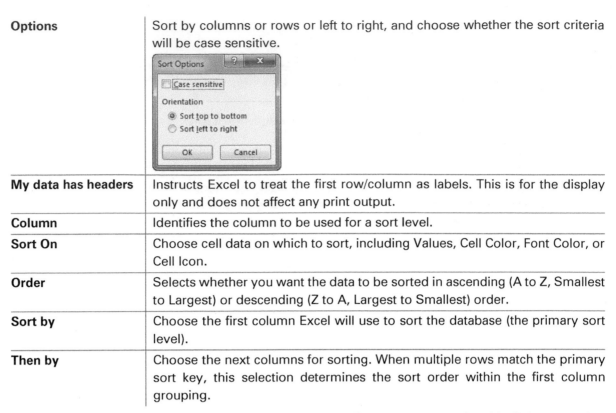
My data has headers	Instructs Excel to treat the first row/column as labels. This is for the display only and does not affect any print output.
Column	Identifies the column to be used for a sort level.
Sort On	Choose cell data on which to sort, including Values, Cell Color, Font Color, or Cell Icon.
Order	Selects whether you want the data to be sorted in ascending (A to Z, Smallest to Largest) or descending (Z to A, Largest to Smallest) order.
Sort by	Choose the first column Excel will use to sort the database (the primary sort level).
Then by	Choose the next columns for sorting. When multiple rows match the primary sort key, this selection determines the sort order within the first column grouping.

You can choose up to 64 columns or rows as sort levels if the primary sort level includes repeating values. The data in each sort level sorts in ascending or descending sequence.

If the range of cells being sorted does not contain column or row headers, turn off the **My data has headers** option. Use this option to prevent the header data from being included with the data to be sorted; they will remain in their places as headers.

EXERCISE

In this exercise, you will sort the inventory list by different criteria.

1. Open the *Inventory to Sort* file and save as `Inventory to Sort - Student`.

2. Click in cell **A2**. Then on the Data tab, in the Sort & Filter group, click **Sort**.

3. Click the arrow for the **Sort by** field.

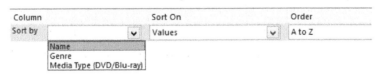

4. Click **Name** as the column to use for the sort and then click **OK**.

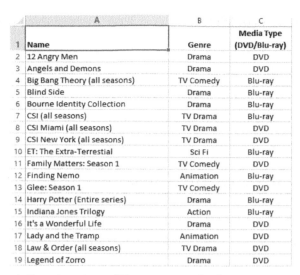

Now let's set up two different sort criteria.

5. On the Data tab, in the Sort & Filter group, click **Sort**.

6. Click the arrow for **Sort by** and click **Genre**.

7. Click **Add Level** to enter another sort criteria.

8. Click the arrow for **Then by** and click **Name**. Click **OK**.

The inventory list is now sorted by genre and then by the title.

Add one more sort level to sort the inventory list by media type, then by genre, and finally by the title.

9. On the Data tab, in the Sort & Filter group, click **Sort**. Then set the options as shown in the following:

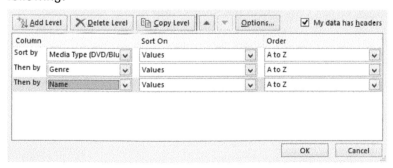

10. Click **OK**.

Your results should appear similar to the following:

	A	B	C
1	Name	Genre	Media Type (DVD/Blu-ray)
2	Indiana Jones Trilogy	Action	Blu-ray
3	Lord of the Rings Collection	Action	Blu-ray
4	Finding Nemo	Animation	Blu-ray
5	Lion King	Animation	Blu-ray
6	Little Mermaid	Animation	Blu-ray
7	Monsters Inc	Animation	Blu-ray
8	Toy Story Collection	Animation	Blu-ray
9	Up	Animation	Blu-ray
10	Mr. Poppa's Penguins	Comedy	Blu-ray
11	Blind Side	Drama	Blu-ray
12	Bourne Identity Collection	Drama	Blu-ray
13	Harry Potter (Entire series)	Drama	Blu-ray
14	Ocean's Eleven Collection	Drama	Blu-ray
15	Pirates of the Caribbean Collection	Drama	Blu-ray
16	Tree of Life	Drama	Blu-ray
17	ET: The Extra-Terrestial	Sci Fi	Blu-ray
18	Star Wars Trilogy	Sci Fi	Blu-ray
19	Big Bang Theory (all seasons)	TV Comedy	Blu-ray
20	CSI (all seasons)	TV Drama	Blu-ray
21	Lost (all seasons)	TV Drama	Blu-ray
22	Top Gun	Action	DVD
23	Lady and the Tramp	Animation	DVD

11. Save the document.

Filtering Information

Finding information in a large or unorganized worksheet can be simplified by sorting; however, you still have to look through all the records in the database. Another way to locate information quickly is to use a filter to hide the records you are not interested in. Filtering does not change the content of your worksheet or the sequence of the information, only what you see.

The quickest and easiest way to filter data in Excel is to use the AutoFilter tool. When you activate this tool, Excel places AutoFilter icons on the right side of each column or field name. Use these icons to select the conditions for the records you want displayed. Initially all information is shown.

The AutoFilter can find rows where a cell is equal to a specific value or set of values. Other selection criteria give you the flexibility to find almost anything you need, including values that are not equal, greater than, less than, greater than or equal to, less than or equal to, and between. Certain types of fields have additional selection criteria (discussed later):

Numbers	Includes top 10, above/below average.
Dates	Includes today, tomorrow, yesterday, this/next/last week, this/next/last month, this/next/last quarter, this/next/last year, year to date.
Text	Includes begins/ends with, contains, does not contain.

To activate the Filter command, on the Data tab, in the Sort & Filter group, click **Filter**.

	A	B	C
1	Name ▾	Genre ▾	Media Type (DVD/Blu-ray ▾
2	Indiana Jones Trilogy	Action	Blu-ray
3	Lord of the Rings Collection	Action	Blu-ray
4	Finding Nemo	Animation	Blu-ray
5	Lion King	Animation	Blu-ray

When the filter command is activated, Excel places arrows on each column heading that you can use to filter the information in the worksheet. Use these arrows to filter the information and show only the data you want to view.

To clear a filter, use one of the following methods:

- On the Data tab, in the Sort & Filter group, click **Clear**; or

- click the **AutoFilter** button for the filtered data and then click **Clear Filter From**.

EXERCISE

In this exercise, you will use the Filter feature to narrow the search to only show data you are interested in viewing currently.

1. Ensure the *Inventory to Sort – Student* file is active on the screen.

2. On the Data tab, in the Sort & Filter group, click **Filter**.

   Arrows should appear at the bottom right of each column heading in the report.

3. Click the **AutoFilter** button for **Genre**.

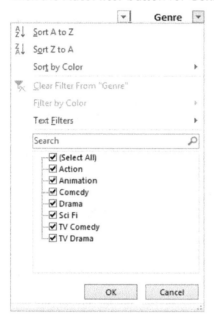

Notice that Excel gives you the option to sort the data, as needed, in addition to setting conditions to find a specific piece of data using the Text Filters. Point to Text Filters to see the available options:

In the bottom half of the menu is a list of the items that appear at least once in the report. You can set the filter using one of these options.

4. Click **Select All** to turn off this option and then click **Animation**. Then click **OK**.

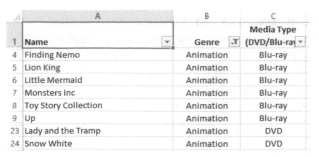

You should now be able to see only the titles that are listed as Animation. Notice that the filter button changes to appear as ⊤ from ▼. This is a visual indicator that a filter has been applied in the worksheet.

5. On the Data tab, in the Sort & Filter group, click **Clear**.

    You should now see the entire inventory list again.

6. Click the AutoFilter arrow for **Media Type**. Click **Select All** to turn this off, click **Blu-ray** and click **OK**.

7. Click the AutoFilter arrow for **Genre** and click **Select All** to turn this off. Click **Action** and **Drama**. Click **OK**.

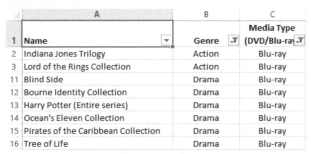

8. Save and close the worksheet.

Working with Charts

 Exam 2 - Objective 3.2

A chart is a pictorial representation of data in a worksheet. A chart can be a more descriptive way of representing your data, as it can clearly illustrate trends or patterns in the data.

You can create a chart by selecting data from the worksheet, and then select the type of chart to insert into the worksheet. Once you have created the chart, you can save it with the workbook. You can create an embedded chart that displays on the same sheet as the data, or you can create charts on their own sheets.

Each set of data in a chart is a series. The chart's horizontal line is the X-Axis, and the chart's vertical line is the Y-Axis. You can apply labels for both axes. If the information contains several data series, you can add a legend to explain the meaning of each series.

To ensure you get the best results when printing charts on a black-and-white printer, try using gray shades, monochrome, or the black/white options to differentiate the data on your chart.

To create a chart, select the cell range(s) for the chart and then, on the Insert tab, in the Charts group, click the chart type.

Once the chart has been created, it should accurately reflect any patterns or trends in the worksheet and show that information in a picture format. Remember that the chart is created based on the cells you select prior to activating the chart feature; if the data in the chart does not match your analysis of the data, you will need to check the series used in the chart (both the items being charted and any time intervals). You can also try changing the chart type to one that will better reflect the type of data you are trying to illustrate. For example, a line chart can show a significant increase in product sales at a glance better than a bar chart would, while a pie chart may do a better job of contrasting sales figures for a product during a specified period. A pie chart can emphasize the total revenue of each location for the year as it compares the values as a whole. A column or bar chart can display the same information as a comparison or ranking in a side-by-side format.

When a chart is on screen, you can select it to display the Chart Tools ribbon, which consists of two tabs with additional options for modifying or customizing the chart.

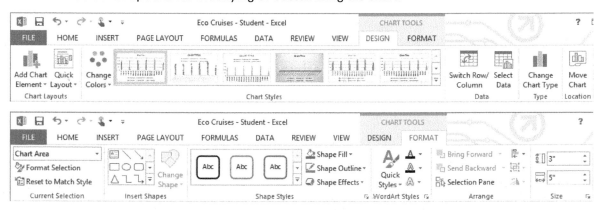

Selecting Chart Types

As noted previously, the type of chart you select will depend on what you are trying to show. Line charts are better for trends, bar charts are better for volume, and pie charts are best for showing portions of a total.

Excel provides a variety of chart types and several subtypes within each major type:

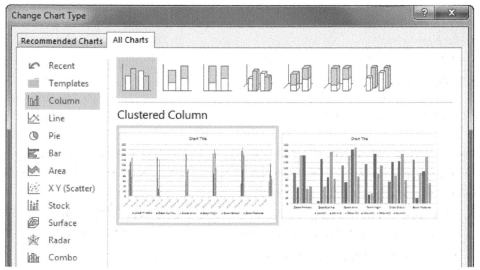

Column	Compares values over time or categories in a vertical presentation.
Line	Compares continuous trends.
Pie	Compares series that make up a whole.

Bar	Compares values over time or categories in a horizontal presentation.
Area	Compares a continuous change in volume.
X Y (Scatter)	Determines data patterns.
Stock	Displays high-low-close data; requires at least three sets of data.
Surface	Displays trends in values with a three-dimensional presentation and a continuous surface.
Radar	Determines patterns or trends with points matched up by lines.

You can create any of these charts in two-dimensional or three-dimensional form; the latter can be more interesting to look at, but may be more difficult to interpret. Alternatively, if you would like a recommendation for a chart type of use, click the Recommended Charts tab to review samples of how each chart type will appear with the data.

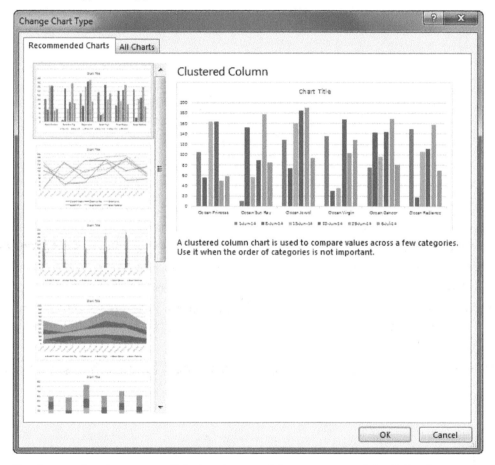

To change the chart type, click the chart and then use one of the following methods:

- Under Chart Tools, on the Design tab, in the Type group, click **Change Chart Type**; or
- right-click the plot area of the chart and then click **Change Chart Type**.

Changing the Chart Layout

Excel generates a chart using standard defaults. Modify the layout to create exactly the look you want. Use commands on the Chart Tools ribbon to manipulate items on the chart.

Chart Title	Add a title for the chart.
Axis Titles	Add titles to the horizontal and vertical axes; you can also customize items for the chart, such as the units used in the vertical axis.
Legend	Include a legend and position it in relation to the chart.
Data Labels	Include data labels on the chart.
Data Table	Display the chart data beneath the chart.
Axes	Include labels on the horizontal and vertical axes.
Gridlines	Include gridlines on the chart.

Excel provides a variety of pre-built layouts that you can apply to your chart, or use the Quick Layouts option to display some common layouts used for charts.

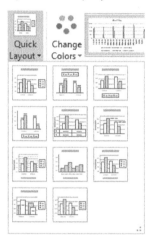

You can further modify the chart with your own layout changes, using one of the following methods:

- Click the chart element you want to modify and then click the appropriate options to change the chart element; or

- on the Format tab of the Chart Tools ribbon, in the Current Selection group, click the arrow for the chart element field to select the item, and then click appropriate options on the Chart Tools ribbon to modify the chart element, or

- Click ⊞ **(Chart Elements)** at the right of the chart to display a menu with more options for selection.

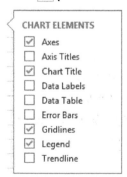

By default, Excel will place the chart in the same worksheet as its source data. You can move this chart to its own sheet, back to its original worksheet, or to a different worksheet using the **Move Chart** command, or perform a cut and paste of the chart from one sheet to another.

EXERCISE

In this exercise, you will create a simple chart and add elements to the chart to make it more effective in determining if there is a pattern for cruise ship preferences.

1. Open the *Eco Cruises* file and save it as `Eco Cruises - Student`.

2. Click the **Enable Editing** button and then the **Enable Content** button to disable the messages.

3. Select cells **A1** to **G7**. Click the **Insert** tab, in the Charts group, click **Insert Column Chart** and then **Clustered Column** in the 2-D Column area.

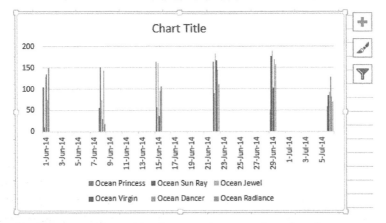

Similar to working with pictures, there are handles that you can use to size the chart object; these are represented by small squares instead of circles. To move the chart object, position the cursor anywhere on a blank area of the border around the chart and when you see ⬚, you can then drag the chart to a different location on the worksheet.

4. Position the mouse cursor on a blank area of the top border of the chart object and drag it to below the data table.

5. Position the mouse cursor on the bottom right corner of the chart object and drag to resize it so it fits within **row 27** and **column J**.

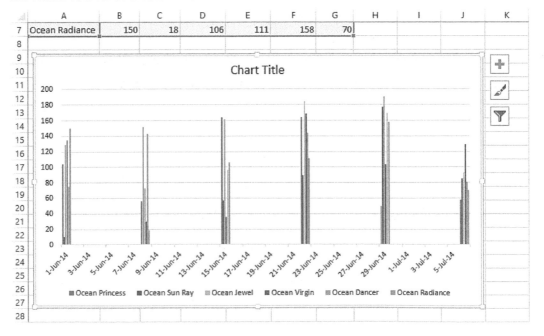

Notice how as you resize the chart, more text appeared across the bottom of the chart, or the horizontal axis. As such, the bars are now too thin to view; you may also want to switch the data so the cruise ships appear across the horizontal axis instead.

6. Under Chart Tools, on the Design tab, in the Data group, click **Switch Row/Column**.

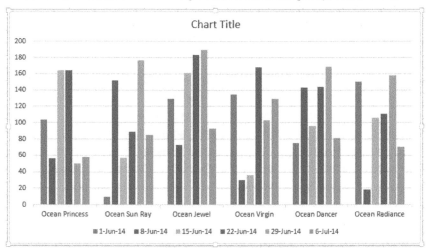

The way you display the chart data will depend on what your focus is; in this case, the current layout represents the data in a more effective manner as we can then see quickly which cruise liners seem to be doing the most business, as well as during which time frame. You can also modify the scale for the horizontal axis if you prefer the previous display. For this exercise, we will leave it with the cruise ships listed in the horizontal axis.

7. Under Chart Tools, on the Design tab, in the Chart Layouts group, click **Add Chart Element**, **Chart Title**. Then click **Above Chart**.

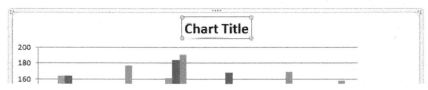

8. Type: `June Bookings` and then press (Enter).

Let's change the chart type to give the chart more impact.

9. Under Chart Tools, on the Design tab, and in the Type group, click **Change Chart Type**.

10. Click the **3-D Clustered Column** chart type (fourth chart type). Click **OK**.

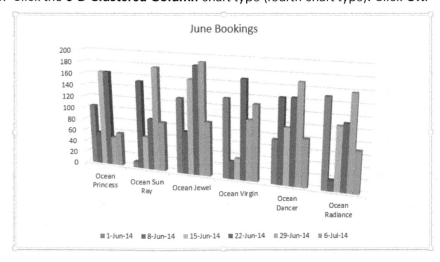

The chart type has changed but also has tilted the chart slightly as part of the chart design to show perspective.

11. Resize the chart approximately 2" (5 cm) larger so you can see how it affects the chart.

12. Save and close the worksheet.

Getting Ready to Print

 Exam 2 - Objective 1.1, 1.3

As you begin working with large worksheets, you may find that the data extends further than what the screen shows. Accordingly, Excel provides you with the ability to change how it displays the worksheet. For instance, if you are performing some "What-if" evaluations, you may want to view distant sections of one large worksheet or workbook on the screen at the same time. As a result, you may experience difficulty working on your large worksheet because you cannot see the row and column headings when making entries. By changing the view to display the values you want to work with in the worksheet, you can determine what options you may want to set prior to printing, such as whether to print the entire document onto a larger paper size, or to select only a specific cell range for printing.

The View tab offers a number of tools to facilitate different views:

Zoom	Change the magnification percentage to zoom closer or further away from the worksheet.
100%	Force the zoom back to 100% immediately.
Zoom to Selection	Zoom into the selected block of cells on the worksheet.

You can also use the zoom options at the bottom right of the status bar to adjust the view.

New Window	Open a new window containing a copy of the worksheet.
Arrange All	Arrange all the windows on the screen in one of several layouts: tiled, horizontal, vertical or cascade.
Freeze Panes	Lock in place the rows above and the columns to the left of a selected cell, while you scroll in the worksheet. This option is useful to keep the headings visible when you are working in cells located far from those headings.
Split	Split the worksheet into two or four panes.
Hide	Hide the active window; this is useful when you are working with multiple windows and you want Excel to display only specific windows.
Unhide	Display a dialog box listing windows which are currently hidden so that you can select individual windows and redisplay them.
View Side by Side	Place two open workbooks side by side in the Excel application window. You can place the workbooks side by side in a vertical or horizontal orientation.
Synchronous Scrolling	Scroll through the worksheets in each pane simultaneously.

| **Reset Window Position** | Reset the displayed worksheets to equal sizes. |
| **Switch Windows** | Present a list of open workbooks. Excel numbers the workbooks; simply click the one you want to view. |

Even though you may have multiple workbooks open at the same time, only one can be active at any given time. That is, you can work on only one workbook at a time; if you need to update two of them at essentially the same time, you must switch back and forth between workbooks to perform the required tasks.

To increase the amount of display area, you can also minimize the Ribbon temporarily.

⌐ ‒ ‒ ‒ ‒ ¬
‖ MMM ‖
‖ Where is the ‖
Money
Going?
‖_ ‒ ‒ ‒ _‖

Customizing the Printout

As you prepare to print a worksheet, Excel determines where the pages will break on the printed output. Excel uses soft page breaks to determine when it has run out of print area for the height and width of the report. To preview where these breaks are located, click **File** and then click **Print**.

A preview of the file appears, giving you a quick look at how the document will print. You can adjust page breaks using the Breaks option in the Page Layout tab. The position of the active cell prior to selecting the Breaks option controls where the page break occurs.

To remove a page break, select the same cell, and then on the Page Layout tab, in the Page Setup group, click **Breaks**, and then **Remove Page Break**. If you want to remove all page breaks in the worksheet at the same time, use **Reset All Page Breaks**.

Excel ignores page breaks if you use Fit to in the Page tab of the Page Setup command when previewing on screen or printing.

Page Break Preview is a special view of the worksheet in which the page numbers are highlighted on the screen. You can drag the page breaks to a new position and Excel will make the necessary adjustments. To use Page Break Preview, on the View tab, in the Workbook Views group, click **Page Break Preview**. Alternatively, click ▦ **(Page Break Preview)** from the view buttons on the right side of the status bar.

You can also change page settings using different options for the page setup. To display these options, use one of the following methods:

• On the Page Layout tab, in the Page Setup group, click the option to change; or

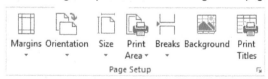

• on the Page Layout tab, in the Page Setup group, click the **Page Setup** dialog box launcher to display the Page Setup dialog box for more options.

Page Settings

Options on the Page tab of the Page Setup dialog box enable you to change the page characteristics for your printed output.

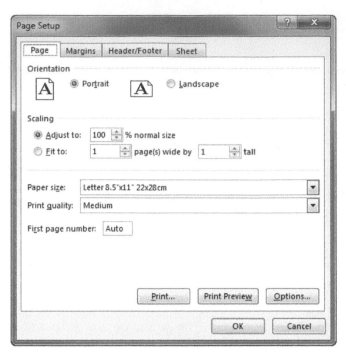

Orientation	The page orientation options are **Portrait** (vertical) or **Landscape** (horizontal). You can also select this command in the Page Setup group of the Page Layout tab.
Scaling	This option enables you to enlarge or shrink the size of the worksheet proportionally, or to use the automatic scaling feature to fit the worksheet into a specified number of pages. You can also select this command in the Scale to Fit group of the Page Layout tab.
Paper size	This option allows you to specify paper size. The options are limited by the capabilities of your printer; also, you must remember to load the appropriate paper or select the correct tray from which to print. You can also select this command in the Page Setup group on the Page Layout tab.
Print quality	This option determines the density of the print characters. Generally, the higher the print quality, the more slowly your printer will produce the document.
First page number	You can use this option to specify the starting page number for the printed worksheet. This may be useful if you are inserting Excel output into another printed document and you want to keep the page numbering sequential. Note that this is effective only if you include a page number in a header or footer.

Margins Tab

Use the Margins tab on the Page Setup dialog box to set the margins and position the print output on the page.

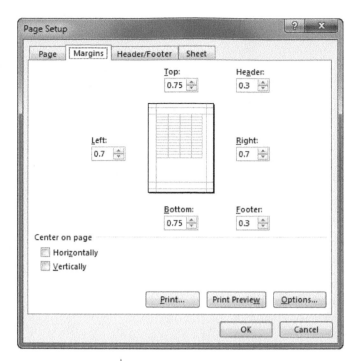

Margins	The Top, Bottom, Left, and Right options set the amount of white space (measured in inches) from the edges of the page around the printed area of the worksheet. The Header setting sets the distance between the Header and the top edge of the page, while the footer setting sets the distance between the Footer and the bottom edge of the page.
Center on page	Center the worksheet horizontally or vertically on the page, or both.

Alternatively, use one of the following methods to change the margins:

- On the Page Layout tab, in the Page Setup group, click **Margins**; or

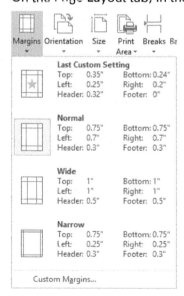

- click the **File** tab, click **Print**, click ⊞ **Show Margins** and then drag the line for the margin you want to adjust.

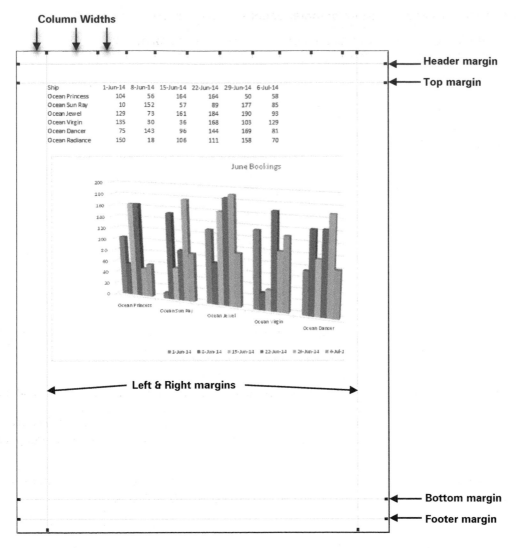

Header/Footer Tab

A *header* is text that is printed at the top of every page of the worksheet. A *footer* is text that is printed at the bottom of every page. By default, there is no text specified for the header or footer.

Excel provides several standard header or footer options, or you can create your own.

When you access Custom Header or Custom Footer, you will see the following:

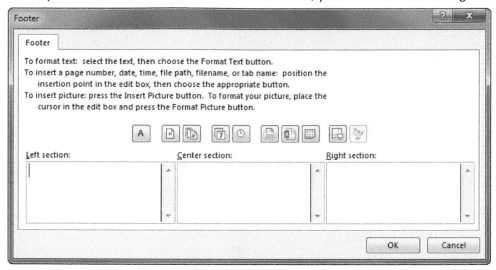

Each header or footer consists of three sections: Left, Center, and Right, which represent the left, center, and right parts of the header or footer. Use the buttons to insert commonly used variables into the header or footer.

A	**Format Text**	Changes the font and size of the text entered into one of the three sections.
	Insert Page Number	The code &[Page] displays in the selected section of the header or footer; page numbering automatically starts at 1 unless you change the starting page number in the Page tab.
	Insert Number of Pages	The code &[Pages] displays the total number of pages in the document; this is often used with the Page number code (Page 1 of 4).
	Insert Date	Inserts the current date into the report; displays as the code &[Date].
	Insert Time	Inserts the current time into the report; displays as the code &[Time].
	Insert File Path	Inserts the current path and file name into the header or footer; displays as the code &[Path]&[File].
	Insert File Name	Inserts the name of the file into the header or footer; displays as the code &[File].
	Insert Sheet Name	Inserts the name of the current worksheet; displays as the code &[Tab].
	Insert Picture	Inserts a picture into the header or footer; displays as the code &[Picture].
	Format Picture	Changes the properties for the picture.

Sheet Tab

The last of the tabs in the Page Setup dialog box is the Sheet tab. It enables you to specify how the worksheet will print.

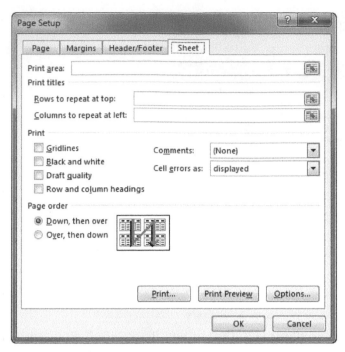

Print area	Selects the portion of the worksheet you want to print; this is useful when you want to print only parts of the worksheet. If left empty, a rectangular section of the worksheet containing all data and cell formatting will be printed.
Print titles	Repeats the column or row titles on each printed page; this is useful when you have many rows and columns of data that span more than one page. You can also select this command in the Page Setup group of the Page Layout tab.
Print	Choose to print specific worksheet items, such as row and column headings or gridlines, in the report. You can also select these commands in the Sheet Options group of the Page Layout tab.
Page order	Changes the order in which multiple pages are numbered and printed.

If you open the Page Setup dialog box from the Print Preview screen, you cannot make changes to the Print area or Print titles section of the Sheet tab.

Printing the Worksheet

To print a worksheet, click the **File** tab, and click **Print**.

Excel displays both the print options as well as a preview of the worksheet with the existing print options applied.

The total number of pages in the printout displays at the bottom left of the preview. If the number of pages exceeds or falls short of what you expected, you may need to revisit and/or change the page setup before printing.

A chart in the worksheet previews or prints based on where it is positioned in the worksheet. You can move the chart to a new worksheet, or insert a page break between the data and the chart. If you are using a monochrome printer, the chart will print in varying shades of gray; it will print in color only if you have a color printer.

Once you have previewed the worksheet on the screen and made sure it is ready to print, you can select the **Print** option.

By default, Excel prints only the current active worksheet in the workbook. You can also specify to print all worksheets in the workbook, a selected group of worksheets, or only a selected range of cells.

EXERCISE

In this exercise you will preview a worksheet and take appropriate action to produce the best result when printing.

1. Open the *Stock Prices* file and save as Stock Prices - Student.

    The file has the data in the first two columns but the rest of the file is a chart that shows the trend for the stock.

2. To determine how the worksheet would print, click **File** and then click **Print**.

Because the chart is cut off at the right side, you need to change the location of the page breaks, and modify some of the page layout options. Your customizations will be determined by what you want to emphasize in the report. In this case, we want the chart to print on its own page.

3. Click **Back** to exit the preview, click the **Page Layout** tab and then click cell **D1**. In the Page Setup group, click **Breaks** and then click **Insert Page Break**.

    You should now have a dashed vertical line between columns C and D to show this is where Excel will stop when it is printing page 1.

4. In the lower right corner of the status bar, click the ▥ **Page Break Preview** button.

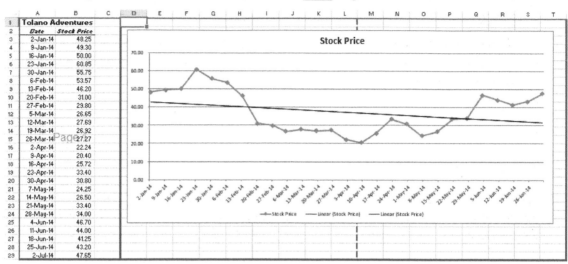

The preview shows that a page break will occur between columns C and D, and also at columns L and M. As you do not want the chart to be printed on two pages, you will need to customize the page setup.

5. On the Page Layout tab, in the Page Setup group, click **Orientation** and click **Landscape**.

6. On the Status bar, click the ▬ and ✚ buttons until you are pleased with the view size.

    You should notice that even though you changed the orientation of the report, the chart is still too big to fit on one page. You can reduce the size of the chart or change the scale for the printed report.

7. Click **File** and then click **Print**.

8. In the list of print options, click the **No Scaling** box and then click **Custom Scaling Options**.

    The Page tab of the Page Setup dialog box appears.

9. Click the incremental button for the **Adjust to** field until it reads 75%. Click **OK**.

10. At the bottom left of the preview portion on the screen, click the ▶ to go to page **2**.

Now try changing the margins to see if this will allow you to increase the scaling for the chart.

11. Click the **Normal Margins** option and change this to **Narrow Margins**.

12. Click the **Custom Scaling** option and click **Custom Scaling Options**. Change the scaling to **85** and click **OK** to see the impact it may have on the chart preview.

    Even though you increased the chart size by 10% (and in fact, you may be able to make it a bit bigger) the smaller margin size allows the chart to fit on one page. This is an example of how you can tweak options to enhance or change elements in the report.

13. Try changing the scaling slightly to see how it appears in the preview.

14. If available, try printing the report to see how it appears in hard copy.

Now let's add a footer to the report so we know where to find this file as well as display a page number.

15. Click the **Back** button to go back to the worksheet.

16. On the Page Layout tab, in the Page Setup group, click the **Page Setup** dialog box launcher.

17. Click the **Header/Footer** tab and click the **Custom Footer** button.

18. In the box at the left, click the ⬚ button to insert the file and path. Click in the middle box and type your name. Select your name and then click the ⬚ button.

19. Change the size to **9** and then choose a color of your choice. Click **OK**.

20. Click in the box at the right and then click the ⬚ button to insert the page number. Click **OK** twice.

21. Preview the report to see if you need to adjust the font size for the footer text. If so, make the appropriate change.

22. If available, print the report once more to include the footer in the printout.

23. Click **Back** to return to the worksheet, then save and close the file.

Lesson Summary

In this lesson you were introduced to the basic skills for working with a spreadsheet application. You learned to enter and format text and formulas, navigate and manage worksheets, filter and sort data, create and modify charts and set printing options. You should now be familiar with:

☑ adding or changing numbers and labels   ☑ sorting and filtering data

☑ entering simple formulas   ☑ creating and manipulating charts

☑ managing worksheets   ☑ customizing the page setup

☑ formatting data

Review Questions

1. A cell is:
   a. The field below the ribbon that shows a reference
   b. The grey boxes at the top or left of the worksheet identifying the columns or rows
   c. The intersection of a column and a row
   d. All of the above
   e. a or c

2. Which steps should you take to display a list of workbook templates?
   a. On the Quick Access toolbar, click New.
   b. Click the File tab, click New.
   c. Press (Ctrl)+(N).
   d. Click the Blank Workbook link on the Getting Started task pane

3. How can you adjust the width of a column?
   a. On the Home tab, in the Cells group, click Format, click Column Width.
   b. On the Home tab, in the Cells group, click Format, click Row Height.
   c. Click and drag the line at the right of the column heading.
   d. Any of the above
   e. a or c

4. When you insert a new row, where does it go?
   a. Above the current row
   b. Below the current row

┌─ ─ ─ ─ ─ ┐
│ **MMM** │
│Go online for│
│ Additional │
│   Review   │
└ ─ ─ ─ ─ ─ ┘

5. How can you enter a cell address into a formula?
   a. You can type it in manually.
   b. You can select the cell and continue typing the formula.
   c. You can click the cell to be included in the formula instead of typing its address.
   d. Any of the above
   e. a or c

6. Look at the following table of information, and then indicate what conclusion you can make from the data:

Production	Week 1	Week 2	Week 3	Week 4
Widgets	80	85	90	80
Gadgets	150	175	200	180

   a. It takes longer to produce widgets than gadgets in the month.
   b. The greatest amount of production occurred during the third week of the month.
   c. Approximately twice as many gadgets are being produced than widgets.
   d. Any of the above
   e. b or c

7. Why might you want to set the Last Name field as the primary sort key and the First Name field as the secondary sort key?
   a. All sorting operations must include at least two sort fields.
   b. You want to group all people with the same first name.
   c. You want to alphabetize people with the same last name.
   d. You want to filter the data to show all people with the same last name.

8. What does the term "Series" refer to?
   a. A set of data being used in the chart.
   b. The type of chart being created.
   c. The group of charts available for the different types of data being charted.
   d. The title for the chart.

9. If you wanted to plot a continuous trend, which type of chart would you create?
   a. Column   c. Line
   b. Bar   d. Pie

10. Why would you want to preview a worksheet prior to printing?
    a. To see how it will appear when printed.
    b. To prevent wasting paper if changes are needed.
    c. To determine whether changes are necessary for the layout of the report.
    d. Any of the above

11. How can you insert a page break?
    a. On the Insert tab, in the Setup group, click Page Break.
    b. On the Insert tab, in the Break group, click Page.
    c. On the Page Layout tab, in the Page Setup group, click Page Break.
    d. On the Page Layout tab, in the Page Setup group, click Breaks, Insert Page Break.

12. Which of the following buttons would you use to insert the file name into a header or footer?
    a. [A]   d. [7]
    b. [ ]   e. [ ]
    c. [ ]   f. [ ]

Lesson 10: Microsoft PowerPoint

Lesson Objectives

In this lesson you are introduced to basic skills for working with an application designed to manage presentations delivered in various mediums. You will set up presentations, and create and edit slides that include text, images, charts, tables, or multimedia. When you have completed this lesson, you will be familiar with the following:

☐ general structure and guidelines for creating presentations

☐ creating new blank presentations or using a template to create a new presentation

☐ saving, closing, or opening presentations

☐ changing the view display for the slides

☐ inserting, deleting or duplicating slides

☐ changing the slide layout or design

☐ adding or manipulating text on the slides

☐ adding or manipulating tables and charts on the slides

☐ adding or manipulating multimedia objects such as pictures, movies, music files

☐ setting up and running the slide show

☐ creating notes or handouts to accompany the slides

☐ printing slide items

What is PowerPoint?

PowerPoint is a presentation program that you can use to create, edit, and manipulate slides for on-screen presentations, sending via email, or promoting products or services on a web page. These presentations can be delivered to live audiences, or viewed individually (self-directed) by others at their convenience.

You can enter text, draw objects, create charts, or add graphics. You can choose to print a presentation or share it over the Internet.

Consider the following tips when creating a presentation:

- Use bullet points or numbers to show procedural steps. Keep the number of points on each slide to a minimum (no more than six recommended), thereby keeping the text brief.

- Set up tables to summarize data, and make sure the data within the tables is legible.

- Include charts to show data patterns or trends, and also show the data sheet for reference.

- Include pictures of varying types. For instance, you might want to include the organization logo on every slide, or a picture of a new product with bullet points on its features and benefits.

- Customize the master slide with the company logo, web site address, and contact information to remind the audience of who you are and what you are presenting. You can then distribute copies to your audience with key points from your presentation.

PowerPoint includes many features to enhance the look of presentations, including the ability to set font and size, background color of each slide, animation, or transitions that will help maintain consistency throughout your presentation. As with other design programs, use design elements with discretion to prevent the presentation from becoming difficult to view; for example, it can be difficult to read content if it's on a dark background even if the text is in a bright color. Animations that occur too quickly can also be distracting. On the other hand, some design elements can help you put some of your information into pictures – which can convey a great deal of information quickly and concisely.

After creating a presentation, always consider having someone else review it to ensure you have the best content, design elements, and timing for your targeted audience.

What Does a Presentation Include?

PowerPoint is used to build a presentation slide by slide. Those slides, shown in order, make up your presentation. Different slide types serve different functions.

Title Slide

This is the opening slide that introduces the subject of the presentation. The title slide usually includes the title or topic, and a subtitle. The subtitle might be the presenter's name or the presenting organization's name, or it might be the date and location of the presentation.

Agenda Slide

This slide usually lists the titles of all the slides in your presentation. The agenda slide is often the second slide in a presentation. It provides an overview of what will be covered, and can help the viewer grasp the flow of the presentation.

Title and Content Slide

This type of slide is the most frequently used layout. The layout controls which placeholders appear on a slide. A title and content slide is commonly referred to as a bulleted-list slide because it includes a title and a bulleted list. The list includes the key points the speaker wants to make about a specific topic. Bullet points should be brief, concise, and clear.

Support Content Slides

You can add various kinds of content to your presentation using different content layouts. Content can include text, design elements, diagrams, videos, tables, charts, sounds, animation, or special transitions from slide to slide.

Summary Slide

The summary slide is the last slide in the presentation. It reviews your presentation, reinforces the key messages, and provides contact information for further details.

Each slide includes placeholders—a dashed-line box with a tip that tells you what you can use the box for. The blank slide layout, however, does not include placeholders.

You can click inside a placeholder to insert text or an object.

When you see a placeholder like the one at the right, click an icon in the box to insert that particular type of object.

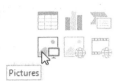

As you position the mouse pointer over an icon, PowerPoint displays a screen tip indicating which type of object will be inserted when you click it.

To move from one placeholder to another on a slide, click the placeholder or press Ctrl + Enter.

Working with Presentations

 Exam 2 - Objective 1.3, 4.1

When PowerPoint starts, it opens in Backstage where you can choose to create a new presentation or open an existing presentation.

Creating Presentations

There are three common methods to create a presentation in PowerPoint, depending on the purpose of the presentation:

Blank Presentation	Provides a blank presentation with only a title slide (no colors or design elements); you add your own content and apply your own colors, backgrounds, images, and so on.
Templates	Use a pre-designed presentation with suggestions for text and application of colors, backgrounds, images, and so on; you can type the text and make design changes.
Reuse Slides	Insert one or more slides from an existing presentation to the current presentation. You can also choose to have the formatting used in the existing presentation to be inserted with the slide, as required.

Create a blank presentation using one of the following methods:

- Click the **File** tab, click **New**, and then **Blank Presentation**; or
- press Ctrl + N.

Before creating your presentation:

- Plan your presentation in draft form before creating it on the computer. This can save you time and keep you on track.

- Keep the text consistent in format and layout – too many variations can be distracting. Remember that text is generally read from left to right, top to bottom.

- Keep the number of colors used to a minimum. Too many colors on one slide can be distracting and detract from the message.

- Use contrast to emphasize a message, such as dark text on a light background.

- Keep the number of bullet points per slide to a minimum; the standard is six points per slide. Make your points brief as you want the audience to pay attention to what you're saying, not what you're displaying.

- Be consistent with special effects.

- For graphs or charts, keep the information to a minimum or split the information onto several slides. Remember the rule: "If it takes you a long time to create the slide, it will take just as long for the audience to read and understand it."

- Add pictures or tables only when relevant or for emphasis. Too much information can be distracting and cause confusion.

- Ensure that the presentation clearly identifies you to the audience.

The appearance and delivery of the presentation can determine how successful you are in reaching and influencing your audience.

Entering Text in the Outline Tab

Use the *Outline View* to insert most or all of the text for the presentation in a separate pane before inserting any illustrations or design elements. You can enhance the presentation using the Slide pane. The Outline View can be activated from the Presentation Views group of the View tab.

1 ☐ **Life Through the Eyes of a Camel**
Traveling via Camel Train

2 ☐ **Planning the Tour**
• What is involved?
• How much are these tours?
• How do they compare to other adventures?
• What's different than a regular sight-seeing tour?

The first line next to the ☐ **(slide icon)** is always the title of the slide. As you type here, the text appears in the Title placeholder box. If you press ⎡Enter⎤ after typing the title on the first slide, a new slide with the Title and Text slide layout will be added to the presentation.

- To insert text for the next text placeholder on the same slide, press ⎡Ctrl⎤+⎡Enter⎤. If you press ⎡Enter⎤ after typing the title on any other slide layout, a new slide with the same slide layout will be added to the presentation.

- To move into the Bulleted List placeholder, on the Title and Content slide, press ⎡Ctrl⎤+⎡Enter⎤ after the title line. After typing in the first point and pressing ⎡Enter⎤, a new bullet line appears.

- To move in a level or create a sub-point, move the insertion point to the beginning of the bullet and press ⎡Tab⎤. This is also known as increasing the indent level.

- To move back to the previous level, move the insertion point to the beginning of the bullet and press ⎡Shift⎤+⎡Tab⎤. This is also known as decreasing the indent level.

- To create a new slide after entering all the points in a bulleted list, press ⎡Ctrl⎤+⎡Enter⎤.

- To select the contents of the entire slide, click the slide icon for the slide.

  1 ☐ **Life Through the Eyes of a Camel**
  Traveling via Camel Train

  2 ⊹ **Planning the Tour**
  • What is involved?
  • How much are these tours?

To exit the Outline View, switch to Normal view.

Entering Text in the Slide Pane

Use the Slide pane to insert or modify items on slides. Placeholders clearly appear on the slides, and serve as a guide concerning where to enter text. You can add formatting to existing items on the slide, or simply add another item for the slide.

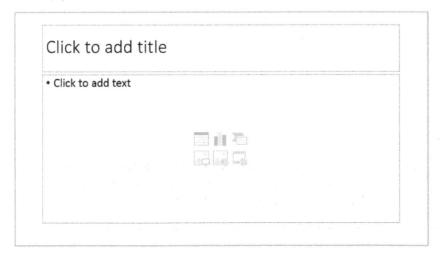

Note that the Slide pane and the Slide Thumbnails pane are two different areas with different purposes.

The Slide Thumbnails pane displays miniatures (also known as thumbnails) of your slides so you can see how the information flows or appears in different areas of the presentation. You cannot make changes directly to the slide in this view as this is an "instant preview" of the contents in the presentation only.

This is the default view for the slide contents.

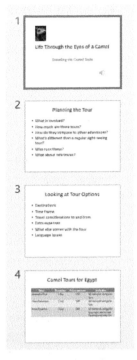

Use the split bar between the Slide Thumbnails pane and Slide pane to show more or less of each pane. For example, to display more slides in this pane, drag the split bar to the left to shrink the size of each miniature slide and fit as many slides as can fit based on the size of the PowerPoint application window.

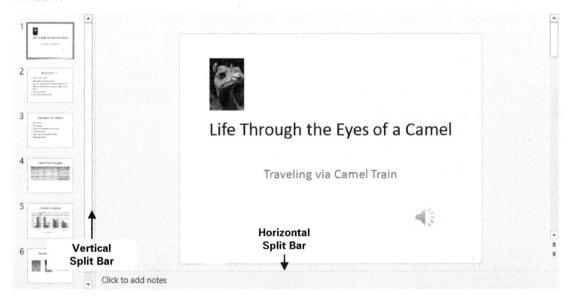

Saving a Presentation

It is important to save your presentations as you work. PowerPoint automatically assigns a .pptx extension to your files. You can also save the presentation as a .ppsx, which makes it a PowerPoint show that can play on a computer that does not have PowerPoint installed.

To save a new presentation or to save changes to an existing presentation, use one of the following methods:

- Click the **File** tab and then click **Save**, or

- on the Quick Access toolbar, click the 🔲 **Save** button, or
- press (Ctrl)+(S).

Select the location where the presentation file will be saved and then the folder, as available. You can also use the Browse button to navigate to a folder not in the Recent Folders list.

The first time you save a presentation, the Save As dialog box will open.

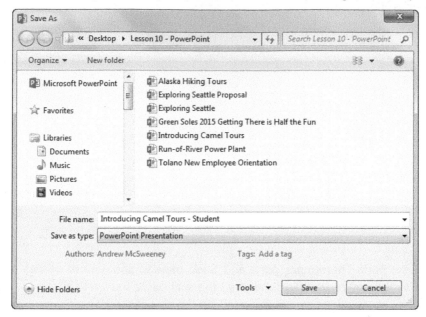

When you first save a new presentation PowerPoint suggests a file name based on the text entered on the title slide; you can accept this name or enter another name. PowerPoint also displays the default folder (such as My Documents in the Documents library), or a folder designated by your school or organization.

To save an existing file with a new name, click the **File** tab and then **Save As**.

If you need to save the file in another format, in the Save As dialog box, click the arrow for the Save as type field and then select the appropriate file type:

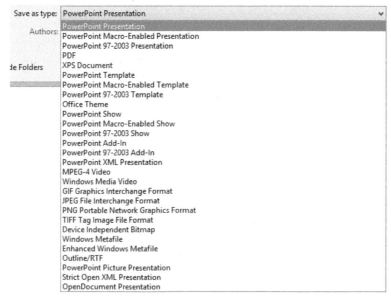

By default, PowerPoint saves presentation files using the .pptx file name extension, although you can change the file type as may be needed by someone who cannot open the 2013 file format type.

Closing a Presentation

Once you have finished working with a presentation, save and close it to clear the screen. To close a presentation, use one of the following methods:

- Click the **File** tab and then click **Close**, or
- Press Ctrl+W or Ctrl+F4, or
- Click the ☒ **Close** button for the application.

When the last open presentation has been closed using one of the first two methods, the application window becomes gray and the only ribbon tab available is the File tab. You use the File tab to open or create a new file.

Opening a Presentation

You can open a presentation file using one of the following methods:

- Click the **File** tab, click **Open**, click the location where the file is saved, and click the file from the list of **Recent Presentations**; or
- click the **File** tab, click **Open**, click the location where the file is saved, click **Browse** to navigate to the folder where the file is saved, select the file and then click **Open**, or
- press Ctrl+O, click the location where the file is saved, click **Browse** to navigate to the folder where the file is saved, select the file and then click **Open** or
- open it directly from Computer or File Explorer.

If the file was saved in a different file format than PowerPoint 2013, click the All PowerPoint Presentations button to choose another file format:

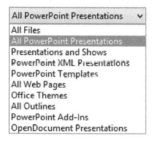

If you open a file that was saved from an attachment in an email, **Protected View** will display an information bar requesting you to enable editing in the file before you can make changes to it (see below). The Protected View feature protects you from the possibility of opening a file that may contain a virus; always save and scan any attachments you receive via email before opening the file in the application program. Alternatively you can apply this feature when opening a presentation to prevent any accidental changes being made to the file.

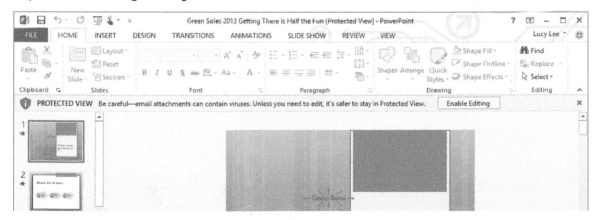

EXERCISE

In this exercise you will create new presentations, open existing presentations, make changes and then save the changes.

1. Start Microsoft PowerPoint, if necessary. Double-click **Blank Presentation**.

2. In the Slide pane for the new blank presentation, type: `Travel Has No Age!` and then press `Ctrl`+`Enter` to move to the sub-title placeholder.

    The text you just entered should appear in the placeholder for the main title of the presentation.

3. In the sub-title placeholder, type: `Andrew McSweeney` for the text, and then click anywhere away from the placeholder.

You will now enter text for the next few slides.

4. Click the **View** tab and in the Presentation Views group, click **Outline View**.

5. At the end of Andrew McSweeney line of text, press `Ctrl`+`Enter` to create a new slide.

    1   **Travel Has No Age!**
          Andrew McSweeney

    2 |

6. Type: `Agenda` as the main title and press `Enter`.

    1   **Travel Has No Age!**
          Andrew McSweeney

    2   **Agenda**

    |3 |

    PowerPoint assumes you want to stay at this level and create a new slide. As you want to enter the bulleted text for this slide instead, you need to press `Tab` to have PowerPoint set the proper level for the text.

7. Press `Tab`.

    1   **Travel Has No Age!**
          Andrew McSweeney

    2   **Agenda**

8. Type: `Introduction` and press `Enter`.

    PowerPoint places you at the same level so you can continue to enter text.

9. Continue entering the rest of the text as shown in the following:

    2   **Agenda**
         • Introduction
         • Picking a Destination
         • Looking at all the Options
         • Go on Your Own or in a Group
         • Using a Travel Consultant vs
           Booking Trip Yourself

10. Press `Tab` to tell PowerPoint you want to enter text at a sub-level for the last bullet point entered.

11. Type: `Advantages and disadvantages` and press `Enter`.

    PowerPoint keeps you at the same level as this sub-text.

12. Type: `Cost differences` and press (Enter).

13. Press (Shift)+(Tab) to move up one level so the text for the upcoming bullet point is at the main level.

14. Type: `Preparing for the Trip` and press (Ctrl)+(Enter) to create a new slide.

15. On the Quick Access toolbar, click 🔲 (**Save**). Click **Computer** as the location and then click **Browse** to navigate to where the student data files are located and then to the Lesson 10 folder. In the Save As dialog box, click at the end of the file name in the File name field. Type: `- Student` and then press (Enter) to save the file.

Now create a new presentation using a template provided in PowerPoint.

16. Click the **File** tab and then click **New**.

17. In the search field, type: `certificates` and press (Enter).

18. Click the **Certificate, Employee of the month (blue chain...)** and then click **Create**.

If this template is not available, choose a certificate from the choices available on your system. It isn't important which certificate you use; the focus here is seeing how PowerPoint provides some pre-designed templates you can use to enter data as required.

You are now ready to save the file with a new name and make changes to the presentation.

19. Press Ctrl + S to save the presentation. Click **Computer** as the location and then click the **Lesson 10 – PowerPoint** folder from the list of Recent Folders.

20. Type: Green Soles Certificate - Student as the new name and then click **Save**.

21. Triple-click where the text *Raffaella Bonaldi* appears to select this text and type: Irma Greenwood.

22. Select the date and type in today's date.

23. Save the certificate again. Then press Ctrl + N to create a new blank presentation.

24. Point at the PowerPoint icon on the Windows taskbar.

    You should have at least three preview windows, one for each open presentation (the number of windows may vary depending on how many presentations you have open or created during this exercise).

25. In the window with the blank presentation created in step 23, click the **Close** button.

26. Press Ctrl + W to close the next presentation.

27. Click **File** and then click **Close** to close the last presentation (repeat this step if you have other presentations open).

    The PowerPoint application window should be empty.

28. Press Ctrl + O to display the Open dialog box and navigate to where the student data files are located.

29. Select the *Alaska Hiking Tours* file to open it.

30. Click **File**, click **Open**, and then in the Recent Presentations list, click the *Travel Has No Age! - Student* presentation.

    You should now have two presentations open.

31. Click **File**, click **Open**, click **Computer** and click **Lesson 10 – PowerPoint**.

32. Ensure you are viewing the student data files location, and then select the *Green Soles 2015 Getting There is Half the Fun* file.

33. Press Ctrl + W to close the *Travel Has No Age* and the *Green Soles 2015* presentations, leaving the *Alaska Hiking Tours* presentation open.

Displaying Information in the Presentation

You can change the view to see more or less of the slide contents. Each view changes the way PowerPoint displays your slides.

To change the view of the presentation, on the View tab, in the Presentation Views group, click one of the following options:

Normal	Consists of three areas: Slide Thumbnails pane, Slide pane, and Notes pane.
Outline View	Displays the Outline pane where you can enter text for the slides.
Slide Sorter	Displays multiple miniature slides on one screen; use this view to rearrange or sort your slides.

Notes Page	Allows you to add text, graphics, or audio to your speaker notes. You can type your notes into the Notes pane of Normal view, and then change to this view to add graphics and audio. Alternatively, you can use this view to enter all items for the speaker notes.
Reading View	View the show in full screen so you can view the contents of each slide in a manner similar to how your audience will view it.

Alternatively, you can click one of the following buttons at the bottom right-hand side of your screen to select any of the options described previously, with the exception of Notes Page.

▣	**Normal**	Displays the Slide Thumbnails, Slide and Notes panes.
⬚	**Slide Sorter**	Shows multiple miniature slides on one screen for rearranging or sorting.
▤	**Reading View**	Displays the slide full screen with the title bar across the top and the status bar across the bottom.
▱	**Slide Show**	Runs the slide show for your review or for you to present to your audience.

You can also change the magnification for the presentation using one of the following methods:

- On the View tab, in the Zoom group, click **Zoom**; or

- on the status bar, use one of the view options for zoom; or

- click ▣100% **(Zoom level)** to set a specific percentage level for the view; or

- click ▣ **(Fit slide to current window)** to have PowerPoint automatically resize the slide to fit within the current window.

Moving Around in the Presentation

To navigate between slides in the presentation, use one of the following methods:

- Click the ▲ **(Previous Slide)** button or press (PgUp) to move to the previous slide in the presentation; or

- click the ▼ **(Next Slide)** button or press (PgDn) to move to the next slide in the presentation; or

- in the Outline View or Slide Thumbnails pane, click the slide you want to move to in the presentation; or use the (↑) or (↓) keys to move between the slides; or

- in the Slide Sorter view, double-click the slide you want to view.

EXERCISE

In this exercise you will use different views, and then move around in the presentation.

1. Ensure the *Alaska Hiking Tours* presentation is active on the screen.

   The Slide Thumbnails pane displays all the slides in the presentation and you can use the scroll bar to move up or down to determine which slide you want to view.

2. If necessary, in the Slide Thumbnails pane at the left of the screen, click **Slide 4** to view the contents of this slide.

3. Click the **View** tab and in the Presentation Views group, click **Slide Sorter**.

Slide Sorter view can be advantageous when you want to view the entire presentation and assess the flow of information. Slide Sorter view is designed to allow you to quickly rearrange the slides by dragging them to a new location. To view the contents of a slide you may want to change, double-click the slide.

4. Scroll in the view and then double-click **Slide 11**.

Slide 11 displays in Normal view so you can make changes to it as necessary.

5. On the View tab, in the Presentation Views group, click **Reading View**.

This view is beneficial when you want to take advantage of the full monitor size to view the slides.

6. At the lower right of the Status bar, click the (**Slide Show**) button to change the view to how the slides will appear when you deliver the presentation.

7. As you point at the lower left corner of the screen, navigation icons appear; click them to move around the presentation.

> **Tip:** The navigation icons do not appear in color until you point at the icon.

8. Press (Esc) to exit this mode.

9. On the View tab, in the Presentation Views group, click **Notes Page**.

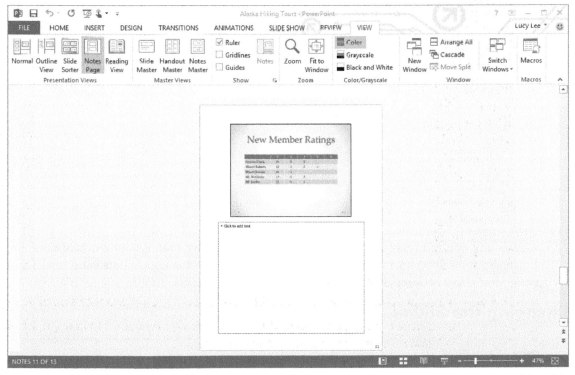

This view is beneficial when you want to see or add speaker notes or comments on slides. You can zoom in or out of the notes, as needed.

10. Use the ⬇ and ⬆ buttons to move from slide to slide.

11. On the Status bar, click the 🔳 (**Normal**) button.

12. Close this presentation file by pressing Ctrl+W.

Managing the Slides

)C³ Exam 2 - Objective 4.2, 4.3

As you begin to work with a presentation, it will likely evolve. For example, you may need to insert new slides, copy a particular slide and paste it into a new location, delete or hide a slide, or reorganize slides for better flow.

Inserting New Slides

You can insert a new slide into your presentation at any time; the new slide will be inserted directly before the currently selected slide. To insert a new slide, use one of the following methods:

- On the Home tab, in the Slides group, click **New Slide**; or
- to insert a new slide with a specific layout, on the Home tab, in the Slides group, click the down arrow for **New Slide**, and then click the layout required; or
- press Ctrl+M; or
- on the last placeholder (usually at the bottom or far right), press Ctrl+Enter; or
- right-click the slide in the Outline View or Slide Thumbnails pane and then click **New Slide**.

Notice you are presented with a variety of slide layouts that follow the standard layouts for a presentation; that is, start with a title slide, and then choose the appropriate slide based on the content being discussed on each slide you want to insert into the presentation.

Changing the Slide Layout

By default, a new presentation starts with a Title Slide layout. You can change the layout of this or any slide at any time.

To change the layout for a slide, use one of the following methods:

- On the Home tab, in the Slides group, click **Layout**; or
- right-click the slide in the Slide Thumbnails pane or the Slide pane and then click **Layout**.

Deleting Slides

When you no longer need a slide, in the Slide Thumbnails pane or Outline View, select the slide and use one of the following methods to delete it:

- press (Delete); or
- right-click the selected slide, and then click **Delete Slide**.

Rearranging the Slides

As you work with a presentation, you may want to change the order of the slides to achieve better flow of information for different speakers.

Use one of the following methods to rearrange the order of the slides:

- In the Slide Sorter view, click and drag the slide to its new location; or
- in the Outline View, click the slide icon to select the entire slide and drag to the new location; or
- in the Slide Thumbnails pane, click and drag the slide to the new location.

Changing the Theme

A *theme* is a set of unified design elements, such as backgrounds, effects, colors, fonts, and graphics, which provides a consistent look for all slides in a presentation. Themes also influence objects such as images, charts, and tables. The theme for a presentation can be changed at any time.

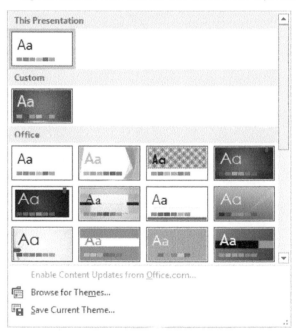

To apply a theme to all slides, click the **Design** tab, in the Themes group, click the desired theme. Alternatively, click **More** to display all the themes. You then have the option of choosing a **Variant** for this theme from the group immediately to the right on the ribbon.

Modifying Themes

You can customize individual aspects of a theme, such as the colors and fonts, while still retaining the other design elements. You can also create your own theme that you can reuse on other presentations.

To change only the theme colors, on the Design tab, in the Variants group, click the **More** arrow and click **Colors**. PowerPoint displays a list of preselected color palettes. Point the mouse at the color palettes to preview the effect on the presentation.

You can also customize the background of a theme by changing other variants in this gallery such as the fonts, effects or the background styles. These variants can be applied over top of the applied theme to produce a specific look for your presentation.

To change the background for one or all of your slides, use one of the following methods:

- On the Design tab, in the Customize group, click **Format Background**; or

- On the Design tab, in the Variants group, click **Background Styles**, then click **Format Background**, or

- right-click a blank area of the slide, and then click **Format Background**.

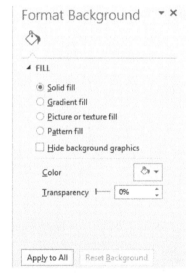

EXERCISE

In this exercise you will open a presentation, add slides, enter text, and then change the layout and design for the entire presentation.

1. Click **File**, click **Open**, click **Computer** and then click the student data files location. Select the *Tolano New Employee Orientation* file to open it.

2. Click **File,** click **Save As**, and then click **Lesson 10 – PowerPoint** in the Recent Folders list. In the File name field, press the (End) key and type: - Student for the new file name. Click **Save**.

3. In the Slide Thumbnails pane, click **Slide 3**.

4. Add the last bullet point to the slide:

    ## Company History

    - Started seven years ago
    - Reduce environmental impacts in businesses
    - Offer variety of services to assist businesses to go green
    - Offer travel adventures focused on leaving minimal carbon footprint

5. On the Home tab, in the Slides group, click **New Slide**.

    PowerPoint inserts a Title and Content slide layout for you. You will change the slide layout.

6. On the Home tab, in the Slides group, click **Layout** and then click **Title Only**.

7. Type: `Tolano Inc.` as the title and click anywhere away from the title placeholder.

8. In the Slide Thumbnails pane, click **slide 5** and then on the Home tab, in the Slides group, click **New Slide**.

9. Add the following text to this slide:

    ## Other Resources

    - Jeff Chou, Human Resources Manager, New York office
      - Obtain Company handbook
      - Manage employee records
      - Contact for training catalog

Now try duplicating a slide as you notice there are too many bullet points on slide 9.

10. Click **Slide 9** in the Slide Thumbnails pane and then press Ctrl + D to create a duplicate of the slide.

    PowerPoint inserts a duplicate of Slide 9. You can now edit the text on both slides to make each slide unique.

11. Click **Slide 9** and in the Slide pane, delete the points from *Disability/Life* … onwards.

12. Click **Slide 10** and in the Slide pane, delete all the text before *Disability/Life*.

13. After the *Training/educational opportunities* point, add a new bullet point and type: `Extended health coverage for out-of-country`.

    Although it appears as if each of the edited slides now contains too little text, you can change the text size or add pictures to make them appear more balanced.

14. Click the **Design** tab, in the Themes group, point at different themes to see how the current slide would look with a theme applied. Click the down arrow in the gallery to see more themes and preview each as you point at them.

Notice that as you move from one theme to another, typeface, font size, font color and backgrounds change.

15. Click a theme of your choice (we chose Organic in our example).

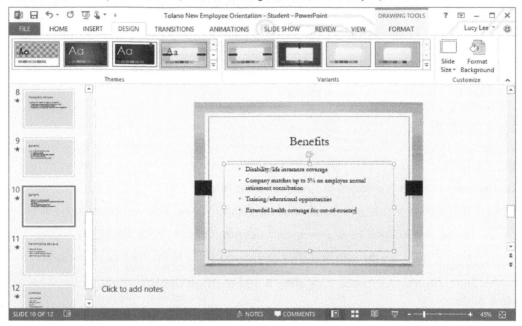

16. Save the presentation.

Now take a look at the presentation flow to see if the information on each slide is correct and fits in that location.

17. On the bottom right of the Status bar, click the ▦ (**Slide Sorter**) button.

18. Review the slide content.

You should notice that Slide 6 seems out of place in its current location, and would make more sense if you reposition it after Slide 11 (before Summary).

19. Scroll the screen so you can see the rows that contain these two slides. Click **Slide 6** to select it and then drag it between Slides 11 and 12.

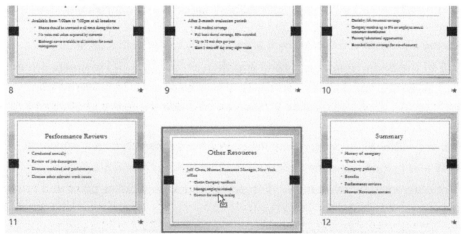

20. When the slide appears between the two slides (as seen above), release the mouse to place the slide here.

The Other Resources slide should now be in the Slide 11 position.

On further review of the presentation slides, you realize Slide 4 is no longer needed.

21. Right-click Slide 4 and then click **Delete Slide**.

    The slides in the presentation flow in a more logical sense now.

22. Click the (**Normal**) view button on the Status bar.

23. Save and close the presentation file.

Managing Slide Objects

IC³ Exam 2 - Objective 1.1, 1.2, 1.4, 4.1

An object is any shape, picture, media clip, chart, or text box inserted into a slide. To make changes to an object, first select or highlight it, then you can:

- delete it
- add tab positions
- indent text

- cut, copy or paste it into another location
- add formatting
- add bullets or numbers

Using Select Versus Edit Mode

The circles that appear around a selected object are called *handles*; they verify that the object is selected and you can make changes to it.

You can size the object using one of the following methods:

- Click one of the handles on the horizontal or vertical sides and then drag to adjust the width or height; or
- click one of the corner handles to size two adjacent sides of the object.

When the border around a text box is a dashed line, you are in Edit mode and you can select specific areas of the text in the box for changes.

When the border around a text box is a solid line, you are in Select mode and can affect the entire contents of the object. To activate Select mode quickly, position the mouse pointer on one of the borders of the placeholder, and then click when you see ⁺↖ (mouse pointer with four-headed arrow).

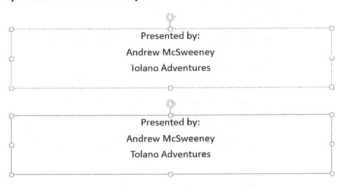

To select specific text within the placeholder, click and drag to select the text. When Edit mode is active, you can also select non-consecutive pieces of text by pressing the (Ctrl) key as you select each piece of text you want.

To select multiple placeholders, click the first placeholder and press (Shift) or (Ctrl) as you click to select other placeholders.

When you select other objects, the handles appear with a solid border, similar to Select mode for a text placeholder. The yellow diamond handle enables you to alter the existing shape of the object, as shown in the following example. The original shape was a rectangle with square corners, and it has been changed to a rectangle with rounded corners:

Manipulating Text

PowerPoint provides many ways to manipulate or edit selected text or placeholders, such as inserting additional text or deleting existing text.

- To insert text, click in the placeholder to display the blinking insertion point and then move to where you want to enter the new text.

- To delete text, use the (Backspace) or (Delete) keys.

Occasionally you may want to insert text into your presentation from another presentation, or from another location in the current presentation. Instead of retyping the information, you can use the Cut, Copy, and Paste commands.

PowerPoint uses the Clipboard to temporarily store any cut or copied items such as text or graphics to be pasted wherever you choose. When active, a notification appears in the taskbar to show the number of items collected on the Clipboard.

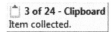

Checking the Spelling

The Spelling feature in PowerPoint provides various options when checking for spelling errors, including custom dictionaries for special terms.

The Spelling feature works in the background to check for spelling mistakes as you type. When PowerPoint detects a mistake, a wavy red line displays underneath the text. You can correct the mistakes immediately, or wait until you are finished creating the presentation.

PowerPoint also displays the ▨ **(Proofing icon)** in the status bar to indicate when words are not recognized by the current dictionary; this icon appears after PowerPoint detects the first spelling error. The icon appears as ▨ if there are no spelling errors or words PowerPoint does not recognize in the dictionary.

The Spelling feature can use two dictionaries at once:

- a main dictionary in the language of choice
- a custom dictionary of special terminology (such as company names, medical or legal terms, or abbreviations).

You can use either or both dictionaries during a spelling check.

To activate the spelling feature for the entire presentation, use one of the following methods:

- On the Review tab, in the Proofing group, click **Spelling**; or
- press (F7).

To check the spelling of individual words, use one of the following options:

- Right-click the word with the red wavy line and then click the appropriate spelling in the shortcut menu; or

- click the ▨ to move to the first word considered to be misspelled and then click the correct spelling for this word.

Remember that performing a spell check checks only the accuracy of the spelling in your slides; you should still proofread your presentation to ensure you are using the correct words.

Formatting Text

Formatting refers to the process of changing the appearance and position of objects on a slide.

The Font dialog box provides basic formatting options and additional options not found in the Font group on the Home tab; you can also use it to select or preview multiple formatting changes at once. To display the Font dialog box, on the Home tab, in the Font group, click the **Font** dialog box launcher.

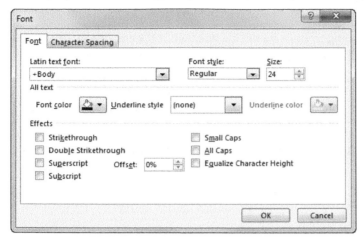

The Font group in the Home tab enables quick, easy access to commonly used character formatting options directly from the Ribbon:

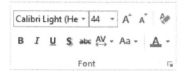

The Mini toolbar provides similar access to commonly used formatting options, and provides a mixture of character and paragraph formatting. This toolbar appears only when you select text; once you move the mouse pointer away from the selection, you will need to select the text again to display this toolbar.

You can also use Quick Styles to apply formatting attributes that are commonly used for specific types of text, such as titles, headings, bullet points, and so on. You can preview the effect a Quick Style will have on text by pointing at the style in the list. To choose a Quick Style, on the Home tab, in the Drawing group, click **Quick Styles**.

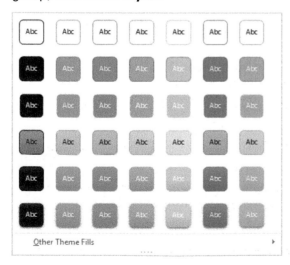

Any formatting changes you make to text on the slides override formatting options applied to the master slide. If you decide to change text on all slides, you can do this in the master slide. Master slides are discussed later in this lesson.

Aligning Text

Each built-in slide layout aligns according to defaults set for that layout. Occasionally, you may want to change text alignment. You can use the same methods as you would in Word:

- On the Home tab, in the Paragraph group, click the appropriate alignment option; or

- On the Home tab, in the Paragraph group, click the **Paragraph** dialog box launcher and then click the appropriate option from the **Alignment** list; or

- in the Mini toolbar, click the appropriate alignment option; or

- press the shortcut keystroke for the alignment required.

EXERCISE

In this exercise you will format text in a presentation.

1. Open the *Run-of-River Power Plant* file and save as `Run-of-River Power Plant - Student`.

2. Click in the title placeholder on **Slide 1** and select the entire title.

3. On the Home tab, in the Font group, click **Bold**. Click the arrow for **Font Size** and click **54**. Click the arrow for the **Font** and point at different fonts to preview the change.

    Notice as you preview the font, the size will vary based on the type of font it is – san serif fonts tend to be appear slightly larger than serif fonts such as Times New Roman or Cambria.

4. Select a font of your choice.

5. On the Home tab, in the Drawing group, click **Quick Styles**. Point at different ones to see how each style affects the slide.

    Notice that certain styles change the color automatically.

6. Click a Quick Style of your choice.

7. Point the mouse cursor at the title placeholder until you see 🔖 near the border. Then click to select the entire placeholder.

8. On the Home tab, in the Font group, click the arrow for **Font Size** and click one size larger than currently set.

9. Click the **Review** tab, in the Proofing group, click **Spelling**.

10. Click the correct spelling for the first error and then click **Change**.

11. When PowerPoint shows the error Tolano, which is the name of the company, click **Add** to add this word to the custom dictionary.

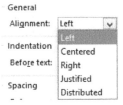

12. Continue correcting the spelling for each error PowerPoint detects, making changes as appropriate.

13. Save the presentation once the spell check is complete.

Now change the alignment for bullet points to see how they appear on a slide.

14. In the Slides tab, click **Slide 4** and then click the contents placeholder.

15. Click the **Home** tab, in the Paragraph group, click **Justify**.

This is an alignment option that is commonly used for text, although primarily in business documents rather than presentations. Notice that the justified text in a slide can be harder to read than left- aligned text.

16. On the Home tab, in the Paragraph group, click **Align Text Left**.

17. Save and close the presentation.

Creating and Using Tables

A table is a grid made up of rows and columns where data can be entered. The intersection of a row and column is called a cell. Entering text in a table is a quick way to ensure the text lines up in columns. Once you create a table, you can format it.

To insert a table, use one of the following methods:

- To add a table to a slide with a content placeholder, click the **Insert Table** icon in the placeholder; or

- to add a table to a slide without a content placeholder, on the Insert tab, in the Tables group, click **Table**, and then drag in the grid for the total number of rows and columns needed for the new table; or

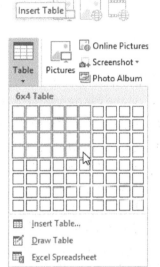

- to insert a table using a command to enter specific numbers for rows and columns, on the Insert tab, in the Table group, click the arrow for **Table** and then click **Insert Table**; or

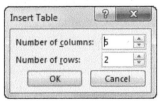

- to draw a table with rows, columns, or diagonal lines, on the Insert tab, in the Tables group, click the arrow for **Table** and then click **Draw Table**; the mouse pointer will change to a 🖊 (pencil) with which you can draw lines as if using pencil and paper.

Formatting the Table

You can format selected data in the table or the entire table. Formatting a table refers to manipulating the cells and the contents within the cells. Formatting options include:

- adjusting the width of columns or the height of rows
- merging cells to form larger cells
- splitting cells to form smaller cells
- adding, changing, or removing the border for selected cells
- adding, changing, or removing shading or fill backgrounds for selected cells

Before you change any part of the table, select the appropriate part of the table, (entire column, one cell, multiple cells). Select items individually using the mouse or keyboard, or use the Table Tools ribbon tabs for the appropriate selection.

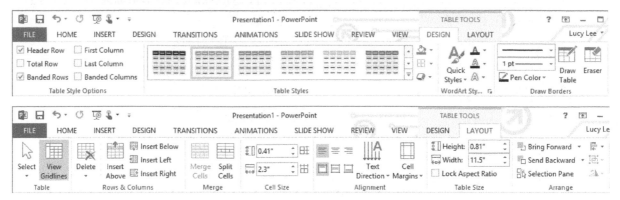

EXERCISE

In this exercise you will create a small table for a presentation to display comparison statistics for a tour.

1. Open the *Introducing Camel Tours* file and then save it as `Introducing Camel Tours - Student`.

2. In the Slides tab, click **Slide 3** and then on the Home tab, in the Slides group, click **New Slide**.

3. Type: `Camel Tours for Egypt` as the title.

4. In the Content placeholder, click the **Table** icon.

5. Type: `4` for both the number of columns and number of rows. Click **OK**.

6. Click in the first cell at the top left of the table and type: `Tour`.

7. Press (Tab) and type: `Duration`. Press (Tab) and type: `Price`. Press (Tab) and type: `Includes`. Press (Tab) once more to go to the next row.

    You have entered the titles that will identify the contents of each column.

8. Enter the rest of the information for the table, pressing (Tab) to move from one column to the next, or if you prefer, click in each cell to enter the data:

Tour	Duration	Price	Includes
Alexandria Port	1 Day	$99	All transport and guide fees
Shore Excursions	1 Day	$85	All transport and guide fees
Great Pyramids	1 Day	$60	All transport and guide fees; does not include Pyramids entrance fee

Now make changes to the table.

9. Click in the cell with *Price* and type: `/person`.

10. Select the entire row with the column titles. Then on the Home tab, in the Paragraph group, click **Center**.

11. Select the cells with data for *Duration* and *Price/person* and on the Home tab, in the Paragraph group, click **Center**.

12. Position the mouse cursor on the vertical line between *Tour* and *Duration*. When you see ┅ drag the vertical line approximately 2 or 3 characters to the right.

    You have widened the Tour column.

13. Adjust the width for the other two columns to your preference.

14. Click anywhere on the border for the table to select the entire table.

15. On the Home tab, in the Font group, click the arrow for **Font size** and change it to **20**.

16. Select the row with the column titles and change the font size here to **24**.

17. Make adjustments to the column widths to accommodate the changes in font size.

    Your table should appear similar to the following:

Tour	Duration	Price/person	Includes
Alexandria Port	1 Day	$99	All transport and guide fees
Shore Excursions	1 Day	$85	All transport and guide fees
Great Pyramids	1 Day	$60	All transport and guide fees; does not include Pyramids entrance fee

18. Save the presentation.

Creating a Chart

Charts (also referred to as graphs) present numerical data in a manner that makes trends or patterns clearly visible. Create charts by importing the information from a spreadsheet application, or by entering the data into a datasheet in PowerPoint.

Consider the following when working with data charts:

- Charts may include a title and possibly a subtitle.
- Bar and line graphs include horizontal (X) and vertical (Y) axes, which can also have titles.
- A series is one set of data.
- If a chart displays more than one series of data, each series is displayed in a legend.
- Each data point in a series can have a label displaying the value at that point.
- A graph can display grid lines and tick marks on the axes.
- Changing the type of chart can produce a more effective presentation.

To insert a chart, use one of the following methods:

- On the **Insert** tab, in the **Illustrations** group, click **Chart**; or
- click the **Insert Chart** icon in the **Title and Content** layout.

Once you activate the chart feature, PowerPoint prompts you to choose the chart type and displays a window similar to the following:

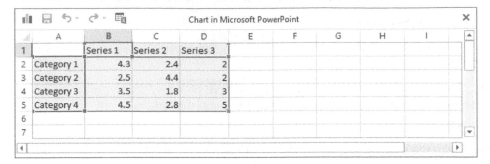

You can enter data for the chart using the Microsoft Chart tool, which simulates an Excel spreadsheet, and uses the same terminology as worksheets.

In PowerPoint, the Chart Tools ribbon tabs appear so you can quickly manipulate or format the chart and its contents on the slide:

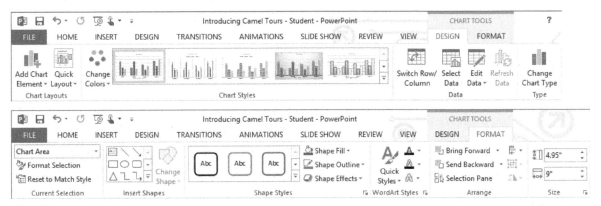

The chart placeholder contains an example of the graph based on the data entered in the datasheet window. As you make changes in the datasheet window, the graph will change also.

A *datasheet* is similar to a table in that it consists of rows and columns filled with sample data. A cell is the intersection of a column and a row, and is identified by its column letter followed by its row number. For example, cell B5 is located at the intersection of column B and row 5.

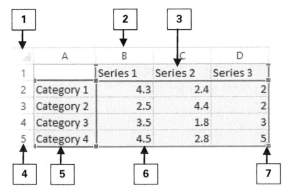

1   Select All

2   Column Address

3   Axis Headings

4   Row Address

5   Categories

6   Y Axis Values

7   Sizing Handle

Select All Button	Selects every cell in the datasheet.
Column Address	Represents the column where the value or label resides.
Axis Headings	Column headings of the data series that appear in the Legend.
Row Address	Represents the row where the value or label resides.
Categories	Lists the names of items being charted. These headings appear on the X axis.

Y Axis Values	Lists the values in the Y axis.
Sizing Handle	Expands the data table to include additional columns and rows if necessary.

Selecting Items in a Datasheet

Prior to executing a command or procedure, you must indicate what part of the datasheet you wish to affect with the command.

A range selection can be as small as a single cell or as large as the entire datasheet. The datasheet keeps the cells highlighted until you change or remove the selection. Click a cell or use an arrow key to remove the selection.

A datasheet displays the selected range by reversing the color of the cells. Within the selected range, there is one cell in normal color; this is the active cell in that range.

To select a range using the mouse:

A single cell	Click the cell.
Extend the selection	Click the cell and drag to the end of the desired range; you can also click the first cell and then press (Shift) as you click the end cell in the range.
An entire row	Click the row header.
An entire column	Click the column header.
The entire worksheet	Click **Select All**.
Non-adjacent columns, rows or columns	Click the cell, column, or row, press (Ctrl), and then click to select the next cell, column, or row; you can also drag to select multiple cells.
Multiple rows	Click the first row number and drag for the number of rows.
Multiple columns	Click the first column letter and drag for the number of columns.

Changing the Chart Type

The type of chart you use will depend on the type of data you are charting. To activate the Chart Type feature, use one of the following methods:

- Under Chart Tools, on the Design tab, in the Type group, click **Change Chart Type**; or
- right-click the chart and then click **Change Chart Type**.

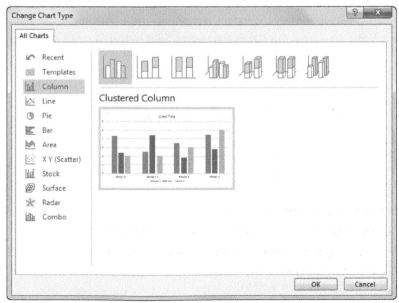

Adjusting the Data Series

You can change the data series properties, such as bar shape, fill attributes, line style, using one of the following methods:

- Select the data series and click the command to apply to the data series from the Design or Format tab of the Chart Tools ribbon; or

- Double-click the selected data series to display the Format Data Point pane; or

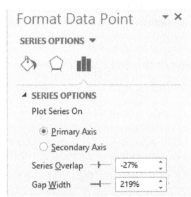

- Right-click the selected data series and click an option from one of the two menus to adjust the data series.

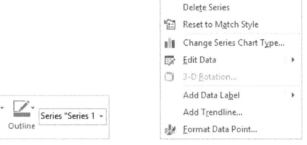

Depending on what is being adjusted, a pane may also appear to the right of the chart element for further options.

You can also use one of the icons at the right of the chart to adjust the appearance of the chart:

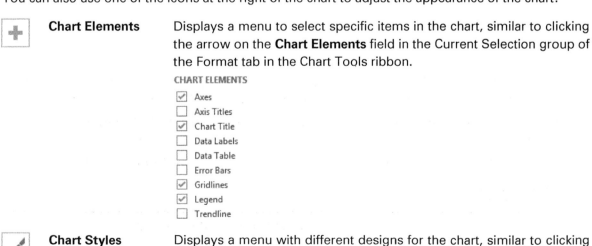

Chart Elements   Displays a menu to select specific items in the chart, similar to clicking the arrow on the **Chart Elements** field in the Current Selection group of the Format tab in the Chart Tools ribbon.

CHART ELEMENTS
- ☑ Axes
- ☐ Axis Titles
- ☑ Chart Title
- ☐ Data Labels
- ☐ Data Table
- ☐ Error Bars
- ☑ Gridlines
- ☑ Legend
- ☐ Trendline

Chart Styles   Displays a menu with different designs for the chart, similar to clicking a style from the Chart Styles gallery in the Design tab of the Chart Tools ribbon. You can also adjust the colors for the chart, similar to using the Change Colors option.

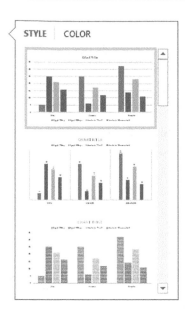

 Chart Filters   Displays a list of chart elements that can be displayed on the chart.

The number of formatting options available depends on the type of chart you select. Keep in mind that it is best to limit the amount of information or formatting included in a chart because:

- The more information there is for the audience to read, the less likely they are to pay attention to you.

- Too many distracting items on the chart can make the chart confusing to read.

EXERCISE

In this exercise you will add a slide that contains some statistics on the types of requests received from customers.

1. Ensure the *Introducing Camel Tours – Student* file is active on the screen and that you are at the last slide in the presentation.

2. On the Home tab, in the Slides group, click **New Slide**.

3. Type: `Customer Response` for the title. Then in the Content placeholder, click the **Insert Chart** icon.

4. Ensure the **Clustered Column** chart type is selected (first type in first row) and then click **OK**.

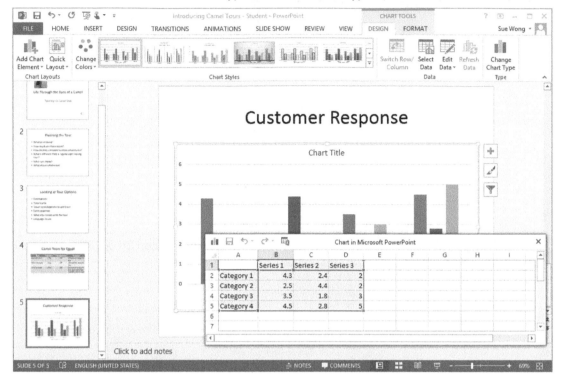

5. Click the **Select All** button at the left of column A and then press (Delete) to delete the existing data. Then click and drag the small blue box at the bottom right corner in column D and drag this to cell **E4** to resize the data location.

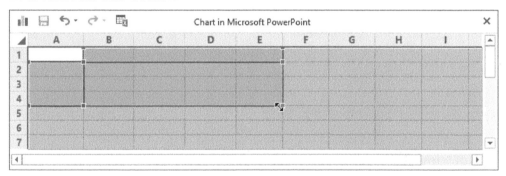

6. Type the following data for the chart, pressing (Tab) to move from one cell to the next or (Enter) to move to a new row (we have made the columns wider for you to enter the data; the titles will be truncated as you type):

	A	B	C	D	E	F
1		Egypt 1-Day	Egypt 5-Days	Australia - Perth	Australia -	Queensland
2	Men	5	25	21	16	
3	Women	25	6	17	12	
4	Couples	32	14	23	11	
5						

7. Close the Chart in Microsoft PowerPoint application to return to the chart and PowerPoint.

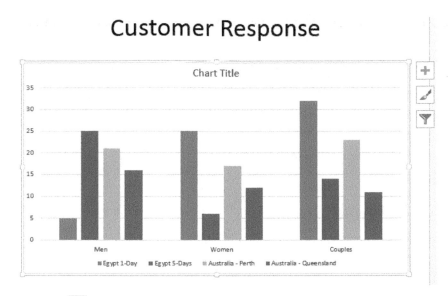

8. Click the icon at the right of the chart and point at various styles to see the effect on the chart. Then click a style of your choice (we chose Style 14).

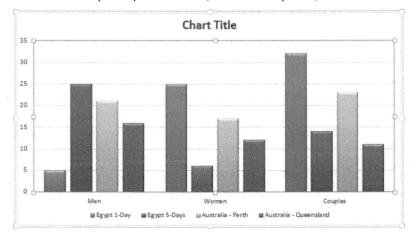

The data in the chart displays which tour was the most popular by the participant type; suppose you want the chart to show the number of participants for each tour group instead.

9. Under Chart Tools, on the Design tab, in the Data group, click **Select Data**. Then in the Select Data Source window, click **Switch Row/Column**, click **OK**, and then close the Chart in Microsoft PowerPoint application.

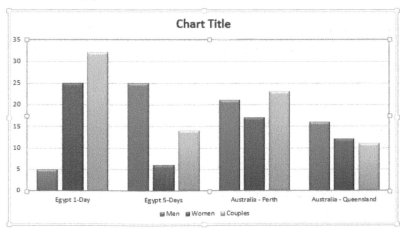

Which chart do you think has the most impact? The final decision depends on what you want to emphasize to your audience. For example, the current chart shows which tours were of most interest. The previous chart showed which tours held the most interest for specific groups of people.

One chart element you do not need on this chart is a separate title. In this case, it is not needed as the title of the slide explains the purpose of the data; in other instances, you may want a separate title such as if you needed to show four other customer responses to a tour/service.

10. Click the Chart Title box in the chart and press (Delete).

11. Save the presentation again.

Inserting Pictures or Clip Art Images

You can easily add pictures to any slide using the Pictures command. Pictures can come from a variety of sources, such as the Clip Organizer, saved picture files, scanned photographs, the Microsoft Office web site, and so on.

To insert a picture file, use one of the following methods:

- On the Insert tab, in the Images group, click **Pictures**; or

- when creating or changing a slide layout, select one that contains a Content placeholder; then click **Pictures** to insert a picture from a saved location.

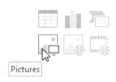

In addition to choose a picture saved on your computer/network, you can also insert pictures from online sources such as Microsoft Office's web site or choose another online location. Take note that pictures obtained from online sources are copyrighted and you should follow the rules for copyright (as well as Fair Use principles).

To insert Clip Art, position the mouse pointer on the slide at approximately the location where you want to add the graphic, and then use one of the following methods:

- When creating or changing a slide layout, select one that contains a Content placeholder. Then click the **Online Pictures** icon; or

- on the Insert tab, in the Images group, click **Online Pictures**.

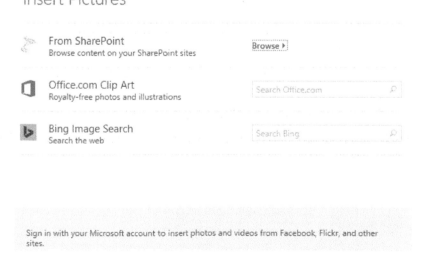

Manipulating the Pictures

Manipulating pictures refers to sizing, moving, or otherwise modifying pictures.

When you select a picture, the **Picture Tools Format** tab displays tools to help manipulate parts of the picture.

Consider the following when working with pictures in PowerPoint:

- You must select the picture in order to display its handles, before you can make changes to it.

- To increase or decrease the size of a picture, click and drag one of the handles.

- To move a picture, position the mouse pointer anywhere inside the picture and, when you see ⃗, click and drag the picture.

- To rotate the picture, click and drag the green handle to the angle required.

- To insert a picture without using a picture placeholder, you may need to reapply an appropriate slide layout, or adjust the individual placeholders on that slide.

- You cannot wrap text around a picture; you can either put the picture in a separate placeholder or manipulate the text so that it appears to wrap around the picture.

EXERCISE

In this exercise you will insert pictures onto different slides in the presentation.

1. Ensure the *Introducing Camel Tours – Student* presentation is active and that you are viewing the last slide (chart).

2. On the Home tab, in the Slides group, click **New Slide**. Type: `Egyptian Camel Tours` for the title.

3. In the Content placeholder, click the **Pictures** icon. Navigate to the student data files folder and select the *camels* file to insert.

Egyptian Camel Tours

Add a few more pictures to this slide.

4.   Click anywhere away from this picture. Click the **Insert** tab, and in the Images group, click **Pictures**.

5.   In the student data files location, select *alexandria* as the file to add to the slide.

6.   Ensure the mouse cursor is somewhere in the selected picture and drag this picture to the left of the first picture.

> **Hint:** As you drag the picture, you may see red dashed lines to guide you to align the picture in relation to the other picture on the slide. These guides are called Smart Guides.

7.   Click anywhere away from this picture. Click the **Insert** tab, and in the Images group, click **Pictures**. In the student data files location, select *camel train* as the file to add to the slide.

8.   Drag the selected picture to the right of the middle picture, making sure the picture still fits on the slide even though it may overlap the middle picture (you will adjust this shortly).

9.   With the camel train picture still selected, point the mouse cursor at one of the corner handles and resize it to approximately two-thirds its original size. Repeat for the other two pictures.

10. Select all three pictures and then on the Format tab, in the Arrange group, click the arrow for **Align** and click **Align Middle**.

11. With the three pictures still selected, on the Format tab, in the Arrange group, click the arrow for Align and click **Distribute Horizontally**.

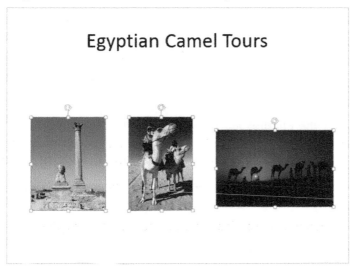

Egyptian Camel Tours

12. Move to **slide 1**. Then click the **Insert** tab, in the Images group, click **Online Pictures**.

13. In the search field for Office.com Clip Art, type: `camel` and press (Enter).

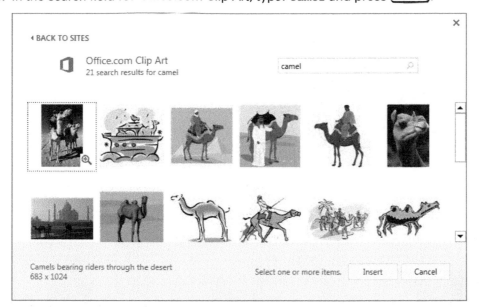

Notice how the results may be limited in choice, especially if you were looking to include some photographs. The number and type of items that appear in this list will vary based on the fact that Microsoft updates their gallery of images frequently.

Try searching for the same item using Bing.

14. Click **Back to Sites**. In the search field for Bing Image Search, type: `camel` and press (Enter).

Notice that the results are a combination of drawn images and photographs. You should notice also that there is an information bar reminding you about how online images can be used.

15. Click the ✖ to close this information bar. If a web page appears on the screen, close the web browser.

16. Scroll through the results and when you see a picture you want to insert, double-click it.

17. Resize the graphic appropriately and then move it to the top left corner above the main title, similar to the following:

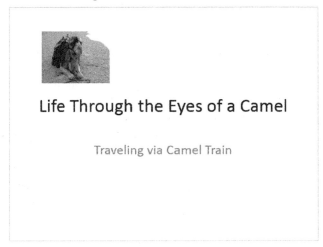

18. Save the presentation again.

Creating Drawing Objects

You can enhance slides by creating your own shapes and drawings using the **Shapes** tool in the Illustrations group of the Insert tab.

Create most objects by clicking at the top left of where you want to position the object and dragging the mouse to specify a size for the object. The exception to this procedure is when you are drawing lines and arrows, which generally require you to click the start point and then at the end point.

Once the object is drawn, you can manipulate the object's shape, color, or effect.

When selecting a shape from the Shapes menu, point at a shape to see the ScreenTip indicating its name. Use the group names as a guide to the type of shape object to create.

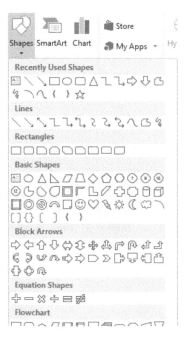

Formatting Objects

Formatting drawing objects is similar to formatting text placeholders. You must select the object before applying the formatting feature. The Drawing Tools Format tab provides a number of features you can use to change the color, style, or fill of the object.

You can access these options and more by using one of the following method:

- Click the appropriate Dialog box launcher buttons; or

- right-click the shape to choose the options you want to apply.

The Format Shape pane appears at the right with further choices for adjusting the shape or text in the shape. The options that appear will vary based on the type of shape or text you want to format.

Arranging Objects

As you add objects and text to the slides, you may want several objects to share the same attributes, or you may want to move objects around the slide.

You may also need to control the stacking order of objects. As you create an object on a slide, it may appear to be in front of another object. You can move it backward or forward. Once you place objects in relation to each other, you can group them and move them as a group, so that their placement and stacking order do not change.

To arrange objects on a slide, use one of the following methods:

- On the Home tab, in the Drawing group, click **Arrange**; or

- Under Drawing Tools, on the Format tab, in the Arrange group, click the option required.

Inserting Multimedia Objects

One advantage of using presentations is the ability to include multimedia files such as videos, music, or links to Web pages that provide more information. To insert a media file, use one of the following methods:

- Select a slide layout that contains Content as part of the slide layout, and then click the **Insert Video** icon to insert a movie or sound clip; or

- on the Insert tab, in the Media group, click **Video** or **Audio**.

Once you insert a media file, a new ribbon appears with two tabs for the media file (the first two screens are for an audio file, and the latter two screens are for a video file):

EXERCISE

In this exercise you will insert objects onto a slide and then change their appearance.

1. Ensure *Introduction to Camel Tours – Student* is active on the screen and that you are on Slide 1.

2. Click the **Insert** tab, and in the Media group, click **Audio**, click **Online Audio**.

3. In the Office.com Clip Art search field, type: camel and press Enter .

Note: If this file is no longer available, choose from another one that may be available. It does not matter which audio file you use here in the demonstration. The focus is on how to insert and manipulate the audio file once it is inserted into the presentation.

4.   Click this item to insert an audio clip onto the slide.

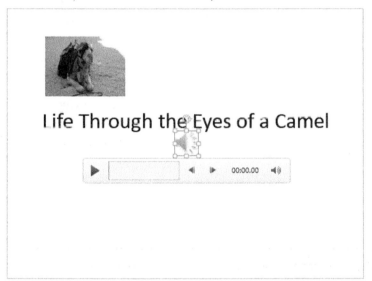

You have inserted a media file from an online source. You can now manipulate this audio file as needed for the presentation.

5.   Position the mouse cursor over the speaker icon and drag to the lower right corner of the slide.

6.   Under Audio Tools, click the **Format** tab, in the Adjust group, click **Color**.

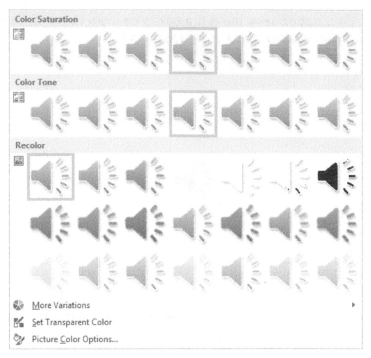

7. Click **Olive Green, Accent Color 3 Dark** (fourth row, middle color).

In this instance you recolored the audio icon as a quick reminder that the slide includes a sound clip you can play, as required. If you were to apply a theme to the presentation, you might need to change the color of the icon to coordinate with the theme.

8. Go to **slide 5**. Click the **Insert** tab, in the Illustrations group, click **Shapes** and then click the ⬊ button.

9. Starting above the top gridline in the chart and approximately midway between the green bar for **Egypt 1-Day** and the blue bar for **Egypt 5-Days** bar, drag to the top of the green bar, as seen in the following:

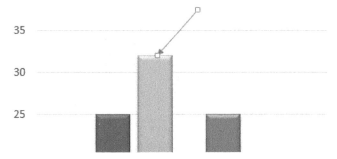

10. Click anywhere away from the arrow, then click the arrow again to select it and on the Format tab, in the Insert Shapes group, click the ▣ (**Text Box**) button.

11. Click at the right of the top part of the arrow and draw a text box wide enough to enter the word `Great!`.

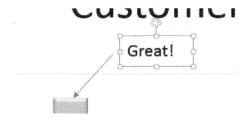

12. Using the mouse or the arrow direction keys, move the box to be more center aligned with the arrow and bar and closer to the arrow. Click away from the text box.

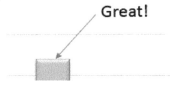

Great!

13. Save and close the presentation.

Creating a Master Slide

You can use a master slide to add items that repeat on each slide, such as a company logo, background color, slide title color or size. To work with a master slide, you must change to a master view; on the View tab, in the Master Views group, click one of the following:

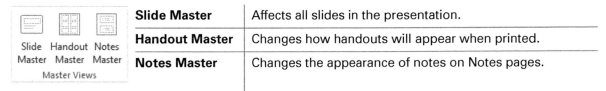

Slide Master	Affects all slides in the presentation.
Handout Master	Changes how handouts will appear when printed.
Notes Master	Changes the appearance of notes on Notes pages.

Note that any changes you make directly to an individual slide will override the formatting you have specified on a master slide.

Inserting Headers and Footers

A header or footer repeats on every slide, either at the top (header) or the bottom (footer). Slides can display only footers, whereas Notes and Handouts can display both headers and footers.

Insert headers or footers by selecting the command from the Insert tab, in the Text group.

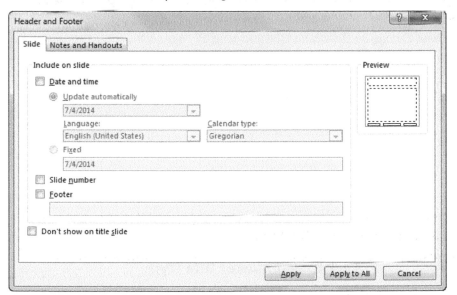

Date and time	Uses either a static date of your choosing or the current date (the current date updates automatically).
Slide number	Includes the page or slide number.

| **Footer** | Repeats text in the Footer placeholder on every slide. |
| **Don't show on title slide** | Suppresses the footer on the title slide. |

The following items appear on the Notes and Handouts pages only:

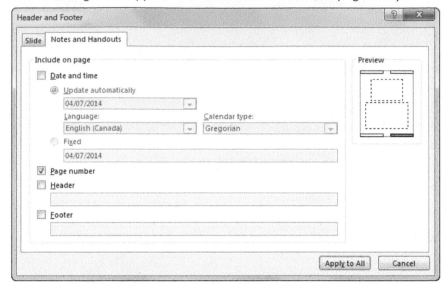

| **Header** | Repeats text in the Header placeholder of every Notes or Handouts page. |
| **Page number** | Enters a page number in the same location as with slides but for Notes or Handouts pages. |

EXERCISE

In this exercise you will work with the slide master to add the logo to every slide in the presentation; you will also format specific placeholders.

1. Open the *Tolano New Employee Orientation* file and save as `Tolano New Employee Orientation (master) - Student`.

2. Click the **View** tab and in the Master Views group, click **Slide Master** to change to this view.

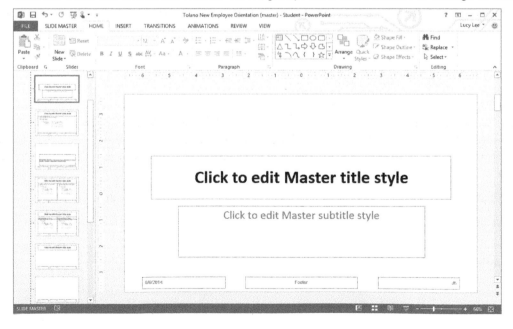

The Slide Master Ribbon displays at the top of the screen. The list of slide layouts available for the presentation appears in the Navigation pane as reference. We will make changes to the Title and Content slide master.

3. Click **slide 1** (the first slide at the top of the pane) in the Navigation pane if necessary. Then click the border of the title placeholder in the Slides area and press Ctrl + B to apply the bold attribute to the contents of this placeholder.

4. Click the **Home** tab and in the Font group, click the arrow for **Font Size** and change to one size larger than the current setting. Click anywhere away from the placeholder.

Now add the company logo so it appears on every slide.

5. Click the second slide in the navigation pane (Title and Content layout). Click the **Insert** tab and in the Images group, click **Pictures**. Navigate to the student data location, if necessary, and select the *tec logo* file.

6. Move and resize the logo so it fits in the center of the Footer placeholder, similar to the following:

7. Click the **Slide Master** tab and in the Close group, click **Close Master View**.

8. Scroll through the slides to observe how the changes were applied.

For now, these are the only changes we will make to the slide master. If you later apply a theme to your presentation, you may revisit the slide master view to make any appropriate changes.

9. Save and close this presentation.

Animating Objects

 Exam 2 - Objective 4.3

You can animate objects and text to increase the effectiveness of your slide shows. You can also customize how the text, objects, and graphics enter (or become visible) when the slide displays, or how they exit (disappear from view). You can also use animation to emphasize objects on the slide.

To add animation, use one of the following methods:

- On the Animations tab, in the Animation group, click **More** to display the Animation Gallery, or

- on the Animations tab, in the Advanced Animation group, click **Add Animation**

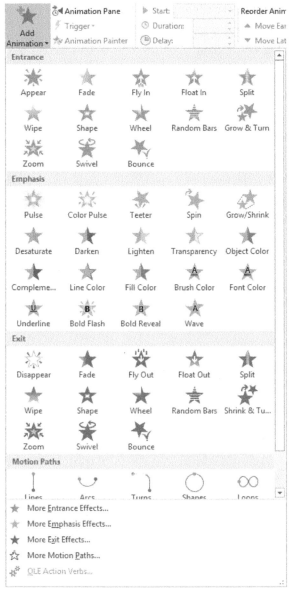

Once you choose an animation, you can set specific options for the animation using the **Timing** group:

Try to be consistent in the number and style of animation schemes used on the slides. Consider your audience and choose the speed and effects accordingly. Too many variations can be distracting.

Customizing the Animation

You can adjust or customize how animation will occur during the presentation, as well as the speed and direction of animations, and order in which text or objects appear on the slide. For instance, you may want the bullet points to appear one bullet at a time so your audience does not focus on the other text on your slide. You can also set an item to dim after it appears on the slide.

To customize the animation, on the Animations tab, in the Advanced Animation group, click **Animation Pane**.

As you select each element to be animated, PowerPoint provides options that control when or how the element will appear.

Be careful which effects you use for different elements in your presentation. Some options, such as Motion Paths, create a special type of animation effect, but they also require that you set up further options. Be sure to check the speed and timing of the animation (when it should start), and then play it to be sure it works well.

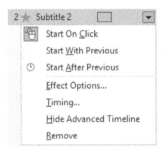

As you apply animation to elements on the slide, PowerPoint places numbered boxes on the slide to indicate the order in which the items will appear; the Animation Pane will also list the animations in numeric order. You can rearrange the elements by using the ▲ or ▼ **Re-Order** arrows near the top of the pane; alternatively, you can drag the item to the required location. The numbers for the animations on the slide automatically reset themselves accordingly.

Animation options vary with the effect used. Use care when adding custom animation; and always play or preview the animation and the order in which it appears. Regardless of whether you animate all or only some of the elements on the slide, ensure that the slide displays in the manner you want before you show it to your audience. You may want to keep some elements, such as titles, static during the show to provide a focal point.

You can customize animation using the **Effect Options** commands for each animation type. The number or types of effects vary with the **Effect** command chosen. Be sure to test each animation prior to setting up for final presentation.

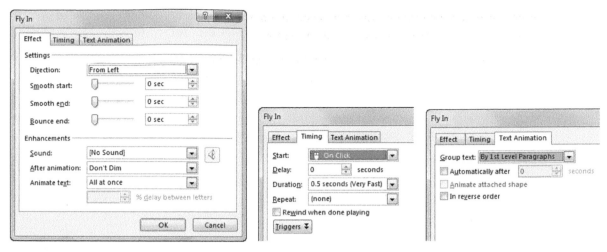

When you no longer want or need an animation, remove it from the Animation Pane list.

Applying Slide Transitions

Slide transitions are special effects that you can apply as you move from one slide to the next during a slide show. Try not to use too many different slide transitions, and be consistent in the type of transitions you use between specific types of slides (such as bulleted lists or charts), as too much variation can distract your audience.

To apply a slide transition, on the **Transitions** tab, in the **Transition to This Slide** group, click a transition style from the gallery.

As with other galleries, you can click **More** to display the entire gallery, and then point at a transition to preview it for the slide.

You can customize the transitions by adding sound or changing the speed; you can also apply a transition to one slide only or to all the slides in the presentation.

Use the options in the **Timing** group to set how your presentation will run, such as with or without a speaker. This option can be useful for self-paced training purposes, or to capture the interest of viewers as they walk by your exhibition booth at a trade show.

EXERCISE

In this exercise you will add a variety of animations to slides and individual objects.

1. Open the *Exploring Seattle* file and then save it as Exploring Seattle - Student.

2. Go to **slide 2** and review the contents on this slide.

    This slide is primarily text with two image objects, one of which should appear with the title; the other should appear with the bulleted text.

3. Click the border for the content placeholder. Then click the **Animations** tab, and in the **Animations** gallery, point at different animation styles.

Notice as you point and watch the animation preview that the graphic for one bullet point appears first before any of the bulleted text. We will change this after setting how the text is to appear.

4. Click **Fly In** as the animation style. Click the **Effect Options** button to the right of the gallery and click **From Left**.

5. On the Animations tab, in the Advanced Animation group, click **Animation Pane**.

6. In the Animation Pane, click the arrow for the **Content Placeholder** and click **Effect Options**. Click the **Text Animation** tab and then click the arrow for **Group text**.

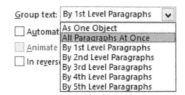

This field determines how the bullet points appear on the slide and by which levels. We would like the bullet points to appear one line at a time, regardless of level so we need to choose the lowest level in the contents placeholder.

7. Click **By 4th Level Paragraphs** and then click **OK**.

The preview should confirm each bullet point flying in from the left one at a time.

8. On the slide, click the star graphic. On the Animations tab, in the Animation gallery, click **Fly In**. Click **Effect Options** and then click **From Left**.

The graphic should now fly in from the left during the preview. However, look at the numbers at the left of the contents placeholder. These numbers confirm the order the items will appear.

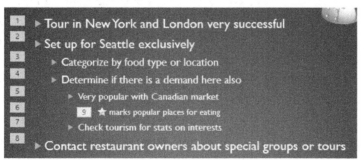

9. In the Animation Pane, click the expansion double arrow below the **Contents Placeholder** animation.

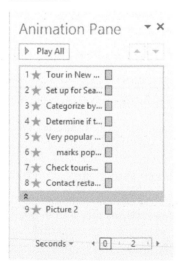

10. Click the **Picture 2** item and then click the **Up** re-order arrow near the top of the Animation Pane until it appears after the bullet point starting with *Very popular* ...

11. In the Animation Pane, click **Play From.**

    As you watch the preview play, you should notice the star appears for the line appropriately but it still appears before the text. You want to change this to occur at the same time as the text.

12. In the Animation Pane, click the *marks popular* text, then click the arrow for the *marks popular* text and click **Start: With Previous**. Click **Play From** to watch the preview.

Now change the entrance speed of the bulleted text content.

13. Click the **double arrow** to hide the individual parts of the Content Placeholder. Then click the arrow for the **Content Placeholder** and click **Timing.**

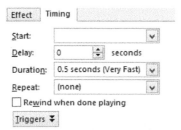

14. Click the arrow for **Duration** and then click **1 seconds (Fast)**. Click **OK.**

    The bullet points appear quickly but not as fast as before. When determining the duration or speed of the content, keep in mind how the presentation will be delivered. In this scenario, we are modifying the presentation based on the fact that it will be delivered by a speaker who will click to present each point. If this presentation was to be shown on a computer and run on its own, the duration time should be set for longer so the audience can read the bullets without feeling rushed.

15. Go back to slide 1. Click the **Transitions** tab and then in the Transition to this Slide gallery, click different transition styles. Then select one of your preference.

Slide Sorter view allows you to see the transitions and animations applied to your slides all at once.

16. Switch to Slide Sorter view. Notice that a small icon displays under the lower left corner of Slides 1 and 2. You can click these icons to view the transition/and or animations applied to each slide.

17. Click the transition/animation icon for Slide 1 to view the transition you applied in Step 15.

18. Click Slide 2, then click the transition/animation icon for Slide 2 to view the animations you added.

You can also add transitions in Slide Sorter view.

19. Click Slide 2 if necessary, then on the Transitions tab, in the Transition to this Slide gallery, click a transition to apply it to the slide.

20. Click the transition/animation icon for Slide 2 again to preview the transition and animations.

21. Click Slide 3, press and hold (Shift), then click Slide 7 to select all the remaining slides in the presentation, then click a transition to apply it to all the selected slides. Slides 3 through 7 now all use the same transition.

22. Click an empty area in Slide Sorter view, then click Slide 4 and change the transition.

23. Change the transition for Slides 5 and 6 as well.

24. Double-click Slide 1 to return to Normal view.

25. Time permitting, apply animations of your choice to the remaining slides in the presentation.

26. Save and close the presentation when done.

Running the Slide Show

There are two options for viewing the slide show: printing the slides directly onto transparencies, or displaying them directly from the computer.

Most people combine other media such as movies or sound with their slide shows, and then deliver the presentation to a live audience or as a self-running show on the computer.

Use features from the Slide Show tab to set up options for the slide show:

Setting Up the Presentation

You can set up options for how the presentation will appear before or after you create your presentation. To set up options for your slide show, on the Slide Show tab, in the Set Up group, click **Set Up Slide Show**.

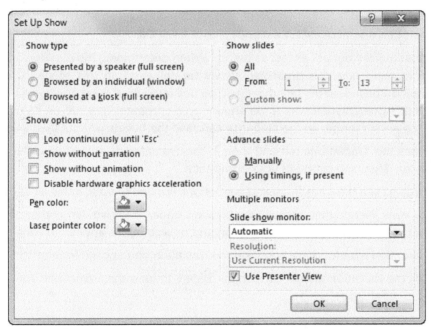

Use the options here to specify how you want to deliver your presentation, such as with a speaker, run on a computer at your booth, or in a window within a Web browser. You can also configure the presentation to support multiple monitors.

Viewing the Slide Show

Start a slide show using one of the following methods:

- On the Slide Show tab, in the Start Slide Show group, click to start the show from the beginning or from the current slide; or
- click ▣ (**Slide Show**) from the view buttons in the status bar; or
- press (F5).

The slide show displays in full screen mode. By default, at the end of the slide show, PowerPoint displays a black screen with the message "End of slide show, click to exit" at the top, indicating that the slide show has ended.

When running a slide show, you can set PowerPoint to advance the slides automatically at set time intervals, or you can advance the slides manually. To advance slides manually, use one of the following methods:

- Click to move to the next slide or to display bullets points or objects on the slide; or
- press (Enter), (Spacebar); or
- press (PgUp) or (PgDn).

To display a menu that you can use to navigate to different areas of the presentation or to use presentation tools, such as a pointer or a pen, during the slide show, use one of the following methods:

- Right-click anywhere on the slide show, or
- Point at the lower left and click (···).

Consider the following when running the slide show:

- Use (◁) or (▷) to go to the previous or next slide in the presentation.
- Use (⊞) to show all slides on the screen, similar to using the Slide Sorter view. You can then click the slide you want the audience to see.
- Use (◎) to zoom into an area of the slide during the slide show.

- Use (✎) to point to, write or emphasize specific items during your presentation. You can also adjust the settings for the pen, such as changing the ink color or thickness. Be sure to test those before your presentation to ensure the colors do not clash and can be seen from anywhere in the room.
- If there are any links in the slides, during the show you can click the link to move quickly to that item, such as a Web site, another slide or a video. Depending on how the link was set up, you may be able to click another link to return to where you were before you activated the link. Otherwise, you may need to close that application, as applicable, to return to the slide show.

To display a slideshow on a second monitor or a LCD projector connected to your computer or notebook, do one of the following:

- On the Slide Show tab, in the Set Up group, click **Set Up Slide Show**, then click the arrow for **Display slide show on** and select the second monitor, and click **OK**.
- on the Slide Show tab, in the Monitors group, click the arrow for **Show On**, and select the second monitor.

When you run the slide show, it will appear in full screen on your second monitor (or LCD projector) while your primary monitor stays in PowerPoint mode.

If you turn on the **Use Presenter View** with your secondary monitor, your primary monitor will change from PowerPoint display mode to the view shown in the following figure when you run the slide show:

Notice the icons below the slide that you can use as the presenter rather than try to find the icon at the lower right of the monitor that the audience is viewing. These icons are the same as the full screen with the slide show, so you can activate an option as needed during the slide show. This view is very useful as it shows you the contents of the current slide as well as the contents of the next slide so you can see the flow of the presentation, or make adjustments as questions from the audience arise.

Use to change how the screen displays; for example, you may want to display a black screen while the audience takes a short break. You can also display speaker notes or enter additional information provided by the audience.

To stop the slide show at any point, use one of the following methods:

- Right-click and then click **End Show**; or
- press Esc.

EXERCISE

In this exercise, you will run a presentation as a slide show, review content and animation flow.

1. Open the *Alaska Hiking Tours* file and save it as Alaska Hiking Tours – Student.

2. Press F5 to go into Slide Show view and then click to view the contents of several slides.

3. Point at the lower left corner to see the navigation tools and click the arrow buttons to move from one slide to another.

4. Click the **Previous** and **Next** buttons to move to different slides.

5. Click the ⬭ button and choose a pen style. Try to write or highlight something on the current slide, or move to another slide to use the pen.

6. When done viewing the slide show, press (Esc) to return to Normal view for PowerPoint. Note that you may need to press (Esc) twice and that you will be prompted to save or discard any screen annotations.

The presentation was originally set up to be delivered by a speaker. Suppose you are now asked to set this presentation on the company Web site so internal and external clients can view it on their own.

7. Click the **Slide Show** tab, in the Set Up group, click **Set Up Slide Show**.

8. In the Show type area, click **Browsed by an individual (window)** and then click **OK**.

9. Press (F5) to begin the slide show.

10. Use the arrows at the lower right corner of the screen to move from one slide to another. Click anywhere on the slide to move from one slide to the next slide.

11. Press (Esc) to exit the slide show view.

12. Save and close the presentation.

The following steps are applicable only if you completed the previous exercise for Animating Objects.

13. Open the *Exploring Seattle – Student* file, then click the **(Slide Show)** view button and progress through the slide show.

The presentation should play with the animations and transitions you set up in the previous exercise. What is your opinion when the presentation finishes? How did you find the transitions plus the animations? Where did you find the focus or impact of the presentation start to change? This is an example of why most presentations are limited to one or two styles for the animation or transitions. This will vary with the audience type and most presentations include some animation effects but often without transitions.

14. Make changes to the animations or transitions as required. Then save and close the presentation.

Previewing or Printing the Presentation

IC³ Exam 2 - Objective 1.1

There are a number of ways to print or preview a presentation. You should always preview your presentation on screen to ensure everything works the way you expect. You may also want to preview the presentation using the traditional print preview to see how the slides in the presentation will appear if you print them as slides or as notes pages. Printing slides can help you evaluate how the presentation topics flow and how well they convey the message you are trying to deliver.

As you begin to finalize a slide show, you can add speaker notes to help you during the presentation. You can also use a variety of formats for printing handouts. Handouts are printed versions of the presentation you can distribute to the audience.

Creating Notes

Notes can help you organize your thoughts about the information you present on each slide. You can create notes at the same time you create your slides, or after you have finalized the content for the presentation. You add notes to a slide using the Notes pane.

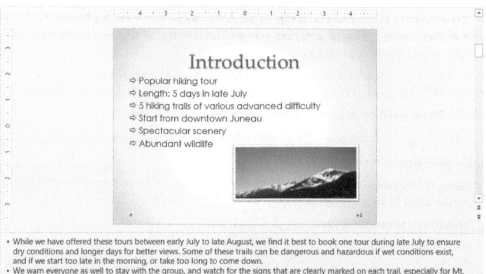

To see more of the Notes pane in Normal view, point to the top border of the Notes pane; when you see ↕, drag it until the pane is the size you want. You can enter only text in the Notes pane, but you can apply basic formatting to the text in this view.

To see a miniature of the slide and view or enter notes to accompany it, switch to the Notes Page view, where you can also add drawing objects or pictures in the Notes area; you will need to adjust these within the Notes area as they will be floating objects. When you return to Normal view, only the text will display.

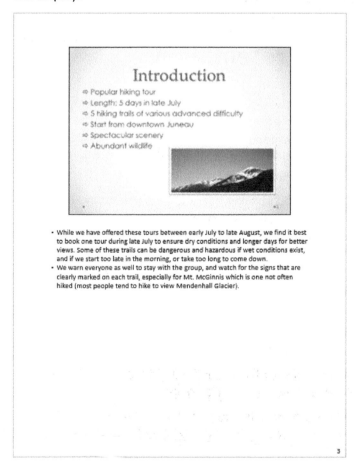

Depending on the amount of information in the notes area, you may have to change the font size or the size of the placeholder to fit the information in the default text box provided. You can also set up these options using the Notes Master feature.

Creating Handouts

Handouts are printed copies of the slides in your presentation, usually intended for distribution. You can specify how many slides to print on each page, up to a maximum of nine per page.

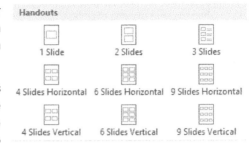

Print handouts using the **Print Layout** option, in the Settings area of Print in Backstage view. The three-slides-per-page option prints with lines at the right of each slide so the audience can write notes during the presentation. The greater the number of slides per page, the smaller the view of each slide will be on the printout.

Printing Items

You can print anything created in PowerPoint, whether slides, notes, or handouts.

* If you are using a monochrome laser printer, all colors in the presentation will print in varying shades of gray.

* If you are printing to overhead transparencies, be sure to use the transparency sheets designed for your printer type; otherwise, the colors may "bleed" or smudge as they are printed and handled.

You can preview your print settings using the Print panel.

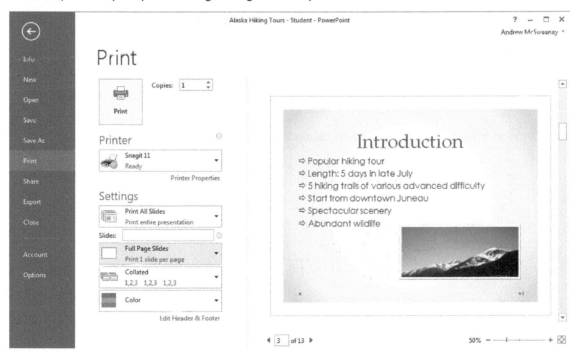

Use the different options in the Print panel to select what you want to print or how you want the items to print such as slides, notes, or handouts; print in color or grayscale.

Notice that PowerPoint gives you a preview with the print options. You can use the arrows at the lower left of the preview to move from one slide to another, as well as zoom in or out of the slides.

Preview your presentation to view items that you are distributing to the audience, or to verify that the elements on the slides appear in the manner intended. The preview will always match the printer type selected.

EXERCISE

In this exercise you will add notes to a presentation and then print (or preview) the presentation in Notes Page view and for handouts.

1. Open the *Exploring Seattle Proposal* file and save as `Exploring Seattle Proposal - Student`.

2. On **slide 1**, click in the Notes pane area and type the following:

   `Proposal for Nick to approve the plan to explore new office area for expansion of West Coast restaurant tours. We can start with Seattle and expand to Vancouver, BC which apparently has also been visited by the hosts of these shows.`

   `Vancouver is a 3-4 hour drive from Seattle and could work well for building a multi-day tour package that could feature a meal that includes venison, buffalo or ostrich in northern BC.`

3. In the Slides tab, click the appropriate slide and then in the Notes pane, type the following:

Slide #	Comment
2	So far we have nothing for the West Coast due to the small exposure; it may well be worth the effort to explore this, especially given the number of tourists they get from Asia-Pacific.
	With Vancouver being so close, we should contact vendors to see about partnering with some of their tours.
3	We found these shows were the most popular and fun for customers, partly due to the variety of food types and prices.
	Each show has taped episodes featuring a Seattle restaurant as well as other cities on the West Coast.

4. Click the **View** tab, and in the Presentation Views group, click **Notes Page**.

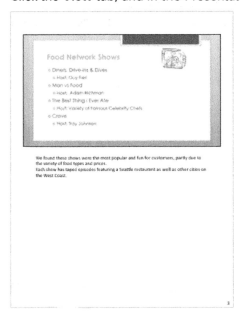

5. On the **View** tab, in the **Master Views** group, click **Notes Master**.

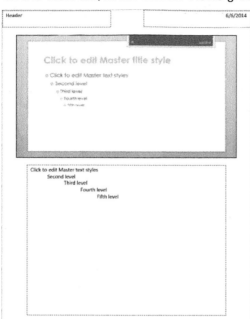

6. Zoom into the content placeholder for the notes and then click anywhere in the first line of text.

7. Click the **Home** tab, and in the Paragraph group, click **Bullets**.

8. Click the **Notes Master** tab, and in the Close group, click **Close Master View**.

9. Scroll through the first few slides to see that the notes have bullets with the text.

You will now print the slides. Check with your instructor to ensure a printer is available; if not, use the tools in the Preview mode to view the slides.

10. Click **File** and then click **Print**.

The appearance of the presentation depends on the printer you have selected; for instance, the slide may appear in black and white if the selected printer is currently set to print in Grayscale. If you do not have access to a color printer, color will be available only when working on the slides.

11. At the bottom of the Settings section, click the arrow for **Grayscale** or **Color** (depending on your particular setup) to view the available settings. Most printers will print in color, grayscale or pure black and white. Click **Color** if the option is available.

12. Click the arrow for **Full Page Slides**.

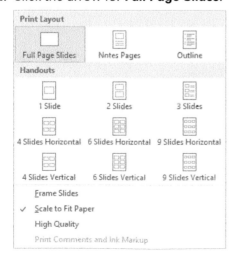

13. Click **Notes Pages** in the Print Layout section.

14. Click **Print** to print the slides using the Notes Pages option.

15. Click **File** and then click **Print**. Click the arrow for **Notes Pages** and click **3 Slides** in the Handouts section. Click **Print**.

16. Save and close the presentation, then exit PowerPoint.

Lesson Summary

In this lesson you were introduced to basic skills for working with an application designed to manage presentations delivered in various mediums. You set up presentations, created and edited slides that include text, images, charts, tables, or multimedia. You should now be familiar with the following:

☑ general structure and guidelines for creating presentations

☑ creating new blank presentations or using a template to create a new presentation

☑ saving, closing, or opening presentations

☑ changing the view display for the slides

☑ inserting, deleting or duplicating slides

☑ changing the slide layout or design

☑ adding or manipulating text on the slides

☑ adding or manipulating tables and charts on the slides

☑ adding or manipulating multimedia objects such as pictures, movies, music files

☑ setting up and running the slide show

☑ creating notes or handouts to accompany the slides

☑ printing slide items

Review Questions

1. Which method can you use to create new presentations?
   a. Blank presentation
   b. My templates
   c. New from existing
   d. Themes
   e. Any of the above
   f. a, c, and d

2. What is generally considered to be the maximum number of bullet points you should include on a slide?
   a. 6
   b. 8
   c. 10
   d. There is no limit

3. Which view button would you use to view multiple slides?
   a.
   b.
   c.
   d.

4. How can you insert a new slide?
   a. On the Home tab, in the Slides group, click New Slide.
   b. On the Quick Access toolbar, click New Slide.
   c. Press Ctrl+M.
   d. Right-click the slide in the Outline or Slides tab and then click New Slide.
   e. Any of the above
   f. a, c, or d

5. To change the slide layout, you can:
   a. On the Home tab, in the Slides group, click Layout.
   b. On the Design tab, in the Slides group, click Slide Layout.
   c. Right-click the slide in the Slides tab or the Slide pane and then click Layout.
   d. Any of the above
   e. a or c

6. To insert a table onto a slide, you can:
   a. On the Insert tab, in the Tables group, click Table.
   b. Change the slide layout to the Title and Table layout.
   c. On the Insert tab, in the Tables group, click Table, Insert Table.
   d. Any of the above
   e. a or c

MMM
Go online for
Additional
Review

7. List the methods you can use to insert a chart onto a slide.
   a. On the Insert tab, in the Illustrations group, click Chart.
   b. Change the slide layout to the Title and Content layout, click Insert Chart icon.
   c. On the Insert tab, in the Illustrations group, click Chart, click Insert Chart.
   d. Any of the above
   e. a or b

8. Which handle on a selected image allows you to resize the image by two sides at the same time?
   a. One of the corner handles.
   b. The middle top or bottom handle.
   c. The middle left or right handle.
   d. The green circle.

9. How can you customize the animation for a placeholder?
   a. On the Animations tab, in the Advanced Animation group, Animation Pane.
   b. On the Animations tab, in the Slide Show group, Animation Pane.
   c. Right-click the placeholder and then click Animation Pane.
   d. Any of the above

10. What types of effects can you set up for an object?
    a. Entrance   d. Exit
    b. Motion Paths   e. a, b, c, and d
    c. Emphasis   f. a or b only

11 When you add notes to a presentation, how can you use them?
    a. As Speaker notes to remind you of what you want to say as you present each slide.
    b. As reminders of tasks you still want to perform while creating/modifying the presentation.
    c. As a way to organize your thoughts as you work on the presentation.
    d. Any of the above

12. Why would you want to create handouts?
    a. To distribute to the audience for reference after the presentation.
    b. To allow the audience to take notes during the presentation.
    c. To use as a hard copy of the slides in your presentation.
    d. Any of the above
    e. b or c

Lesson 11: Microsoft Access

Lesson Objectives

In this lesson you will be introduced to a relational database management tool you can use to organize and retrieve large amounts of information. On successful completion of this lesson, you should be familiar with:

☐ what a database is

☐ how to create, save, open or close a database

☐ how to create and modify records

☐ how to use simple queries

☐ how to create and use reports

What is Access?

Microsoft Access is a database management system (DBMS) and a complete application development environment. Unlike some DBMS programs, Access includes the tools you need to develop user-friendly interfaces and reports. For users who are interested only in setting up databases and managing data, Access provides a user-friendly environment that allows you to accomplish database tasks very quickly even without prior knowledge.

Any interaction among a user, program and database takes place through the use of structured query language (SQL). In Access, the actual SQL code that controls and manipulates the data is used behind the scenes; users interact with a graphical environment which allows them to create tables, queries, reports and other database objects.

Access has been used by thousands of organizations to manage simple lists or design complex multi-user database applications over local area networks and the Internet. Access provides a powerful set of tools that enable you to create a database and start entering, organizing, searching, sorting, tracking, reporting and sharing information in a systematic way.

Access Database File

An Access database is a container for a variety of database objects; it can contain one table or a collection of tables, forms, reports and queries. For example, an order tracking system that uses four tables is not four databases; it is one database that includes four tables: most likely one for customer information, one for order information, one for order detail information and one for product information.

An Access (version 2007 and above) database stores its objects in a single file with the .accdb file name extension. Previous versions of Access used the .mdb file name extension. In Access 2013, you can open and work with both .mdb and .accdb databases. You can also use Access to create new databases and save the databases as .accdb or .mdb files for backward compatibility with earlier versions (for example, Access 2000 and Access 2002-2003).

Database Objects

An Access database can contain various types of database objects, including tables, queries, forms, reports, macros and modules. The following sections briefly introduce database objects. All database objects can be accessed from the Access Navigation Pane.

Tables

The basic building block of any database is a table. A database table is similar in appearance to a list or spreadsheet, in that the data is stored in rows and columns, as shown in the following:

The row and column layout is called a datasheet. Each row in the table is a record. Each record consists of one or more fields, and each column in the table is a field. The preceding figure shows the Datasheet view of a table named "Vendors." The table contains six records (rows), and each record is about a specific vendor. Notice that each field (column) contains a specific category of information, such as name, address, phone number and so on for each vendor.

The main difference between storing your data in a spreadsheet and storing it in a database is in how the data is organized into tables. In a spreadsheet, all the data is stored in one table. In a database, data is organized into separate tables. For example, data about products will be stored in a products table, while data about orders will be stored in an orders table, and so on.

A complex database might contain a dozen or more tables, many of which might be related to each other by a common field. The ability to work with multiple related tables is a feature of relational databases. Different types of relationships can be created.

Forms

Forms are commonly used as data entry screens. They are user-friendly interfaces for working with data, and they often contain elements and command buttons that make entering data and performing various other tasks quick and easy.

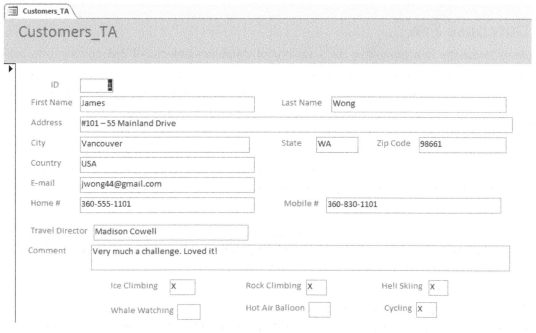

While you can enter and edit data in datasheet view, most database users prefer user-friendly forms for viewing, entering, editing and deleting data in the underlying table.

Reports

You use reports to print and summarize data. For example, a report such as the one shown below can group customers by country, and then list pertinent contact information. Each report is formatted to present the information in the most readable way possible. You can format any report to fit your requirements and you can create custom reports as well.

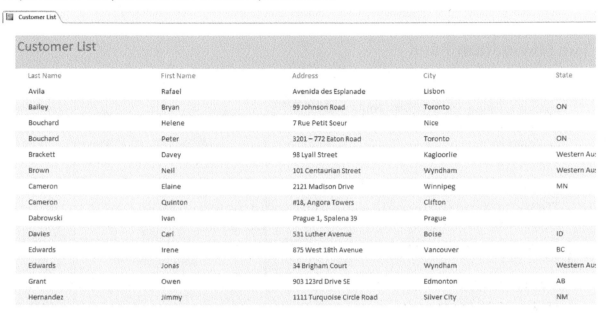

You can run a report at any time and it will always reflect the current state of the data in the database. Generally, you will print reports, but you can also view them on the screen, export them to another application, or send them as email messages.

Queries

You use queries to extract subsets of data from one or more tables. The data you want to retrieve may be stored in several tables, and a query allows you to view data from several tables in a single datasheet. In addition, because you generally do not want to see all the information at once, queries allow you select certain fields and add criteria to retrieve only specific records.

The result of a query is called a record set or result set. You can view the result set on the screen, print it, copy it to the clipboard, or use the output of the query as the record source for a form or report.

Object Views

In Access, there are a variety of views you can use when you work with database objects. Database designers and administrators generally use the built-in "design" views when structuring tables and designing other objects, such as queries and forms. In contrast, database users generally use a view that allows them to work directly with the data.

When you double-click an object in the Navigation Pane to open it, the object opens in its default or "open" view. The open view for tables and queries is Datasheet view. The open view for forms is Form view, and the open view for reports is Report view.

Interface Components

The Access 2013 user interface provides the ability to work with a database as a complete file, and the ability to work with individual database objects. The three main components to the Access 2013 user interface are:

Ribbon	Common to all Microsoft Office applications, the Ribbon is a panel of command buttons and icons organized into a set of tabs. The Ribbon appears across the top of the program window. Each tab on the ribbon contains groups of commands related to specific database tasks.
Navigation Pane	A pane on the left side of the program window that displays database objects.
Backstage view	A collection of commands on the File tab of the Ribbon.

The Navigation Pane

Located on the left side of the screen, the Navigation Pane is a central location from which you can create and use any type of database object.

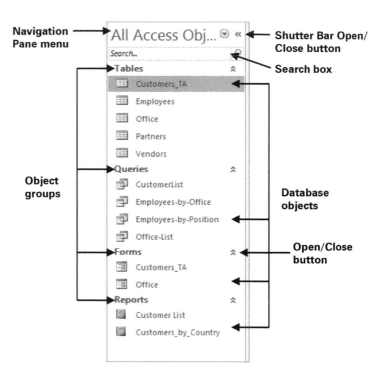

The Navigation Pane includes the following components:

Navigation Pane menu	Click the drop-down arrow to open a menu that allows you to specify which objects to show. The default selection is All Access Objects.
Open/Close buttons	Collapses the Navigation Pane so only its Open/Close button and shutter bar display. Collapsing the pane provides more space on the screen for working with an object. To reopen the Navigation Pane, click its shutter bar.
Object groups	Organize the objects in a database, allowing you to find what you are looking for. Each object group includes an Open/Close button, which you can use to collapse or expand the list.
Database objects	The tables, queries, forms and other objects that exist in the database. Each object appears in its appropriate group.
Search box	You can type the name of an object for which you are looking and the objects that display in the Navigation Pane are filtered to match the name you enter.

Backstage View

You use Backstage view to create, open, save, print and manage databases. In contrast to Backstage view is the Access client view, which you use to work with the objects within a database. For example, you use Access client view to create tables, add records, or modify a form.

Backstage view shows the commands and options available on the File tab of the Ribbon.

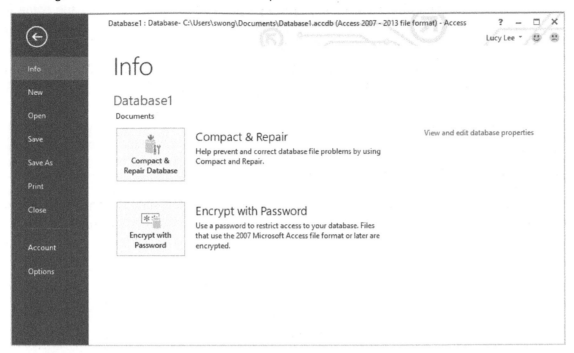

The tabs within Backstage view are: Info, New, Open, Save, Save As, Print, and Close. Each of these tabs includes commands and options that appear in the right pane of the window when the tab is selected. Backstage view also includes the Account tab to update your profile and the Options tab which opens the Access Options dialog box.

Managing Database Files

 Exam 2 - Objective 1.3

As with other applications in the Office 2013 suite, file management tasks in Access are performed in Backstage view. The commands and options available here are related to things you can do with an entire database as an entity.

Creating a New Blank Database

New databases are created from database templates. The Blank database template creates an empty database file; that is, it creates a database that does not contain any database objects.

To create a new blank database, click **Blank desktop database** in the template gallery on either the startup screen or the New tab of Backstage view. Access opens a dialog box and suggests a name (Database#.accdb) and location (the Documents folder) for the new database file.

You can specify your own name for the database in the File Name box. You can also click the **Browse for a location to put your database** button 📁 to specify where you want to save your database file. When you click this button, the File New Database dialog box opens. Once you have specified the desired location, select the text in the File name box, type a name for the new database and click **OK**.

When choosing a name, consider the following:

- The file name can be a maximum of 255 characters (including the drive and folder path), and may not include these characters: / \ : * ? " < > |
- Give the file a name that will help you identify its contents quickly.

- Access automatically assigns the .accdb file name extension. (The default database type for Access 2013 is the Microsoft Access 2007 – 2013 Database.) You need to type only the name for the database.

Creating a Database from a Template

Access ships with several database and app templates, and provides quick links to templates on the Office.com Web site. Some templates include sample data.

Templates enable you to create new databases quickly. A template is a model or boilerplate of a typical database that contains all the table, query, form and report objects required to perform a specific function. For example, templates are available to track assets or inventory, manage tasks or contacts, and administer projects.

To create a database that contains ready-to-use objects, click a template in the gallery. If you do not see the template you want, click a link in the Suggested searches area, or type a keyword in the Search box and click ⌕ to locate templates online.

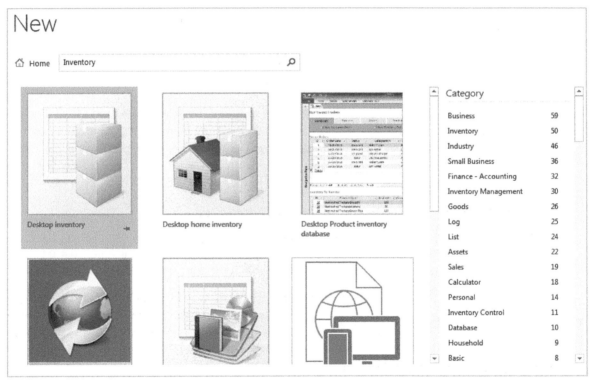

Click options in the Category list box to refine your search. Click the template you want to use, specify a name and location and then click **Create** to create the new database. Once you have created a database based on a template, you can enter data and customize the database to meet your requirements.

Saving a Database

When you first create a database, you enter the file name in the File Name box. It is not necessary to save the database file after you have given the database a file name; as you work in the database, you will save the individual database objects. Whenever anyone adds, modifies, or deletes data, Access will save these changes to disk immediately.

However, you can use the **Save As** command if you want to save the database with a different file name, save it as another file type, or save it in a different location, such as to a network folder or a OneDrive folder. This command is accessible in Backstage view when a database file is open.

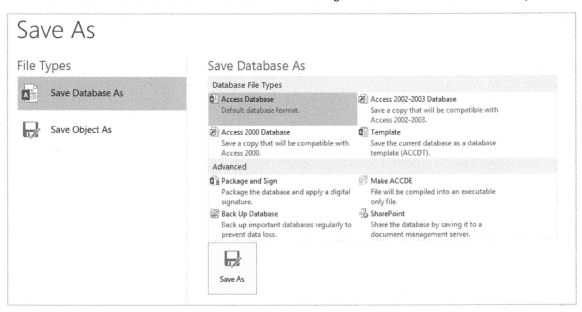

Clicking the **Save As** command opens the Save As dialog box.

Use the options in the Save As dialog box to change the name or location of the database file.

Closing a Database

When you have finished working with a database, you can close the database and still keep Access open to work with other databases. You must close the current database file before you can view or edit another database file. To close a database you use the **Close** command in Backstage view.

Opening an Existing Database

As you begin to use Access, recently used database files display in the Recent list in the Startup screen and on the Open tab of Backstage view. You can specify the number of files to display in the list to a number between 0 and 50 (inclusive). To open a database that appears in the list, simply click the database name.

You can also click the **Open** tab to open a database.

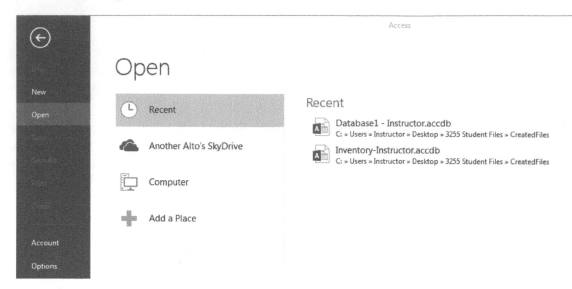

The Open tab is arranged in three sections. The left section shows the tabs of Backstage view; the middle section displays various storage locations connected to the system; and the right section lists the files located in the currently selected storage location. Click a database file to open it.

When you select a storage location other than the Recent file list, you may see icons for folders and/or a **Browse** button.

Clicking a folder icon or the Browse button opens the Open dialog box, which should be familiar to anyone who has used a Microsoft application.

You can click the folders in the dialog box to navigate the directory tree on the computer. When you locate the file you want, you can double-click the file name or click the file name and then click the **Open** button.

You can work with only one database at a time in Access. If you open a database and then open a second database, the first database will automatically close. To work with two open databases, you must start separate sessions of Access and work with one database in each session. In the vast majority of situations, you will work with only one database at a time.

EXERCISE

In this exercise, you will create, save, close and open databases.

First, you will create (and then close) a new, blank database.

1. Click **Start, All Programs, Microsoft Office 2013, Access 2013**.

    Access opens in Backstage view and displays the startup screen.

2. Click **Blank desktop database** in the list of templates.

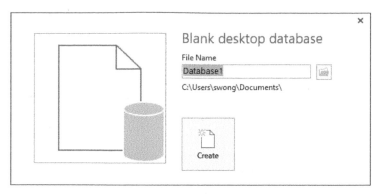

3. Click at the end of the File Name and type: - Student. Then click the **Browse** button to navigate to the *7318 Student Files* folder, then the *Lesson 11 – Access* subfolder.

4. Click **OK** to save your specifications.

    The new file name and file location should display in the right pane of the window.

5. Click the **Create** button to save the blank database in the specified location.

    Access saves the database and opens a blank datasheet with the suggested name *Table1* on the datasheet tab. You have successfully created a new, blank database.

6. In the Ribbon, click the **File** tab to return to Backstage view, then click **Close** to close the blank database.

Next, you will create a database from a template.

7. Click **File** and in the list of categories below the search field, click **Contacts**.

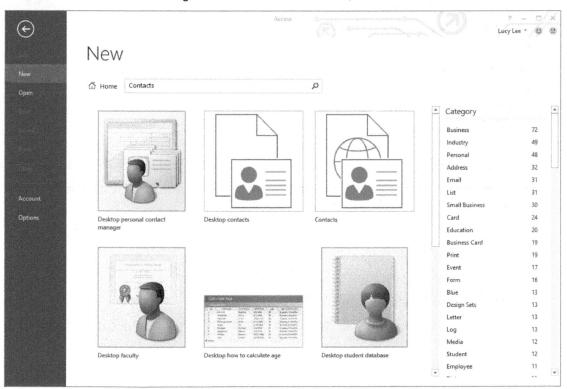

8. Click **Desktop contacts**. In the **File Name** field, type: `Contact Manager - Student` as the new name for this file.

9. Click the **Browse** button, then navigate to the **Lesson 11 - Access** subfolder within the *7318 Student Data* folder and click **OK** to specify a location for the new database.

10. Click **Create**.

    Access downloads the template, and creates a new database based on the template. Access also opens a Help window called Getting Started with Contacts that displays information on how to use the template. (Note: The Getting Started window may be hidden behind the Access application window. If it is hidden, access it.)

11. Read the information that Access provides to help you with understanding how to use this type of database. If time permits, click the Play button to watch a video.

12. When you are finished, close the Getting Started window.

    Notice that the new database contains several database objects that were created automatically from the template. Notice also that the file is opened in Protected mode because the template was downloaded from the Internet. Files that open in Protected mode are read-only until you specifically enable the content.

13. In the security warning, click **Enable Content** so you can work with the database objects. (If the Getting Started window displays again, close it.)

14. Switch to Backstage view, then close the database.

15. Click ✕ to exit the Access application.

Next, you will open a database and save it with a new name.

16. Start Access again. Click **Open Other Files**.

17. Click **Computer** from the location area and then click **Lesson 11 – Access** folder from the list of Recent Folders.

18. Select **Tolano Inc** as the file and then click **Open**.

19. Click **Enable Content**, click **File** and then click **Save As**.

20. Ensure **Access Database** is selected in the Save Database As area and click **Save As**. In the File name field, press (End) to move the cursor to the end of the existing text, press (Backspace) once, then type: - Student.

21. Click **Save**.

    Access saves the file as *Tolano Inc – Student* and opens it.

22. Click **Enable Content** to turn off the security warning and enable editing of the database.

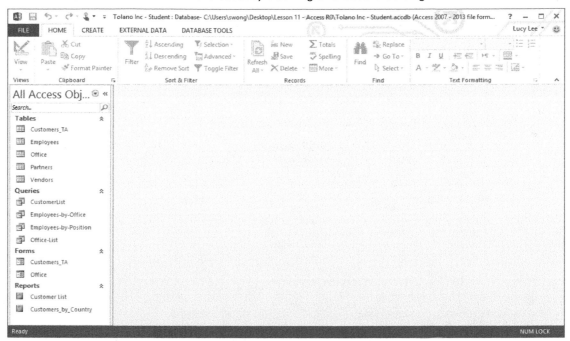

23. Leave the database open for upcoming exercises.

Table Basics

 Exam 2 - Objective 5.1

As you have already learned, a database uses tables to store data. A table is a collection of information about a specific topic, and the data is organized into rows and columns. The following figure shows a portion of a typical database table containing contact information.

Field   Record

In a table, each column is called a field and each row constitutes a record. A *field* is a category of information within a table and a *record* is a collection of information consisting of one or more fields pertaining to a specific entity, such as a person, product or event.

In a database table, each record should be unique; no two records in a table may be exactly the same.

Working with Records

Many people use Datasheet view when they work with table records. Datasheet view includes a record selector, record navigation buttons and a record number box which indicates the number of the current record.

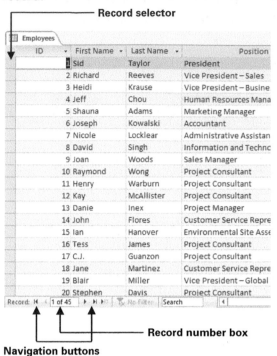

In Datasheet view, the record selector appears highlighted for the current record. In the preceding screen, Record 1 is the current record. Notice that the entire row is displayed in a different background color as well. At any given time, only one record can be the current record.

Navigating a Datasheet

In Datasheet view, the record number box shows the record number of the current record. You can type a number in the record number box to move to a specific record, or you can use the navigation buttons to move through the datasheet. The navigation buttons are:

⏮	**First record**: moves the cursor to the first record in the table and keeps the cursor in the same field.
◀	**Previous record**: moves the cursor to the previous record in the table and keeps the cursor in the same field.
▶	**Next record**: moves the cursor to the next record in the table and keeps the cursor in the same field.
⏭	**Last record**: moves the cursor to the last record in the table and keeps the cursor in the same field.
⏭	**New (blank) record**: creates a new record at the end of the table and moves the cursor to the first field of the new record.

You can also move through a datasheet by pressing the keyboard directional keys, pressing (Tab) or clicking anywhere in the datasheet.

Entering and Revising Records in Datasheet View

Entering records into a datasheet is much like entering data into a spreadsheet. You can use the arrow keys, the (Tab) key and the mouse to move from field to field in a table.

To add a new record, either click the **New (blank) record** button ( ) to create a new blank row, or click in the last field of the last record, and the press (Tab) to create a new blank row.

As you enter new or revised data into a table record, a pencil icon displays in the record selector to indicate that the record contains unsaved changes. When you reach the end of a record, you can press (Tab) or (Enter) to move the cursor to the first field of the next record, and the edited record is automatically saved.

You can also press (Ctrl)+(S) to save changes from anywhere in the Datasheet.

Deleting Records in Datasheet View

When you delete (or remove) a record from a table, you delete all the fields for the record. You cannot Undo a record deletion.

To delete a record, click the record selector for the record you want to delete (Access highlights the entire row), then on the Home tab, in the Records group click **Delete**. You can also delete a record by right-clicking the record selector, and then selecting **Delete Record** in the shortcut menu. When you delete a record, Access displays the following message box.

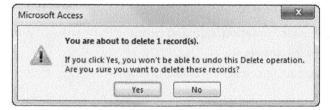

Click **Yes** to delete the record.

EXERCISE

In this exercise you will add, edit and delete records in the Partners table. The Partners table is designed to store contact information (name, address, phone, and so on) pertaining to Tolano's partners.

1. In the Navigation Pane, in the **Tables** group, double-click **Partners** to open the table in Datasheet view. The table is currently empty, and the first field (ID) for a new record is highlighted. The ID field in the Partners table is a special type of field that automatically generates an ID number. You cannot enter data into this field.

2. Press (Tab) to move to the PGiven field, then type: Baradoch.

3. Press (Tab) and type: Brochanan as the surname.

    Notice that a pencil icon displays in the record selector, indicating that the record has not yet been saved.

4. Enter the rest of the data for the first new record as indicated below.

Partner	Green Soles Adventures Club
PAddress1	16 Hiker's Way
PAddress2	Suite F
PCity	Chicago
PState	IL
PZip	60626
PWork	773-909-4550
PEmail	bbrochanan@greensoles.com

When you get to the end of the record, press (Tab) once more to create a new record. Notice that when you move to the next record, the first record is automatically saved.

5. In the second new record, press (Tab) and type: Vivienne as the given name. Enter the rest of the data as indicated below. When you get to the end of the record, stop and do not press (Tab).

PSurname	LeClaire
Partner	Valley'n Peaks Medical Clinic
PAddress1	1800 Cottonwood Drive
PAddress2	103
PCity	Brooklyn
PState	NY
PZip	11211
PWork	718-657-2157
PEmail	medaid@valleynpeaksmc.com

When you get to the end of the record, notice the pencil icon in the record pointer.

6. Press (Ctrl)+(S) to save the record.

7. In the Navigation buttons, click ▶※ to create a new record.

8. Press (Tab) and then enter your own contact information, skipping over the Partner field. When you reach the end of the record, press (Ctrl)+(S) to save it.

9. In the last record (which contains your contact information), click the Partner field, type: GS4 Class and then press (Ctrl)+(S).

10. In the last record, select the value in the PCity field, replace it with the name of another city, then save the record. Editing a record is as easy as selecting the existing value, and typing in a new one.

11. Click the record selector for the last record, on the Home tab, in the Records group, click **Delete**, and click **Yes** to confirm the deletion.

Access deletes the last record in the Partners table.

12. Leave the table and the database open for upcoming exercises.

Adjusting the View

IC³ Exam 2 - Objective 1.1, 1.3

You will have noticed by now that working in Access is a little bit different than working in other Office applications. In most applications, you work with a single file and any changes you make to the file can be either saved or abandoned at the end of (or at any point during) the session.

In Access, you work with the individual objects within the single database file, and at the end of an Access session, you don't save the database file; instead you save changes to the individual objects as you work with them.

As you have already seen, each database object opens in its own window. You cannot, however, resize the object windows, and you cannot increase the zoom setting for an object window. (You can adjust the zoom setting when previewing reports, and you will learn more about that later in this lesson.)

The Access application window itself, like any other application window, can be minimized, maximized or restored. When you restore or maximize the application window, the windows for any open objects are resized accordingly.

Switching between Open Objects

Because a database file is a collection of objects, you can open and work with several objects simultaneously. Each object displays in its own window, and only one object can be the active object at any given time. To make an object the active object, simply click its window tab.

The following figure shows three open tables (Partners, Employees, Office), one open form (Customers_TA), and one open report (Customer List) in the Tolano Inc – Student database. The Partners table is the active object.

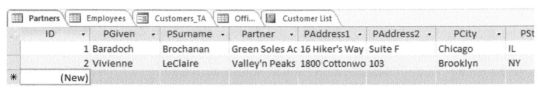

Manipulating a Datasheet

At times you may want to change the appearance of a datasheet or rearrange the columns to suit your needs. For example, suppose the datasheet contained 20 or more fields. The screen is not large enough to display all the fields at once. If you need to work with data in fields 1, 2 and 17, it would be cumbersome to scroll horizontally to reach field 17.

There are several techniques you can use to make your work easier. You can:

- **Hide or unhide columns** – to temporarily hide fields that you do not need to edit so that they no longer take up space on the screen. To hide a field, right-click the column heading in the datasheet and select **Hide Fields**.

- **Resize fields** – to display more or less data as required. You can resize a field by positioning the mouse pointer over the right border of the field in the heading row. The mouse pointer will change to a resizing icon (✛), indicating that you can resize the field. Click and hold the left mouse button and drag the right border left or right, as required.

- **Rearrange fields** – you can physically drag a field to another position in the datasheet so the fields you need to edit are adjacent to one another. To move a field, click the column heading to select the field, position the mouse pointer over the heading for the selected field, then click and hold the left mouse button until a thick blue line appears along the left boundary of the field. Drag the field into the desired position, and then release the mouse button.

- **Freeze and unfreeze fields** – you can freeze the first one or several fields in a table so they do not scroll out of view when you scroll the datasheet horizontally to the right. To freeze a field, right-click in the column heading, then select **Freeze Fields**.

EXERCISE

In this exercise you will open multiple objects, switch between open objects, adjust the amount of viewing space, and manipulate a datasheet.

1. In the Navigation Pane, in the **Tables** group, double-click **Employees** to open the Employees table in Datasheet view.

    Now both the Partners and Employees tables are open.

2. In the Navigation Pane, in the **Tables** group, double-click **Customers_TA** to open the Customers_TA table in Datasheet view.

    Now three tables are open.

3. In the workspace just below the Ribbon, click the **Employees** tab to make the Employees table the active object.

4. At the right edge of the workspace, click the **Close** button to close the Employees table.

    The Customers_TA table should now be the active object.

5. At the upper-right corner of the application window, click the **Maximize** button to maximize the Access window.

    Notice that the available workspace increases, and you can now see more of the Customers_TA table.

6. At the top of the Navigation Pane, click the **Shutter Bar Open/Close** button to collapse the Navigation Pane and display even more of the table data.

7. Click the shutter bar for the Navigation Pane to open it once again.

8. At the upper-right corner of the application window, click the **Restore Down** button to restore the Access window.

9. At the upper-right corner of the application window, click the **Minimize** button to minimize the Access window.

    The window disappears from the screen and displays only as a button on the task bar.

10. Click the Access button in the taskbar to restore the window.

11. At the right edge of the workspace, click the **Close** button to close the Customers_TA table.

    The Partners table should now be the only open object.

Now try resizing some of the columns so you can see more of the data or specific areas of the data.

12. Place the mouse cursor on the vertical line between the ID and the PGiven column titles.

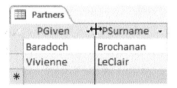

13. Drag the mouse cursor to the left to resize the width of the ID column. Size to your preference.

14. Place the cursor on the vertical line between Partner and PAddress1 and then double-click to automatically resize the column so that it will display the entire organization name.

15. Adjust the column width for other columns in the datasheet, as needed.

16. When done, click the **Save** button on the Quick Access toolbar.

17. Click the **Close** button at the far right of the table to close it.

18. Minimize the Access window to keep the database open, but out of sight.

Finding the Data You Want

 Exam 2 - Objective 1.1, 1.3, 5.1

Access databases are ideally suited for storing large quantities of complex data. However, if there were no way to retrieve the specific data you need, databases would not be very useful.

Depending on the number of records a table contains, finding the data you want may be a simple matter of scanning a small table. However, if a table includes hundreds or thousands of records, browsing the table to locate specific information would be time consuming and inefficient.

Access provides several methods for finding exactly the data you want. These methods include entering the appropriate record number in the Record Number box in the navigation buttons, using the Find feature, sorting records, filtering tables and using queries.

Finding Records

You can use the Find feature to locate records that contain a specific value or text string in a particular field. For example, you could find records in an inventory tracking database for all products that begin with "s" or find all products that cost $14.95. The Find feature searches the datasheet and moves the record selector to the first record that matches the value or text you specify. You can click the **Find Next** button to move through the Datasheet viewing each record that meets the criteria.

You access the **Find** feature in the Find group on the Home tab. When you click this command, Access opens the Find and Replace dialog box:

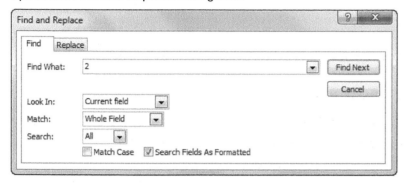

Use the **Find** tab to locate records that contain a specific text string or value. Type the string or value you want to find in the **Find What** text box, and specify where to search, how to determine a match, and the direction in which to search.

The value in the **Look In** drop-down list determines where Access will search. If the value is set to Current field, Access will search only the current field in the datasheet. The current field is the field that contains the cursor. You can specify to search the current field or the entire datasheet.

The value in the **Match** drop-down list determines how Access will evaluate whether a record matches the string or value in the Find What text box. You can specify **Whole Field, Any Part of Field**, or **Start of Field**.

By default, searches are conducted from the current record downward, and loop back to the beginning of the datasheet if necessary to ensure that all records are examined. That is, if you have a table with 1000 records and record 61 is the current record, the search will commence from record 61 downward to the end of the datasheet and then proceed to the top of the datasheet and back down to record 61.

You can control how Access conducts a search by changing the value in the **Search** drop-down list. The possible values are **Up, Down** or **All** (the default). Specifying Down will cause the search to proceed from the current record downward. The search ends once the bottom of the datasheet is reached. Specifying Up will cause the search to proceed from the current record upward, and the search ends once the top of the datasheet is reached.

Additionally, you can perform a case-sensitive search by turning on the **Match Case** option. By default, this option is not turned on. You can also specify to search fields as formatted. This setting instructs Access to find only data that matches the same pattern of characters as what you entered into the **Find What** text box. For example, if you are searching for the value $3,500.00 in a cost field with this option turned on, then you must enter 3,500.00 with the comma, period, and two decimal digits. If you turn the option off, then you can enter just 3500 into the **Find What** text box. By default, this setting is turned on.

Sorting Records

You can sort records in Datasheet view to display them in order by the values in any field. For example, you might sort the Employees table by the Office field to see all employees listed by the office in which they work. To see an alphabetical listing of employees, you could sort by the LastName field.

To sort a datasheet, click in any record in the column you want to use for the sort order, then click either the **Ascending** or **Descending** button in the **Sort & Filter** group on the **Home** tab of the Ribbon. You can also right-click any cell and select one of the available sort options from the shortcut menu.

Click the **Remove Sort** button in the Ribbon to turn off the sort order.

Sorting affects the way records display in a datasheet, but does not affect the physical order of the records in the table.

You can also sort by more than one column. When you sort by more than one column, the first column selected is the secondary sort key. The last column selected is the primary sort key.

Filtering Records

While you can use sorting to rearrange data in a datasheet, filtering enables you to isolate the specific records with which you want to work. Filters use a set of conditions called *criteria* to test records and determine whether or not they should be displayed. When a filter is applied, only a subset of the records display in the datasheet. However, once you remove the filter, all the records display again.

When you define criteria for a filter, you can specify that matching records match one single value or fall within a range of values. For example, you can create and apply a filter that displays only those records for orders that have not shipped.

Filter by Selection

There are a variety of filtering methods. For example, Filter by Selection will filter records that contain or do not contain identical data in a specific field, such as filtering out all records that equal or do not equal the value "WA" in a state field. To filter by selection, place the cursor in the column that you want to filter and on the Home tab, in the Sort & Filter group, click **Selection** and select an appropriate option.

In the example, if you click Equals "WA", then only records where the value in the state field equals WA will display in the subset.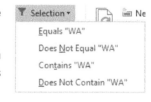

If you click Does Not Equal "WA", then only records where the value in the state field does not equal WA will display in the subset. Selecting this option is also known as Filter Excluding Selection.

Alternatively, on the Home tab, in the Sort & Filter group, click **Filter** or click a column-heading arrow. Next, select check boxes with the values you want and clear the check boxes with values you do not want in the list.

If the field is a text field, click **Text Filters** and select an appropriate option:

If the field is a number field, click **Number Filters** and select an appropriate option:

When you apply a filter, a filter symbol displays in one or more of the column headings.

In addition, the Filtered button displays on the status bar.

If you click the Filtered button, you can remove and re-apply the temporary filter and the Unfiltered button will display on the status bar.

You can also temporarily remove and reapply a filter by clicking **Toggle Filter** in the Sort & Filter group on the Home tab.

EXERCISE

In this exercise you will find, sort and filter records.

First, you will find records.

1. Open the Employees table in Datasheet view.

2. Click in the **First Name** column in Record 1. Then on the Home tab, in the Find group, click **Find**.

3. Type: Richard in the **Find What** box and press (Enter).

    Access locates record 2 (the first matching record) and selects it.

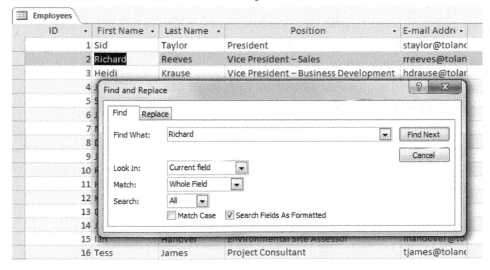

4. Click **Find Next**.

       Access locates and selects the next matching record, record 25.

5. Click **Find Next**.

       Access displays a message indicating that the search item was not found. Records 2 and 25 are the only matching records.

6. Click **OK** to close the message box.

7. Click in the **Find What** text box, type: `Tokyo`, then click **Find Next**.

       Access displays the item not found message.

8. Click **OK** to close the message box.

9. Display the Look In drop-down list, then select **Current document**. You are specifying that Access should search the entire datasheet.

10. Click **Find Next**.

       Access selects the first matching record – one that contains the text Tokyo in the Office field.

11. Click **Find Next** as many times as necessary to reach the end of the search, then close the message box.

12. Close the Find and Replace dialog box.

Next, you will sort records.

13. Click any field in the **LastName** column, then in the Sort & Filter group on the Ribbon, click **Ascending** to reorder the records in ascending alphabetical order.

       Notice that the sort ascending symbol (upward facing arrow) appears in the LastName column heading.

14. In the Ribbon, click **Descending** to reorder the records in descending alphabetical order.

       Now the sort descending symbol displays in the LastName column heading.

15. In the Ribbon, click **Remove Sort** to remove the sort and reorder the records by the ID field.

16. Right-click any field in the **FirstName** column, then select **Sort A to Z** in the shortcut menu to sort the records in alphabetical order by first name.

17. In the Ribbon, click **Remove Sort**.

18. Right-click any field in the **LastName** column, then select **Sort A to Z** in the shortcut menu to sort the records in alphabetical order by last name.

19. Without removing the existing sort, right-click any field in the **Office** column, then select **Sort A to Z** in the shortcut menu to sort the records in alphabetical order by office.

       The records are now sorted first by office, then by last name, allowing you to view an alphabetical list of employees in each office.

20. In the Ribbon, click **Remove Sort**.

Next, you will filter records.

21. Click in the **Office** field of any record where the value in the Office field is "London".

22. In the Sort & Filter group on the Ribbon, click the **Selection** button, then select **Equals "London"**.

Access hides all records where the value in the Office field is not equal to London. The remaining five records constitute the filtered subset. Notice that the Filtered button displays on the status bar and that the Record indicator reads Record 1 of 5.

23. In the Sort & Filter group, click the **Toggle Filter** button to remove the filter.

24. Click the **Toggle Filter** button again to reapply the filter.

25. Right-click any field in the **Office** column, then select **Does Not Equal "London"** in the shortcut menu.

    This action applies a second filter, and there are no records in the subset. If you want to view all records for offices other than London, you must first remove the Equals "London" filter and then apply a new filter.

26. Right-click the blank field in the **Office** column, then select **Clear filter from Office** in the shortcut menu.

    Access clears the filter and all table records display.

27. Right-click the **Office** field of any record where the value in the Office field is "London", then select **Does Not Equal "London"** in the shortcut menu.

    Access shows the 40 records where the value in the office field is not equal to London (and hides all records where the value in the Office field is equal to London).

28. Right-click the **Office** field for any record, then select **Clear filter from Office** in the shortcut menu.

29. Right-click the **Office** field for any record, then in the shortcut menu click **Text Filters**, then click **Begins With.**

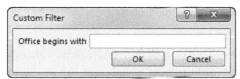

30. Type: s in the **Office begins with** text box, then click **OK** to apply the filter.

    There are nine records in the filtered subset.

31. In the Sort & Filter group on the Ribbon, click the **Filter** button, then select **Clear filter from Office** in the shortcut menu.

32. Click in the **Office** field of any record, then click the **Filter** button in the Ribbon to open the shortcut menu shown below.

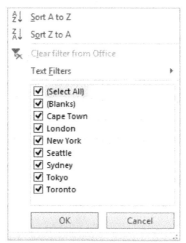

33. Clear the **Seattle** and **Sydney** check boxes in the shortcut menu, then click **OK** to apply the filter.

The filtered subset displays the 36 records for which the Office field is not equal to Seattle or Sydney.

34. In the Sort & Filter group on the Ribbon, click the **Filter** button, then select **Clear filter from Office** in the shortcut menu.

35. Close the Employees table, and click **No** if prompted to save changes to the design of the table.

36. Minimize the Access window.

Using Queries to Find Data

Another method for viewing specific data from a table is to run a query. A query asks a question of a table, such as "Which customers live in Washington?" and selects records from the table which answer the question. The selected records are displayed in a datasheet, where you can view, analyze, sort and print them.

You can use a query to answer a simple question, perform calculations, combine data from different tables, or to add, change or delete table data. Queries that you use to retrieve data from a table or to perform calculations are called *select queries*. Queries that add, change or delete data are called *action queries*.

A select query is a specialized instruction which selects and displays specific information from a table. It is stored as a database object and can search one or more tables in a database. In most cases, the database designer creates queries to retrieve specific information, and a database user simply runs the query to view the information. When you open a query, the result set displays automatically (that is, the query runs when you double-click it in the Navigation Pane).

If you open a query in Design view, you can run it by clicking the **Run** button in the Results group on the Design tab of the Ribbon.

The resulting set of records from a query is called a result set or a *dynaset* (dynamic subset). A dynaset is not a static snapshot of records, but a dynamic changing subset of records. As you make changes to a table, the results of a query based on that table change accordingly to reflect the table's current condition.

Additionally, when you run a query, you can filter or sort the result set using the filtering and sorting techniques you have already learned.

EXERCISE

In this exercise you will run queries and sort and filter the result sets.

1. Restore the Access window. In the Navigation Pane, in the **Queries** group, double-click **CustomerList** to run the query and display the result set.

   The query displays information from selected fields in the Customers_TA table.

2. Open the Customers_TA table in Datasheet view and scroll to view all the fields.

   Contrast the table's datasheet with that of the query. If you were looking for only name and address information, which might you find easier to use?

3. Close the Customers_TA table.

Sort the query result set by the Country, then LastName, and then FirstName fields.

4. In the result set datasheet, click in the **FirstName** field for any record, then on the Home tab, in the Sort & Filter group, click **Ascending**.

5. In the result set datasheet, click in the **LastName** field for any record, then on the Home tab, in the Sort & Filter group, click **Ascending**.

6. In the result set datasheet, click in the **Country** field for any record, then on the Home tab, in the Sort & Filter group, click **Ascending**.

7. In the Quick Access toolbar, click the **Save** button, then close and reopen the query.

   Notice that the sort order you created remains in effect.

8. In the Navigation Pane, in the **Queries** group, double-click **Employees-by-Position** to run the query and display the result set.

   The query displays information from selected fields in the Employees table.

Filter the query result set to show only the positions for the Cape Town office.

9. Right-click the Office field for any record with the value "Cape Town" in the Office field, then select **Equals "Cape Town"** in the shortcut menu.

10. Close the Employees-by-Position query without saving the changes.

11. Close the CustomerList query.

12. In the Navigation Pane, in the **Queries** group, right-click **Employees-by-Office** and then select **Design View** in the shortcut menu to open the query in Query Design view.

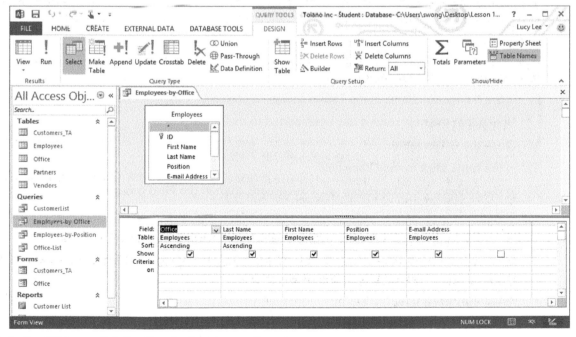

13. In the Ribbon, click the **Run** button to run the query.

14. Close the query without saving, then minimize the Access window.

Working with Data in Form View

IC³ **Exam 2 - Objective 1.3, 5.1**

Forms can make data entry a more comfortable experience for novice users than working directly in a datasheet, and many database designers create forms specifically for this purpose.

In most cases, forms display one record at a time instead of rows and rows of records. Forms also allow the designer to display all the table fields for a record on one screen, eliminating the need to scroll horizontally.

The same navigation tools and techniques that you use with datasheets can be used with forms.

EXERCISE

In this exercise you will work with records using a form.

1. Restore the Access window.

2. In the Navigation Pane, in the **Forms** group, double-click **Office** to open the Office form in Form view.

   This form displays records from the Office table. Notice the familiar navigation buttons at the bottom of the window.

3. In the navigation buttons, click **Next record** to display the data for the next record in the table.

4. In the navigation buttons, click **Last record** to display the data for the last record in the table.

5. In the navigation buttons, click **First record** to display the data for the first record in the table.

6. In the navigation buttons, click **New record** to display blank fields for a new record you will add to the underlying table.

7. Press (Tab), type: `Seattle`, press (Tab), type: `88 Piermont Drive`, press (Tab), type: `Seattle`, press (Tab), type: `WA`, press (Tab), type: `98117`, press (Tab), type: `206 555 6262`.

   The record has not been saved yet.

8. On the Quick Access toolbar, click **Save**.

9. In the Navigation Pane, in the **Tables** group, double-click **Office** to open the table in Datasheet view.

   Notice that the new record has been added to the table.

10. Close the Office table.

11. In the form, click in the Office field.

12. In the Ribbon, click the **Home** tab if necessary, then in the **Find** group, click **Find** to open the Find and Replace dialog box.

13. In the Find What text box, type: `Toronto` then press (Enter).

    Access locates the record for the Toronto office and displays it in the form.

14. Close the Find and Replace dialog box.

15. Close the Office form.

16. Minimize the Access window.

What is a Report?

 Exam 2 - Objective 1.3, 5.1

Reports are database objects that take the raw data stored in a database and present that data in meaningful ways. Reports present data visually. For example, if you want to use charts or graphs, you use a report.

In contrast to forms, which are designed for on-screen use, reports are designed to be printed. Although you can print tables or forms, you can create reports that are designed to be printer friendly and visually appealing. Using a report, you can group and sort data effectively, add formatting to enhance visual appearance, and even display calculations to analyze and summarize the data.

Report Views

There are four views for reports: Report view, Print Preview view, Layout view and Design view. You use Report view and Print Preview view to view or print report data.

Layout view and Design view are advanced views used to modify the design (structure) of a report. Working with reports in Design view is an advanced skill, and is beyond the scope of this lesson.

Report view is the open view for a report. When you double-click a report in the Navigation Pane, it opens in Report view, allowing you to view the data. Although you can click or tab to controls in Report view, you cannot edit the data and you cannot modify a report's design in Report view.

Customers_by_Country

Country	City	Last Name	First Name	Address	State	Zip Code	E-mail	Home #
AU								
	Canberra	Macintosh	Katey	23 Pine Valley Lane	New South Wales	26101	Kmac44@newsouth.net	61 2214 5563
	Kagloorlie	Brackett	Davey	98 Lyall Street	Western Australia	6430	2brackett@gmail.com	61 8 5514 8756
	Wyndham	Brown	Neil	101 Centaurian Street	Western Australia	650216	neil_brown@gmail.com	08 9161 3214
	Wyndham	Edwards	Jonas	34 Brigham Court	Western Australia	650216	Jedwards45@wyndham.net	08 9161 9876
	Wyndham	O'Brien	Kelly	80 Pretoria Crescent	Western Australia	650216	kobrien@wyndham.net	08 9161 4785
	Wyndham	Peterson	Jenny	44 Pretoria Crescent	Western Australia	650216	jcpeterson@whyndham.net	08 9161 555
CA								
	Edmonton	Grant	Owen	903 123rd Drive SE	AB	T3R 9N1	ogrant55@rogers.com	780 321 5555
	Halifax	Lewis	Larry	#77 – 3311 Pender Lane	NS	B0P 2N3	llewis@sprint.ca	514 325 6598
	Lethbridge	Smithers	Frank	55 125th Ave SW	AB	T2J 5A4	smithers-f@gmail.com	
	Surrey	Johnson	Adam	342 125th Avenue	BC	V2H 4Y1	afj25@gmail.com	604-520-0066
	Surrey	Johnson	Patricia	342 125th Avenue	BC	V2H 4Y1	patricia_j@hotmail.com	604-520-0066
	Toronto	Bailey	Bryan	99 Johnson Road	ON	M3V 8W1	bb6661@bell.ca	613 874 1452
	Toronto	Bouchard	Peter	3201 – 772 Eaton Road	ON	M1M 8T6	pbouchard@bell.ca	416 666 9099
	Vancouver	Edwards	Irene	875 West 18th Avenue	BC	V6J 2Y7	iedwards@shaw.ca	604 654 1224
	Vancouver	Lim	Geoff	#25 – 606 Burrard Street	BC	V7K 2P9	glim9966@hotmail.com	604 665 4455

Print Preview

While it is possible to right-click a report in the Navigation Pane and select **Print**, it is considered best practice to preview a report before printing. The Print Preview view allows you to preview exactly how the printed output will look. In a multiple-page report, you can view one, two, four, eight or twelve pages on one screen.

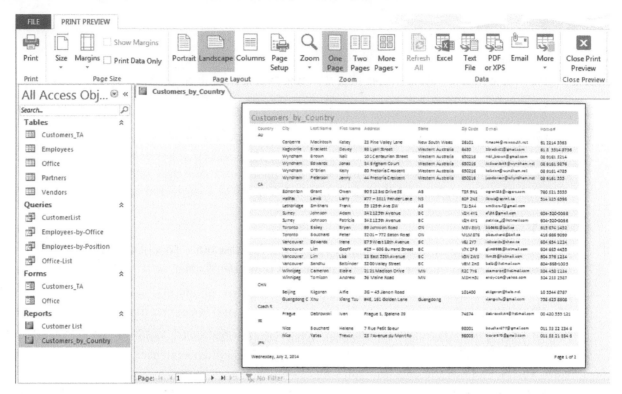

Print Preview is the only view that allows you to adjust the Zoom setting. Drag the zoom slider at the lower-right corner of the window to zoom in or out, or click the Zoom button in the Ribbon to adjust the zoom setting. The ability to zoom in on report details is useful if you merely want to read some of the report data without having to print it.

Print Preview also provides the opportunity to make last minute adjustments to the report, including:

- Specifying paper size
- Adjusting margins
- Changing the page orientation
- Specifying to print only the data (without titles or headings)
- Directing output to a specific printer
- Exporting the report output to a file such as an Excel spreadsheet, a text file, a PDF or XPS file, a Word document, or an HTML document. You can also specify to export the report output to a file and attach the generated file to an email message.

Print Preview is also the only report view that provides access to the Print command.

Layout View

Layout view is table-based. The report fields and their labels are positioned within cells in the layout. Layouts are guides that align controls horizontally and vertically to give the report a uniform appearance. A *control* is a graphic object that displays information in a report. Each cell in the layout is either empty or contains a single control.

Customer List				
Last Name	First Name	Address	City	State
Avila	Rafael	Avenida des Esplanade	Lisbon	
Bailey	Bryan	99 Johnson Road	Toronto	ON
Bouchard	Helene	7 Rue Petit Soeur	Nice	
Bouchard	Peter	3201 – 772 Eaton Road	Toronto	ON
Brackett	Davey	98 Lyall Street	Kagloorlie	Western Australia
Brown	Neil	101 Centaurian Street	Wyndham	Western Australia
Cameron	Elaine	2121 Madison Drive	Winnipeg	MN
Cameron	Quinton	#18, Angora Towers	Clifton	
Dabrowski	Ivan	Prague 1, Spalena 39	Prague	
Davies	Carl	531 Luther Avenue	Boise	ID
Edwards	Irene	875 West 18th Avenue	Vancouver	BC

When you view a report in Layout view, each control displays real data, offering a useful view for setting the size of controls, or performing other tasks that affect the visual appearance of the report.

EXERCISE

In this exercise you will open a report and adjust the view.

1. Restore the Access window.

2. In the Navigation Pane, in the Reports group, double-click **Customers_by_Country** to open the report in Report view.

3. Drag the vertical scroll box to view all the report data.

4. In the view buttons at the lower-right corner of the window, click **Print Preview** to change to Print Preview view.

5. In the Zoom group in the Ribbon, click **Two Pages** to view both pages of the report.

6. Drag the zoom slider at the lower-right corner of the window to zoom in on the report details.

7. In the Zoom group in the Ribbon, click the **Zoom** button to return to the previous zoom setting.

8. In the Zoom group in the Ribbon, click the arrow at the bottom of the Zoom button, then in the drop-down menu, click **150%** to increase the magnification.

9. Use the Zoom button to increase the magnification to 200%.

10. Use the Zoom button to set the magnification to 100%.

11. In the Print group in the Ribbon, click the **Print** button to open the Print dialog box.

    You can send the report to a printer using this command.

12. Click **Cancel** to close the Print dialog box.

13. In the Page Size group in the Ribbon, click **Print Data Only** to show only the table data in the report.

14. Click **Print Data Only** again to return the report to its previous setting.

15. In the Page Layout group in the Ribbon, click the **Page Setup** button to open the Page Setup dialog box. You can use the tabs in the Page Setup dialog box to adjust the margins and change the page orientation.

16. Click **Cancel** to close the Page Setup dialog box.

17. Close the Customers_by_Country report.

18. Minimize the Access window.

Designing Reports

To design a report that is meaningful and easy to understand, begin by deciding on the data you want to include in the report, and how you want to arrange the data. Then you can decide on a layout.

Report Layouts

Access provides two basic layouts for reports:

- **Tabular** layouts resemble spreadsheets, and are best used when you need to present your data in a simple list format. Tabular layouts always span two sections of a report; whichever section the controls are in, the labels are in the section above.

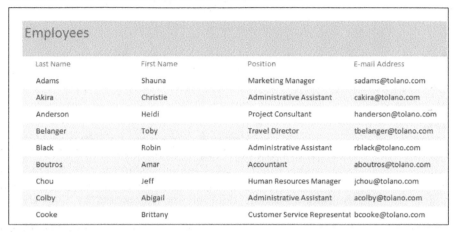

- A **stacked** layout displays data arranged vertically, as you might see on a paper form with a label to the left of each control. Use a stacked layout when your report contains too many fields to display in tabular form. Stacked layouts are always contained within a single report section.

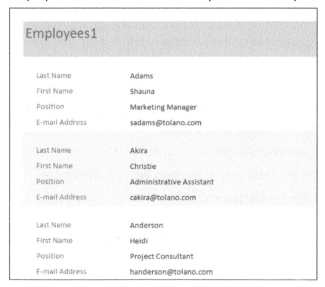

Creating Reports

There are several ways to create a report in Access. You can:

- Use the Report tool, which is an automated report-generating tool that creates a tabular report based on all the fields of a selected table or query.

- Use the Report Wizard, which presents a series of dialog boxes that prompt you for input. After you have specified the necessary options, the wizard creates the report based on your specifications.

- Create a report from scratch using the Blank Report command button. A blank report is an empty canvas that is not initially attached to an underlying table or query. You can create reports from scratch using Layout or Design view. Creating a report from scratch is an advanced skill, and is beyond the scope of this lesson.

Using the Report Tool

Creating a simple report with the Report tool is the quickest method of creating a report. When you select a table or query and click the Report tool, Access creates a tabular report that includes all the fields from the selected table or query. The new report opens in Layout view, where you can modify it if necessary.

To create a report using the Report tool, click a table or query in the Navigation Pane that you want to use as the data source for the report. Click the **Create** tab, and in the Reports group, click **Report**.

Creating a Report Using the Report Wizard

If you want control over which fields appear on a report, or you need to use data from multiple tables or create a complex layout, you can create a report using the Report Wizard. The wizard also lets you define how the data is grouped and sorted, and you can use fields from more than one table or query (provided that you have defined the relationships between the tables and queries in the Relationships window).

After you have completed the wizard, Access creates the report based on your specifications and opens the report in Print Preview.

EXERCISE

In this exercise you will create reports.

First, you will create a report using the Report tool.

1. Restore the Access window.

2. In the Navigation Pane, in the Queries group, click **Office-List** to select the query. Do not open the query.

3. Click the **Create** tab in the Ribbon if necessary, then in the Reports group, click **Report**.

    Access creates a report called Office-List and opens the report in Layout view.

4. Click the **Page Setup** tab in the Ribbon, then in the Page Layout group, click **Landscape** to change the page orientation.

5. Click the **Save** button in the Quick Access toolbar, and click **OK** to accept Office-List as the name for the new report.

6. Close the Office-List report.

Next, you will create a report using the Report Wizard.

7. In the Ribbon, click the **Create** tab if necessary, and in the Reports group, click **Report Wizard**.

8. Display the Tables/Queries drop-down list, then click **Table: Employees** to specify that you want to base the report on data stored in the Employees table.

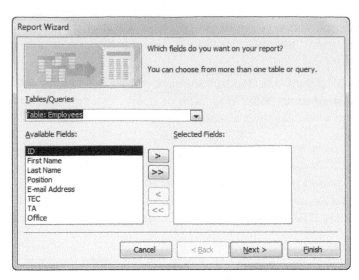

9. In the Available Fields list box, double-click **First Name**, **Last Name**, and **Office** to add these fields to the Selected Fields list. Click **Next**.

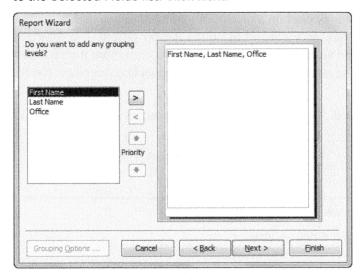

This report is quite small so no grouping is necessary.

10. Click **Next**.

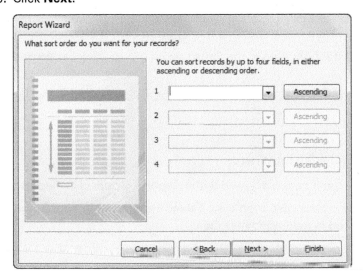

11. Click the arrow for **1** and click **Last Name**. Leave **Ascending** as is and then click **Next**.

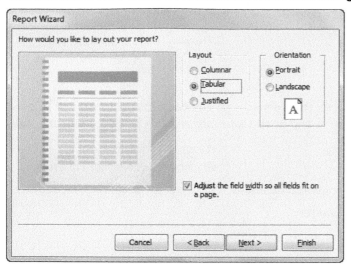

12. Click **Tabular**, if necessary, and then click **Next**.

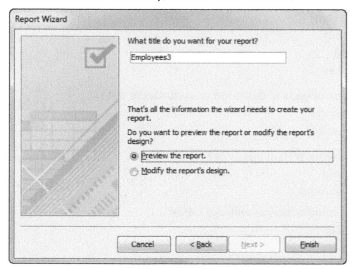

13. Change the report title to: Employee List and click **Finish**.

Access displays the report in Print Preview.

14. Close the Employee List report.

15. Click the **File** tab in the Ribbon, and then click **Close**.

16. Click **Close** to exit Access.

Lesson Summary

In this lesson you were introduced to a relationship database tool you can use to organize large amounts of information for reports, find or sort information, as well as manage the database. You should now be familiar with:

☑ what a database is

☑ how to create, save, open or close a database

☑ how to create and modify records

☑ how to use simple queries

☑ how to create and use reports

Review Questions

1. What does DBMS stand for?
   a. Database Management System
   b. Data Base Marketing System
   c. Data Bits Memory Services
   d. Database Marketing Services

2. Which of the following database objects is designed to summarize data?
   a. Tables   c. Reports
   b. Forms   d. Queries

3. How many databases can you work with at any time?
   a. Two   c. Three
   b. One   d. Unlimited

4. Which table item is a category of information within a table?
   a. Table   c. Field
   b. Record   d. Query

5. Which navigation button creates a new record in the table?

   a.    d.

   b.   e.

   c.

6. Which type of query retrieves data from a table or performs calculations?
   a. Select   b. Action

7. Which button will add a field to the Selected Fields list for a report?
   a. >   c. <
   b. >>   d. <<

8. Which report layout displays the data in a vertical format?
   a. Tabular   b. Stacked

┌──────────────┐
│ **MMM**   │
│ Go online for │
│ Additional   │
│ Review   │
└──────────────┘

Lesson 12: World Wide Web

Lesson Objectives

In this lesson, you will prepare to browse the Internet by reviewing how web sites are organized, and identifying common web page elements. You will also learn how to perform basic tasks using a web browser. On completion, you will be familiar with:

- ☐ the difference between the Internet, the World Wide Web, and browsers
- ☐ the structure of a URL
- ☐ identifying common web page elements
- ☐ the basic functions of web browsers

- ☐ navigating in a browser
- ☐ using tabbed browsing
- ☐ working with bookmarks
- ☐ viewing the history

The Internet, Browsers and the World Wide Web

 Exam 3 - Objective 1.1

Although people often use the terms Internet and World Wide Web (WWW) interchangeably, they are in fact separate but related things.

The Internet

The Internet is a vast global network that functions in much the same way as your school or company network. A network is an arrangement of computers that are connected in such a way that they can communicate and share information with each other. Networked computers use special networking hardware to form the connections that make communication possible.

The Internet is comprised of many smaller networks which are connected together so that they can communicate and share information. The hardware used to connect a computer to the Internet is the same hardware used to connect a computer to a company or school network, and the hardware that forms the core of the Internet is not much different.

In fact, the Internet is a collection of hardware. It consists of wires, routers, switches, microwave links, servers, and communication protocols. Because the Internet is so large, companies, schools and individual users do not connect to it directly; instead, they connect through a middleman called a service provider.

When you purchase (or subscribe to) Internet service, you pay an *Internet Service Provider* (ISP) for a connection to the Internet. (You actually connect to the ISP's network, which in turn is connected to the Internet.) The ISP provides the connection, and the connection provides access to the Internet (and all the smaller networks connected to it).

Clients and Servers

It is important to understand that on the Internet (as on any network), some computers function as clients and others function as servers. A *client* is any computer that requests a service or resource (such as a document or web page) from another computer on the network. A *server* is any computer that provides services or resources to other computers (clients) that request them.

There are many types of servers used on the Internet. Perhaps the most familiar is the web server. A *web server* hosts or stores a company's or an individual's web site. A *web site* is a collection of interconnected pages that contain information about a company, person, product, or service. The web site may be one of many hosted on a particular web server. Many organizations own and maintain their own web servers and host their own web sites. As an alternative, many Internet Service Providers (ISPs) host web sites for their subscribers.

When you connect to the Internet and visit a web page, your computer and your browser software act as clients – the computer requests Internet access from your ISP and the web browser requests web pages from the web server hosting the web site that you are visiting. You will learn about browsers shortly.

A Brief Introduction to Connection Hardware

Note: You will learn more about connections and hardware devices in in a later lesson. The concepts introduced here will help you differentiate between hardware (Internet) and software (the World Wide Web).

Once you purchase Internet service through a service provider, you must use networking hardware designed to allow to you to connect to the Internet.

Internet connections can be dial-up or direct. Dial-up connections use standard analog telephone lines and a device called a modem, which is installed inside the computer. The modem physically connects to the telephone network using a standard telephone wire. The modem dials the access number required to connect to your ISP. When a modem at the ISP "answers" the call, a connection is established. If you use a dial-up connection, you must establish a connection each time you want to access the Internet. Once your Internet session is complete, you disconnect (hang up).

In contrast, direct connections are always "on." That is, you do not need to establish a connection and then disconnect when you are through. Most users make direct connections to the Internet using a digital subscriber line (DSL) or a cable Internet connection. If you connect to the Internet at your school or company, you most likely make that connection through your organization's local area network (LAN), which in turn connects to an ISP.

Direct connections require that a network interface card (NIC) be installed in your computer. The NIC sends and receives data back and forth between your computer and the network. There are a wide variety of NICs available; some connect to a network using a wire called a network cable, and some connect to a network wirelessly. If the NIC uses a network cable, one end of the cable is inserted into the NIC and the other end is inserted into the network connection port on a networking device, such as a hub, switch or router. In some offices, the cable plugs into a network connection port on a wall plate. If the NIC uses a wireless connection, it sends and receives radio signals to and from a wireless access point somewhere in the vicinity.

EXERCISE

This exercise assumes that your computer is connected to a classroom network, that an Internet connection is available and that the organization's firewall does not block outgoing ping requests. At the time of this writing, the yahoo.com and ccilearning.com web servers all respond to ping requests.

In this exercise you will locate the hardware that connects your system to the Internet, and use a simple utility to test whether your Internet connection is functioning.

First, locate your network interface card (NIC) and see what type of connection it uses.

1. If the physical location of your computer permits, try to locate your network interface card (NIC). Ask your instructor for assistance if necessary. Does your NIC connect your computer to the network using a wire, or is the connection wireless?

   _____

2. If your NIC uses a wire, where does the wire connect to the network? Is there a box with connection ports near your desk? Do you plug into a wall jack?

   _____

   If your NIC connects wirelessly, can you see the wireless access point?

   _____

3. Look at your NIC. Does it include a light that flashes on and off periodically? Most NICs include an indicator light to let you know that the device is sending and receiving data.

Next, use a simple network utility called ping that will indicate whether you are connected to the Internet.

4. Click the **Start** button, type: cmd in the Search box and press (Enter) to open a command prompt window.

5. In the command prompt window, type: ping www.yahoo.com then press (Enter).

   If you are connected to the Internet, your screen should resemble the one shown below. Any line that begins with the word "Reply" is a response from the yahoo.com web server. If the server replies to you, then you are connected to the Internet.

   ```
   Administrator: C:\Windows\system32\cmd.exe

   Microsoft Windows [Version 6.1.7601]
   Copyright (c) 2009 Microsoft Corporation.  All rights reserved.

   C:\Users\Andrew McSweeney>ping www.yahoo.com

   Pinging ds-any-fp3-real.wa1.b.yahoo.com [206.190.36.105] with 32 bytes of data:
   Reply from 206.190.36.105: bytes=32 time=28ms ITL=53
   Reply from 206.190.36.105: bytes=32 time=27ms ITL=53
   Reply from 206.190.36.105: bytes=32 time=25ms ITL=53
   Reply from 206.190.36.105: bytes=32 time=28ms ITL=53

   Ping statistics for 206.190.36.105:
       Packets: Sent = 4, Received = 4, Lost = 0 (0% loss),
   Approximate round trip times in milli-seconds:
       Minimum = 25ms, Maximum = 28ms, Average = 27ms

   C:\Users\Andrew McSweeney>_
   ```

6. In the command prompt window, type: ping www.ccilearning.com, then press (Enter).

   ```
   Administrator: C:\Windows\system32\cmd.exe

   C:\Users\Andrew McSweeney>ping www.ccilearning.com

   Pinging www.ccilearning.com [192.254.188.8] with 32 bytes of data:
   Reply from 192.254.188.8: bytes=32 time=145ms ITL=52
   Reply from 192.254.188.8: bytes=32 time=135ms ITL=52
   Reply from 192.254.188.8: bytes=32 time=149ms ITL=52
   Reply from 192.254.188.8: bytes=32 time=141ms ITL=52

   Ping statistics for 192.254.188.8:
       Packets: Sent = 4, Received = 4, Lost = 0 (0% loss),
   Approximate round trip times in milli-seconds:
       Minimum = 135ms, Maximum = 149ms, Average = 142ms

   C:\Users\Andrew McSweeney>
   ```

   Again, you should receive four reply messages from the ccilearning web server if you are connected to the Internet.

7. Close the command prompt window.

The World Wide Web

While the Internet is a network comprised of hardware connections, the World Wide Web is a system of interlinked documents that are accessible on that network called the Internet. There are countless millions of documents hosted on web servers – and if you can access a document by typing its address into a web browser, or by clicking a link that takes you to it, that document is part of the World Wide Web.

Documents hosted on web servers are generally referred to as web pages, and web pages usually contain links (called *hyperlinks*) to other pages located on web servers around the Internet. If you have ever visited a web site and clicked a link that took you to another web site (or to another page within the same web site), then you have used a hyperlink. These hyperlinks form the connections that make the World Wide Web possible – web pages around the world are connected to one another by hyperlinks.

The Internet is the network (that is, the hardware) that allows users to access documents on the World Wide Web, and the World Wide Web is the vast collection of "connected" documents available on the network known as the Internet.

Web Browsers

As you saw in the previous exercise, an Internet connection allows you to contact a web server and receive a reply. But in and of itself, this is not terribly interesting. To actually view web pages and navigate web sites, you need more than simply an Internet connection – you need a web browser.

A web browser is a program that enables you to view and navigate web pages on the Internet, and to experience the amazing rich media that is available on the World Wide Web. That is, a web browser is software. Web browsers are highly sophisticated programs. Their most basic function is to display pages created with hypertext markup language (HTML). HTML is a special language that web page designers use to add text, hyperlinks, applications, video clips, sound and animation to web pages. When web pages are designed properly, visitors can "point and click" to launch applications, navigate to specific areas of the web site, or visit related web sites – all within a web browser window.

EXERCISE

In this exercise you will visit the Yahoo and CCI Learning web sites using the Internet Explorer web browser. Later in this lesson, you will learn about browser features and functionality in depth.

1. Click the **Internet Explorer** icon in the taskbar to open the browser.

2. Click in the browser's address bar to select the current text, then type: www.yahoo.com and press Enter .

   Your browser window should resemble the following figure.

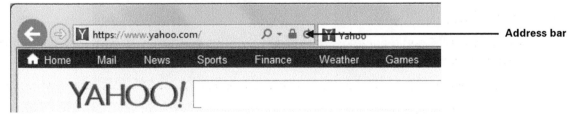

This is the same web site you pinged in the previous exercise. Notice all the pictures and formatted text. Notice the wide selection of articles and stories on the page.

3. Click in the address bar to select the current text, then type: `www.ccilearning.com` and press `Enter`.

4. Scroll the page to examine its layout.

    Notice that it includes a banner, pictures, logos, and various navigation tools (such as tabs) to move around the web site. A web browser provides a mechanism for interacting with an amazing variety of media on the Internet.

5. Close your browser.

Understanding Web Site Addresses

 Exam 3 - Objective 1.2

In the previous exercise, you entered a web site address into the browser address bar. Every web page on the Internet has a specific address. This address is called a *Uniform Resource Locator (URL)*. It is the global address of documents and other resources on the World Wide Web. A URL consists of two basic parts: a protocol identifier and a resource name. The protocol identifier and the resource name are separated by a colon (:) and two forward slashes (//).

Protocol identifier

http://www.ccilearning.com

Resource name

Web Site Protocols

Web browsers use various networking protocols to communicate with web servers (and other types of servers) around the Internet. A *protocol* is simply a set of rules that enable computing devices to communicate with one another. The protocol used to request web pages from a Web server is *HyperText Transfer Protocol (HTTP)*. Web servers also use HTTP to send web pages to the computers that request them.

Browsers assume that you want to use the http protocol when you enter a web address. This allows you to simply type: "www.yahoo.com" instead of "http://www.yahoo.com." Some web browsers display the http:// protocol identifier in the address bar and others do not.

While http is the protocol used to view web pages, browsers also support protocols for functions such as transferring large files, viewing news group articles, or sending and retrieving email. *File Transfer Protocol (FTP)* is a protocol commonly used to transfer large files between a user's computer and a special type of server called an FTP server. If you want to use your web browser to access an FTP server to transfer a file, you must specify the ftp protocol in the browser address bar; for example: ftp://aeneas.mit.edu.

Resource Names

The resource name portion of a URL specifies the location of a particular web page or file. The location is referred to as a *domain name*.

A typical domain name consists of three labels separated by periods or dots as shown below:

Server Name	Identifies the name of the web server
Registered Domain Name	Identifies the organization that owns the domain name. Each domain name is unique and is registered with the Internet Corporation for Assigned Names and Numbers (ICANN).
Top-level Domain	Identifies the category of the registered domain name.

Domain names are arranged into specific categories. These categories are identified by the top-level domain. You can generally determine what type of information a web site contains (or what it is meant to do) simply by reading the top-level domain. The original top-level domains are:

.com	Represents commercial or company sites. Most web sites in this domain sell a service or product, usually through an "online store" or web page from which you can purchase items directly. The .com domain is considered a generic top level domain and can be registered by anyone.
.net	Another type of commercial web site. It is generally hosted on a network managed by an Internet Service Provider (ISP).
.edu	Represents an education site created to share information about an academic institution, its curriculum, and other activities. This category may also be associated with research organizations.
.gov	Refers to a site associated with a local, regional, or national government. (Depending on the country, there may be additional levels included in the URL to identify specific areas such as states, municipalities, townships, etc.)
.int	Refers to international organizations.
.mil	Refers to military organizations.
.org	Identifies a site dedicated to a non-profit organization that may promote a specific cause such as foundations for heart and stroke, cancer, etc.

An advantage of using these top-level domains is the ability to present your organization as global since the domain category does not identify where your web site is hosted. For example, although .com indicates that the site is commercial, the company that owns it could be in any country, or could have its headquarters in one country while its web site is being managed by an ISP somewhere else.

Other top-level domain names use a two-letter abbreviation and are meant to identify the state or country in which the web site is hosted; examples include:

au Australia	**fr** France	**jp** Japan
br Brazil	**il** Israel	**mx** Mexico
ca Canada	**in** India	**tw** Taiwan
cn China	**it** Italy	**uk** United Kingdom
dk Denmark		

For example, an academic institution may be based in one country while maintaining schools in other countries, such as the web address of www.phoenix.edu. This address is the University of Phoenix campus located in Phoenix, Arizona, USA whereas the web address of www.university-of-phoenix-adult-education.org/university_of_phoenix_canada.html is for the university's campus located in Vancouver, BC, Canada. Each school can manage its own web site in its own country and also display information from the web server at the school's main location. To view general information about the school, you may need to enter `www.abc-school.com`, and then be re-directed to *www.abc-school.cn* to see the curriculum offered in China, or *www.abc-school.fr* for the school in France.

Some URLs include the path and filename of a specific page stored on the web server. For example the URL http://www.opera.com/browser/tutorials/mail/setup/#account-setup displays a page called #account-setup stored in the /browser/tutorials/mail/setup folder on the web server named "www" at opera.com.

Common Web Site/Page Elements

 Exam 3 - Objective 1.2

Typically, the first page you see when you access a web site is the top level page, called the *home page* or index page. The home page serves as the "starting point" for a web site. Usually, a home page contains links to all the other pages on the web site – allowing you to navigate to different areas. In a well-designed web site, each lower-level page includes a "home" link that will return you to the web site's home page with a single click.

Regardless of whether you are viewing the home page of a web site, or a page buried deep within the web site structure, the page likely contains a number of common elements. Some of the most common are pointed out in the following image:

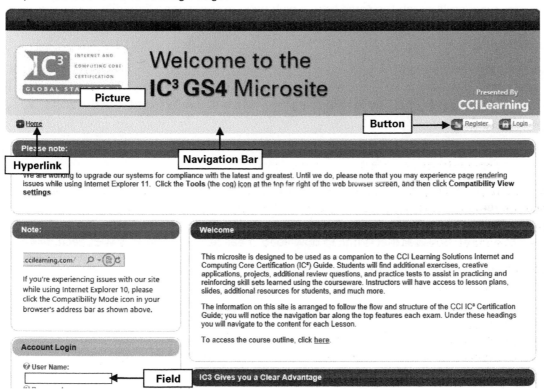

Navigation Bar	Well-designed web pages include a navigation bar (usually down the left side or across the top of the page) that provides links to various areas of the web site. A navigation bar is similar to a table of contents for the site and may be called a *site map*. The web page shown in the preceding image includes a navigation bar across the top.
Picture	Web pages often contain graphics or photographs. Pictures may be static (unchanging) or dynamic (a slide show of several pictures displays in the given location). Some web page designers use pictures to animate pages, or to launch actions, such as running a video. Some designers also use pictures as links to other web pages.

Field	Many web pages contain forms with fields or blank spaces where you can enter information. The information you enter is then sent to the web server for processing. Most web pages contain at least one field, usually to allow you to search for an item on the web site. In the web page shown in the preceding image, you are required to enter your registered user name and password before you can access items on the site.
Button	A button is an interactive graphic that performs an action when you click it. In the web page shown in the figure, clicking the button sends the login information to the server.

Browser Features and Functions

 Exam 3 - Objective 1.2

There are a wide variety of browsers freely available for various operating systems. Browsers commonly used on Windows systems include Microsoft Internet Explorer, Mozilla Firefox, Google Chrome, Opera and Safari. The following images show each of these browsers. Note that although the browsers function in much the same way, a web page may appear a little differently in each browser. This is because a browser's coding determines how it interprets the HTML code used to define a web page.

Microsoft Internet Explorer

Developed by Microsoft in 1995 and was one of the first graphical user web browsers, Internet Explorer (IE) continues to be very popular for browsing the Internet as it is included with the Windows operating system.

Mozilla Firefox

Firefox was originally developed by Mozilla Corporation and Mozilla Foundation in 2004. As it is an open source web browser that is free to download, it has gained popularity with each new release.

Google Chrome

Chrome was developed and released as a stable product in 2008. It was originally available as freeware although a large portion of its code was released in 2008 as an open source project called Chromium; newer releases of Chrome are based on this version.

Opera

Opera Software releases its web browser as an individual product for download or as part of an Internet suite of products. It is one of the original web browsers introduced in 1994 and now is available for a number of computing devices, including several mobile devices.

Safari

This web browser was originally designed for the Apple computer and is the most commonly used one for any Apple computing device. Safari is also available in a Windows version.

Notice that even though the appearance of each is slightly different from the others, all of them include many of the same basic features, such as an address bar, a Home button, a bookmark button, and Forward, Back and Refresh buttons.

You will examine these features shortly.

Browser Functions

Browsers perform several functions. Among other things, they retrieve and display web pages, allow users to navigate around the World Wide Web, play media files, and support encryption to allow for secure web transactions. In the following section, you will examine a few of the basic functions of a browser.

Addressing

As you have already learned, you enter a URL into the address bar in the browser to indicate which web site you want to visit. When you type a web site address into the address bar, the browser sends a request to the appropriate web server. The server receives the request, retrieves the appropriate web pages, and then sends them back to your browser. The browser then formats and displays the web pages for you within the browser window.

The address bar displays the URL of the page currently displayed in the browser window. You can visit any web page by typing its URL into the Address bar and pressing ⌷Enter⌷.

As you navigate to other pages within a web site (or as you visit pages on other web sites), the URL shown in the Address field updates to show the address of the current page. Most browsers maintain a history of URLs that you can access from the address bar. Clicking a URL displayed in the address bar history list has the same effect as entering the URL directly into the address bar.

In addition to displaying the URL, the address bar often includes several buttons. The Internet Explorer address bar is shown below:

The Internet Explorer address bar includes the following buttons:

Search	You can search directly from the Address bar in Internet Explorer, instead of first accessing a search engine page. Enter your search criteria in the Address Bar and then click the ⌕ **(Search)** button or press ⌷Enter⌷ to view a list of web sites related to your search criteria.
Show Address	Click the ▾ **(Show Address)** button to display a history of the URLs of previously visited web sites.

Refresh/Go	Click the ↻ **(Refresh)** button to re-display or refresh the contents of the current web page. Click → **(Go to)** after typing in a web site address to go to that site.
Stop	Click the ✕ **(Stop)** button to halt the downloading of information for a web page. The Stop button appears only while a page is loading.

As you become more familiar with various online communication methods, you may decide to use a service to shorten a URL. Shortened URLs are easier to work with when addressing email messages or posting updates to a blog.

Uploading and Downloading

The terms uploading and downloading refer to the process of sending information from your computer to a server (uploading), and the process of receiving information from a server (downloading).

Downloading is the process of copying a file from a server on the Internet to your computer. Many people think of downloading as the act of copying specific files, such as music files, application files, document files, etc., from a web site to their computers. While this is true, it is also true that every time you visit a web site, one or more pages from the web site are downloaded to your computer.

Most web pages include several pictures, and these pictures are not part of the page itself, but are stored separately on the web server. The web page itself contains "placeholders" where the pictures will be inserted when you download the page from the web server to your browser. If pictures are excessively large in file size, they may take longer to display than the surrounding text. The same is true for multimedia elements such as audio or video files.

These elements are downloaded automatically, but separately, when your browser loads the web page, and these downloaded elements are stored on your hard drive in a special folder designed to hold temporary Internet files. Each browser includes a temporary Internet files folder for this purpose.

In contrast, *uploading* is the process of sending information from your computer to a server on the Internet. The most basic example of uploading is typing a URL into a browser's address bar. When you press (Enter), the browser sends (or uploads) a request for the specified web page to the web server that hosts the page.

Other examples of uploading include entering a user name and password for a web site, or submitting information through a web form, or posting to a blog. Sometimes you may upload files or pictures that you want to share with others to a shared folder on the Internet, or to an FTP site.

Most users download much more information than they upload. Accordingly, most ISPs provide service that downloads information much faster than it uploads. Most home and small business owners purchase broadband Internet service – either cable Internet or Digital Subscriber Line (DSL) service. (You will learn more about these services later in this courseware.) The term "broadband" is used loosely, and generally applies to any direct high-speed connection. Broadband Internet service provides two speed measurements:

- **Downstream (download)** — Data moves downstream as it reaches you from a web server. Residential cable Internet service generally provides download speeds between 1 and 6 Mbps. Users can purchase DSL service with downstream speeds of 8, 12, or 24 Mbps.

- **Upstream (upload)** — Data moves upstream when you send or upload information. Residential cable Internet usually provides upstream speeds between 128 Kbps to 728 Kbps. Users can purchase DSL service with upstream speeds of 640 Kbps, 1 Mbps, or 3 Mbps.

Hyperlinks

As you have already learned, you can click a hyperlink in a web page to move to another (connected) web page or to a particular section within the current web page. A hyperlink is a reference to data that is located somewhere other than the present location. A hyperlink can point to a whole document or to a specific element within a document.

Generally, a hyperlink consists of an anchor (which is the location within a document from which the link can be followed), and a target (which is the destination web page or specific area within the current web page).

Hyperlinks often display as underlined or colored text. However, hyperlinks are not limited to text; pictures or icons or even specific areas on a graphic can be hyperlinks as well. When you view a web page in a web browser, hyperlinks behave in a specific manner. When you hover the mouse pointer over a hyperlink, the mouse pointer changes to a pointing hand ( ) icon. When you click a hyperlink, you move to the web page that is designated as the target of that hyperlink. The web page may be part of the same web site, or may be a page on a different web site.

Some web pages contain links that are not readily visible on the screen until you position the mouse pointer over them, but once you see a , you know that you have found a hyperlink.

CCI Learning courseware please click here.

Sometimes hyperlinks are configured to open the target web page in the current browser window, while others open a new tab and then display the target web page within the new tab. Web developers also create hyperlinks that will download or copy files from a server onto your computer.

If you return to the anchor page after clicking a hyperlink, the hyperlink often displays in a different color, indicating that it has already been followed.

Other hyperlinks you will see on a web page are sponsored by companies who have paid to advertise on that web page. For instance, once a results list appears for search criteria, there will be links usually at the right side that list different organizations or services that may have information or products you can purchase.

Searching

While there are several well-known search engine sites on the Internet (you will learn how to use a search engine site later in this courseware), many modern browsers include a search box in the address bar, which allows you to search for information without first having to navigate to a search engine site.

In Internet Explorer, you can search directly from the address bar. Simply click in the address bar and start typing. If you enter a complete URL, you will go directly to the web site. If you enter a search term or an incomplete address, click a search provider in the menu to launch a search using the currently selected search engine.

A list appears with suggestions of search criteria for selection; this is the **Turn on suggestions** feature that is on by default. You can change this using the options command for the web browser.

You can also click the **Add** button in the drop-down menu to add search providers (such as Google or Ask.com) from the Internet Explorer Gallery web site.

Typically, a search engine returns tens of thousands of results. You can use the following techniques to narrow the number of results:

- Choose specific key words. For example, typing *lemon sharks* will show fewer results than simply typing *sharks*.

- Put quotation marks around a phrase or a group of keywords to force the search engine to look for occurrences of those words together rather than searching for each of those words individually.

- Use Boolean operators. Popular Boolean operators you can use with searches are the words AND, OR and NOT.

- Even if you do not type Boolean operators, most search engines interpret a space between keywords as an implied Boolean AND. That is, if you type *nuclear radiation* in the address bar, the space between the keywords is interpreted as a Boolean AND, and the results will include both words.

EXERCISE

In this exercise you will use hyperlinks to move around a web site.

1. On the taskbar, click the Internet Explorer icon.

2. Click in the address bar, type: `www.tolanoadventures.com` and press (Enter).

    You should be viewing the Tolano Adventures home page.

    Take a few moments to move the mouse cursor around the screen to see if you can find links on the page. The only links on the page are in the navigation bar. The fours links are: Home, About Us, Services and Contact Us. Notice that these links do not appear with underlines, and the mouse pointer changes when you hover over them. The appearance of links is left to the discretion of the web page developer.

3. Position the mouse pointer on the **Services** link in the navigation bar, and then click the link.

    You are now viewing a list of services that Tolano Adventures provides.

4. Move your cursor to point at the **Biking/Cycling Tours** link in the list and then click this hyperlink to move to this page to view its contents.

    Notice that, as you click each hyperlink, the web browser navigates to the web page specified as the target for that link.

5. Click the **Home** link in the navigation bar to move to the home page for the web site.

Now try searching for information using the address bar in the web browser.

6. Click in the address bar, then type: `elements`. Observe the list box that displays beneath the address bar. If *Turn on suggestions (send keystrokes to Bing)* displays in the list box, click the link to display suggested search terms.

7. Click **elements** in the list box to display the first page.

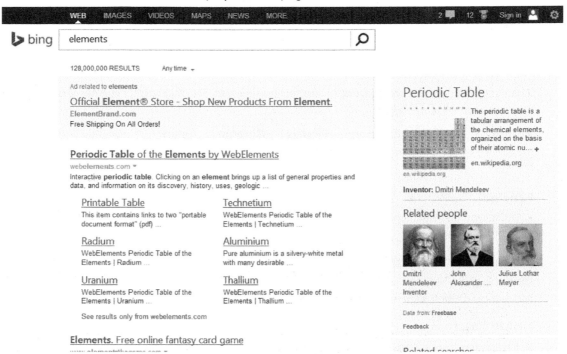

Notice the number of results that display; this number will change over time as more items are added to the Internet. Also notice the list at the right side that lists different types of results for the search criteria – these items are links that have been sponsored by organizations who hope you will click the link to their site with the intent to view or purchase.

8. Click in the address bar, type: `elements periodic table` and press ⟮Enter⟯.

Notice that the search returns fewer results. Each of the listed results includes the words elements, periodic and table. A Boolean AND is implied by the spaces between the words.

9. Click in the address bar, type: `"periodic table of elements"` and press ⟮Enter⟯.

While the results list appears similar to the last search criteria entered, notice that because you included quotation marks, each of the listed results includes the exact phrase "periodic table of elements."

10. Click in the address bar, type: `hydrogen+oxygen`, then press ⟮Enter⟯.

11. Click in the address bar, type: `hydrogen+oxygen NOT H2O`, then press ⟮Enter⟯.

Did the number of returned results decrease?

12. Close the browser.

Browser Features

Browsers include several features which make them easy to use and easy to customize. Browser features help make browsing the World Wide Web efficient and fun.

Back, Forward and Refresh Buttons

Although web pages often provide their own navigation tools, every browser includes buttons that allow you to navigate among the sites you visit within any given browser session.

- The Back button moves back one page. The back button becomes active once you click a link or visit a different page by typing a URL in the address bar.

- The Forward button moves ahead one page. The forward button becomes active once you move back one page.

- The Refresh button reloads or re-displays a page. You may want to refresh a page if the content changes continuously, or if part of the page failed to load correctly.

The symbols used for these buttons are fairly universal. The following table illustrates how the buttons appear in various browsers.

Button	Internet Explorer	Firefox	Chrome	Opera
Back				
Forward				
Refresh				

If a menu bar is available in the web browser, it can usually be displayed using the (Alt) key. You can then use the View menu to go to a specific page or to refresh the screen. In general, the menu bar is hidden by default as the buttons enable you to navigate or access options faster.

Home Page

A browser's home page is the page that is displayed by default when you open the browser. Most browsers are configured with a default home page when you install them. For example, the default home page for the Internet Explorer browser is the www.msn.com page.

However, you can set the home page for your browser to any page you want. For example, users set their home page to a search engine or to their favorite web site. If you visit a site frequently, it can be efficient to set that site as your home page. It should be noted, however, that many companies prefer that employees set their home page to the company web site.

You can also set most browsers to display a blank page as the home page.

All web browsers include a button that will quickly return you to your default home page, no matter how many other web sites you have visited. Each browser uses its own version of a House symbol.

Tabs

Modern browsers allow for tabbed browsing. That is, you can view different web sites simultaneously – each in its own tab. Opening a new tab is the same as opening a new browser window. Browser tabs are similar to buttons in the Windows taskbar. You can open a separate web page in each tab, and switch between them by simply clicking on the tab. Only one tab can be the active tab at any given time.

Working with multiple open tabs allows you to compare information from different web sites, or copy and paste information from one web page into another.

To create a new tab, use one of the following methods:

- Click the **New Tab** button, or
- press (Ctrl)+(T), or

- right-click an active tab and then click **New tab**, or
- if the Menu bar is displayed, click **File** and then click **New tab**.

In Internet Explorer, when you open a new tab, the browser displays thumbnails of the sites you visit most often.

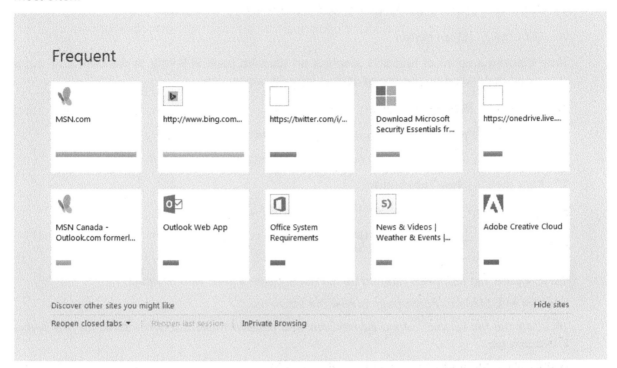

You can click a thumbnail to open that site in the active tab.

You can also right-click a tab and select **Duplicate tab** in the menu to open a new tab that displays the same web site. For example, if you are viewing the MSN web site, you could read one article in one tab, open a duplicate tab, and then click a link to view a different article on the MSN site in the other tab.

To view a link on a web page in another tab without leaving the web page, right-click the link and then click **Open in new tab**. You can then view the contents of two different pages for the same web site.

To close a tab you no longer want to view, click the ✖ **(Close Tab)** button on that tab. If you have multiple tabs open, you can right-click the active tab and specify to close the tab, or close all the other open tabs.

If you have multiple tabs open, and you click the **Close** button for Internet Explorer, you will be prompted to specify whether you want to close the current tab or close all the open tabs.

EXERCISE

In this exercise you will use various features in the Internet Explorer browser.

1. Click the **Internet Explorer** icon in the taskbar.

2. Click in the address bar, type: `www.ccilearning.com`, and then press (Enter).

3. Click in the address bar, type: `www.google.com`, and then press (Enter).

4. Click the ⬅ **(Back)** button to move back one page (to the CCI Learning page).

5. Click the ● (**Forward**) button to move forward one page to the Google page.

6. Click in the address bar, type: `wikipedia`, and then press (Enter).

7. Click the 🏠 (**Home**) button to return to the browser home page.

8. Click in the address bar, type: `www.disney.com` and press (Enter).

9. Click the ✕ (**Stop**) button.

Note that the amount of text and graphics on the web page will vary at the time you stopped the download depending on the speed of your Internet connection.

10. Click the ↻ (**Refresh**) button.

11. Click the 🏠 (**Home**) button to return to the home page.

Now try viewing two or more web sites and navigating between the web pages.

12. Click the ▢ (**New Tab**) button.

13. In the address bar, type: `www.cnn.com` and press (Enter).

14. Press (Ctrl)+(T) to open a new tab and type: `www.tolanoadventures.com` in the address bar. Click → (**Go**).

15. Click the first tab, which should be the home page of your web browser.

    The web browser home page is now the active tab.

16. Click the tab for the Tolano Adventures web page to make the home page for this web site the active tab.

17. Click the **CNN** tab and then click ✕ (**Close Tab**).

    You should now have only two tabs open: the home page for your web browser and the Tolano Adventures home page.

18. Click the tab for the home page of your web browser and click ✕ (**Close Tab**).

    You should now have only one open tab, the Tolano Adventures home page.

19. Minimize the Internet Explorer window.

Favorites/Bookmarks

If you visit a site frequently, you can "bookmark" the site so that you can visit it without having to enter its URL. When you bookmark a site, you save the URL in a folder created specifically for storing bookmarks. Various browsers give different names to their bookmark folders. In Internet Explorer, bookmarks are stored in a folder called Favorites.

You can work with Favorites in Internet Explorer by opening the Favorites center. The Favorites center includes three tabs – one for bookmarks, one for news feeds and one for the browsing history.

*   To display the Favorites Center, click ☆ (**View favorites, feeds, and history**), or

*   press (Alt)+(C).

The number of folders or web sites displayed in the Favorites pane will vary, depending on the web browser version and on previously set bookmarks. You can organize bookmarks into folders, move them, or remove them.

You can expand or collapse folders ("open" them to see a list of the contents or "close" them to see only the folder) by clicking the folder.

You can have the web browser place each of the links in a folder as a separate tab by clicking the arrow to the right of the folder name (or pressing Ctrl + Enter):

You can share your favorites with others online through web sites, such as social networking sites, where you save the bookmarks and then apply keywords for that bookmark. This is known as *social bookmarking* and works like a resource center where people can find addresses for sites devoted to particular topics using these shared bookmarks or favorites. You must, however, first register with a social networking site.

Adding Favorites

To add a web site to the list of favorites, use one of the following methods:

- Click the ☆ (**View favorites, feeds or history**) button and then click **Add to favorites**, or

- on the Menu bar, click **Favorites** and then click **Add to favorites**, or

- press Alt + Z , and then click **Add to favorites**

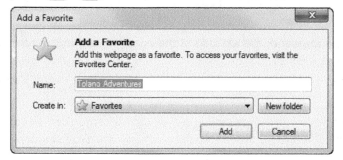

You can create a new folder for the link, move it into another folder, or choose to have it appear at the main level on its own.

Once you add a web site to the Favorites list, access it by clicking it in the Favorites list.

You can also use the Favorites bar to add favorites you want to access frequently. Right-click anywhere in the blank area by the tab, click **Favorites bar**, and then click ☆ (**Add to Favorites bar**).

Deleting Favorites

To remove a bookmark in the Favorites list, use one of the following methods:

- right-click the bookmark, then click **Delete** from the shortcut menu, or
- select the bookmark, press (Delete) and then click **Yes** to confirm the deletion.

To delete an item from the Favorites bar, right-click the button and then click **Delete**.

Organizing the Favorites List

The web browser gives you the option to choose where the Favorites link will appear. As you begin to add favorites, you may want to organize these links.

To organize the Favorites Center, use one of the following methods:

- Activate the Favorites Center and then drag the link to a new location, or
- activate the Favorites Center, click the arrow for **Add to favorites** and click **Organize favorites**, or
- activate the Menu bar, click **Favorites** and then click **Organize favorites**.

You can then choose any of the options in the dialog box to organize (or reorganize) the list of favorites.

If you choose to use the first method, as you drag the link to a new location, a thick horizontal black line appears to guide you in placing the link.

EXERCISE

In this exercise you will work with bookmarks.

1. Restore the Internet Explorer window.
2. Click in the address bar, type: `www.ccilearning.com` and press (Enter).
3. Click ☆ **(View favorites, feeds, and history)** to display the Favorites Center. Click 🖈 **(Pin the Favorites Center)** to keep the pane open.

    The Favorites Center should now appear at the left side of the window, and occupy the full height of the screen.

4. Click **Add to favorites**.
5. Ensure the text shows as: `CCI Learning` for the **Name** and click **Add**.

    The Favorites Center should appear similar to:

Now try adding other sites to your Favorites Center.

6. In the **Address** field, type: `www.foodnetwork.com` and press (Enter).
7. Click **Add to favorites**, type: `Food Network` as the name and then click **Add**.

    The web site has been added to your list of favorite sites.

8. In the **Address** field, type: `www.travelchannel.com/tv-shows` and press ⌷Enter⌷.

   This URL points to a specific page on a web site other than the web site home page. By including the "/tv-shows" in the address, you can go directly to this page on the web site, instead of having to navigate there from the web site home page.

9. In the list of links for More Shows, click the **Bizarre Foods** link.

10. Click **Add to favorites**, and then click **Add**.

11. Click **Back** to return to the previous page.

12. Scroll further down In the More Shows list of links, click **Truck Stop USA** (should be near the end of the list of shows).

13. Click **Add to favorites**, and then click **Add**.

    Notice how both pages on the Travel Channel web site are now bookmarked for later use.

Now that you have some favorites, you need to organize the links by topic.

14. Click the arrow for Add to favorites and then **Organize favorites**.

15. Click **New Folder**. Type: `Restaurant Tours Research` and press ⌷Enter⌷.

16. Click the *Food Network* link in the list and then click **Move**.

17. Click the *Restaurant Tours Research* folder and then click **OK** to move the Food Network link into the Restaurant Tours Research folder.

18. Repeat steps 16 to 17 for the *Bizarre Foods* link and the *Truck Stop USA* link.

19. Click **Close** to exit the Organize Favorites dialog box.

Now try moving a link by dragging it to a different location.

20. Click the *Restaurant Tours Research* folder and drag it upwards to organize folders in alphabetical order.

The horizontal black bar that appears as you drag the folder indicates where the folder will be placed when you release the mouse button. Folders or web site links can also be reorganized within a folder.

21. Release the mouse button at the appropriate location.

    Notice that the folders are listed in alphabetical order.

22. If required, drag the CCI Learning Solutions link into its appropriate alphabetical position in the list of favorites.

23. Minimize the Internet Explorer window.

Checking the History

Every browser includes a history function that stores the URLs of web sites you have visited in the browser's History folder.

The History folder stores the URLs of sites you have accessed within a defined period of time, and provides a convenient way to revisit web sites, especially if you cannot remember the exact URL. In Internet Explorer, the default amount of time to keep pages in History is 20 days. If you use the web for a lot of tasks, the History folder can become unmanageably large. A large History folder can be difficult to use, uses considerable disk space, and can slow the browser speed. You can, however, adjust the time period for storing pages, and you can empty the folder manually.

To display the history, activate the Favorites Center and then click the **History** tab.

Within the History tab, you can click the arrow for the **View By Date** drop-down to choose among various view options:

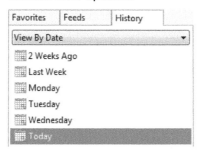

Once the list of sites appears in the preferred view, you can do one of the following:

- To go to a site, click the site link in the list.
- To see other pages you may have visited within a given site, right-click the link and then click **Expand**.
- To collapse the list of web pages for a site, click the site link.
- To delete a site from the list, right-click the link and then click **Delete**.

To delete the entire history, use one of the following methods:

- Click ⚙, click **Safety** and then click **Delete browsing history**, or
- on the Menu bar, click **Tools** and then click **Delete browsing history**.

EXERCISE

In this exercise, you will work with the History folder.

1. Restore the Internet Explorer window, ensure the Favorites Center is open and then click the **History** tab.

2. Click **Today**.

    You should see a list of all the sites you visited today.

3. Click the arrow for the **View By Date** drop-down.

4. Click **View By Site**.

    Notice how the history list appears. The number of sites listed here will vary depending on who else may have used the web browser recently.

5. Click ✖ **(Close the Favorites Center)**.

6. At the top right edge of the Internet Explorer window of the screen, click ⚙, click **Safety** and then click **Delete browsing history**.

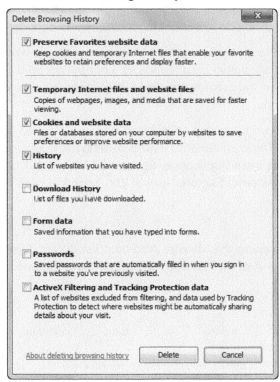

7. Examine the settings listed in the dialog box. Can you predict what will happen when you click the Delete button?

8. Click **Delete**.

    When complete, the web browser displays a screen similar to the following:

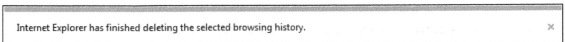

9. Close the message box, then open the Favorites center and click the History tab if necessary. The history tab should now be empty.

10. Minimize the browser window.

Plug-ins/Add-ons

In order to present the interactive multimedia so abundant on the web today, a browser requires applications called plug-ins or add-ons. *Plug-ins* are programs that extend the capabilities of web browsers. When you visit a web site and your browser encounters a file type that it cannot natively support, you may be prompted to download and install a plug-in so you can view the web page properly.

Plug-ins are associated with a specific operating system (such as Windows or Macintosh) and sometimes with a specific browser (such as Firefox or Internet Explorer). In Firefox, plug-ins are generally referred to as add-ons. Adobe Flash Player, Windows Media Player, and Real Networks RealPlayer are examples of popular plug-ins.

Plug-ins generally have a particular file type associated with them. For example, Windows Media Player can be used to play files that include the .wma (Windows media audio) and .wmv (Windows media video) file name extensions. The player also supports several video and audio file formats (such as .avi, .mpeg, .midi, .wav).

Internet Explorer and Firefox both include several native plug-ins. These are automatically installed with the browser. However, as you browse the Web, you may be prompted to download and install new plug-ins or update the plug-ins that are already installed. It is good practice to occasionally upgrade plug-ins because upgrades frequently include increased functionality and security updates.

To install or upgrade a plug-in, it is often best to go to the vendor's site because that is where you will find the latest version of the plug-in. Vendor sites also usually include information on the minimum system requirements (operating system version, hard disk space, RAM, processor speed, etc.) required for the plug-in as well as installation instructions.

In Internet Explorer, toolbars and ActiveX controls are also considered add-ons. ActiveX controls are small programs that are used on the Internet. They can enhance your browsing experience by allowing animation or they can help with tasks such as installing security updates at Microsoft Update. When you visit a site that uses an ActiveX control, Internet Explorer asks if you want to install the ActiveX control.

Managing plug-ins/add-ons

You can manage plug-ins and add-ons by opening the Manage Add-ons dialog box. Click the **Tools** button, and then click **Manage add-ons**. Under Add-on Types, click **Toolbars and Extensions**.

Display the **Show** drop-down list and select to view currently loaded add-ons, all add-ons, add-ons that are pre-approved by Microsoft (select the **Run without permission** option to view these), or ActiveX controls (select **Downloaded controls** to view these).

To turn an add-on on or off, click the add-on in the dialog box, then click either the **Enable** or **Disable** button.

To delete installed ActiveX controls, select the **Downloaded controls** option in the Show drop-down list, click the ActiveX control you want to delete, then click **More information**.

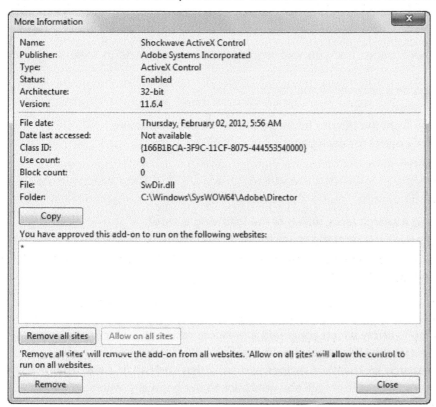

In the More Information dialog box, click the **Remove** button.

Lesson Summary

In this lesson, you reviewed how web sites are organized, and identified common web page elements. You also learned how to perform basic tasks using a web browser. You should now understand or be able to:

☑ the difference between the Internet, the World Wide Web, and browsers

☑ the structure of a URL

☑ identify common web page elements

☑ the basic functions of web browsers

☑ navigate in a browser

☑ use tabbed browsing

☑ work with bookmarks

☑ view the history

Review Questions

1. Which statement properly defines the concepts of Internet, Browsers and the World Wide Web?
    a.   The Internet and the World Wide Web are two names for the same thing; and all pages of the Internet are viewed through browsers.
    b.   The Internet is a network that hosts the linked pages which form the World Wide Web, and these pages are viewed through browsers.
    c.   The World Wide Web is a network, and browsers are another name for the Internet.
    d.   Any of the previous
    e.   a or b

2. If there are several web pages that you visit regularly, what can you do to make accessing them more efficient?
    a.   Define each page as a browser Home page.
    b.   Bookmark each page.
    c.   Delete each page from the History folder so that it will become active.
    d.   Install an ActiveX control for each page.
    e.   Any of the previous
    f.   a or b
    g.   a or c

3. If you use a phrase as a search term, which of the following is true?
    a.   The search engine will interpret the space between each word in the phrase as a Boolean AND.
    b.   The search engine will interpret the space between each word as a Boolean OR.
    c.   The search engine will interpret the space between each word as a Boolean NOT.
    d.   The search engine will reject the phrase because you cannot use more than one word as a search term.

4. Ann visited a site last Tuesday which contained a meatloaf recipe that she really wants to try, but now she can't remember the URL. What should she do?
    a.   Conduct a new search for meatloaf recipes and hope that she can find this one recipe again.
    b.   Click the browser's Back button until she gets back to the page she wants.
    c.   Click the browser's Refresh button.
    d.   Look for the URL in the History folder.

5. Which is the fastest method to use to view two or more web sites in your web browser?
    a.   Start another session of the web browsers.
    b.   Set up a separate monitor to open a new window for the web browser.
    c.   Open a new tab and enter the web site address.
    d.   Type the new site address into the address bar at the current page.

6. When you post information to a personal Web site to share with others, which action are you performing?
    a.   Uploading   b.   Downloading

MMM
Go online for
Additional
Review

Lesson 13: Getting Connected

Lesson Objectives

In this lesson you will examine the hardware, media and configuration settings that are required to connect to an organization's network or to the Internet. On successful completion, you will be familiar with:

☐ the advantages of networking

☐ common network speeds

☐ common networking models

☐ the role of TCP

☐ local area networks (LANs)

☐ how wired and wireless connections work

☐ addresses used on the LAN

☐ wide area networks (WANs)

☐ analog and digital signaling

☐ methods for connecting to the Internet

☐ the role of the domain name system (DNS)

☐ the need for security

☐ the role of firewalls and gateways

☐ the use of virtual private networks (VPNs)

☐ basic troubleshooting techniques

Defining a Network

 Exam 3 - Objective 2.1

Today, the word "network" is used almost daily in reference to a wide range of technologies. At its very basic definition, a network is a system for moving objects or information.

For example, the Pony Express of 1860-1861 was a U.S. network of stations, riders and horses that moved information (delivered mail) across a 2,000-mile trail that stretched from St. Joseph, Missouri to Sacramento, California. Another example is the public switched telephone network (PSTN), which has been moving information (by way of voice) from coast to coast and around the world since 1915.

In modern computing terms, a network is a group of two or more computers connected in such a way that they can communicate, share resources and exchange data with one another. This definition can include a small business network in one room, or a worldwide network connecting millions of users, such as the Internet.

Advantages of Using a Network

The advantages of using a network include the ability to:

• share files

• use network resources (such as printers)

• access the Internet

Before the days of modern networking, if you wanted to share a file with another user you had to save the file to removable media (in the past this was usually a floppy disk), and then deliver the media to the other user. In an office, you could walk down the hall and hand the disk to someone else. But this method of file sharing was particularly inconvenient if another user was miles (or countries) away.

Sharing resources like printers saves money and allows people to be productive without being overcrowded by redundant equipment.

Network Speeds

A network's speed is determined by its capacity to move information. Capacity is measured in bits, and the speed or data transfer rate of a network is measured in bits per second (bps). As with storage capacities, data transfer speed is often measured in thousands, millions or even billions of bits per second, as shown in the following table:

Measurement	Equal to...
bps	Bits per second
Kbps	Thousand bits per second
Mbps	Million bits per second
Gbps	Billion bits per second

Many factors affect the speed at which data travels across a network. These include:

- type of transmission media (copper wire, fiber-optic cable, free space)
- the network standard used (different standards support different speeds)
- amount of traffic on the network
- speed of networking devices on the network (network card, modem, hub, switch)

A network's capacity for transferring data is also referred to as its bandwidth. Throughout this lesson you will learn about network speeds and factors that can affect performance.

Networking Models

Two networking models have been in common use for several years. These are the client/server model and the peer-to-peer model. A third networking model – the Web-based model – is emerging and becoming more prevalent as the Internet stretches to the far reaches of the globe.

Client/Server Model

Many corporate networks are structured using the client/server model. These networks are also called *server-based* networks. In a server-based network, individual computers and devices interact with one another through a central server through which they are all connected.

In a typical server-based network, the individual PCs are *client* systems. These are the systems used to browse the Internet, check email or print to a network printer. The services requested by the client systems (such as Internet access, email or access to network resources) are provided by the server. The *server* is more powerful than the clients connected to it.

Server-based networks are generally more secure than peer-to-peer networks because a central server controls access to all the network resources. To access the network from a client system, users must log on to the network by providing a user name and password.

Peer-to-Peer Model

A *peer-to-peer network* is one in which all the participating computers are more or less equal, and there is no central server. In a peer-to-peer network, each computer connected to the network is called a *host*. Hosts in a peer-to-peer network can share files, an Internet connection, a printer, a scanner or other peripheral devices. A Windows 7 HomeGroup (or in previous versions of the Windows operating system, a Microsoft Windows Workgroup) is an example of a peer-to-peer network.

Web-based Model

Today, because of the global availability of the Internet, companies and individuals can use the Internet as their network "backbone" and connect with other people around the globe. Networking over the Internet is called internetworking, and is becoming more and more common.

Individuals need only a browser and an Internet connection to share files, download applications, watch videos or participate in distance learning.

TCP/IP and Networking

In order for any computing device to communicate with any other device, the two devices must have a common communication scheme. This communication scheme is called a *protocol*. A protocol is simply a set of rules that enable devices to communicate with one another in an agreed-upon manner.

All major operating systems (Windows, Mac OS, UNIX/Linux) support a networking protocol called *Transmission Control Protocol/Internet Protocol (TCP/IP)*. TCP/IP is the standard protocol for both local and wide area networking, and is required for Internet access.

TCP/IP is a collection or suite of protocols that provide services for many things users do on the Web— from downloading email to following hyperlinks and downloading data from an FTP site. The component protocols of the TCP/IP suite are also commonly referred to as a protocol stack. Any network that uses TCP/IP as its networking protocol is referred to as a TCP/IP network.

Local Area Networks (LANs)

 Exam 3 - Objective 2.1, 2.2

A *local area network (LAN)* is a group of computers that are connected within a relatively small geographic area, such as a home, office or small group of buildings. A LAN can consist of as few as two computers, or any number of systems up to hundreds of computers and servers. LANs are commonly used for communication between users within an office.

A home network consisting of two computers and a shared printer is a common example of a small LAN. Usually, there is no server involved in a home network and the connected PCs are generally peers.

A corporate office within a building is an example of a larger LAN. Usually, corporate LANs are server-based networks. Users must log on to the network providing a recognized user name and password. Once logged on, a user gains access to the network services and resources.

The majority of LANs in use today adhere to a networking standard known as Ethernet. Ethernet is a family of networking technologies for local area networks.

Connecting to the LAN

Whether your LAN is a server-based network or a peer-to-peer network, you must connect to it in order to participate. A connection to the LAN requires:

- a network interface card (NIC)
- a transmission medium (wired or wireless)

Network Interface Card (NIC)

Also called a *network adapter card*, the NIC is a device that serves as the interface between the computer and the network (that is, it provides the physical connection between the computer and the network cabling or wireless signal).

Modern computers include NIC hardware integrated into the motherboard, but it is still common to find NICs that reside in a motherboard PCI expansion slot too. NICs come with USB and FireWire interfaces as well. Laptops often use PCMCIA NICs, which are NICs that you can insert into a special slot on the laptop.

A NIC includes a port for connecting a network cable. A network cable connects the NIC to the network. The other end of the network cable plugs into a port that leads into the network. NICs also come in wireless varieties, allowing you to connect to a Wi-Fi network. Wireless NICs do not include a port for connecting a network cable.

Transmission Medium

In order to send and receive data, a transmission medium must exist. In corporate environments, the most common medium is copper wire in the form of a twisted pair cable (although coaxial and fiber optic cable can also be used). In home networks, a wireless medium is commonly used.

Common LAN Devices

The transmission medium (network cable) provides the physical pathway for information to travel around the network. One end of a network cable plugs into the NIC on a computer; the other end plugs into a port on a connection device on the LAN. LAN connection devices provide a central point of communication, and make it possible for systems connected to it to communicate with one another.

Connection devices can connect individual systems to one another, and can connect separate networks to one another.

The following are common connection devices found on the LAN.

Switches/Hubs

A hub connects computers in a network so they can exchange information. A hub has several ports and each computer attached to the network plugs into a port on the hub using a network cable. Hubs are an old and slow technology, and have largely been replaced by switches or by switch/hub combination devices.

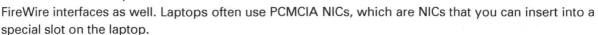

A switch connects either individual systems or multiple networks. Switches include multiple Ethernet ports and different sized switches offer a varying number of ports. The figure shows a 24-port switch.

Routers

Routers can be used to connect networks to one another. Within a LAN, internal routers connect separate portions of the LAN. At the edges of a LAN, a router is used to connect to a public carrier (phone company or Internet Service Provider). That is, a router receives the connections that form a wide-area network (WAN) link. You will learn about WANs shortly.

Because a router connects different networks, it serves as the entry point and exit point for each network, and is aptly referred to as a *gateway*.

An organization typically has one router that connects to a public carrier's lines to access the Internet. This type of router is called an *access router* because it provides access to the Internet. The access router provides the path outside the LAN. Because it acts as the gateway to the Internet, this router is referred to on the network as the "*default gateway*."

Wired Connections

Wired LANS use a cable to connect systems to the network. The most common type of cable used in an Ethernet wired LAN is called a twisted pair cable. Other common names for twisted pair cable include: Ethernet cable, patch cable, straight-through cable, network cable and RJ-45 cable.

This is the cable that you plug into your NIC. You plug the other end of the network cable into a network port in order to connect to the network. Depending upon the setup of your LAN, the network port may be located on a wall jack, or located on a hub, switch, broadband router, or DSL or cable modem.

Regardless of the location of the network port, the key is that computers connect to a central device that makes communication possible. For example, in a home network consisting of two PCs, each user might plug in to a port on a broadband router. The broadband router is the central device that makes communication between the two systems possible. In a corporate office, two or three users might connect their PCs to a port on a switch or hub.

Wired Ethernet LANs can move data at rates of 10 Mbps (million bits per second), 100 Mbps, 1 Gbps (billion bits per second), or even 10 Gbps. Wired connections are more secure than wireless connections which are subject to eavesdropping and other illicit activity.

Wireless Connections

In wireless LANs (WLANs), the open air is the connection medium and wireless signals are radio waves sent through the air. Because WLAN signals are radio waves, they can be easily intercepted by unauthorized users, and many network administrators do not allow wireless connections to their corporate LANs. Proper steps must be taken to secure a wireless network. You will learn about WLAN security later in this lesson.

Many modern laptops include built-in wireless NICs, although it is still quite common to see removable wireless NICs in the form of PCMCIA cards and USB devices.

Computers (PCs and laptops) that include a wireless NIC also include a standard NIC that uses a network cable, allowing you a choice in the way you connect. Many users will use a wireless connection when they are computing in a remote area (that is, an area in which there are no network ports available), and then switch to a wired connection when they are back in their office space.

Just as wired connections must ultimately terminate at a central device, wireless LAN connections use a central connection point as well. In wireless LANs, a wireless access point is the central device through which wireless systems connect to the network. The wireless access point itself, however, connects to the LAN through a wired connection.

Wireless connections are most common in homes and small offices, and they are convenient because users can access the network from different locations within the home or office, allowing the user greater mobility. However, wireless connections are slower than wired connections. Common speeds for today's wireless networks are 11 Mbps, 54 Mbps and 300 Mbps, depending on the WLAN standard in use.

Addressing on the LAN

In order for the computers connected to a network to communicate with one another, each computer requires a unique address. There are two types of addresses that are used on a LAN—a MAC address and a network (IP) address.

MAC Address

Every NIC has a unique address permanently burned into it by the manufacturer. This address is the *Media Access Control (MAC) address*. This address is also referred to as the physical address or the hardware address. MAC addresses are used for addressing only by devices within the same LAN, not outside the LAN. For data to be sent outside the LAN, an IP address is used.

Internet Protocol (IP) Addresses

It is a useful and common practice to connect one LAN to another LAN. While MAC addresses are used for addressing by devices within the same LAN, an Internet Protocol (IP) address is used for addressing between devices on different LANs.

Internet Protocol (IP) is the protocol in the TCP/IP suite that is responsible for addressing. Each computer on a TCP/IP network (or on the Internet) has an Internet address that distinguishes it from all other computers on the network. This Internet address is called an *IP address*.

There are two versions of Internet Protocol (IP)—version 4 (IPv4) and version 6 (IPv6). The differences between the versions are not important to our discussion, and IPv4 is still used predominantly.

All addressable devices on a network, including network printers, routers, etc., must have an IP address.

Following are some important points to understand about IP addresses:

- An IPv4 address is a 32-bit address written as a series of numbers divided into four segments with each segment separated by a dot. A sample IPv4 address might be: 200.168.212.226.

- An IP address is not permanent; IP addresses are leased to computers on the network for a specified period of time. If you were to move a computer from one network to another, its IP address would change.

- An IP address provides two pieces of information: it identifies the network on which the host resides, and it identifies the particular host on the network.

- A computer must have an IP address to connect to the Internet.

- An IP address must be unique within the network. When a system is connected to the Internet, its IP address must be unique on the Internet.

Network and host portions

An IP address identifies the network on which a host resides, and it identifies the particular host on the network. To identify these elements, an IP address includes two portions:

- A **network** portion – also called the network identifier, the network ID, or the network prefix. The network portion is indicated by a certain number of bits (starting from the left-most bit).

- A **host** portion – the remaining bits (after the network prefix) identify the specific host on the network.

A special notation called slash notation can be used to indicate how many bits are used for the network prefix. For example, in the IP address 200.168.212.226/24, the network prefix is 200.168.212 (the first 24 bits), and the host ID (consisting of the remaining 8 bits) is 226.

Networking devices use the network and host portions of an IP address to determine on which network a particular host resides, and to determine whether that network is local or remote.

What determines an IP address?

A system's IP address is determined by the network on which it resides. That is, all hosts on the same network share the same network address, but must have a unique host number. For example, three nodes on the 200.168.212 network might be 200.168.212.226, 200.168.212.228 and 200.168.212.300.

IP addresses may be manually assigned and configured by a network administrator, or they can be assigned and configured automatically through a service called *Dynamic Host Configuration Protocol (DHCP)*. Many networks (including home broadband networks) use the DHCP service to automatically assign IP addresses to their hosts. In most cases a host leases an IP addresses from a DHCP server when it logs on to the network.

Where do IP addresses come from?

A company or individual cannot merely select an IP address and begin using it. To ensure that each user on the Internet has a unique IP address, addresses are issued by the Internet Corporation for Assigned Names and Numbers (ICANN).

The ICANN allocates blocks of IP addresses to Internet Service Providers (ISPs), which in turn allocate addresses to their customers. When you purchase Internet service, you purchase the right to use a specific IP address (or in the case of a large company, a range of IP addresses) that has been allocated to your service provider.

Other required addressing information

In addition to an IP address, each host on a network must be configured with the following information:

Subnet Mask	A 32-bit number (similar to an IP address) that networking devices use to determine whether a destination system is local (on the same LAN) or remote. If an incorrect subnet mask is specified in a system's network configuration settings, the system will not be able to communicate with other systems on the network.
Default Gateway	Default gateway – this number is the IP address of a networking device that provides access outside the local LAN. The default gateway is usually a router. In order to access the Internet, your system must know the address of the default gateway – the router that leads to the Internet.

Reserved Address Ranges

The ICANN is in charge of assigning and coordinating IP addresses around the world, and the IP addresses allocated to service providers for distribution to their customers are public IP addresses. Public IP addresses can be used to access and participate on the Internet.

The ICANN has also reserved specific ranges of IP addresses as private IP addresses. A private IP address is an IP address that can be used for communication within the confines of a LAN, but is not routable or addressable over the Internet. Private IP addresses are for local use (*local* means within the LAN).

The following address ranges are reserved as private IP addresses:

- 10.0.0.0 to 10.255.255.255
- 172.16.0.0 to 172.31.255.255
- 192.168.0.0. to 192.168.255.255

Most residential networks use private addresses in the 192.168.0.0. to 192.168.255.255 range.

Private Addresses and Connecting to the Internet

It may be difficult at first to see the advantage to using private IP addresses on your LAN or home network if these addresses cannot be used on the Internet.

In a typical residential LAN setting for example, the home owner purchases Internet service from an Internet Service Provider, and one Internet-addressable IP address is included with the purchased Internet service. The Internet service comes into the home through either a DSL or cable modem or modem/router combination. The modem/router performs several functions, including (but not limited to) the following:

- It assigns private network addresses to the systems connected to it (usually 192.168.1.x), thus establishing an internal LAN.

- It uses a technology called network address translation (NAT) to replace the private IP address used by a system on the LAN with the Internet-addressable IP address that was provided with the purchase of Internet service.

Private network addresses are also commonly used inside corporate LANs. A corporation likely leases several public IP addresses that can be used on the Internet, and then translates private network addresses into public ones when Internet access is required. Network address translation occurs in the same way as it does on a home network, although a corporate LAN might use different hardware (proxy servers, firewalls, etc.).

Connecting LANs Together

It is often useful to connect one LAN to another LAN. For example, if different divisions of a company within a large business each have their own LAN, connecting the LANs allows the divisions to share data and resources.

LANs can be connected to one another using privately-owned communication lines, or they can be connected using communication lines provided by a public carrier such as the phone company or an ISP. When two or more LANs are connecting using a public network, a WAN is created.

Wide Area Networks (WANs)

 Exam 3 - Objective 2.2

A *wide area network (WAN)* consists of two or more LANs that cover a wide geographic area (for example, a city, state or country), and are connected using the lines of a public carrier. A public carrier is a telecommunications service provider that is regulated by the government. Examples of public carriers in the United States include AT&T, MCI and Western Union.

Consider a large business with offices in several locations worldwide. Each office has its own LAN which it can use to share resources and data locally. However, if the company needs to share resources with other offices, the LANs can be connected using communication lines provided by a public carrier (such as the phone company or an Internet service provider). When two or more LANs are connected using a public network, a WAN is created. The largest WAN on the planet is the Internet.

The main features that distinguish LANs from WANs are:

- A LAN is confined to local cabling that you install in your home, or that an IT department has routed through the office. In a LAN, the organization owns all the components. In a WAN, an organization leases some of the necessary components that are required to transmit data (such as high-speed telecommunications lines).

- LANs are also usually much faster than WANs. For example, most Ethernet cards transfer data at 10 or 100 Mbps, and in installations using Gigabit Ethernet, data moves at 1 Gbps. A typical WAN connection might run at 1.5 Mbps – 44.736 Mbps.

Public carriers provide services that allow you to send messages and documents over a telephone line to other users.

Public Switched Networks

 Exam 3 - Objective 2.2

A public switched network is any carrier network that provides switched services for the purposes of sending communications messages. Phone companies, Western Union and cellular providers all maintain public switched networks. They hire their services out to the public.

The Public Switched Telephone Network (PSTN)

No discussion of networking can ignore the importance of the PSTN. The *public switched telephone network (PSTN)* provides telephone service around the world and is integral to wide area networking because of its infrastructure. Infrastructure is the basic underlying physical structure or framework needed for the operation of a service or enterprise.

Telecommunications companies worldwide have been building the infrastructure of the PSTN for nearly a hundred years installing countless thousands of miles of telephone cable, switches, trunk lines and fiber optic cable. Internetworking depends on connections which are provided by the infrastructure built by these telecommunications providers.

Public carriers often lease their lines for private use to companies or individuals. These leased lines offer high speed data transfer and guaranteed capacity (bandwidth). While Internet Service Providers (ISPs) provide access to the Internet to their customers, this access is often made available through high-speed lines that are leased from public carriers. Usually transparent to the individual user, public carriers furnish most of the long-distance connections that power the Internet

Analog and Digital Signals

Two types of signals are used to transfer information electronically – analog and digital.

Analog signals are electrical signals that vary in amplitude and frequency. These signals are measured in cycles per second, or Hertz (Hz). Broadcast radio and television, and cable TV traditionally use analog signals. And originally, all telephone service was analog as well.

Digital signals are electrical signals that contain one of two values – 1 or 0. Digital signals are measured in bits per second (bps).

Digitizing is the process of converting analog signals into digital signals. Hardware devices such as modems, or signal processing software can easily digitize analog signals.

The Digital Phone Network

Today, the PSTN is almost entirely digital, except for the small portion that extends from the telephone company's central office (CO) to users' homes and offices. The central office is a building where subscriber telephone lines are connected to switching equipment for local and long-distance calls. The small portion of the network that extends from the CO to users homes is called the local loop or the "last mile" and is usually an analog line that provides what is known as plain old telephone service (POTS).

On a POTS line, a telephone conversation begins with an analog signal as voice information is spoken into the receiver. The analog signal travels down the local loop until it reaches the CO. Here, the analog signal passes through a switch and is digitized and sent into the digital heart of the telephone network.

The information remains in its digital format until it reaches the CO for the party receiving the call. Here is it modulated back into an analog signal and sent down the local loop to the receiving party.

Circuit Switching

Circuit switching is a technology that uses a dedicated physical path to send and receive information. The PSTN uses circuit switching.

Consider what happens when you make a phone call.

1. You pick up the receiver and open a connection to the local telephone switch.

2. You dial a number, and the switch then connects to other switches along the PSTN, forming a physical pathway between your telephone and the telephone of the person you are calling. This pathway will be used to transfer voice information back and forth between the two telephones.

3. When the person you are calling answers the phone, a circuit is established and will remain open for the duration of your call. As long as the circuit remains open, no one else can use the telephone line. All the switches and wire pathways involved in the connection remain in use for the entire duration of the call. All the voice information that is exchanged between the calling party and the receiving party travels along this same path (circuit).

4. When you hang up the phone, the circuit is disconnected, and the switches and wire pathways that had been dedicated to your phone call are now free again for other people to use.

Several Internet connection technologies use circuit switching. These include: POTS, ISDN, and leased lines.

Packet Switching

Packet switching is a technology for transferring information which does not rely on a dedicated physical path. In a packet switched network, information is broken down into discrete units called "packets" and addressing information is included in each packet, allowing the packet to be routed to its intended destination. All packets are routed through the network based on their addressing information.

Data networks use packet switching to transfer information between hosts on the network. The Internet also uses packet switching to transfer information between hosts.

Two familiar Internet connection technologies – Digital Subscriber Line (DSL) and cable Internet – also rely on packet switching.

Connecting to the Internet

 Exam 3 - Objective 2.1

As you have learned, the Internet is the largest WAN on the planet. As such, you must use a WAN connection to participate on the Internet.

You can purchase a connection through either a telecommunications company or an ISP. Some providers offer dial-up connections, and most offer direct connections through DSL or cable.

Dial-Up Connections

Dial-up connections are very slow and rarely used anymore. However, some users still use dial-up because it is the least expensive method of obtaining Internet access.

POTS Connection

As you have learned, the local loop to users' homes and offices is usually an analog POTS line, which operates at 64 Kbps.

Dial-up connections on a POTS line require the use of a modem which enables computers to transmit data over the analog telephone line. A modem converts (modulates) digital data from a computer into an analog signal which is transmitted over the local loop. (This analog signal is then digitized at the CO and sent through the digital portion of the phone network. When it reaches the CO at the receiving end, the digitized signal is modulated back into an analog signal and sent up the local loop.) The analog signal then passes through another modem on the receiving end of the connection. The receiving modem converts the analog signal back into a digital signal (demodulates) and transmits it to the receiving computer. This type of modem is called a traditional or analog modem.

> **Note:** Today the term modem is widely used and refers to any device that adapts a computer to a telecommunications line or cable TV network.

The modem physically connects to the telephone network using a standard telephone wire. When you use a dial-up connection, your computer uses the modem to dial the access number required to connect to your ISP. When a modem at the ISP "answers" the call, a connection (circuit) is established and maintained for the duration of the data transfer. That is, the phone line remains in use until you disconnect. When you finish your online session, you disconnect from the ISP by hanging up the line.

If you use a dial-up connection, you must establish a connection each time you want to access the Internet. Once your Internet session is complete, you disconnect (hang up).

The maximum possible speed for data transfer over a standard analog telephone line (allowing time for modulation and demodulation) is 56 Kbps.

Integrated Services Digital Network (ISDN)

An *Integrated Services Digital Network (ISDN)* line is a digital telephone line. Because the line is digital, no conversion from analog to digital is required. However, you must still establish a connection when you want to access the Internet, and then hang up when you are done. ISDN transfers data at 128 Kbps.

ISDN has been available throughout most of the world. Today, ISDN has been largely superseded by cable and DSL services.

Direct Connections – Broadband

In contrast to dial-up connections, which require activation for each usage, direct connections provide continuous access to the Internet through permanent network connections. That is, direct connections are always active.

Direct connections are more desirable than dial-up connections because they are generally capable of handling high bandwidth. Direct connections can be obtained in various ways, including leased lines, cable Internet service, digital subscriber lines, and LAN connections.

Often direct connections are referred to as broadband connections. Broadband is a technology that divides the available media bandwidth into multiple channels, and each channel carries a separate signal. This allows a single wire to carry several communications such as voice, fax, or data simultaneously. At one time, broadband systems carried only analog signals. Today, broadband signals can be analog or digital.

Today, the term broadband is used loosely to describe any connection that is always "on" and that provides speeds of 1.544 Mbps or higher.

Leased Lines

A leased line is a permanent connection between two or more locations that consumers can lease (rent) from a phone company. When you lease a line, you do not share it with other consumers; it is available exclusively to you. Typically, leased lines are used by businesses to connect offices that are geographically far apart. Leased lines are also commonly used by companies for Internet access because they offer high bandwidth and are cost-effective for heavy Internet traffic.

Because leased lines are private, they provide a company with a way to expand its private network beyond its immediate geographic area by forming a secure wide area network. Leased lines are reliable and secure, but they are expensive. Competing technologies such as DSL and cable are more cost-effective for small businesses.

Digital Subscriber Line (DSL)

A *digital subscriber line (DSL)* is a high-speed all-digital connection that uses digital phone lines and a DSL modem. DSL service is provided by the phone company. Several channels are carried over a single wire. DSL service can run on existing copper telephone lines if the lines are in good condition. DSL is a broadband technology; it divides the media bandwidth into multiple channels through multiplexing. DSL is offered by the phone company or telecom provider and is the main competitor to cable Internet connections.

DSL and other broadband modems are not modems in the traditional sense; that is, they do not convert digital signals to analog ones. Broadband modems provide a way to attach a computer to a public carrier's network. These devices are called "modems" because they connect computers to the phone network or to a cable TV network (which have traditionally carried analog signals).

DSL service provides users with a dedicated connection to the provider's digital network. When you have a dedicated connection, you do not share the available bandwidth with anyone else; the connection is all yours. For this reason, DSL subscribers do not experience a slowdown in network response time when more users connect to the network (as is the case with cable Internet subscribers).

Inside the customer's premises, a DSL modem is used to connect to the digital telephone circuit using a telephone cable. The modem also includes an Ethernet port. You attach the modem to your computer using an Ethernet cable by plugging one end of the cable into the Ethernet port on the modem and the other end of the cable into the Ethernet port on your NIC. (Some DSL modems also include a USB port for connecting to the computer.) The picture on the right shows a typical DSL modem.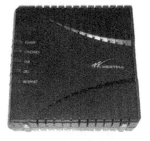

DSL Availability

Your distance from the provider's central office determines whether you can receive DSL service. If your home or office is too far away from the central office, DSL service will not be available to you. The distance limit for ADSL service is 18,000 feet (5,460 meters).The telephone company's use of loading coils and bridge taps to provide service to a remote area can also disqualify that area for DSL service, as these devices are not compatible with DSL equipment. You must check with a service provider to find out if DSL is available in your area.

DSL Speeds

Different speeds are available with DSL service, depending upon the type of service you use and how far you are from the provider's central office. The farther you are, the more the signal quality decreases and the slower the connection speed gets. The quality of the copper lines also affects signal quality and speed.

There are two speed measurements for DSL service – downstream and upstream. Data moves downstream as it reaches you from another location (for example, when a web server sends a web page that you have requested). The term downloading refers to the downstream flow of data. Data moves upstream when you send or upload information (for example, when you enter a URL in the browser's address bar or submit an online form).

Asymmetric DSL (ADSL)

Asymmetric DSL (ADSL) is the type of DSL service used by most homes and small businesses. ADSL divides the frequencies available on the line in an unequal manner—providing more frequencies for downloading than for uploading. Accordingly, when you use ADSL, your download speed is usually much faster than your upload speed.

ADSL can provide a maximum download speed of 8 Mbps (at 6,000 feet from the central office), and a maximum upload speed of 640 Kbps. In general usage, download speeds are closer to 1.5 Mbps, and upload speeds vary between 64 and 640 Kbps.

Some enhanced services such as ASDL2 and ASDL2+ improve performance. ASDL2 increases download to 12 Mbps and upstream to 1 Mbps, and ASDL2+ improves downstream to as much as 24 Mbps and upstream to 3 Mbps.

Symmetric DSL (SDSL) service is also available, and is used mainly by businesses. This type of service does not allow you to use the phone at the same time, but the upstream and downstream speeds are the same.

Cable

Cable Internet service is another broadband technology and is a direct competitor to ADSL. Instead of copper phone lines, a cable TV (CATV) system uses coaxial ("coax") cables to transmit signals. You can connect to the Internet through the CATV system using a cable modem.

Outside the customer's premises, the cable modem connects to the provider's cable modem termination system (CMTS), which generally supports several subscribers within the neighborhood. The CMTS connects a group of cable subscribers to the Internet.

Inside the subscriber's premises, the cable modem attaches to the cable service via a coaxial cable (the same type of cable you attach to your television set). The cable modem includes a jack for the coax cable and it also includes an Ethernet port. You attach the modem to your computer using an Ethernet cable by plugging one end of the cable into the Ethernet port on the modem and the other end of the cable into the Ethernet port on your NIC.

The picture to the left shows a cable modem. Although you cannot see the ports, the modem is connected to the cable service through a standard cable TV coaxial cable.

Cable providers generally route a coax loop through a neighborhood to support the subscribers in the general vicinity. Because cable modem users share this network loop (that is, they share the available bandwidth), performance slows down as new users come online.

Cable modem technology will theoretically support speeds of around 30 Mbps. However, actual speeds vary widely. Most providers offer services between 1–6 Mbps downstream, and 128–768 Kbps upstream.

Broadband Routers

In residential and small office networks, the DSL or cable modem provides the connection to the service provider's network, and therefore, to the Internet. These devices are considered routers because they connect a computer or network to the Internet, and are often referred to as residential gateways.

In many cases, these modems allow several users to share one Internet connection. These modems include more than one Ethernet port (or support wireless connections), allowing multiple users to plug in an Ethernet cable and connect to the Internet.

If your DSL or cable modem includes only one Ethernet port (allowing just one connection), you can purchase a separate broadband router and use it on your network to allow multiple users to share one Internet connection.

A broadband router, such as the one shown in the following figure, includes several Ethernet ports. One port is designated as the WAN port (or Internet port). You connect the router to your modem by attaching one end of an Ethernet cable to the router's WAN port, and the other end of the cable to the Ethernet port on your DSL or cable modem. This connection allows the router access to your Internet service.

The other Ethernet ports on the broadband router are LAN ports. When you want to connect other computers to the network, you attach them (via Ethernet cable) to the LAN ports.

Other Factors Affecting Performance

While various WAN technologies (DSL, cable, POTS) determine the top theoretical connection speed, several factors can affect the actual performance of your Internet connection. These include:

- Network traffic – if several users are sharing an Internet connection simultaneously, then the available bandwidth must be shared. This is especially noticeable to cable users. Usually an entire neighborhood shares a cable loop. As more users come online, performance can decrease dramatically.

- Wireless vs. Wired connections – most wireless LANs transmit at 54 Mbps, which is substantially slower than the average 100 Mbps rate for a wired Ethernet connection. Some older WLANs transmit and receive data at 11 Mbps. Newer wireless LANs (called "Wireless N LANs" or "802.11n LANs) operate at 300 Mbps.

- On slower connections, especially dial-up connections, large files such as photographs or audio or video files can seriously slow the loading of a web page. Some dial-up users configure their browsers to suppress the display of images in order to speed up page loading.

- Multiple open tabs – browsers provide for tabbed browsing, which means that you can have several web pages open at one time. Each open web page represents an open connection with a web server, and as such, each open tab uses a certain amount of network resources. On slow connections, working with multiple open tabs can decrease browsing speed.

Addressing on the Internet

 Exam 3 - Objective 2.2

You already learned that every computer connected to the Internet must have a unique IP address. This means that web servers (the computers that host web sites) must have IP addresses too.

IP addresses are required if systems on the network are to communicate. For any one computer on the Internet to communicate with another computer on the network, it must know the IP address of the computer with which it wants to communicate.

Have you ever typed an IP address into the address bar of your browser? Chances are you haven't.

Most people type a URL into the browser address bar. The typical URL consists of a protocol identifier and a domain name. How then, does your computer know the IP address of the desired web server when all you type into the address bar is the domain name?

The answer is by using DNS.

Domain Name System (DNS)

The Domain Name System (DNS) is a service that maps unique domain names to specific IP addresses. These mappings are stored on records in a DNS database. Every domain consists of DNS records. A *DNS record* is an entry in a DNS database.

DNS resolves IP addresses into their text-based names. For example, you can access the CCI Learning Solutions web server at IP address 96.53.76.108 by typing: *www.ccilearning.com* in your browser's address bar. In other words: 96.53.76.108 = www.ccilearning.com.

Both the domain name and the IP address refer to the same resource, but the domain name is easier to remember. Without DNS, you would need to enter an IP address any time you wanted to access a resource on the Internet.

DNS Servers

The DNS service is made possible through DNS name servers, which are servers on the Internet whose sole function is to resolve domain names into their IP addresses. For example, when you enter a URL such as www.ccilearning.com into your browser's address bar, the browser contacts a domain name server to obtain the IP address related to this domain name. When the browser receives the IP address 96.53.76.108 from the domain name server, the CCI Learning Solutions site displays on the screen.

Aside from being an integral part of the Internet infrastructure, DNS servers are also used in both enterprise and small business networks. When home users enter a URI into a browser address bar, the host names are resolved to IP addresses by the ISP's DNS server.

If a DNS server is unreachable, you will not be able to navigate to a web site by entering its URL in the browser address bar. You can, however, still reach the site if you know its IP address.

The Need for Security

 Exam 3 - Objective 2.1, 2.2

Remember that a LAN is a private network. The systems within a LAN can communicate with one another, but cannot communicate with any system outside the LAN. Systems outside the LAN cannot communicate with a system inside the LAN. All of this changes, however, when a WAN link is added.

Once a LAN is connected to a WAN link, the LAN is connected to the outside world. The systems inside the LAN can communicate with systems outside the LAN, and systems outside the LAN can communicate with systems inside the LAN. This makes the systems inside the LAN vulnerable to malicious activity.

For example, unauthorized users might try to access the network and its resources, or steal data, or introduce viruses to systems within the LAN. Any person who attempts to gain unauthorized access to a computer system is known as a *hacker*. Hackers employ many different methods to obtain what they want. For this reason, network administrators must focus on keeping systems within the LAN secure from unauthorized access and unwanted activity. To combat these risks, IT professionals design and implement specific policies related to security.

When you connect a computer to a network, the information stored on that networked computer can, in theory, be accessed by any computer connected to the network. When you connect a computer to the Internet, you have connected it to the largest network on earth. In theory, any other user on the Internet can (try to) connect to your computer.

As an individual Internet subscriber, you must also take steps to protect your systems from unwanted connections or attack.

Private vs. Public

The systems within a LAN are part of a private network, and are considered trusted systems. However, any system outside the LAN is not trusted. Any system connecting to the LAN over the Internet is especially untrusted.

Because the Internet is not centrally controlled or owned, anyone can access it. For this reason, the Internet is referred to as "the public network." Because there is no central control or ownership over the Internet, no one can "police" the Internet to protect the people who use it. For this reason, the Internet is also referred to as "the open network" or "the untrusted network."

In network diagrams, the Internet is often represented by a cloud, because its contents are unknown.

Authentication and Access Control

Network administrators use authentication and access control to manage network resources and keep the network secure.

Authentication is the process of verifying the identity of a user who logs on to a system or network. The simplest method of authentication is the use of user names and passwords. Access control is the process of controlling who may access particular network resources or services. Access control is usually accomplished by associating specific permissions to each user account. For example, Alice may have permission to access the company web server and the company personnel database, while Bob may have permission to access only the Accounting folder on the network.

Authentication and access control provide a measure of security within the LAN, but most network security measures are focused on preventing outsiders from accessing the LAN illegitimately.

Firewalls/Gateways

Network professionals use firewalls to protect the LAN from unauthorized access from outside.

A *firewall* is a security barrier that controls the flow of information between the Internet and a private network. A firewall can be a dedicated computer system, a specialized firewall appliance, or it can be implemented on a networking device such as a router. In a home or small office networking environment where a broadband router is used, a firewall is usually built in to the broadband router.

A firewall protects your network from malicious activity coming from outside your network, and provides a "door" through which people can communicate between a secured network (the LAN) and the open, unsecured Internet. A network firewall is most commonly placed between a corporate LAN and the Internet.

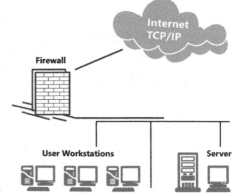

By connecting to the Internet through corporate firewalls, no computer on the LAN is actually connected to the Internet, and any requests for information must pass through the firewall. This feature allows users on the LAN to request information from the Internet, but to deny any requests from outside users for information stored on the LAN.

Gateways and Packet Filtering

You have already learned that routers are referred to as gateways. Remember, a router is the entry point into a network, and all incoming traffic comes through the router. From a security standpoint, a gateway is a router that has been configured to protect the network by examining each packet coming into (or out of) the network. The gateway can check each packet against a defined list of rules for what should be allowed in and what should be rejected.

Gateways use a process called *packet filtering* to determine what should be allowed into the network, and what should be rejected.

A packet filtering gateway inspects each data packet as it arrives and then uses simple rules to determine whether that packet should be allowed to pass through to the network. For example, you could examine packets coming from a specific IP address, or destined for a specific IP address. Packet filtering is fast and inexpensive, but it is not a particularly flexible method, nor is it foolproof. Packet filtering is therefore considered the first line of defense in protecting the network.

Advanced Firewall Functions

While gateways can be configured to perform packet filtering only, firewalls can use other methods (in addition to packet filtering) to control traffic flowing in to and out from the network, including:

Stateful Inspection	Stateful inspection firewalls build upon packet filters by having the firewall maintain information about the state of each active connection. When a new packet arrives at the firewall, the filtering mechanism first checks to determine whether the packet is part of a current active (and previously authorized) connection. If the packet is not on the list of active connections, then the firewall checks it against its rules and determines whether the packet should be allowed in. Stateful inspection firewalls are very efficient and cost-effective and the most commonly used firewalls in enterprises.
Proxy service	A proxy replaces the internal network IP addresses with a single IP address which multiple systems can use. Through network address translation (NAT), you can effectively hide the systems connected to your internal network from the outside world.

Desktop Firewalls

Firewalls can also be implemented through software. Also known as personal firewalls, desktop firewalls offer protection for an individual system instead of an entire network. Tools such as Norton 360 or ZoneAlarm Internet Security Suite can detect and respond to attacks on a computer system.

Desktop firewalls offer many firewall features, such as inspection of all incoming transmissions for security threats. When a firewall is used in conjunction with antivirus software, a personal computer is very secure, provided that the user updates these applications frequently.

Many operating systems now include built-in (native) desktop firewall software. Windows, for example, includes Windows Firewall which is enabled by default. You can customize the settings for Windows Firewall just as you can for third-party firewall applications.

Firewall Ports

One of the ways that firewalls determine whether specific data packets should be allowed into the network is by examining the source and destination port of the packet.

Computers use ports for communication, and ports are numbered from 0 to 65,535. Specific applications and services (such as HTTP, DNS, or email) use a specific port number. For example, any request or response for a web page uses the HTTP protocol, and HTTP communications use port 80. Any requests or responses for DNS services use port 53.

One way of securing a network is to block all incoming ports on the firewall, and then to open only the specific ports that correspond to the types of communications the network administrator wants to allow into the network. If users inside the LAN will be allowed to view web pages, then the administrator must open port 80 on the firewall. Since DNS helps us locate web pages, the administrator will also have to open port 53.

The configuration of the firewall ports affects all communications coming into and going out from the LAN. An improperly configured firewall can block out phone service, prevent web access, block video and audio from web sites, or disallow instant messaging communications.

Firewall Challenges

Firewalls can present challenges to network users. Sometimes firewall settings block access to particular web sites, or block streaming audio or video from coming into a network. If your corporate system is behind a firewall and you have difficulty connecting to specific Internet sites or services, you may need to contact a network administrator, who can then adjust the firewall configuration.

You may also learn, however, that the service or web site you want to access conflicts with your organization's security policy.

Virtual Private Networks (VPN)

Network administrators put a lot of effort into blocking unauthorized connections from the outside into the LAN. However, they must also provide a method for allowing authorized connections from the outside. Connecting from outside the network is known as remote access.

Security is an especially important component of remote access because communication across a public network (such as the Internet) is vulnerable to interception or eavesdropping. For this reason, remote access methods must provide for authentication and encryption. Authentication is the process of confirming the identity of a user or computer system. Encryption is the process of converting data into an unreadable form of text, which then requires a decryption key in order to be read.

In the past, remote access was provided through remote access servers, modems and dedicated phone lines. In most modern networks, however, access is obtained using a virtual private network (VPN) connection.

A VPN is an encrypted connection between two computers. VPNs allow secure communications across long distances using the Internet as the pathway for communication instead of using a dedicated private line.

VPNs make it possible for telecommuters and traveling employees to establish a secure connection to the company network from outside the company premises. VPNs also make it possible for a company with several satellite offices to establish secure connections between all their locations.

Using VPN

In order for a network to support VPN connections, a VPN server must be set up to receive incoming connections. Any user who wants to make a VPN connection from a remote location (for example, from home or from a hotel room) must install and then launch VPN client software to open a connection with the VPN server.

Users must log on (authenticate) using a valid user name and password, just as if they were logging on to the network from inside the corporate office.

Wireless Security

Because wireless networks use radio waves to send and receive information, they are susceptible to eavesdropping and unauthorized access. For example, a hacker who is within range of your wireless transmissions can intercept them. User names and passwords should never be sent over unencrypted wireless communications.

Additionally, an unauthorized user can obtain "free" Internet access through your wireless access point if you do not take steps to secure it. Securing your access point and your transmissions is accomplished through wireless encryption.

Wireless Encryption

As you read earlier, encryption is the process of converting data into an unreadable form of text. If a hacker intercepts an encrypted transmission, the encrypted data is useless to him. Decryption is the process of converting encrypted data back into its original readable form.

Encryption and decryption are accomplished through keys. A key is a mathematical algorithm. The more complex the key, the harder it is to decipher the encrypted message without access to the key.

When you configure encryption on a wireless access point, each wireless client that wants to gain access to the wireless network must present an appropriate passphrase when first connecting to the access point. The presentation of the correct passphrase is like entering the correct password when you log on to a network. Only wireless clients that have been configured to supply the correct passphrase will be granted access to the network. The process of gaining access to the wireless network is called authentication.

During the authentication process, the appropriate keys are exchanged so that encrypted transmissions can take place.

Wireless encryption mechanisms include the following:

Wired Equivalent Privacy (WEP)	The original security mechanism for wireless networks. WEP encrypts all data packets sent between the client and the access point, but uses unencrypted exchanges during the authentication process. Today, WEP is considered obsolete and administrators use more advanced security schemes. However, some very old wireless hardware will not support advanced security schemes, and so WEP is the only alternative.
WiFi Protected Access (WPA)	WPA provides better security than WEP, without requiring that wireless networking hardware (NICs and access points) be updated. That is WPA works with most older wireless devices.
WiFi Protected Access 2 (WPA2)	WPA2 provides the most secure encryption, however it requires modern wireless equipment. All new wireless networking hardware supports WPA2 (and some older hardware supports it as well).

You should always use the strongest encryption mechanism supported by your wireless hardware whenever possible.

Network Troubleshooting

 Exam 3 - Objective 2.3

Troubleshooting is the process of resolving problems by logically eliminating possible causes, and then finding and correcting the actual cause of the problem. Understanding how network hardware, network addressing and DNS work may help you troubleshoot some common Internet connectivity problems.

If you successfully eliminate the possible causes of a problem at your end of the connection and still cannot connect to the Internet, the problem may lie with your service provider. Call your ISP to see if there is a service outage, or to report one if they are unaware of a problem. If your service provider cannot verify that there is a service outage, you will most likely be connected to a Help Desk professional who will walk you through additional troubleshooting steps to help you resolve your connectivity issue.

Reviewing the Basics

This section will review the concepts covered in this lesson.

- In order for any computer to participate on a network, it needs a valid IP address.

- IP addresses are allocated to ISPs, who in turn allocate them to subscribers. When you (or your organization) purchase Internet service, your ISP gives you an IP address (or a range of IP addresses) to use. The IP address may be configured on the computer manually, but is generally leased to hosts automatically through the use the Dynamic Host Configuration Protocol (DHCP). Most server-based networks such as those used in companies and organizations support their own DHCP server. In home networks, the broadband modem or broadband router provides DHCP service and leases addresses to the systems connected to it automatically, so the user does not have to configure the address.

- Other required addressing information includes the default subnet mask and the address of the default gateway. The networking devices use the subnet mask to determine on which network a particular host resides. If the subnet mask is configured incorrectly, the computer will not be able to communicate with other hosts on the network. The address of the default gateway is the address of the device (usually a router) that leads outside the network. A system must know the address of the default gateway in order to access the Internet.

- In order for a computer to participate on an IP network, it needs a way to connect to the network. This is accomplished through a network interface card (either wired or wireless) and a transmission medium (either a cable or the open air).

- Network hosts connect to one another through a central connection device. In office or school settings, this is often a switch, switching hub or port in a wall jack. In home network settings, the central connection device is often a broadband modem or router. Most broadband modems and routers offer both wired and wireless connectivity.

- Domain Name System (DNS) is a service that allows you to enter user-friendly URLs instead of IP addresses into a browser address bar in order to locate web sites on the Internet. DNS maps domains to IP addresses. If the DNS server on your company network (or on your ISP's network) is down, you will not be able to navigate to web sites using URLs.

- To check if you are connected to a network, you can use the Network Sharing Center to view what connections are available to you and the status of the networks. Within this feature of the Control Panel, you can also view the IP address or DNS Server, as well as change the connection from one network to another, such as LAN to wireless. You will learn about the Network Sharing Center in the following exercise.

EXERCISE

In this exercise you will use the Network Sharing Center to check on the status of the connection for your computer, and view general information about the connections. The images provided in this exercise are meant for demonstration and comparison purposes; they will differ from what has been set up on your computer.

1. Click the **Start** button and click **Control Panel**. Then click **View network status and tasks**.

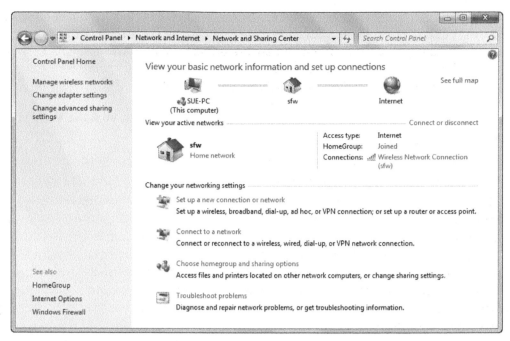

2. If there are any wireless connections available for your computer, click **Manage wireless networks** from the options in the left panel.

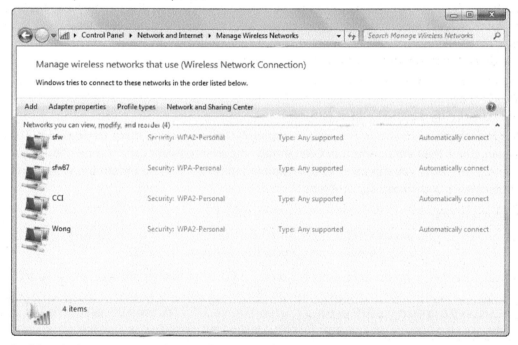

In this window, you can change the order of available wireless connections, add a new wireless connection, or view or change properties for the connection. Notice in our example that each of the connections has security set up where a password is required to be able to connect when within connection range.

3. Click the **Back** button to go back one window.

4. Click **Change adapter settings** from the options in the left panel.

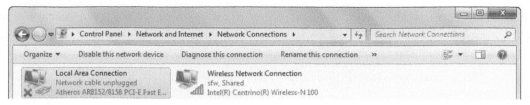

5. Click an active connection in the list and then on the Command bar, click the **View status of this connection**.

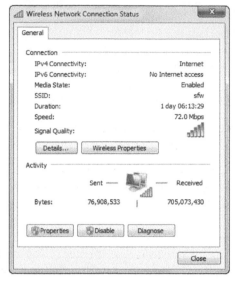

6. Click the **Details** button to view more information on the status of your connection.

7. Click **Close** to exit all windows.

Troubleshooting Hardware Issues

Although network hardware is required to support Internet access, most users seldom examine the devices to which they are connected. Even though the average user cannot repair hardware that is not functioning properly, anyone can examine simple indicators to help determine what particular issue might be causing a connectivity problem.

Indicator Lights

Almost all networking devices (NICs, hubs, switches, broadband routers/modems) include one or more indicator lights that relay information about how the device is performing.

Every NIC includes a green light emitting diode (LED) that flashes intermittently as information is transferred to and from the computer through the NIC. If you are unable to access the network, you can first visually examine the NIC to see if it is functioning. USB NICs are the easiest to see, and laptops and netbooks also include an indicator (usually on the keyboard) that is illuminated when the wireless NIC is active.

Most hubs and switches include an LED indicator for each connection port, and the indicator lights up when a device is properly connected to a port (through a network cable). Most broadband routers also include a green LED for each wired port, and the indicator lights up when a device is plugged into the port. If you are experiencing connectivity problems, trace your network cable to the router and ensure that the LED is lit on the port to which you are connected. If it is not, unplug the cable and plug it in again to create a secure connection. If the port LED still does not light up, try connecting to a different port. Depending on whether you are working on an organization's network or your home network, you should either notify someone in the IT department about the connection problem, or plan to purchase a new broadband router.

If a broadband router also functions as a wireless access point, the WLAN indicator light will be illuminated when the wireless function is turned on. If your wireless device cannot find the access point, make sure that the access point is turned on.

Broadband modems also include indicator lights for the following conditions: power on, sending signal, receiving signal, PC activity (this light comes on when the computer is connected to the modem), and Online (this light indicates that the modem has negotiated a successful connection with the provider's network). Visually inspect the modem to ensure all appropriate lights are on.

Firmware Updates

When you use a direct connection, such as DSL or cable, it is not uncommon for your service provider to periodically send firmware updates to your modem. Firmware updates affect the way in which hardware functions. Sometimes the modem will not function correctly after the installation of a firmware update until the device is powered off and then restarted. This process is similar to rebooting a computer system; power off the modem, wait a few moments, and then power it back on again.

There is no easy way to tell when a firmware update has been installed; therefore, if a modem was functioning properly and then suddenly stops working, the solution may be as simple as restarting it.

If you find it necessary to restart your broadband modem, it is considered best practice to also restart any other networking hardware devices connected to it – including broadband routers and VoIP devices or analog phone adapters.

Signal Quality Issues

The transmission of network signals is dependent on the transmission medium. The connections between the wires in an Ethernet cable and the contacts in the connector can sometimes work loose, or a wire may break somewhere in the middle of the cable. A damaged cable will not transmit signals. If you suspect that a cable is damaged, replace it with a new one. Ethernet cables are relatively inexpensive, and connecting and disconnecting an Ethernet cable is a simple matter of plugging it in or pulling it out (just like a telephone cord.)

An Ethernet cable that is not fully and securely connected cannot transmit signals correctly either. If you are experiencing network connectivity issues, a simple troubleshooting measure is to check the connections. If the cable is not plugged in properly, disconnect it and then reconnect it.

Certain conditions can also affect the strength and quality of wireless signals. Wireless signals can pass through office walls in most buildings, but the environment in which a wireless device operates limits its range. For example, a wireless access point operating in the open air might have a range of between 120 and 200 meters, but in a closed environment where signals must pass through wood or brick walls, the range is reduced to between 15 and 25 meters. In an environment where the signal must pass through metal reinforced walls, ceilings and elevator shafts, the signal range is reduced to 10 meters, and in some cases, the access point may not be able to sustain a connection at all.

In a corporate environment, the IT staff may consider adding more access points, placed at strategic positions throughout the workplace to boost the wireless signals. In a home environment, if you find that the wireless signal is not strong enough, you can try repositioning the antennas on the access point or moving the wireless client closer to the access point.

Wireless communications are also subject to interference from other devices (for example, microwave ovens, garage door openers, baby monitors) operating in the same frequency range. If you believe other devices are interfering with your wireless signals, avoid operating these devices, and/or move your wireless client further from the sources of the interfering signals.

To test what may be affecting your connection to the Internet try to connect to a LAN using an Ethernet cable only. If you can connect to the Internet in this way, then there may be an issue with the wireless router and you can begin troubleshooting steps to determine and resolve the issue.

Troubleshooting Addressing Issues

In order to participate successfully on the Internet, a computer must be configured with the proper IP address, subnet mask and default gateway. Together with other values, these three items constitute your system's network configuration settings.

End users do not normally specify these settings, and seldom make changes to them. In most cases, a computer automatically obtains these settings from a DHCP server. You may, however, be asked by a member of the IT staff or a member of your ISP's Help Desk team to view these settings and report on their current values. You can check your network configuration settings using a utility called IPCONFIG.

```
C:\Windows\system32\cmd.exe

Microsoft Windows [Version 6.1.7601]
Copyright (c) 2009 Microsoft Corporation.  All rights reserved.

C:\Users\AnotherAlto>ipconfig

Windows IP Configuration

Ethernet adapter Bluetooth Network Connection:

   Media State . . . . . . . . . . . : Media disconnected
   Connection-specific DNS Suffix  . :

Wireless LAN adapter Wireless Network Connection:

   Media State . . . . . . . . . . . : Media disconnected
   Connection-specific DNS Suffix  . :

Ethernet adapter Local Area Connection:

   Connection-specific DNS Suffix  . :
   Link-local IPv6 Address . . . . . : fe80::f96d:6d2:31ba:74fe%11
   IPv4 Address. . . . . . . . . . . : 192.168.1.2
   Subnet Mask . . . . . . . . . . . : 255.255.255.0
   Default Gateway . . . . . . . . . : 192.168.1.1
```

To use the IPCONFIG utility, perform the following steps:

1. Click **Start**.

2. In the Search box, type: cmd and press (Enter).

    This step opens a command prompt window.

3. In the command prompt window, type: ipconfig and press (Enter).

4. Look for the line that begins "IPv4 Address ..." to find the three required settings.

Even though you may not know what your IP address should be, you can easily recognize two IPv4 addresses that indicate a problem. These are:

0.0.0.0

169.254.x.x (where x can be any number between 0 and 255)

The 0.0.0.0 address is a special initialization address a system uses when it is trying to obtain an IP address from a DHCP server. If your system is using 0.0.0.0 as its IP address, it means that it was unable to reach the DHCP server and does not have a valid IP address.

If your system is using 169.254.x.x as its IP address (along with the subnet mask 255.255.0.0), it means that it was unable to reach the DHCP server and it has configured itself with an IP address using the Windows Automatic Private IP Addressing (APIPA) feature.

The APIPA address range (169.254.0.1 through 169.254.255.254) is a range of private IP addresses that cannot be used on the Internet. The system uses the self-configured IP address until a DHCP server becomes available.

If you check your configuration settings and see that your system is using either an initialization address or an APIPA address, it means that your system is unable to contact the DHCP server on the network.

Check first to ensure that your network cable is plugged in. If the cable is plugged in, and you are connected to your organization's network, your next step should be to the IT department. If you are working on a home network, you may need to restart your broadband modem or router.

Testing Connectivity with Addresses

In the previous lesson, you used the PING utility to test Internet connectivity. If you receive one or more reply messages, then connectivity is confirmed.

You can ping specific addresses to help determine where a break in connectivity may lie.

For example, if your NIC and network cable are functioning correctly, you should be able to successfully ping your own IP address.

If the NIC and cable are good and your network configuration settings are correct, you should be able to successfully ping other computer systems on the local network, and you should be able to ping the default gateway.

Further, if your Internet connection is functioning, you should be able to ping your ISP or your favorite web site by its IP address, assuming that the web site is configured to respond to ping requests. At the time of this writing, the web servers at Yahoo.com (www.yahoo.com) and CCI Learning (www.ccilearning.com) are configured to respond to ping requests, and you can ping them to test for Internet connectivity.

If you cannot ping the Yahoo or CCI Learning servers by domain name, try pinging them by IP address. The IP address for Yahoo is 72.30.38.140. The IP address for CCI Learning is 96.53.76.108. If you can successfully ping a web site by its IP address but not by its domain name, then the network (or ISP) DNS server is not functioning or is unreachable.

To use the ping utility, perform the following steps:

1. Click **Start**.

2. In the Search box, type: cmd and press (Enter). This step opens a command prompt window.

3. In the command prompt window, type: ping [ip_address] (where ip_address is the IP address of the system you are trying to reach) and press (Enter).

4. Look for reply messages to verify connectivity.

Troubleshooting Security Settings

Security settings can also cause connectivity issues.

Wireless Security

Most wireless LANs use an encryption scheme to protect access to the network and the network resources. Even hotels that offer free WiFi to guests may require that you enter a passphrase when attempting to connect to the network.

If you are having difficulty gaining access to a wireless network, make sure that you know the correct passphrase and that you are entering it correctly.

Participating on an encrypted wireless network requires that both the client and the access point are using the same encryption scheme (WEP, WPA or WPA2). Some wireless clients require that you specify which encryption scheme to use. Be sure that you specify the correct scheme. Ask the network administrator is you need assistance.

Firewall Configuration

Firewalls protect a computer system by blocking potentially dangerous communications from the outside. Determining what is "dangerous" is often a matter for the network administrator.

If you are using a system at your school or workplace and cannot use particular Internet applications, such as Instant Messaging, or cannot view videos from the Internet, ask the network administrator if these applications are blocked.

Depending on the company security policy and your ability to justify your need to use these blocked applications, the administrator may adjust the firewall settings to allow you to use these applications.

On a home network, you decide what is allowed through the firewall. When you install Internet-based programs, the installation procedure often opens the appropriate ports on the Windows firewall (assuming you have sufficient rights to install software).

If you experience problems using Internet-based applications, you can look on the vendor's web site for information on known issues concerning firewall settings, and then make the appropriate changes to the firewall.

EXERCISE

In this exercise, you will troubleshoot basic connectivity issues in your classroom. You will also consider specific scenarios and describe the steps required to resolve the problems described in each one.

Optional: During a break, your instructor will create connectivity problems for certain classroom systems. If your instructor has elected not to perform this part of the exercise, begin at Step 5.

1. As a class, work with your instructor to identify the problem on each of the affected systems.

2. Use the process of elimination to try to isolate the cause of each problem.

3. When you have isolated the cause of each problem, take the required steps to resolve the problem.

4. Test each system to confirm that the problem has been resolved.

5. As a class, consider the following scenarios, and identify the required steps to identify and resolve each problem.

    Scenario 1: Your home Internet connection has been functioning for months, and then one morning you discover that you cannot connect to the Internet.

    Use the ipconfig command to discover the IP address, subnet mask and default gateway. Make sure that the system is not using an initialization address or an APIPA address. If your system is using either of these addresses, try rebooting the modem, router and computer system.

If your system has a valid IP address, ping other systems on the local network or ping the default gateway to make sure the local hardware is functioning properly.

If you can ping other systems on the network or your default gateway, try to ping your ISP. If you can ping the default gateway, but not your ISP, try rebooting modem, router and the computer system.

If you reboot all the devices and still cannot obtain Internet access, call your ISP.

Scenario 2: You have just begun working for a new company. On your first day at work, you successfully log on to the network, and then successfully get out to the Internet. You download and install Skype, but when you try to log in to Skype, you cannot connect to the Skype server.

Since you can log on to the network and to the Internet, you already know that the networking hardware is functioning properly and that Internet connectivity is not the issue.

Ask your supervisor or someone in the IT department if instant messaging applications are allowed in the workplace. If they are not, you can to make a case for why they should be allowed.

Scenario 3: Your company has just expanded its office space and your entire department has been relocated to a different floor in the building. When you get to your new office, you discover that you cannot log on to the company network or get on to the Internet.

See if your co-workers are having the same problem. If more than one person is having connectivity problems, the problem may lie with some of the networking devices.

If no one else is having difficulty, check your network cable to make sure it is connected properly. If only one person in a local group is experiencing connectivity problems, it is likely that the problem lies with the individual computer system. After a moving an entire department, it is possible that an IT staff person forgot to connect your network cable.

Lesson Summary

In this lesson you examined the hardware, media and configuration settings that are required to connect to an organization's network or to the Internet. You should now be familiar with:

☑	the advantages of networking	☑	wide area networks (WANs)
☑	common network speeds	☑	analog and digital signaling
☑	common networking models	☑	methods for connecting to the Internet
☑	the role of TCP	☑	the role of the domain name system (DNS)
☑	local area networks (LANs)	☑	the need for security
☑	how wired and wireless connections work	☑	the role of firewalls and gateways
☑	addresses used on the LAN	☑	the use of virtual private networks (VPNs)
		☑	basic troubleshooting techniques

Review Questions

1. Which of the following data transfer speeds is the fastest?
    a. 3 Gbps   c. 300 Kbps
    b. 300 Mbps   d. 3,000,000 bps

2. Which of the following statements is true of an IP address?
    a. It is permanent.
    b. It is burned onto a NIC by the manufacturer.
    c. It identifies the network on which a host resides, and it identifies the particular host on the network.
    d. It is not required for Internet access.

3. Which of the following statements is true of a wide area network (WAN)?
    a. A WAN is usually confined to a small geographic area.
    b. A WAN is formed when two or more LANs are connected using a public network.
    c. A WAN is almost always faster than a LAN.
    d. A WAN is confined to the local cabling you install in your home or office.

4. What do POTS, ISDN and leased lines have in common?
    a. They all use circuit switching.
    b. They all use packet switching.
    c. They are all dial-up connections.
    d. They are all direct connections.

5. The term broadband refers to:
    a. any high-speed connection that uses circuit switching.
    b. any high-speed connection that is always "on".
    c. any high-speed dial-up connection.
    d. any type of connection that provides access to the Internet.

6. Which of the following can improve browsing performance on a dial-up connection?
    a. Suppressing the display of images.
    b. Opening multiple browser tabs to distribute the page loading task.
    c. Sharing the dial-up Internet connection with several computers.
    d. Opening an instant messaging application while browsing.

7. Which service enables users to access web sites by domain name instead of by IP address?
    a. DHCP   c. DSL
    b. DNS   d. APIPA

8. Which of the following statements accurately describes gateways and firewalls?
    a. Gateways use packet filtering to protect a network; firewalls can use packet filtering as well as more advanced techniques for controlling traffic flow.
    b. Firewalls use packet filtering to protect a network; gateways can use packet filtering as well as more advanced techniques for controlling traffic flow.
    c. Firewalls protect network resources while gateways protect sensitive information.
    d. Gateways protect network resources while firewalls protect sensitive information.

9. What does a virtual private network (VPN) provide?
    a. A security barrier that blocks incoming communication requests.
    b. Secure access into a private network from the outside.
    c. Security for wireless networks.
    d. An increase in web browsing performance.

10. Which wireless encryption scheme provides the strongest level of protection?
    a. WEP   c. WPA
    b. WEP2   d. WPA2

MMM
Go online for
Additional
Review

Lesson 14: Digital Communication

Lesson Objectives

In this lesson you will be introduced to different communication methods and means of sharing information, with an emphasis on using electronic mail. On completion, you will be familiar with:

- ☐ different types of electronic communication
- ☐ identifying users on communication systems
- ☐ different communication methods
- ☐ appropriate uses for electronic communication
- ☐ advantages of electronic communication
- ☐ how an email address is structured
- ☐ identifying email components
- ☐ using attachments effectively
- ☐ understanding how to deal with junk mail
- ☐ common problems with electronic communication

How Can I Communicate with Others?

 Exam 3 - Objective 3.1, 3.2, 4.1

Communication refers to any process that enables you to interact with others. Electronic communication is simply communication that involves using an electronic method such as email, instant/text messaging or video conferencing.

There are two essential time frames for communication: real-time and delayed. In real-time communication, information is sent and received instantly. A face-to-face conversation is an example of real-time communication. If Mary and Bob are having a face-to-face talk, then as soon as Mary says something, Bob hears it. Additionally, Bob can respond immediately. And as soon as Bob says something in reply, Mary hears his reply.

In delayed communication, there is a time delay between the sending and receiving of information. A mailed letter is an example of delayed communication. Mary writes Bob a letter. She puts the letter in an envelope, addresses and stamps the envelope and drops it off at the post office. In a few days, a letter carrier delivers Mary's letter to Bob's mailbox. When Bob comes home from work, he checks the mail, brings it inside, and then opens and reads Mary's letter.

In this lesson, you will explore methods of electronic communication that occur in real time, and you will explore methods that incur a delay.

Electronic Mail (Email)

Like postal mail, a valid address is required to send messages; however, the messages are sent electronically using an account provided by an ISP or your organization. Email is also similar to postal mail in that just as the recipient of a letter need not be at home in order for the mail to be delivered, an intended email recipient need not be logged on to an email program in order to receive an electronic message. An email Inbox is very much like a postal mail mailbox. Letters sit in a mailbox until the recipient opens the box and brings in the mail. Email messages sit in a recipient's Inbox until that person logs on and checks for messages.

Email is a standard and popular method for exchanging business communications and personal messages when a response is not urgent. Some popular programs used for email include Microsoft Outlook, Google Gmail, or Apple Mail. Email is likely the most popular means of electronic communication as it provides businesses (and individuals) with a documented trail of the communications that have taken place between one or more contacts. Email is also tremendously popular as a means of sharing files sent as email attachments.

Instant Messages

Sometimes called IM, this type of electronic communication allows two or more participants to "converse" with one another in real time by typing messages into the window of an instant messaging program. Instant messaging programs such as Microsoft Lync, Skype, ICQ, Google Talk, or Yahoo! Messenger enable people to "chat" with each other, regardless of where they are located. For example, two participants may be working on different floors of the same office building, and a third participant might be working in an office across town. Instant messaging is a very useful means of communication to use when an answer is needed quickly.

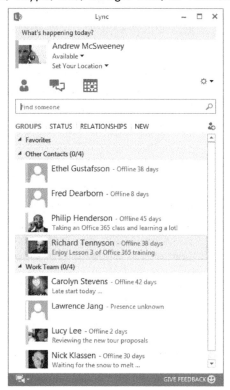

In order to use an instant messaging program, you must create an account with a username and password. Many instant messaging clients are associated with online services, such as an email account. For example, if you have a Microsoft Account, you can use your username and password to sign into Microsoft Lync (a program included with Microsoft Office 365), or you can message someone in the Contacts list of Outlook.com using the one account.

The figure is an example of the popular Microsoft Lync communications program commonly used in a business environment, and a quick look at this program. You will find that all instant message programs share similar features and it is a matter of determining where the command is located in that program. For instance, the Yahoo! instant messaging program refers to contacts as Buddies.

Information Bar	Enter a brief description of what you are working on, something you want to draw attention to, such as an upcoming company event or the release of a new product.
Profile	Name of person signed in along with a picture and two fields identifying your availability status and your location.
View Icons	The first three icons enable you to view contacts, view conversations, or view any meetings scheduled for the current day.
Options Icon	At the far right is the gear icon that allows you to change settings for how Lync works.
Show Menu button	Click this button to display other actions you can perform such as sign out of the program and start an online meeting with someone else. You can also choose to display the menu bar at all times.
Display Options	Choose the tab to view the contacts, such as in groups, by status, relationship, or the new contacts you added but have not organized as yet.

Add Contact	Add a contact to your list of people you want to share instant messages.
List of Contacts	Displays the contacts in noted categories, starting with Favorites and other groups you can create.
Primary Device Icon	Icon indicates which input and output devices are available. In this example, we have both a PC microphone and speakers available.

Many people consider instant messaging to be less intrusive than a phone call, because even though the message recipient sees the message instantly, he or she is not required to respond immediately. For example, suppose Carolyn sends an instant message to Andrew asking about the location of a particular file. Andrew receives the message, but is currently speaking with a colleague. Andrew can send a quick instant message to Carolyn indicating that he is currently on the phone, but will be with her in a few minutes. Andrew can then conclude his phone call, and send an instant message to Carolyn indicating that he is now available to assist her. The instant message conversation can proceed from there.

Some instant message programs enable you to chat with contacts regardless of the operating system, but you will not be able to connect using different messaging programs. You can however choose to import the contacts from one program into the common program you and your contacts will be using. For example, if you used to chat via MSN Live Messenger, the list of contacts can be imported into Outlook.com for instant messaging; likewise one of your contacts can import their list of contacts from Yahoo! Messenger into Outlook.com so the two of you can chat.

Be very careful not to share or give out passwords or credit card numbers in an instant message. Exchanges made through instant messaging programs travel across the Internet, and these communications are not always secure. In addition to sending instant messages, most IM programs allow you to:

- share web links
- chat face-to-face with other users who have a webcam
- send pictures or videos

- send files
- play sounds
- use the computer as a telephone (if you have a headset)

Using Multimedia Features

Most IM programs also allow live audio and video to be exchanged in real-time. Programs such as Skype, iChat, FaceTime or Google Talk include features that support live video-conferencing. These programs are immensely popular when you want to "visit and share" with people globally in a very cost effective manner.

You need to have an account that you can use to log into a service before you can use these types of programs, as well as have the proper hardware such as a webcam, microphone, and speakers installed before you can see or hear others. If only one party has the appropriate equipment, video and sound can still be transmitted from that computer but the other party will be limited to text only conversation.

Depending on the device you use to communicate with someone else, you may be using the mouse or keyboard to activate features or push physical buttons, such as a device within a car or a cellular phone.

OPTIONAL EXERCISE

In this optional exercise, you will watch a few videos that demonstrate instant messaging.

1. Your instructor will decide whether to show each video to the class on a main viewing screen, or to allow each student to view individually. If you do watch these videos individually, be sure to use your headset so that you will not disturb other students in the class.

2. In the web browser type the following addresses into the address bar, one at a time to watch the presentations:

URL	Title	Length (mins)
http://www.youtube.com/watch?v=X 5f4fj7GfM8	What Is I.M. or Instant Messaging?	1:12
http://www.youtube.com/watch?v=Y 02zsfrG_PA	Microsoft Lync: Instant Messaging, Telephony, Video Conferencing and Meetings	1:48
http://office.microsoft.com/en-us/videos/video-instant-messaging-in-lync-2013-VA104023130.aspx?CTT=5&origin=HA104030774&client=1	Instant Messaging in Lync	00:50

Text Messages

Text messages are similar to instant messages except they are sent over a cellular provider's network using a protocol called Short Message Service (SMS). Text messages are created and sent from cellular phones (or other similar mobile devices). As the name of the protocol implies, the number of characters allowed per message is limited (about 100 to 200 characters per message, depending on the service provider). You can send a text message to one person or to many people, however the message may take longer to reach certain recipients, depending on the cellular network involved. The figure shows six text messages that form a conversation.

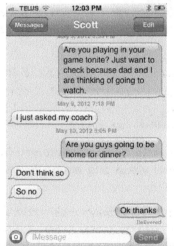

In addition to Short Message Service, many cellular providers offer Multimedia Messaging Service (MMS), which provides a standard way to send messages that include multimedia content to and from mobile phones or other suitably equipped mobile devices.

This service allows users to send photographs and video to other users, as well as mobile updates such as breaking news or weather updates As with plain text messaging, you can send multimedia messages to one or more people, but the speed for sending and receiving may be slower depending on the size of the message or the speed of service provided by your cellular provider.

Text messaging can be useful when no other forms of communication are available or when the intended recipient cannot be reached through a phone call. For example, if you just found a supplier of specialized paper for printing marketing materials, you can text a colleague at the office to continue printing on existing stock until you return with the new supply.

Crossing Over

Electronic messages can in many instances be ported from one method of communication to another. For example, you can send an SMS message to a cell phone using email.

Most cell phone providers have a special email address that you can send a message to, which then gets forwarded as a text message to the cell phone. For example with Verizon in the U.S., you can email cellnumber@vtext.com, where "cellnumber" is the recipient's 10 digit cellular number. The message will be sent as a text message to that phone. Other carriers typically have some type of equivalent and/or a web page from which you can send a text message to one of their phones. Several are listed in the following table:

Provider	Email address
Alltel	cellnumber@message.alltel.com
AT&T	cellnumber@txt.att.net
Bell	cellnumber@txt.bell.ca
Boost	cellnumber@myboostmobile.com
Nextel	cellnumber@messaging.nextel.com
Rogers	cellnumber@pcs.rogers.com
Sprint PCS	cellnumber@messaging.sprintpcs.com
T-Mobile	cellnumber@tmomail.net
Virgin Mobile	cellnumber@vmobl.com

Additionally, many cell phone providers will allow you to enter a text message on their web site and send it to a cell phone on their network.

Cell phones can be used to send email messages and to send and receive instant messages; however, the phones must be Internet capable, and you must be subscribed to an Internet data plan.

VoIP

Voice over Internet Protocol (VoIP), allows you to make voice calls using a broadband Internet connection instead of a traditional (analog) telephone line. VoIP, also known as *Internet telephony* or *Voice over Broadband (VoBB),* converts analog voice signals into digital data packets, adds addressing information to each packet, and then sends the packets across a data network (such as the Internet). Many businesses use VoIP services because they are less expensive than traditional telephone services, especially for long-distance calling.

You can make or receive a VoIP call on your computer using special software called a softphone application and a headset. You can also use a dedicated VoIP phone, or even a traditional telephone in conjunction with a special analog telephone adapter. In each case, you must be connected (either through a wired connection or wirelessly) to a network that provides VoIP services.

Residential consumers can purchase VoIP phone service through their ISP (if the services are offered), or through a third party service provider such as Vonage. The provider will usually supply the required equipment.

Many businesses choose to implement their own VoIP solutions by modifying their existing data networks to support phone services. While implementing VoIP can help businesses realize a substantial cost savings, there is often a steep learning curve involved, and in many cases the existing data network must be substantially modernized to support the demands of carrying voice.

Video Conferencing

Video conferencing allows people in geographically distant locations to participate in a conference with one another. Attendees at each location gather around a table in a room equipped with a video camera, microphone, video screen and speakers. (In some setups, only cameras and screens are used, and audio information is relayed over a conference telephone.)

Video cameras at each location record the attendees, and the videoconferencing software sends the recorded data (usually over the Internet) to the other locations in real time, much like a live broadcast. The intention of videoconferencing is to allow participants to see nonverbal communication and has often been advertised as "the next best thing to being there."

In practice, however, most videoconferencing systems are nothing like being there. The videocast images are too small, or the cameras do not capture hand and arm motions, or the participants appear to be looking away from the camera.

Some manufacturers, such as Cisco systems, offer *telepresence* systems to enable long-distance business meetings over high-speed networks. Telepresence systems are reported to be a vast improvement over standard videoconferencing systems. They require the following:

1.   A camera that is optically aligned with the eyes of the person on the screen.
2.   A life-size image with upper body arm gestures clearly visible. For desktop conferencing, smaller images are acceptable but no less than about 70% of life-size.
3.   Correct cultural distance where the image of the person is at table height and the image resides just beyond that, as if sitting on the other side of a meeting table.
4.   Image that is broadcast quality or better in resolution.
5.   Audio quality that is superior – voices sound crisp and clean, free from distortion.

Although business telepresence systems can save money on travel, these products are expensive to purchase and install, and are not in wide use.

In some systems, control of the screen can be assigned to someone in the audience. This is a useful way to conduct online training sessions or meetings that include employees in remote locations. In fact, some systems allow you to record the session so you can then share it with others.

Another feature of telepresence programs is the ability to give permission or grant access to someone else, as in the case of allowing someone to take a presenter role until you take back control. This feature is very beneficial when you are conducting online training sessions and someone at a remote site needs to show something about a product to the rest of the audience.

EXERCISE

In this exercise you will watch some videos with general information regarding online presentations, and how to use conferencing tools for various purposes.

1.   Your instructor will decide whether to show each video to the class on a main viewing screen, or to allow each student to view individually. If you do watch these videos individually, be sure to use your headset so that you will not disturb other students in the class.

2. In the web browser type the following addresses into the address bar, one at a time to watch the presentations:

URL	Title	Length (mins)
http://www.youtube.com/watch?v=yU0kYO2UAgU	What Is Microsoft Lync Online	2:01
http://office.microsoft.com/en-us/videos/video-make-a-video-call-in-lync-2013-VA104027273.aspx?CTT=5&origin=HA104030774&client=1	Make a Video Call in Lync	01:21
http://office.microsoft.com/en-us/lync-help/video-share-desktop-and-programs-in-lync-2013-VA104036199.aspx?CTT=5&origin=VA104036814	Share Desktop and Programs in Lync 2013	01:21
http://www.youtube.com/watch?v=n-BdHXv80fY	Web Conferencing vs. Video Conferencing	1:17

3. Close the web browser when finished.

Chat Rooms

Chat rooms are designated areas on the Internet where people with similar interests can communicate with each other by typing on a keyboard. Participating in a chat room is similar to using instant messaging; however, when you join a chat room, any message you post to the chat room will be visible to all members of the chat room. That is, you cannot direct a message to only specific individuals within the chat room.

People from anywhere in the world can join a chat room and most chat rooms are categorized by topic, so users can find conversations that interest them. A chat room may include a moderator who monitors the content of the conversation in order to prevent abuse.

Most chat rooms are text based although some newer versions use video as well; others offer games for multiple players. An example of how you could use a chat room in business would be to conduct a survey with existing customers about potential new products and then set up different chat rooms for discussion on specific products.

Social Networking Sites

Social networking sites are web sites you can join to connect with people you know and to meet new people as well. You must create an account on a social networking site before you can use it. To create an account, you select a username and password. You will use this username and password to log into your account, and these are associated with your personal profile.

When you create a profile on a social networking site, the site creates a page for you. You can then post pictures, video, or text about yourself on your page. Many social networking sites also include games you can play by simply allowing the game application to access your profile information.

You can invite other people to display links to their profiles on your page, and other people can invite you to do the same. You can access your page from anywhere in the world that has an Internet connection, giving you the option to update your page at any time.

Some people use social networking sites to find old friends and keep in touch with current ones; other people use business networking sites to widen their professional contact lists. A company may also set up a page on a social networking site to promote a service or product they offer, as in the case of a radio station with a dedicated page for popular radio personalities.

Examples of different social networking sites used around the world include Myspace, Facebook, Badoo, Skyblog, Twitter, LinkedIn, Orkut, Flixter, Friendster, Migente, Bebo, Studivz, Xing, etc.

Facebook is currently the most popular social networking site and is estimated to have over 900 million users worldwide. Each user can customize his or her site to share text or photos, as well as play games with others online.

EXERCISE

In this exercise you will navigate to various social networking web sites so you can see how the information is designed to be shared by multiple people.

1. In the Address field of the web browser, type: `www.facebook.com` and press `Enter`.

2. If you already have an account with Facebook, log in and view the contents on the home page.

   What type of information is displayed on the page? How does the information for your login differ from others in the class who may also have an account with Facebook?

3. In the Address field, type: `www.pinterest.com` and press `Enter`.

   Pinterest is a different type of social networking site, considered a pinboard, where members can upload anything they find interesting and people can then comment on it. This site has been very popular for gathering ideas for decorating, wedding, or menu planning.

4. In the Address Bar, type: `www.livejournal.com` and press `Enter`.

   Live Journal is a social networking site that has over 37 million users globally where you can keep a blog, diary, or journal of a topic of interest to you. As you can see, there are numerous other topics or features you can access once you have an account in addition to keeping the journal for your own interests.

5. Leave the web browser active for the next exercise.

Blogs

Blogs are online journals that include a communications element. Generally, the blog creator publishes or "posts" an article about a specific topic, and others can then post comments in response. Blogs can also include links to other peoples' blogs. These links are sometimes called trackbacks.

To create a blog, you simply navigate to a blog site and create an account. Most sites include templates that enable you to start posting articles immediately. To post an article to your blog, you must sign in using the username and password you select when you create the account. You can also send a link to your blog to other users.

Below are several blog sites you can visit to create your own blog:

- Blogger   www.blogger.com
- WordPress   wordpress.com
- Tumblr   www.tumblr.com
- Xanga   www.xanga.com
- Weebly   www.weebly.com

Creating and maintaining a blog can help an individual become a recognized authority about a specific topic or within a specific field, and you can search blog sites for answers to questions on almost any subject.

A company may set up a blog area on its web site to encourage customers to offer suggestions for improvements, discuss problems regarding a service or product or share fixes for issues. Often, you are required to register with a blog site before you can submit comments.

In addition to the more popular blog sites noted earlier, many larger web sites such as Disney or sites for television stations include an area for blogging.

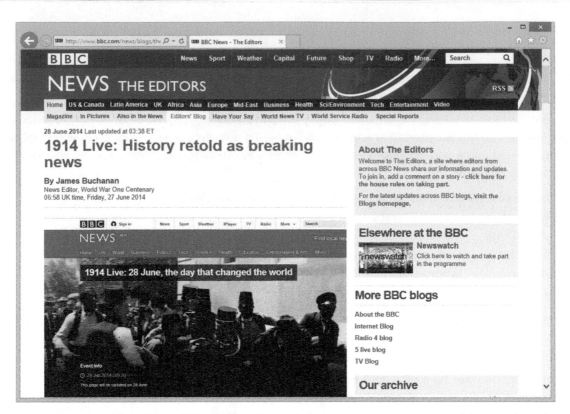

The term, *microblogging*, refers to the process where you can update your blog entries. An example of this would be Twitter where people can enter a small amount of text to publish an update to their status or to express/reply to an opinion. These small messages can also be referred to as *microposts.* The status update option in a social networking site such as Facebook is another example of microblogging.

Twitter is a popular social networking service; however it has a restriction of no more than 140 characters that can be entered as a text-based message known as a "tweet". When you need to include a URL in a post but it causes you to exceed the maximum characters, you can shorten the URL using a service such as bitly.com or Tiny URL. This effectively shortens the URL for the audience but still links to the full URL address when clicked. For instance, to tweet a post that included a link to the CCI web site to view information available for the IC³ certification, the full address for this URL is: http://ccilearning.com/solutions/ic3-digital-literacy/. Using a service that shortens the URL, this would become http://bit.ly/1rjFMPE. This link is much shorter to include in the tweet.

Shortening the URL for a web address does not have to be for a microblog only; another reason someone might shorten the web address is to change the display of the original address as in the case of someone or a small business whose web site is set up on an ISP. In this case, the owner may wish for clients to use a link that displays the company name instead. Shortened URLs can also be used in emails as well as other social networking sites such as Facebook. These types of services are usually free and may require you to create an account to use the service. Some services offer the option to view statistics based on the type of feedback you receive on shortened URLs you create.

EXERCISE

In this exercise you will look at some of the more popular blog sites to learn how they gather or share information through the interactions of blog members. Notice that each site may require you to set up an account before you can post comments.

1.   In the Address field of a web browser, type: `www.huffingtonpost.com` and press (Enter).

The Huffington Post is a very popular blog site for the most recent news or postings for local or world news.

2. Scroll through the page to see what other information you can view.

3. In the Address field, navigate to: `www.pinterest.com`.

4. In the Address field, navigate to: `www.businessfinder.com`.

Now try navigating to a blog created by a commercial enterprise. As seen with some of the social media sites, some business may require you to set up an account before you can post anything.

5. Navigate to: `http://ccilearning.com/blog`.

6. Scroll to view any of the articles and notice how you can enter comments about the blog.

In this case, CCI Learning is interested in getting feedback from you but does not require you to register your information prior to making a comment or viewing information or feedback from other people. You should also notice the tabs at the left side of the screen that will link you to other media sites to post information, such as Facebook, Twitter, or LinkedIn.

7. Navigate to: `http://blogs.office.com`.

This blog site is similar to the CCI Learning blog site in that you can make comments or navigate to other social media sites to post your comments there instead.

Let's now take a look at one of the sites that offers a service to shorten URL addresses.

8. In the Address field, navigate to: `www.bitly.com` and press (Enter).

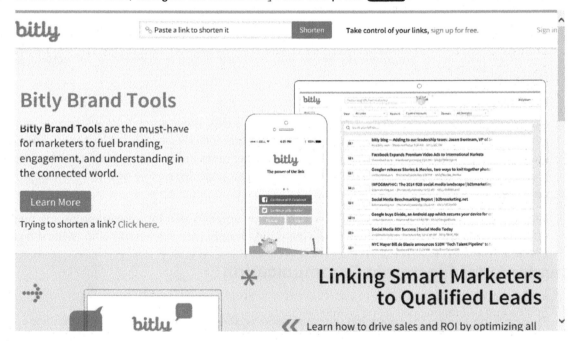

9. Review the content on this page to understand how this service works.

This type of service is very useful when you want to include a link to a web address that may be long in length; given that many social media sites have a limit on the number of characters you can use for each post, it is helpful to be able to shorten the address link. Notice how you can set up an account to be updated on news with this organization, but you don't need to create an account to shorten an address link.

10. Close the web browser.

Presence

When used in the context of communication applications, presence refers to the ability to determine the status of your contacts at a given time. In other words, you can tell at a glance whether someone you want to communicate with is online and available. In cases where a contact is not available, you may be able to determine the reason for the unavailability, and perhaps even the duration.

In instant messaging programs, presence indicators include Online (available for communications), Busy (currently engaged in other activities), Away (not at the desk or not in the office), and Do Not Disturb (in but not available at the moment). You can manually change your status at any time.

Some options, such as Be Right Back or Out to Lunch, are more specific and give others an idea of how long you'll be unavailable. You may also be able to enter a custom status message, such as "Be back on Tuesday." or "Gone for the day."

Many programs allow you to make yourself appear to be offline when you're actually online. This allows you to see which of your contacts are online, but prevents your contacts from interrupting you. Appearing offline is akin to being invisible while you are logged on. You can then change your status to "Available" or "Online" when you are ready to receive communications.

Your presence indicator may also tell others whether you have a Webcam for video calling/conferencing. Most programs will detect if a Webcam is available for video and will provide the option to turn it off any time during the conference – preferably before it starts so the audience isn't surprised when video is no longer available.

You may also be able to configure your communications software to change your status automatically. For example, you can configure Outlook.com to set your status to Away if you're inactive for a specified period of time or to automatically show you as Busy if you're running a full-screen program or presentation.

Social Media and Access Control

Some social media sites include presence indicators that show when you are online (and therefore available for chat). An example of this is Facebook that includes a chat option; you can change your chat status to offline although you may be doing other tasks in Facebook. Most social media sites also give you a fair deal of control over who can view your page (everyone or only friends/contacts), who can view your profile information, and who can post comments on your page.

When you post comments on someone else's page, you can also indicate whether you want to share your comment with everyone who views the page, or only with the person who owns the page.

Standards for Electronic Communication

 Exam 3 - Objective 4.1

There are no fixed rules regarding communications; there are, however, some guidelines and widely accepted standards to consider when using electronic communications. These include:

- Email should never completely replace another form of communication; before you choose email, think about the purpose of your message, the response you are seeking, and how quickly you need it. For instance, if you need technical support on a software issue immediately, it may be faster to call the vendor or the IT department than to send an email. If a situation is best resolved by speaking to someone directly, use the telephone or seek a face-to-face meeting.

- Keep in mind that email or text messages are not real-time communication. Email messages (and responses) can be subject to delay – especially if the recipient is away from their device for any length of time.

- When writing a message, think about your audience. For instance, a business or school email should have a professional tone and follow general business practices for correspondence. Even when writing a simple text or instant message to a friend, give some thought to what and how you are writing. For example, are you using acronyms or shortened versions of words (such as using "u" instead of "you"), and will the recipient understand these? Are you including punctuation in the message? If the recipient uses the same format as you do for messages, they will understand what these mean whereas a recipient who does not send a lot of text messages may find it difficult to comprehend the message content.

- Be as clear and concise as possible.

- Always check spelling and grammar before sending your message, especially when sending messages to business contacts. Proofread the message to be sure it makes sense and is easy to understand. If the message includes hyperlinks, test the links to ensure that they work properly. Remember that your email represents your organization or school and should reflect the appropriate image.

- Consider the length of your message; for email, if the message requires you to scroll more than two screen lengths, it may be best to send it as an attachment, provide a link to further information, or contact the person directly. Additional details such as pricing lists, assignments, or catalog items should be provided as secondary references. The same principle holds true for text and instant messages; if the message requires much explanation, it may be best to call the person directly. The intent of messaging is to send information in a concise manner. When replying to a message, consider how much of the previous message needs to appear in your reply. For instance, if this is the fourth time you've replied to the same message, this reply will contain the entire history of this communication (or the entire email "string" or "thread"). In some cases, you may want to keep this as an official record; in other situations, it may not be necessary to show the history and you can delete the earlier responses from the body of the message.

- Remember that business emails are official company correspondence; file and archive them using the appropriate folders in your email program. This applies to all messages you send or receive using an email address provided by your organization or academic institution. This may also be true if you are sending messages using a mobile device that is owned and paid for by an organization.

- Use discretion when sending messages to multiple people. Does everyone need to receive this message? What is the purpose of this message and who needs this information?

- When replying to a message that was sent to several recipients, consider whether it is necessary for everyone who received it to read your reply; you may need to respond to the originator only. For example, suppose your supervisor sends an email reminding you to submit your travel budget so he/she can complete the department budget; he/she might Cc the Accounting department as a courtesy, to show them that more information is needed. In this case, your reply should be sent only to your supervisor.

- If the message contains confidential or sensitive information, or requires a signature for approval, consider which the best method of communication is, and whether using a traditional hard copy might be better.

- Be careful sending messages with personal jibes, ethnic jokes, or bad language, even to people you know, as they can easily be misinterpreted or forwarded to other people who may take offense.

- Avoid "flaming" people. A *flame* is an email or chat room message that personally attacks the recipient. Such messages have no place in business or school communication, informal or personal communication, or instant messaging. If you have been flamed, it is best to ignore it. If you respond in kind, this may lead to an escalation which is referred to as a "flame war."

- Refrain from using all uppercase letters in your message as this is considered "shouting". Use shouting with utmost discretion. ALL CAPITALS is hard to read; if you want to indicate emphasis, use bold text instead. Whenever possible, use the correct casing for the message text, and use appropriate punctuation so everyone understands what is being said in your message or post.

- Avoid making false or malicious comments about a person as this is considered libel. This is also true regarding bullying or harassing someone in any manner.

- Refrain from using abbreviations and acronyms in business or school communications, even when sending personal messages or using an instant or text messaging program. As not everyone is familiar with these, it can lead to misinterpretation or confusion. This includes *emoticons,* which are symbols that attempt to convey to the recipient the sender's emotion.

Common Text Acronyms	
411	Information request
brb	Be right back
i<3u	I heart or love you
l8r	Later
lol	Laugh out loud
np	No problem
ppl	People
rofl	Rolling on floor laughing
tmi	Too much information
ttyl	Talk to you later

- Remember that sites that encourage you to join and contribute personal information such as photos or videos are accessible by the general public, particularly via the many social networking sites and blogs available on the Web. Keep this in mind when deciding what you want to post about yourself (or others) and who might see it.

- Use *netiquette,* or good manners, in all electronic communication, whether it is for business or personal purposes. Remember that electronic modes of communication tend to be very open to misinterpretation. Always remember that the recipient cannot see your face, and that it is very difficult to convey tone in a written message. For example, a sarcastic remark meant as a joke can easily hurt someone's feelings. Try to treat others in the same manner that you want to be treated, online or in person.

- Always try to respond to messages in a timely manner. Not all messages require an immediate response, but when a message contains a question or requires further action, be sure to send an appropriate reply.

- Consider the frequency of your posting – how important is the information, and how many people have responded to the first post?

- Always follow the rules and guidelines established by your school or organization (and local, regional and national laws if appropriate) regarding electronic communications.

Working with Email

 Exam 3 - Objective 3.1

In order to use email, you must have an email account. An email account can be provided by your ISP, provided by your school or organization, or provided by a Web-based email provider such as Outlook, Live, Hotmail, iCloud, Zoho, Yahoo! or Gmail.

An email address is structured as follows:

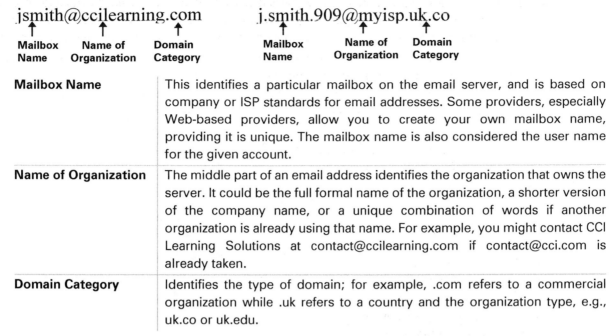

Mailbox Name	This identifies a particular mailbox on the email server, and is based on company or ISP standards for email addresses. Some providers, especially Web-based providers, allow you to create your own mailbox name, providing it is unique. The mailbox name is also considered the user name for the given account.
Name of Organization	The middle part of an email address identifies the organization that owns the server. It could be the full formal name of the organization, a shorter version of the company name, or a unique combination of words if another organization is already using that name. For example, you might contact CCI Learning Solutions at contact@ccilearning.com if contact@cci.com is already taken.
Domain Category	Identifies the type of domain; for example, .com refers to a commercial organization while .uk refers to a country and the organization type, e.g., uk.co or uk.edu.

The *jsmith@ccilearning.com* address indicates that the address belongs to someone at a commercial company called CCI Learning. A fairly common company standard for mailbox names is to use your first initial followed by your last name. In the example email address, the user's first name begins with "J" and the user's last name is "Smith."

The j.smith909@myisp.uk.co email address suggests this address belongs to someone with the same first initial and last name as many other people; the number "909" helps to make this address unique. The account is with a company called My ISP, which is located in the United Kingdom.

Other common domains include .edu for education sites, .gov for government, or .org for non-profit organizations. Take note that not all commercial companies use .com and may use a domain code to represent the country of origin. For example, an email address that ends in ebay.ca is an indicator that this person works at the Canadian office of eBay, whereas an email address that ends in louvre.fr indicates this person works at the Louvre in France. You must be precise when you enter a person's email address if you want to ensure that your message will be sent to the intended recipient. Every email address within a given domain must be unique. For example, suppose both Jane Smith and John Smith want to create a Hotmail account. John creates his account first, and uses the address jsmith@hotmail.com. Jane cannot create her account at Hotmail using the same name. She could, however, create an account using the address jsmith747@hotmail.com (assuming no one else has already created an account using that address). Jane could, however, use jsmith if she were to create her account on a different domain. For example, she could be jsmith@yahoo.com or jsmith@live.com.

Usernames, Passwords and Credentials

Once you create an email account (or have one created for you by a network administrator), you will be required to log in to the account before you can send or receive email.

To log in to an email server, you must supply a valid user name and password. On most company accounts and ISP accounts, the user name is the mailbox name (for example, jsmith). In some Web-based email accounts the user name is the mailbox name, and in others the entire email address including the domain name (jsmith@hotmail.com) constitutes the user name. All mail servers have the ability to detect if the email address you chose has been used before and you may find you will need to add some characters or be creative in the name selection. There are standard guidelines you can follow when choosing a username; most companies will require you to follow company policy or choose one on your behalf. For personal accounts, consider what type of messages will be sent or the purpose for setting up this account. For example, if you want to create a web-based email account that will store potential junk messages from subscriptions or purchases made online, you may want to create a username that doesn't clearly identify you, similar to an alias, such as am123890, 4sports-now, h33holland, and so on.

You should follow standard guidelines for creating a password for an email account; in fact, many email programs list the requirements you must meet to create a password. Most require a minimum number of characters and specify that one or more must be non-alphabetic characters. Some programs even display a scale indicating the strength of the password as you create it.

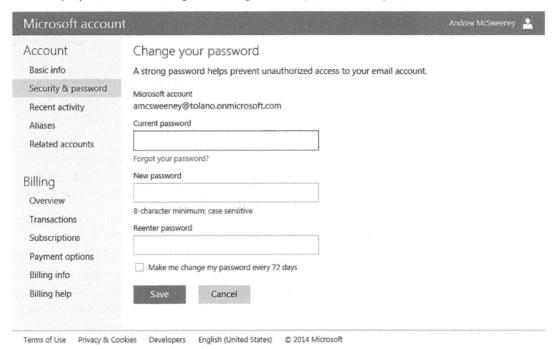

When selecting a secure password consider the following:

- Use a minimum of six characters in length (or based on standards set up by the school or organization.)

- Include a mixture of numbers, casing, or a symbol within the password, such as amc-1983:08, 55DrewM.

- Avoid using names of people close to you such as a spouse, child, or pet; if someone knows you well enough they will try to guess your password using these names first.

- Try to choose a password that is logical but not obvious so you can also remember it; as you begin to create accounts for yourself on a variety of web sites, you will want to be able to remember which password is associated with which account.

- Avoid using the same password for every account; at most, try to have approximately five different passwords, or choose one that will be long and difficult to guess such as aM:20154-D77M.

- Avoid using a variation of a password that may be easy to guess, such as Password-Jan, Password-Feb, password001, password 003, DrewJ12, DrewF12, pa$$w0rd, etc.

Together, your user name and password constitute your email credentials. Credentials must be presented to the email server when you log on to check or send email.

It is highly important to keep your user name and password confidential. No one except you and the email server should know your password – not even the network administrator. Keeping your username and password confidential protects not only your email account but any online account or social media application that is associated with your email account.

Consider for a moment all the things you do online. Do you do your banking online? Pay credit card bills online? Subscribe to newsletters? How many of these activities are tied to your email address?

Many email client programs provide settings that allow the program to store your username and password so that all you need to do to log in is launch the application. The email client automatically sends the stored username and password to the email server. This is considered a safe practice within a company email system, but is not a particularly safe practice for Web-based email accounts. If you use a public computer, or share a computer with other users, you should never select the option to remember your password, as other users can log in to your email if they know your username.

The following demonstration illustrates that the email server checks the credentials for a user before the user is allowed to log into the account, or make any changes for that account. This example uses Outlook.com as the main email program and the user (Andrew McSweeney) will add a previously established personal email account as an alias to his Outlook.com account so that messages from both email servers are delivered to one location and can be viewed on any computing device connected to the Internet.

1. Start the web browser and navigate to: `www.outlook.com`.

2. At the sign in screen, enter the Microsoft account ID and password.

   Microsoft has reviewed and validated the information provided by this user as a registered account on their email server.

Now let's take a look at how Andrew can combine his personal email into this location.

3. At the top right of the screen, click your name and click **Account Settings**. In the panel at the left, click **Aliases**.

4. If you have recently created the account or share the computer with other users, you will see a screen similar to the following asking you to verify your account before it will show you any aliases associated with your account:

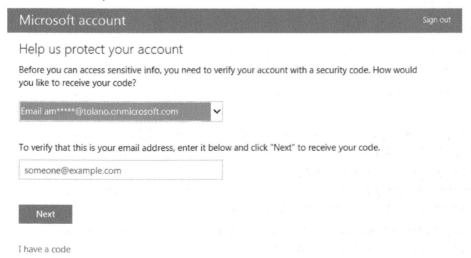

Enter your email address to verify the account and click **Next**.

You will now need to obtain the code from a message sent by Microsoft before you are able to view any aliases. Once you enter the code into the preceding screen, click **Submit**. Notice how you can also click the **I sign in frequently on this device. Don't ask me for a code.** if you are the main user of this computer.

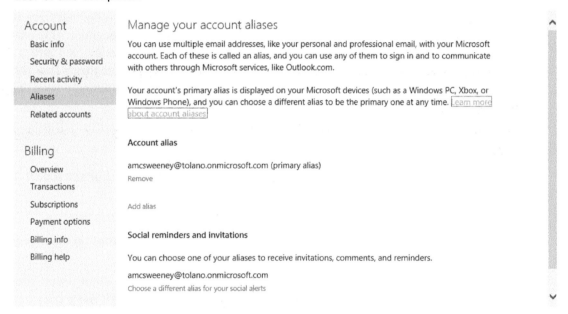

5. Click **Add alias**.

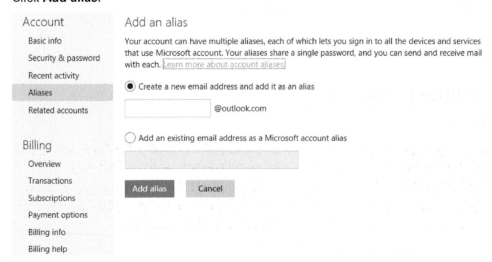

6. Choose the option for the alias you would like to add.

    In this demonstration, we will create a new account that Andrew can use that doesn't require as much typing as the original account.

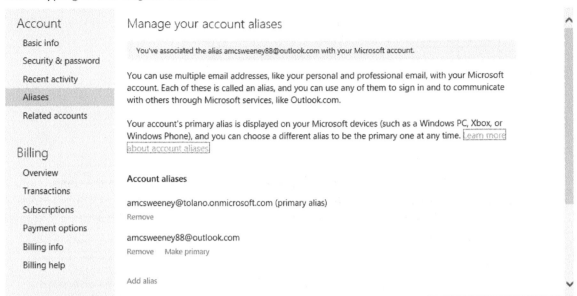

Notice how you can also remove an alias, as needed, or as indicated with our demonstration, you can click **Make primary** to have this account set up as the primary address to use when signing into Outlook.com

7. Click **Related accounts** in the panel at the left to see what other options are available for this account.

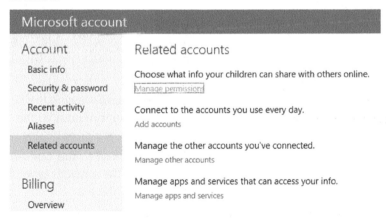

8. Sign out of Outlook.com and then close the web browser.

Using Microsoft Outlook

 Exam 3 - Objective 3.1

> **Note:** Although many email programs are currently available, for the purpose of this courseware we will use Outlook 2013. Remember that the concepts remain the same regardless of the email program; the differences lie in where the commands and features are located in each program.

Microsoft Outlook is a popular program for managing email, and it also includes modules to manage information such as appointments, contacts, project notes and task lists.

When you open Outlook, your screen will look similar to the one shown below:

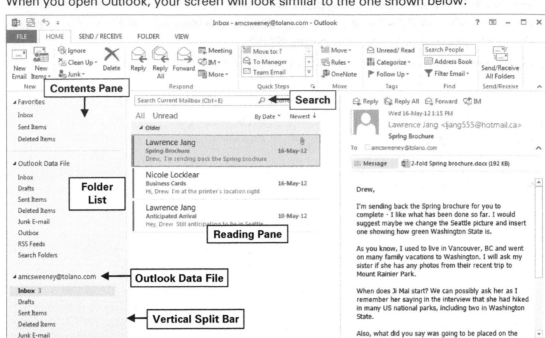

Contents Pane	Displays the contents of the selected item for the active module in the Navigation Pane. For instance, if Mail is active, the Contents Pane lists the messages for the selected folder; if the Contacts module is active, you will see a list of contacts in the Contents Pane.
Search	Enter search criteria and see the results display while you type.
Outlook Data File	Shows the folder list for the current Outlook data file. In the preceding image, there is a data file for the default Outlook data file and then one for the student data file being used in this courseware.
Folder List	Displays information for each module or folder, similar to viewing the Folders pane in Windows explorer. Each module has slightly different options in the Navigation pane, with Mail showing the most folders (you can create or edit folders).
Reading Pane	Displays the contents of any email message highlighted in the Content pane. By default, the Reading Pane is displayed on the right of the email or tasks list when in Mail or Tasks mode, but it can be repositioned below the list.
Vertical Split Bars	Drag to show more or less of the pane on either side (in this case, folders or modules). All vertical panes on the Outlook screen are separated by vertical split bars. When you position the mouse pointer over a split bar, it becomes a split symbol that you can then click and drag to adjust the size of the desired panel. If you maximize the screen, Outlook adjusts the size and number of items you can see in either portion of the Navigation Pane.
Peeks Bar	At the bottom of the Navigation pane, this bar shows icons or text for the other Outlook modules. You can switch between the views by clicking the ellipsis (...), click **Navigation Options** and then click **Compact Navigation**.
Navigation Pane	Move between different modules or components of Outlook, or navigate between the folders in the Mail module of Outlook.

The illustration on the previous page shows the Outlook screen in its default configuration when the application is first installed. Because many of the screen sections can be resized, minimized, or turned off, your screen may not look like the example shown.

Outlook consists of several modules or components that enable you to perform a variety of tasks:

Mail Calendar People Tasks ···

Mail	Compose, send, read, and manage email messages.
Calendar	Schedule appointments, meetings, or events.
People	Manage your contact list, much as you would in an address book.
Tasks	Track and prioritize your activities.
Notes	Enter brief notes, similar to sticky notes.
Folders	Display all folders in the top portion of the Navigation Pane.
Shortcuts	Display any shortcuts Microsoft or you may set up for places you want quick access to, such as Microsoft Online, or your company's SharePoint site.

You can enter information into the individual modules or you can integrate one Outlook feature with another. For example, you can send an email message directly to a contact while you are working in the Contacts module. This lesson focuses on the email module of Outlook only.

Creating New Messages

Sending an email message is similar to mailing a traditional letter. You write the body of the message, add address information and then send it. You must have an active email account before you can send or receive mail. To send mail, you must know the email address of each intended recipient. Sending a message follows these steps:

1. Create a new mail message.

2. Address the message to the recipient.

3. Type the text for the subject, and then type the message, applying any formatting as required, such as bold text or indented paragraphs. If you need to email someone a file, attach it to the mail message.

4. Use the spell checker and proof read your message to eliminate spelling or grammatical errors.

5. Send the message.

Once you click the **Send** button, the message may be temporarily stored in the *Outbox* folder until you specify to send the message to the email server for delivery. This is handy when working offline as you can store all outgoing messages until you are ready to send them. You can also configure Outlook to automatically send messages directly to the email server when you click the **Send** button.

To create a new message, from the main Outlook window, use one of the following methods:

*   On the Home tab, in the New group, click **New Email**, or

*   On the Home tab, in the New group, click the arrow for **New Items** and then click **E-mail Message**, or

*   press (Ctrl)+(N).

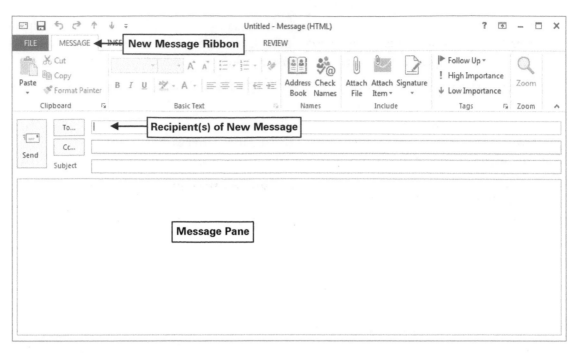

Once the new message window appears, type in the email addresses for the intended recipients or choose names from the list of contacts stored on your system. Regardless of the email program, the components of an email message are the same.

An email message includes:

- Addressing information – you must enter at least one email address for an intended recipient. You may send a message to several recipients by specifying more than one address.

- A subject line – the text you enter in the subject line lets the recipient know what the message is about. A subject line is not required, but most email programs prompt you to enter one if you try to send a message that does not include a subject line. It is, however, good business practice to always include a subject line.

- Body – this is the main text of the email.

- Signature – this is a block of text that includes your name, title, and possibly your contact information. A signature is added to the end of an email message. A signature is not required, but it is good business practice to include an email signature.

- Attachment(s) – these are files that you send along with an email message. Attachments can include pictures, videos, or documents. Attachments are optional, and can greatly increase the size of an email message.

The following figure shows a newly composed email message. This message includes the address of the recipient, a subject line, the body of the email, and a signature.

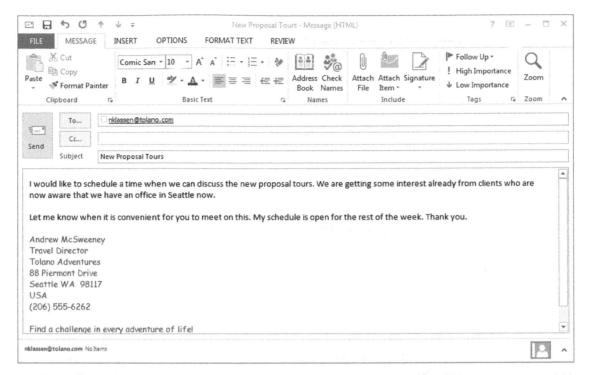

At the bottom of the message, Outlook displays the recipient's name in a small pane with a picture (or photo icon), of the recipient at the far right. This is known as the People pane where you can view more information about the recipient, or any items you've exchanged recently with this contact. This can be useful if you are tracking the conversation or *thread* of a message.

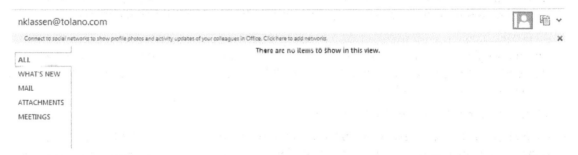

Use the  or ^ to expand or collapse the pane; you can also use the icon to switch between the two different views for the people pane.

You can also position the cursor on the bar between the message content pane and the People pane and drag up or down to size the pane.

Addressing

The addressing lines are very important as they identify who will receive the email message.

To	This identifies the primary recipient(s) of the email. You can send the email to one or several recipients by separating their unique addresses with a semicolon or comma. The default separator for most email programs is a semicolon; you can set the separator to a comma in the Outlook program options.
Cc	This stands for "carbon copy" and indicates people who will receive a copy of this email for information purposes only.
Bcc	Bcc stands for "blind carbon copy" and provides a way to hide certain recipients; it prevents their addresses from appearing in the email address fields when another recipient opens and views the message. Any person whose address you enter in this field will receive a copy of the message, but other recipients will be unaware of any recipients listed in this field. For example, you might send an email confirming a dinner date with your sister, and Bcc the friend organizing her surprise party.

Using the Address Book

An email address book (or Contacts list) is a directory of contact information. Most entries include at least a name and email address. Using the address book is a fast and accurate way to insert email addresses into an email message. To access the list of contacts from the new message window, click the ▢ To... ▢ or ▢ Cc... ▢ buttons.

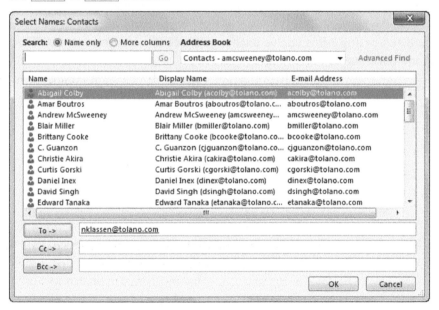

Use one of the following methods to select multiple contacts, then click the appropriate address button:

- To include everyone in a range of names, click the first name in the list, and then press and hold the (Shift) key as you click the last name you want. Everyone from the first to the last name is selected.

- To select individual names distributed throughout the contact list, click the first person you want to receive the message, and then press and hold the (Ctrl) key as you click the name of each individual contact you want to select.

You can select the names for each address field. Remember that names listed in the Cc field appear in this area of the message when received; names in the Bcc field do not appear anywhere in the message as seen by the recipients. Individuals who receive a Bcc message will see the names of other recipients listed in the To and Cc fields, but will not see their own name listed at all.

Many email programs allow you set up group lists (or distribution lists) in your address book. For example, if Denise, Tina, Ken, Mike and Ron are members of your study group, and you regularly send email messages to your entire study group, you can create a group list called "StudyGroup" that includes the email addresses for Denise, Tina, Ken, Mike and Ron. You can then simply enter the name of the group list in the To: field and a message will be sent to all five members of the study group.

The Subject Line

Be brief and concise, when entering text in the Subject field. Choose a few words that will sum up the purpose of the message for the recipient. Do not send a message without an entry in this line to ensure the message is not blocked by the recipient's server as suspected junk mail. Also, remember that subject lines are visible in the email list window. Do not use embarrassing or inappropriate words or phrases in the subject line – or anywhere in an email message.

The Message Body

This is where you type the body of the message. Some email programs provide formatting features, such as bold, italics, or underline, which you can apply to the text for emphasis or enhancement. You can also include pictures, sounds, slide shows, and so on, that will appear with the text, as well as hyperlinks that will connect the recipient directly to another email address or a web site.

The New Message Ribbon tab contains formatting features you can apply to text in the New Message pane.

The Format Text tab contains the same basic formatting plus additional, commonly used Word program features.

Formatting features can be applied either as you type or after the text is entered. If you choose to add the formatting after the text is typed, be sure to select the text first.

Applying formatting features gives the message a more professional appearance and can be used to emphasize specific areas. Be careful about the features you add as the message text can become distracting. Some users configure their email programs to display messages in plain text. If a recipient uses the Plain Text mail format, he or she will not see your formatting.

Proofing Your Message

Outlook can check for misspelled words or words not commonly found in a dictionary, such as names, computer terms, medical terms, abbreviations, and so on. If changes to the message text are necessary, you can use tools such as the thesaurus to find alternate wording to convey your message. To activate this feature or other proofing tools, click the **Review** tab and then click the appropriate option in the Proofing group:

Always try to maintain a professional manner in your messages, even with people you know very well. This reflects well on you and your company, as well as the products or services you provide.

To activate the spelling feature, use one of the following methods:

- On the Review tab, in the Proofing group, click **Spelling & Grammar**, or

- press (F7).

Sending the Message

Once the information for the message has been entered into the Address and Subject lines, and the body of the message, click **Send** at the left of the address fields.

EXERCISE

In this exercise you will learn how to address, enter and format an email message and then send it.

> **Note**: To perform the following exercises, an Outlook email account must be already set up on your system. In order to work with the exercises in this lesson an Outlook data file for Andrew McSweeney has been provided with the student data files for this courseware. If this file has not been added to Outlook prior to this exercise, please add it now. Start Outlook, click the **File** tab, click **Open & Export**, and click **Open Outlook Data File**. Navigate to the student data files location and click the *Andrew McSweeney - Student.pst* file. This will then add the data file only, meaning that any messages you send or receive will be stored in the email account set up on your system.

1. On the Home tab, in the New group, click **New Email**.

2. In the **To** address field, type: `dsingh@tolano.com`.

3. Click in the **Subject** field and type: `Computer Equipment`.

4. Click in the body of the message and type the following:

   > We received notice that the computers were delayed due to an accounting error. The vendor called to let us know that there was a problem with the credit card used. Could you look into this for us at your earliest convenience?
   >
   > Thanks!
   >
   > Drew

5. Click and drag to select the two words, *accounting error* in the first sentence.

6. On the Message tab, in the Basic Text group, click **A ▾** (**Font Color**) to apply red to the selected text.

7. With the text still selected, on the Message tab, in the Basic Text group, click **B** (**Bold**).

8. Click anywhere away from the selection to view the formatting changes just applied.

9. On the Review tab, in the Proofing group, click **Spelling & Grammar** to ensure there are no spelling or grammatical errors in the message. Click **OK** when the check is complete.

10. Click the **Send** button.

Now send a message to multiple people.

11. On the Home tab, in the New group, click **New Email**.

12. In the **To** address field, type: `nklassen@tolano.com; ljang55@outlook.com`.

13. Click in the **CC** field and type: `dsingh@tolano.com`.

As you begin to type the characters for David's email, you may notice a list appear below the field. This is known as the AutoComplete option where Outlook recognizes you have used this email before and provides it in a list for easy selection. To accept this suggestion, click the name or use the ⬇ arrow to move to the name and then press `Enter`.

14. Click in the **Subject** field and type: `Office Setup Delay`.

15. Click in the message area and type the following:

    ```
    We will be experiencing a delay in setting up the computers for the
    new office. We received notice this morning about a problem with
    delivery of the computers and David has been notified of this issue.

    I have also called the IT vendor to notify them of a possible delay.
    As we did not set a firm date for installations, we will be able to
    continue with other tasks for the new office in the meantime.

    Contact me if you have any questions on the aforementioned.
    ```

16. Click the **Send** button to send the message to these recipients.

Receiving Messages

Most email programs will automatically check for new messages as soon as you log into the program. You can also customize the time interval to check for new messages in Outlook.

To check if you have received any messages, use one of the following methods:

- On the Send / Receive tab, in the Send & Receive group, click **Send/Receive All Folders**, or
- press `F9`.

When Outlook finishes sending and receiving all messages, new messages appear in the Contents Pane of the Outlook window. The *Inbox* folder also displays a number that indicates the total number of new messages received in the Folders list.

Outlook shows the contents of a message in the Reading Pane. A new message has a colored bar at the left of the message that disappears once you view the contents of the message. Use the split bar between the Contents Pane and the Reading Pane to show more or less of each pane.

You can also double-click a message to view its contents. Open a message to see the message in full, or to access options to reply to the message.

If you are using the Reading Pane to reply or forward a message, you can choose to enter the message text directly in this pane. Alternatively, you can also click **Pop Out** to open a window for this message. Notice you can also choose to discard the message if you decide you do not want to send it.

Replying to a Message

When you open a message to read it, options for replying appear in the Ribbon. You choose to read a message in the Reading pane on the main Outlook window, or open the message to read it in a separate window.

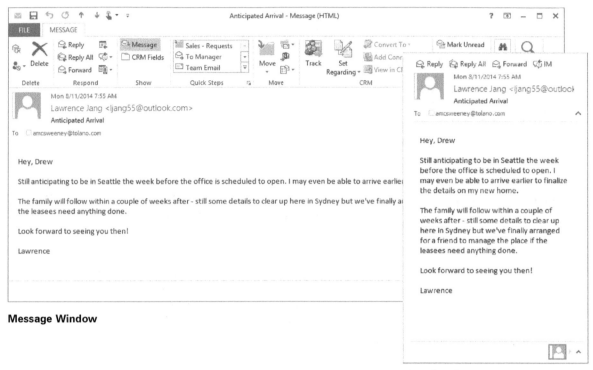

Message Window

Preview Pane

Once you have read a message, you can reply to the sender or to all recipients of the original message. When choosing the Reply or Reply All options, decide whether to reply only to the sender or to all parties who received the original message.

To reply to the sender of a message, use one of the following methods:

- On the Home tab, in the Respond group, click **Reply**, or
- press (Ctrl)+(R), or
- if viewing the message, on the Message tab, in the Respond group, click **Reply**.

To reply to everyone addressed in the original message, use one of the following methods:

- On the Home tab, in the Respond group, click **Reply All**, or
- press (Ctrl)+(Shift)+(R), or
- if viewing the message, on the Message tab, in the Respond group, click **Reply All**.

When you select the Home tab method to reply to a message, the Reading pane changes to display the original message and includes the option to pop out or display the full Reply window, as well as to discard the message if you change your mind about sending a reply. You can type your reply in the body text area, directly above the message sent to you, as seen in the following:

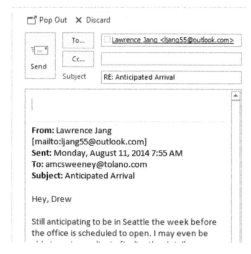

If you choose the keyboard shortcut or the Message tab reply option, Outlook creates a new message and within it, displays a copy of the original message as a reference.

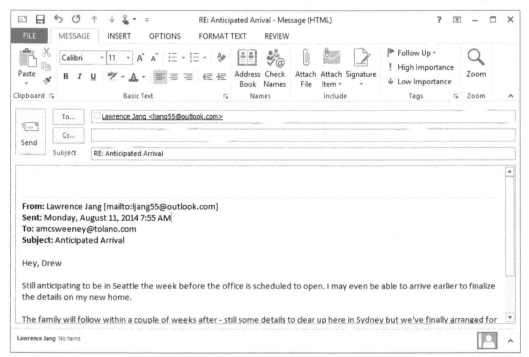

Any method to create a reply adds RE: to the beginning of the subject line to identify this message as a reply. Outlook also automatically lists the appropriate address(es) in the Address fields allowing you then to focus on the message text. You can customize how the original message appears in a reply using the Mail Options in the **File** tab.

Once you have replied to a message, Outlook displays ⤺ next to the message in the Inbox to indicate that you replied to this message. The icon is the same regardless of whether you replied to the original sender or everyone addressed in the message. Notice the arrow in the icon points in the same direction as appears on the **Reply** and **Reply All** buttons in the Ribbon.

Forwarding a Message

Use the **Forward** option to send a message that you have received to someone else. For example, suppose you and a colleague are working together on a project. You have received an email message concerning the next scheduled production meeting, and you notice that your colleague is not included in the list of recipients. You can forward the message to your colleague, who will then have all the necessary information. When you forward a message, your copy of the message remains in your Inbox.

To forward a message, use one of the following methods:

- On the Home tab, in the Respond group, click **Forward**, or
- press (Ctrl)+(F), or
- if viewing the message, on the Message tab, in the Respond group, click **Forward**.

As with the Reply feature, when you click the Home tab option to forward a message, the Reading pane changes to include the Pop Out or Discard options, and you can enter the text in the body text area directly above the original message.

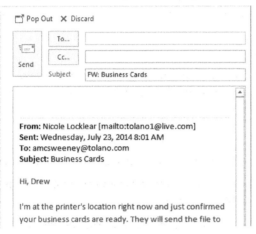

If you choose the keyboard shortcut or the Message tab to forward the message, a new window appears for you to enter the recipients as well as the message text:

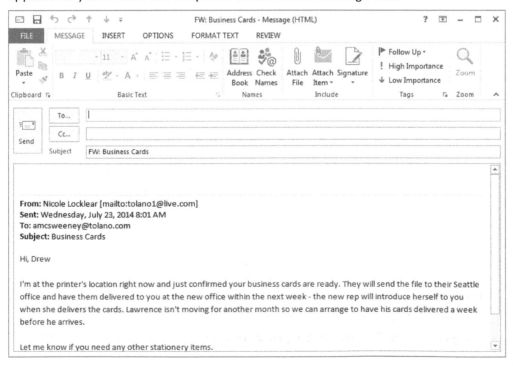

Regardless of the method chosen, Outlook automatically creates a copy of the message and adds a FW: to the original message Subject line. The address fields remain blank so you can enter the addresses of those who should receive the forwarded message.

After forwarding a message, Outlook displays ⊠ next to the message in the Inbox to indicate you forwarded this message to someone else. Notice the arrow in the icon points in the same direction as the icon on the **Forward** command button.

EXERCISE

In this exercise you will be replying to and forwarding messages appropriately. There should be three messages in the Inbox for the Andrew McSweeney data file.

1. Double-click the *Anticipated Arrival* message from Lawrence and read the message.

2. On the Message tab, in the Respond group, click **Reply**.

   Outlook creates a new message, addressed to Lawrence Jang, and inserts a RE: into the subject line, indicating this message is a reply.

3. Click in the message area and type the following:

   ```
   Don't worry about anything here, although if you do manage to get here
   per your original date, let me know so we can order your business
   cards for the opening.

   Drew
   ```

4. Send the message, correcting any spelling errors that appear, and then close the original message.

   The icon at the right of this message in your Inbox should now show an envelope with a purple arrow pointing to the left indicating you replied to this message.

5. Double click this message to open it in its own window, and view the information bar that appears above the address field.

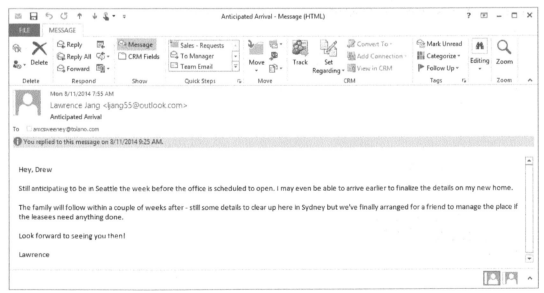

6. Close the message.

7. Click to select the message from Nicole Locklear.

8. On the Message tab, in the Respond group, click **Forward**.

Notice how the subject text now includes FW: to indicate you are forwarding this message to someone else in the Reading Pane.

9. Click in the **To** field and type: `ljang55@outlook.com` (you are sending this message to Lawrence using his personal email as he has taken time off from work to pack for the move to Seattle).

10. In the message area (above the existing text), type the following:

    ```
    FYI - let me know if your arrival dates are changing so we can
    reschedule some of the earlier events for the office opening.

    Drew
    ```

11. Click **Send** and close the original message from Nicole.

    You should now notice that the icon at the right of the message shows an envelope with a blue arrow pointing to the right indicating the original message was forwarded to someone.

Working with Attachments

Sending attachments with your email enables you to share information. However, consider the following points regarding attachments:

- Keep the attachment file size as small as possible. The size of an email message includes the size of any attachments. One way to reduce attachment size is to convert the original document into a format that reduces file size; for example, you can save a Word document as a PDF file. (Using this format can also protect your document from being changed by the recipient.) The larger the message size, the longer it will take to deliver to the recipient(s).

- Consider including a hyperlink or a URL link in the body of your email instead of sending a large file as an attachment. For example, if you have access to a video demonstration of a product, place a copy of it on your web site and provide the URL in the message to the customer. This is more interesting than receiving an attachment with words and pictures describing the product.

- Consider what the attachment is and whether email is the best way to send it. The more secure or confidential a document is, the more you should protect it from being accessed and used by others online. For example, a legal contract requiring handwritten signatures may be better sent as a printed document via courier. You can still send an email, without including an attachment, confirming that the document will be arriving by courier for signatures.

- Consider the file type and whether the recipient has a program that will recognize and open it. In an effort to screen out spam or junk mail and minimize security risks, some organizations or schools set their mail servers or readers to block email messages with certain types of attachments.

- Some email servers are configured to block messages that include graphics or URLs. If you send a message containing these extra elements and do not hear back within the expected period of time, consider sending a follow-up email inquiring whether the first message was received. Alternatively, contact the person by telephone for an immediate response.

- Attachments are notorious sources of viruses and other malware. Always set your antivirus program to automatically scan and check all incoming and outgoing mail to prevent any viruses from entering your network, or being sent from your computer to others.

To attach or insert a file in an email message, on the Message or Insert tab, in the Include group, click **Attach File**. This option is available regardless of whether you are creating a new message in its own window or from the Reading Pane.

You can then navigate to the appropriate location and select one or more files to attach to the message. Repeat the steps as necessary to add more attachments from different locations.

If you decide not to send (or no longer want) the attachment, use one of the following methods to remove the attachment from the message:

- Select the file name in the Attached field and then press (Delete), or
- right-click the file name in the Attached field and then click **Remove**.

Viewing Attachments

When you receive a message with an attachment, Outlook displays a 📎 next to the new message. The Reading Pane also displays the name of the attached file.

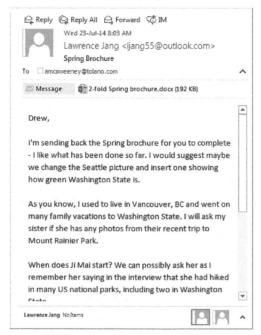

You can right-click an attachment to display options for handling it:

- Click **Preview** to preview the attachment in the Reading Pane or the message window. You can also preview the attachment simply by clicking its name. To view the message contents again, click the **Message** icon at the left of the attachment. Once you preview the attachment, a new ribbon appears to assist you with further tasks:

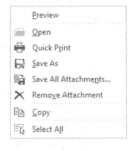

- Click **Open** to open the file in a program that recognizes the file type.
- Click **Save As** to save the attachment to a location on the local drive or a network drive. This can also help to protect your system as you can scan this file for viruses prior to opening it.

There will be occasions when a **Preview file** button appears in the preview for the attachment, as seen in the following:

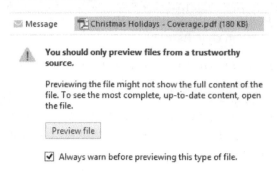

Messages such as these indicate that you may want to save the file and scan it before opening it. Alternatively, you may need to select a program that enables you to preview the contents of the attachment.

EXERCISE

In this exercise you will view and then open an attachment included in a message from Lawrence Jang. The Reading Pane is turned on by default but may have been turned off by another user. If you do not see the Reading Pane, click the **View** tab, and in the Layout group, click **Reading Pane**. Then click the position where you want the Reading Pane to display (at the right or below the list of emails).

1. Click the message from Lawrence Jang that displays a paper clip icon at the left.

2. In the Reading Pane, read a bit of the message and then click the attachment name above the message contents to view the contents of the attachment in the Reading Pane.

3. Click the **Message** box to return to viewing the message contents.

4. Double-click the attachment name to open the file in Word.

    You should notice that the Protected View is active with this document because it was sent via email.

5. Close Word without saving the document.

Managing Spam

Spam refers to any unsolicited message; often they promote products and services, or convey specific political/religious views. Spam mail is the same as junk mail. People or companies who send these types of messages are called *spammers.*

Spammers buy email address lists from companies that specialize in email marketing. It is natural for companies to want to market their products and "keep you informed." Reputable companies will ask for your email address and ask for permission to give your address to other companies who sell associated products and services. Companies must make their privacy policy available for viewing; the privacy policy must describe how your personal information may be used or shared. Companies may use and share your information only if you give your consent.

Most email programs include a filtering feature to block spam or other junk email. Many ISPs also run active spam filters on their mail servers to block the most common types of spam mail before they reach your email Inbox. You can also download and install a variety of programs to help block any spam messages that sneak by your ISP.

Following are some ways to avoid being placed on a list that results in you receiving spam messages:

- Do not allow your email address to be added to any marketing address lists. When you visit a web site that asks for your email address, be sure to read the company's privacy policy. Provide your email address only if you are sure the company will not sell it or share it.

- Set up an additional email account, separate from your main, personal account, with a Web-based email service that you can use for these types of requests. This separates the email you want from the email you don't want; when you check your Web-based account, you can delete all the junk messages at once.

- Do not reply to any email that you consider junk even if the message says that your name will be removed from their list if you respond as indicated. In all likelihood you are simply confirming that your email address is valid, which can then result in you receiving even more spam mail.

- Avoid putting your name and email address on any public lists, such as adding your name to a mailing list at a seminar or signing an online petition.

- Avoid disclosing your email address on any online forums or newsgroups as they commonly exchange information. If you must indicate an email address in one of these online areas, try to use an alias, or disguise the address by changing the structure with extra text. For example, you might type out j_smith at outlook dot com or j-smith-nomorespam@outlook.com.

- To prevent your messages from being flagged as spam by email servers, follow the general guidelines for sending email. Always include appropriate text in the Subject line. Many spam filters search for Subject lines that include Hi, Re: Your Order, and so on.

- You can also receive junk mail through other electronic communication devices such as cellular phones and PDAs. With text messages you may be able to stop receiving spam by sending a text message with the word "Stop" to the originator.

Dealing with Junk Mail in Outlook

Outlook provides a Junk Email Filter to detect potentially undesirable email messages and place them directly in the *Junk E-mail* folder rather than the *Inbox* folder. There are two parts to the Junk E-mail Filter: the Junk E-mail Lists and the special Microsoft-developed filter technology used to evaluate whether an unread message should be treated as junk email.

To set up the junk email options, on the Home tab, in the Delete group, click **Junk** and then **Junk E-mail Options**.

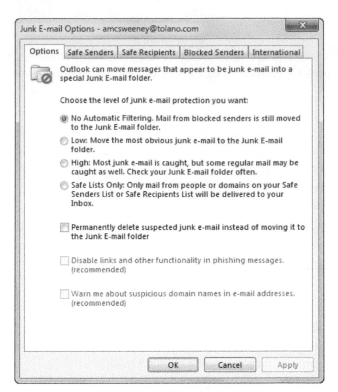

No Automatic Filtering	No action is taken for an incoming message, unless the sender is in the Blocked Senders list.
Low	Filters out messages that include obvious junk mail characteristics.
High	Aggressively filters out messages that include more subtle as well as obvious junk mail characteristics.
Safe Lists Only	Sends all messages to the Junk E-mail folder unless the sender is in the Safe Senders or Safe Recipients list.

Outlook also contains a system to detect and protect against phishing messages. *Phishing* is a term used to describe email messages that try to obtain details of a bank account, credit card or PIN number from the recipient. If Outlook detects a potential phishing attempt in an email message, Outlook converts it to plain text format, disables all links in the message and places it in the *Junk E-mail* folder.

There are four junk email lists you can use to filter out different types of messages considered to be junk messages:

- Click **Safe Senders** to view those email addresses you consider safe and want to receive messages from; this list is often called a *white list*. You can specify to automatically trust messages that come from people included in your Contacts list.

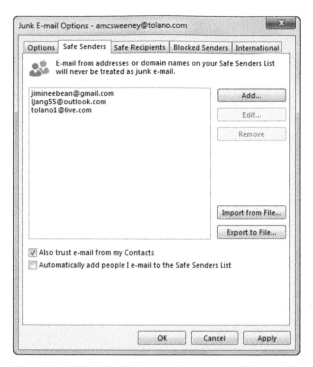

- Use the **Safe Recipients** tab to specify email addresses you regard as safe recipients. Any messages that you send to users on your Safe Recipients list will never be treated as junk mail by your email server.

- Use the **Blocked Senders** tab to list specific senders from whom you do not want to receive messages. Messages from any blocked sender are automatically put into the *Junk E-mail* folder. You can include global addresses for a domain; for example, *@hotmail.com would block any messages sent by any email address from @hotmail.com unless they are included in the Safe Senders list.

- Use the **International** tab to block messages from specific foreign domains such as those with language encodings (character sets) you do not want to receive. You can block messages that come from domains in specific countries such as .au or .fr), and you can block messages written in specific languages (such as Cyrillic or Greek).

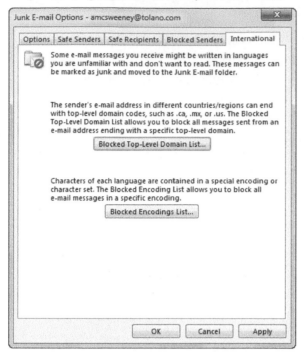

You can enter these addresses manually or import lists from earlier versions of Outlook. You can easily remove email addresses from any of the Outlook junk email filter lists by selecting the address and then clicking **Remove**.

Marking Messages as Junk

When you receive a message that Outlook considers to be junk, the message is automatically moved to the *Junk E-mail* folder. If you receive a message that you want to mark as junk, you can choose how you want the message to be treated, such as moving it to the *Junk E-mail* folder, or blocking the sender or blocking future messages from the domain or organization.

To mark a message as junk:

- On the Home tab, in the Delete group, click **Junk**, and click the appropriate option, or
- Right-click the **message**, click **Junk** and then click the appropriate option.

Content in a message sent to the *Junk E-mail* folder changes to text-only format so that no harmful content can be activated.

To unmark a message as junk:

- On the Home tab, in the Delete group, click **Junk**, and click **Not Junk**, or
- Right-click the message, click **Junk** and then click **Not Junk**.

Outlook then moves the message to the Inbox where you can view it in its original format.

Emptying the Junk E-mail Folder

You can delete messages in your *Junk E-mail* folder in the same way you would delete messages in any other folder except that these are permanently deleted.

To remove selected messages in the *Junk E-mail* folder:

- On the Home tab, in the Delete group, click **Delete**, or
- Press (Delete) or (Ctrl)+(D).

To empty the entire *Junk E-mail* folder, right-click the folder and then click **Empty Folder**.

EXERCISE

In this exercise, you will examine options for junk email protection. You may not have any junk email if filters are active on your mail server, or if someone else has emptied the *Junk E-mail* folder. The instructor may need to demonstrate how to remove junk mail.

1. On the Home tab, in the Delete group, click **Junk**, and then click **Junk E-mail Options**.

    Note the default settings for Junk E-mail Options.

2. Click **High** and click **OK**.

3. Right-click the message from Nicole Locklear, click **Junk** and then click **Block Sender**.

> **Note:** If this is the first time the Junk E-mail options have been set, the screen above will appear to remind you of the action. If you do not see this message, then the Junk E-mail options have been set previously and the message is moved to the *Junk E-mail* folder automatically. You can then proceed to step 5.

4. Click **OK**.

5. Click the *Junk E-mail* folder to view how this message now appears in the Reading Pane.

    Outlook has automatically inserted a note about disabling any links or other features that could cause harm to your system.

6. Right-click the message, click **Junk** and then click **Not Junk**. Outlook displays a message box describing the action(s) it will take. Click **OK**.

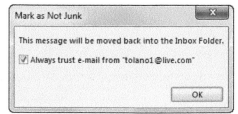

The message is moved back to the Inbox.

Archiving Messages

To keep all your messages but also keep the Outlook data file small, archive your old messages. Archived messages are moved from the main Outlook file and stored in a separate file. To view one of these messages later, click the archive file to view the archived contents.

To archive messages manually, click **File**, and with Info selected at the top of the left pane, click **Cleanup Tools** in the right pane and then click **Archive**.

Click the folder you want Outlook to archive. For instance, you may want to archive your messages only, or create a copy of the entire Outlook data file. Depending on the number of messages and how long you want messages to be available from the Inbox, set the archive date to be six months or older so you have only the most recent messages in the Inbox.

After setting options for the archiving process, the status bar displays ARCHIVING ⊗ to indicate that the archiving process is taking place in the background. On completion, a new folder called *Archive Folders* appears in the Navigation Pane. You can expand this folder to show the structure of the items you included in the original archive. You can also choose to close this folder from the Navigation Pane; in this scenario, you are changing only the display of the Navigation Pane (the original archive file is saved in the Outlook Files folder in the Documents library).

To automatically archive items, use one of the following methods:

- Click the **File** tab, click **Options**, and in the Advanced category, click **AutoArchive Settings**, or

You can specify how often to run the AutoArchive feature. The preceding figure shows that by default, AutoArchive is configured to run every 14 days. The default settings also specify that Outlook will display a prompt asking if you want to AutoArchive your messages before running the feature. You can elect to proceed, or you can cancel the operation.

• click the **Folder** tab, in the Properties group, click **AutoArchive Settings**.

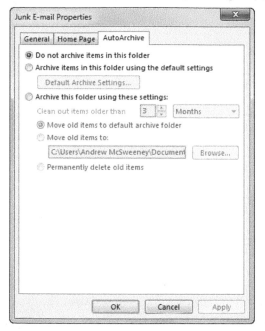

EXERCISE

In this exercise you will change a setting for AutoArchive.

1. In the main Outlook screen, click the **File** tab, click **Options**, click **Advanced** in the panel at the left then click **AutoArchive Settings**.

2. Ensure **Run AutoArchive every** is turned on, and set the number of days to be **45**.

3. Click **OK** to accept this change and then click **OK** once more to leave the Outlook Options window.

   You have configured Outlook to automatically archive your personal folders once every 45 days. All archived messages are moved to a folder in the Navigation Pane named *Archive Folders*. Outlook will add newly archived items to the Archive Folders file unless you specify otherwise.

Automating Outlook

Every email program is customizable; that is, you can set options for how your email is handled. Outlook provides a number of features to help you customize and maintain your program to function in the most effective and efficient manner for you.

Using Signatures

A signature is a block of text that is automatically added to the end of your messages whenever you create a new message. This saves having to enter your name and information or a product slogan each time you send a message. You can create as many signatures as required, but only one can be designated as the default signature.

To create a signature, select **File**, **Options**, and in the **Mail** category, in the Compose messages area, click **Signatures**.

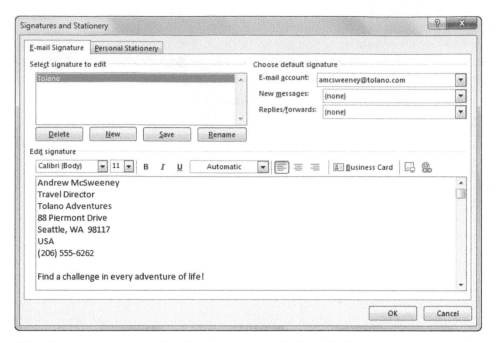

Click **New**, enter a name for the signature and click **OK**. You can then enter the text for the signature and format it as required.

You can create several signatures at once, or you can add new signatures as you need them. Many people use separate signatures for business or personal use, or perhaps for a volunteer role. You designate a signature to be the default signature that appears in every message, or specify to use different signatures for replies and forwards. To use a signature other than the default signature in a new message, on the Message tab, in the Include group, click the arrow for **Signature** and then click the appropriate signature.

EXERCISE

In this exercise you will create two signatures and set default options for new messages.

1. Click the **File** tab, click **Options** to open the Outlook Options window, in the left pane click **Mail**, then in the right pane click **Signatures**.

2. Click **New**.

3. Type: `Tolano` for the name of this signature and then click **OK**.

4. Type the following information in the box area, as shown:

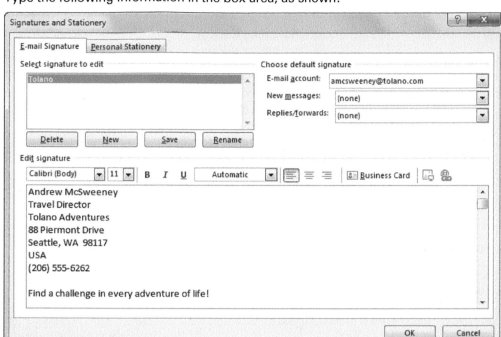

5. Select all the text and click the arrow for the font color to select a color of your choice.

6. Select the last line in the signature and then click the **Bold** button.

7. Click **Save** and then click **New** to create a new signature.

8. Type: `Personal` for the name of this signature, click **OK** and enter the following text:

    Andrew McSweeney
    (883) 788-0808
    Drewm808@gmail.com

    Notice how the text is in bold based on the feature that was last chosen before starting this signature.

9. Select the entire text block and then click the **Bold** button to turn off this feature.

10. Click **Save** and then click **OK** to exit this feature. Close all other open windows for the Outlook options.

11. Create a new message.

    Notice how the Tolano signature automatically appears in the area for the body of the message. You can begin typing your message, and the signature will move down to make space. The Tolano signature is currently set as the default signature. If you want to change the signature in this email message to another one, you need to delete this text and then insert the other signature.

12. Select all text for the signature and press (Delete).

13. On the Message tab, in the Include group, click **Signature** and then click **Personal**.

    Andrew's personal signature now appears in the message. You can click at the top of the message area and type the body of your email message.

Now let's navigate to the Signatures window to see which options we can set as default for new messages.

14. Close the new message without saving it, then click the **File** tab, click **Options**, click **Mail** in the left pane if necessary, and then click **Signatures** in the right pane.

Examine the Choose default signature section in the Signatures and Stationery dialog box. Notice that Tolano appears in the field for New messages.

15. Click the arrow for this field to see what options are available.

The signature you select to use for new messages will depend on how you want to manage your messages. In general, people will set up a default signature to match the majority of email that will be sent. That is, if you send more business email than personal email, you would probably specify a business signature as the default signature. If you send more personal email than business email, then you would likely specify a personal signature as your default signature. You can also specify (none) for this setting. If you specify (none), then no signature will be automatically appended to new messages, but you can always add one on a per-message basis. This is a good choice for people who regularly use two or more different signatures.

16. Display the list for New messages, then click **(none)**.

17. Click **OK** twice to close the options windows.

18. Create a new message. Notice that no signature is added.

19. Click in the message area, press ⌈Enter⌋ a few times, then in the Message tab in the Include group click **Signature**, then select one of the signatures to add it to the message.

20. Close the new message without saving it.

Sending Out-of-Office Notices

As a business practice and out of courtesy, if you plan on being away from the office, send a message in advance to those you deal with regularly to inform them. Even if you plan to retrieve your messages while you are away, inform people of your absence and offer them the name of a colleague who can assist them.

Out-of-office notices should provide details regarding the dates you will be away and who will be handling your work during your absence. Try to send the notice at least two days prior to your departure. You can also set up your messages to automatically be forwarded to someone else to handle during your absence.

Sending an away notice to personal contacts is at your discretion.

Some email programs and mail servers provide the option to send an out-of-office response automatically to anyone who sends you an email during this time. You set up the option from your system, and the mail server automatically generates a response and sends it out every time it detects a new message arriving in your Inbox.

The main downside to this is that the response will be sent regardless of who the sender is; it could be a company that generates junk or spam mail and your response could tell them that your email address is valid.

Note that you will not have access to this feature unless you are connected to a dedicated mail server such as Microsoft Exchange.

To set up or remove an out-of-office notice, click **File** and with the Info category selected in the left pane, click **Automatic Replies** in the right pane. Then click **Send automatic replies**.

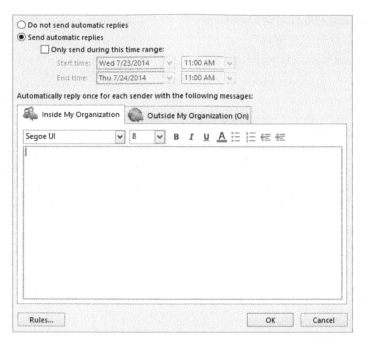

You can now set the time frame for your absence using the Start time and End time boxes. Click in the blank box to type the message you want the server to send. You should include information about your dates of absence, the date/time of your expected return, and include contact information for a colleague who can assist during your absence. This message is then sent automatically to anyone who sends you email during your absence. You can also format the message and then copy it to the **Outside My Organization** tab so both internal and external contacts will receive the auto-response.

EXERCISE

In this exercise you will examine out of office notices. If you are not connected to a dedicated mail server such as Exchange, you will not have this option available. If this is the case, review the following steps to familiarize yourself with how this feature works.

1. Click the **File** tab, select **Info** in the left pane if necessary, then click **Automatic Replies**.

    Note that you can create out of office replies for people both within your organization and external to your organization. In most cases, you can use the same message for both scenarios; however, situations may arise in which you need to use a different message for each. For example, if you will be away attending a conference, you may want your message to internal contacts to include the name of the conference, while your message for external customers might simply indicate that you will be gone for a set length of time. You can format the text in a similar manner to creating a new message.

The following figure shows a sample out-of-office message.

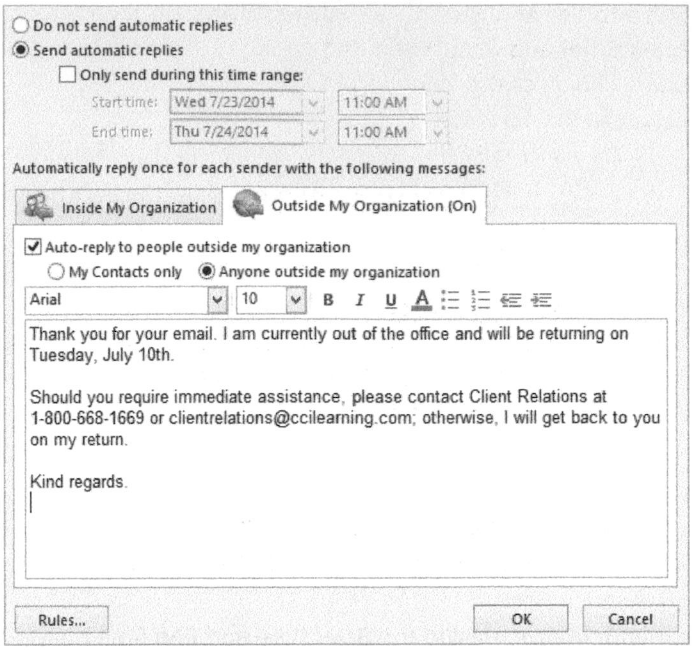

```
○ Do not send automatic replies
● Send automatic replies
     ☐ Only send during this time range:
        Start time:   Wed 7/23/2014  ∨   11:00 AM  ∨
        End time:     Thu 7/24/2014  ∨   11:00 AM  ∨
Automatically reply once for each sender with the following messages:

   [icon] Inside My Organization    [icon] Outside My Organization (On)

☑ Auto-reply to people outside my organization
    ○ My Contacts only   ● Anyone outside my organization
 Arial          ∨  10  ∨   B  I  U  A  ≣ ≣ ≡ ≡

 Thank you for your email. I am currently out of the office and will be returning on
 Tuesday, July 10th.

 Should you require immediate assistance, please contact Client Relations at
 1-800-668-1669 or clientrelations@ccilearning.com; otherwise, I will get back to you
 on my return.

 Kind regards.


  Rules...                                        OK            Cancel
```

2. Close the window without entering or saving anything.

Lesson Summary

In this lesson you were introduced to different communication methods and means of sharing information, with an emphasis on using electronic mail. You should now be familiar with:

☑ different types of electronic communication

☑ identifying users on communication systems

☑ different communication methods

☑ appropriate uses for electronic communication

☑ advantages of electronic communication

☑ how an email address is structured

☑ identifying email components

☑ using attachments effectively

☑ understanding how to deal with junk mail

☑ common problems with electronic communication

Review Questions

1. What types of electronic communications are available?
    a. Email
    b. Video conferencing
    c. Text messaging
    d. Chats
    e. Any of the above
    f. a or c

2. In the following email address, which part represents the mailbox name?
    p.f.92fallon@yahoo.com
    a. yahoo
    b. @
    c. p.f.92fallon
    d. com

3. Alice sent an email message to Gail, Susan and Kelly. When Gail opened the message, she saw that the message was addressed to her and Susan. When Susan opened the message, she saw that the message was addressed to her and Gail. When Kelly opened the message, she saw that it was addressed to Gail and Susan. Which of the following statements is true?

    a. Alice listed all three addresses in the To field.
    b. Alice listed Kelly's address in the To field while Gail and Susan were listed in BCC field.
    c. Alice listed Gail's address and Susan's address in the To field, and listed Kelly's address in the BCC field.
    d. Alice listed all three addresses in the BCC field.

4. Why is it important to include something in the Subject line?

    a. To provide the recipient with a quick description of the message contents.
    b. To prevent an email server from marking this message as potential junk mail.
    c. Because it is mandatory to fill it in when sending a message.
    d. Any of the above
    e. a or b

5. What's the difference between replying to a message and forwarding a message?

    a. Reply is when you respond to the sender and Forward responds to the sender and also sends a copy of your message to you.
    b. You can reply to one or more people whereas you can only forward the message to one person.
    c. Reply is when you respond to the sender and Forward is sending the message to someone else.
    d. Nothing

6. When might you want to use a hyperlink instead of attaching a file in an email?

    a. When the attachment is large and the file can be downloaded from a specific area on a web site.
    b. When your recipients cannot view text formatting.
    c. When including the email address for a colleague or customer.
    d. When you are sending messages from a web-based email server.
    e. Any of the previous
    f. a or c

7. What does spam refer to?

    a. Unsolicited messages that promote products, services or political/religious topics.
    b. Messages from companies where you signed up to receive their newsletters.
    c. Pictures in messages from friends.
    d. A virus in a message.

8. What does it mean to archive your messages?

    a. Outlook will move messages received prior to a specific date into the Deleted Items folder.
    b. Outlook will move messages received prior to a specific date into a separate data file.
    c. Outlook makes a backup of the Outlook data file and stores it in another location automatically.
    d. Outlook tracks every action taken with a message in a summary file every 60 days.

9. Why might you want to create a signature?

    a. So you don't need to create a picture of your handwritten signature each time you send a message.
    b. To create a new message automatically every time you start Outlook.
    c. To include standard information such as your contact information on every new message.
    d. To automatically copy yourself whenever you send a message.

10. Why should you set up a notification that you will be out of the office for a period of time?
    a.   Business courtesy.
    b.   Allows people to know who to contact during your absence.
    c.   It's good business practice.
    d.   Any of the previous
    e.   a or c
    f.   b or c

Lesson 15:
Digital Citizenship

Lesson Objectives

In this lesson, you will examine the practices of good digital citizenship and online safety. On completion, you will be familiar with:

- ☐ the standards for professional communication
- ☐ how to avoid inappropriate behavior while online
- ☐ intellectual property, copyright and licensing rules
- ☐ ergonomics and how to set up a your workstation
- ☐ protecting your computer from software threats
- ☐ what viruses are and how to prevent them from damaging your computer
- ☐ how to protect yourself when conducting e-commerce or purchasing online

Identifying Ethical Issues

 Exam 3 - Objective 4.1, 4.2

As it becomes easier to contribute information to the Internet, the feeling of anonymity can cause some people to do things online that they might not do offline, or to disregard copyright laws or privacy issues.

Perceived anonymity, however, does not absolve individuals of responsibility for their online behavior, whether it is creating or modifying information, or communicating with others on a web site, Weblog, wiki, or chat room. Protect yourself and practice the same respect and common sense online as you would in face-to-face communications.

Understanding Intellectual Property, Copyrights and Licensing

Information on the Internet is freely available for you to read, listen to, or otherwise enjoy. People create web sites for many reasons – to advertise, to educate, to entertain, to intellectually challenge. However, simply because information is presented on a web site which you can access freely, that does not imply that information is free for you to copy, use, distribute or present as your own.

Intellectual Property

Any created work or invention is considered to be the *intellectual property* of the person (or organization) who created it. Essentially, anything created by an individual or group on their own behalf is owned by that individual or group; anything created by an individual or group under contract to an organization belongs to the organization that paid the "fee for service."

Estimating the true value of intellectual property is not an easy or straight-forward task. For example, suppose ABC company develops a training course on creating laser pointers. How much is this intellectual property worth? Is it worth the cost of one book? The cost of enough books for an entire class? The cost of conducting the training class itself? The cost of three years of classes? How do you factor in the time and money spent on creating ABC company's particular style and method of instruction? Has the style and method evolved over several years of improving previous works?

As another example, consider that Peter has spent 10 years writing an opera. How do we calculate the value of this creative work? Do we factor in the software he used? Do we factor in years of musical training seminars that helped him refine his approach? Do we factor in the number of people who ask if they may stage and perform the opera?

The point is intellectual property is highly valuable, and it is often equally difficult to calculate the degree of loss or damage incurred by the individual or organization whose property was stolen. While it may seem like a small thing to "borrow" all or part of someone else's intellectual property, misusing it amounts to theft or *piracy*, and in some cases even industrial espionage.

Copyright

Copyright laws were created to protect intellectual property. *Copyright* refers to the protection of any material, published or unpublished, created by an individual or organization. This applies to books, music, videos, essays, white papers, pictures, software programs, web sites, and so on.

A copyright is a law that gives you ownership of your intellectual property. It can cover anything that you create – a painting, a photograph, a song or a book – if you created it, you own it. Copyright law grants you, and you alone, specific rights over your intellectual property. For example, you have the right to make and distribute copies of your work, perform or display your work publicly, or create additional works based on the original.

These are your rights alone. No one can make a copy of your painting, use your web site code on their web page, or perform a song written by you, unless you give your specific consent.

A copyright also gives you the exclusive right to sell your work. While it is difficult to determine the value of a work, the copyright guarantees that you and you alone have the opportunity to sell, lease or otherwise use your work in exchange for compensation.

Registering a Copyright

As soon as an original work is fixed in a material form (a picture is painted, or a poem is printed, or a piece of code is saved to a disk), the work is protected by copyright. Generally, copyright protection begins from the date the work is created, applies for the entire lifetime of the author, and extends fifty years after the author's death.

When you have created an original work, it is advisable to put a copyright notice at the bottom. The notice includes the copyright symbol ©, followed by the date of creation, followed by your name. For example: Copyright © 2014 Andrew McSweeney. This is sufficient for asserting a copyright claim if someone violates your rights. For instance, if someone posts your song on their web site without your permission, you can make a claim and they will be forced to remove it.

However, if you want to be able to sue an offending party for monetary damages, then you should register your copyright with the copyright office in your region. For instance, to register a work with the U.S. Copyright Office, submit a completed application form, a nonrefundable filing fee ($35 if you register online), and a nonreturnable copy or copies of the work to be registered. You can find this form online at http://www.copyright.gov/eco/.

Copyrighted Material on Web Sites

Material presented on a web site is subject to the same copyright rules as information in any other media. As a rule, information is copyright-protected.

You can use copyrighted material only if the creator grants you the right to use it. Depending on the material, this could mean paying a royalty, or it could mean acknowledging the creator when you reproduce that content in your own work. It is your responsibility to determine what is required before using any part of an original work.

When information is published on a web site, you are permitted to view the information but restrictions apply to the way you use it. That is, you are limited to "fair use," which means that you can use portions of copyrighted information for the purpose of criticism or comment without seeking permission from the rights-holders. For example, if you are writing an essay on the results of a particular court case and want to comment on the judge's report, you can copy and paste the report from the web site with quotes and a reference. It does not matter whether your comments are positive or negative; the fair use principle protects you.

Copyright implicitly belongs to the owner of the web site or published material, even if no copyright symbol (©) or text appears on the product. The originator may have a patent on the product or technology, meaning that person has exclusive rights to make, use, or sell this product or technology. They may choose to license or grant you specific rights, but you cannot advertise the product or technology as your own. An example of this would be the Macintosh computer where Apple owns the patent for this computer and licenses out information for the computer to programmers who want to create software for it.

If you wish to use information but are unsure about the copyright situation, send the web site owner an email asking for permission to use the information and describe how you intend to use it.

Some web sites allow you to use the information they provide as long as you quote it accurately and give them credit. However, you must be careful about this as the web site owner may not be the original creator of the information, and therefore does not have the legal right to grant permission.

The following is a list of sources you can research for more information on copyright or trademark laws, and what is applicable in your location:

http://whatiscopyright.org
http://www.copyright.gov (United States Copyright Office)
http://www.copyright.com (Copyright Clearance Center, Inc.)
http://www.tmexpress.com (Trademark Express)
http://fairuse.stanford.edu (Copyright and Fair Use at Stanford University Libraries)
http://strategis.gc.ca/sc_mrksv/cipo (Canadian Intellectual Property Office)
http://www.iipi.org (International Intellectual Property Institute)
http://www.wipo.int (World Intellectual Property Organization)

Legal Ramifications of Copyright Infringement

If you are found to be in violation of a copyright, you will receive a letter from legal sources asking you to remove the content if it is on your web site, or delete any files that were downloaded such as songs, movies, television shows, and so on. You may also find that the ISP has terminated all services for your account, and there is the possibility you may be sued for any damages and have to pay a monetary settlement to the copyright owner.

Licensing

Licensing occurs when you are given permission to use a particular product or service from a vendor. For example, Microsoft displays a license agreement the first time you download clip art or media from one of their web sites for use in your documents. The license agreement states that you will not resell these files or claim these as your own works.

When you purchase a software program, you are purchasing a license to install and use that program on one computer only. This is also known as a *single seat* license. The traditional method of purchasing software is to obtain the program on CDs or DVDs in a package that includes a booklet with instructions on how to install and use the program.

You can also purchase and download software online. In such cases, you pay for the program, usually with a credit card, and then receive separate emails from the vendor confirming the purchase and providing a license number, often called the *product code* or *key code.*

An organization or company with a large number of users for a software program will usually purchase a *network* or *volume license* instead of individual copies. The network administrator will receive one media set (for example, a set of CDs) that contains the software, as well as options such as drivers. The network administrator then copies the program into a folder on the network, from where he/she can install it onto multiple computers and enter the key code to activate the program. The number of systems onto which the software can be installed is determined by the terms of the volume license. This option is cost-effective in reducing the amount of time needed to install a program on many computers. The network administrator can also perform installations from a remote site without needing to carry the software media around, thereby reducing the possibility of damage or loss.

A *site* license grants the purchaser permission to use the software on a network at a single location (site), with an unlimited number of end users. A site license usually allows you to copy and use the software on multiple computers at a single site. It is more expensive than purchasing a single copy but less expensive than purchasing a copy for each computer at the site. There may be a maximum specified number of simultaneous users.

Software is increasingly being sold as a service. Software as a Service (SaaS) or Application Service Provider (ASP) licensing enables you to access and use a software program from your system via a network, the organization intranet, or the Internet. You are required to log on to the appropriate network using a valid ID and password before you can access the software. Once a SaaS contract expires, you can no longer access that software until you renew the license. Managing the licenses can be done by a network administrator in an organization or by an ASP.

Although these are the most common ways to obtain software, there are other legitimate means as well. Other methods of distributing or obtaining software include *shareware, freeware, bundling, premium* and *Open Source.* Shareware are trial versions of software that you can download for free, but usually these programs have limited functionality or provide a limited amount of time that you can access the program. If you like the program though, you pay a nominal fee which removes these restrictions. Freeware programs do not charge a fee and may be shared with others at no charge. A potential drawback to using Shareware of Freeware is that support is often limited or non-existent and you are not automatically entitled to updates.

Software can also be "bundled" with a computer purchase. For example, when you purchase a new PC, the purchase price includes the license for the operating system, and may include a trial version of Microsoft Office, and a number of other programs included with specific vendors for services such as Netflix to view movies or television shows. Some of these programs may require you to purchase a full version of the program or to register online before you have access to the program, while others may include the full version and require no further action on your part. Premium software is an example of the latter and you would download the software from a specific web site offering these services.

Another type of software is Open Source, wherein the programming code is available to anyone who wants to use it. Some Open Source programs are set up like freeware in that they are available at no cost. You can modify the program to suit your needs and also share your version with others; however, you are not permitted to charge anyone for it. The feature that distinguishes Open Source programs is that, by sharing the programming code as well as the program itself, users who like certain programs can build in new functions and also make them available to others.

Whichever way you obtain software, it is your responsibility to ensure you are observing the licensing rules. When you purchase licensed software, you will be notified by the vendor of any updates and you will be able to obtain them at no additional cost. If you do not have a valid license, you will be violating the vendor's copyright and could be subject to legal action. A network administrator is aware of this responsibility and should take the necessary steps to ensure there are enough licenses for each computer in the organization. By accepting the End User License Agreement (EULA) at the time of installation, you further agree to abide by the rules for using this software on the computer.

Creative Commons

Creative Commons (CC) is a non-profit organization that provides six different types of licenses for people who want to share their creative works or knowledge and retain the copyright. These licenses do not replace copyright but help the copyright owner to manage how the creative works can be shared or used.

Using a CC copyright license provides a standard method of allocating permissions on the creative work within the restrictions of copyright laws and also ensures that the copyright owner gets credit for the original creative work. The copyright right owner can decide which license to use:

Attribution	Others will be able to distribute, remix, tweak and build on your work, so long as you are given credit for the original works. This license type is the most accommodating and recommended for maximum distribution and use of the licensed materials.
Attribution – NoDerivs	Others can distribute for commercial or non-commercial purposes but it must be in its original form with credit given to you.
Attribution – Non-Commercial – ShareAlike	Others can remix, tweak or build on your work for non-commercial purposes; they must give you credit and license the new work with the same terms of your license.
Attribution – ShareAlike	Others can remix, tweak, or build on your work for commercial purposes; they must give you credit and license the new work with the same terms of your license. This license type is used by organizations such as Wikipedia who want to ensure the public has the freedom to use, modify or redistribute the original works as well as any derivatives of the original works.
Attribution – Non-Commercial	Others can remix, tweak, or build on your work for non-commercial purposes. You must be given credit on any new work and be non-commercial, they don't need to license the new works using the terms of your original license.
Attribution – Non-Commercial – NoDerivs	Others can only download the original works and share with others provided you are given credit for the original works which cannot be changed or used for commercial purposes.

Licenses are also available where all rights are granted with the intent that the works are being placed in a public domain. In this scenario the owner is giving up all rights to the original works.

By providing an avenue such as Creative Commons to manage how copyrighted materials can be shared or used, this enables organizations such as Flickr, Google, or Wikipedia to make information available to the general public, in most cases without having to worry about violating any copyright laws. Information can be updated and distributed in a fair manner for the copyright owner, as well as the organization utilizing the license.

For further information on what Creative Commons does or how you can support this effort, refer to the following web sites:

http://creativecommons.org/

http://en.wikipedia.org/wiki/Creative_Commons

http://www.youtube.com/t/creative_commons

http://www.flickr.com/creativecommons/

http://freemusicarchive.org/curator/Creative_Commons/

Censorship and Filtering

The Internet does not have a governing body that oversees the content placed online; as such, there are many gray areas of what is considered good or bad material. This gives rise to debates over whether information should be censored or filtered with the intent to protect users from what may be considered offensive or dangerous information (such as how to make a bomb). Accordingly, many ISPs and organizations make use of different tools to help reduce certain types of information from being accessed.

Blockers and Filters

Blockers and filters are software that enable you to control the type or amount of content that can be viewed; these are often used in academic or corporate organizations to limit or block specific information. For instance, in a school environment, the network administrator may set up blockers for anything that refers to pornography, social media or other controversial sites as determined by the school administrators. An organization may set up blockers to prevent employees from spending a lot of time on the Internet instead of working, such as downloading pictures or videos. It may also set up email filters that check for specific words in incoming messages and if detected, then moves the message to a junk or spam folder – or you may not receive the message at all! One reason for blocking some sites is to reduce the possibility of a virus being downloaded to the server and then populating itself to every computer connected to the server, internal or external.

Some social media web sites may also set up blockers on messages or postings that may contain questionable or objectionable material, usually found in the Subject line. These blockers may originate at the ISP once you navigate to the social media site. Other sites such as chat rooms may have an individual who acts as a moderator to monitor the discussions and warns you when he/she deems the conversation to be inappropriate.

Another type of filter is referred to as *blacklisting,* which occurs when you have been flagged or placed on a list of users who are denied access to a particular service, privilege or recognition/credit. A simplified example of this is someone who sends a message often to a large group of recipients and the message is then considered to be spam. In order to have the sender's name removed from the blacklist that person would need to contact the ISP or vendor and explain why he or she should be removed from the list. In some cases he or she may need to send a formal letter requesting removal from the blacklist. In some cases, a user may need to switch ISPs if he or she is unable to get removed from one or more blacklists.

Arguably, the use of filters and blockers can be called censorship; however, one must also consider that an institution or organization has the right to enforce whatever guidelines it deems suitable concerning the use of their equipment and services. While filters and blockers can prevent specific types of information from coming into a network (that is, these tools effect the people within the organization), these tools have no effect on the people outside the organization who share content that is considered questionable.

Additionally, there is much disagreement concerning who should decide what constitutes offensive, dangerous, or exploitive information. For example, some web sites support a particular race or lifestyle and are often considered to be controversial or to promote "hate." The owners of these web sites are choosing to express their views through a medium that is available to anyone with Internet access, and in many countries, they are exercising their right of free expression. Unless a web site is deemed to have promoted an illegal action, the owners of the web site cannot be forced to shut down the site or to change their message.

The world consists of people from various cultures, beliefs, and lifestyles; what one person considers inappropriate or offensive may not be recognized in the same manner by another person. For example, some countries block their users from accessing any religious or spiritual web sites because they feel this is best for their residents while other countries consider this an extreme form of censorship. Note that a governing body that has censored content for the entire country usually has control over all the Internet-connected computers in that country.

Another shortcoming associated with the use of filters and blocks is that sometimes users are able to hack into the blocker or filter software and change the configuration. Vendors of the filtering software must, therefore, constantly upgrade their product to protect against hacking.

Practices to Avoid

For moral, ethical and legal reasons, there are certain online practices that should be avoided.

Plagiarism

Plagiarism is when you use information created by another person and present it as if it were your own, either word for word or with minor changes.

It is easy to find information on the Internet to use in your document, and just as easy for someone else to find it and recognize your use of it as plagiarism. This amounts to theft. It does not matter that it is only a paragraph of text or a single picture; it is regarded as stealing the intellectual property or original work of someone else.

When using information from the Internet, always use it in its original form and cite the source material to ensure you are following fair use principles. By acknowledging that you are borrowing the content and providing the information to find the source, in most cases, you will avoid being accused of plagiarism.

Libel or Slander

Libel is making an untrue statement in writing that "defames" a person's or an organization's reputation. If the defamatory remark is spoken, it's termed *slander.* Any defamed person or organization can sue for damages. The same rules apply to comments written on the Internet.

Ethically and legally, libel and slander are wrong. In practice, people do sometimes share unfavorable thoughts about others in confidence with people they trust. People taking part in chat rooms or Weblogs can fall into the trap of "speaking" freely, forgetting that they are actually writing and that their words are not anonymous. These words can both harm the person who writes them and the person who is being written about. The wisest course to take – both online and offline – is to treat libel in the same manner as you would rumors: do not start, do not listen, and do not respond.

Piracy

Piracy is usually associated with copyright infringement or plagiarism as this act assumes that original works have been reproduced or modified to fit a specific purpose, without the permission of the owner. Piracy also occurs when an item is shared with others at no cost, thereby reducing any compensation to the originator. Examples of piracy include downloading or uploading shared files like music, movies, videos or television shows (even for personal use) where no permission has been provided by the owners. Software is routinely pirated (purchased once and then copied and distributed countless times).

If you allow the downloading of copyrighted material (that you do not own and do not have permission to distribute), you can be sued. In a civil suit, you may have to pay damages to the copyright owner of up to $30,000 USD. If the court determines that the infringement occurred willfully, you may be ordered to pay up to $150,000.

Piracy is considered a federal crime if the court determines you are doing it willfully with an intent to profit. Criminal penalties include up to ten years imprisonment depending on the nature of the violation.

Piracy is also ethically wrong. If you would not steal a DVD from a music or video store, why would you download an album or movie from a web site that is illegally making these items available to the Internet public at no charge? Both actions amount to the same thing – stealing.

To protect yourself against any legal ramifications of accidental piracy, always purchase software from reputable retailers. Avoid downloading free songs or movies from sharing sites on the Internet, and do not install non-licensed copies of software.

Inappropriate Behavior

Some behavior is inappropriate and should not occur online any more than it should in our day-to-day offline life. There may not be laws addressing certain types of behavior, but you are responsible and accountable for your actions online. Consider the following types of inappropriate behavior:

- Pranks can be hurtful and should be avoided. Because of the assumed anonymity, the Internet is a prime arena for pranksters. For example, one person sends another person an email saying the boss is unhappy and wants to see him immediately. Later, the prankster sends another email saying that they were "just joking." Starting a hoax about a nonexistent virus is another kind of prank.

- Bullying online occurs when one or more people are hurt through constant, deliberate, hostile or malicious messages or posts. This includes harassment for any purpose. Bullying is not a harmless electronic action aimed at no one in particular. Bullying is targeted at real people, and it can cause severe stress, distraction and anxiety. In some cases, bullying has led to teenage suicide. Bullying is serious, dangerous and harmful. If you or someone you know is bullied or harassed online it is important to report the incident to the proper authorities. Many countries have existing laws or are drafting new laws to prosecute this type of behavior, no matter the age of the perpetrator.

- Avoid "flaming" people. A flame is an email or chat room message that personally attacks the recipient. Such messages have no place in business or school communication, informal or personal communication, or instant messaging. If you have been flamed, it is usually best to ignore it. If you respond in kind, this may lead to an escalation which is referred to as a "flame war". Like bullying, flaming is not a harmless, faceless action. Flaming is directed at real people, and can cause physical harm. There are documented cases where flaming has escalated into physical violence.

- Avoid spamming people. As you learned earlier, spamming is the sending of unsolicited electronic junk mail. Aside from the fact that people expect to be able to engage in online chat rooms and forums without running the risk of opening themselves up to receiving spam, spam messages can harbor malware, and malware is dangerous.

- Do not share personal information about others, even if all parties involved are well known. If someone has given you confidential or sensitive information, respect their privacy and keep it to yourself. This includes posting pictures or videos on social networking or video sharing sites. Use discretion if you are planning to publish anything to a social media site. Keep in mind that once pictures or videos have been made available online, even if you remove them from your site they may have already been downloaded by someone else who could then post them elsewhere.

- Do not ridicule or dismiss the opinions of others. People come from a variety of different cultures, traditions, and beliefs. Take care not to judge or respond in a negative manner to anything you see or read online. Remember that each person is as entitled to his or her opinions as you are to yours, and this should be respected online as well as offline.

- If you are creating information for online use, provide facts and sources to support the information. Be respectful and accurate, and target your tone and message to your audience appropriately. If the information is for a web page where personal opinions are encouraged, make it clear that the opinions expressed are your own and that you do not represent any institution, agency, religion, or political party.

Keep the golden rule in mind: do unto others as you would have them do to you - both online and offline.

Practicing Good Online Citizenship

 Exam 3 - Objective 4.1

The guidelines you use to be a good citizen in day-to-day offline life should also be extended when you are online. In fact, this may have more impact as the forms of communication you use directly reflect on you or your organization. It should not matter which form of communication you use; to reduce any communications issues, it is important to consider the following while living online:

- Running a spell check should not be the only tool you use to check your communication. It is important to ensure you have not only used the correct spelling but also used the word in the correct context, especially in a business scenario. For example, a prospective employer may not select your resume if he/she reads something that makes no sense grammatically, such as "I develop there policing and proceeds manual" versus "I developed their policies and procedures manual".

- Be very careful when using abbreviations or acronyms in the communications. The recipient should be familiar with the item of discussion in its short form before you include it in any communications. Even if you feel the recipient should know what the abbreviation is, extend the courtesy of providing it at least once in the documentation for a quick reference. For example: "We should contact Charles Martin (Chaz) at the Associated Press (AP) office tomorrow ..." instead of "Should cont Chaz @ AP 2morrow ...". Avoid using uppercase letters whenever possible for all or a majority of the text. This Implies shouting, yelling, or over-emphasis of a topic. Use proper casing instead, along with correct punctuation so someone who may not be familiar with that form of communication can decipher what is being said in the message.

- Always consider the intended recipient or audience of your communications. For business practices, even if you know the business contact very well on a personal basis, stay as professional as possible in your written (and verbal) communications as these are usually kept for archival purposes. All forms of communication whether written (email, text or instant messaging) or oral can be saved or recorded and stored

- Consider what might be the best form of communication for the purpose in question. For instance, it is likely faster to call someone to clarify an urgent issue than to send email or text and wait for a response. On the other hand, someone who may be having a difficult time getting their message across verbally may fare much better in listing the issues or queries in an email instead. It also is not realistic to expect that someone will respond immediately if you post something on a blog or social media site; these types of web sites are not considered to be time-sensitive means of communication. Even if you tend to text message someone frequently, you may want to follow up with a summary in a written letter or email to track what was discussed or decided. This provides you with the advantage of having a project update as well as a record of the communications.

- Try to remember to keep personal feelings out of your communications, especially if they are negative. An angry response sent in haste may lead to more confusion or miscommunication. Even when posting a personal response on a blog or other form of social media, remember that other people may see this information on that site. This may not seem important but many organizations use these sites as a reference source and see your response which could lead to an unfavorable opinion or judgment.

- Apply common sense and good judgment to what you may want to post online, not just in text but also pictures or links from other sites. Many organizations review social media sites such as LinkedIn, Twitter, or Facebook as part of their hiring procedures to research the type of activities you are involved in and if you would be a good fit for their team. Hiring policies generally include information about who you are in addition to your technical expertise, experience and education. For example, you are part of a committee selecting volunteers to help with a fundraiser to build a rehabilitation center. One applicant has posted pictures of himself/herself intoxicated at various parties – how is this likely to affect your decision to consider this candidate?

EXERCISE

In this exercise you will explore the Nine Elements of Digital Communications and then discuss with others these general guidelines and what impact they may have.

1. Start a web browser.

2. In the Address Bar, type: `www.bing.com` and press (Enter).

3. In the Search field, type: `9 elements of digital citizenship` and press (Enter).

4. Click the link that goes to www.digitalcitizenship.net/Nine_Elements.html.

5. Read the contents of this page and then open a discussion regarding each of these points.

   – How relevant are these points and do they apply to how one should behave online?

   – Are there areas where you think more guidelines may be needed?

   – What other areas do you feel should be included or expanded in this list?

6. Go back to the search results page and click other links to see the information provided there such as YouTube or MindMiester for example.

7. In the search field, type: `being a good online citizen` and press (Enter).

8. What results did you get this time? Click a few to read the contents and decide if they enhance what you read in the Digital Citizenship pages. For example, the http://cluna2014.wordpress.com/2014/07/15/being-a-good-online-citizen/ site displays a blog (article) written by someone who wanted to explore what it means to be a good online citizen as well as looking at Creative Commons images/pictures. Decide which stories and videos you want to watch to see if the submissions are helpful in understanding how to be a good online citizen.

9. After visiting a few more sites close the web browser.

Protecting Your Data or Computer

 Exam 3 - Objective 5.1

Storing personal and business data on portable devices such as notebooks or cellular phones raises the question of how to protect these assets. Replacing lost information or the unit itself is expensive and time consuming. The following guidelines can help protect the data and safeguard your work environment.

Theft

For business data, you can purchase systems to lock computers in special cabinets or use durable cables to tie them to the desk. Video camera surveillance is very effective for areas with a large number of computers like central offices and network rooms.

Do not leave portable devices unattended at any time when you are in public areas. For example, don't assume that if you leave your notebook on a table in a coffee shop you visit frequently the store employees or other patrons will watch it while you purchase another coffee. Another example could be leaving your device in your car where it may become attractive to a thief, or the device could be damaged if the car is exposed to extreme heat or cold.

Data Loss

You can lose data through a result of hackers, hardware failure, power spikes, accidental deletions, theft of a device, physical damage to a device, or disgruntled employees. If you provide a critical service, you should have an emergency plan in place to cope with an incident that causes a major loss of your system or its data. This includes having the proper security requirements on the network such as firewalls, enforcing encryption on wireless routers, and using a program to identify all authorized network users.

With portable devices, keep the device near you when you are in public. Consider using a synchronization program to copy the data from the portable device to a dedicated computer as a backup. This is crucial if you use your portable device to store personal information such as passwords, notes, private documents, or sensitive contact information.

To reduce the possibility of someone changing data files, consider adding a password to specific files or remove any shared rights on the files or folders. Work with your network administrator to protect the data, including scheduling regular backups of the data in case of theft, fire or access by a malicious external source.

Data Security

A *hacker* is someone who gains unauthorized access to a computer, generally with the purpose of "looking around", stealing or corrupting data. Take every precaution to protect your system from unauthorized access. A hacker could:

- steal information (such as designs or project information) with the intent of selling it,
- destroy data resulting in your company's inability to deliver products, services, or projects on time,
- change information, causing embarrassment and damaging a company's reputation.

An effective way to protect data is the through the proper use of passwords. You can limit access to critical information by ensuring everyone has a valid user ID and password. Use a strategy to make it difficult for hackers to guess your password:

- Use a formula that is logical enough for you to remember but not obvious enough for someone else to guess, such as your first name and the current month. A password consisting of the company's name and the current month could be considered obvious.
- Avoid using a nickname or the name of your spouse, child, or favorite pet.
- Try to use a combination of letters and numbers, as this is much harder to guess. You may want to create a rule for passwords requiring, for example, a minimum of six characters plus one symbol, or every other character is a number or uppercase character.
- Change your passwords on a regular basis, for example, every three or six months.
- If you are worried about remembering too many passwords, switch back and forth between three to five passwords.

- Use different passwords for confidential files and for logging on the network or the Internet. This will ensure that the files remain protected, even if someone guesses your system password.
- Be very careful if you choose to have the web browser remember your password for individual web sites. When you choose this option, anyone who is using your computer will be able to access the information for that web site. Refrain from activating this option with any web site that contains personal information such as online banking, or credit cards. Use caution even if the site keeps track of reward points only; if you entered any personal information for your login profile, others can gain access to this information as well.

Another way to prevent an unauthorized person from accessing your data is to ensure you install and maintain devices such as firewalls, gateways and specialized software to ensure the integrity of the server. A firewall's main goal is to control incoming or outgoing network traffic and determine whether particular data packets should be allowed through to the network or Internet. Without the security software to validate users, the network is vulnerable to anyone who wants to hack or steal the data.

Data security is a very specialized field. Most companies hire a security consultant to perform a risk assessment and recommend an appropriate security plan for the company. The plan should also include training for the employees.

Backups

You should back up your data regularly and store the copies in another location. You need only back up data files, as application files can always be reinstalled from the original media. Windows includes a backup program for this purpose, although third-party vendors also sell and support this type of service.

Every organization should have a backup strategy. Some key factors to consider are:

- Data should be backed up on removable media like magnetic tapes, portable hard drives or optical discs.
- The more critical the data, the more often it should be backed up. Most network servers are backed up at least once daily using an automated system.
- If users store data files on their local drives, encourage them to make a copy on the server for daily back up or to create backups of their own.
- When working with files, encourage users to save frequently to ensure there is no data loss. Some application programs also include an automated feature to save the files at a set interval.

Many large companies build in backups as part of their disaster and recovery plans and in fact, many companies use the cloud to store the backup copies. This provides not only an off-site location to protect the data but also the ability to restore the data from any location provided there is Internet access. For example, if there were a fire at the company premises, the network administrator can still be restoring the applications and data onto a new server from a remote site. Examples of cloud services include Microsoft OneDrive, iCloud, or Windows InTune.

Identifying Software Threats

Common software threats come in the form of viruses, worms, and spyware. There are numerous tools you can use to protect your computer against these threats; some of these are free while others have a cost. Windows 7 includes built-in spyware protection in Windows Defender. You can also download and install Microsoft Security Essentials, which monitors the system for spyware and viruses.

Spyware/Adware/Cookies

Spyware is a software application that is secretly placed on a user's system and gathers personal or private information without the user's consent or knowledge. *Adware* is a software application that automatically displays or downloads advertisements.

Many Internet-based applications contain spyware. Spyware can also be placed on a user's system by a virus or by an application downloaded from the Internet. Once installed, spyware monitors the user's activity on the Internet and sends that information to the person who created the spyware. That person can then gather web site usage, email and even password information from the user, then use it for advertising purposes or malicious activities.

Cookies are small text files placed on your computer by a server from which you have downloaded a web page. Although cookies themselves are not dangerous, they can be used to store user names and passwords if you click "Yes" when your browser asks you if you want to store this information. Cookies also track browser activities, such as sites you visit and options you select. A hacker who gains physical access to your system or successfully installs spyware can steal your cookies, and with them, any stored user names and passwords

You can download and install freeware spyware/adware detection and removal applications, or you can use Windows Defender to monitor your system for spyware.

Malware

Malware, or malicious software, refers to programs or files whose specific intent is to harm computer systems. Malware is an electronic form of vandalism that can have global implications. IT professionals must be aware of malware to be able to detect and remove malicious code before it harms systems and networks.

Malware includes computer viruses, worms and Trojan horses. Worms are self-replicating viruses that consume system and network resources, and can automatically spread from one computer to another. A worm can reside in active memory and replicate on the network. Worms can spread to all computers connected to a network and are commonly spread over the Internet via email attachments. A *Trojan horse* is a program designed to allow a hacker remote access to a target computer system. The code for a Trojan horse is hidden inside seemingly harmless applications, such as games. Trojan horses are installed on the target system when the user runs the infected application.

Downloading

In general, the term downloads refers to programs or other large files (such as video files) that can be executed or run on your computer after you copy them from a web server. Most browsers give you the option to save downloaded files to the hard drive or to install software directly from the Internet. Executable files in particular are considered to be potentially dangerous because they are often used to transmit malware and spyware.

It is strongly recommended that when you choose to download a file, you save the file to a designated folder on the computer and then scan the downloaded file to check for any potential threats before running the installation. An up-to-date antivirus program will detect any known threats included with the file, at which point you should delete the file and then also remove it from the Recycle Bin.

Be very careful to read the screen carefully before automatically clicking any buttons, especially the Accept or OK button. While the majority of programs are safe to download, it is important you read the End User License Agreement to see how your information can be used. Before automatically running an installation, perform a scan to ensure the installation file has no viruses, malware, or spyware. For instance, downloading a free song or music could lead to the installation of a virus on your system.

Be sure to also update the operating system (and other programs) to protect your data against any new viruses or threats from malware or spyware. Program and operating system updates often include security enhancements.

Personal Firewall Settings

When you work at a system owned by a school or organization, that system is protected by the organization's firewall. A firewall filters information coming into and going out of the network. Companies and schools use hardware firewalls to protect their computer systems. A hardware firewall is a physical device (such as a computer or router) whose function is to inspect all incoming and outgoing information, and to block any communications that are considered to be dangerous. The network administrator sets up rules that the firewall uses when making that determination.

A personal firewall performs the same basic function – it protects a computer from potentially incoming threats you may get on your personal computer, such as viruses, malware, spyware, or attempts at unauthorized accesses. Personal firewalls are software applications. Windows includes a built-in firewall, but you can purchase third-party firewalls if you want to take advantage of some specific features that they offer. Only one software firewall should be in effect at any given time. If you attempt to use two personal firewall programs at the same time, they can have the effect of canceling each other out.

Personal firewalls generally monitor communication requests coming in to your system from the Internet, and communication requests going out from your system. For example, programs (such as antivirus programs) which are designed to automatically download and install updates must connect to a server to search for available updates. These communications are designed to take place in the background so that they do not interfere with the user. However, a personal firewall may block these communications if it does not recognize that a particular program has permission to send and receive communication requests without the user's express knowledge.

You can check and adjust the personal firewall settings by selecting Windows Firewall from the Control Panel. If you are unsure what settings to use, work with a technical specialist. This should be one of the first items to configure for your computer when you have access to the Internet, in addition to ensuring you have an antivirus/spyware/malware program installed that scans all incoming or outgoing data files.

Updates

It is critical to update the operating system in order to protect against any known security issues. New viruses are created regularly and some of these are designed to exploit potential security risks in the Windows software. As such, Microsoft releases updates on a regular basis to protect systems against these software threats. When you receive notice of available Windows updates, you can check to see what the updates include and install the ones that address security issues. In most cases, even if some of the updates do not seem relevant to your system, run the update anyway to ensure you have the latest security updates to protect your system and data files.

Residual Files

Be aware that there can often be residual files left on any storage device (such as a hard drive, flash drive or portable drive), after you uninstall an application program, such as a game or trial version of a program.

While residual files in themselves are not dangerous, they can contain personal information which may be exploited if your system is compromised. For example, if you used an accounting program to track your bank accounts, the residual files may contain your account information, or your passwords. These files are generally stored in the program's folder on the hard disk.

After you uninstall a program, examine the hard disk to see if any of the program's folders remain. If you find any, you can manually delete them.

Some programs that do not uninstall completely can leave erroneous entries in the Windows Registry. The Windows Registry is a database in Windows that keeps track of configuration settings and installed software. Partial or erroneous entries in the Registry can cause performance issues in some cases. If you experience performance issues or receive error messages after uninstalling a program, you can use a third-party uninstaller program that can search for "left-over" Registry entries and delete them. You can also manually delete Registry entries. It is highly advisable to refer this type of issue to a specialist who has experience working with the Registry.

Residual files can also remain after you delete data files. Remember that files deleted from the hard drive are stored in the Recycle Bin. If you delete sensitive files, be sure to empty the Recycle Bin so that the files cannot be restored.

If you will be donating an old computer system that once held personal information, you should use a specialized utility program called a "shredder" that will destroy all data on the hard drive. Formatting the hard drive is not sufficient. Formatting the drive makes the storage space available once again, but does not destroy the data written on the disk, and that data can be recovered by knowledgeable users with a recovery tool. Shred the files on the hard drive, or remove the hard drive from the system before you donate it.

If you use portable storage devices (USB drives, SD cards or external hard drives), always be vigilant if those devices contain sensitive information. Do not leave them where unauthorized users may access them. When you no longer need to store sensitive information on these devices, be sure to remove the information completely.

Cookies

A cookie is a small text file that gets stored on your hard drive when you visit a web site. The web server that hosts the web site places the cookie on your machine, and the cookie is used to share information between your computer and the web server. The information contains the web site address and some codes that the web browser shares with the web site whenever you visit again. Cookies in general are not harmful or dangerous, and usually they do not contain personal information. These can be very helpful if you register on a web site and then want to log into your account each time you visit the site.

The disadvantage of this type of cookie is that anyone using your computer, who knows your account ID and password, will be able to log in and make a purchase using your account information. Another disadvantage is that a cookie can be used to identify certain purchasing habits or interests and this information can be sold to another vendor who will then market their products to you.

Cookies can be removed by clearing them from the web browser using the Tools command. How often you choose to clear the cookies is a personal choice although you should set a frequency if you want to reduce the amount of junk or spam mail you receive.

Understanding Viruses

A *virus* is a malicious program designed to damage computer systems. Specifically, a virus is a program that takes control of system operations, and damages or destroys data. Viruses are loaded onto your computer without your knowledge and run without your consent. All computer viruses are human made and are often designed to spread to other computer users through networks or email address books.

Viruses can be transferred via email attachments, program or file downloads, and by using infected disks, CDs, or flash drives. If you pass an infected drive to a co-worker, that co-worker's system can also be infected. Similarly, a colleague might inadvertently send you an email attachment infected by a macro virus. If you attempt to open or print the file, the virus will engage. Email attachments have become the most effective way to spread viruses.

A virus can:

- Display harmless messages on the screen.
- Use all available memory, thereby slowing or halting all other processes.
- Corrupt or destroy data files.
- Erase the contents of an entire hard disk.

There is only one way a virus can infect your computer – you let it! All viruses come into your computer through files such as email or instant messaging attachments, sharing files on a removable storage device, or downloads from a network or the Internet.

> **Tip:** Spyware and adware programs are not as potentially harmful to the computer as a virus; however, if the antivirus program installed includes protection for spyware or adware, be sure to activate these features and run checks or scans at the same time you check for viruses.

Viruses target both PC-type and Mac computers. Exercise caution no matter which type of system you use.

A common type of virus aimed at corporate networks comes in the form of an email attachment. Opening the attachment releases the virus, which then sends copies of itself via email to everyone in your contact list. This type of email virus does not damage data, but consumes network resources as messages are generated and sent automatically from every corporate system that has received the message and opened the virus attachment.

Consider a large corporation which uses a global email address book for all its employees. If one employee receives an infected message and opens the attachment that contains the virus, the virus will copy itself, and send an email message containing the virus to every address listed in the global address book. This process is repeated every time an unsuspecting employee opens the message (most employees trust messages received from people within their own company), and the entire company network can crash because of the dramatically increased volume of email traffic.

As you have already learned, some viruses are much more destructive. They can erase data files, cripple programs, and re-write entries in the Registry. In short, they can make a system completely unusable and corrupt all of its data.

Using an Antivirus Program

An easy way to protect against malware is to use antivirus software to scan email attachments and files for known viruses, and to eliminate any viruses that are discovered. All versions of antivirus software include free and frequent updates to the virus definition files that enable the program to recognize and remove the latest viruses. Always keep your antivirus program updated.

If your computer is infected with a virus, even if the antivirus program detects it, you may not be virus free without completing a full scan on the computer. Depending on the virus and its severity, the antivirus program may not be able to clean it from your computer but will quarantine the virus. It may also provide you with a link to the vendor's web site for other options. This is why it is extremely important to have an antivirus program installed on your computer and set up to run whenever the computer starts to protect your system from any virus causing damage to every file on your system.

Consider the following indications that you might have a virus:

- You see messages, prompts, or displays on your screen that you've never seen before.
- You notice the computer seems to be running slower or you are suddenly having problems with programs.
- Certain software applications no longer work, or programs are starting automatically.
- You hear random sounds or music that you've never heard before.
- Names of your disk, volumes, or files seem to have changed, and you did not make the changes.
- Your computer seems to contain many more or fewer files than you used to have.
- You see error messages indicating that a file is missing, usually a program file.
- You get messages with attachments from people you do not know.
- You begin to get many messages with attachments from people you know but the subject line has a "RE:" or "FW" prefix, even though you have not sent those people anything.

If you are concerned that your antivirus program may not catch everything on your computer, here are some things you can try:

- When you put a flash drive or CD into your computer, use the antivirus program to scan the portable device, even if there are no programs on it. Although a CD generally has a read-only setup for files on that CD, there may have been a virus in one of these files at the time it was burned onto the CD.
- If you receive email with attachments, never open the attachment without first scanning it. Even if the message comes from someone you know, check the attachment.
- If you suspect you might have a virus on your system, try going to the antivirus program's web site and running an online scan of your computer. The web site scan program contains all the latest virus definitions, as such, is able to catch anything that is on your system that may have been missed by your antivirus program (especially if it is not up to date). Using an online version of the antivirus program can also be useful if the virus prevents your antivirus program from running.
- You can also take the computer to a technical specialist who will be able to work with you to scan the drives in the system for any potential viruses, and then look for resolutions to quarantine and then remove the viruses.

Removing Viruses from the Computer

When an antivirus program is running, it will scan the files you select; when it finds a virus or threat, it will notify you and give you the option to quarantine or remove the threat.

- If you choose quarantine, the antivirus program will place the file with the virus in a quarantined or vault area where it can be prevented from infecting other files. Quarantined items can generally be deleted at a later date if required.
- If you choose to remove the file, the antivirus program will permanently delete it from your system. You usually do not need to do anything else.
- If the antivirus program finds a virus that cannot be removed, it will still quarantine the file. Make a note of the virus name and, when the scan is complete, go to the antivirus program's web site to find a removal tool for the virus. This generally involves downloading a file and then following the instructions to remove that virus from your system.

Occasionally, view the virus history on your machine and examine the files in the quarantine area. Delete any files with viruses that may still exist on your computer.

EXERCISE

In this exercise, you will examine your current security settings.

1. Open the **Control Panel**, click in the **Search** box and type: `security status`.

2. When the **Check security status** item appears in the Start menu, click it.

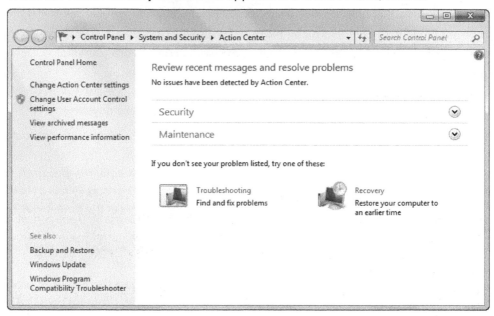

3. Click the arrow for **Security**.

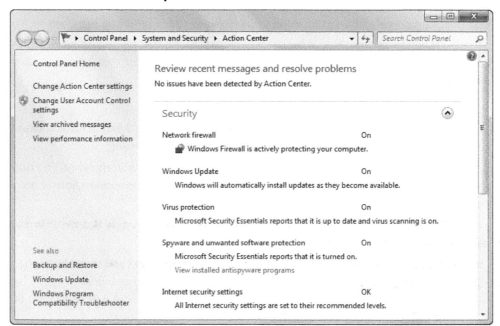

The information listed on the screen will vary based on which programs have been installed on your system for protection.

4. Scroll through the list to see which options are active on your system.

5. Close this window.

You will now look at the antivirus program available from Microsoft called Security Essentials. If there is a different antivirus program installed in the classroom or computer, please activate that program through the Start menu to view the options available with your antivirus program.

6. Click **Start** and in the search field, type: `security essentials`.

7. Click the **Microsoft Security Essentials** item at the top portion of the Start menu.

8. Click the **Update** tab.

Depending on how the program is configured on your system, you should check for updates to ensure that you always have the latest protection against viruses. The screen shown in the preceding figures indicates that the computer checks for updates automatically. In most corporate environments, computers are configured to automatically look for updates when the user logs on to the network.

9. Click the **Home** tab. Ensure the Scan Options are set to **Quick** and then click **Scan now**.

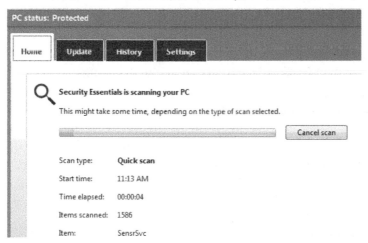

The length of time the scan will take depends on when the last scan was performed and how big the hard drive is on the computer.

10. As time permits, allow the scan to finish or click **Cancel scan** to exit this feature.

11. Close the antivirus program.

Preventing Personal Injuries

 Exam 3 - Objective 5.2

While computers can make our lives more productive, their use also brings certain safety issues into play. Safe computing involves adopting methods and techniques to avoid strain and discomfort while working, avoiding personal injury and protecting yourself from health hazards.

Working Safely and Comfortably

Repetitive stress injuries (RSIs) become commonplace as users begin to work on their computers for long periods of time. RSIs are conditions that occur gradually over time and are caused by too many uninterrupted repetitions of an activity or motion, particularly if the activity or motion is unnatural or awkward. RSIs for computer users usually affect the hands, wrists and arms, but can also affect other joints such as the elbow or neck.

To combat RSIs, users can use ergonomically designed furniture and proper techniques for safely using the computer. *Ergonomics* is the science of designing equipment that maximizes safety and minimizes discomfort. Measures you can take to prevent RSIs when using your computer include:

- Sit in a chair that provides lower back support, armrests and adjustable height.
- Use an ergonomic keyboard, which allows your hands to rest in a more natural position when you type than a standard keyboard does.
- Tilt the monitor up about 10 degrees to prevent neck strain.
- Use a padded wrist support to support your wrists when you are not typing.

To prevent eyestrain or headaches, you can:

- Position your monitor from 24 to 30 inches away from your eyes.
- Adjust the monitor resolution so text and icons are large enough to see clearly.
- Ensure that the monitor does not flicker. The refresh rate should be at least 72 Hz.
- Avoid staring at the display screen for long periods of time.

If you work at a computer for several hours a day, keep *ergonomics* in mind. First and foremost, <u>never</u> work at the computer without taking regular breaks. Get up once every hour, stretch, and walk about to get the circulation going and to rest your eyes. The following are some other points to keep in mind when considering how to create and use a computer workstation.

- The work surface should be stable; everything on the work surface should be resting flat.
- The monitor and keyboard should be directly in front of you, not at an angle.
- The top of the monitor should be about 2 to 3 inches above your eyes. You should not need to tilt or crane your neck to view the contents of the screen.
- There should be no glare or reflection on the screen. Where possible, ensure you have natural light with blinds that enable you to reduce or block any glare or reflection. Alternatively, have a lamp with appropriate wattage that enables you to identify images clearly in a darker room.
- Ensure there is appropriate lighting to read the screen clearly at any time of day. There should be a light source directly above the monitor, whether it is fluorescent lighting or a desk lamp. Where possible, try to pick a light source that simulates natural light.
- Place any documents that you will be looking at as you type in a document holder in line with the monitor.
- When seated comfortably, position your arms so that your wrists are straight and flat, and your arms are close to your body.
- Keep your feet flat on the floor and your thighs and forearms parallel to the floor. If your feet do not reach the floor, use a foot rest. This will help with blood circulation as you sit for a period of time.
- The keyboard should be in a comfortable position so your arms are not straining to reach up or down to the keys on the keyboard. This is also true for the mouse. In some cases, you may want to place the keyboard and mouse on a lower level than the level of the desk. Ensure the keyboard and mouse are close to you so you are not straining to reach them.

- When typing, try not to bend the wrists. Your wrists should be relatively parallel to the keyboard and if possible, use the entire arm to help with typing rather than just the fingers or the hand.
- If you feel strain on the wrist, arm or fingers when using the traditional mouse, try switching to a trackball, a larger mouse, or consider using a device that uses touch technology.

These guidelines also apply to notebook users, although an advantage of a notebook is the ability to take it with you anywhere, including the beach or in a vehicle. If you plan to put the notebook on your lap, ensure you are sitting appropriately as described in the guidelines, and where possible, use a tray or something sturdy to place the notebook on as you work. This will ensure a flat surface for the notebook as well as reduce the amount of heat, generated from the notebook, on your lap.

It is to your advantage to consider ergonomics when you work with a computing device for long stretches of time. Even with a portable device, think of how you are sitting and using the device as well as getting up periodically to stretch your muscles. Strains on your body can lead to more than just physical pain, but also lead to a reduction in mental alertness, low productivity, errors in your work, or absences from work or school from physical ailments.

EXERCISE

In this exercise you will assess how you are positioned in front of the computer and what you may want to correct to reduce potential ergonomic concerns.

1. Stand up and stretch your body, reaching high with your arms to stretch your back.
2. Take a closer look at the chair you are sitting in and note where the handles or levers are located. Find the one that adjusts the height of the chair and make the appropriate adjustments for yourself.
3. Look straight at the monitor and determine if it is at eye level. If possible, tilt the monitor so you can see it better without having to strain your neck.
4. Pull the keyboard close enough to you so you are not stretching your arms or back to reach the keys.
5. Repeat step 4 with the pointing device for your computer.
6. Now work with someone in the class to review how you are positioned in front of the computer and whether there are things that could be adjusted to provide a better working environment.

Protecting Yourself While Online

 Exam 3 - Objective 5.1

As mentioned previously, the Internet has no one governing body determining what is appropriate behavior by individuals or companies. Accordingly, you need to be careful while online and take steps to protect your personal information. One guideline you can always apply is ensuring the passwords you use are as secure as possible. Also, periodically change your passwords to ensure further protection of your personal information.

For sites where you want to register for further information, consider using an alternate email address such as an account with a Web-based provider such as Yahoo!, Google or Outlook.com to help reduce the number of potential junk messages you may receive in your main email account. You may want to use your main email address only for those sites where you actually purchase items and as your general Inbox.

Buying Online

How safe you feel conducting transactions such as banking or making a purchase online will determine how much e-commerce (electronic commerce) or online shopping you do. Many web sites have taken appropriate steps to ensure their customers' security, but there are additional steps you can take to protect yourself.

If a company offers a deal that seems too good to be true, research that deal. Take the same precautions you would take if someone made that offer offline—would you give a large sum of money to a person without researching the product or service they are selling? Research the company's credibility by calling the contact numbers listed on the site, look for a client list or customer references.

Check the web address to see if they have any security options included for their site. For instance, if you wanted to see which products Amazon has to offer, you would type: www.amazon.com in the address bar of the web browser, which then displays the following in the address bar:

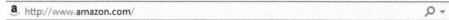

Notice how the address shows http://www.amazon.com, even though it wasn't added to the web site address you entered. Remember that http is a protocol used to recognize instructions sent to the web server so it can understand how to respond to your request from your computer. In this case this is a general page of information for this vendor. Once you decide to set up with an account for the vendor and sign in, the web address changes to display as:

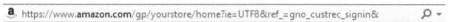

Whenever you see https, this means you are in secure portion of the vendor's web site to make a financial transaction. When a site displays a lock icon and it is activated, this means you are in a secure area of the vendor's web site to review any previous or new transactions made.

Secure portion of the Amazon web site   **Security Icon**

When you submit your personal information to an e-commerce site, you connect over a *secure connection*, as indicated in the URL (https) as well as the 🔒. This indicates you have a connection that uses the *Secure Socket Layer (SSL)* protocol instead of the unsecured Hypertext Transfer Protocol (HTTP). SSL is an encryption technology developed to secure web transactions. SSL was the predecessor to Transport Layer Security (TLS), the latest encryption method used to secure online transactions.

Most web transactions are secured using encryption. Encryption is the process of converting data into an unreadable form. Decryption is the process of converting encrypted data back into its original form. Encryption and decryption are made possible through the use of keys. A key is simply a mathematical algorithm.

There are various models of encryption. Public-key encryption is the model used for securing web transactions. In public-key encryption, electronic information is encrypted using a public encryption key before the information is sent over the Internet. The public key is known to all sending and receiving parties. When a party on the other end receives the encrypted information, a private encryption key is applied to the information to "decrypt" or unscramble it and convert it back into its original, readable form. The public and private key are mathematically related, and the private key is known only to the receiving party.

Do not give out your credit card information indiscriminately. You would not give this information over the phone to a stranger, so take the same care online. You can sign up for an account with a vendor without making a purchase so you don't need to provide a credit card at that time. There are also other options to make payments for online purchases without using a credit card, such as using a service like PayPal.

Be sure the web site is a well-known and reputable company, for example, Amazon, Apple, Dell or Disney. If the company has a good reputation based on its retail stores, its sites will be well protected for e-commerce. If the company is not known to you, be sure to research it before purchasing anything from them online. Your research should also include information about others who sell the same product or service, as well as organizations that track good and bad reports about companies, such as the Better Business Bureau (BBB).

Note also that when you purchase an item, once you click the appropriate button to indicate the actual purchase with a credit card, the vendor will then perform the transaction at their end. This may take a few moments to finalize. As the transaction is taking place, do not click any buttons until you see the page telling you the transaction was successful. Clicking the Back button to try and submit the purchase again may result in the vendor charging you for a second purchase of the item.

Choose e-commerce sites carefully. When you begin a transaction such as a purchase, look for the lock icon indicating that the transaction is secure. A legitimate e-commerce site will also have a privacy policy or statement included on its front page. Be sure to look for this statement and read it to see what conditions or requirements you will be subject to if you choose to do business with this vendor.

When you navigate to a site to purchase something, check that the web site address is spelled correctly, and that the site is set up the way you would expect from the company. This can help you determine if you are at the correct site for that vendor. For example, if you wanted to purchase another copy of this book from CCI directly, the site address to navigate to would be shop.ccilearning.com; you could also type the registered web site address of www.ccilearning.com and then click the Shop Online feature from the home page. If you were to type www.cci.com/shop you would be directed to a completely different type of business than CCI Learning Solutions. To determine which may be the correct web site, you may want to start by visiting the vendor's home site initially and look for a link to their e-commerce site.

Phishing for Information

Phishing refers to the process of gathering personal information from someone with the intent to commit a criminal offense. *Spoofing* is when a person or web site appears to be a legitimate organization but in reality has simulated the screen to look like the legitimate company and will gather your personal information behind the scenes for illegal purposes.

One of the dangers of being online is the possibility of identity theft. This happens whenever personal information is obtained without the owner's permission. Identities are stolen for the purpose of committing fraud or other criminal activities resulting in getting credit, other financial gains, or impersonating someone. Once the criminal has your personal information, he or she can obtain additional identification, using your credentials, such as a new social insurance card, credit cards, or other pieces of personal identification.

An example of how phishing works is if you receive an email or see an advertisement asking for contributions to a worthy cause; be sure to check the validity of this charity. Never send checks or money orders, offer credit card information, or use any electronic form of transferring money to this organization unless you have absolute confirmation of its validity. Call the organization or go to the local branch of that charity directly to confirm the information in the email. If you contribute and later find out that the charity is fraudulent, it is extremely difficult to get your monies back, or worse, any personal information you may have provided during the transaction.

Spoofing can occur if you receive an email from a financial institution asking you to click a link in the message to update your personal information. Never click the link without calling the financial institution first to determine if you do need to update the information. In a scenario such as this, criminal elements have created a web page that looks very much like the authentic financial organization's web site. However, once you click the link in the message, you are actually directed to a web site where your personal information will be gathered and then used for fraudulent purposes, such as transferring funds to their own accounts, gaining access to your PIN codes or creating new cards with your identity. This is another example of how identity theft can occur without you being aware that your personal information has been stolen. In this scenario, you could be held responsible for any purchases or fraudulent acts committed with your identity, and your credit rating could be damaged.

Another example of a phishing exploit is this: you receive a telephone call from someone claiming to be a well-known vendor such as Microsoft, and this person indicates that they have detected an issue with your computer. Do not share any personal or financial information with them. Do not give them access to your computer and verify the call by asking for a telephone number so you can return the call. Also, be sure to research the number before you return the call. Beware of any hoaxes of this type (such as a warning about a problem with your social networking site) as you may be directed to a spoofed site asking for personal information.

How Much Information Should I Share?

The amount and type of information you wish to share will be at your own discretion. As there are no definitive rules or guidelines for Internet use, you need to apply your own filter as to what you want to share and with whom. Remember that the information you find on a web site about a company, or profile page about someone, may not be totally accurate, and in some cases may be totally fraudulent. It therefore becomes your responsibility to use common sense when deciding how much information you should share with others. Always consider what you would do in your offline life and extend this to your online life.

For instance, refrain from sharing or trading personal information with anyone you chat with online. There is no way of determining whether they may fraudulently use your ID and password. This also includes sharing any financial information in an IM transmission or chat room with people you know very well. Information sent in instant messages or chat sessions is not secure, and can be intercepted by anyone who is illegally monitoring conversation traffic. Once your information has been compromised, there is no easy way to determine who is using your information.

Be careful who you trust online. Even though they appear to be friendly, they may not be who they say they are. For instance, a personal friend may have had their login ID and password compromised and someone else is using the compromised account and pretending to be that friend. They could be looking to gain personal information from anyone in the contact list connected to that account.

Avoid posting personal information such as your age, gender or phone number, online and never agree to meet someone you met online alone. This may seem harmless but for your safety, always try to pick a public place and take a friend or parent with you who will be able to help you should the circumstances turn negative.

In the same theme, don't broadcast on any social networking or chat programs if you are going away for a length of time. Even if you don't show your address anywhere in your profile, be careful about sharing personal details that could allow someone to determine where you live or spend your time, such as a picture of the front of your home, or of the unique street signs.

Seriously consider the types of pictures or text you post on social networking sites. What you may consider to be harmless and inconsequential may result in different responses than anticipated. Remember that the world consists of diverse cultures and beliefs and as such, everyone is entitled to their own opinions and judgments. What may be accepted in your country or social circles may not be considered appropriate by prospective employers or other countries or industries. For example, if one of your interests is collecting unique insects, sharing pictures of these may be fun for your friends but others may respond with less favorable comments.

Protecting Your Privacy

Infringement of your privacy occurs when personal information about you is shared with or sold to others without your knowledge. Any time you visit a web site, some information about your activity is left on your computer. There is no such thing as total or absolute privacy when you surf the Internet.

Others can track information whenever you visit Internet sites through methods such as online forms, cookies, history of sites visited or your temporary Internet files. Some sites track your activities during the time you are visiting their sites (for example, which pages you go to, which links you click, how often you visit). In most cases, this is harmless as it is most often used to improve target marketing.

One of the best ways you can protect yourself is to read the privacy statement on the web site. The privacy statement should clearly state what information they seek and how they plan to use it. Some web sites can gather information about the hardware and software on your computer by asking specific questions when you download an item or fill in a form.

In addition to some of the methods to protect yourself mentioned previously, some other steps you can take to protect your privacy include:

- Do not fill in any forms unless you really want something from that web site. If you cannot go any further into the web site without registering, be sure that this is a reputable company, you have read their privacy statement or policy, and you understand how they plan to use the data. You can also ask the company not to use your name in any manner although this may be ignored by the company.

- If you do register with a web site, be sure to not select options that indicate you would be interested in receiving email from third-party companies on related products or services. If the web site provides you with the option to share your information with their partners, consider carefully whether you want this.

- Delete the history for sites you have visited. Use the options in your web browser to clear the history immediately or set a frequency period for when the browser clears the history.

- *Shoulder surfing* is the practice of obtaining sensitive information by looking over someone's shoulder. Shoulder surfing can happen while you are standing at an automatic teller machine, entering the PIN for your debit card at the grocery store, entering your email password on your Smartphone, or entering your user name and password on your laptop at an airport WiFi spot. Be aware and take notice of who is around you and where they are standing. If necessary, cover your screen or move to a more secluded area when entering sensitive information.

- Purchase third-party software that directly addresses privacy issues. Many of these programs contain more features than those available with your web browser. An example is CyberScrub Privacy Suite that will enable you to permanently erase the Internet history on your system. Another software program with similar features is WinSweeper.

- Be careful to avoid including any add-ins or toolbars when you download a program for evaluation or entertainment. Additional toolbars may permit the collection of information about your web surfing habits. Watch that you do not inadvertently download an unwanted application or toolbar when downloading software, particularly free software – read the screens carefully when downloading.

While on the Internet, the easiest rule to follow is to use your common sense. Companies on the Internet operate very similarly to the way they do in in their brick and mortar stores; any special offers or services that are not a direct part of the original service or product lead to receiving mail from other companies that you may not be interested in. If you are asked for information that you are not comfortable giving, follow your instincts and do not share that information.

There is a wide range of sources on the Internet that discuss and explain privacy issues more thoroughly and offer suggestions on how you can protect yourself and your family when living online. There are also various initiatives to prevent people from obtaining information or contacting you, such as keeping your telephone numbers off a list that can be used by telemarketers, or sharing information gathered in cookies. One such initiative is the Opt-out Tool developed by the Network Advertising Initiative that will scan your computer to identify any member companies that may have placed an advertising cookie file on your computer. You then have the option to "opt out" of any advertising by removing any cookies left by that company. Other programs of this type include the Internet Advertising Bureau and Digital Advertising Alliance that help to develop industry standards and research different advertising strategies for online use. To read more information about these types of organizations, navigate to the following sites:

http://en.wikipedia.org/wiki/Interactive_Advertising_Bureau

http://www.aboutads.info/ (Digital Advertising Alliance)

http://www.ghostery.com/

http://en.wikipedia.org/wiki/Ghostery

http://en.wikipedia.org/wiki/HTTP_cookie#Privacy_and_third-party_cookies

EXERCISE

In this exercise, you will apply your research skills to help determine how to identify ways you can protect yourself and any data files you may have on your computer.

1. In a web browser, navigate to www.disneyworld.disney.go.com.

Notice how the web address shows the https protocol, which means you have accessed a secure area of the Disney web site. The lock icon is available to view more information about the security on this site.

2. Click the lock icon.

3. Click **Should I trust this site?**.

Certificate errors: FAQ

Internet Explorer 10 ⌄

Occasionally you'll get an error message telling you there's a problem with a website's security certificate. A site's certificate enables Internet Explorer to establish a secure connection with the site. Certificate errors occur when there's a problem with a certificate or a web server's use of the certificate. Internet Explorer helps keep your information more secure by warning about certificate errors.

What do certificate errors mean?

Error message	What it means
This website's security certificate has been revoked	You shouldn't trust this website. This error often means that the security certificate was obtained or used fraudulently by the website.
This website's address doesn't match the address in the security certificate	This error means that a website is using a certificate that was issued to a different web address. This error can occur if a company owns several websites and uses the same certificate for multiple websites.

4. Read a part of the screen and then close it.

5. Close the popup window regarding certificate errors if one is open.

6. On the Disney page, scroll to the bottom of the page and click **Privacy Policy/Your California Privacy Rights**.

7. Read the first few paragraphs to see what Disney does with information you provide if you register on this site.

8. In the address bar, type: `www.apple.com` and press ⌈Enter⌋.

    Notice here that Apple does not have any security as this is their front page to inform the user of what products and services Apple has to offer.

9. Click the **iTunes** tab to move to this page.

    Apple still does not show the lock icon to indicate a safe site even though you can download the software from this page. This is because iTunes is an example of a product that is copyrighted to Apple but is made available at no cost to everyone through a Creative Commons license.

10. Scroll to the bottom of the page and click the **Privacy Policy** link.

11. Read the privacy policy here to see how Apple deals with information it may obtain from any submissions or purchases.

12. In the address bar, type: `10 things you should not share on social networks` and press `Enter`.

13. Click one of the results (such as the one from computer.howstuffworks.com) and navigate the page to read about the listed items. Then try some of the other results to see what their list contains.

    As you view each page, note the date the article was published on the web site and how some items still apply for today's social networking sites. Again, how much information you choose to share is at your discretion but do give consideration to how some of the items here may affect your life or those of friends and family.

14. In the Search field, type: `risks of buying online` and press `Enter`.

15. Scroll through the results list and then click one of interest to you, such as a link giving you tips on how to purchase items online.

16. Research other topics covered in this lesson to see how trends or behaviors may have changed since certain sites came online. For example, how many video stores are still in business in your location versus people using Netflix to watch movies? Or the number of new blogs or forums you can join or favorite sites that now have an area for you to chat to other members.

17. Close the web browser when you are finished.

Lesson Summary

In this lesson, you looked at the practices of good digital citizenship and online safety. You should now be familiar with:

- ☑ the standards for professional communication
- ☑ how to avoid inappropriate behavior while online
- ☑ intellectual property, copyright and licensing rules

- ☑ ergonomics and how to set up a your workstation
- ☑ protecting your computer from software threats
- ☑ what viruses are and how to prevent them from damaging your computer
- ☑ how to protect yourself when conducting e-commerce or purchasing online

Review Questions

1. When sending email to a prospective employer, what type of writing style should you apply for the cover letter and resume?
   a. Business and professional
   b. Casual
   c. Combination of a with some business humor
   d. Combination of a and b

2. You wrote an exceptional research paper on the economic conditions in 2013. A teacher now reads another report with exact portions from your research paper. What is this an example of?
   a. Copyright infringement
   b. Fair use
   c. Plagiarism
   d. Creative commons

3. How does libel differ from slander?
    a. Libel applies only when speaking about celebrities.
    b. Slander occurs when the false statement is spoken verbally whereas libel is defamation in writing.
    c. Slander results in a larger fine.
    d. There is no difference.
    e. a or c

4. In choosing a secure password, what guidelines should you consider?
    a. Maximum 8 characters.
    b. Combination of upper and lowercase characters.
    c. Use all numbers.
    d. Add at least one symbol.
    e. Minimum 8 characters.
    f. All of the previous.
    g. b, d & e

5. What are residual files?
    a. Files that stay on the computer all the time.
    b. Operating system files to help you install printer (or other devices).
    c. Files that identify and validate your network id and password.
    d. Files that are left on a storage device after an application program is uninstalled.

6. Before you add any extra features to a newly installed antivirus program, what should you do?
    a. Get the network administrator to help.
    b. Automatically download the file you want to install on the computer.
    c. Scan the computer for any existing viruses, spyware or adware.
    d. Reboot needed only.

7. What are some ways you can protect your privacy while online?
    a. Do not fill in any forms where you may not be interested in getting information from the company.
    b. Use an alias when on public forums or blogs.
    c. Do not check the option to receive information from retail partners of the company.
    d. Any of the previous.
    e. a or b

MMM
Go online for
Additional
Review

Lesson 16:
Finding Information

Lesson Objectives

In this lesson, you will conduct research and evaluate information you find on the Internet. On completion, you will be familiar with:

- ☐ finding items on the Internet
- ☐ evaluating search results
- ☐ searching for an item on a specific web site
- ☐ what a search engine is and how it works
- ☐ narrowing a search using the search engine
- ☐ evaluating information on the Internet

Searching for Information

 Exam 3 - Objective 6.1, 6.2, 6.3

Millions of web servers worldwide are connected via the Internet. On average, each server hosts one thousand or more web pages.

No organization monitors the information on the Internet, which means you will find both good and questionable information there. Use your own discretion to determine what is appropriate viewing or what information is valid.

One of the main purposes of creating a web site is to share information with others. The design of the pages on a site will vary depending on the organization and the purpose of the business or service. Many sites include a search field somewhere along the top or along the left side of their web pages. You can use this search field to search the web site for specific information. Using the search field on a web page searches only the web site to which the page belongs; this is different from searching the entire Internet for information on a specific topic.

Additionally, different types of sites contain different types of information:

- Business web sites usually include pages that describe the company and its products or services, as well as areas for feedback or online purchases. Depending on the business, there may also be pages with interactive or entertainment options to make the experience with that web site more enjoyable; examples might include Disney, a television station, or Apple.

- Government web sites tend to include pages for each department, and additional pages with links to files or forms that you can download. Depending on the department, you may also find that the government will provide you with numerous statistics for topics such as census or employment. There may also be pages with lists of resources and contacts to other organizations that deal with this government agency.

- Social networking sites such as Facebook or Twitter enable subscribers to share photographs, games and videos, chat online, or post simple messages. Many of these sites offer the ability to create simple pages dedicated to specific topics or people such as musicians or bands, worthy causes such as the environment or cancer research, or general interest topics like scrapbooking, sport teams, or specific themes. Other people have created applications such as games or quizzes designed to run in the social networking environment; site members are encouraged to install these applications and play with or against others registered on the site.

- Blogs allow individuals to enter comments or information on pages devoted to specific topics. These sites provide an easy way to create or modify content and share it. For instance, a student living abroad may set up a blog as a journal where he/she can post updates, photographs, or videos. His or her family and friends can visit and make comments on the blog to stay in touch and to find out more about the student's life away from home. A blog can increase its credibility when it includes links to other blog sites and those sites contain links back to this blog site.

- Wiki sites are used as sources of information and provide tools that enable individuals to add, edit or rearrange information on the site. The changes can be tracked by users of the site to see who entered the information and how valid, accurate and up to date it is. Because of this "public editing" process, wikis tend to be fairly reliable sources, as long as there is a high number of contributors to that wiki site.

- Other sites allow individuals to upload multimedia items such as photographs, video, audio and podcasts. For example, YouTube includes both professional and amateur created videos. Material can be uploaded only by registered users, but registration is not difficult and is free. However, the site enforces terms and conditions regarding the type of videos that can be uploaded to provide viewers with some protection against questionable content.

- YouTube also welcomes uploads in the form of *podcasts*. Anyone with an appropriate multimedia program can record audio, video, or both and save the files in a format that will be recognized as a podcast. These files can be viewed on the web site, as well as on a computer or portable media player such as a Zune, iPad, Galaxy or iPod.

- A news feed site distributes press releases as stories occur rather than at set times as on television, radio, or in print. Individuals can subscribe to a news feed at no cost to get these updates, which may be viewed via a newsreader or newsgroup either in your email program or on the news web site. These sites typically encourage viewers to respond to news items. News feed sites are somewhat like bulletin boards in that you can view and comment on the feeds without providing your email address.

- Sites that are designed to provide reference links can be found on individual web sites or set up as part of a search engine web site. Many of the aforementioned types of web sites include a page with links to other pages or sites providing information on the same topic. For instance, suppose you visit the web site for the Louvre museum in France and view a page about a special exhibition of Egyptian artifacts. That page may include links to web sites describing other exhibitions of Egyptian artifacts as well as a link to the Egyptian government agency that manages the transportation and protection of Egyptian artifacts being shown around the world.

- There are numerous education web sites available on the Internet although the ones with a .edu domain are generally associated with an accredited school such as a university, high school, or college. These sites contain a wealth of information pertaining to curriculum planning, lesson plans, examples of reports or exams in addition to a list of resources for particular course types, such as mathematics, biology or history. You may want to search a .edu site if you were looking for information on how to structure a class project.

When searching for information, also consider using traditional sources such as the public library or a local university. Traditional sources like these still offer a wide variety of information in the form of periodicals, microfiche, reference books, and other types of publications that may not be available online.

All these methods to search or find information are designed to provide you with alternatives when researching or acquiring knowledge on a specific topic. As you will see in forthcoming portions of this lesson, you can search for items on a global basis or narrow the search to target a specific subject. It is recommended that you compare information found on various sites to determine the accuracy before making use of any of the information. In fact, in some cases, you may want to verify the information you find online with information found in a traditional source such as an encyclopedia or journal, especially if the topic is fact-based and easily verifiable.

Searching a Specific Web Site

One of the fastest ways to search for information is to use a search engine or search field on a particular web site. Any criteria you enter in a particular web site's search field will provide results from this web site only. This can make it much easier to search for information on a specific topic, service or item that is sold or provided by this company.

The location of the search field will vary from site to site, although it is generally located near the top of the web page.

EXERCISE

In this exercise you will look for specific information in one web site to see what kind of results you receive.

1. Start the web browser and in the Address Bar, type: `www.microsoft.com/office` and press `Enter`.

    You should now be at the main page for Microsoft Office products. Notice that the **Search** field is quite close to the top of the page, enabling you to enter text for what you want to see on the Microsoft Office site.

    Suppose you want to find information about Office 365, a cloud solution promoted by Microsoft.

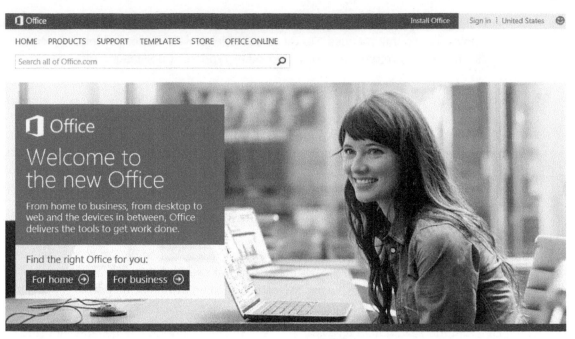

2. In the **Search** text field, type: `office 365` and press `Enter`.

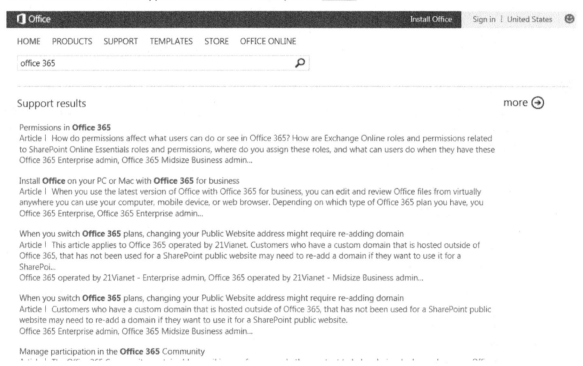

3. Click one of the results to see the information returned for your search. Click **Back** to return to the results page.

4. Now change the search criteria to: `office online`.

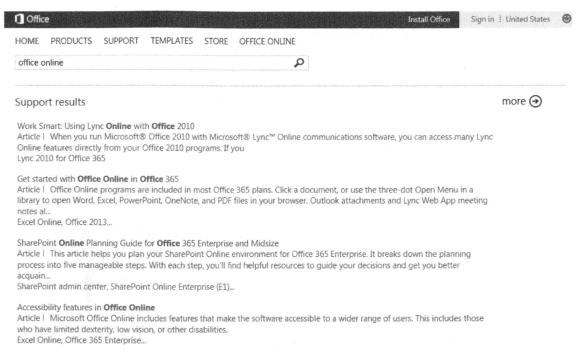

Notice how Microsoft displays results for the new search criteria but still in relation to Office, given that you started with the Microsoft Office site.

5.   Click the **Home** button to return to the home page of the web browser.

Using Search Engine Technology

The purpose of any search engine is to provide an easy and fast way to research information stored on other web sites in order to find answers to questions posed. An Internet search engine has three basic tasks it can perform:

- Search the Internet based on the search criteria entered
- Keep an index of the words found, and
- Display where to find information stored in these indexes

A search engine web site specializes in making it easy to find information on any topic, located anywhere on the Internet. Some commonly used search engines at the time of writing are Google™, bing™, Ask® and Yahoo® Search!.

Although the services provided by these companies vary, they all use similar technology. The search engine consists of a database of Internet URLs; each record in the database includes the URL, a short description, a title, keywords, and other site information. Users access the URL database via the search engine company's web site, as shown in the diagram.

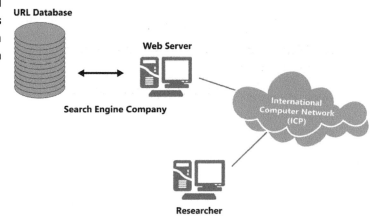

A search field on the search engine company's web site works in the same way as a search field on an organization's web site. The difference is that the search engine company's web site searches its database, compiles a list of records matching the keywords, and returns a list formatted as a web page, which may look similar to the one shown below:

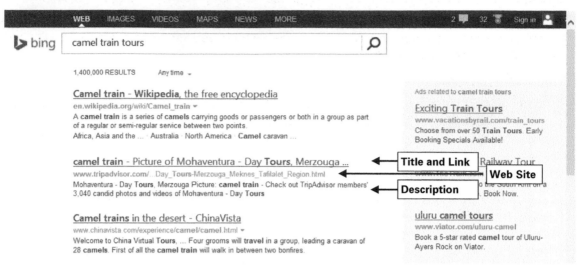

Most search engines rank the URLs they retrieve by how closely the information associated with that URL matches the keywords entered in the search field. However, sometimes web sites are written to include hidden keywords or tags and may appear in a list of results even though they do not seem to be related to the keywords or search criteria entered.

Understanding How Search Engines Work

Although search engine companies use similar technology, they differ in the features offered and in search effectiveness. Be aware of these differences so you can select the search engine that will return the results best suited to your specific research requirements.

The content in search engine databases is partly determined by how the companies capture the URL information. The standard process is for the site owner to submit the URL to the search engine company (SEC), which then uses its software to extract information automatically from that site. The number of URLs in the database depends on the diligence of the web site owners and developers in submitting their URLs for inclusion in the database.

Some SECs, such as Yahoo!, use human operators rather than software to extract URL information. This is a slower process but may result in more accurate data.

Rankings used to be set from the number and type of keywords you submit to the search engine company. Most companies would like their web site to be ranked near the top as most users tend to click on one of the first five results and don't scroll down to see if other results might be more relevant or have reliable information. Rankings are now determined by the content and also by how frequently others link to you.

SECs use indexes, which reduce the amount of time it takes you to find information regardless of whether you are looking for text, video, or audio. These indexes may also include directories or lists that include other links as well as FAQ (Frequently Asked Questions) pages, where people can submit content regarding topics of common interest. Another option for an SEC is using shared bookmarks, which is referred to as a *social search engine.*

Some SECs have moved to a more collaborative search engine model where an online chat option allows you to search for items and also chat with someone at the SEC who may notice that you need assistance in narrowing the search criteria.

Another option for finding information is to use link lists, indexes, shared bookmarks, or other suggested links that appear on a variety of web pages, such as wikis, social networks, or blogs. Some organizations may also provide links from a page on their web site to other web sites with additional information for the topic matter.

Using Search Engines

To start a search, enter your search criteria or *keywords* in the search field on that search engine's web page. There are different ways of using keywords to find more or fewer matches, and each page on the search engine web site will contain a search field, so you can broaden or refine your search at any time.

Depending on your web browser, the options selected, and whether the keywords you enter are similar to any you have entered previously, as you begin to enter text a list will appear below the search field. If one of these items matches what you want to find, you can select it in one of the following ways:

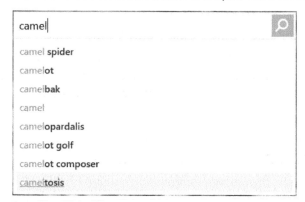

- Click the item in the list, or
- use the ⬇ or ⬆ key to move to and select the item, then press ⬚Enter⬚ to accept the selection.

Once the text appears in the search field, you can press ⬚Enter⬚ or click the button to the right of the search field to begin the search. This is referred to as an *AutoComplete* option where the web browser can be set to remember all entries until and unless they are deleted.

You can also narrow your search to include only specific file types such as images, news, or videos. This is advantageous when you want to focus on a particular file type, such as videos on how to fix a cell phone, pictures of a famous 17th century painting, and so on. An alternative to searching for a new product on a search engine is to navigate to sites where reviews can be found for that new product. In many cases, these sites also enable you to download items, as in the case of a trial edition of a software or a freeware/shareware program. Examples of these types of sites include cnet.com, tucows.com, softpedia.com, sourceforge.com, or filehippo.com.

Narrowing the Search

Search engines are a tool for finding items on the Internet, but the results are not always useful. If you type in only one or two keywords, the search engine will look for all matches of either word, and that will return tens of thousands of matches, most of which will not be relevant! You can narrow the search by choosing more specific keywords; for example, typing *satellite images of great wall of china* is an effective way to narrow the search and produce better results than just typing *great wall of china*.

You can also narrow your search by using keywords to find a specific item; for example, entering *lemon dessert recipes* will bring results for this topic, whereas *lemon recipes* will bring results for any type of recipe that uses lemons.

The following contains popular Boolean operators you can use to further narrow the search criteria:

AND	Connect keywords with "AND" when you are searching for multiple terms in a single document; your search will include only documents with all your search terms. Notice that it is not necessary to use quotation marks; in fact, quotation marks serve a different role in searches. Take a look at the following examples: Great paintings AND louvre exhibitions Great paintings AND "louvre exhibitions"
	When you put quotation marks around a phrase or a group of keywords, the search engine looks for occurrences of those words together rather than searching for each of those words individually. So a search on the first example will return a broader range of results, which may be what you need if you're not completely certain what you're looking for. But if you're very clear about your criteria, quotation marks around groups of keywords can bring you more specific results.
OR	Search for documents that include one or another of your search terms. This can be useful if you are searching for information on a topic that might be indexed in two or more different ways. For example, the company IBM is nicknamed "big blue"; entering "big blue" OR "IBM" will return all results on IBM even if, in some places, it is referred to only by its nickname. You can also type "/^"instead of the "OR" to activate the same functionality.
NOT	Use in conjunction with "and" if you want to exclude certain results from your search. For example, "tennis NOT Wimbledon" will return any pages about tennis except those that refer to Wimbledon.
NEAR	Use to look for terms in the same document that are within ten words of each other. For example, *cancer* NEAR *breast* will return documents containing "studies on breast cancer" and also "studies of cancer of the breast".

Another method to narrow the search for information is to use a search engine's advanced features. For instance, the following figure shows the advanced search features for the Yahoo! Search engine. Notice the various fields you can use to find specific information:

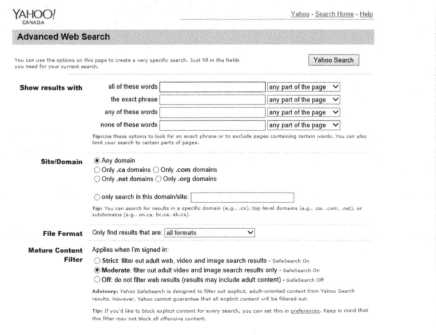

You can specify search criteria such as file format, domains, text characters, web sites, or file size. Note the number or type of fields you can use to narrow the search will vary from one search engine to another.

Another method to narrow the search is to use HTML objects as part of the search criteria. Since most information searched comes in the form of web pages using HTML, it is possible to use some of the HTML objects in searches. Some examples would include:

anchor	`adventure tours anchor:camel` will find pages with hyperlinks to any adventure tours featuring camels.
host	`samsung host:rogers.com` will find pages about any Samsung product with the phrase "rogers.com" in the host name of the web server.
image	`volcanos image:mount st. helens` will find web pages containing images for the Mount St. Helens volcano.
link	`ic3 certification link:ccilearning.com` displays any pages about the IC3 certification with links to CCI Learning Solutions.
site	`surface site:Microsoft.com` displays any pages about the Surface tablet from Microsoft's web site.

EXERCISE

In this exercise you will use different search engines to find items and then narrow the search results.

1. Type the following URL: `www.yahoo.com` and press (Enter).

    Notice the directory listing of categories of general interest topics, as well as the location of the Search field. Also notice that this search engine provides options such as email. You should also see a feature called *Answers* (this link will vary in location depending on when Yahoo! updates the pages for its web site).

2. Scroll the page until you see and can click **Answers** in the left panel or the top navigation bar.

    Yahoo! now displays a web page that enables you to enter a question about what you are searching for, which may be another way to narrow your search. This web page also includes an area where you can share the information you find with others on the Yahoo! site. You may be required to register prior to being able to post a question and have others respond to it.

3. Click the **Back** button to return to the Yahoo! home page.

Try viewing the contents of one of the other categories.

4. From the Yahoo! sites area, click **News**.

    You should now be viewing a page of current news events. Having categories available is very advantageous when you may be looking for something specific, for example, election results, earthquake, shopping site, and so on.

5. Click **Back** to return to the main Yahoo! screen. In the search field near the top of the screen, type: `unique foods`.

    Notice some of the options that appear below the search field to help you narrow the search.

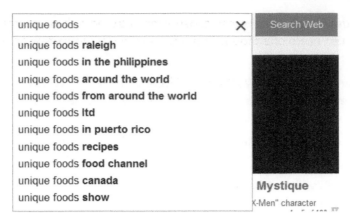

6. Complete the search criteria by typing: of the world and then click the **Search Web** button.

    A page with a list of results should now appear on the screen. By narrowing down the text, you are asking the search engine to focus on a specific topic instead of displaying a list of any web site that might contain the words, unique foods.

7. Scroll the page to see the list of results.

8. Click the **Images** link to the left of the search results.

    Yahoo! now displays a page of pictures only. This is different from the previous web page as this search narrows the results to include only pictures matching the search criteria, not text

Let's now try searching the same criteria in another search engine to see what options are available for narrowing the search using this search engine.

9. Click to create a new tab in the web browser. Then in the Address bar, type: www.google.com and press ⌐Enter⌐.

10. In the Search field, type: unique foods of the world and click **Search** (or press ⌐Enter⌐).

    Notice the number of results in the list. Suppose you want to see the images instead.

11. Click the **Images** link.

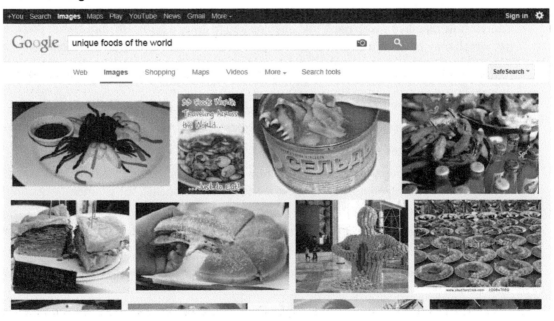

Notice how some of the images here are similar to those seen with the Yahoo! search engine. Differences between search engines are often found in the tools they offer to narrow down search results.

12. Click the tab for the Yahoo! search results page and review these links.

13. Click **Latest** to show more recent images for this search criteria.

The number of images that appear will vary based on when you perform this exercise.

14. Click **Back** to return to the previous screen, or if you had narrowed down the search several times and want to return to the original display of screens, click **Web**.

One thing you may have noticed as part of the search links is the Safe Search option near the top of the links list. In this case, it has been turned on (default) to prevent any inappropriate types of images appearing as part of the search results. When you turn this feature off, you will be asked to accept a set of terms indicating you are at least of legal age and also agree to the terms of service. Each web browser has an option similar to this to prevent inappropriate types of information being displayed automatically when a search is performed.

15. Click the Google search tab. Then click the **Safe Search** button at the far right of the navigation bar above the images.

16. Click **Filter explicit results**.

The number of images you have on the screen should be reduced. Again, depending on when you perform this exercise, you may see different images than shown currently in this courseware.

Now try entering a search of a different topic and then reducing the number of results using the Google search engine.

17. Click **Back** to return to the results page. Then in the search field, replace the text with: `camel tours` and press `Enter`.

Notice the number of results that display on your screen. You should be able to see a number near the top of the results list that tells you how many matches Google found for this criterion.

18. In the search field, click at the end of the existing text and type: `egypt OR australia`. Press (Enter) to begin the search.

The results page should include a fewer number of results than the first search, and should include only results related to camel tours in either Egypt or Australia. Take note that in some cases you may get more results; remember that rankings are based on what keywords are submitted to find content or linked references to specific sites.

Suppose you only want to show camel tours that are offered in Egypt or Australia and also include a long trek as part of the tour.

19. In the search field, click at the end of the existing search text, type: `AND long treks`. Press (Enter).

Notice now that you may have fewer results than previously.

Now try setting up an advanced search.

20. In the search field, type: `Caravaggio site:louvre.fr` and press (Enter) to begin a search of any collections by Caravaggio that may be displayed in the Louvre Museum of France.

Notice the list of results shows only those results that match the preceding search criteria.

21. Click the **Images** link at the top of the screen.

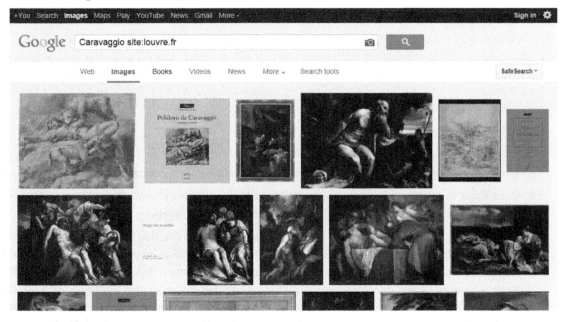

22. Click **Search tools** to display a new bar of options to help narrow the search.

23. Click **Size** and then click **Medium**.

Did the list of images change? The more criteria you add in the search, the more finite the list can become.

24. Close the web browser.

Evaluating the Information

With web design software becoming easier to use, it is now possible for virtually anyone to quickly create and publish information on a web site. However, with no international body to apply quality control to this information, it is up to the user to evaluate the quality of the information they find on the Web.

Web sites of well-known organizations usually present accurate information as their reputation is at stake. However, it is important to be alert to bias via omission of opposing views. Web sites of lesser-known organizations or individuals can sometimes present novel ideas or perspectives, but problems with accuracy and (to an even greater extent) bias must be considered.

When researching information on the Internet, do some "comparison shopping." Similar to shopping for a home appliance where you would compare products sold by a number of retailers before buying, always visit a variety of web sites and compare the different information they provide on similar subjects. After researching and finding certain facts repeated on several web sites that seem reliable, you may want to go to the local library to find documents, sources, journals, or reference materials to validate your Internet research. In general, consider the Web an excellent place to begin, and think of printed materials as providing support for what you've learned online.

So how can we evaluate the quality of information found on the Internet? As part of your evaluation, include factors such as accuracy, authenticity, objectivity, currency (how up to date is the information) and coverage, or AAOCC.

Reliability and Relevance

You can tell a lot about a web site by looking for obvious errors in facts, statistics, grammar, spelling, or language use. For instance, if the web site of a company contains numerous spelling errors you might conclude that not much effort has gone into web site creation, which may lead you to question the effort that has gone into researching the information provided.

How current a web site is provides another indication of the effort that went into constructing it, as well as the quality of the information. Check when the site was last updated. It may be fine that a web site for a company that sells seasonal items hasn't been updated recently, but a reputable news site or travel agency should be updating their information at least daily. If they are not, you have reason to question the reliability or relevance of the information.

Validity and Authenticity

If a web page is offering facts and statistics, one way to determine their accuracy is by checking the author's and publisher's qualifications. The author of a page showing facts and statistics should always be identified, and the web site should provide information about what else he/she has written on this topic and how long he/she has been working in this field. Who published this author's work and what is the relationship between the author and publisher?

You should be able to find much of this information by visiting the About Us, Mission, Philosophy, Corporate Profile, and Background sections of the web site. You should also follow links in the content to review additional information that assists in authenticating the author's credentials and the material presented. Links that are broken or lead to pages that are no longer available may call into question how up to date the information is. Other links that appear legitimate may actually take you to a page or site that contains offensive content or sells another product or service. The Webmaster or person in charge of the web site should be checking links occasionally to maintain the company's credibility and reliability.

Use the URL as a guide to whether the web site is affiliated with a recognized organization or institution instead of a group or individual without established credibility. If a reputable organization reproduces information from other sources, it is more likely to ensure the information is faithful to the original than to be found altering material, either out of carelessness or a desire to support a certain viewpoint. For example, you want to volunteer at a local charitable organization that provides services to single parent families but you rarely see patrons at the site. As a result you want to research this organization to see if it is legitimate and how it operates. The first place you might check is the list of registered charitable organizations to see if this one has registered. The next place to check could be a search engine to see if you can find information about this local charity whether it be news articles the charity has been featured in, or fund raising drives they have sponsored. If they have a web site, check the information on the site to see where it may point visitors for more information. If the charity is registered, explore the information a bit more to see if they have one or more branches and where these are located. What other information can you find out about the charity from this site, such as is the charity affiliated with another organization or is it sponsored by a specific company? Does the web site use the .org domain or is it a .com site, indicating it may do business online either as a fundraiser or for personal profit. The more links you can find of people or organizations with favorable reviews on this charity, chances are this charity is a reputable one.

Similarly, the presence or absence of source references can help you assess the authenticity of material on the Web. If a web site "quotes" information on a subject without providing the source of the information so you can check up on it, you have to wonder if the content has been altered or if it is being quoted out of context and without the original author's permission. Be sure to research any articles listed as well to determine if they are factual; articles can be written for a variety of reasons, and are not necessarily based on facts. They could, for example, be an unbiased review of products or services or they could instead represent the writer's personal preference of products or services. A trustworthy article will also be referenced by other people or organizations on their web sites.

If a site claims to offer technical expertise, check the source references if available. For example, if a site addresses problems and solutions for a specific Microsoft product, they should have a reference to the Microsoft Knowledge Base which is a huge database of technical issues and resolutions Microsoft maintains. Specific articles or reference papers do not need to be referenced; but including a link to this type of official source lends credibility to the web site.

Finally, if you are viewing blog or wiki content, remember that authors need no qualifications to contribute. Even though wiki content is reviewed by members of the public for accuracy, it is always wise to "comparison shop" and try to verify the information on more than one blog or wiki, as well as on related web sites.

Objectivity and Bias

It is unlikely that you will come across information from any source that contains no bias of any type. However, reliable authors and web sites strive to inform their audience with accurate facts and statistics. A bibliography or source list with links to other sites is a good indicator of the openness and objectivity of the information. Be sure to check a few of these links, even if available only in traditional paper format, and read the full articles to determine if the information here is fact or fiction. Articles usually also contain a reference list of the sources they used to gather the information. For example, if you were looking for information on a political leader, be sure to check the sources, for both date of publication and objectivity. Some older sources may be written to promote the leader's controversial actions but do not provide information on the outcome of those actions, favorable or otherwise. A more recent source may be more objective and provide details on any positive or negative impact of these actions for the country or global economy.

Look for depth of coverage of the topic, supported by other types of information. Is the web site or author associated with other reputable organizations? Do these organizations have certifications that support their ability to provide unbiased information? What types of sponsored advertisements or links appear on the site? Who owns the products or services being advertised on this web site?

Many organizations offer accurate information on their web sites, but their agendas are well known to be biased and the information they provide is unbalanced. There is nothing wrong with stating an opinion as long as it is represented as such. Any arguments should be supported with documentation; if the topic is controversial the presentation should provide viewpoints on both sides of the issue. Check if the site offers an area called a *forum* where people can leave messages or posts. Read some of the posts to see if there is a balance of positive and negative comments, people offering facts versus opinions. In general people sign up on forums that are of interest to them; however, it doesn't guarantee that you are speaking to someone who is an expert in that field, having both factual experience and education to back up their comments.

You can often tell if opinions or viewpoints are being presented as fact by the tone of the message. Is the page factual and informative or does it seem more persuasive? If humor is used, do you find it effective or does the tone seem sarcastic or exaggerated?

Another consideration is advertising. Is there advertising on the page, and if so how much? Do the ads seem independent of the content or are they selling similar or complementary products or services? Is this really a site that provides objective information, or is there a commercial bias? Ads are usually an indicator that a vendor wants to attract your interest in their products, which means they have paid the organization in order to be able to advertise on this site. In some cases this may not influence you but it may also cause you to be more discriminating about doing business with this organization.

How did you find the site? If a site has a good ranking in many search engines, this may indicate effort invested in the design and maintenance of the web site. However, this is not necessarily a reliable indicator of information quality as some organizations pay to get good rankings.

If you have any questions or doubts about the content on a web site, check to see If the author or publisher can be reached by phone, mail, or email and contact them directly with your concerns.

EXERCISE

In this exercise you will take a look at how different search results can display a variety of information that may or may not be relevant to the topic you are searching.

1. Open a web browser, if necessary. In the address bar, type: `www.bing.com` and press (Enter).

2. In the search field, type: `earth summit` and press (Enter).

   A list should appear with a variety of results, ranging from information about this summit on Wikipedia to sites who may be involved with or promote Earth Summit. If you look at other links on subsequent pages, you may also see a link regarding a horse named Earth Summit.

3. Click the link that will navigate to the Wikipedia site and then read some of the information there.

   Wikipedia is an example of a site where information and reference links can be found but the contributors of the information are individuals who want to share information on a topic. As a result, there is no guarantee that the information is current or totally accurate. For example, if you were to search for a famous person on Wikipedia, most of the information there will be accurate but there may also be some misinformation based on unverified events in that person's life, for example, alleged illegal actions by the military in the 1600s.

Note that this step asked you to click the link that Wikipedia has for the term, earth summit. Another link to Wikipedia provides information on a horse that was named Earth Summit (http://en.wikipedia.org/wiki/Earth_Summit_(horse)); you may not see this link until you go to the next page of results.

Let's now take a look at how Wikipedia could have helped you research the term "earth summit".

4.   In the search field, type: `earth summit`, but do not press `Enter`.

Wikipedia now displays a list of suggestions in a similar manner to a search engine. This is an example of how you could use a wiki site to help you research information as you can narrow the search criteria within a site that is considered an online encyclopedia.

To demonstrate how different domains can display different types of information, try navigating to a different web site for the same topic. Suppose you had come across a site when researching but wanted to read the information in the wiki site first; now you are ready to view the information on the alternate site.

5.   In the address bar, type: `www.encyclopedia.com/topic/Earth_Summit.aspx` and press `Enter`.

6.   Scroll through the page to see the contents and compare it to what you read in Wikipedia.

This is an example of how checking the domain for a site can give you an indicator about whether one site may provide more information than others.

Now let's try entering search criteria for a topic that would be considered controversial but could be a project you may be asked to complete for a Sociology or Political Science course.

7.   Navigate to: `www.bing.com` and type: `oldest US laws in effect` as the search criteria. Press `Enter`.

8.   Take a moment to review the results for the search criteria to determine which ones might contain accurate information and which ones might be based on opinions or judgments of society.

9.   Click **Images** at the top of the screen to narrow the search to show only image files.

Even when viewing images, some of these may seem to be have a different agenda than what was being searched. Remember that the results are based on your keywords and entries in the search engine database; you may see images that don't seem to fit the search criteria.

10. Click **Videos** to take a look at the video files that meet the search criteria.

Notice how you can narrow the search by using an option above the videos (such as video length, or source). How accurate do these videos appear in relation to the search criteria?

11. Click **Web** once more and click one of the results there, such as the link for old laws still in effect. Then look at some of the links above the article (or elsewhere on the page) to see what or who they might reference.

When researching information, it is important to look at all the different sources available to you so that you can compile a fair and accurate report. You may find that viewing some of the videos may reveal a different perspective on the topic and open other areas you may want to include in the report. This is an example of why you want to ensure you have as many resources as possible to help you evaluate information for its validity, reliability, and credibility.

12. Close the web browser.

Lesson Summary

In this lesson, you will conduct research and evaluate information you find on the Internet. You should now be familiar with:

☑ finding items on the Internet

☑ evaluating search results

☑ searching for an item on a specific web site

☑ what a search engine is and how it works

☑ narrowing a search using the search engine

☑ evaluating information on the Internet

Review Questions

1. How can you find items using a search engine?

2. To narrow the search to find information on hiking trails that do not include those offered in Alaska, which word should you include in the search criteria?
   a. AND   c. NOT
   b. OR NOT   d. OR

3. You are looking for information to help you decide whether to purchase a PC or an Apple notebook. You've found a web site created by someone who has used both types of computers previously and seems to favor the Apple environment. What could you check for on the web site to determine if his issues with the PC are accurate?
   a. Forum where people have contributed their opinions.
   b. Any sponsored advertisements.
   c. References to technical sources such as the Microsoft Knowledge Base.
   d. Some information about who the author is and his credentials.
   e. Any of the previous
   f. a or c

MMM
Go online for Additional Review

4. Why should you be cautious of accepting the opinions of people on a forum?

5. How can ads be a deterrent when researching information on a particular web site?

6. How could you verify a solution offered by someone claiming to be a technical expert?

IC3® Internet and Computing Core Certification Guide

Using Windows 7 &
Microsoft® Office 2013

Appendix A: Courseware Mapping

Appendix B: Glossary of Terms

Appendix C: Index

Courseware Mapping

Computing Fundamentals

	Objective Domain	Lesson
1	**Operating System Basics**	
	1.1 What is an OS and what does it do?	1, 3, 5
	1.2 Manage computer files and folders	1, 2
	1.3 Manage computer configuration, Control Panel, OS drivers	4
2	**Computer hardware and concepts**	
	2.1 Common computer terminology	3
	2.2 Types of devices	3
	2.3 Computer usage	3
3	**Computer software and concepts**	
	3.1 Software management	5
	3.2 Licensing	5
	3.3 Software Usage	5
	3.4 Software Tools	5
4	**Troubleshooting**	
	4.1 Software	5, 6
	4.2 Hardware	6
	4.3 Devices and Peripherals	6
	4.4 Backup / Restore	6

Key Applications

	Objective Domain	Lesson
1	**Common Application Features**	
	1.1 Common Features and Commands	7, 8, 9, 10, 11
	1.2 Formatting	8, 9, 10
	1.3 Navigating	7, 8, 9, 10, 11
	1.4 Working with multimedia files	8, 10
2	**Word Processing Activities**	
	2.1 Organizing data	8
	2.2 Layout	8
3	**Spreadsheet Activities**	
	3.1 Spreadsheet Layout	9
	3.2 Data Management	9
4	**Presentation Activities**	
	4.1 Inserting content	10
	4.2 Slide Management	10
	4.3 Slide Design	10
5	**Basic Database Interactions**	
	5.1 Record Management	11
6	**Collaboration**	
	6.1 Comments	8
	6.2 Sharing files	7

Living Online

Objective Domain	Lesson
1 Browsers	
1.1 Internet vs. Browsers vs. WWW	12
1.2 Navigation	12
2 Networking concepts	
2.1 Internet Connection	13
2.2 Network types and features, capabilities	13
2.3 Network troubleshooting	13
3 Digital Communication	
3.1 Email communication	14
3.2 Real-Time communication	14
4 Digital Citizenship	
4.1 Communication Standards	14, 15
4.2 Legal and responsible use of computers	5, 15
5 Safe Computing	
5.1 Securing online communication or activity	15
5.2 Ergonomics	15
6 Research Fluency	
6.1 Using Search Engines	16
6.2 Evaluate search results	16
6.3 Using advanced features of search engines	16

Glossary of Terms

AAOCC – Refers to authentic, accuracy, objectivity, currency, and coverage, or the guidelines you can use to help evaluate information you find on the Internet.

Access Permission – A rule associated with an object (usually a folder, file, or printer) to regulate which users can have access to the object and in what manner.

Active Cell – The cell in which you are entering information, or the current location of the cell pointer.

ActiveX – A programming tool that enables Web designers to embed small programs on a Web page that become active when you "point and click".

Address Bar – A field used to enter a path to find a file, folder, or Web address. This field appears in Windows Explorer as well as the Web browser.

Administrator – Network Administrator; a person responsible for setting up and managing the domain or local computers and their user and group accounts, assigning passwords and permissions, and helping users with networking issues.

Adware – Software that automatically displays or downloads advertisements.

Alignment – The positioning of text or the contents of a cell; for example, left, right, or centered.

Analog – Representation of data that is continuous when received, for example, sound.

Animation Effects – Feature that allows you to add an animation effect to an object in the current slide.

Application – Programs are referred to as applications, and perform certain functions such as word processing. An application program is usually a collection of programs and data files that work together for a specific purpose.

Archived Files – A file that has been designated as a file that is older than a specific date and placed in a separate area to reduce the size of the Outlook data file. Could also refer to a file that has been compressed for storage purposes using program such as WinZip or WinRAR.

ASP – Application Service Provider. See SaaS.

AutoCorrect – A feature that automatically corrects common spelling, punctuation, or capitalization errors as you type.

AutoFill – A method of copying data and formulas or creating data series by dragging the lower right corner of a cell or range.

AutoFit – A feature that automatically adjusts the width of a column or the height of a row so that the cells are just wide or high enough to display the values in those cells.

AutoSum – A tool that quickly inserts a SUM function into the current cell, and determines the appropriate cell range to use.

Baseline – The "base" where the bottom of most characters are aligned. The baseline is used as the base from which to measure line spacing.

Bcc – Blind carbon copy; a field in the header of an email message. Other recipients of the message will not see who was named in the Bcc field.

Blockers/Filters – Special software that can be installed to control the type or amount of content that can be viewed on a computer.

Blog – An online tool in which you can write information on a topic, similar to a journal. Some blogs enable others to post a comment on your entries.

Bold – Dark or highlighted text.

Bookmark – Marks a location of an item such as a help topic so that you can quickly return to it later. Also known as Favorites.

Boolean Operators – Words or symbols you can use to narrow the search criteria.

Booting – The process of turning on the computer and loading the operating system.

Borders – The feature that enables you to add lines or borders to selected data.

Breadcrumb Trail – The method Windows uses to display the file path where each piece of text in the Address Bar is an active control.

Bridge – A network device used to connect network segments to handle network requests but do not analyze or re-route messages.

Broadband – Direct connections that provide continuous access to the Internet through permanent network connections.

Browse – View available network resources by looking through lists of folders, files, user accounts, groups, domains, or computers. Browsing enables users on a Windows network to see what domains and computers are accessible from their local computer. May also refer to the process to view items on the Internet – see Web Browser.

Built-in Functions – Pre-programmed formulas that perform specific calculations. You can type these functions in or use the Insert Function wizard to assist.

Button – An icon in a Ribbon group or Dialog box representing a specific feature or function. Click on the button in order to activate the feature or function.

Bus – An internal device that connects hardware to the motherboard.

Cable – A connector device for attaching hardware to your computer; in terms of the Internet, this is a broadband technology that provides continuous service to the Internet using coaxial cable to transmit signals.

Calendar – A feature in Outlook that enables you to enter and keep track of appointments or events.

Card Readers/Writers – Devices used to read flash memory cards to transfer the contents to a computer.

Cc – Carbon copy; a field in the header of any email message. Other recipients of the message will see who was named in this field.

Cell Address – The location description that specifies an individual cell.

Cell Range – A section of a worksheet containing two or more cells.

Cell Reference – The use of a cell address or cell range address in a formula.

Cell Styles – A feature that enables you to apply many different formatting characteristics to one or more cells with a single command by choosing from a selection of format templates; see Quick Styles or Table Styles also.

Cellular Telephones – Also called mobile or handheld devices for voice or data communications over a network of specialized stations, or cell sites. Many mobile devices can also handle activities such as text messaging, email, paging, or searching the Internet.

Center – Text placed in the center of two margins or at a tab setting.

Character – A character can be a letter, number, or other piece of data.

Chart – A pictorial representation of the data you enter in a worksheet.

Chat Rooms – Designated areas on the Internet where people with similar interests can communicate with each other by typing on a keyboard.

Check Box – An option in a dialog box used for selecting or activating items or features. If checked, the feature is activated. If unchecked, the feature has been turned off.

Circular References – A type of error that occurs when one or more cells refer to each other directly or indirectly in the formula.

Circuit Switching – A technology that uses a decided physical path to send and receive information.

Clear – Removes information (or formatting and comments) from selected cells and leaves the cells blank.

Click – Point the mouse at the item and then quickly press down and release the mouse button.

Clip Art Graphic – Pictures made from vectored or drawn objects that you can insert into documents.

Clip Art Pane – A window that displays whenever you want to insert clip art. Items can be inserted from this pane, imported from other programs, or downloaded from the Internet.

Client – A computer that may access shared network resources provided by another computer, called a server.

Clipboard – A temporary storage location used to transfer data between documents and between applications.

Close – To shut down a document window or application window from the Desktop; could also be used to close a window, dialog box, or task pane.

Column – A vertical arrangement for text or numbers, separated from other columns by a grid line, and denoted with alpha letters per column. Excel has a maximum of 256 columns, denoted from A to IV.

Columns – A feature that enables you to format the layout of your document into one, two, or three columns of text.

Command Bar – The bar below the Address Bar in Explorer that displays a list of commands to view or manage your files.

Command Button – A Command button may have a picture or icon, or a word appearing on the button. It is used to perform a specific function, such as OK, Cancel, Close, or Print.

Comments – Similar to a sticky note where you can enter information for yourself or others to review.

Compatibility Mode – A feature that allows you to create documents in Office 2013 that do not contain new or enhanced features unique to Office 2013, so others using previous versions of Office will have full editing capabilities.

Compressed File – A process that reduces the size of one or a set of files for sharing purposes.

Contact – An entry in Outlook containing information about a person or organization, including the name, address, telephone numbers, or other relevant information such as a picture, email address, IM address.

Contact Group – A list of contacts grouped into a named email list address that can be used to send a message to every contact in that list at the same time.

Contextual Spelling – An option in the spell checker that detects and corrects the types of errors that previously got through spell checkers because the word was spelled correctly but was the incorrect word for the context (for example, misuse of the word "there" in place of "their").

Contextual Tabs – The tabs that appear on the Ribbon according to the type of object you have entered or selected in a document.

Controls – Features that enable you to create and design a form or dialog box, for example, text box, check box, radio button, drop-down menu, and so on.

Control Icon – The icon appearing on every application that runs a window.

Control Menu – The menu appearing on every application that runs in a window.

Control Panel – Where you can view and manipulate basic system settings.

Cookie – A tiny file placed on your computer by a Web site. This may be used so that you can log onto frequently used sites quickly.

Copyright – The law that governs ownership of original works to the author or publisher, published or unpublished.

CPU – see Microprocessor Chip.

Creative Commons – A non-profit organization that provides six different types of licenses for people who want to share their creative works or knowledge but also retain the copyright.

Credentials – The process the email server uses to check and validate an email address and the password.

Cursor – A cursor marks the position in a document on the screen where text or a graphical object will be placed. A cursor can appear in many different forms: an Insertion Point, a blinking underline, or a blinking square.

Cut – The editing process of transferring selected text or items to the Clipboard so that you can move them from one location and place them into another.

Data Transfer Rate – The speed at which a computer can move data from one place to another.

Default – The standard settings that are in effect unless you change them. You can usually adjust the defaults for most commonly used settings.

Delete – Removes the selected item closes in data from a selected direction.

Desktop – The screen background for Windows where windows, icons, and dialog boxes appear.

Device – A hardware item that is referenced or accessed by the user from an application program, such as a mouse, scanner, a hard disk, CD-ROM drive, or a modem.

Device Driver – A program that enables Windows to communicate with your device.

Dial-up Connection – A method to connect to the Internet where you dial a specific number provided by the ISP.

Dialog Box – A window where additional items may be selected or activated.

Dialog Box Launcher – The small 'x' at the bottom of a group of commands on a Ribbon Tab that displays a dialog box or a task pane for further options.

Digital – Representations of data that can be retrieved in intervals, such as data on a disk.

Directories – Contains a list of URLs that have been classified according to subject matter.

Disk Operating System – The original operating system developed for the PC, known as DOS. This was text-based software where you entered single line commands to perform tasks such as managing files or starting programs.

Document – A file such as a letter, memo, or budget, presentation, report, photo album, cash flow report, and so on.

Document Properties – A tool you can use to view or add information about a file, such as the author name, document statistics. You can also add keywords to assist in finding this file later.

Domain – A collection of computers defined by the administrator of a Windows network. A domain provides access to the centralized user accounts and group accounts maintained by the administrator. Each domain has a unique name.

Domain Name System (DNS) – A service that maps unique domain names to specific IP addresses.

DOS – see Disk Operating System.

Double-Click – The process of clicking the left (or primary) mouse button twice quickly.

Download – When you connect to another computer, or web site, and transfer files from there to your own computer.

Drag – This means to point the mouse pointer at the selected item, then press and hold down the left mouse button as you move or drag the mouse pointer to another location. Release the mouse button when the mouse pointer is over the new location.

Drag Select – This means to point the mouse pointer at one corner of the area to select, then press and hold down the left mouse button as you move or drag the mouse pointer to the opposite corner. Release the mouse button when the area is selected.

Drop-Down List – Displays additional choices when you click the arrow for the list.

DSL – Digital Subscriber Line; a high-speed all-digital connection that uses digital phone lines with a modem to connect to the Internet.

E-Commerce – The process of purchasing online from a web site.

Edit – The process of manipulating (adding, removing, formatting, and so on) text or objects.

Electronic Book Readers – A specialized electronic device that enables you to read a book; these types of book files can be purchased and then downloaded from specialized sites.

E-learning – A training tool designed to provide learning concepts online; may include audio, video, or could be mostly text.

Email Address – This is the name you are known by on the Internet. A typical email address for an Internet user might be user@yourcompany.com

Email – Electronic Mail; the most widely used application of the Internet. An Internet user can transfer files and write messages to other users simply by knowing their email address.

Embedded Operating Systems – Manage and control operations on the specific type of equipment for which they are designed, such as in a vehicle.

Encryption – Makes information indecipherable. Files, folders or email messages can be encrypted so that unauthorized people cannot view or use the information.

Ergonomics – The study of humans in a workplace environment and how to maintain or prevent workplace injuries.

Extension – The last part of the name given to a file. It can be up to three characters and usually describes the "type" of file (for example, .PDF for portable document files; .EXE for executable program files; .XLSX for Excel files; etc.).

Extranet – A server at a company designed to allow internal and external users access to that server, such as for e-commerce.

FAQ – Frequently Asked Questions; a list of commonly asked questions by new users. The FAQ is usually set up as a link on a Web page.

Fair Use – The policy that states you can use information from a variety of Web sites provided it is for research or information gathering purposes only. You must also identify where the information was found.

Favorite Links – An area within Explorer where frequently used folders can be placed to enable easy one-click access.

File – A basic unit of storage for a group of data that belongs together and has been given a name, such as a document, a spreadsheet, or a database.

File name – The name of a file. There are two parts to a file name, the name and the extension.

File Path – The location where a file is stored on the computer. This typically includes the Drive letter and Folder and perhaps Sub Folders where the file is saved.

Fill – The process of selecting a color or pattern to fill a shape such as a rectangle, line, or star.

Firewall – A security barrier that controls the flow of information between the Internet and a private network.

Flags – An option in Outlook that allows you to mark or flag an Outlook item for follow up or another type of action. You can also set a reminder of when this item is due.

Flaming – When you send a message that personally attacks the recipient.

Flash Device – A portable storage device that usually appears as a long stick with a USB connector; these can be purchased in various sizes; also known as a memory key, flash card, or thumb drive.

Folder – A container that stores files and other folders; also known as a directory or subdirectory.

Font – A graphic design or typeface applied to numerals, symbols, and characters.

Font Size – The vertical measurement used to identify the size of proportionally printed characters (72 points equals 1 inch).

Footer – Text that repeats at the bottom of every page and may include page numbers.

Format – Instructions to the program as to how it should display such as number styles, fonts, colors, etc.

Formula – Used in a cell to calculate new result values to display; composed of values, cell references, arithmetic operators and special functions. These results may be used in other formulas located in other cells.

Formula Bar – A field on the screen that displays the formula in the active cell. It can also be used to make entries into the worksheet.

Freeware – A program you can download and use for no cost and can be distributed to other users.

FTP Site – A computer location on the Internet that has files available for downloading to your computer.

FTP Server – A computer location on the Internet that has files available for downloading to your computer.

FTP – File Transfer Protocol; used to exchange and manipulate files over a computer network, or the internet.

Function – A feature designed by Excel that enables you to quickly perform a calculation or formula using a specialized function.

Game Systems – A device that enables one or more people to interact in a gaming program, such as an Xbox, Wii, PlayStation, or DS System.

Gateway – A separate computer used to route information from or to the Internet within a company. Gateways may often be used as a proxy server or firewall as it checks the information flowing to or from the Internet.

Gadgets – Mini-programs that display on the Windows Sidebar. Examples of gadgets include a calendar, clock and contacts, weather tracker, or RSS feeds.

Global Address Book – An address book set up the network administration that lists the names of employees or groups that can be used to address an email.

Group Collaboration – An application program that enables several people to work, interacts, and share files in real time, similar to having a meeting.

GUI – An acronym for Graphical User Interface; Windows is a GUI.

Graphics – Illustrations that can be inserted into a document such as pictures, clip art, charts, text boxes, shapes, etc.

Hacker – A hacker spends his time trying to understand the intricacies of a program or a system. A hacker usually knows almost all there is to know about what they use.

Handheld Operating Systems – Used on PDAs and Smartphones.

Handouts – A PowerPoint feature that allows you to print miniature slides for distribution to the audience.

Hard Disk Drive – Main form of storage for data on the computer; can be available in traditional models or solid state drives.

Header – Text or graphics that repeat at the top of every page. A header may include page numbers.

Help – A reference function that summarizes the capabilities of program features, and helps you find answers to questions about program usage.

Hibernate – The sleep mode that is available only to notebooks to put the notebook into a mode that draws no power.

Highlighted – Indicates that an object or text is selected and will be affected by the next action or command.

History – The option that captures and lists the web sites you visited over a frequency of time. This can be deleted using the appropriate command in the web browser.

Home Page – A page of information found on a web site located on the World Wide Web.

HTML – Hypertext Markup Language; a 'language' used to create/save web pages to the Internet. HTML creates a page with graphics, tables, hyperlinks and multimedia.

HTML Objects – Specific words you can use to narrow the search criteria such as anchor, host, or site.

HTTP – Hypertext Transfer Protocol; the system used to connect computers to domains on the Internet. These letters at the beginning of an address indicate where to look for a location on the Internet.

Hub – A network device that connects PC's together to form a network where all users share equal transfer speeds from the total network connection speed.

Hyperlinks – Words or phrases, usually underlined, that indicate a location that you can access from the page you are currently viewing.

Icon – A graphical representation of various elements in Windows, such as disk drives, applications, and documents.

Indent – A temporary left and/or right margin, usually in effect for one paragraph at a time.

Insert – An editing function that enables you to add text between other text, including entire columns or rows.

Insertion Point – The place where text inserts when typed.

Insert Worksheet Tab – The tab at the end of the worksheet tabs on the lower left corner of a workbook to assist in inserting/creating a new worksheet at the current location.

Instant Messages – Communicating with someone else in real time using a program that enables you to enter text or by activating a multimedia feature to view each other.

Internet – A global network of computers. It is a large non-administered collection of computers that no one person or organization owns or is responsible for.

Intranet – A company's private network used to share information, operating systems and/or services and which is accessible only to employees or authorized users.

Instant Messaging – A program designed to allow people to chat to each other in real time, albeit one line of text at a time.

Intellectual Property – Any created work or invention by a person or.

IP Address – A set of numbers that identify the address of an Internet Web site, using TCP/IP protocol.

ISP – Internet Service Provider; a company that offers the use of its computers and facilities to access the Internet for a fee.

Junk Mail – Unsolicited mail received from people promoting or selling products or services.

Justification – The alignment option that displays text with even wrapped edges at the left and right margins, similar to a block or rectangle of text.

Labels – Text entries that consist of alphabetic and numeric characters, plus most printable symbols. This type of data is not generally used in calculations, except for text functions.

LAN – Local Area Network; a group of computers in one location that are all connected together with a common wiring system.

Legend – A box on a chart that explains the meaning of each line in a line chart, or bar in a bar chart.

Libel/Slander – The process of writing or saying something untrue to defame or ruin an individual's or organization's reputation.

Linking – The process of referencing cells or worksheets in one file to another, so that changes made on one file will automatically change in the linked file.

Linux – UNIX-like operating system that is freely available and modifiable. Linux is widely used on supercomputers and high-end servers, and is very popular with entrepreneurial software developers.

Licensing – When you are given permission to use a product or service from a vendor.

List Box – A rectangular box with a list of choices that can be selected.

Log Off – To stop using the network and remove your user name from active use until you log on again.

Log On – To provide a user name and password that identifies you to the network.

MAC Address – Media Access Control; the unique address permanently burned into the NIC by the manufacturer. Also referred to as the physical or the hardware address.

Malware – Malicious software created with the intent to harm the computer through viruses, adware or using malicious code that disrupts a computer's operations.

Margin – The white space or area from the edge of the paper to the text.

Master – A slide that contains all the consistent formatting or elements that PowerPoint uses on all slides in the presentation. You can create masters for slides, notes, handouts and outlines.

Maximize Button – The small box at the right of the title bar used to display the window full screen to occupy the entire desktop.

Media – A term that can refer to any audio or video device or file.

Menu Bar – The horizontal bar containing the names of all the application menus.

Menu – A list of items used to execute commands, display dialog boxes, or display another menu.

Microblogging – Refers to the process where you can update your blog entries, such as updating your status on Facebook or Twitter.

Microprocessor Chip – Often called the "brain" of the computer as this is where calculations and logical operations are performed; also referred to as the Central Processing Unit (CPU).

Minimize Button – The first small box at the right of the title bar used to temporarily close the window, replacing it as a button on the taskbar.

Mini Toolbar – A contextual toolbar that appears only when you select text. As you move the mouse pointer over the toolbar, it becomes a functioning toolbar with commonly used text formatting options.

MMS – Multimedia Messaging Service; similar to SMS but provides a standard way to send messages that include multimedia content from one mobile device to another.

Mouse Pointer – Usually shown as an arrow on the screen that follows the movement of the mouse on the screen, regardless of the pointing device used, such as a mouse or touchpad.

MP3 Player – A portable music or media device that stores music files; in some cases, the player may also be able to store video or picture files.

Multitasking – The ability of a computer to perform more than one task at a time.

Name Box – This box displays the cell address of the active cell. It is located on the left below the toolbar.

Newsgroup – A discussion group on the Internet.

Newsreader – A software package used to access Newsgroups where you can read information about specific topics, as well as send information to other users as individuals or groups.

Network – When computers want to communicate with each other, they connect together with via a network. Special programs can allow one computer to request data from another computer. One computer in a network may be at the corporate head office, another in the next office. This transferring of data can reduce paper and mail, and help to make the business run better. Networks can be wired together or set up with a wireless router.

Network Interface Card (NIC) – Hardware that must be installed on your computer before you can send or receive data between your computer and the network.

Network/Volume License – When an organization buys a set number of licenses to install the software on computers that may be in any location where the organization does business.

Non-printing Characters – Codes provided by Microsoft to help identify certain features or actions in the document, for example, ¶ displays when the (Enter) key is pressed, → displays when the (Tab) key is pressed, etc.

Notes – A PowerPoint feature that allows you to enter notes on the current slide as reference during the creation of the presentation.

Notification Area – Found on the right side of the taskbar and includes a clock and icons that communicate the status of certain programs and settings.

Office Clipboard – A place to store data temporarily, pending retrieval.

Open – The function that enables you to transfer a file from a storage device to the screen.

Open Source Software – Application programs created by programmers with the intent of making the programming codes available to anyone at no cost. When modifications are made to open source programs, these are then made available as well at no cost.

Operating System – A software program that controls all hardware and application software on the computer.

Optical Drive – Designed to read a flat, circular disc such as a CD or DVD; data can be written to the disc using a laser to read or write the data.

Option Button – A selection that appears in a dialog box that allows a user to choose one item in a group of choices.

Orientation – The direction of the paper for text flow; Portrait takes advantage of the length of the paper vertically whereas Landscape uses the length of the paper horizontally.

Packet Switching – A technology for transferring information which does not rely on a dedicated physical path.

Page – The number of lines designated to create a page of data. Word automatically divides the document into pages based on the margin settings, the line spacing and the size of text.

Page Break – The division between two pages.

Page Setup – The feature that determines how the program displays and/or prints the file, that is, margins, headers, footers, gridlines, and so on.

Paragraph – A set of text or items from one paragraph mark to another.

Paste – The editing function of placing cut or copied data into a new location.

Password – A security measure that restricts logons to user accounts, computer systems and resources. A password is a unique string of characters that must be provided before a logon or access is authorized.

Patches – File or programming code inserted into an existing program as an immediate solution to a particular programming problem.

PDF – Portable Document Format; a file format commonly used to share documents with others, generally to view, save, or print.

Pinned Programs – An area of the Start Menu where frequently used programs can be 'pinned' to enable easy access to programs.

Phishing – A method that fraudsters will employ in order to obtain your log in credentials for secure Web sites.

Piracy – Occurs when a copyrighted item is shared at no cost or sold to someone without the owner's permission.

Plagiarism – The process of passing off someone else's work or idea as your own without crediting the source.

Plug-ins – Also known as Add-ons; a small application that extends the capabilities of web browsers.

Podcast – An audio or video file you can upload to play or broadcast from a media player or a Web site. Podcasts can also be broadcast in real time from your computer with a Webcam.

Power Plan – A collection of hardware and system settings that manages how the computer utilizes power.

Presence – Refers to the ability to determine the status of your contacts at a given time.

Print – The process of sending a file to the printer, complete with printer instructions for the format and type of text.

Privacy – Protecting one's information when online. Check the privacy statements of web sites prior to giving any personal information to that site.

Program Options – A feature within a Microsoft Office program that enables you to set options for this program, such as units of measure, number of recently used documents to display, AutoCorrect entries, and so on.

Proportional Spacing – The space used for an individual character and is measured in point size. With proportional spacing five WWWWW's take up more space than five IIIII's.

Protocol – A set of rules that enable computers to communicate with one another.

Public Switched Telephone Network (PSTN) – Provides telephone service around the world and is integral to wide area networking.

Quick Access Toolbar – Located above the File tab and contains popular commands such as Save, Undo, and Redo. This toolbar can be customized for those commands you use frequently.

Quick Styles – A feature that enables you to apply formatting characteristics to a block of text, a table, or an illustration by choosing from a selection of format options. The number and type of commands vary with the feature and Ribbon available. See Cell Styles or Table Styles also.

Random Access Memory (RAM) – Functions as an electronic memory pool where the computer holds working copies of programs and data. This type of memory is volatile which means it is cleared from the memory when the computer is shut down.

Recycle Bin – A temporary storage area for deleted files. Deleted files remain in the Recycle Bin until the deleted files are restored or the Recycle Bin is emptied.

Replace – A feature that enables you to find and then replace specified text throughout the document.

Remote Storage – An area off site where you can store data such as a virtual drive on an ISP's server, a network server in a different location from you, an external hard drive, and so on.

Research – Reference books and research Web sites that can be accessed through Office programs via the Review tab on the Proofing group.

Residual Files – These are files that can be left on any storage device after you uninstall an application program, which can contain personal information that could be potentially exploited.

Resource – Anything that you use on your computer, such as a folder, printer or scanner.

Restore Button – You can use this button to reduce or enlarge the window.

Ribbon – A collection of tabs located directly below the title bar, providing quick access to commands you must use to complete a task.

Ribbon Tabs – Relates to a type of activity, organizing command buttons into logical groups. The group name appears on the Ribbon tab below the group of command buttons.

Read Only Memory (ROM) – Stores data that can be read and used but not changed; stores instructions that control the basic functions of the computer.

Read Only Memory Basic Input Output Setup (ROM-BIOS) – A group of integrated circuits and chips hardwired to the motherboard that loads instructions into memory and then executes the instructions. This process happens only when you start or restart the computer.

Router – Connects different networks serving as the entry point and exit point for each network; also referred to as a gateway.

Ruler – Located below the Ribbon in Word or PowerPoint; the ruler displays icons that allow you to perform functions such as changing margins, tabs and indents quickly.

SaaS – Software as a Service; a subscription service where you purchase licenses for software that expire at a certain date.

Save – The process of storing or copying the information in the memory to a disk. If you turn the computer off without saving to a disk, you lose all the information you have entered in the memory.

Search Engine – A database program designed to work with a web browser to help find information. A search engine database will search for matching information from other search engines such as Yahoo, Google, Bing, etc.

Section Break – The division between two different sections or areas of text, indicating a change that affects only that section or area, such as portrait versus landscape orientation, different headers and footers, etc.

Select All Button – Clicking this button will select all cells in the current worksheet. It is located to the left of the column headings and above the row headings.

ScreenTip – A text box that displays helpful information on the purpose or function of a button or text box.

Screen Saver – If selected, displays a picture that will appear when you do not use the mouse or keyboard for a specified period of time.

Scroll Bars – Scroll bars automatically appear in a window if the contents are not entirely visible. A vertical or horizontal scroll bar may appear.

Series – Each set of data used in a graphical chart.

Server – A main computer that provides services and access to common files in a group of computers. A dedicated computer that holds all email is called the Mail Server.

Service Packs – Collection of updates typically released after enough updates have accumulated to warrant a new release.

Shared Folder – A folder that can be shared by other computer users. You can share folders on a network or on a local hard drive.

Shareware – A type of application program that can be downloaded and used for an evaluation or trial basis. If you like the program, you can then pay the nominal cost of this program which will remove advertisements or provide more features in the program.

Shortcut – A shortcut is a quick way to start a program or open a file or folder without having to go to its permanent location. Shortcuts are especially useful for programs, files, and folders you use frequently.

Shortcut Keys – The commands activated by pressing the Ctrl key with another key to perform a specific task, such as pressing Ctrl + P will display the Print menu.

Shortcut Menu – The menu that appears when you click the right mouse button.

Shouting – When you send a message using all capital letters.

Shut Down – The command to use from the Windows Start menu when you no longer want or need to use the computer.

Signatures – A piece of text that appears at the bottom of an email that includes contact information on who sent the message.

Single Seat License – When you purchase a software program that will be installed on one computer only.

Site License – When an organization buys a license that entitles them to install the software on an unlimited number of computers at one site only.

Sleep Mode – The power option that consumes less power as the display turns off and puts the computer to sleep.

Slide Layout – The process of determining what should be on the slide (that is, the title text, text and chart, organization chart, and so on). PowerPoint provides a number of pre-designed layouts from which you can select for each slide.

Slide Sorter – The view that displays multiple miniature slides on one screen; use this view to rearrange or sort your slides.

SMS – Short Message Service; a protocol used by cellular providers to enable text messages to be sent from one mobile device to another.

Social Networking – A select type of network on the Internet that you can join, usually for social purposes such as meeting new people, playing games, sharing photos or videos.

Solid State Drives – Use memory chips to read and write data; no moving parts so these are less fragile than traditional drives in addition to being silent.

Spacing – Refers to the amount of white space between individual characters, words, lines or columns of text or objects.

Speaker Notes – A PowerPoint feature that allows you to create notes of each slide in the presentation and then print these for your reference during the presentation.

Spelling & Grammar – A feature that checks the spelling and grammar of the document and usually provides a list of corrections for any error it finds.

Spoofing – The act of pretending to be an individual or organization with the intent to defraud people who come to the web site.

Spreadsheet – Used for entering and analyzing data (for example, financial forecasting, cash flow, auditing, and so on). See also Worksheet.

Spyware – Software that is secretly placed on a computer and gathers personal and private information without the user's consent or knowledge.

Status Bar – Located at the bottom of the screen. The status bar displays messages, cursor location, page number, section number, and whether specific features are active.

Start Button – The Start button displays the Start menu. The Start button is the single most commonly used feature in Windows.

Start Menu – The Start menu is the primary means of starting programs. It also contains the Start Search box.

Start Search Box – A component of the Start menu that enables you to search for files, folders and programs.

Switch – Connects computers (either individual systems or multiple networks) in a network so they can exchange information.

Style – A combination of formatting features you can save and apply as a set.

Subnet Mask – A 32-bit number that networking devices use to determine whether a destination system is local or remote.

Symbol – A character that can be inserted into a document, either as a text character or for a bullet or numbering style.

Tab – Depending on the context used, it may refer to the `Tab` key on the keyboard, a page of options in a dialog box, a menu command on the Office 2013 Ribbon, or an option to display another page for further actions. The latter three are analogous to an index tab protruding from a file folder.

Table – A feature that enables you to create a grid layout for content consisting of columns and rows, similar to how a worksheet appears.

Table Styles – A feature that enables you to apply many different formatting characteristics to a table with a single command by choosing from a selection of format templates; see Cell Styles or Quick Styles also.

Task Notification Area – Found on the right side of the taskbar and includes a clock and icons that communicate the status of certain programs and settings.

Task Pane – A window displayed at the side of the screen that appears when specific commands are activated such as the Office Clipboard, PivotTable options.

Taskbar – The area at the bottom of the screen that runs horizontally and contains the Start menu and other frequently used programs, folders or files.

Taskbar buttons – These display on the Taskbar whenever you have activated a program to display the contents of a file or program in a window.

Tasks – A feature in Outlook to set up a list of tasks you need to accomplish. Alternatively, you can assign tasks to others to complete.

TCP/IP – Transmission Control Protocol/Internet Protocol; the standard protocol for both local and wide area networking, and required for Internet access.

Template – A pre-designed form created by Microsoft, a third party vendor, or a user to create a specific type of document. Setting up a template enables documents of that type to have a consistent look.

Text – Alphabetic and numeric characters, plus most printable symbols. See also Labels.

Text Messaging – Similar to instant messaging but generally sent over a cellular provider's network.

Thesaurus – The feature that allows you to look up words with similar or opposite meanings.

Touchpad – The small rectangular area on a notebook that enables you to select and use the mouse pointer on the screen.

Tracking Changes – A process that displays all changes made to the file, including editing actions and formatting changes.

Transition – A feature that allows you to determine how text and objects are built on a slide, as well as how each slide will advance to the next slide.

Trendline – A common method of analyzing data using charts or graphs based on the data in a worksheet.

Theme – A collection of appearance settings sorted as a theme. For example, color and appearance, color schemes, screen savers, sound schemes and mouse pointer schemes.

Title Bar – The horizontal bar located at the top of a window and containing the title of the window or program.

Troubleshooting – The process of determining what may be causing an issue on the computer and then finding a resolution for the issue.

UAC – User Account Control (See User Account Control)

Undo – The feature that enables you to reverse the last action performed.

UNIX – One of the first multi-tasking multi-user operating systems originally developed for use on large mainframe computers and servers.

Updates – Files or collection of software tools that resolve security issues and improves performance.

Upload – The process of sending data from your computer to server, such as video, pictures.

URL – Uniform Resource Locator. The entire address that is recognized "universally" as the address for an Internet resource.

URL Shortening – A service that enables you to shorten the length of a URL address to insert into a message or post such as on Twitter.

USB Drive – Flash memory data storage device integrated with a USB connector.

User Account Control (UAC) – A general term for the way administrative and standard user accounts work within Windows. The account type determines the level of access that the user can have to the computer.

User Name – A unique name identifying a user account to Windows. An account's user name cannot be identical to any other group name or user name on its own domain or workgroup.

Values – Numeric, date, or time values you enter directly into a worksheet cell. This type of data is not only used to show information in a spreadsheet but is used to calculate other values on the same or other spreadsheets.

Video Conferencing – Enables people in distant locations to participate to communicate with one another using the internet and audio/video technology.

View Options – Different ways of being able to view a document, usually to assist in working with the text, page layout, web layout, an outline, or reading.

Virus – A small program written for the purpose of destroying information on a disk or the entire computer.

Virtual Private Network (VPN) – An encrypted connection between two computers.

VoIP – Voice over Internet Protocol; a means of communicating with two or more people using a telephone connected to a network using Internet protocol.

Web Browser – Software needed to navigate through the web. For example, Internet Explorer, Mozilla Firefox and Safari are web browsers.

Web Content – The content on a Web page.

Web Site Address – Specific address assigned to a web site that is entered in the URL to navigate to the site.

Wiki – A dedicated Web site that enables one or more people to enter information on a specific topic. These are often compared to encyclopedias although there is no guarantee the information is completely accurate or up to date, as these are managed by individuals.

Wireless Network – The ability to have a network of computers and/or resources that are connected without the use of cables.

Word Wrap – A feature that moves text from the end of a line to the beginning of a new line as you type.

World Wide Web (WWW) – System of interlinked documents accessible on the Internet.

WYSIWYG – Refers to "What You See Is What You Get", a display mode that shows the document exactly as it will appear when you print it.

Working Offline – Doing work or creating data on your computer while it is not connected to the network or to an online service such as the Internet.

Workstation – Any networked computer using server resources.

WWW – World Wide Web; a multimedia service on the Internet. The WWW contains a collection of online documents with text, images, sound, or video. The documents are stored on Internet servers around the world.

X-axis – The horizontal edge of a chart, marking the scale used there.

Y-axis – The vertical edge of a chart, marking the scale used there.

Index

A

AAOCC, 575
Absolute Addresses, 306
Access
    Action query, 422
    Database files, 401
    Dynaset, 422
    Field, 411
    Filter, 183
    Finding records, 417
    Forms, 402
    Navigation buttons, 183
    New, 405
    Queries, 403
    Rearranging the datasheet, 415
    Record, 411
    Reports, 403
    Search, 183
    Split bar, 183
    Tables, 402
    Work Area, 183
Access client view, 404
Access Work Area, 183
Accessibility Settings, 79
Action Query, 422
Active Cell, 285
Active Directory, 89
ActiveX, 454
adapter, 460
Add-ons, 454
Address Book, 508
Addressing, 441, 461, 470, 508
    Internet protocol, 462
    Mac, 462
    On the Internet, 470
    Testing connectivity, 481
    Troubleshooting, 480
ADSL. See Asymmetric Digital
    Services Line
Advertising, 577
Adware, 112
Aligning
    Text, 224
Alignment, 310
    Tables, 274
Animation, 383
    Customization, 385
Antivirus, 112
Anti-virus Program, 548
anti-virus software, 548
APIPA. See Windows Automatic
    Private IP Addressing
Application Service Provider, 92,
    536
Applications Tab, 173
Archiving, 524
Articles, 576
Asymmetric DSL, 469

Attachments, 516
    Opening, 517
    Opening attachments, 517
    Preview file button, 518
    Previewing, 517
    Saving attachments, 517
Authentication, 475
    Wireless security, 475
Authenticity of Information, 575
AutoComplete, 569
Auto-forwarding, 528
Avoiding viruses, 158
Axes, 327
Axis titles, 327

B

Backstage, 181, 191
Backstage view
    Tabs, 405
Backstage View, 404
Backups
    Locations, 147
Basic Terminology
    Active cell, 285
    Cell, 285
    Cell address, 285
    Formulas, 288
    Labels, 288
    Values, 288
    Workbook, 285
    Worksheet, 285
Blacklisting, 538
Blank Database, 405
    Creating, 405
Blockers, 538
Blogs, 493
    Microblogging, 494
Bookmarks, 448
Boolean Operators, 444, 570
Booting, 7
Borders, 273, 312
Breaks
    Page, 251
Broadband, 467
    Routers, 470
Broadband router
    WAN port, 470
Brower Functions
    Hyperlinks, 442
Browser Features, 445
    Active-X add-ons, 454
    Add-ons, 454
    Back, forward or refresh
        buttons, 445
    Favoriites or bookmarks, 448
    History, 452
    Plug-ins, 454
    Tabs, 446
Browser Functions, 441
    Addressing, 441
    Searching, 443

Bullets and Numbering
    Customizing, 231
Bundling, 92, 536
Buttons, 440

C

Cable, 469
    Modem, 469
Cable modem, 469
CATV. See Cable
CD Drives, 58
CD Writers, 59
Cell, 285
Cell Address, 285
Cell Addresses
    Absolute, 306
    Relative, 306
Cell Styles, 314
Cells
    Deleting, 299
    Inserting, 298
Censorship, 538
    Blacklisting, 538
    Blockers, 538
    Filters, 538
Changing the Folder, 32
Changing the View, 33
Character Formatting, 223
Chart
    Types, 325
Chart Layout, 326
Chart legend, 327
Chart titles, 327
Chart Tools Ribbon, 325
Chart Types, 325, 367
Charts, 324, 365
    Adjusting the data, 368
    Axes, 327
    Axis titles, 327
    Chart layouts, 326
    Data labels, 327
    Data table, 327
    Datasheet, 366, 367
    Gridlines, 327
    Series, 324
    Titles, 327
    Types, 367
Chat rooms, 491
Circuit Switching, 466
Client systems, 458
Client/Server, 458
Client/Server Networks, 458
Clients, 433
Clip Art, 372
Close
    Database, 407
    Documents, 215
    Workbooks, 291
Close Button, 24
Cloud, 147
Collapse Button, 29

Colors, 314
Column Headings, 182
Column Width, 275
Column Widths, 297
Columns, 253
    Breaking, 254
    Changing the Number of
        Columns, 254
    Deleting, 299
    Inserting, 298
Command Bar, 24
Comments, 279
Communicating with Others
    Blogs, 493
    Chat rooms, 491
    Electronic mail, 485
    Online conferencing, 490
    Social networking sites, 491
    Text messages, 488
    Weblogs, 493
Communicating with Others
    Shortening the URL, 494
Communicating with Others
    Email, 498
Computers, 51
    Electronic book readers, 54
    Hand-held, 53
    Laptop, 52
    Media players, 53
    Mobile, 53
    Music players, 53
    Netbook, 52
    Notebooks, 52
    Personal, 51
    Tablets, 52
Connecting to the Internet, 466
    Dial-Up Connections, 466
    Other factors affecting
        performance, 470
Connection Hardware
    Bandwidth options, 434
    Modem, 434
Content Creation
    Programs, 104
    Templates, 104
Content Creation Software, 104
Contents Pane, 504
Control Buttons, 24
Control Panel, 69
    Accessibility settings, 79
    Changing the date or time, 74
    Changing the language, 76
    Customizing the Desktop
        display, 71
    Power options, 81
Cookies, 545
Copying and Moving, 42
Copyright, 533
    Fair Use, 535
    Licensing, 535
    Sources of information, 535
Creating
    Database from a template, 406
    New blank database, 405

Cropping, 265
Cursor and Numeric Keypad, 63
Cut, Copy or Paste, 294

D

Data Labels, 327
Data Loss, 543
data repetition, 99
Data Storage, 145
    Cloud, 147
    External Hard Drive, 147
    Offiste, 147
Data Table, 327
Database, 401
    Action query, 422
    Closing, 407
    Creating from a template, 406
    Database vs Spreadsheet, 98
    Dynaset, 422
    Field, 411
    Finding records, 417
    Forms, 402
    Opening an existing, 407
    Queries, 403
    Record, 411
    Reports, 403
    Saving and publishing, 407
    Tables, 402
Database Management, 97
Database Management System,
    401
Database Templates, 406
Datasheet, 366, 367
    Manipulating, 415
    Navigating, 412
    Rearranging, 415
Date & Time, 74
DBMS. *See* Database
    Management System
Default Gateway, 463
defragmentation, disk, 114
Deleting Files & Folders, 47
Design
    Themes, 355
Desktop
    Customizing, 71
    Display, 71
Desktop Firewalls, 473
Desktop Publishing, 96
Device Drivers
    Firmware, 142
    Updates, 143
DHCP. *See* Dynamic Host
    Configuration Protocol
Dialog box launcher, 185
Dial-Up Connections, 466
    ISDN, 467
    POTS, 466
Digital Subscriber Line, 468
    DSL availability, 468
    DSL modem, 468
    DSL speeds, 468

Direct Connections, 467
    Broadband, 467
    Cable, 469
    Digital Subscriber line, 468
    Leased lines, 468
Disk Cleanup, 114
Disk Compression, 114
Disk Defragmenter utility, 114
Disk Maintenance Programs, 114
DNS. *See* Domain Name System
DNS Records, 471
DNS Servers, 471
Domain, 437
Domain Category, 499
Domain Name System, 471
    DNS records, 471
Domain Name Systems
    DNS servers, 471
Domains
    Top level categories, 438
DOS, 1, See Disk Operating
    System
Downloading, 442, 545
    Downstream), 442
Draft, 218
Draw Borders, 274
DSL. *See* Digital Subscriber Line
DSL Availability, 468
DSL Speeds, 468
Dynamic Host Configuration
    Protocol, 476
Dynaset, 422

E

Ease of Access, 79
E-Commerce, 554
Edit Mode, 359
Editing, 192
Effects, 223
Electronic Book Readers, 54
Electronic Mail, 485
Email, 498
    Address book, 508
    Addressing, 508
    Archiving, 524
    Attachments, 516
    Auto-forwarding, 528
    Automating, 525
    Domain category, 499
    Junk, 519
    Mailbox Name, 499
    Marking messages as junk, 522
    Message body, 509
    Organization Name, 499
    Proofing, 509
    Replying to messages, 512
    Signatures, 525
    Spam or junk mail, 519
    Subject line, 509
    Threads, 507
E-mail, 198
Emptying the Recycle Bin, 48

7318-1 v1.00 © 2014 CCI Learning Solutions Inc.

Encryption, 475
  WEP, 475
  Wireless, 475
  WPA, 475
  WPA2, 475
End User License Agreement, 93, 121
Entering Data, 288
  Dates, 288
  Numbers, 288
  Text, 288
Entering Text
  Slide pane, 344
Ergonomics, 551, 552, 553
  Repetitive stress injuries, 552
Ethernet, 461
Ethical Issues, 533, 541
  Copyright, 533
  Libel, 539
  Plagiarism, 539
  Slander, 539
  Unethical behavior, 540
EULA. See End User License
  Agreement, See End User
  License Agreement
Evaluating Information, 574
  Advertising, 577
  Articles, 576
  Authenticity, 575
  Forums, 577
  Knowledge Bases, 576
  Objectivity, 576
  Reliability or relevance, 575
  Sponsored links, 577
Excel
  Absolute or Relative
    addresses, 306
  Basic terminology, 285
  Cell styles, 314
  Changing data, 293
  Chart tools ribbon, 325
  Chart types, 325
  Charts, 324
  Closing workbooks, 291
  Column headings, 182
  Column widths, 297
  Common Built-in Functions, 305
  Creating a new blank
    workbook, 286
  Creating a workbook from a
    template, 286
  Customizing the page setup, 331
  Cut, copy or paste, 294
  Deleting rows, columns or
    cells, 298
  Entering data, 288
  Filtering data, 322
  Formatting, 309
  Formula Bar, 182
  Formulas, 303
  Insert Function, 182

Inserting or deleting
  workbooks, 301
Inserting rows, columns or
  cells, 298
Moving around, 289
Name Box, 182
Naming workbooks, 301
Office Clipboard, 294
Opening workbooks, 290
Page breaks, 331
Previewing or printing
  workbooks, 336
Protected View, 290
Row headings, 182
Row height, 298
Saving workbooks, 289
Sorting data, 319
Spelling errors, 318
Split bars, 182
Tab scrolling buttons, 182
Undo or Repeat, 294
Views, 330
Zoom, 330
Exiting the Computer, 8
Expand Button, 29
Eyestrain, 552

F

Fair Use, 535
FAQ. See Frequently Asked
  Questions
Favorites, 448
  Adding, 449
  Deleting, 449
  Favorites center, 448
  Organizing, 450
Favorites Center, 448
Field, 411
Fields, 439
File Extensions, 39
File Tab, 181
File Transfer Protocol, 437
Files, 27, 191
  Application, 27
  Closing, 215
  Common problems, 49
  Copying, 42
  Data, 27
  Deleting, 47
  Extensions, 39
  Finding, 46
  Managing in Microsoft Office, 191
  Moving, 44
  Renaming, 45
  Restoring from Recycle Bin, 48
  Saving in Word, 210
  Selecting, 41
  System, 27
Filter, 183
Filter by Selection, 418
Filtering, 322
Filters, 538
Find feature, 417

Finding Files, 46
Finding Items, 243
Finding Records, 417
Firewall Challenges, 474
Firewall Ports, 473
Firewalls, 472
  Advanced functions, 473
  Challenges, 474
  Desktop, 473
  Ports, 473
  Troubleshooting the
    configuration, 482
Firmware, 142, 479
Flaming, 497
Flash drives, 59
Folders, 27, 29
  Changing, 32
  Copying, 42
  Creating, 29
  Deleting, 47
  Finding, 46
  Moving, 44
  Renaming, 32, 45
  Restoring from Recycle Bin, 48
  Selecting, 41
Font Command, 224
Font Size, 223
Fonts, 312
Footer, 333
Footers, 334, 381
  Page numbering, 252
Formatting, 223, 309, 360
  Aligning, 224
  Aligning text, 362
  Borders, 312
  Cell Alignment, 310
  Cell styles, 314
  Characters, 223
  Colors, 314
  Decimal Digits, 309
  Effects, 223
  Excel, 309
  Font command, 224
  Font Size, 223
  Fonts, 312
  Numbers, 309
  Objects, 377
  Paragraphs, 224
  Patterns, 314
  Sizes, 312
  Styles, 235
  Tables, 273, 363
  Text, 360
  Text characters, 223
Formatting Codes, 208
Forms, 402
Formula Bar, 182
Formulas, 303
  Creating, 303
  Errors, 303
  Identifying, 304
  Mathematical operators, 303
Forum, 577
Forwarding a Message, 514

fragmentation, disk, 114
Freeware, 92, 536
Freeze panes, 330
Frequently Asked Questions, 568
FTP. *See* File Transfer Protocol
Function Keys, 63
Functions, 305
   =AVERAGE, 305
   =COUNT, 305
   =MAX, 305
   =MIN, 305
   =SUM, 305

G

Gateway, 460
Gateways, 472
   Default, 461
gigabyte (GB), 56, 458
Gridlines, 327
Group Policy, 89
   Active Directory, 89

H

Hacker, 471, 543
Hand-held Computers, 53
   Electronic book readers, 54
Handheld Operating Systems, 5
Handles, 260
Handouts, 395
Hard Disk Drives, 58
Hardware, 142, 478
   Connections or Cables, 142
   Other types of issues, 144
   Replacing, 142
   Updates, 142
Header, 333
Headers, 334, 381
   Page numbering, 252
Help, 167, 181
   Additional technical support,
     169
   Help Toolbar, 188
   Knowledge Base, 171
   Microsoft Office, 181
   Microsoft Office program, 187
   Search Options, 188
   Table of Contents, 168
   Toolbar, 188
   Topics, 188
   Windows, 167
Help Button, 24
Help Toolbar, 188
Hibernate, 81
Hide window panes, 330
History, 452
Home Page, 439
   Site map, 439
HTML. *See* hypertext markup
   language
HTML Objects, 571
HTTP. *See* Hypertext Transfer
   Protocol
Hub, 460
Hubs, 460

Hyperlinks, 442
   Pointing hand, 443
HyperText Markup Language.
Hypertext Transfer Protocol, 437

I

ICANN. *See* Internet Corporation
   for Assigned Names and
   Numbers
Illustrations
   Handles, 260
   Using Bing to search, 262
Indenting
   Paragraph command, 230
Indents, 230
   Adjusting, 231
Index Page, 439
Indicator Lights, 478
Input Devices
   Keyboard, 61
   Microphones, 64
   Mouse, 63
   Stylus, 64
   Touchpad, 64
Input/Output Devices, 61
   Pointing Devices, 63
Insert Function, 182
Inserting
   Cells, 298
   Columns, 298
   Objects in Word, 264
   Pictures in Word, 260
   Rows, 298
   Slides, 365
   Tables in Word, 271
Inserting Cells, 274
Inserting Columns, 274
Inserting Rows, 274
Insertion Point, 182, 207
Installing a New Program, 120
Integrated Services Digital
   Network, 467
Integrated Suites Software, 96
Internet, 433
   Connecting to, 466
   Domains, 437
   Ethical issues, 533, 541
   Evaluating the information, 574
   Home page, 439
   HyperText Markup Language.
   Internet Service Provider, 433
   Protocols, 437
   Search engines, 567
   Searching for information, 563
   Uploading or downloading,
     442
   URL, 437
   Web browsers, 436
   Web pages, 436
   Web server, 433
   Web site, 433
   Web site addresses, 437
Internet Corporation for Assigned
   Names and Numbers, 463

Internet Explorer
   Favorites list, 450
Internet Protocol (IP) Addresses,
   462
Internet Service Provider, 433
Involate
   Card readers and writers, 60
   Optical drives, 58
   USB drives, 59
Involatile
   Hard disk drives, 58
   Solid state drives, 58
IP Address, 462
   Default gateway, 463
   Determining, 462
   Host portion, 462
   Reserved ranges, 463
   Subnet mask, 463
   Who issues these, 463
IP Addresses
   DNS, 471
   Private, 463
IP Addressing
   DNS servers, 471
   Dynamic host configuration
     protocol, 476
IPCONFIG, 480
ISDN. *See* Integrated Services
   Digital Network
ISP. *See* Internet Service
   Provider

J

Junk Email
   Emptying, 523
Junk Mail, 519
   Marking messages, 522

K

Keyboard, 12, 61
   Cursor and numeric keypad, 63
   Function keys, 63
   Typewriter keys, 62
Keywords, 569
kilobyte (KB), 56, 458
Knowledge Base, 171
Knowledge Bases, 576

L

LAN. *See* Local Area Networks
Language, 76
Laptop, 52
Layout View, 426
Leased Lines, 468
Libel, 539
Licenses, 91, 535
   Single Seat, 91, 535
   Site, 92, 536
   Volume, 92, 536
Licensing, 535
Line Spacing, 234
List Information, 231
Lists
   Tables, 277

Local Area Networks, 459
   Addressing, 461
   Common LAN devices, 460
   Connecting to, 459
   Connecting together, 464
   Gateways, 460
   Hubs, 460
   Routers, 460
   Switches, 460
   Wired connections, 461
   Wireless connections, 461
Looking at the Screen
   View buttons, 182

M

MAC Address, 462
Mac OS, 4
Mailbox Name, 499
malware, 157, 545
Malware, 112, 157, 545
Manipulating Pictures
   Smart Guides, 374
Margins, 250, 332
   Boundaries, 250
   Setting, 250
Master Slide, 381
Mathematical Operators, 303
Maximize Button, 24
Media Players, 53
megabyte (MB), 56, 458
Memory, 56
   Random Access, 57
   Read Only, 56
Memory card reader, 60
Merging Cells, 275
Message Body, 509
Messages
   Archiving, 524
Messages
   Address book, 508
   Addressing, 508
   Attachments, 516
   Body text, 509
   Checking for new, 511
   Creating, 505
   Forwarding, 514
   Junk mail, 519
   Marking as junk, 522
   Proofing, 509
   Replying, 512
   Sending, 505, 510
   Spam, 519
   Subject line, 509
Microblogging, 494
Microphones, 64
Microprocessor Chip, 55
Microsoft Office
   Backstage, 181
   Editing tools, 192
   Exiting a program, 178
   Getting help, 187
   Help, 181
   Preferences, 183, 191
   Starting a program, 177

Microsoft Windows
   Command bar, 24
   Control buttons, 24
   Start button, 12
   Taskbar, 14
Mini toolbar, 223
Mini Toolbar, 361
Minimize Button, 24
Modem, 434
Monitor, 65
More Button, 184, 237
Mouse, 63
Moving, 268
Moving a Window, 25
Moving Around
   Presentations, 351
   Word, 208
   Worksheets, 289
MP3, 53
Multimedia, 105, 260
Music Players, 53

N

Name Box, 182
Narrowing the Search, 569
   /^, 570
   and, 570
   HTML objects, 571
   not, 570
   or, 570
Navigation Bar, 439
Navigation Buttons, 183
Navigation Pane, 186, 404, 504
Navigation Pane Split Bar, 504
Netbooks, 52
Network, 457
   Advantages, 457
   Definition, 457
network adapter card, 460
Network Interface Card, 434, 460
Networking Models, 458
   Client/server, 458
   Peer-to-peer, 459
   TCP/IP, 459
   Web-based, 459
Networks
   Access control, 472
   Authentication, 472
   Firewalls, 472
   Fundamentals, 457, 459, 464,
      465, 466, 470, 471, 475
   Gateways, 472
   Local area, 459
   Packet filtering, 473
   Private vs public, 472
   Public switched, 465
   Security, 471
   Speed, 458
   Troubleshooting, 475
   Troubleshooting hardware
      issues, 478
   Virtual private, 474
   Wide area, 464
   Wireless security, 474

New
   Database files, 405
   Database from a template, 406
   Documents, 213
   Messages, 505
   Presentations, 343
   Workbook from templates, 286
   Workbooks, 286
   Worksheet, 301
NIC. See network interface card
Notebooks, 52
Notes, 393
Notes Pane, 183

O

Objectivity of Information, 576
Objects, 372
   Animating, 383
   Arranging, 377
   Clip Art, 372
   Drawing, 376
   Formatting, 377
   Multimedia, 377
   Pictures, 372
Office Clipboard, 222, 294
Online Conferencing, 490
Open
   Database, 407
   Workbooks, 290
Open Source, 92, 536
Opening
   Word documents, 216
Operating System, 1
   Embedded, 5
   Power options, 6
   Updates, 144
   Updates and versioning, 156
   Windows 7, 4
   Windows desktop, 11
Operating Systems
   Advantages and
      disadvantages, 6
   DOS, 1
   Handheld, 5
   Unix, 5
Opt-out Tool, 558
Orientation, 249
   Landscape, 249
   Portrait, 249
Outline, 218
Outline Tab, 182
Outlook
   Addressing messages, 508
   Archiving, 524
   Automating, 525
   Checking for messages, 511
   Contents pane, 504
   Forwarding a message, 514
   Junk Mail, 519
   Marking messages as junk, 522
   Modules, 505
   Navigation Pane, 504
   Opening attachments, 517
   Out-of-Office notices, 528

Previewing attachments, 517
Proofing messages, 509
Reading pane, 504
Replying to messages, 512
Saving attachments, 517
Search, 504
Sending messages, 505
Signatures, 525
Spam messages, 519
Split bars, 504
Threads, 507
Out-of-Office Notices, 528
Output Devices
Monitor, 65
Printers, 65
Projectors, 65
Speaker, 66

P

Packet Filtering, 473
Packet Switching, 466
Page Break Preview, 331
Page Breaks, 251, 331
Page Numbering, 252
Page Settings, 331
Page Setup, 248
Customizing, 331
Header/Footer tab, 334
Margins, 250, 332
Orientation, 249
Page breaks, 331
Page settings, 331
Paper size, 248
Sheet tab, 335
Paper Size, 248
Paragraph Command, 230
Paragraph Spacing, 234
Patches, 18
Patterns, 314
Peeks Bar, 504
Peer-to-peer model, 458
Peer-to-peer network, 459
Personal Computer
Booting, 7
How it works, 66
Shutting down, 8
Personal Computers
Input/Output devices, 61
Looking inside, 54
Microprocessor chip, 55
Monitors, 65
Printers, 65
Software, 91
Starting, 7
Storage systems, 57
Personal Firewall, 546
Phishing, 555
Picture, 439
Pictures, 260, 372
Changing properties, 267
Clip Art, 261
Cropping, 265
Files, 260
Manipulating, 264

Moving, 268
Properties, 267
Rotating, 266
Sizing, 265
Using Bing to search, 262
Wrapping Text, 267
Piracy, 539
Placeholder, 182
Placeholders, 342
Plagiarism, 539
Plain Old Telephone Service.
Plug-ins, 454
Pointing Devices, 12, 63
Mouse, 63
Stylus, 64
Touchpad, 64
Pointing Hand, 443
Portable PCs
laptop, 52
POTS. *See* Plain Old Telephone
Service
POTS Connection, 466
Power Options, 6, 81
PowerPoint, 341
Align text, 362
Animation, 383
Chart datasheet, 366
Charts, 365
Clip Art objects, 372
Closing a presentation, 347
Customizing animation, 385
Delete a slide, 355
Format text, 360
Formatting tables, 363
Handouts, 395
Headers or footers, 381
Insert slides, 354
Master slides, 381
Moving around, 351
Multimedia objects, 377
New presentations, 343
Notes, 393
Notes pane, 183
Open a presentation, 347
Outline tab, 182
Picture objects, 372
Placeholder, 182
Presentation structure, 342
Presenter view, 392
Print options, 395
Printing presentations, 393
Protected View, 347
Quick Styles, 361
Rearrange slides, 355
Saving a presentation, 345
Select vs Edit mode, 359
Setting the slide show up, 390
Shape objects, 376
Slide layouts, 354
Slide pane, 183, 344
Slide shows, 390
Slide transitions, 387
Slides tab, 182
Spell Checking, 360

Split bar, 183
Split bars, 345
Tables, 363
Text objects, 360
Themes, 355
Zoom, 351
Pranks, 540
Premium, 92, 536
Presentation Manager, 341
Presentations, 103
Aligning text, 362
Animation, 383
Changing the view, 350
Chart datasheet, 366
Charts, 365
Checking the spelling, 360
Clip Art objects, 372
Closing, 347
Creating, 343
Deleting slides, 355
Formatting tables, 363
Formatting text, 360
Handouts, 395
Headers or footers, 381
Inserting new slides, 354
Master slides, 381
Moving around, 351
Multimedia objects, 377
Notes, 393
Opening, 347
Picture objects, 372
Presenter view, 392
Print options, 395
Printing, 393
Quick Styles, 361
Rearranging, 355
Saving, 345
Select vs Edit mode, 359
Setting up, 390
Shape objects, 376
Slide layouts, 354
Slide shows, 390
Slide transitions, 387
Structure, 342
Tables, 363
Text objects, 360
Themes, 355
Previewing, 336
Documents, 256
Print Layout, 217
Print Options, 395
Print Preview, 425
Printers, 65
Printing, 330, 336, 393
Customizing the page setup,
331
Documents, 256
Handouts, 395
Header or footer, 334
Margins, 332
Print options, 336
Print Options, 395
Sheet, 335

Privacy, 557
    Opt-out Tool, 558
Private IP Addresses, 463
Processes Tab, 174
Projectors, 65
Proofing, 509
Properties, 267
Protected View, 218, 290, 347
Protecting Your Data or
    Computer, 542
    Viruses, 547
Protecting Yourself, 553
    Buying online, 554
    E-commerce, 554
    Phishing, 555
    Spoofing, 555
Protocols, 437
    Dynamic host configuration,
        476
    File transfer.
    Transmission control, 459
    Web site, 437
PSTN. *See* Public Switched
    Telephone Network
Public Switched Networks, 465
Public Switched Telephone
    Network, 465
    Analog and digital signals, 465
    Circuit switching, 466
    Digital phone, 465
    Packet switching, 466
Public switched telephone
    network (PSTN)
    POTS connection, 466

Q

Queries, 403
    Dynaset, 422
Quick Access Toolbar, 181, 184
    Customizing, 184
Quick Styles, 237, 361

R

RAM. See Random Access
    Memory
Random Access Memory, 57
Read Mode, 217
Read Only Memory, 56
Reading Pane, 504, 511
Receiving Messages
    Checking, 511
Record, 411, 412
Records
    Finding, 417
Recycle Bin, 47
    Restoring items, 48
Recycling Bin
    Emptying, 48
redundant power supplies, 53
Reinstalling a Program, 133
Relative Addresses, 306
Reliability or Relevance, 575
Renaming a Folder, 32
Repeat, 221, 294

Repetitive Stress Injuries, 552
Replacing Items, 243
Replying to Messages, 512
Report, 424
    Creating, 428
    Designing, 428
    Layout View, 426
    Layouts, 428
    Report views, 425
Report Tool, 429
Report View, 425
Report Wizard, 429
Reports, 403
Research Tools, 246
Residual Files, 546
Resource Names, 437
Restore Down Button, 24
Restoring a File or Folder, 48
Ribbon, 181, 184
    Chart Tools, 325, 366
    Displaying dialog boxes or task
        panes, 185
    Drawing Tools, 377
    Format Text, 509
    Gallery lists, 184
    Groups, 184
    More button, 184
    New Message, 509
    Picture Tools, 265, 373
    Table Tools, 271
    Tabs, 184
Ridicule, 540
Rights and Access, 88
Risks
    Hacker, 543
    Privacy, 557
    Protecting yourself, 553
    Viruses, 547
ROM. See Read Only Memory
Router
    Access router, 461
Routers, 460
    Broadband, 470
    Gateways, 460
Row Headings, 182
Row Height, 275, 298
Rows
    Deleting, 299
    Inserting, 298
Ruler, 208
    Setting indents, 230

S

SaaS. *See* Software as a Service
Safe Mode, 166
Save
    Workbooks, 289
Save to Web, 200
Saving
    Documents, 210
    File types, 406
    Naming conventions, 405
Screen Elements
    Access, 181

Accessing commands and
    features, 183
    Excel, 180
    File tab, 181
    Help, 181
    Insertion Point, 182
    PowerPoint, 180
    Quick Access toolbar, 181
    Ribbon, 181
    Ribbon, 184
    ScreenTips, 183
    Status Bar, 182
    Title Bar, 181
    Word, 179
    Zoom Slider, 182
ScreenTips, 183
Scroll Bar, 209
Scroll Bars, 25
Search, 183
Search Engine Company, 568
Search Engine Features, 568
Search Engine Technology, 567
Search Engines, 567
    Features, 568
    Keywords, 569
    Narrowing the search, 569
    Technology, 567
Search Options, 188
Searching, 443, 563, 565
    AAOCC, 575
    AutoComplete, 569
    Evaluating the information, 574
    Narrowing, 569
    Purpose or type, 563
    Specific Web Site, 565
SEC. *See* Search Engine
    Company
Secure Socket Layer, 554
Security, 471
    Access control, 472
    Authentication, 472
    Firewalls, 472
    Gateways, 472
    Hackers, 471
    Packet filtering, 473
    Private vs public networks, 472
    Protecting your data or
        computer, 542, 551, 553
    Software threats, 544
    Troubleshooting settings, 481
    Virtual private networks, 474
    Wireless networks, 474
    Wireless settings, 482
Select Mode, 359
Select Query, 422
Selecting, 209, 293
    Cells, 293
    Consecutive text, 209
    Selection Bar, 210
    Table items, 273
Selection Bar, 210
Series, 368
    Adjusting the data, 368
Server-based networks, 458

Servers, 433
Service Packs, 18
Service Tab, 174
Shading, 273
SharePoint, 201
Shareware, 92, 536
Sharing documents
    E-mail, 198
    Save to Web, 200
    SharePoint, 201
Sharing Information
    Comments, 279
    Tracking changes, 280
Sharing Personal Information,
    540
Sheet Setup, 335
Shortening the URL, 442, 494
Shouting, 498
Shut Down Options, 8
Shutting Down the Computer, 8
Signal Quality, 479
Signatures, 525
Single Seat, 91, 535
Site License, 92, 536
Site Map, 439, *See* Navigation
    bar
Sizes, 312
Sizing, 265
Sizing a Window, 25
SkyDrive, 200
Slander, 539
Slide Layout, 354
Slide Layouts, 354
Slide Pane, 183, 344
Slide Show, 390
    Navigating, 391
    Running, 391
    Setting up, 390
    Viewing, 390
Slide Sorter, 355
Slide Transitions, 387
Slides
    Animating objects, 383
    Charts, 365
    Deleting, 355
    Inserting new, 354
    Rearranging, 355
    Tables, 363
    Transitions, 387
Slides Tab, 182
Smart Guides, 374
Social Bookmarking, 449
Social Engines
    Social search engine, 568
Social Networking Sites, 491
    Social bookmarking, 449
Social Search Engine, 568
Software, 91, 155
    Adware, 112
    Antivirus, 112
    Application Service Provider,
        92, 536
    Bundling, 92, 536

Checking the system
    requirements, 93
Choosing an application
    program, 95
Content creation, 104
Database management, 97
Desktop publishing, 96
Disk cleanups, 114
Disk compression, 114
Disk maintenance, 114
End User License Agreement,
    121
Freeware, 92, 536
Hardware implications, 95
Installing a new program, 120
Licenses, 91, 535
Malware, 112
Managing programs, 120
Multimedia, 105
Obtaining, 1, 23, 91
Open Source, 92, 536
Premium, 92, 536
Presentations, 103
Reinstalling, 133
Shareware, 92, 536
Software as a Service, 92, 536
Spyware, 112
Suites, 96
System protection, 112
Types, 95
Uninstalling a program, 130
Updates to programs, 155
Updating, 136
Updating the operating
    system, 156
Using, 14
Viruses or malware, 157
Web applications, 96
Windows 7 Upgrade Advisor,
    156
Software as a Service, 92, 120,
    536
Software Threats, 544
    Cookies, 545
    Downloading, 545
    Malware, 545
    Operating system updates, 546
    Personal firewall, 546
    Residual files, 546
    Spyware, 545
Solid-State Drives, 58
Sorting, 319
Spam, 519
Speakers, 66
Spell Checker, 318
Spelling, 241, 360
Split Bar, 29, 183
Split Bars, 182
Split worksheet, 330
Splitting Cells, 275
Sponsored Links, 577
Spoofing, 555
Spreadsheets
    Database vs Spreadsheet, 98

spyware, 157
Spyware, 112, 545
SQL. *See* Structured Query
    Language
SSD. *See* Solid State Drives
SSL. *See* Secure Socket Layer
Start Button, 12
    Start menu, 13
Start Menu, 13
Starting the Computer, 7
    Booting, 7
    Windows desktop, 11
Status Bar, 182
Storage Systems, 57
    Card readers and writers, 60
    CD drives, 58
    CD writers, 59
    Hard disk drives, 58
    Solid state drive (SSD), 58
    USB drives, 59
    Zip drives, 59
Structured Query Language, 401
Styles, 235, 314
    Automatically Update, 239
    Quick Styles, 237
    Styles pane, 239
    Styles Window, 238
Styles Pane, 239
Styles Window, 238
Stylus, 64
Subject Line, 509
Subnet Mask, 463
Supporting Facts, 541
Switches, 460
System Protection Tools, 112
System Requirements, 93

T

Tab Scrolling Buttons, 182
Tab Selector Box, 226
Table Selector, 271
Table Tools, 271
Tables, 271, 363, 402
    Adjusting the width or height,
        275
    Aligning items, 274
    Formatting, 363
    Inserting, 272
    Inserting rows, columns or
        cells, 274
    Merging or splitting cells, 275
    Organizing lists, 277
Tabs, 446
Task Manager, 173
    Applications tab, 173
    Processes tab, 174
    Service tab, 174
Taskbar, 14
TCP/IP. *See* Transmission Control
    Protocols/Internet Protocols
Technical Support, 169
    Displaying the Windows
        version, 170
Template, 286

Templates, 104, 343
    Word, 213
terabyte (GB), 56
Text
    Aligning, 362
Text Messages, 488
Text Objects, 360
The Computer Feature
    Changing the view, 33
Theft, 543
Themes, 355
    Colors, 356
    Modifying, 355
Thread, 507
Title Bar, 181
TLS. See Transport Layer
    Security
Toolbars
    Mini, 223
    Quick Access, 181
Touchpad, 64
Tracking Changes, 280
Transmission Control
    Protocol/Internet Protocol, 459
Transport Layer Security, 554
trojan, 545
Troubleshooting, 141, 475
    Addressing issues, 480
    Basics of network
        troubleshooting, 476
    Connections or cables, 142
    Firewall configuration, 482
    Firmware updates, 479
    Hardware, 142
    Hardware issues, 478
    Identifying viruses or malware,
        157
    Indicator lights, 478
    IPCONFIG utility, 480
    Keeping copies of data, 145
    Other hardware issues, 144
    Printers, 145
    Replacing hardware, 142
    Security settings, 481
    Signal quality issues, 479
    Software, 155
    Updating device drivers, 143
    Updating hardware, 142
    Updating the operating
        system, 144
    Using Safe Mode, 166
    Wireless security, 482
    Wireless signals, 479
Typewriter Keys, 62

U

UAC. See User Account Control
Undo, 220, 294
Unethical Behavior, 540
    Piracy, 539
    Pranks, 540
    Ridicule, 540

Sharing personal information,
    540
    Supporting Facts, 541
Unhide window panes, 330
Uniform Resource Locator, 437
    Resource names, 437
Uninstalling a Program, 130
UNIX, 5
Updates, 18, 546
    Automatic updating, 19
    Categories, 19
    Device drivers, 143
    Hardware, 142
    Operating system, 144, 156
    Software, 155
Updating Software, 136
    Installing, 137
Upgrade Advisor, 156
Uploading, 442
    Upstream), 442
URL. See Uniform Resource
    Locator
USB Storage, 59
User Account Control, 85
User Accounts, 84
    Create a new account, 86
    Setting accounts and rights, 84

V

View Buttons, 182, 218
Views, 330
    PowerPoint, 350
    Presenter view, 392
    Read Mode, 217
    Slide Show, 390
    View Buttons, 218
    Word, 217
Virtual Private Networks, 474
virus, 547
Viruses, 157, 547
    Anti-virus program, 548
    Avoiding, 158
Voice Over Internet Protocol, 489
Volatile, 57
    RAM, 57
VPN. See Virtual Private
    Networks

W

WAN. See Wide Area Networks
Web Applications, 96
Web Browser, 436
    Favorites list, 450
    Searching for information, 563
Web browsers, 446
Web Browsers, 436
    Downloading, 442
    Features and functions, 440
    Functions, 441
    HyperText Markup Language,
    Uploading, 442
    Uploading or downloading,
        442
Web Layout, 217

Web Page, 436, 439
    Buttons, 440
    Fields, 439
    Navigation bar, 439
    Pictures, 439
Web pages, 436
Web Server, 433
    Domains, 437
    Protocols, 437
Web Site, 433
    Protocols, 437
Web Site Addresses, 437
Web Sites
    Authenticity of information,
        575
    Evaluating the information, 574
    Home page, 439
    Index page, 439
    Objectivity of information, 576
    Reliability or relevance, 575
    Searching, 565
    Web page, 436
WEP, 475
Wide Area Networks, 464
Wide Area Networks (WANs), 464
Window
    Moving a window, 25
    Scroll bars, 25
    Sizing a window, 25
Windows
    Operating system updates, 546
Windows Automatic Private IP
    Addressing, 480
Windows Desktop, 11
    Keyboard, 12
    Mouse, 12
    Navigating, 12
    Recycle Bin, 47
    Start button, 12
    Taskbar, 14
Windows Explorer
    Collapse button, 29
    Copying and moving items, 42
    Expand button, 29
    Renaming Items, 45
    Selecting files or folders, 41
    Split bar, 29
Windows Help and Support, 167
Wired connections, 461
Wireless Connections, 461
Wireless Security, 474
    Encryption, 475
Word
    Align text, 224
    Aligning table items, 274
    Blank Lines, 207
    Clip Art, 261
    Column break, 254
    Columns, 253
    Comments, 279
    Contextual errors, 242
    Create from a template, 213
    Creating a new blank
        document, 213

Cropping objects, 265
Customizing views, 217
Cut, copy or paste, 221
Deleting text, 207
Find and replace, 243
Font command, 224
Formatting codes, 208
Formatting text, 223
Grammatical errors, 242
Indents, 230
Indents set in the Paragraph
    command, 230
Insertion Point, 182, 207
Line spacing, 234
List - customizing, 231
Lists - organizing, 231
Manipulating pictures, 264
Margins, 250
Moving around, 208
Multimedia, 260
Multimedia objects, 264
Office Clipboard, 222
Opening documents, 216
Orientation, 249
Page breaks, 251
Page numbers, 252
Page setup, 248
Paragraph spacing, 234

Pictures, 260
Preview and print, 256
Print Settings, 257
Quick Styles, 237
Repeat, 221
Research tools, 246
Rotating objects, 266
Ruler, 208
Selecting table items, 273
Selecting text, 209
Selection Bar, 210
Sizing objects, 265
Spelling errors, 241
Styles, 235
Table Selector, 271
Table Tools ribbon, 271
Tables, 271
Tracking changes, 280
Undo, 220
Word Wrap, 207
Wrapping text around pictures,
    267
Zoom, 218
Workbook, 285
Workbooks, 286
    Close, 291
    Creating new blank, 286
    Opening, 290

Previewing, 336
Printing, 336
Saving, 289
Template, 286
Working with a Program, 14
Worksheet, 285
Worksheets
    Deleting, 301
    Inserting, 301
    Naming, 301
    Navigating the worksheet tabs,
        300
World Wide Web, 435
    Domains, 437
    Internet, 435
    Web pages, 436
    Web server, 433
    Web site, 433
    Web site addresses, 437
WPA, 475
WPA2, 475

Z

Zip Drives, 59
Zoom, 218, 330
    PowerPoint, 351
Zoom Slider, 182, 218

7318-1-00-00-MAN